Literature in the Making

OXFORD STUDIES IN AMERICAN LITERARY HISTORY

Gordon Hutner, Series Editor

Family Money
Jeffory A. Clymer

America's England
Christopher Hanlon

Writing the Rebellion
Philip Gould

Antipodean America
Paul Giles

Living Oil
Stephanie LeMenager

Making Noise, Making News
Mary Chapman

Territories of Empire
Andy Doolen

Propaganda 1776
Russ Castronovo

Playing in the White
Stephanie Li

Literature in the Making
Nancy Glazener

Surveyors of Customs
Joel Pfister

The Moral Economies of American Authorship
Susan M. Ryan

After Critique
Mitchum Huehls

Unscripted America
Sarah Rivett

Forms of Dictatorship
Jennifer Harford Vargas

White Writers, Race Matters
Gregory S. Jay

Anxieties of Experience
Jeffrey Lawrence

The Civil War Dead and American Modernity
Ian Finseth

The Puritan Cosmopolis
Nan Goodman

Realist Poetics in American Culture, 1866-1900
Elizabeth Renker

The Center of the World
June Howard

Not Quite Hope and Other Political Emotions in the Gilded Age
Nathan Wolff

History, Abolition, and the Ever-Present Now in Antebellum American Writing
Jeffrey Insko

Literature in the Making

A HISTORY OF U.S. LITERARY CULTURE
IN THE LONG NINETEENTH CENTURY

Nancy Glazener

UNIVERSITY PRESS

Oxford University Press is a department of the University of Oxford. It furthers
the University's objective of excellence in research, scholarship, and education
by publishing worldwide. Oxford is a registered trade mark of Oxford University
Press in the UK and certain other countries.

Published in the United States of America by Oxford University Press
198 Madison Avenue, New York, NY 10016, United States of America.

© Oxford University Press 2016

First issued as an Oxford University Press paperback, 2019

All rights reserved. No part of this publication may be reproduced, stored in
a retrieval system, or transmitted, in any form or by any means, without the
prior permission in writing of Oxford University Press, or as expressly permitted
by law, by license, or under terms agreed with the appropriate reproduction
rights organization. Inquiries concerning reproduction outside the scope of the
above should be sent to the Rights Department, Oxford University Press, at the
address above.

You must not circulate this work in any other form
and you must impose this same condition on any acquirer.

Library of Congress Cataloging-in-Publication Data
Glazener, Nancy.
Literature in the making: a history of U.S. literary culture in the long
nineteenth century/Nancy Glazener.
 pages cm.—(Oxford studies in American literary history)
Includes bibliographical references and index.
ISBN 978-0-19-939013-7 (cloth)—ISBN 978-0-19-094005-8 (paper)
ISBN 978-0-19-939014-4 (updf)
 1. American literature—19th century—History and criticism.
 2. Literature and society—United States—History—19th century.
 3. Literary movements—United States—History–19th century. I. Title.
PS201.G56 2015
810.9'355—dc23   2015005674

For Ben and David Foster

{ CONTENTS }

Acknowledgments   ix

Introduction: Literary History as the History of "Literature"   3
Scholarly Supports for This Study   7
Literature as Modern and Antimodern   12
How This Study Proceeds   16

1. Organizing Literature   20
Looking for Literature in the Eighteenth Century   21
The Problem with Poetry   24
Phillis Wheatley and the Transformation of Poetry   29
The Genres of Literature   36
The Two Canons   43

2. Literature, Civil Society, and the State   53
Print, Aesthetic Autonomy, and the History of Censorship   54
Literature in the Marketplace   63

3. Studying Literature   71
Shakespeare, Modern and Antimodern   74
Where Shakespeare Was Studied   83
How Literature Was Studied   95
Taste, Belles Lettres, and the Sublime   106
Coleridge, Emerson, and the Legacies of Moral Philosophy   109

4. Lost Episodes from Public Literary Culture   119
The St. Louis Movement and the Concord School   120
Dueling Bards   128
The Browning Society in the United States   136
A Library of American Literature   148

5. Literary Species and Academic Toolkits   161
Clash of the Titans: Novels versus Poetry   165
Crafting Conflicts   179

6. Disciplinarity and Beyond   193
Literature as Disciplinary   195
Literature as Interdisciplinary   205
Literature as Antidisciplinary   210
Coda   217

Notes   225
Index   313

{ ACKNOWLEDGMENTS }

This book interrupted and then absorbed parts of an earlier book project on which I had been working for some time, so there are many people whose advice and support have helped me along the way and whom I am eager to thank. Some of them helped in more than one capacity. I hope that anyone I missed here knows I am grateful.

Several generous readers reviewed most or all of the manuscript and offered excellent advice. James R. Kincaid moved to Pittsburgh just in time to become my most hardworking and judicious reader close at hand, reading this book in a couple of incarnations and offering crucial encouragement and advice. Deidre Shauna Lynch, who has been one of my best readers since our days in graduate school, offered astute suggestions about the whole manuscript and shared with me her wonderful book *Loving Literature* in manuscript. I am fortunate to have had the very best press readers for this book imaginable, Stephanie Foote and Elizabeth Renker. Their detailed suggestions about my long manuscript and their attention to its best possibilities, along with Gordon Hutner's wise counsel, have made it a better book. Any errors that remain are Jim Kincaid's fault.

Many other interlocutors offered valuable advice and feedback on stretches of this book or projects that ended up contributing to this book: Susan Balée, David Bartholomae, Dale M. Bauer, Troy Boone, Marah Gubar, Jayne Elizabeth Lewis, Daniel Morgan, Shalini Puri, James Seitz, Sandra Siegel, Susan Harris Smith, Angela Sorby, John Twyning, Jennifer Waldron, Courtney Weikle-Mills, Mary Saracino Zboray, and Ronald Zboray. A conversation with Brenda Glascott transformed my thinking about how the fields of composition and rhetoric might figure in this book. Alison Escher and Amanda Godley helped me identify and access current high school literature textbooks relevant for my work in chapter 5. Katie Homar offered me excellent ways to develop this project's connections to British Romantic writing and scholarship. I've been especially fortunate to have Marianne Novy's advice about navigating Shakespeare scholarship from an early stage of this project, and I've benefited as well from interchanges with other generous Shakespeare scholars: Curtis Breight, Jonathan Burton, Peggy Knapp, Zachary Lesser, John Twyning, Jennifer Waldron and Michael Witmore.

I am grateful for Don Bialostosky's ongoing intellectual camaraderie and his thoughtful responses to drafts of this project, offered while he has been a busy department chair and I've been director of graduate studies. The administrative workload has sometimes been overwhelming, so it has been wonderful to have a channel open for talking about ideas.

My work was furthered by the efforts of two excellent research assistants: Schuyler Chapman and Lisa Schwartz. I have benefited as well from being in dialogue with a number of people whose work on overlapping or adjoining topics has shaped my thinking: Mark Lynn Anderson, Jonathan Arac, Amy Blair, Jean Ferguson Carr, Stephen L. Carr, Neil Doshi, Carolyn Elliott, Jane Feuer, Jaime Harker, Hannah Johnson, Katherine Kidd, Andrea Lapin, Tara Lockhart, Christine Mahady, Elizabeth Oliphant, Kellie Robertson, Gayle Rogers, Mariolina Rizzi Salvatori, William Scott, Jennifer Schell, Clare Sigrist, Philip Smith, Swathi Sreerangarajan, and Brook Thomas. I am also grateful to several scholars who allowed me to read their then-unpublished scholarship that informed my work here: Sydney Bufkin, Margreta de Grazia, Beth Driscoll, Karin Hooks, and Erin A. Smith. At Oxford University Press, I benefited from the patient editorial support of Brendan O'Neill and Claudia Dukeshire.

The love and encouragement of many friends and relatives have made my labors lighter. I want to thank the extended Glazener and Foster families for being diplomatic and kind about the book that took forever. Jayne Lewis, Deidre Lynch, Jennifer Pasternack, Shalini Puri, and Katie Trumpener were especially closely involved with my work on this book, as intellectual project and long-term life challenge, and it truly might not have been finished without them. Phil and Slu Smith have enriched my life in many ways, not least by modeling high standards of scholarship and teaching and great professional generosity. D'Ann Moutos and Shirley Shadix nourished my ambitions early in my life and have never stopped inspiring me. I am also grateful to more friends than I can name who have kept up my morale and made life more fun.

The people whose support was most crucial lived with this book every day: Paul, David, and Ben Foster, who made sure that I took time out for bike rides and board games. Paul took over many tasks that made it possible for me to devote time to this book on top of teaching and administrative duties, and he was a good sounding board for every incarnation of this book as well as the project it interrupted. My sons, Ben and David, cheered me on and took an interest in my work. Ben honed his excellent style by proofreading and editing some of my work here, and David inspired and guided my interest in the worlds of fan fiction and Internet reading cultures. This book is dedicated to Ben and David with the hope that they will always find what they need in order to work on what's important to them.

I am grateful for permission to include here material that has been published in other forms. Chapters 1, 2, and 4 have drawn on my essay about "Women in Literary Culture during the Long Nineteenth Century" in *The Cambridge History of American Women's Literature*, edited by Dale M. Bauer (New York: Cambridge University Press, 2012). Chapter 2 has adapted material from my discussion of "The Novel in Postbellum Print Culture" in *The Cambridge History of the American Novel*, edited by Leonard Cassuto, Clare Eby, and Benjamin Reiss (New York: Cambridge University Press, 2011). Chapter 4 features analyses tried out in "Print Culture as an Archive of Dissent: Or, Delia Bacon and the Case of the Missing Hamlet," *American Literary History* 19.2 (Summer 2007), and in "The Browning Society in U.S. Public Literary Culture," published in "Lessons from the Past: The History of Academic English," ed. Leigh Dale, Jennifer McDonell, and Marshall Brown, a special issue of *Modern Language Quarterly* 75.2 (June 2014). The costs of the index were defrayed by support from the Richard D. and Mary Jane Edwards Endowed Publications Fund.

Literature in the Making

Introduction

LITERARY HISTORY AS THE HISTORY OF "LITERATURE"

Literature in the Making does not offer an account of how works of literature were written. It examines instead how the phenomenon "literature" came into being, seeking to uncover how strange literature is: a peculiar amalgam, not something self-evident or elemental. By examining how literature emerged—and how recently—I hope to loosen its hold on us and highlight our choices about what we wish to carry forward from or as literature as well as to examine features and effects of literature that ought to give us pause. I don't mean to debunk the whole idea of literature or the texts that have counted as literature. However, the rhetorical drumroll that usually accompanies testimonials to literature can make it hard to notice how the category shapes our encounters with things we read and with each other. Suspending the drumroll, *Literature in the Making* will examine literature as a collective invention and an institution.

Literature is a collective invention in the way that writing, money, voting, picnicking, and torture are: social practices that involve material resources and that are developed and refined in complex ways over time. Literature is also an institution supported by laws and organizations, built on the practice of writing in the way that banking, democracies, municipal parks, and national intelligence agencies are built on the collective inventions of money, voting, picnicking, and torture. In other words, literature is an institution insofar as it is supported not just by custom and personal discretionary participation but also by the state (through its support and monitoring of education, libraries, and the arts) and other established concerns (publishing houses, booksellers, foundations). Institutions can change or end, but they enjoy inertia because they are embedded in the design of collective life.

As invention and institution, literature has some specificity but no settled definition. Indeed, it's hard to define without begging the very methodological questions that are most important to keep open. Does literature consist primarily of a set of texts? a kind of reading experience? a cultural commitment? a marketing label? Wittgenstein proposed that an overloaded word may take on significance as the site of "a complicated network of similarities overlapping and criss-crossing," even if it can't be defined in a consistent way.[1] In support of this understanding of language, he offered the analogy of family resemblances: some members of the family X have snub noses, some have sharp cheekbones, some have dark hair, but perhaps no single member has all these features. Nonetheless, people who know the family recognize its members.

Just as families have networked characteristics, the ways in which literature means something and matters are networked. "Literature" may be consequential without being determinate. Indeed, some of the most potent terms are unwieldy in this way, as in the case of many of the supercharged terms with which literature is often associated (culture, civilization, humanity, enlightenment). During the first half of the nineteenth century, the kinds of writings widely understood to count as literature—its repertoire, in effect—narrowed, so that literature came to be associated with a particular set of imaginative genres rather than the tapestry of learned culture it had designated before. This narrowing marked the invention of literature in the sense familiar today. The invention of literature shaped and was shaped by literature's material infrastructure (print culture), its characteristic social practices and venues, and its most important institutional supports (the development of literary studies in higher education, the development of formal public education incorporating literature, and laws affecting the ownership and dissemination of literary works). As the century continued, the ways in which literature ought to be circulated, read, studied, and valued were further elaborated. Literature took on new meanings (which were also new effects) as it came to be absorbed into the forms of collective life and institutionalized in specific ways. Literature's initial embodiment in print meant that it continued to be affected by developments in the publishing industry and by the culture's ideological investments in print, although it also extended beyond print. *Literature in the Making* tracks literature's narrowing and subsequent elaboration over the course of the long nineteenth century, examining some of the most important claims and controversies that developed along the way.

Literature affects writers and readers worldwide, but literature began as an important component of modern European culture, one of the apparatuses of imperial civilization that was gradually appropriated by many who had been excluded from it. It is presently being renegotiated by an expanded set of proprietors. In its broadest uses, literature includes a variety of texts (including oral and manuscript compositions now available in print and digital formats) produced throughout the world over many centuries. Literature initially designated a body of valued texts, and this sense persists as well in the academic practice of the "literature search," which can apply to topics ranging from art history to epidemiology to mathematics. In this book, I detail and analyze the process by which literature was given more specific significance: associated with a particular set of imaginative genres; identified as a measure of excellence for works in those genres; made an index of the health and strength of a people; credited with fostering modes of public reflection crucial to civil society; entrusted with values and forms of experience believed to be at risk in modern life; and held to play a special role in readers' intellectual, moral, and emotional development. Each of these criteria could generate its own canon, and my list is not exhaustive. Indeed, the canon wars of the late twentieth century recycled some long-standing differences of opinion about what counts as literature or the best literature.

More important than the boundary work of determining what counts as literature is the question of what it means to encounter something as literature.[2] Literature can offer knowledge, certainly, but it is usually characterized by its capacity to offer something else: wisdom; enhanced attunement to certain registers of human experience; exposure to core national values or problems; sharper awareness of the capacities of language as a medium; or intense, transformative experiences. Instructive texts can count as literature if their style or design is aesthetically significant, as can texts central to the intellectual life of an era and texts relevant to other disciplines—say, Plato's *Phaedrus* and Marx's *Capital*. But reading the Bible as literature is not the same as reading the Bible as revelation; reading the work of Plato and Marx as philosophy or reading *Capital* as a work of economic theory is not the same as reading these works as literary texts.

There's also an ugly side to literature. Literature has not stopped being aligned with civilization against barbarism, even if the barbarians keep changing, and the power relations of imperial modernity are still at work in it. In many academic quarters and public venues, the canon has expanded, perhaps even dissolved, but literary studies has not managed to forge an identity independent of canonicity. The publicity accorded to identity politics in the canon wars continues to impact the terms in which different works get valued. Is Hawthorne's *The Scarlet Letter* a great novel but Chesnutt's *The House Behind the Cedars* a great novel about the African-American experience? Is Whitman's poetry great but Lydia Sigourney's only interesting?[3] The policing of literature usually involves the distribution of honor and contempt so that texts in the border zones, such as genre fiction or texts that resurfaced in the canon wars after long neglect, risk dismissal or condescension. Self-published works confront similar questions of literary value, since not securing commercial publication throws into question the value of a work even though nobody thinks that everything that gets published commercially is worthwhile. Questions of literary value circulate incessantly, inside and outside academia. One of my women friends thinks men write the best novels, a private opinion pitched as an irritable rejoinder to canon revision. I once heard two scholars of British literature agree informally that the United States had produced nothing much worth reading—banter at a cocktail party, but imperially condescending. The reading world is full of transactions in which people assign value to certain books or traditions and thereby to the people who read and write them. I've offered anecdotes rather than documentation not because literature's embroilment in status transactions and power relations can't be documented, but because its capacity to confer and withhold value reverberates unexpectedly in daily life.

In spite of these continuing skirmishes, *Literature in the Making* is a retrospective account made possible in part because literature's cultural centrality has been shaken, so that we are less likely to take it for granted now than we were fifty years ago. Now that academic literary scholars routinely investigate texts that didn't count as literary a few decades ago, we are in a position to notice things we never did before. We learn more about literature when we acknowledge its blurry boundaries as well as what's connected with it. New technologies are also changing our relationship to literature, which may be moving beyond its long intimacy with the book, and this possibility draws attention to ways in which our sense of literature has been shaped by the material features of books. In addition to working across disciplines to understand literature in conjunction with its longstanding sister arts, we're still absorbing the force of some of the newer media that outstrip literature's reach. Beginning in the twentieth century, cinema and television have offered modes of narrative absorption, metanarrative play, lyrical reverie, and cultural analysis similar to those valued in literature. The new Charles Dickens might well be Mira Nair or Joss Whedon. Film and media studies hasn't displaced literary studies from core curricula, but film, television, and digital media that incorporate images and sound are restructuring the terrain of culture so that print texts occupy a narrower tract.

Moreover, a world in which higher education is too expensive for many and in which secondary education may not leave graduates or dropouts robustly literate is a world in which literature will matter less. As I'll discuss, literature was promoted in the nineteenth-century United States in tandem with many forms of education that people pursued on their own time. Universal literacy seemed like a plausible goal, vaguely combined with the fantasy that everyone in the United States might someday be middle-class. But many live in poverty in the United States and throughout the world, and people who are poor—hungry, unsafe, and likely to use most of their energy just surviving—will not find it easy to concentrate on reading, in or out of school.[4] Literature depends on literacy education, and literacy education depends on people's material security. There are remarkable people who have sought out demanding educations in spite of great adversity—indeed, this book will inventory some of the resources available for self-education and mutual education in the nineteenth-century United States. There will always be people who manage to wring possibilities out of the bleakest circumstances, but they have never been the majority. If literature is a social good, then it's one of the many that cannot thrive among people who are barely subsisting. A good way to support literature would be to end poverty, although this book will focus on a more limited set of factors affecting literature's circulation and import.

Within higher education, expanding or dissolving the canon and its study has revitalized the work of departments of modern languages and literatures, but this expansion has also meant that it gets harder and harder to specify the "literature" part. Critical theory and cultural studies made literary studies deeply interdisciplinary, offering cross-disciplinary objects such as discourse, textuality, culture, and power-knowledge. The critique of the nation-state as a rubric organizing intellectual and cultural production has brought into view literature's transnational dimensions, which are investigated sometimes under the auspices of comparative literature but more often and awkwardly within departments defined by national and imperial languages.[5] In practical terms, literature departments are still mainly sites where novels, plays, poems, and essays are studied—these being the core genres around which the narrower version of literature cohered in the nineteenth century—and literature courses and scholarship still attend to matters of form, style, and interpretation that were formulated before the canon wars and critical theory shook up the landscape. But it is less and less the case that "literature," in the sense that initially defined departments of modern languages and literatures, is a good way of naming the object of literary studies.[6] Either literary studies has expanded beyond literature, or literature itself has expanded profoundly. However we understand this change, we need to take it on board as a vital renovation within the discipline, not a loss.

Scholarly Supports for This Study

Precisely because the idea of literature has become so flexible (in the optimistic version) or has been put at risk (in the fearful version), we can examine it in new ways. A wave of collective invention is under way in literary studies, and *Literature in the Making* has taken inspiration from it. Building on the theoretical interventions and historical recovery work launched in the 1970s, literary studies turned its attention to many more kinds of texts, working out terms of value and modes of analysis that depart from older models of canonicity and literary interpretation but also benefit from them. Popular and middlebrow literatures have become part of the mainstream of literary studies, informing its approaches as well as providing new objects.[7] More importantly, many critics have been working to bridge the gap between expert and lay reading practices (neither of which is monolithic) without simply valorizing either.[8] The most promising two directions, in my view, are studies of affect and the commons, which revisit traditional dimensions of literary value but pursue them differently. Affect studies reframes aesthetic apprehension as sensual, emotional, and bodily, never divorced from cognition and collective life, and the development of the commons as a touchstone for political analysis and action offers a new way to consider the public-oriented dimensions of literature.[9] This study benefits from both but is not fully aligned with either.

Literature in the Making is a work of cultural history orchestrating four strains of scholarship: aesthetics, print culture studies, the disciplinary history of English literary studies, and the history of public literary culture. Built into these four domains are two methodological tensions. One pits the idealizing, universalizing tendencies bequeathed by eighteenth-century aesthetic philosophy against the contingent material and economic history of print culture studies. The second methodological tension plays the compact academic genealogy of English literary studies against the variety of nonacademic forums in which people have studied literature. The way I've named the confrontations suggests that print culture and public literary culture will have the upper hand, as the messy operations of the publishing industry smudge the clean lines of aesthetic theory and as the varied activities of lay readers point to the narrowness and conjectural nature of academic reading protocols. That's correct: attending to print culture and public literary culture challenges the received wisdom about literature in important ways that have not yet been absorbed sufficiently, so these approaches will get extra attention here.

To grant print and public literary culture precedence is not to dismiss aesthetics and disciplinary history, though. The study of print culture necessarily decenters literature, positioning literary print culture within a large and diversified publishing industry that was continually adapting to new conditions. This displacement is illuminating for literary studies, but the fact that literature has mainly taken the form of print does not mean that literature's significance is reducible to the facts of its print production and circulation. The aesthetic conversations taken up here offer a range of ideas about how encounters with art and literature could be formative or transformative, and these ideas had real effects.[10]

It's not surprising to position print culture studies and aesthetics as contending fields, but the disciplinary history of literary studies has not previously been positioned within the larger history of public literary culture. Within the disciplinary history of literary studies, I focus on the history of English literature in the United States, exemplified by the formation of English departments (which came to include U.S. literature) but reflected also in the development of English and U.S. literature as core subjects in secondary education. Although I track English in the United States, my account draws on the larger history of English literary studies that traces its formative development to the edges of the British Empire (mainly Scotland and India) and to dissenting educational institutions in England, sites where English literary studies was both a vehicle for imperial domination and an imperial resource that could be appropriated.[11] In keeping with this history, the study of U.S. literature was a special emphasis of nonelite U.S. higher education in the nineteenth century and an adjunct to U.S. imperial ambitions in the twentieth century.[12] That the academic study of English and U.S. literature negotiated national and imperial agendas has been persuasively established: Anglophone literary studies was shaped profoundly by geopolitics.[13]

Academic English literary study in the United States was not based solely on academic precedents, however. It also drew heavily on public literary culture. I build here on the work of Anne Ruggles Gere, who argued as early as

1997 that members of women's clubs in the late nineteenth century "created the preconditions for professionalizing literary study while offering an alternative to its university instantiation."[14] Indeed, for most of the century, academic literary culture was a subset of public literary culture, and in this arena where women and men were both active, forms of literary analysis were developed that English departments later selectively adopted. By public literary culture, I mean the channels through which people who claimed a stake in literature collaborated with each other and pursued their commitments to literature. These channels included clubs, opportunities for formal and informal education, and books and periodicals along with lectures, readings, and elocutionary and theatrical performances.

For most of the nineteenth century, while the modern version of literature was cohering and during the decades when it was relatively new, academic literary offerings—lectures, courses, and publications—operated as part of public literary culture, accruing some authority from their connection with higher education without being segregated in expert-specialist channels. Only after the reorganization of knowledge around credentialed expertise, which stabilized at the very end of the nineteenth century, did academics effectively come to determine what counted as literature and literary studies. English became a core discipline within higher education and secondary schooling only because there was widespread popular support for the importance of literary studies, but as a result of this transformation, academic literary culture was segregated from public literary culture.[15]

Folding the history of academic English into the history of public literary culture before the research university model became dominant, I argue that public literary culture included some approaches to literary studies that were richer than those institutionalized in early English departments. We have in recent decades been reclaiming some of these approaches, usually without knowing they had been part of literary studies before. I will also explain how the adoption of the research university model led to English departments' appropriating some ingredients of public literary studies and excluding others; the previous development of these ingredients in public literary culture even dropped out of the historical record. Chapter 6 acknowledges the Internet's challenge to the authority of experts and its potential to renew the collaboration between academic and lay readers that was widespread before the end of the nineteenth century. The Internet's capacity to provide collaborative spaces and commons outside of academic channels, in addition to the egalitarian potential of its do-it-yourself ethos, is another reason why we need to understand the public's share in developing English literary studies in the first place.[16] In keeping with repeated scholarly calls for literary studies to work on better ways of collaborating with the public, *Literature in the Making* contributes to our understanding of what was possible before the expert-amateur divide reconfigured literary studies.[17]

The domains I'm bringing together draw on intellectual history, material and economic history, and social and cultural history; they address ethics and politics as well as aesthetics, it possible to consider literature as idea, object, commodity, practice, and experience. Such a broadly synthetic approach means that this study is bound to reduce and simplify some of the scholarly conversations it takes up. I hope that the value of having a large-scale account integrating a number of important fields of scholarship will offset what has been lost through compression and elision.

Given the conceptual breadth of my inquiry here, it may seem bizarre—either imperially arrogant or stubbornly provincial—that I'm focusing on the United States in the long nineteenth century (roughly, from the U.S. Revolution through the 1910s).[18] I am not claiming that literature was invented or most importantly developed in the U.S. I claim only that the United States is as good a site as any for examining how literature as we know it cohered. The history of literature was national as well as transnational, since nations are both distinct geopolitical entities and nodes in global networks. Rodrigo Lazo has posited that the "history of the modern archive is inextricable from the establishment of nation-states," and his work is designed to promote scholarly attention to "migrant archives" that are not part of these "official spaces of archivization."[19] Taking up the obverse inquiry, I delve here into the production of a U.S. national ideology and archive of literature that highlighted certain transnational channels (even though the privileged channel to Great Britain also caused anxiety) but obscured or disavowed others. Nineteenth-century literary culture was organized nationally even though it tended to be cosmopolitan in outlook; the dominant stretches of U.S. literary culture, understood inside and outside the United States as representing the nation, were Anglophone, even though many languages contributed to U.S. literature and even though Anglophone literary culture was deeply enmeshed with other literatures and literary cultures. Although this study takes up a number of figures whose literary investments were multilingual (including George Ticknor, Henry Wadsworth Longfellow, Denton J. Snider, William Torrey Harris, and the prolific translators and editors of *Poet-Lore*, Helen A. Clarke and Charlotte Porter) and keeps multilingual exchange in view, it cannot substantively address U.S. literary culture as an enterprise bigger than the English language or unfold its transnational dimensions beyond familiar kinds of traffic.

The idea of literature that had cohered by about 1850 was initially formulated in Europe and Europe's colonies and former colonies through a set of cultural channels I'll characterize as "Euro-American." The United States is the site I'm investigating, but the channels reached the Americas at large.[20] The version of Euro-American culture I examine was specifically Anglophone and oriented toward England, though informed by European currents of thoughts that circulated across nations and languages.[21] This Euro-American version of literature encountered other ways of valuing legacy texts as it traveled and was imperially enforced. Various practices of cultural translation and adaptation resulted in our current sense that literature includes the epic of Gilgamesh, the Ramayana, and Basho's haikus, as well as many European texts from long ago. No doubt literature was changed by its travels, including those within U.S. immigrant and minority cultures; no doubt in some ways it also resisted being changed. These travels exceed the scope of this study.[22] There is also much more to be learned about how literature and literary culture mattered in cultures of letters that were not part of the networks of literary culture I examine here, most of whose participants were white and economically privileged or stable. As is the case with many other beliefs embedded in European imperialism, literature was understood as a human accomplishment and value at which Europe excelled and to which other parts of the world ought to aspire, universal in scope but taking distinctive national forms. These beliefs add to the importance of examining transnational literary culture as it was refracted and organized within a particular national literary culture, since readers in the long nineteenth century were constantly navigating national literary boundaries.

The practical reasons for my focus on the United States are that I have been trained as a scholar of nineteenth-century U.S. literature and culture and that much of the scholarship relevant to this study has been organized nationally, even if that scholarship concerns exchanges between nations (such as the influence of Scottish and German models of higher education in the United States). The geopolitical power of the United States in the twentieth and twenty-first centuries adds to the interest of understanding U.S. literary culture in particular, since the U.S. academy and U.S.-based media conglomerates currently wield a disproportionate influence on literary publishing and literary studies throughout the world.[23] My working assumption, which this study can't in itself prove or disprove, is that the history of literature in the United States has much in common with the history of literature in the rest of the world, mainly because literature emerged when the world was becoming rapidly more interconnected and when even local singularities were likely to be framed in global terms. The example of the United States cannot simply be generalized to stand for the larger history of literature, but neither is it likely to be utterly anomalous.

Literature in the Making focuses on the United States and contributes to U.S. literary studies, most importantly by insisting that the history of literature in the United States cannot be confined to works of literature that were written by authors born or residing in the United States.[24] U.S. literary history has mainly focused on the production and early reception of U.S.-based writings considered literary, but literature began as a category valuing older texts, legacy texts out of which canons were forged. Most of the legacy texts that circulated in the United States were British and Anglophone, supplemented importantly by an international supercanon (Homer, Dante, Shakespeare, Cervantes, Milton, and Goethe). Among national literary traditions, English literature was the best known, best loved in the United States during the long nineteenth century, and

Shakespeare was the most important author. "We can only naturalize a French, Italian, or German work, by translation, but an English book is, as it were, born a citizen of the United States," noted a reviewer who participated in the dominant fantasy that the United States was monolingual and culturally oriented toward Great Britain.[25] It would be too neat to say that readers in the United States defined literature on the basis of English texts and then appropriated that model for U.S. writings, but that model is closer to the truth than the assumption that they developed an understanding of literature on the basis of U.S. writings. Although *Literature in the Making* features a number of well-known U.S. authors (Phillis Wheatley, Charles Brockden Brown, Washington Irving, Ralph Waldo Emerson, Herman Melville, Charles Chesnutt, Pauline Hopkins, William Dean Howells, Mark Twain, Henry James, Edith Wharton, Frank Norris, and others), they will be important mainly as authors who participated in literary culture.

What, then does this project offer to U.S. literary studies? It extends the work of transnational literary studies, positioning U.S. literary culture as a set of U.S.-marked traces within transnational literary circuits. Coleridge's interpretation of Shakespeare, Browning's poems, and Ibsen's plays were events in U.S. literary culture, events that need to be incorporated into our study of texts authored by U.S. residents. In particular, this book further elaborates the complex relations between the United States and Great Britain examined in recent studies such as Christopher Hanlon's *America's England: Antebellum Literature and Atlantic Sectionalism,* Meredith McGill's *American Literature and the Culture of Reprinting, 1834–1853* and Elisa Tamarkin's *Anglophilia: Deference, Devotion, and Antebellum America.*[26] *Literature in the Making* also suggests that it's impossible to examine U.S. literature without taking into account the dynamic and paradoxical development of literature itself, which our disciplinary protocols have oversimplified. Every author we've been accustomed to locate in U.S. literature during the long nineteenth century encountered literature as a strange compound of aesthetics, property, public thought and feeling, and wood pulp (among other things), so *Literature in the Making* is designed to deepen our understanding of the complications at work in an author's "literary aspirations" or "literary judgment." This study also develops some of the intricacies of public reception that our familiar objects navigated in the nineteenth century. Finally, it examines the nineteenth-century foundations of academic literary scholarship and contributes to our understanding of the circumstances that shape our research and teaching as Americanists.

Literature as Modern and Antimodern

Because literary culture perpetually generated claims about literature's value for readers facing modern conditions, the version of literature that emerged by about

1850 was inflected by ideas about modernity. The Modern Language Association and departments of modern languages and literatures were named "modern" mainly in contrast to ancient languages and writings, but throughout the long nineteenth century, ideas about literature lived in close proximity to ideas about what it was to be modern.[27] Without claiming that this version of literature simply *was* modern, I argue that hopes and fears and longings about literature paralleled constructions of modernity, thereby throwing into relief how thoroughly our thinking and even our experience of literature are still shaped by this paradigm.

In the wake of the quarrel of the ancients and moderns, "modern" often named a set of interrelated historical transformations believed to make life qualitatively different from premodern life, which first meant ancient—before the "middle" ages—but then accommodated a number of more recent thresholds. Modernity was associated with a set of ideas, institutions, and technologies: individualism, the nation-state legitimized by popular sovereignty, social mobility, capitalism, industrialism, print, and (in the United States) democracy and Protestant Christianity.[28] Many claims and assumptions about literature's significance were keyed to features associated with modernity: individualism and nationalism, most conspicuously, but also capitalism and print. Nevertheless, the distinctive feature of modernity was that it named the cumulative effects of these innovations or perhaps some mysterious underlying force at work in all of them: that it designated a wholesale transformation, not a set of discrete innovations. As Michael Löwy and Robert Sayre explain, modernity was influentially perceived "as a whole whose multiple aspects are interrelated and interlocking: an all-encompassing civilization, a world in which everything holds together."[29] Modernity was cast as a qualitative change in human experience, "planar," as Perry Anderson has characterized Marshall Berman's influential presentation of it.[30] It was affective as much as intellectual, and it involved new ways of experiencing being a self or belonging to collectives.

We can register the import of modernity's formulation without believing modernity to be an epoch, force, or comprehensive worldview, though. In *We Have Never Been Modern*, Bruno Latour points out that the designation of our world as modern is "only the provisional result of a selection made by a small number of agents in the name of all."[31] In a similar vein, Talal Asad has proposed that modernity "is a *project*—or rather, a set of interlinked projects—that certain people in power seek to achieve."[32] Latour proposes that the networks that circulate modern practices and beliefs have all along been contemporary with networks keeping alive "nonmodern" or "amodern" beliefs and practices. Like Raymond Williams's heuristic schema of dominant, emergent, and residual practices, Latour's approach emphasizes the heterogeneity of contemporary phenomena and discourages teleology.[33] Arjun Appadurai similarly characterizes our world as one "in which modernity is decisively at large, irregularly self-conscious, and unevenly experienced" and in which the belief in modernity may represent something new without representing the kind of rupture posited by understandings of modernity as an epoch.[34] Building on these perspectives, as well as the work of scholars who have called attention to the equal and opposite distortions at work in designating beliefs and practices as "traditional," I want to underline that I'm not claiming that literature *was* modern.[35] Rather, literary culture overwhelmingly took modernity to be a meaningful paradigm for Euro-American experience in the long nineteenth century. The new version of literature that emerged by the mid-nineteenth century was a networked set of ideas and practices that were commonly configured as supports for modernity or bulwarks against it. Modernity is a paradigm, not an empirical reality, but belief in the paradigm of modernity was a structuring and consequential feature of U.S. public literary culture during the long nineteenth century.

Literature was shaped not only by ideas about how culture and social life were modern but also by modern-coded emotional responses.[36] The paradigm of modernity organized history, creating not only a "Great Divide" between ancients and moderns but also a structure of feeling about that divide.[37] The most prominent structure of feeling responded to the "fortunate fall," a Romantic trope interpreting and extending the biblical story of how Adam and Eve were expelled from the Garden of Eden after they ate from the Tree of Knowledge.[38] Being cast out of Eden was fortunate because it brought about self-knowledge and self-determination, after all. An influential rendition of the fortunate fall was Friedrich Schiller's account of the transition from the "naïve" to the "sentimental."[39] He distinguished the direct and unselfconscious relationship that ancients purportedly enjoyed with nature (another impossibly overloaded value), which he called "naive," from the reflective, self-conscious relationship of moderns to nature, which he called "sentimental." Schiller argued that moderns have lost something valuable, a fresh and direct relationship to the world often figured as childlike, but that this loss is the necessary precondition for something better, a stance in which our separation from nature allows us greater freedom of thought and action. Both the grief of loss and separation, which might take the form of nostalgic fantasies about childhood or primitivism, and the compensatory satisfactions, which might include an emotional tolerance for complexity and an ethical-aesthetic privileging of maturity, are emotionally resonant in Schiller's account, and both could be heard in discussions of art and culture during the long nineteenth century.[40] The feeling-tone of modern loss could form a chord with the tone of celebration of boundless modern possibilities, as they were imagined.

An important characteristic of modern great divides is that they are made to be bridged. No sooner did Schiller periodize the naïve and the sentimental than he transmuted them into subjective stances or qualities available to moderns. From the naive, we can take "a sober spirit of observation," "a firm attachment to the uniform evidence of the senses," and "a resigned submission to the necessity ... of nature"; from the sentimental, "a restless spirit of speculation in theoretical things...[and] a moral rigorism in practical things which insists on the absolute in the actions of the will."[41] Other stories of modernity similarly posit epochal divides but convert them into sets of contrasting vantage points that modern individuals can access. Just as Hebraism and Hellenism were available to non-Jewish, nonpagan readers of Matthew Arnold, modern culture was perpetually allocating values and ideas to particular populations and periods, then offering them to everybody.

The version of literature established in the nineteenth-century United States played out both celebratory and mournful versions of the modern. Literature was valued for shoring up modern subjects and guiding modern projects, but it was also valued for stockpiling antidotes to modernity. Not only individualism but also characteristically modern ideas of self-development were embedded in the admiration for Shakespeare's prolific creation of compelling characters, insofar as Shakespeare seemed to enact imaginatively the characteristically modern idea that a person might become anything or anyone—that our internal possibilities are boundless. However, the contrasting idea that poetry and drama were ancient forms of expression, emerging originally from primitive tribal experiences, made it possible to envision Shakespeare's works as shelters for long-standing experiences or values, keeping them alive in (what was taken to be) a modern world hostile to them.[42] In both framings, literature was designed to serve modern readers: readers fulfilling modern possibilities and readers being fortified against modern deprivations.

Somewhat paradoxically, then, the construction of literature as modern and the construction of literature as antimodern both conformed to the paradigm of modernity, since antimodernity tended to present itself as a "modern critique of modernity."[43] Laying the intellectual foundation for these constructions were the dominant traditions of eighteenth-century European philosophy, Scottish Common Sense Philosophy and German aesthetic philosophy. Common Sense Philosophy, a product of the Scottish Enlightenment though broadly influential in nineteenth-century Europe and the United States, posited capacities and perceptions that people shared but could develop individually, including taste and a moral sense.[44] As put forward by Francis Hutcheson, Thomas Reid, and the neighboring philosopher Adam Smith, Common Sense Philosophy treated literature, or some of the genres on their way to becoming literature, as a shared resource for self-discipline and socialization, locating it in civil society and harnessing it to modern projects. Thinkers in the Common Sense tradition valued imaginative writings as practice grounds for moral responsiveness and taste, casting novels in particular as extensions or simulations of the social world. Scottish philosophy mobilized mimetic texts for practices of ethical invigilation but also valued their expression and reflection of collective life. Along with writings by Montesquieu and Johann Gottfried von Herder that formulated how cultures could be shaped by national conditions and histories, Common

Sense Philosophy provided underpinnings for literary nationalism and for the nineteenth-century sense of literature—especially novels—as a medium for the ongoing representation and analysis of social life in a national framework.[45]

Literature was invented in the contact zone between Common Sense Philosophy and the now better-known traditions of German aesthetic philosophy represented by Kant and Schiller. For heuristic purposes, we can contrast the modernizing (civic, civilizing) view of literature developed in Common Sense Philosophy with the antimodern (transcendent, anti-instrumental) view of literature developed in German aesthetic philosophy, which defined aesthetic value in opposition to art's capacities to be sold or put to worldly uses, even civic-minded and sociable uses. Yet because literature was an ensemble, a complex phenomenon involving texts and reading practices and the circumstances of print's circulation, it could sustain relationships with both these traditions, which provided the starting intellectual infrastructures for literature's public-oriented and aesthetic rationales. Indeed, these contradictions generated the problems and controversies that became the stuff of literary culture.

Over time, literary culture generated many ways of reconciling public-oriented and aesthetic understandings as well as ways of picking one over the other. These ways developed beyond the original Scottish and German positions, which had been from the start disseminated, appropriated, and transformed in casual use. The opposition between modern and antimodern rationales for literature did not always line up neatly with the opposition between public-oriented and aesthetic rationales for literature's value, but literary culture kept producing new possibilities within this matrix. In this study, I'll call the narrower version of literature associated specifically with imaginative genres "modern literature," to differentiate it from broader understandings of literature, but the phrase most usefully designates literature's complex and dynamic relationship with the paradigm of modernity. Modern literature, in this sense, affected ancient as well as recent texts.

How This Study Proceeds

The chief argument of this study is embodied in its approach: I'm arguing that it's important to bring together aesthetic theories, print culture studies, disciplinary history, and the history of public culture in order to understand literature as an invention and institution, and, further, that the paradigm of modernity was formative in all these domains.

Accordingly, *Literature in the Making* offers a history of how the foundational components of literature and literary studies came together in the form we mainly recognize today: literature's characteristic assemblage of genres and its division between poetry and prose, its national and international canons, the author-function, toggling versions of aesthetic autonomy, and the forms of literary history, aesthetic interpretation, philological investigation, and textual criticism that still constitute core practices within academic literary studies. It should not be surprising to learn that each piece of standard literary equipment today is the fossil remains of a significant problem or controversy, although I believe most readers will be surprised by some of the stakes and players. I hope this account will be broad enough to help students and scholars determine how literature has impinged on a variety of particular texts and authors of interest. Effectively, then, I argue that the changing history of literature has to be taken into account within any investigation of U.S. literature, and I advance along the way claims about the impact of specific features of literature and watersheds in its conception and institutionalization, especially with regard to literature's fundamental but complex relationship to modernity.

As a history, the book moves in mainly chronological fashion from the period of modern literature's earliest emergence to the period in which its academic institutionalization was secured, examining some of the key factors involved in this process and explaining the roles they played. This kind of explanatory work has now mainly been consigned to multiauthored "companion" volumes and literary histories, as the ever-more-streamlined monograph is expected to maximize its surprises rather than offer a comprehensive scholarly account. However, the belief that literary scholarship should only concern itself with the startling is one of the orthodoxies I hope to overturn here: I offer a capacious explanation that addresses many of the factors that readers would expect to be involved in literature's history, in addition to offering some particular arguments that may be startling. The book traces an arc from the late eighteenth century to the early twentieth century that proceeds in three steps, each occupying two chapters. The first two chapters set out important features of literature's emergence in the new, more specific sense: the creation of an interlocking system of genres and canons, in chapter 1, "Organizing Literature," and the legal elaboration of literature as intellectual property subject to market conditions and state censorship, in chapter 2, "Literature, Civil Society, and the State." Together, the chapters investigate literature's infrastructure, homing in on the ways in which the idea of literature was conditioned by the development of some of the apparatuses involved in its institutionalization. These chapters take a panoramic view, emphasizing literature's large-scale, virtually systematic effects but also the gradual, unsystematic adjustments by which it acquired its familiar supports.

Collective inventions often appear uncanny because they exceed determinate human intentions, resulting instead from the cumulative effects of many actions and circumstances. The middle two chapters highlight some particular, deliberate ways in which people took up the possibilities for engagement generated by the new version of literature. Chapter 3, "Studying Literature," launches the argument that nineteenth-century public literary culture in the United States developed some of the core practices of U.S. academic literary studies as well as important kinds of literary reading and responsiveness excluded until recently from the academy. The chapter brings together the social history of public literary studies with its intellectual infrastructure. As the foundational author of modern literature, Shakespeare was the centerpiece of U.S. public literary culture, and the reading practices and forms of scholarly caretaking developed for his plays helped define how readers could participate in literature. Chapter 4, "Lost Episodes from Public Literary Culture," takes up some instructive dead ends in public literary culture, all of which were connected with Shakespeare studies. Three of these episodes connected literature with philosophy and social thought: the St. Louis movement, which valued literature as part of a Hegelian commitment to self-education and public education; the Browning Society, which valued Browning as an interpreter of modernity; and the Baconians, who were wrong about the authorship of Shakespeare's plays but held important views about the plays' significance. The fourth episode concerns an unusual literary anthology whose history registers changes in literary culture brought about by the stratification of the publishing industry and the increasing cultural authority of academics at the end of the century. Collectively, the four episodes point to some remarkable directions in nineteenth-century public literary culture that were excluded from early academic literary studies.

The final two chapters take stock of literary culture at the end of the century and develop the argument that literary studies was diminished by being installed as a discipline in the research university, an argument for which all the earlier chapters laid groundwork. Chapter 5, "Literary Species and Academic Toolkits," picks up the history of literary genres begun in chapter 1, focusing on ways in which evolutionary thinking (including social Darwinism) and the instrumentalizing tendencies of academic instruction affected late-century relations between novels and poetry, on the one hand, and between drama and short stories, on the other. The establishment of academic English studies has often been treated as the culmination of literature's cultural aspirations, but one of its effects was to impose on a lively and varied literary culture a brittle divide between credentialed academic experts and everybody else, who could only be amateurs. Chapter 6, "Disciplinarity and Beyond," examines English literature's installation in higher education toward the end of the nineteenth century, emphasizing the losses brought about by the creation of academic experts and the separation of academic literary culture from public culture. The chapter argues that even though early academic literary studies was intensely disciplinary, sometimes rigidly so, it was also interdisciplinary and antidisciplinary, precisely because it incorporated tendencies developed within public literary studies. Since conventional literary studies and the model of disciplinarity on which it was based are both in need of renovation, the contradictions built into academic literary studies from the beginning may be some of our most valuable resources as we consider how best to move forward.

Like any complex analysis, my discussion highlights certain factors rather than others, partly because the factors I highlight have been missed before and partly because they resonate with present interests and concerns. My inquiry was set in motion initially by the surprise of coming across nineteenth-century critics who pursued the kind of political and philosophical questions that I thought had not entered literary studies before the late twentieth century. I discovered that many people had thought deeply about literature before it was commonly taught in universities, and that the development of academic literary expertise disenfranchised some learned people, such as the Shakespearian editors Helen A. Clarke and Charlotte Porter and the literary-philosophical polymaths Denton J. Snider and Thomas Davidson. The answers to all our problems can't lie in the late nineteenth century—the era of robber barons and the onset of Jim Crow—but learning more about nineteenth-century public literary culture can help us stay open to rethinking the public missions of higher education, the liberal arts, and literary studies. There were serious readers in all walks of life when literary authority was more decentralized. Recognizing that nonacademics can contribute to literary studies would probably be a good way to build cultural alliances, and it might change the role of literary studies in higher education and beyond.

{ 1 }

Organizing Literature

We might consider literature's transformation between the middle of the eighteenth century and the middle of the nineteenth to be the analytic refinement of a category that was previously conglomerate or miscellaneous. In eighteenth-century Anglo-American usage, "literature" designated learned writings, usually those available in print. Literature meant letters, in the sense of "republic of letters" or "man of letters," and it might refer specifically to valued Latin and Greek works.[1] The kinds of imaginative works that we associate with literature today were included in this baggy category, but so were treatises in any area of learning: Sophocles's *Oedipus Rex* and Lucretius's *On the Nature of Things* and Francis Bacon's *Great Instauration* were all literature in 1750. By around 1850, however, writings such as *Oedipus Rex* that were imaginative or fictive or the objects of taste—explanations varied—were sorted out of the jumble and allowed to keep the mantle "literature," while writings such as *On the Nature of Things* and *Great Instauration* migrated to other fields of knowledge. Once winnowed, this new category of literature, which is likely to strike us as more coherent than its predecessor, could be better examined and understood. It could be organized into national and international canons and into genres, periods, and movements. New modes of reading and study appropriate to it were developed.

The account I've just given is true, but it is also a modern fable: a fable about how modern processes and ways of thinking straighten out the tangled messes left by previous eras and make possible new and more productive uses of whatever has been untangled. As Jon Klancher has pointed out, the modern way is not just to classify but also to organize, and organization reveals or creates logical and structural relationships that generate new opportunities for human involvement.[2] Once literature began to be defined in a modern way, organizing literature could become an ongoing task generating forms of comparison, elaboration, and evaluation that affected how literature was read and also how it could be connected to other endeavors. The emergence of literature was marked by passionate manifestos about literature, art, poetry, and the imagination. Amid this clamor, the apparatuses of genres and canons quietly and consequentially slipped into place.

The development of literary genres and canons offered ways of distributing modern and antimodern dimensions of literature so that literature could both advance modern projects and offset modern failings. Long-standing genres were retooled within the ensemble of literature, and literary canons retrofitted legacy texts with literary features. These apparently modest, stealthy conversions, along with the slippage between the old and new repertoires of the term "literature," concealed the magnitude of the transformation under way.

This chapter spotlights some of the most important conversions bundled into the invention of literature, conversions that can be grasped most readily in the case of poetry. What poetry included, before the nineteenth century, is remarkably similar to what literature came to include by about 1850. By tracing the transformation that turned poetry into a division within literature, rather than an umbrella term for the chief fictive genres, we can examine the larger set of generic negotiations that cumulatively contributed to the new version of literature. This transformation affected not only the literary ambitions of poets going forward but also how earlier poets were integrated into the history of poetry. The changing fortunes of Phillis Wheatley's poetry are illuminating in this regard, because the distorting terms on which her body of work was first devalued and then revalued were both keyed to the version of literature that cohered after her death.

Taking the eighteenth century as its springboard, then, this chapter analyzes the adaptation and reconfiguration of the genres that came to define literature by 1850. Literature's contradictory relationship with modernity was negotiated in the interplay among these genres, and this interplay underlines how important it is to consider not only how individual works participated in genres but also how genres cohabited within the ensemble of literature. There was a similar interplay between the national and international canons that were consolidated during the nineteenth century. These interlocking mechanisms of genres and canons made literature run, and texts that might be literary were fitted into the machinery, made to jam the machinery, or used to design new parts.

Looking for Literature in the Eighteenth Century

The earlier understanding of literature that was mainly superseded in the nineteenth century did not emphasize connections with taste, the imagination, or the fictive. Rather, as Sandra Gustafson has underlined, "Any formal written work—for instance, a scientific treatise, a sermon text, a work of philosophy, or an ethnographic narrative—counted as 'literature.'"[3] The many U.S. periodicals of the early national era identifying themselves as literary repositories, literary journals, literary cabinets, literary museums, and so forth did not usually link their literariness specifically to imaginative writing or to the genres that later formed the core of literature. Literature could be found wherever books, periodicals, or manuscripts circulated during the early national period, and even forms of practical wisdom could count as literature if they were written down or printed. As late as 1829, for example, Samuel L. Knapp's *Lectures on American Literature* identified "newspapers" as the "species of literature" in which "we surpass all other countries," although he noted that he meant literature "in its extended sense."[4] The term "literature" was gravitating toward written texts, especially print texts, and this increasingly strong association between literature and print also linked literature to official knowledge. Oral compositions such as sermons, orations, and educational lectures could be treated as literature, but the classification usually came to bear once they were printed.

In spite of the difference between the capacious sense of literature current in the eighteenth century and the more restrictive one dominant in Anglophone cultures by about 1850, some important features of the broader understanding were carried forward in the narrower one. One carryover was the assumption that literature had a collective value, contributing to various grand and large-scale projects such as culture, learning, and civilization. Consider for example James Bowdoin's 1780 address to the newly formed American Academy of Arts and Sciences. Klancher's history of the institutions promoting (and thereby defining and elaborating) the arts and sciences emphasizes the distinctively modern authority of such institutions, which organized, divided up, and legitimized fields of knowledge.[5] The American Academy began with an expansive mandate characteristic of the period before these institutions began to sort arts from sciences. Bowdoin quoted in his address the academy's official purpose: "to cultivate every art and science, which may tend to advance the interest, honour, dignity, and happiness of a free, independent, and virtuous people." As the academy's first president, he invited the "sons of literature" to start cultivating the "wide and extensive field" that included the "fountain-heads of science." He opened up to them a grab bag of learned pursuits: the study of antiquities, natural history, divinity, morality, "knowledge of the Hebrew scriptures, and of the oriental and other languages," mathematics, natural and experimental philosophy, "the medical art," and "the belles lettres."[6]

In the narrowed sense of literature that would soon prevail—the version I call "modern literature" because it was shaped powerfully by the paradigm of modernity, as the introduction explained—the only items in Bowdoin's list that would count as literary are knowledge of languages (as a support for literary reading), the pursuit of belles lettres, and perhaps the study of the Hebrew scriptures. Yet Bowdoin's grand vision for the academy harnessed literature to the Enlightenment in ways that would persist. One way linked national interests to the betterment of the world at large. Institutions such as the American Academy are meant to benefit both "*America* and the world in general," Bowdoin emphasizes, and they create associative links that extend people's sociable "affections" outward from their immediate communities to the nation and beyond. In a now-familiar imperial move, Bowdoin implicitly redefines the "world in general" as the "civilized," European-influenced world, contrasting Europe—"the most improved, and best accommodated, of mankind"—with Africa, whose Hottentots, like the "aboriginal natives of *America*," are inferior because of their "want of civilization, and improvement, and in particular their total want of literature"—presumably, their having no written body of knowledge, according to Euro-American criteria.[7]

A nonsectarian religiosity within a tacitly Christian context was also part of Bowdoin's charge to the academy, and it conformed to the long-standing tendency for U.S. public discourse about education and culture to be implicitly, if not explicitly, Christian. Contemplating "the works of nature" will lead the academy's members to reverence "the idea of a SUPREME MIND, the consummately perfect author of them," Bowdoin proclaims; he later references the "LORD GOD," veering from an elastic deist formulation to a conventionally Christian one. In other words, admiring the works leads to seeking and revering the author, a pattern that would be adapted for literary studies. Bowdoin's designation of "Supreme Mind"—better than our little minds but still something like ours—clinches the sublime circuit in which humans, confronting some immense Other, are both humbled and ennobled, achieving mastery through their capacity to reflect on the encounter. Put otherwise: Bowdoin models a way of experiencing the overwhelming magnitude of the universe, a magnitude encountered not only through direct observations but also through speculative awareness ("unnumbered worlds revolving in the immeasurable expanse; systems upon systems composing one boundless universe"). The tone of awe provides Bowdoin's crescendo, but his emphasis throughout on human intellectual capability establishes the moment of awe as a structuring counterpoint to humans' ability to grasp features of the universe. A taste for the sublime, an aesthetic fundamental to the narrower version of literature, was already at work in Bowdoin's evocation of the pursuit of the arts and sciences. The motives for pursuing study and scholarship woven together by Bowdoin would all accrue to the modern version of literature in place by 1850: the disinterested pursuit of knowledge; eagerness for practical applications of knowledge; the simultaneous cultivation of personal advantage, collective advancement, social affiliation, national progress, and world improvement; the pursuit of a higher form of civilization; and spiritual awe.

This older, broader sense of literature and the newer, narrower one I call modern both circulated in the latter part of the eighteenth century. Around the same time that Bowdoin identified literature with learned pursuits, it was also being associated more specifically with belles lettres or poetry and endowed with slightly different values and uses. Consider this excerpt from Adam Ferguson's *History of Civil Society* (1767), which was reprinted in the *Royal American Magazine* under the title "Of the History of Literature" in 1774, an instance of the continual circulation and reprinting of British texts in British America and the early United States. Ferguson identifies literature with the spontaneous productions of "genius" and sets out an understanding of literature as fueled by collective life rather than learning:

> Before many books are written, and before science is greatly advanced, the productions of mere genius are sometimes complete: The performer requires not the aid of learning where his description or story relates to near and contiguous objects; where it relates to the conduct and characters of men with whom he himself has acted, and in whose occupations and fortune he himself has borne a part.[8]

The bardic origin of poetry in tribal life was a familiar touchstone in eighteenth-century culture, establishing poetry as long-standing (in contrast to prose, which Ferguson and others identified with the time-bound progress of knowledge).[9]

Ferguson's Romantic-leaning account of literature was written and published earlier than Bowdoin's address, a reminder that periodization is a crude heuristic obscuring the complexities of historical change. Moreover, disturbing the periodizing myth that Romanticism emancipated those in thrall to rigid neoclassicism, Ferguson did not support the American Revolution, whereas Bowdoin was active in it.[10] Romantic-sounding ideas about literature in the eighteenth century did not necessarily conform to the next century's best-known versions of literary Romanticism. In keeping with his book's goal of celebrating civil society, Ferguson holds that "literary talents" (the ones necessary for creating "poetry") are best nourished by active participation in collective life rather than private study or pastoral retreat: "The most striking exertions of imagination and sentiment have a reference to mankind: They are excited by the presence and intercourse of men: They have most vigour when actuated in the mind by the operation of its principal springs, by the emulations, the friendships, and the oppositions, which subsist among a forward and aspiring people." Ferguson goes on to insist that "liberal endowments bestowed on learned societies, and the leisure with which they were furnished for study, are not the likeliest means to excite the exertions of genius," effectively opposing the institutional promotion of literature but still embedding literature in civil society.[11] Both Bowdoin's and Ferguson's versions of literature were oriented toward modernity, connecting literature with advances, forward motion, and aspiration. Their sense of literature as one of many modern accomplishments redounding to a nation or a protonational people also registered the emerging practice of organizing literature into national traditions.

The Problem with Poetry

One of the reasons why the narrower version of literature—modern literature—could present itself as long-standing is that it annexed the history of poetry.

During the long nineteenth century, it was commonly assumed that the earliest literary compositions were poems taking the form of songs or chants.[12] Since poetry became literature's anchor genre, and since it had been for Aristotle and others the metacategory comprehending other literary modes or genres (epic, lyric, and dramatic), poetry's history could be treated as literature's history.[13] In this spirit, René Wellek argued that poetry was the "confusion of literary genres," an ore from which the genres we know were gradually refined (and he thereby offered an early telling of the modern fable I rehearsed at the beginning of this chapter).[14] Poetics was one of the most important tributaries that fed into the theories of taste and aesthetics that shaped modern literature, and it later became as convenient to identify poetics with literary or aesthetic theory as it was to identify poetry with literature.

The history of poetry and poetics is important to literature, but the conflation of poetry with literature obscures the fact that poetry was transformed when it was turned into one literary genre among others, even though it is still often treated as the most literary. I'll be using the term "genre" loosely to indicate any formal distinction made between types of literature, since so many schemas of genres, modes, and subgenres have been put forth. Within modern constructions of literature, poetry was part of two schemes of classification. One divided literature into enduring genres: most often, poetry, drama, novels, and essays. The history of poetry was incorporated within literature when poetry became a literary genre and, within poetry, all poetic genres also became literary. In the other, newer scheme of classification, literature was divided into poetry and prose, bigger and looser categories given new classificatory importance. This division could bypass poetic genres and take the crudely empirical form of equating poetry with verse, so that writings might be sorted on the basis of line breaks alone. However, the scheme equating poetry with verse jostled uneasily with the sense that writings in verse or prose might count as poetic insofar as they were powerfully imaginative, regardless of their arrangement on the page.

Here and in chapter 3, I argue that we can learn something important about literature by considering why some of its important predecessors—poetry, rhetoric, and belles lettres—did not take on the role that literature came to play in the nineteenth century. In the case of poetry, as we've seen, an important issue was whether poetry ought to be defined primarily by the technical attribute of being written in verse or by an animating purpose that transcended the distinction between verse and prose. This ambiguity was vividly at work as early as Sir Philip Sidney's "A Defence of Poesie" (1579). Sidney famously formulated poetry's defining goals, adapted from Horace: "to teach and delight." The delights of poetry could make dry or challenging topics more palatable, and Sidney lists many authors from the classical curriculum who offered knowledge in the form of poetry (verse): "So Thales, Empedocles, and Parmenides, sang their naturall Philosophie in verses. So did Pythagoras and Phocillides, their morall Councels. So did

Tirteus in war matters, and Solon in matters of pollicie, or rather they being poets, did exercise their delightfull vaine in those points of highest knowledge, which before them laie hidden to the world."[15] Works of science, moral philosophy, military strategy, and governance could all be poetry if they were rendered in verse, although Sidney acknowledges that some critics would exclude these works because they are "wrapped within the fold of the proposed subject" rather than allowing the writer to follow "the free course of his own invention." (Concern about the kind of knowledge properly offered by poetry surfaces here, as well as the question of whether poetry requires unfettered authorial initiative.)

Elsewhere in his argument, though, Sidney identifies poetry with "feigning" and fictiveness, the activities of the poet as "Maker," rather than with "ryming and versing." He cheerfully disqualifies Plato's critique of poetry as deception by pointing out that even Plato's dialogues were effectively poetic, that is to say, fictive. Poetry's distance from verse is underlined by Sidney's turning to a discussion of eloquence on the part of Cicero and others. He chides himself for "straying from Poetrie, to Oratory," marking the distinction (authorized in part by Aristotle's twin treatises on poetics and rhetoric) but betraying the larger implications of the idea that poetry was defined by projects—imitation, delight, instruction, and the shaping of language—that need not be confined to verse or even to traditional poetic genres and that overlapped with eloquence, the domain of rhetoric.

Even Aristotle defined poetry ambiguously, arguing that it was grounded in two human instincts. One was the instinct of imitation (*mimesis*), assimilating poetry to the visual arts. The other instinct was a proclivity for "music and for rhythm."[16] Although the *Poetics* doesn't focus on this differential, the imitative possibilities of language far exceed the specific formal requirement of metrical composition, just as the pleasures of rhythm and other harmonizing uses of sound (rhyme, alliteration, assonance) can be employed for projects other than imitation. Since the kinds of mimetic enterprises and formal generic constraints that Aristotle goes on to consider could be satisfied in verse or prose, considerable instability was built into the definition of poetry.[17]

Sidney's defense circulated in eighteenth-century Anglo-American print culture, as did the problem of whether poetry meant verse or something more. Restrictions of diction and topic were also sometimes attributed to poetry, leading to William Wordsworth's famous pledge to include "ordinary" objects and language that had previously been excluded but were central to the poetics he and Coleridge unfurled in *Lyrical Ballads*.[18] In a U.S. periodical essay of 1789, for example, the anonymous author rejected the dictionary-style definition of poetry as "*the art of making verses, of lines or periods that are in rhyme or metre*" and followed one impulse in Sidney and Aristotle (without attribution) in inviting readers to "form a more noble and more rational idea" of poetry: that "*poetry is the art of expressing our thoughts by fiction.*" With this move, under the sign of rationality, the boundaries of poetry expanded:

> Every work...where the thoughts are expressed by fictions or images, is poetic; and every work where they are expressed naturally, simply, and without ornament, although it be in verse, is prosaic. The difference, therefore, between verse and prose, is perhaps not so great as between poetry and prose; for we frequently see prosaic verses, but never prosaic poetry, for that would imply a contradiction.[19]

Having distinguished poetry from verse, the writer goes on to reconnect them, insofar as verse offers some of the greatest pleasures of poetry. The argument that poetry can't be limited to verse but that the highest form of poetry is verse, also floated in Sidney's "Defence," would continue to be influential.

Verse as a formal feature draws attention to the material registers of manuscript or print as a medium: to visual layout and to sound. Verse thereby highlights the fact that language can never be reduced to an immaterial semantic or cognitive content. What our anonymous author calls the prosaic would often later be identified with the referential qualities of language, bypassing ways in which the sounds of words operate both as sensory inputs and as traces of the complex linguistic interrelationships by which particular words become meaningful. To the extent that it is still a compliment to call prose poetic, poetry is still associated with the richest possibilities of language as a medium, including its aesthetic potential.[20] Yet the association of poetry with invention persisted, as in Richard G. Moulton's iconoclastic proposal, in *The Modern Study of Literature* (1915), that poetry is defined by creating something new, so that modern novels "are in the fullest sense poetry" whereas "prose is limited to the discussion of what already exists."[21] Moulton's move shows that the earlier sense of poetry as a project bigger than verse (even free verse) continued to be available to challenge merely instrumental use of the categories of poetry and prose.

In hindsight, indeed, we might conclude that the more expansive claims made for poetry reached toward a way of distinguishing the aesthetic dimensions of written texts from the specific formal properties of verse. This tension within the category of poetry was managed, though not permanently resolved, by the invention of literature. The dyad of prose and poetry managed the flow of literature by confining poetry to verse and equating literature, in prose or poetry, with the operations of imagination and taste.[22] The category "prose" surfaced as an organizing category within literature at least as early as the 1780s, when Vicesimus Knox published the first of his blockbuster anthologies, *Elegant Extracts: Or Useful and Entertaining Passages in Prose* (1784) and followed it in 1789 with *Elegant Extracts: Or, Useful and Entertaining Pieces of Poetry* (and then in 1790 *Elegant Epistles*, so that the three great divisions in the composite version of *Elegant Extracts* were, oddly enough, poetry, prose, and epistles).[23] Later anthologies such as Rufus Wilmot Griswold's *The Poets and Poetry of America* (1842) and Henry Wadsworth Longfellow's *The Poets and Poetry of Europe* (1845) focused on poetry-as-verse and omitted writings that were not verse. Longfellow's

Poets and Poetry of Europe includes excerpts of dramas written in verse, in keeping with drama's long history as a poetic genre.[24] However, the anthology does not feature essays, novels, or short stories, with the result that Cervantes is identified in a headnote as "the immortal author of *Don Quixote*" but is represented in the anthology by an excerpt from his verse drama *The Tragedy of Numancia* and a set of poems extracted from *Don Quixote*.[25] Griswold's *Poets and Poetry of America* (1842) spun off his later *Prose Writers of America* (1846), just as Frederic H. Hedge's *Prose Writers of Germany* (1847) cast itself as a (partial) companion piece to Longfellow's *Poets and Poetry of Europe*.[26] The pairing of poetry and prose could also be used to regulate literary reading, as in Henry Reed's advice to keep "one's reading well proportioned in the two great divisions, prose and poetry," which he mapped onto the "admirable combination of the practical and the poetical" in the "Anglo-Saxon character." Reed drew support for his prescription from the Bible's combination of poetry and prose.[27]

Anthologies organized by genre and nation are designed to make classifications such as "poetry" and "American" operational, of course, not necessarily to inquire deeply into the nature of poetry or nationality. Nevertheless, collections such as Griswold's, Longfellow's, and Hedge's contributed to the process of analytic narrowing that eventually made literature rather than poetry the basis of departments of modern languages and literatures, and they implicitly set criteria for literary value keyed to excellence in poetry or prose.[28] A countervailing current at odds with the promotion of formal aesthetic criteria for anthology-making was the national project—grounded in the older sense of literature—of including cultural treasures and eloquent writings relevant to national life in national literary anthologies. For example, Evert and George Duyckinck's *Cyclopaedia of American Literature* (1855) announced the expansive purpose of "exhibit[ing] and illustrat[ing] the products of the pen on American soil" (a locution that allowed the editors to claim works written in the United States but published abroad).[29] The Duyckinck brothers' elaborate justification of this practice suggests that they recognized more selective criteria for U.S. literature, but they provided an influential model: indeed, their selection principles bear some resemblance to those of the Heath and Norton anthologies of U.S. literature, now that we have recovered an expanded canon.[30]

The midcentury practice of dividing literature into poetry and prose might be understood as the middle phase in a three-phase transformation of poetry during the long nineteenth century:

> 1. Poetry began as a conglomerated category identified with verse but often extended to other imaginative, fictive, or eloquent writings. There was no question that Philip Freneau's or Phillis Wheatley's works in verse were poems, during their lifetimes, but there was room for many opinions about what qualities made for the best poetry and about whether prose that shared these values could count as poetry.

2. In the second phase, a more uniform category of poetry defined as verse literature (including verse dramas) was distinguished from prose literature, and the more expansive characteristics previously attributed to poetry were attributed to literature. Lofty claims were still made about poetry's special imaginative status, but there was no question that prose could be imaginative and eloquent and (therefore) literary.

3. In the third phase, poetry was narrowed further by being identified with the lyric.[31] No one denied that narratives or dramas in verse were poetry, but poetry's most characteristic or most highly valued features became the features epitomized by lyric poetry. Complicating this paradigm, experiments in free verse (notably Whitman's) and prose poetry (especially by French poets) expanded the possibilities for what could count as verse and as poetry, but they continued to be formatted differently from mainstream prose.

This third phase caught momentum in the last decades of the century. As early as the 1840s, though, the tendency to identify poetry with rarefied aesthetics and luxury pointed toward a division of labor in which poetry (as ever more lyric) was figured in increasingly ethereal terms versus novels, which were cast as weightier, public-oriented, and designed to help readers live in society.[32] In this way, the division of poetry and prose helped to manage contradictions within the very idea of literature: aesthetic understandings of literature gravitated toward poetry, while public-oriented understandings gravitated toward fiction. And poetry—especially lyric poetry—continued to be the favorite literary champion pitted against utilitarianism and the sciences by literature's defenders because it best exemplified literature's aesthetic function of counteracting instrumental rationality, whereas novels became increasingly important conduits of public culture and signs of national cultural prowess.

Phillis Wheatley and the Transformation of Poetry

Modern literature's organization of literary genres and periods changed how readers read, giving them powerful incentives to forge relationships with some texts but not others. Once literature was projected backward as a way of organizing legacy texts, William Shakespeare became the type specimen of a literary author, and the English Renaissance was often treated as the birthplace of modernity, including modern versions of literature. Eighteenth-century works did not fare as well. The Romantics, who put their stamp on many ideas about literature, defined themselves against the previous era of literary production, even though they also relied on aesthetic philosophy from the seventeenth and eighteenth centuries. Shorthand versions of literary periodization commonly contrast Romantic beliefs in rule-breaking individual genius, organic form, and inspirations drawn from natural settings and simple people with neoclassical devotion to rules, the authority of tradition, highly conventional genres, and the forms of artifice and social pressure at work in the built world (cities and the court). However, this periodizing account appears to trace a change of aesthetics within a stable tradition of literature, whereas instead the nineteenth-century consolidation of modern literature retroactively demoted eighteenth-century writings within an anachronistic system of literary value. The practice of periodizing literary history meant that eighteenth-century U.K. and U.S. texts continued to be included in national canons, since every era needed to be part of this history, but the new literary dispensation that enshrined Shakespeare and wondered if we'd ever see his like again tended to hope that Alexander Pope and Ann Radcliffe would have no successors.[33]

Poetry was the genre through which nineteenth-century literary culture most vigorously distanced itself from eighteenth-century cultures of letters. Therefore, the distance between eighteenth-century poetry and nineteenth- and twentieth-century readers highlights the ways in which the invention of literature developed certain reading practices and tastes at the expensive others. The example of Phillis Wheatley's poetry is especially instructive because the late twentieth-century expansion of the canon gave readers incentives to reconsider her work, even though the Romantic-coded ideas about literature they had inherited fit eighteenth-century texts poorly.

In the 1970s and 1980s, reconsiderations of Wheatley focused mainly on two questions: whether she had "espouse[d] in any way the plight of her race," as R. Lynn Matson put it in 1972, and whether her poetry was aesthetically accomplished.[34] As I discuss below, the first question adapted a long-standing criterion for national literary canons before U.S. literary studies became "hypercanonical," as Jonathan Arac has put it.[35] Some of the best-known nineteenth-century literary anthologies included public-oriented writings that were eloquent or memorable writings bearing on important phases of national life.[36] Within the expanded U.S. literary canon of the late twentieth century, the value of Wheatley's poetry increased insofar as she could be recognized as offering testimony about slavery and racial oppression, fulfilling public-oriented literary purposes.[37]

"On Being Brought from Africa to America" was the Wheatley poem that most often troubled readers seeking testimony because it cast her enslavement as a "mercy" taking her away from her "*Pagan* land" and offering Christian salvation to her "benighted soul." Her use, here and elsewhere, of conventional imagery patterns valorizing light over dark compounded the danger that Wheatley's poetry would reveal that she was trapped in a "slave mentality."[38] As a result, for some readers of the 1970s and 1980s, Wheatley's writings offered a different but also valuable kind of testimony by vividly manifesting the power of slavery and white supremacy to warp the perceptions even of a prodigy, "Phillis Miracle Wheatley," as June Jordan called her.[39] Others proposed that apparently submissive features of the poems may have been ironic or strategic. They highlighted in "On Being Brought" other phrasings, such as Wheatley's reference to "our sable race," that might have signaled African solidarity and dissent from white perspectives.[40] Critics seeking such testimony have weighted heavily Wheatley's letter to Samson Occom, a prominent Mohegan leader, proposing that "in every human Breast, God has implanted a Principle, which we call Love of Freedom," a letter now routinely anthologized along with Wheatley's poems.[41]

Whether their Wheatley was brilliantly veiling subversive sentiments or tragically conveying the damage of slavery, readers in search of testimony tended to cast her as a lyric poet manqué whose expressive desires exceeded her opportunities, including the opportunities provided by neoclassical practices. The expressive desires at stake were expected to involve criticizing slavery, as if we know in advance not only why the caged bird sings but what she must be singing about. A poem such as "On Being Brought From Africa to America" can in this way be envisioned (Romantically) as the intimation or perhaps the ruin of the more fully and authentically resistant or angry lyric poem that might have been.

The assumption that writers of color must constantly perform race, including orthodox versions of race politics, has often been criticized, but the tendency to privilege their writings about race persists.[42] The omnipresence of the Occom letter in instructional anthologies offers it to readers as an interpretive key: Wheatley's poetry may not reveal as much about her experience of slavery as readers wish, but her letter to Occom offers a substitute instance of authentic personal expression.[43] Seldom do anthologies or scholarly treatments address the significance of the fact that this letter from February 1774 was published in several Connecticut and Massachusetts newspapers in the following two months. Rather than being a private communication between two people of color evading white scrutiny, the letter (in an era when letters often operated as news releases, official reports, and position papers) was made public soon after it was received and may have been designed for publication.[44] Even if it was not, the letter points to the difficult problem of assessing the pressures affecting Wheatley's treatment of slavery in her poetry compared with the publication of some of her views in another form. Wheatley's letter to Occom might strengthen the interpretation that "On Being Brought" presents white racism ironically, but it also raises questions about why the poem's treatment of slavery and racism was so tightly laced.

The other literary criterion engaged during Wheatley's late twentieth-century recovery was the aesthetic value of her poems. Really, though, the two questions were intertwined: the more likely it was that Wheatley was strongly critical of slavery but expertly encoded these sentiments in her poetry, the more satisfying late twentieth-century readers were likely to find her poems, grasped as dissident writings artfully evading censorship. Indeed, this approach made Wheatley's poetry much richer than other colonial and early national poems, which many late twentieth-century scholars of Wheatley found unappealing. "Phillis Wheatley was not a great poet; but then neither was the American poetry of the eighteenth century a remarkable literature," Matson observed.[45] Terence Collins, who thought Wheatley succumbed utterly to the dominant culture's "demean[ing of] blackness," judged that her poetry was "[o]nly occasionally worth reading for its aesthetic value (like indeed most Colonial poetry)."[46]

These critical judgments were very much like the judgments made of Wheatley's poetry in the nineteenth century. The century's consensus seemed to be that her poetry was as good as any other eighteenth-century early American poetry, all of which was not very good. References to Alexander Pope's pervasive influence seemed to sum up the problem, effacing the variety of eighteenth-century poems. The Duyckincks' *Cyclopaedia* treated Wheatley's work favorably but treated all eighteenth-century poetry with condescension. "Phillis Wheatley is a very respectable echo of the Papal strains [the influence of Alexander Pope]," they offered, including in their collection two poems from her published volume and three that had appeared in periodicals; they also praised Wheatley for being "for the time a kind of poet-laureate in the first domestic circles of Boston."[47] Griswold's *Female Poets of America* (1848) offensively noted, "If not so great a poet as the abbé Gregoire contended, she was certainly a remarkable phenomenon." However, even Griswold judged her poems "quite equal to much of the contemporary verse that is admitted to be poetry by Phillis's severest judges" (the use of Wheatley's first name marking racist disrespect).[48]

Clearly, though, Griswold doubted whether eighteenth-century poems counted as poetry in any way that mattered to him or his readers. Griswold and the Duyckincks included Wheatley as a canonical U.S. poet but marked the distance that mid-nineteenth-century readers felt from eighteenth-century poetry, and this distance was registered throughout the century.[49] The principal eighteenth-century U.S. poet admired by nineteenth-century readers was Philip Freneau (1752–1832), who outlived Wheatley (1753–1784) and was remembered for Romantic-leaning poems such as "The Wild Honeysuckle" (written two years after Wheatley's death).[50]

Racism certainly affected critics' treatment of Wheatley, in large ways and small, during her lifetime and in every generation after. The eighteenth-century conversation in which the Abbé Gregoire praised Wheatley as a representative of her race and Thomas Jefferson dismissed her on the same grounds (to be in turn dismissed by Gilbert Imlay, who was "ashamed" of Jefferson's "disgraceful prejudices") kept reverberating, and questions of her "imagination" (which Jefferson deprecated) and "genius" usually veered toward assessing Africans' capacity for creativity.[51] But the difficulties Wheatley presented to nineteenth- and twentieth-century readers were in many ways those that her eighteenth-century contemporaries presented, except that her contemporaries were not being scrutinized so intently because the stakes of their revaluation were not so high. These are the difficulties that led David Shields to ask provocatively, "Why is belles lettres the most profoundly dead of all the literatures produced in British America?"[52]

The late twentieth-century revision of the literary canon was designed to correct the exclusivity of the hypercanon, cultivating appreciation for the achievements of authors who had been excluded or marginalized. However, canon revision sometimes meant that the aesthetic criteria of old-style canonicity were simply applied to works by women, minority, and working-class writers that had once received literary attention but had more recently been marginalized. Not surprisingly, one strand of Wheatley's recovery highlighted her poetry's commonalities with Romantic aesthetics. For instance, in his 1988 preface to Wheatley's collected works, John C. Shields emphasized her work's attention to the imagination and its cultivation of sublime effects. Shields points out that in Wheatley's poem "On Imagination," the imagination, figured as an "imperial queen," is the primary capacity honored, whereas fancy and memory are both figured as subordinate faculties in a way that anticipated Coleridge's elevation of imagination. Wheatley's attraction to the sublime, nourished by her admiration for Milton, surfaces in her eloquent presentations of divine glory, vastness, flight, and other experiences of boundlessness that anticipated Kant's emphasis on magnitude as a characteristic of the sublime.[53] Wheatley's Romantic possibilities figure strongly in Shields's case for her work's literary value.

To be sure, Wheatley valued the imagination and had a penchant for the sublime. It's only the idea that these qualities are leading indicators of her poetry's value that I would dispute. Read as proto-Romantic poetry, Wheatley's work may not be very satisfying; neither is Pope's work or Freneau's work from the same years as Wheatley's. As Virginia Jackson has pointed out, eighteenth-century women poets did not write simply "poetry," in the presumptively lyric sense that came to predominate in the next century: "they wrote circuit-of-Apollo poems and imitations of Tibullus's elegies, *apologeia*, thankful or hopeful or regretful or devotional hymns, sonnet cycles, fragments, friendship poems, devout soliloquies, locodescriptive poems about particular places, and odes to particular friends or lovers or patrons."[54] That is, they wrote in a rich array of genres that were mainly eclipsed, in the course of the next century, by the homogenizing ideal of the Romantic lyric.

If we do not adjust our frame of reading to the culture of letters that Wheatley navigated, then we lose the opportunity to connect with the intellectual and affective pleasures Wheatley was likely to have valued and sought. I don't mean that we can recover an authorizing intention of Wheatley's, nor that Wheatley's poems must be confined to the late eighteenth century, where we can read them only if we first assume the mental equivalent of period costumes. But if we believe that texts in imaginative genres are valuable only insofar as they are literary in the narrower modern sense, then we don for reading mental equipment designed in the nineteenth century and marketed as aggressively as designer jeans. I'd argue instead that the value of Wheatley's writings (and that of many other imaginative writings, including recent ones) ought to be understood quite apart from the category of literature. Paul Giles, who has for similar reasons argued that "questions about sincerity and authenticity are the wrong ones to be asking" about Wheatley's work, proposes a fruitful reframing of her work: "Like Pope, Wheatley works not through autobiographical expressiveness but through ironic intertextuality and the subversion of formal genres, a process entirely consonant with the multidimensional capacities of prerevolutionary America, which traded off its position as a reflexive mirror of more established cultures."[55]

There are still important questions to consider about the power relations of race and gender that shaped Wheatley's career, but scholarship about Wheatley no longer has to be waylaid by questions of whether her work deserves to be taught and studied.[56] Scholars attending to eighteenth-century cultures of letters and the many poetic genres operating in eighteenth- and nineteenth-century culture have offered new ways of valuing Wheatley's work and entering into its pleasures. It's worth noting, however, that two of the most obvious ways in which her poetry departed from Romantic aesthetics were particularly significant for her as an enslaved African American female author:

1. Wheatley wrote many poems in conventional public genres: most notably, odes to famous people (including the Earl of Dartmouth, King George III, and George Washington) or prominent groups (students at Harvard) and elegies on the deaths of public figures (such as the evangelical minister George Whitefield). Her poetry was emphatically and legibly Christian, aligned with an established branch of Methodism. On Wheatley's visit to London in 1773, the lord mayor presented her with a copy of a valuable folio of Milton's *Paradise Lost*: the choice may well have registered not only her poetic stature but also her explicitly religious sense of her poetic vocation, which meant that she wrote to and on behalf of Christians (especially Protestants, especially Methodists).[57] The desire for a poet to voice collective sentiments on public occasions persists today, most notably in the role of poet laureate, but the Romantic sense that authentic poetry must be stamped by individual subjective experience—especially unorthodox, fugitive experience—has sometimes made it hard for readers to appreciate commemorative poetry. Hegel, who held "so called *pièces d'occasion*" to demonstrate "[p]oetry's living connection with the real world and its occurrences," nonetheless warned that the occasion must be only a "stimulus which makes the poet abandon himself to his deeper penetration of the event and his clearer ways of formulating it." Otherwise, poetry "seems...to fall into a position of dependence."[58]

2. Wheatley's elaborate classical allusions distinguish her poems from the personal revelations and vivid natural settings prized by the Romantics who followed her. Classical allusions—or at least the kind of ritualized allusion common in neoclassical poetry, allusions often criticized in the

next century as extraneous and ornamental—were sometimes treated as a form of unnatural constraint from which the Romantics had heroically emancipated themselves: Hazlitt's *Lectures on the English Poets* (1818) even proposed that Wordsworth and company turned the sentiments of the French Revolution against the tyranny of Alexander Pope, ending "servile imitation" and recognizing "a classical allusion...as a piece of antiquated foppery."[59]

I've emphasized Hegel's charge of dependence and Hazlitt's of servility because they highlight the special irony of Wheatley's situation. Exactly the qualities dismissed within Romantic aesthetics for marking a lack of artistic independence—Wheatley's assumption of public authority and her poetic performance of classical learning—were the qualities by which she registered her poetry's seriousness and resisted being defined by her enslavement. In late eighteenth-century North America, writing poetry was a form of public reflection and educated participation in civic life as well as a personal accomplishment that could become the currency of sociable exchange.[60] This is not to say that writing poetry, especially poetry steeped in classical learning, was not a form of serious artistic ambition, just that it was not an ambition set apart from public engagement and social contact.[61] Even James Bowdoin—president of the American Academy of Arts and Sciences, merchant, scientist, and statesman—wrote poems and published a book of poetry, and that volume of poetry, *Paraphrase on Part of the Oeconomy of Human Life*, was couched as a response to a prose treatise rather than as the product of spontaneous inspiration.[62] The position of college class poet was also an honor tuned to poetry's public significance, and a number of eighteenth- and nineteenth-century men of letters earned early public recognition in this way. For example, Hugh Henry Brackenridge delivered "The Rising Glory of America," a poem that he had written with Philip Freneau, at the 1771 commencement for the College of New Jersey (later Princeton), and Joel Barlow, graduating from Yale in 1778, delivered his original epic "The Prospect of Peace."

Wheatley's poetry demonstrated that she—African, enslaved, and female—could participate through her writing in public life and in social circuits of learned civil exchange.[63] Coming to terms with Wheatley's body of work requires readers to acknowledge poetic ambitions that were not cordoned off from other kinds of eloquence and even linguistic play. For example, Griswold reported that Wheatley "wrote with singular fluency, and that she excelled particularly in acrostics and in other equally difficult tricks of literary dexterity."[64] An example of this investment in poetry in the service of intellectual discipline—perhaps akin to the intellectual discipline conventionally derived from learning Latin and Greek—was her verse answer to a verse "Rebus" (1773). The rebus offers six clues in three stanzas, and the first letters of the correct six answers spell out "Quebec," referencing the 1759 Battle of Quebec, a decisive British victory against the French. The rebus has been attributed to James

Bowdoin, and the reprinted rebus and Wheatley's answer were the culminating pieces in Wheatley's published volume of poetry.[65] Wheatley's response—a play of wits involving recent history—was, arguably, an example of civic sociability conducted among people for whom verse could be a stimulating medium of interchange as well as a vehicle of freestanding reflection and envisioning. The invention of modern literature effectively truncated poetry's eighteenth-century repertoire.

The Genres of Literature

Modern literature was an ensemble of genres. Each genre was shaped by the ensemble as a whole and configured within it, perhaps in more than one arrangement. For example, in one arrangement, poetry and drama were the most venerable and prestigious genres, novels and essays more recent and lower in literary standing. In another arrangement, poetry and novels were becoming exclusively literary, since they could be judged good or bad as literature but had no other home base, and therefore especially literary, whereas drama was divided between (print) literature and theatrical performance, and essayistic writings were divided among literature, journalism, and many fields of knowledge. Just as poetry was reworked to become a genre and division within modern literature, essays, novels, and plays were retooled to operate within the complex of modern literature.

Perhaps because of the tacit premise that literature properly took the form of books, the design of books was registered in many beliefs about literature. The durability of books embodied the sense that literature was lasting. The way that postures of reading folded books into the space of the body, with books perched in a lap or settled on a table or desk, over the legs and oriented toward the curve of chest and head, contributed to the sense that books were personal prosthetics organizing an individual's intimate space. The gradual, layered encounter with the pages of a codex no doubt contributed to the persistent association of literary value with depth and fine discriminations. The accumulation of books led to libraries, and libraries pose the question of what is to be included in them, according to Roger Chartier: "The division between the books that one absolutely must possess and those that might (or must) be left aside is only one of the ways to mitigate the problem of the impossibility of a universal library."[66] Following this logic, literary canons may have developed as a way of regulating desires for possession and mastery stimulated by the material, collectible nature of books.

The stable holdings of a library are at odds with the dynamism of performance, however, and this tension complicated the place of drama within the ensemble of literature. The reflective, contemplative experience of private individual reading was prescribed as an antidote to the volatility of live performance, which brought the dangers of mobs and riots. Jean-Jacques Rousseau's 1758 critique of the theater may have been "perversely contrarian, penned at a time when theaters had become integral to urban cultural landscapes," as James Melton argues, but the charge that powerful collective emotions elicited by plays might be dangerous was often reiterated.[67] That theatergoing might stir up audiences fit the (public-oriented) conception of literature as a medium of national thought and feeling, but it made the authorities nervous. "The powerful nature of such an engine for bad or good purposes has in all times drawn the attention of the legislature to the drama," August Schlegel noted, and he warned of "dangerous abuses" in spite of his commitment to drama.[68] A famous instance of this danger was the Astor Place Riot of 1849, in which twenty-five people were killed in a violent conflict stimulated by competing performances of *Macbeth* in New York City.[69] Even William Dunlap, playwright, actor, and theatrical producer, argued that the U.S. government should follow Germany's example of sponsoring and regulating theaters in order to counteract the prevailing "licentiousness" displayed by prostitutes and drunks in the audience and vulgar spectacles onstage.[70] Antitheatrical prejudices channeled elite distaste for mixed-class audiences.[71]

Through a peculiar sleight of mind, Shakespeare—and specifically Shakespeare as dramatist—became the keystone author of modern literature around the same time that drama was moved to the fringes of U.S. literary culture, taking on the status of "bastard art" that Susan Harris Smith has examined.[72] By the latter part of the nineteenth century, commercial productions of Shakespeare's plays had been mainly sequestered within elite-controlled theaters maintaining strict decorum, and productions of Shakespeare's plays had become highly valued as resources for readers with a literary investment in the plays.[73] Even earlier, though, Shakespeare's plays were claimed for literature by being detached from performance, since many men of letters declared the plays were best savored in private silent reading, as if they were novels. Schlegel proposed in 1808 that "a dramatic work may always be regarded from a double point-of-view—how far it is *poetical*, and how far it is *theatrical*," as if the two strained against each other.[74] The literary enshrinement of Shakespeare's plays treated them as freestanding print texts rather than blueprints for performance. Shakespeare and other dramatists from earlier centuries were included in literary histories and literary anthologies, but drama after Richard Sheridan's *The School for Scandal* (1777) tended to be marginalized within the version of literature and literary history that was dominant after midcentury. (One important exception was Royall Tyler's *The Contrast* [1787], perpetually honored as the first U.S. play.)[75]

Just as nineteenth-century poetry departed from neoclassical practices, nineteenth-century drama left behind the last vestiges of classical regulation. One of the hallmarks of modern drama, clinched by what Sir Walter Scott called the "adoration" of Shakespeare at the turn of the nineteenth century, was the decisive abandonment of the classical unities, which continued to regulate

French theater long after their influence had dissipated elsewhere. The powerful influence of Aristotle in most matters made it especially important to find a way to bracket rather than disavow his authority on this one. Scott's "Essay on the Drama" (1818) rehearsed the reasons why the classical unities of time, place, and action were appropriate to the ancient stage (though, Scott points out, not always observed even there) but not to the modern, in which innovations in staging could accommodate changes of location and lapses of time.[76] Scott also moved away from Aristotle and Plato in insisting that whereas ancient audiences might have been deceived by the "illusion" of the stage, the obtrusive social and commercial machinery of modern theatergoing meant that audiences could not forget themselves: "dramatic representation does not present the illusion of reality" anymore.[77] Waving toward Aristotle's emphasis on *katharsis*, Scott reiterated that even without illusions, drama's "effects are produced by the powerful emotions which it excites in the minds of the spectators."[78] The belief that literature might be characterized by the power and intensity of the responses it provoked, registered most influentially in De Quincey's 1847 distinction between the "literature of power" (his focal point) and the "literature of knowledge," aligned the drama with other literary genres in spite of its anomalies.[79] Yet even William Dunlap's *History of the American Theatre* (1832) characterized the history of the theater as merely "connected with the history of our literature and manners," marking also a separation.[80]

U.S. drama began the nineteenth century as mainly poetry and ended the century as mainly prose, contributing to the growth of literature's prose sector. A knotty complication posed by prose, however, was that it was not simply a precinct *within* literature but also included many kinds of writings that were coming to be located *outside* literature. Griswold's preface to his anthology of prose announced that he conformed to William Ellery Channing's practice of counting "books of every description, whether devoted to the exact sciences, to mental and ethical philosophy, to history and legislation, or to fiction and poetry, as literature; though it is common thus to distinguish none but such as have relation to human nature and human life": here, in the context of prose, we see literature identified broadly with the book and the humanities. But Griswold went on to explain that in this anthology, "I have confined my attention chiefly to the department of belles lettres, only passing its boundaries occasionally to notice some of our most eminent divines, jurists, economists, and other students of particular science, who stand at the same time as representatives of parties and as monuments of our intellectual power and activity."[81] Such boundary crossings in and out of the most restrictive category of literature indicate that prose overflowed the boundaries of literature in a way different from poetry, which might be good or bad literature but had no recognized place outside of literature. Considered as not-verse, prose sprawled alarmingly.

Over the course of the nineteenth century, however, the category of prose was stabilized, and its relationship to literature was routinized. These things were accomplished through an intricate historical process that, like the transformations in poetry, might be broken down into three overlapping phases:

    1. Phase 1 was the distancing of rhetoric and oratory from literature, so that literature came to be associated primarily with print genres and with forms of interpretation focused on authors' intentions rather than audiences' experiences. Chapter 3 examines this shift more closely, but it was work in the tendency as early as the eighteenth century to identify literature with learned print texts.

    2. The second phase was the increased specification of the core genres of modern literature: poetry; drama; the novel and romance, which were taking on special significance as the overlapping flagship genres of national literary culture; and a number of short forms of prose (essays, sketches, tales) that by the end of the century had mainly issued in the short story and the personal essay. Certain long forms of nonfiction prose, especially works of history, sometimes counted as literary, especially if they were credited with narrative shaping and stylistic beauty, but they tended to be loosely appended to literature, not serving to define it or to elicit specifically literary practices of reading and study.

    3. Phase 3 was the reorganization of knowledge that laid the groundwork for the late nineteenth-century establishment of the modern research university and its disciplines. In this reorganization, fields such as history and philosophy became academic disciplines, and literature became a defining object of study within departments devoted to writings in national and imperial languages. As a result, writings assigned to other disciplines were likely to be excluded from literature or marginalized within literary studies. The tendency to differentiate specialized knowledge from literature, in keeping with De Quincey's distinction between the "literature of knowledge" and the "literature of power," can be glimpsed in Henry Reed's proposal in 1850 that "[b]ooks that are technical, that are professional, that are sectarian, are not literature in the proper sense of the term." Literature was addressed "man to man," based on "our common human nature," so it excludes "whatever is addressed to men as they are parted into trades, and professions, and sects."[82]

Essays also straddled the boundaries of literature. As a compositional form harking back to Montaigne, tracing a mind's reflective encounter with its world, an essay could be imaginative and eloquent, satisfying aesthetic criteria for literature. As a form oriented toward civil society and forming popular opinion, an essay could also serve public-oriented dimensions of literature. Moreover, the essay may have been the only literary genre for which nineteenth-century Anglophone culture prized eighteenth-century models: the age of Queen

Anne (from the late seventeenth to early eighteenth centuries) was hailed as the golden age of essays.[83] Many nineteenth-century writers followed Benjamin Franklin's lead in emulating the essays of the *Spectator*; Joseph Addison, who contributed to the *Tatler* (1709–1711) and the *Spectator* (1711–1712), was touted as the best English stylist well into the nineteenth century.

But complicating the status of the essay was the fact that it was, more or less, the medium of journalism, including journalistic staples not usually admired as literary. Standard journalistic forms that shared ground with essays—news reports, editorials—were instrumental, written for pay and often to order, structured fundamentally by the market conditions (and sometimes partisan loyalties) that literature was supposed to transcend. When Griswold praised the essay's high standing in *Prose Writers of America*, he envisioned an authorial stance that was discretionary and leisured, far from that of a working journalist:

> The Essays of a people are among the best indexes to their condition and character. They are often produced by minds transiently released from public affairs, when reflection and speculation employ powers that have been schooled for action. To write just treatises, says Bacon, requireth leisure in the writer and leisure in the reader. The essay is more fit for the nation whose energies and sympathies are lively and diffused. It flourishes most where some degree of cultivation is universal.[84]

Closely related to the essay was the sketch, which might combine narrative, description, and reflective commentary. Sketches, which entered the hypercanon through Irving's *Sketch-Book* and some of Hawthorne's works, were a popular antebellum form mainly displaced or absorbed by short stories later in the century. The essays and sketches most likely to receive literary attention were those that followed a scene or a train of thought—or both—rather than making polemical or scholarly arguments. They were also likely to be authored by writers with reputations in other literary genres, such as James Russell Lowell.

The most surprising literary development of the nineteenth century was that by midcentury the novel—formerly so disparaged—had become a literary mainstay. An anonymous writer in the *Anglo-American* recalled in 1847 an earlier time when "the novel, like the polecat, was known only by name and a reputation for bad odour." During that era (apparently, the stuffy eighteenth century),

> essayists,... over whose dreary pages many of our readers have doubtless yawned in the countless editions and imitations of the 'Elegant Extracts,' sneered magnificently at fiction, as unworthy to occupy the time which a man of intellect must spend in reading, much more in writing it....
>
> This state of things was completely changed in less than two years by the irresistible popularity of Scott. [*Waverley* was published in 1814.] Alike intelligible to all, and appreciable by all, he became at once as much the darling of the milliner's apprentice as of the *bas bleu*.[85]

Not only the elevation of the novel but also the sinking of the essay is at stake in this fable, although the animus is directed at the essayist as reviewer. Within Griswold's anthology of prose, an excerpt from William Ellery Channing titled "Literature of the Age" focused on fiction and poetry, adding to the novel's growing reputation as the most conspicuously literary prose genre.[86] The novel was the "single most important growth industry in the eighteenth-century literary market," according to James Melton.[87] It was credited with various ancestries, traced back sometimes to ancient Greece but more often to medieval Arab texts and European traditions of chivalric romance; Moorish Spain surfaced as an important relay between Asia Minor and Europe, a connection that added symbolic weight to *Don Quixote*'s traditional status as the first modern novel.[88] Whatever its backstory, the novel's significance in the long nineteenth century was bound up with the industrial and commercial nature of print, and concerns about the novel's influence on readers were keyed to the ready availability of print as well as to the absorptive pleasures of the novel form.[89]

As was the case with "literature," the very term "novel" was not really stabilized in the version we recognize today until the nineteenth century. Homer Obed Brown has pointed out that most of the eighteenth-century British works now known as novels were not initially classified that way: Defoe, Richardson, and Fielding "took great pains to distinguish what they wrote from what were then called novels." Fielding's and Richardson's works came to be known as novels "rather late in the eighteenth century," Defoe's works even later.[90] The eighteenth-century English writings we now classify as novels were likely to have been identified on their cover pages as histories or tales or romances or stories or (sequences of) letters, and the same trend held in British America and the early United States. The generic uncertainty registered in these works can be seen in Benjamin Franklin's difficulty, as late as 1771, in naming the technical innovation characterizing works such as Samuel Richardson's *Pamela* (1740), an innovation that Franklin traced back to John Bunyan's *Pilgrim's Progress* (1678) and which he did not confine to works we would now consider novels:

> Honest John was the first that I know of who mix'd Narration and Dialogue, a Method of Writing very engaging to the Reader, who in the most interesting Parts finds himself, as it were, brought into the Company, & present at the Discourse. De foe in his Cruso, his Moll Flanders, Religious Courtship, Family Instructor, & other Pieces, has imitated it with success. And Richardson has done the same in his Pamela, &c.[91]

Brown identifies Sir Walter Scott as the English figure most active in the institutionalization of the novel, especially through his prefaces for Ballantyne's Novelist's Library series: "[W]hat had been innovative but generically and socially problematic writing in the eighteenth century became, with Scott, a recognized genre that could be defined, edited, and collected *in a set*, and then described, imitated, and developed."[92] Scott's prefaces also started sorting what was properly novelistic and literary within earlier works from newly excluded features such as didacticism, which had apparently been quite satisfying for earlier readers.[93]

Scott's biographical prefaces about Richardson, Fielding, Sterne, and other novelists did not clearly distinguish novels from romances, but they discussed these works as developments within romance or developments beyond previous forms of romance.[94] Scott praised novels for moving away from the aristocracy, abandoning "the trappings of romance" in order to trace "the human heart" more intricately; for presenting "circumstantial detail" that contributed an "air of reality" to narrative; and, above all, for depicting vivid and plausible persons, offering an "accurate display of human character."[95] In an essay about romance for the *Encyclopaedia Britannica*, Scott explicitly departed from Samuel Johnson's assumption that the romance and novel were distinguished by subject matter (military fables and adventures in love and chivalry, for the romance; "smooth," less adventurous love, for the novel). Instead, Scott defined the romance as "a fictitious narrative in prose or verse; the interest of which turns upon marvellous and uncommon incidents" and the novel as "a fictitious narrative, differing from the Romance, because the events are accommodated to the ordinary train of human events, and the modern state of society."[96] His account paralleled Johnson's treatment of the novel as modern and the romance as a repository for lost possibilities, although elsewhere Scott participated in widespread uncertainty about whether the forms contrasted or overlapped with each other.

I'm emphasizing the ways in which the novel and romance were both linked and distinguished within Anglophone literary culture in order to rebut in yet another context the idea that an "American romance" tradition could be productively contrasted with the English novel tradition. Scott's essay about Henry Fielding would have given U.S. authors reasons to worry about whether they could succeed on Scott's terms: Scott identified Fielding's *Tom Jones* (1749) as "the first English novel" and praised the quintessential Englishness of Fielding's works, which took advantage of a scaffolding of social positions, roles, and rules that many believed the United States lacked.[97] The twentieth-century romance theory of U.S. fiction was a valuable corrective to a critical tendency to judge every nineteenth-century work of fiction by the model of *Middlemarch*, but it effectively masculinized the U.S. tradition in fiction (creatively reversing the tendency to feminize the romance and masculinize the novel). The writers privileged by the romance theory were men, and their reflections on epistemology and suspicions of cultural orthodoxies were implicitly pitched against a novelistic embrace of social normativity ("the middlebrow," for Richard Chase, who launched the romance theory) that was by reflex action feminized.[98] Even apart from the disturbing gender politics of this account, defining novel against romance in terms of national traditions loses sight of the extent to which the ongoing negotiation of the two was a complex transnational project, one dimension of which was a division of labor between fiction's potential to recuperate ideas and beliefs that had been marginalized or privatized within modernity, on the one hand, and its potential to take up modern concerns and examine modern ways of life, on the other.[99]

Genres set expectations for readers, including critics. Scott's delineation of the romance and novel served many purposes, but one was to establish more flexible standards by which works of fiction might be judged. He wrote passionately in defense of Ann Radcliffe, whose works had sometimes been dismissed as "fare of the nursery... the wild and improbable fictions of an overheated imagination" and found inferior to works by Richardson, Smollett, and Fielding:

> The real and only point is, whether, considered as a separate and distinct species of writing, that introduced by Mrs. Radcliffe possesses merit, and affords pleasure; for, these premises being admitted, it is as unreasonable to complain of the absence of advantages foreign to her style and plan, and proper to those of another mode of composition, as to regret that the peach-tree does not produce grapes, or the vine peaches.[100]

The analogy between genres and biological species would crop up often in nineteenth-century literary culture, and it assimilated the activity of critics and reviewers to the work of naturalists. Of course, the analogy could not explain why the birds that used to eat peaches had stopped liking them, or why the frame of mind in which one ought to eat grapes had come to be so elaborately regulated. In this respect, genres were more like brands than like species. They set readers' expectations and established forms of readerly trust or mistrust, and their fortunes were powerfully affected by reputational factors (including authors' literary standing and their coding as current or classic, outmoded or contemporary, timeless or ephemeral).[101]

The Two Canons

The creation of literary canons was advanced and stimulated by the production of literary anthologies in the eighteenth century. Poetry, the anchor genre, was also the genre whose anthologizing formulated early versions of English national canons. John Bell's edition of *The Poets of Great Britain: Complete from Chaucer to Churchill*, published in one hundred volumes between 1777 and 1789, was one such series; its better-known rival was Samuel Johnson's *Lives of the Poets* (1779–1781).[102] As Margaret Ezell has shown, such series capitalized on earlier publication and marketing strategies, including the practice of publishing miscellanies of poems and songs identified as the "Choicest" or "of the Most General Esteem Either in Town or Court" or (in a different key) as "diverting" and "entertaining."[103] In the last decades of the eighteenth century, series like Bell's and Johnson's became more common, targeting a particular genre within a national tradition and providing editorial apparatuses that located authors and works within a national sequence of historical periods.[104]

These early anthologies in literary genres were intended for commercial success, and it's useful to remember that there were many instructional works circulating before textbooks began to be designed specifically for school use—Quintilian's *Institutes of Oratory*, for instance.[105] The creation of canons, Jonathan Brody Kramnick has emphasized, was the product of an interaction between "restricted and large-scale culture," both of which involved commercial motives as well as somewhat disinterested collective judgments. Even scholars such as Colley Cibber and Lewis Theobald were involved in Grub Street's bookmaking, after all, whereas large sales over time could function as a "means of gauging literary achievement, the very test of time itself," as in the case of Vicesimus Knox's announced principle of compounding his *Elegant Extracts* mainly from works that had been anthologized before.[106] (Knox's *Extracts* nowhere announced a project of forging a national literary tradition, but apart from classical texts, almost all of his selections were by British authors.) These and other British anthologies circulated in the United States, inspiring comparable efforts such as Mathew Carey's *Beauties of Poetry, British and American* (1791) and Elihu Hubbard Smith's *American Poems, Selected and Original* (1793).[107]

As we've seen, poetry was a starter version of literature that became a key constituent of the literary ensemble of genres, each of which shaped and was shaped by the ensemble. The emergence of a transgeneric literary canon—actually, two kinds of canons—was also an important literary development. The novelty of constructing a general canon of literature across genres can be glimpsed in a review published in the Philadelphia-based *Port Folio* in November and December 1802. The reviewer held that Jean-François de la Harpe's published course of lectures on ancient and modern literature offered something "altogether new" insofar as La Harpe treated literature as a unified category of works "addressed to the imagination and taste":

> We have books which investigate the nature of the different species of composition—poetry, history, oratory: and deliver the rules for composing in each, with many excellent criticisms on the different productions of each kind, which have appeared. The plan of La Harpe is different. He supposes the general rules of criticism, and the nature of the different species of composition, to be already known. His purpose is to take the general principles and rules of judgment which have been established by philosophy and taste, and apply these to all the works of literature which are the objects of taste, from the time of Homer to our own.

For La Harpe, the reviewer explained, the set of works addressed to imagination and taste "includes every kind of literary production, excepting only physical philosophy, and the abstract sciences."[108] Literature was still a broad category in which one might expect to find empirical and theoretical sciences unless they were specifically excluded, but La Harpe's work moved toward a narrower category of literature keyed to the receptive faculty of taste.

Very likely, some of the *Port Folio*'s readers would not have found La Harpe's stance so very new, since eighteenth-century works of Scottish Common Sense Philosophy and (less widely circulating) German aesthetic philosophy also formulated taste and the imagination in ways that drew together works across genres. The French term *belles-lettres*, which was taken up in English, and its English adaptation "polite literature" were often used to signal a genre-crossing literary domain. Nevertheless, any major paradigm shift is likely to involve the shock of the new registered repeatedly in different versions, some of which are welcoming and some not, and some of which dispute whether it is even new. This reviewer's stance suggests that La Harpe's approach was new but welcome.

The *Port Folio* review is a good example of the gradual and dispersed invention of literature, in part because of this review's print history. The review was reprinted from an English journal, a common practice. It's curious, though, that exactly the same review of La Harpe's lectures was reprinted a second time in the *Port Folio* seventeen years later, in 1819.[109] There is no way to be sure, but it may have been reprinted because the innovation it praised was still being absorbed.[110] Beyond its foundational gesture of grouping together works that appeal to taste, La Harpe's published course on literature, which was used as an instructional text in France, emphasized two other features important to modern literature: a canon stretching far back in time and, within that canon, a pronounced attention to genres.[111] La Harpe's idea of literature was projected onto the ancients, as the passage above emphasized, and traced through time up to eighteenth-century French literature: Homer, Sappho, Dante, and Molière received extended treatments, aligned as exceptional authors.[112] This approach contributed to the process by which the modern version of literature acquired a long history.

The somewhat peculiar organization of La Harpe's work, which concentrated on ancient texts, French texts from the time of Louis XIV, and recent French texts, conformed to a wider tendency to delineate two complementary canons: an international canon of master authors—typically a small and select group I'll call a "supercanon"—and national canons that were more comprehensive. The attention La Harpe accords to Dante, who doesn't fit into La Harpe's chronological scheme very well, underlines the fact that the international and national canons don't divide neatly into ancients versus moderns.[113] For La Harpe, as for many later literary historians, the international (that is, European) canon offered touchstones for the development of taste: accordingly, the *Port Folio* review ends up checking La Harpe's assessments of various ancient writers. Whereas the international supercanon featured authors accorded the highest aesthetic merit, national canons were likely to manage collective memory, including understandings of the nation's political fortunes. The devotion of La

Harpe's central volumes to writings from the era of the Sun King resembles in this respect English literary histories from the same era that played up Elizabethan literature's associations with national conquest and prosperity. Then as now, national canons located authors and their works not just in history but specifically in narratives of the nation's might and fortunes.

The phrase "literary canon" became routine by the mid-nineteenth century, and it connected criteria for literary value with Christian and classical traditions of canon making.[114] In the Christian tradition as well as traditions of rhetorical instruction, canon making was an institutional enterprise crucial to the transmission of beliefs and practices. Within the Roman Catholic Church, the canon is the set of sanctioned scriptures—the Bible—that has been determined by authoritative councils practicing a high-stakes version of textual criticism and editing.[115] In official bodies such as the Council of Trent (1546), Catholic authorities sought to determine whether a given text was divinely inspired, which version(s) of a text had been transmitted most reliably, and which translations most faithfully captured the best versions. The results affected how believers understood the history and essentials of their faith, determining the founding document (and authoritative interpretive conventions) for believers and outlying representatives of the church, priests and monastics. The associations of biblical canonicity with the sacred, with authoritative rules, and with centralized institutional power (power also exercised through Protestant determinations of the biblical canon) are also legacies important for literary canons.[116] The biblical canon was a body of texts unified by divine inspiration, not a sampler, so it resembled the lofty international supercanon rather than inclusive national canons.

The nonreligious canons bequeathed by the ancient Greeks and Romans were structurally even more similar to modern literary canons, since they were in effect lists of valued writings (including orations).[117] A body of learned men in Alexandria, in the Ptolemaic era and a little after, set about compiling a record of the best Greek writings, establishing also the most accurate versions of the texts and correcting errors in transcription. They called these texts *hoi kānones*.[118] These men have come to be known as the Alexandrian critics, and their project of canonicity emphasized style, operating like the claim circulating in the nineteenth century that Joseph Addison "stood at the head of the literary canon" because he was "the best writer of the English language" (arguably, a rhetorical rather than literary version of canonicity).[119] The other chief ancient source for a canon was Quintilian, whose *Institutes of Oratory* (first century A.D.) urged orators in training to study the best models. *Institutes of Oratory* was rediscovered in the fifteenth century, and "Quintilian's rule" circulated as the injunction to read only the "best authors"; accordingly, Jean-François de La Harpe was sometimes called the "French Quintilian" for his canon-setting efforts.[120] Quintilian's topic was the education of orators, and he urged, "For a long time, too, none but the best authors must be read, and such as are least likely to mislead him who trusts them." He invoked criteria that would be important in modern literature such as "elegance" and "regularity of structure," and he treated works by genre (tragedy, comedy, lyric, elegy, and so forth).[121] The cultivation of virtue and good judgment was as much at stake in his selection as oratorical art, especially when he argued the importance of understanding the causes that famous orations supported. This emphasis on the contexts for eloquence would drop out of many shorthand references to his canon creation, as would his caution, "Nor must he who reads feel immediately convinced that everything that great authors have said is necessarily perfect; for they sometimes make a false step, or sink under their burden, or give way to the inclination of their genius."[122]

The heritage of canonicity offered supports for narrower and broader canons based on stronger and weaker principles of canonicity.[123] In the Christian tradition, some writings excluded from scripture were deemed heretical; unauthorized ways of interpreting the Bible could also be heretical. The sacralization of the literary canon, especially the supercanon, amounted to a strong principle of canonicity. In contrast, the rhetorical tradition's weaker canons were oriented toward practice, seeking to include texts from which speakers and writers could learn and relying on less stark and monumentalizing versions of canonicity. The biblical canon cast itself as permanent, although successive Catholic and Protestant councils revised the canon's contents; conversely, rhetorical canons were designed to admit additions and revisions, even though lasting criteria of oratorical excellence were put forth.

National literary canons tended to be organized into periods, and once periodizing narratives were under way, works were more likely to be considered canonical if they fit readily into the defining features of their period. Anthologies and histories of literary genres organized by nation often served as national archives, registering important phases of national experience or kinds of writing deemed especially representative of the national character (which was usually cast as a unified disposition, laying the groundwork for discordant populations to be marginalized).[124] Considerations of excellence or reputation were not suspended in national anthology making, but the timely vividness of writings was emphasized as well as, or sometimes instead of, their timeless value. For example, in Thomas Warton's *The History of English Poetry* (1774–1781), credited by René Wellek with being one of the earliest histories to focus on poetry in the modern literary sense, we hear that "[t]he first CHANSON A BOIRE, or DRINKING-BALLAD, of any merit, in our language, appeared in the year 1551." Warton excerpts this historic drinking song, which opens, "I cannot eat, but little meat, / My stomach is not good."[125] Long before the Heath Anthology, Warton's history of English poetry presumed that texts could be important because they captured something about collective life. George Ticknor's *History of Spanish Literature* (1849) was similarly structured by literary nationalism, offering a periodized literary history in which Ticknor traced "national" literary tendencies even in medieval texts.[126] Under the classification of "didactic prose," Ticknor included proverbs, works of botany, religious instruction, travel writing, and political philosophy, rhetoric, moral philosophy, and courtly manners, but he was careful to mark this last category as "[t]he last department in the literature of any country, that comes within the jurisdiction of criticism on account of its style."[127]

Anthologies of national literatures sometimes contributed to romantic nationalist efforts to ground the nation in folk cultures that had produced ballads and stories, as in Thomas Percy's influential collection *Reliques of Ancient English Poetry* (1765). They also gave literary attention to officially public collective experience and decision making, incorporating important national documents and speeches and pamphlets. A modern nation-state (as distinct from a dynastic polity binding its subjects primarily through fealty and conquest) was supposed to be defined by its citizens' sharing something—race, language, political culture, traditions—that made it reasonable to unite its population under the same government.[128] In practice, of course, claims for the unity and distinctiveness of any nation's population were ideological fictions that needed to be constantly shored up and adapted, and literature was often one of nationalism's supports.

A notorious early injury to U.S. cultural nationalism was Sydney Smith's volley, in the *Edinburgh Review* in 1820, "In the four quarters of the globe, who reads an American book?" Although the question has figured in U.S. literary history as a direct challenge to the literary ambitions of the United States, Smith wasn't talking about imaginative writings, and books were only one category he considered in an inventory of American culture that included American paintings, statues, medicine, chemistry, astronomy, manufactures, and so forth. Indeed, many Americans today might be sympathetic with Smith's chastising of U.S. pretensions to cultural superiority: he pointed out that European nations by 1820 did not tolerate chattel slavery at home (only in their colonial possessions, as he didn't mention), a fact that undermined Americans' tendency to play up their freedoms and identify the Old World with tyranny.[129] In any case, Smith's question and Americans' wounded resentment of it both took for granted that cultural accomplishments redounded to the nation: that they were indices of the nation's health.[130]

Within U.S. literary studies, Smith's question has been treated indignantly as a calumny refuted by the publication of Washington Irving's *Sketch-Book* that same year (1820): here, the refutation goes, was an American work of literature accorded international respect. Only zealous literary nationalism could credit *The Sketch-Book* straightforwardly to the United States, though. The volume's contents were written while Irving was living in England; the vaunted "American" materials such as "Rip Van Winkle," "The Legend of Sleepy Hollow," and "The Spectre Bridegroom" drew on Dutch and German immigrant cultures; and the volume included a number of essays about England, especially on Shakespeare.[131] Circumstances such as Irving's sojourns in Spain and his investments in literary traditions beyond English used to be treated as exceptions within national traditions, but we now understand them as outcroppings of routine transnational literary traffic.

However, the international supercanon that developed alongside national literary canons was not transnational, in our current usage. It was transcendent, although the writers and works of the supercanon were also assimilated within particular national traditions. The international supercanon guaranteed that literature itself was a stable and universal value operating across nations and cultures. The supercanon was also held to embody a universal standard of taste that could curb national vanities, but it was so selective that it was seldom used in this way. It didn't seem fair to compare most writers with Homer, Dante, Shakespeare, Cervantes, Milton, and Goethe, the writers most often elevated to the supercanon.

Shakespeare was the centerpiece of the international supercanon. Varying combinations of the other authors were included, the ones most likely to be omitted in the nineteenth-century United States being Cervantes (perhaps because his most valued work was a novel, a newer genre still generating controversy in the nineteenth century) and Goethe (a recent writer whose fortunes were bound up with Romanticism, also a subject of controversy).[132] Homer was the ancient and Dante the medieval figure ensuring that the scope and significance of the canon exceeded the merely modern. Dante and Milton were the writers whose inclusion signified that the canon incorporated the best of Christian culture. Molière was occasionally included in the lineup, but the overwhelming identification of Shakespeare with the highest possibilities of modern drama may have contributed to Molière's frequent omission in spite of the diplomatic desirability of representing France in the array.[133]

The supercanon was routinely identified as a set of authors, not of individual writings. These authors had all written large and ambitious works that enhanced their claims to literariness, but the veneration of canonical authors was personal, like that accorded to saints.[134] On the basis of the early starter versions of modern literature, it's possible to imagine an alternate supercanon (say) that would include the best work—if for now we leave aside the question of how "the best" is determined—in each valued genre, within the same Eurocentric context. Such a canon might include the best sonnet (composed, let's say, by the Polish poet Adam Mickiewicz, if the canon could stretch beyond western Europe), the best novel (perhaps still *Don Quixote*), the best tragedy (Sophocles's *Electra*, say), the best sketch (here would be Irving's opportunity!), and so forth. Alternatively, it's possible to imagine an international canon in which each nation was represented by its best-loved, most folk-inspired or folk-friendly work, in keeping with Romantic nationalism: maybe *Song of Roland* for France, Grimms' *Fairy Tales* for Germany, and Chaucer's *Canterbury Tales* for England. What we have instead is a supercanon permeated by the Romantic idea of authorial genius, therefore promoting the use of authors' biographies to regulate their works' interpretation: Foucault's author-function.[135]

Denton J. Snider, a U.S. literary critic whose career later chapters track, marked the sacred quality of the supercanon by calling its contents "Literary Bibles."[136] Variant supercanons had their partisans—Snider's omitted Cervantes and Milton, for example—and some readers were devotees of one or another supercanonical author: Snider mainly studied and taught Shakespeare, for example, but Dante and Goethe were most important for others in his intellectual circle.[137] Snider had studied Latin in high school and ancient Greek at Oberlin, and he spent his life learning modern languages so that he could read his Literary Bibles in the original.[138] Like many readers, though, he began reading the supercanon in translation, since the great U.S. translation efforts of the nineteenth century concentrated on the supercanon: Longfellow's translation of Dante's *Divine Comedy* (1867), William Cullen Bryant's translations of Homer's *Iliad* (1870) and *Odyssey* (1871–1872), and Bayard Taylor's translation of Goethe's *Faust* (1870–1871).[139]

The supercanon points toward the development of "world literature." Goethe's presence in the supercanon advertised that possibility, since around 1829 he had written an essay endorsing the prospect of a "European literature" or even a "world literature." The essay registered the interlocking roles of national and world canons, envisioning "a world literature ... in which an honorable place is reserved for us Germans," a world literature whose poetry is "cosmopolitan" but "shows its nationality." There were also traces of Kant's hope for a peaceable coexistence among nations in Goethe's vision: world literature would be nourished by the contacts already under way among nations, even contacts of warfare, but world literature would come to fruition "when the disputes within one nation are settled by the opinions and judgments of others."[140] World literature, in this vision, was international.

Longfellow labored very much in Goethe's tradition. Two of his most admired poetic projects, *Evangeline* (1847) and *Hiawatha* (1855), were valued at home and abroad as distinctively U.S. productions; *Hiawatha* may have been the best-known appropriation of Native American materials in the long nineteenth century.[141] However, Longfellow, as professor of modern languages at Harvard, was also strongly committed to the importance of studying modern European literatures. His anthology *The Poets and Poetry of Europe* (1845) reprinted works in ten European languages, all of which Longfellow could read at least a little: Anglo-Saxon, Icelandic, Danish, Swedish, German, Dutch, French, Italian, Spanish, and Portuguese. Although the anthology included very old writings, such as *Beowulf* and the Icelandic Eddas, it did not include Latin and Greek classics: Longfellow appeared to have organized his collection by identifying the modern national literatures he considered important and working backward through their vernaculars, offering a composite "literary history ... of various countries."[142] The anthology was loosely periodizing, identifying schools and movements and generalizing about the productions of particular regimes. Longfellow pioneered the approach followed by comparative literature for the next century and more, establishing grounds for comparing works, authors, and movements across nations but embedding works in national traditions.

The reciprocal construction of national and international canons means it should not surprise us that Denton Snider understood his Literary Bibles as a cultural treasure trove for U.S. readers in particular. He even jokingly referred to them as the "American Federal Union of the Literary Bibles."[143] His discussion exemplifies the process by which converting the past into "tradition" turns it into a discretionary personal resource for moderns. As Snider put it, "[T]hese Literary Bibles were finally traditional, handed down to us from the outside, being utterances, in form at least, of the European mind, not directly of ours."[144] It was both a privilege and an obligation for U.S. readers to appropriate the best of this tradition, Snider believed, and a selection such as the Literary Bibles made that task manageable:

> We cannot absorb the vast complex Literatures transmitted to us from the Past, yet we, as their heirs, must somehow get to know their scope, their essence, and appropriate their highest worth. It is impossible for us in our busy age to read so many books; they must be epitomized to their most concentrated values. The tribunal of the centuries has made and seals with its approval the selection of the Literary Bibles, which thus become text-books in the High School of Civilization.[145]

Snider, a former high school teacher, had earned his metaphor, which is cheesier than anything we'd expect from Goethe or Longfellow. Nevertheless, he shared their investment in an international supercanon.

A canon embodies a desire for mastery even though it marks subjection to a discipline. It marks the works one ought to know, since knowing them means taking on some of their power or authority as well as being shaped by them. A canon fends off the fear that too many works might deserve to be read and valued, along with the unsettling possibility that there might not be a surefire approach to becoming educated and cultured. The belief that there are too many books in circulation is often cited as a motive for canon creation in this period, but the excess of books can only cause anxiety in relation to a drive for mastery. Otherwise, having access to more books than you can read is no problem, like having more than enough food available.

As Snider's discussion of the Literary Bibles emphasizes, a canon also manages readers' relationship to history, and in this regard, the relationship offered by a canon might be understood as distinctively modern. A canon establishes the past—or rather, a particular version of the past, since canon setting always has ideological consequences. A canon implies that works of distant times and ages are available, in every way that matters, to the modern reader—available as commodities, however much literature is promoted as something transcending commodification. They can be plucked at will from the stockpile of tradition and made one's own, rather than being sites for volatile encounters in which even competent readers might risk failure or uncertainty, unable to be sure of whether something has been lost in the consumption of the concentrated vitamin-text.

{2}

Literature, Civil Society, and the State

> It is evident that without civil society, there could be
> no regular communication of thoughts, nor even a
> necessity for it; nor should we have manuscripts,
> books, and printing presses.
>
> —THE PORT FOLIO (1820)[1]

An ambivalent relationship to civil society has been built into literature. Woven from language in public circulation, literature has been prized as a medium of public thought and feeling, one inviting especially intense engagement yet offering also a certain reflective distance from the world in which it circulates. Equally, however, literature has been valued for its capacity to transcend its original circumstances and transport readers away from theirs, involving them in timeless universals rather than timely particulars. The interplay between these positions has meant that literature fosters enthusiasm for the creative possibilities of civil society as well as longings to establish a standpoint outside it.

This ambivalent relationship to civil society derives from literature's powerful identification with print, especially books. Some analysts have emphasized civil society's role in facilitating market relations, identifying it with the networks where information circulates and deals are made; others have defined civil society by its functional independence from both state and markets, prizing it as an autonomous domain in which views are exchanged and public opinion is formed.[2] Literature-as-print was affected by the state apparatuses that regulated commerce and allowed for the formulation of intellectual property; literature-as-print was also caught up in the special valorization of print as the lifeblood of the public sphere, which meant that print both sustained popular sovereignty and was subjected to state scrutiny. Print's double life as industrial commodity and vital public medium, oriented to both marketplace and state, has powerfully shaped understandings of literature. In particular, claims about the special protections literature deserves have been shaped by the legal histories of intellectual property and censorship pertaining to print. This chapter examines the peculiar transformation by which championing authors' (and readers') freedom from political and religious monitoring—the early form of aesthetic autonomy—turned into the belief that literature transcended economics and politics. This transformation increased the tension between literature's core supports, its aesthetic value and its power to inform public thought and feeling.

Print, Aesthetic Autonomy, and the History of Censorship

In 1820, Hegel located civil society as a zone of discretionary transactions between the institutions of the family and the state, but civil society had already been celebrated for some time as a self-consciously modern imaginative domain in which people pursued and exercised certain kinds of freedom.[3] Although civil society was forged in monarchies and colonial polities, a republican fantasy of the polis has always animated it. Civil society evokes debate and decision making conducted in person, as in the New England town meetings that Alexis de Tocqueville held to be characteristically American.[4] Yet civil society is also crucially conducted in print, and the informed reflection that is its hallmark resembles stances attributed to accomplished readers: "Read not to contradict and confute; nor to believe and take for granted; nor to find talk and discourse; but to weigh and consider," Francis Bacon advised in one of his aphorisms about judicious reading that circulated widely during the long nineteenth century.[5] The portability of print, far exceeding the scope of oral eloquence or manuscript circulation, allowed it to address and annex readers through their very attention: as Michael Warner has demonstrated, to read a print text is to become part of its public.[6] Given the geographic scale of the new United States, print was crucial for creating a sense of national belonging and circulating ideas and opinions.[7]

Surprisingly enough, civil society's connection with commerce initially counted as one of its benefits. The civility of civil society was cultivated as an antidote to the sectarian violence of the Reformation and Counter-Reformation, and promoters of mercantile capitalism argued that trade relations required and promoted peaceful sociability.[8] The idea that capitalism was rational, a mathematized form of reciprocity safe to practice with strangers, made it politically congenial to many supporters of republics and constitutional monarchies, although disagreements simmered on both sides of the Atlantic about particular economic issues such as free trade, currency management, and the mechanisms of banking. By the time of the U.S. Revolution, the scene was set for free enterprise to count as an important exercise of liberty that might also bring about social advancement and personal improvement. Hopes for civil society were in this way interwoven with ideas about commerce's capacity to improve the quality of life and about the political value of the mode of reflection and exchange known as criticism, which developed public opinion.[9]

Although Hegel's definition located civil society within the nation-state, civil society was also the foundation of the Republic of Letters, a virtual Enlightenment cosmopolity supported by networks of correspondence and print. The Republic of Letters was first mentioned in English by Joseph Addison in a 1711 issue of the *Spectator*, and it was an influential ideal in British North America and the early United States.[10] Devotion to the ideal could have national effects—as it did in the case of Benjamin Franklin, whose gregarious scholarly and political correspondence raised the intellectual reputation of the new United States— but it posited a public that cut across nation-states, even after Latin was no longer a lingua franca.[11] Correspondence was a central practice in the Republic, including correspondence among scholars scattered in different parts of the world who might never meet face to face, and civility was an important ethic shaping both correspondence and sociable exchange in salons, learned societies, and other venues.[12] Print was a crucial resource for the Republic, evidenced by the international circulation of book reviews and bibliographies. For example, Cotton Mather made use of *The History of the Works of the Learned*, an annual bibliography begun in 1699 whose subtitle says it all: *An Impartial Account of Books Lately Printed in All Parts of Europe: With a Particular Relation of the State of Learning in Each Country*.[13] Gordon S. Wood has emphasized how much supporters of the U.S. Revolution were invested in the Republic of Letters.[14] As an ideal that shaped real practices, the Republic also provided an important foundation for the international supercanon and comparative projects such as Longfellow's *Poets and Poetry of Europe*.

Amid this upwelling of investments in civil society, the Republic of Letters, and the frameworks they provided for peaceable and productive exchange, the Scottish Common Sense philosophers formulated theories of taste that were effectively theories about the value of art and literature in civil society. Common Sense Philosophy sounds like practical wisdom, but it was actually named for its assumption that people shared one or more indwelling capacities, in contrast to Locke's *tabula rasa* model of the mind. Locke's individualist, rationalist empiricism, laid out especially in *An Essay Concerning Human Understanding* (1689), raised the problem of how his building blocks, sensation and reflection, could provide a foundation for ethical responses and taste, which appeared to be qualitatively so different from these ingredients. Positing higher-level capacities with which all people were endowed, Common Sense philosophers such as the third Earl of Shaftesbury (Anthony Ashley Cooper), Francis Hutcheson, and Thomas Reid circumvented this problem. Although Common Sense Philosophy could and sometimes did ratify orthodoxies, privileging what those in charge perceived and believed in common, the tradition also valued the social and bodily locations of people's perceptions and responses, including their reading. The capacities and perceptions that people shared in common but could develop individually included taste and a moral sense, both of which mattered for incipient understandings of literature.

Common Sense Philosophy treated imaginative texts as shared resources for self-discipline and socialization. Imaginative works could be practice grounds for moral responsiveness and taste, extensions or simulations of the social world that might provide "instructive moral examples of taste, sympathy, and discreet as well as indiscreet character."[15] Common Sense approaches harnessed mimetic texts to practices of ethical invigilation but also treated them as significant expressions and reflections of collective life. For Adam Smith, whose moral philosophy dovetailed with that of Common Sense, reading added to the store of experiences that allowed people to formulate rules for ethical conduct, so that when we "read in history or romance the account of actions either of generosity or baseness," such accounts are added to our direct experience, eliciting reactions of approval or disapproval and inductively shaping our working ethical principles.[16]

Common Sense provided a philosophical account of the value of imaginative texts in civil society, a rationale aligning with the principle emerging on the Continent that artists, including writers, offered forms of truth and insight that should not be coerced or censored. In his letters in *On the Aesthetic Education of Man* (1794), Friedrich Schiller emphasized the right of artists not to be coerced by political authorities:

> Art, like Science, is absolved from all positive constraint and from all conventions introduced by man; both rejoice in absolute immunity from human arbitrariness. The political legislator may put their territory out of bounds; he cannot rule within it. He can proscribe the lover of truth; Truth itself will prevail. He can humiliate the artist; but Art he cannot falsify.[17]

Schiller's account registers his awareness that art was in fact subject to regulation and censorship, and this context of political repression in Euro-America helps account for the strange transformation by which the principle of aesthetic autonomy, which initially emphasized the rights of art and artists not to be legislated or constrained, somehow developed into the belief that even artists' uncoerced, independent political convictions ought to be excluded from their work.

One context for this shift was the influence of Immanuel Kant's philosophy, which was forged in opposition to Common Sense Philosophy and ultimately eclipsed it. The zone of disputation between Common Sense Philosophy and Kant's philosophy roughly corresponded to the domain of literary culture organized by the tension between public-oriented and aesthetic understandings of literature. Viewed more comprehensively, though, Common Sense theories of taste were also aesthetic theories, just as Kant's project of determining what was universally good, true, and beautiful had the potential to impact public, collective life: I'm offering a heuristic distinction between public-oriented and aesthetic understandings of literature (or dimensions of literary culture) that in practice were often amalgamated.[18] It's important that Kant's aesthetic thought was forged under the regime of Frederick II of Prussia (1712–1786), however. Transplanted to Prussia, where by the latter part of the eighteenth century a British settlement had sprung up to manage the trade in Baltic timber on behalf of the Royal Navy, Common Sense thought entered into not only a different set of philosophical conversations but also a different political world, one where the republican possibilities circulating in Scotland could not be entertained.[19] In contrast to the comparative openness known, in the wake of the Glorious Revolution, as English liberty, Frederick the Great held that "the affairs of government were necessarily opaque and incomprehensible to everyone outside the king and his inner circle (he himself went so far as to arrange the abduction and beatings of foreign journalists who thought otherwise)," according to James Van Horn Melton.[20] Kant endorsed independent thought, but he probably recognized that "enlightenment was progressing [in Prussia] to the extent that Frederick permitted it."[21] Kant's philosophy cannot be reduced to the political exigencies he faced, but his emphasis on the private and transcendent experience of art effectively insulated art from political regulation by insulating it from political import. Through Kant's influence, Anglophone culture may have been impacted by Prussian repression at second-hand.

However, there was no shortage of direct political repression in the United States and Great Britain. From the Revolutionary era through at least the 1790s, U.S. writers and readers had powerful incentives to create nonpartisan print spaces, partly due to the threat of government prosecution but also because political (and religious) culture could be so contentious. Early U.S. law was strongly influenced by British legal codes and common law as well as legal scholarship such as William Blackstone's *Commentary on the Laws of England* (1765–1769), and on both sides of the Atlantic, printed matter was subject to censorship.[22]

In British America, colonial governments prosecuted works they thought would undermine their authority, leading some colonial writers to seek publication in England, where the authorities were not always tuned in to internal colonial politics.[23] The eighteenth-century love of pseudonyms—classical epithets such as "Publius" or fictional personae such as Benjamin Franklin's creation "Silence Dogood"—served many purposes, but protection from prosecution was an important one. In England, "Junius," who criticized the government in a series of anonymous letters published between 1769 and 1772, escaped prosecution only because his true identity was not discovered.[24] Authors were wary, but printers were much more likely to be prosecuted than authors. James Franklin was punished for publishing criticisms of the Massachusetts colonial government in his newspaper, although his strategic response demonstrates that colonists also found ways to evade state control. After he was forbidden to publish the paper, he transferred the proprietorship of the *New-England Courant* to his younger brother Benjamin, igniting Benjamin Franklin's lifelong support for freedom of the press.[25] Royal governors and assemblies in New England had fairly comprehensive powers to censor what was published, so sentiment for freedom of the press was important to supporters of the Revolution.[26]

Nonetheless, state regulation of speech, assembly, and publication continued after the Revolution, aggravated perhaps by the new government's insecurity. The First Amendment to the U.S. Constitution protects all these freedoms, but its early implementation brought only a little loosening of state repression.[27] The crime for which James Franklin had been prosecuted, seditious libel, was prosecuted aggressively and feared on both sides of the Atlantic even after the Bill of Rights was passed. Seditious libel was the publication of subversive ideas and sentiments: ideas that bred insurrection or undermined confidence in rulers.[28] Although we think of libel as blameworthy because it is false or misleading, seditious libel was defamation that unsettled established authority—exciting "discontent" or "tending to disturb the public peace, by vilifying the government, or otherwise exciting the subject to revolt."[29] That the defamation was true did not become a viable defense against seditious libel in the United States until 1803.[30] Because the private reputations of officeholders contributed to the stability of government, published writings that tarnished the reputations of officeholders were thought to weaken government (rather than, say, to strengthen it by exposing corruption).[31] In keeping with this logic, Charles Brockden Brown, during his legal studies in the early 1790s, took up the question "[i]s falsehood necessary to constitute a libel against the chief magistrate of a state?" and prepared a dutifully authoritarian answer (which we can hope did not represent his best thinking about the issue), noting that the libeler has "committed a double injury. He has...endangered the reputation of a private citizen, and hazarded a violation of the public peace."[32] In the authoritarian climate of the 1790s, Brown's friend Elihu Hubbard Smith even worried about being prosecuted under a statute against blasphemy because he read works by irreligious philosophers.[33]

The threatening government scrutiny of print during the 1790s—early in what I'm calling the long nineteenth century—provides an important context for why aesthetic autonomy came to mean literature's staying out of politics. The Terror in France, the Revolution's bloodthirsty form of homeland security, along with rumors of subversive secret societies such as the Illuminati prompted paranoid reactions on the part of governments in Europe and the United States; the Haitian Revolution got less attention, but it contributed to fears of slave insurrections and hemispheric instability.[34] Stricter laws against sedition and treason were passed in England during the 1790s, and the harassment and repression of radicals there intensified.[35] Print was treated as especially dangerous: indeed, there were charges in England and Germany that lending libraries spread "seditious revolutionary propaganda."[36] Authors began to be targeted for prosecution along with printers, no doubt because (as the next section details) their rights to own their compositions threw them into greater prominence. A sign of the growing public sense that authors were more responsible than printers for words that got into print was an English jury's ruling in the case of Henry Woodfall, who had published Junius's letters in his newspaper. Junius's identity being unknown, Woodfall was the only person available to take the fall; the jury's apparently reluctant verdict was "[g]uilty of printing and publishing only," which resulted in legal complications that let Woodfall off the hook.[37] In England, a number of English radical writers, including Thomas Hardy (founder of the workingmen's London Corresponding Society, which the government declared illegal in 1799), William Cobbett, and Thomas Paine (in absentia), were prosecuted in highly publicized trials in the 1790s and early 1800s. Few of these men were punished on the basis of what they wrote, but a number of people involved in the London Corresponding Society and similar organizations were transported or imprisoned.[38]

In the United States around the same time were passed the severe Alien and Sedition Acts of 1798, which also tripped up the Franklin family: Franklin's grandson Benjamin Franklin Bache, publisher of the Jeffersonian newspaper *Aurora*, was arrested and jailed because of his paper's criticisms of President Adams.[39] Short-lived though they were, these laws amounted to a frightening crackdown, and versions of them have been revived in the United States during subsequent times of war.[40] Prosecutions for seditious libel under state laws continued after the Sedition Act lapsed in 1801: even though Jefferson was elected partly in reaction against the severity of the Alien and Sedition Acts, *Port Folio* editor Joseph Dennie was convicted in 1803 of seditious libel because of a paragraph bemoaning the tendencies of implicitly Jeffersonian "democracy" to promote "civil war, desolation, and anarchy."[41]

The print works prosecuted in England and the United States under these laws were mainly newspapers and overtly political books and pamphlets, but contemporary imaginative writings also took up matters of political significance. Many poets wrote straightforwardly as Federalists (such as Timothy Dwight and the Connecticut Wits) or Jeffersonians (such as Philip Freneau and, eventually, Joel Barlow), and in 1808, the teenaged William Cullen Bryant's first publication was a poem opposing Jefferson's embargo of Great Britain and France during the Napoleonic Wars. (The poem lamented the corruptions of "faction" and offered an apostrophe to "Much injur'd Commerce!")[42] Many early U.S. novels announced in subtitles and prefaces that they were patriotic and civic-minded, typically through bland means such as promoting "virtue" which nonetheless emphasized fiction's potential to shape public culture. More volatile were gothic novels, including Charles Brockden Brown's conspiracy-filled novels of the '90s, which played out forms of fear, paranoia, and aggression with political dimensions.[43]

Hawthorne's "Custom-House" preface to *The Scarlet Letter* has been highlighted by Jonathan Arac as a foundational moment in the development of literature because of Hawthorne's boldness in claiming imaginative leeway for his romance, versus the earlier tradition of novels explicitly conscripted for nation building. Although my study points to more widespread and gradual processes at work in literature's invention, Arac is right that Hawthorne's preface registers a project quite different from the civic republican motives registered in many novels of the early national period. I'd argue that the narrowing of aesthetic autonomy prepared the way for Hawthorne's stance, and the narrowing may have been at work in Brown's brief but intense career as novelist, which offers an earlier instructive example.[44]

Brown's novels capture not only the political turbulence of the era but also public concerns about deception and demagoguery. In 1799, almost half a century before Hawthorne was fired from his position as surveyor when the Whigs took power and took up writing romances, Brown's novelistic career made an analogous swerve away from controversy. Brown's first four novels—*Wieland* (1798), *Ormond* (1799), *Arthur Mervyn* (1799), and *Edgar Huntly* (1799)—grapple with the political ideas of William Godwin, whose *Enquiry concerning Political Justice* (1793) shared in the energies of the French Revolution by radically calling into question government itself, laying groundwork for anarchism and libertarianism. Godwin found many features of the liberal status quo pernicious: the institution of individual property, its protection by law and government, and the tendency for law and government to serve wealth and power. Godwin's *Things as They Are; or, Caleb Williams* (1794) was recognized as a fictional "companion volume" to his *Enquiry*, marking the intimacy between novels and politics, and Godwin's novel has long been recognized as an important influence on Brown.[45] A Godwinian attention to abuses of power vies in Brown's novels with an anti-Godwinian depiction of the dangers that result when individuals step utterly outside social ties and conventions (as in the case of the seducer Ormond and the murderous zealot Theodore Wieland, in *Ormond* and *Wieland*). Moreover, these novels frequently highlight connections among the U.S. Revolution, the French Revolution, and the Haitian Revolution, thereby keeping alive a sense of the contingency and disturbing violence of the U.S. Revolution.

Brown's preface to *Wieland* (subtitled *An American Tale*) emphasizes that the events of that novel are "extraordinary" but have real-world precedents: Brown does not claim to have created a world elsewhere but rather to have examined the instructive possibilities of events that are not typical but also not impossible. His four early novels explore politically charged topics such as the relationship between persuasion and seduction, dramatizing anxieties about popular sovereignty and about how individual and collective wills are formed. Brown's later two novels, *Clara Howard* (1801) and *Jane Talbot* (1801), are very different. As Robert S. Levine has pointed out, the narrow time frame in which all Brown's novels are written ought to discourage us from insisting too strongly on periodizing his career.[46] But Brown's shift from novels named for men (assuming that *Wieland* references the murderous Theodore Wieland rather than his sister Clara, the narrator) to novels named for women aligns with the prominence of marriage plots in the later novels, with the result that Brown seems to careen from Ann Radcliffe's neighborhood to Jane Austen's. Brown's trademark international scope and his wild plotting are still in evidence, but the later novels promote prudence and conventional ideas of personal responsibility. For example, the widowed Jane Talbot and her suitor Henry Colden are initially precluded from marrying because their families disapprove of the match and threaten to disinherit them. Various misunderstandings ensue, but the tepid resolution is the marriage of two relatively mature persons who won't be disinherited after all. This marriage plot does not represent an Ian Watt-style important social or political merger, and the book's exploration of the importance and fragility of reputation is not linked to the kinds of potent epistemological, ethical, and political questions that attended it in Brown's earlier novels.[47] Marriage plots need not be boringly conventional, but Brown's are.

Brown's swerve away from Godwin's influence moved his work away from speculative political topics. In the contentious political culture of the turn of the century, he began to minimize controversy and sensation. Jared Gardner has pointed out that what critics have often interpreted as Brown's withdrawal from literature, meaning from novel writing, might more fruitfully be understood as an energetic turn to the magazine, which Gardner presents as a more promising literary form. Brown's magazine editing represented a collaborative endeavor that was a peculiarly appropriate national form, "an attempt to replicate in print the intimacies, conversations, politics, and aesthetics of the club and the coffeehouse."[48] Gardner's argument wonderfully captures the ways in which print was tasked with adapting for large-scale civil society functions that used to be performed in live conversation. And although he doesn't acknowledge that the very category of literature was transforming, he is right to point out the thoughtlessness of treating Brown's novels as more literary than his magazine work.

Magazine work nonetheless also moved Charles Brockden Brown away from the disturbing political speculations of his early novels. As Gardner acknowledges, magazines after the Revolution mainly distanced themselves from the strongly partisan stances of newspapers.[49] The early United States fostered some public forums that were fiercely partisan, such as the gatherings and print circuits that launched and maintained the Federalist and Democratic-Republican Parties, and others that were strictly nonpartisan, spaces in which divisive topics were deliberately ruled out of bounds.[50] *The Constitution of the Free-Masons* (1734), printed by Franklin, forbade Masons to bring into the organization private quarrels about "*Religion*, or *Nations*, or *State Policy*." Likewise, the Tuesday Club of Annapolis (1745–1756) passed a ruling requiring "the membership to laugh down anyone making direct reflections on matters of church or state."[51] The management of the public sphere required venues in which people could develop opinions and find solidarity as well as venues in which people could gather sociably for interchange that left aside their primary political and religious commitments.

Print periodicals provided both kinds of spaces, since newspapers mainly were partisan, as were the major British *Reviews*, and magazines mainly were not.[52] The magazine, an invention of the early eighteenth century, was associated with variety, the term having originally designated a storehouse for goods.[53] The nonpartisan stance announced by the *Port Folio* in 1814 (after Dennie's death) was embraced by many magazines and some reviews: "The work will, as heretofore, consist principally of original and well written papers, in every department of literature and science. Party politics, however, polemical theology, and every topic calculated to inflame the passions and to nurture animosities, rather than to improve the intellect or amend the heart, will be rigidly excluded."[54]

The need to find respite from political polarization may have coincided with the desire to avoid censorship or public opprobrium (which led William Godwin into seclusion), and both may have contributed to Brown's swerve into domestic fiction and then magazine editing. The intense scrutiny of speech, writing, and print under way in the turn-of-the-century United States is registered by Tunis Wortman's *A Treatise concerning Political Enquiry, and the Liberty of the Press* (1800). Wortman powerfully captured the strange character of the times, in which events "attended with terrifying convulsions" were nonetheless "peculiarly calculated to excite the attention, and to awaken the energies of Mind." He urged greater latitude for public thought, in speech and print, among other reasons so that the study of "civil society" could be advanced along with her "sister sciences." He also pugnaciously described "the history of prosecutions for libel" as demonstrating that "[g]overnments are impatient of contradiction; that they are not so zealous to punish Falsehood from an enlightened and disinterested attachment to Justice, as they are ready to smother opinions that are unfavorable to their designs." Nevertheless, even this strong proponent of freedom of the press identified "Literary Associations" devoted to learning and scholarship (apparently not literary in the narrower sense) as potentially dangerous:

> Literary Associations are particularly adapted to discussion: but it is not to be denied that they may be rendered subservient to improper purposes. In the present state of Society they may become the theatres of intrigue and cabal. Wherever they exist their conduct should be vigilantly observed. Still an attempt to suppress them would be highly dangerous and tyrannical. It is not until they burst out into inflammatory conduct, or exhibit violent symptoms of disorder, that the magistrate should exercise coercion; and even then it is to be understood that the outrage, and not the association, is the genuine object of such coercion.[55]

As Paul Keen has argued about British culture in the 1790s, "Central to the claim for the autonomy of literature as a public sphere free from government control was the conviction that rational individuals were capable of exchanging ideas, however radically misconceived, without being tempted into acting on them."[56] Somehow, though, it began to be expected that the works' very design, especially the quality of aesthetic distance, would insulate readers from any very strong or direct promptings to action.

As the requirement that art ought not to be coerced by rulers turned gradually into the requirement that art be untouched by artists' convictions, public-oriented understandings of writing and speech were increasingly subordinated—though never eliminated—within the emerging understanding of modern literature. The revolutions and counterrevolutionary crackdowns of the late eighteenth century contributed to a climate in which people who cared about art tried to protect it from regulation and censorship by declaring it hors de combat: fundamentally incapable of fomenting political unrest or dissent. Guarding a space for imaginative experimentation under governments wary of revolution—and among citizens weary of polarization—seemed to require stipulating that the aesthetic subject was completely separate from the citizen capable of rabble-rousing. In the early nineteenth century, public aesthetic discourse was also shaped by some writers who were horrified by the French Revolution, moved rightward personally, and wished to insulate literature from any complicity with political imaginings that might turn violent: Wordsworth and Coleridge might fit this profile, along with Brown, who wrote an anonymous pamphlet criticizing Jefferson's administration.[57] William C. Dowling argues that the Federalists, having lost their ascendancy, became invested in literature as a refuge from "party passions," so it is possible that the politically dispossessed, left and right, may have cultivated literature's separation from politics because it allowed them to wield cultural authority while enjoying latitude for unpopular views.[58]

Literature in the Marketplace

Aesthetic autonomy was initially put forward to protect art and literature from repression and censorship, even though this protection eventually jammed literature's transmission of public thoughts and feelings. However, aesthetic autonomy was also designed to offset the damaging effects of art's circulation in the form of commodities or commercial exhibits. Indeed, Common Sense's philosophy of taste and Kant's aesthetic philosophy were both designed to enhance and integrate human capacities (in the best tradition of Alexander Baumgarten's *Aesthetica* [1750], which launched aesthetics as the "science of sensual cognition")[59] by providing experiences of the world uncontaminated by desires for acquisition. Shaftesbury in 1711 identified virtuous action with disinterested action and contrasted the capacity to recognize and enjoy beauty with "brutes[']" fixation on getting "their own share."[60] As its name suggests, the ethic of disinterestedness was designed to offset the operations of self-interest, offering a relation to the world that wasn't organized around acquisition and possession.[61] The kind of imaginative projection and cross-checking of judgments invited by the Common Sense tradition tried to bypass self-interest by multiplying the vantage points and sites of identification available to a perceiver. Kant sought disinterestedness another way, distinguishing the perception of true or ideal beauty from mere pleasurable sensations or judgments of what a perceiver finds agreeable (which might be compromised by self-interest) and requiring ideal beauty to be universal.[62] His approach also deemphasized the role of "sensual experience" in aesthetic apprehension, however.[63]

Just as literature was insulated from political scrutiny by being declared apolitical, literature was exempted from the effects of commodification by being declared to transcend it.[64] The legal context in which literary works became property and authors proprietors represented another route through which literature was subjected to state power, and this context also influenced the development of aesthetic autonomy. Belief in aesthetic autonomy led to a delicate doublethink in which serious artists were expected to support themselves by their work but not to design their writings primarily for sale.

Scholars of print culture have long recognized that the legal rights of authors emerged as a result of market competition among printers. Invoking the author's continuing connection to his or her writings was a way of establishing the injustice of perpetual copyright for printers who hoped that other printers' monopolies would end. The emphasis on authors' rights concealed tussles between rival printers.[65] Of course, authorship could only be deployed in this contest because readers were already interested in authors. The interest had long been supported within rhetoric by an attention to *ethos*, the import of a rhetor's character. As early as 1598, an edition of the works of Chaucer had been prefaced by a biographical essay, and biographical prefaces and portraits of authors became more important in seventeenth- and eighteenth-century editions of legacy texts.[66] The influential British copyright legislation of the eighteenth century on which comparable U.S. laws were modeled did not invent authorship, but it developed legal and economic supports for the tendency to attach every text to a single author (or a determinate set of coauthors) and to raise the author-text pair—the author-function, Foucault called it—conceptually above the social circulation of words and ideas and the collective labor of print publication.[67]

Just as print publication was a flashpoint for censorship, it also triggered questions about who owned printed texts and could profit from them. In the early eighteenth century, in Great Britain and British America, printers owned what they printed. An author initially owned a manuscript, but once the manuscript was sold to a printer, the printer owned the ensuing publication as well as the right to print new editions and to launch lawsuits against unauthorized reprints.[68] In the United Kingdom, the members of the Stationers' Guild, once they had procured a work from an author, had a perpetual monopoly on the reprinting of that work. The laws were designed to adjudicate the property rights of printers, not authors.

The two pieces of British legislation that gave authors rights had tremendous impact on the print world in which literature was eventually installed. The first, the Copyright Act of 1709, better known as the Statute of Anne, gave authors rights in their works for delimited time spans and allowed anyone, not just members of the Stationers' Guild, to undertake publication as contracted by authors.[69] The main impact of the Statute of Anne was to end the monopoly of the Stationers' Guild, not to promote the interests of authors; court cases in its wake tended to protect printers' property rights in works they wished to continue selling, and authors' claims were seldom put forward.[70] However, the end of perpetual copyright and the Stationers' Guilt monopoly was important for the development of literary canons because it meant that entrepreneurial publishers could negotiate for the rights to create collected editions of works by dead English authors.[71] Before this statute passed, important works by the same author might be controlled by separate publishers, each of whom effectively held perpetual copyright on part of the author's output (which began to be called a "corpus" in the eighteenth century).[72] After the Statute of Anne these copyrights were of limited duration and could be more readily valued and bartered, so that any printer could open negotiations to assemble, say, Milton's collected works. Many a multivolume edition of an English author's works came to be published in the same format used for the Greek and Latin texts standard within academic studies.[73] Johnson's *Dictionary of the English Language* (1755) defined a "classick" as an "author of the first rank: usually taken for ancient authors," but modern authors' works could be readily packaged as classics after the Statute of Anne.[74]

The 1774 ruling in *Donaldson v. Becket* brought about further development of the rights of authors and the nature of intellectual property.[75] The decision affirmed the sole right of an author to consent to a work's publication, and it emphasized that rights reverted to authors after the period of copyright expired. Works for which there were no living authors or identifiable heirs were therefore out of copyright and available for printing—a circumstance that made it easier still to publish anthologies and editions of an earlier author's collected works. Bell's *Poets of Great Britain* and Johnson's *Lives of the English Poets* (1779–1781), whose canon-making significance chapter 1 considered, were direct beneficiaries of *Donaldson*.[76]

Donaldson established not just the legal rights of authors but also the slippery nature of intellectual property; an edition of James Thomson's poem *The Seasons* (1726) was the work at issue. (The decision was officially published as bearing on "the Question of Literary Property," taking literature in the broad eighteenth-century sense, but the association of literary property with a poem meant that the *Donaldson* ruling has often been analyzed in relation to the emerging modern version of literature.)[77] The rights vested in authors by this decision were not conventional property rights in land or objects: not rights to the original, physical manuscript or rights to the profits on published copies, nor even rights to a particular configuration of words (since that would have allowed printers to take over a published text, change a few words, and reprint it as a new composition). Chief Justice William de Grey identified literary property as a new kind of "claim of property," "abstract and ideal, novel and refined."[78] Words mattered, as Blackstone's *Commentaries* formulated the issue, ideas and sentiments mattered, but what the author owned (or the right that the author possessed—discourses of property rights and more diffuse kinds of personal rights were interwoven in the legal history of copyright) was something in between words and ideas or sentiments.[79] The assumption embodied in *Donaldson* that the value of certain texts lay in a mysterious, sacralized conjunction between an author's intentions or internal experiences and the words on the page became highly influential in literary culture, and it gave legal form to Milton's earlier proposal that a (great) book is the "life-blood of a master spirit."[80] The ruling also implied that interpreting literature meant grasping some significance that lay somewhere between an author's intention and the words on the page. Moreover, it coincided with the Romantic elaboration of "genius," a capacity for creative inspiration often characterized as divine but usually not straightforwardly religious (hence the convenience of invoking muses, demigods of a previous dispensation).[81] As Martha Woodmansee and Mark Rose have emphasized, in spite of the idealizing rhetoric of Romantic ideologies of genius and aesthetic autonomy, these ideas were structurally quite similar to legal conceptualizations of written compositions as copyrightable intellectual property, the preconditions of literature's commodity status.[82]

This definition of literary property would have been unthinkable if the judges in *Donaldson* had believed, say, that there was nothing new under the sun and that the value of a printed work lay in its eloquent fashioning of commonplaces: if they had been on the side of the ancients versus the moderns, or if they had subscribed to a fundamentally rhetorical understanding of writing and print. The emphasis on individual authors' ownership also departed significantly from any belief that what was written and printed was always deeply collaborative because language was shared and dialogic, although the remarks of Charles Pratt, Earl of Camden, in support of the decision underlined the fact that valuable print texts were a shared resource:

> Why did we enter into society at all, but to enlighten one another's minds, and improve our faculties, for the common welfare of the species? Those great men, those favoured mortals, those sublime spirits, who share that ray of divinity which we call genius, are intrusted by Providence with the delegated power of imparting to their fellow-creatures that instruction which heaven meant for universal benefit.[83]

Although Camden emphasized "science and learning," Milton's *Paradise Lost* was his key example of a work whose "real price... was immortality."[84] The ruling thus gingerly balanced authorial ownership, which was cast as a form of stewardship, against the importance of public access to God-given wisdom siphoned into print.

U.S. laws and rulings about copyright mainly followed English ones. The U.S. Federal Copyright Act of 1790 was modeled on the Statute of Anne, similarly dispensing copyrights in multiples of seven years, and many U.S. states had passed similar legislation before 1790. *Wheaton v. Peters*, an 1834 Supreme Court decision, corresponded in many respects to *Donaldson v. Becket*.[85] Moreover, English discussions about print texts as art and property also circulated in British America and the early U.S. periodical culture, shaping North American cultures of letters even before U.S. copyright laws caught up with British ones. The close coordination between U.S. and U.K. treatments of copyright and authorship makes it especially noteworthy that nothing in U.S. law protected the rights of British or other foreign authors until the passage of the International Copyright Act of 1891, commonly known as the Chace Act.

The anxieties often expressed about whether the United States was producing, or would produce, a literature equal in stature to Great Britain's need to be understood in the context of the ready circulation in the United States of reprinted British texts, in spite of the fact that Henry Clay introduced a bill in favor of international copyright as early as 1837; Charles Dickens also publicized the case for international copyright with increasing anger during his 1842 tour of the United States.[86] Meredith L. McGill's work has established the crucial role that reprinted British texts played in nineteenth-century U.S. public culture. Most of the reprinting proceeded without authorization from English authors or publishers, although some U.S. publishers made special arrangements to compensate English authors, and the reprints were usually much less expensive than imported British books.[87] U.S. authors could secure their copyrights in the United Kingdom by traveling there or to Canada around the time of a book's publication; U.K. authors were offered no reciprocal privilege.

A compounding of commercial motives and public-spiritedness not unlike that in *Donaldson* appears to have led to the delay in making any provision for foreign authors' copyrights. Many U.S. publishers wished to keep reprinting British works without paying royalties: Peter Jaczi and Martha Woodmansee emphasize that the Chace Act was passed only when it suited the interests of leading retail publishers, who feared competition from other reprinters if they had no way of protecting their editions' prior claims.[88] The now-familiar reluctance for the United States to sign international agreements that it didn't initiate may also have been at work. However, McGill has argued for the importance of the "strong half-life of the republican understanding of print as public property"—in effect, civic republican support for a commons ethos.[89] Alongside the development of the legal construction of authorship as ownership—and alongside the Romantic ideology of individual genius—there was and is a countertradition in the United States emphasizing that ideas are the creation and property of all. As Emerson suggested in *Representative Men* (1850), "It is easy to see that what is best written or done by genius, in the world, was no man's work, but came by wide social labor, when a thousand wrought like one, sharing the same impulse."[90]

The long delay in ratifying international copyright (or making any special copyright provisions for the British authors so much admired by U.S. readers) had many consequences. One was that the availability of cheap reprints helped support literacy in the early United States, the process by which reading became "a necessity of life," as William J. Gilmore's work demonstrates.[91] The rapid advances in printing technology and the continual expansion of print distribution networks in Euro-America meant that reading matter became ever more readily available across the long nineteenth century. The increased availability of print stimulated appetites for reading, once books and periodicals ceased to be rare and precious and instead became less expensive and widely available. Scholars have moved beyond the oversimple theory that an ethos of "intensive reading"—of the Bible and devotional volumes—gave way in the nineteenth century to a contrasting practice of "extensive reading," but unlicensed reprinting (not technically piracy, McGill points out) contributed to the print abundance that invited many kinds of investments in reading during the era when the modern idea of literature was cohering.[92]

In the absence of international copyright, the ready availability of English-authored texts in literary genres was believed by many to hinder the development of U.S. literature. As I emphasize throughout this book, the category "American literature" obscures important ways in which forms of U.S. literary nationalism voiced and practiced in the nineteenth century coexisted with the formative influence of British publications and British literary culture in the United States. I argued in chapter 1 that the modern organization of literature produced national and international canons that drew boundaries between domestic and foreign texts, even though the European authors of the supercanon were the most greatly esteemed. The burdens of literary nationalism also meant that U.S. readers perpetually worried whether their nation's productions measured up to imported or reprinted "foreign" works.

The British statutes that established copyrights and ended print monopolies, facilitating the publication of anthologies and series, also ushered in more aggressive economic competition in print culture. The idea of "bookmaking"—working up volumes solely for profit—complicated the earlier use of printing to turn into books things that would otherwise have circulated as manuscripts. In the case of periodicals, it was even more obvious that contents had to be cooked up so that newspapers and magazines could publish on schedule. The nineteenth-century explosion of print accelerated the segmentation of print culture, establishing market sectors and, within them, the branding of genres, publishing houses, book series, and authors. After 1856, the famous blue and gold bindings of volumes of poetry published by Ticknor and Fields (and imitated by others) constituted an invitation to literary readers, although any reader might sample and value what was offered; Beadle's series of Dime Novels, which mainly bore yellow covers engraved with dynamic scenes, was branded equally effectively, and the Beadle name also operated as a brand that was compounded by the reputations of particular Beadle authors.[93] The construction of distinctive marketing positions, such as literary poetry and dime novels, as well as the creation of authorial reputations that functioned as brands (for dime novelist Edward S. Ellis as much as for Henry Wadsworth Longfellow) became increasingly important during the course of the nineteenth century.

In *Reading for Realism*, I delineated a set of periodicals, the *Atlantic* group, that had literary standing in the latter part of the nineteenth century. Some of the magazines were owned by book publishers with literary lists, whereas other freestanding magazines declared and enacted their commitment to literature by highlighting questions about what literature did and which works were literary. By and large, these periodicals were oriented toward the idea that literature came in the form of books, although the poetry, essays, short stories, and serial novels they published were presented as literary in quality, pieces that might well end up in books.[94] Although *Literature in the Making* considers an expanded set of stakeholders in late nineteenth-century U.S. literary culture, the *Atlantic* group contributed substantially to literature's association not only with books but even with a specific model of book publication.

Trade publication was the system identified with literary publication: the system by which publishers contract with authors for their manuscripts (usually arranging payment in the form of royalties) and control the printing and marketing of books as well as their distribution to retail outlets. Because trade publication depended on retail outlets, even if they were general stores, it operated mainly in settled parts of the United States and thrived in urban areas. As a result, the modes of distribution that reached rural and remote populations were those with the least power to confer literary value, even though works that had independently been established as literary might also be distributed in these ways. Religious presses such as the American Tract Society were pioneers of print distribution, making Bibles and devotional publications available in newly settled and barely settled areas—indeed, the impossible dream of the society's agents was to "visit *every* abode."[95] The American Tract Society and similar organizations sold through colporteurs, salaried traveling agents, whereas secular publishers tended to use agents who worked on commission, including canvassers who took orders for books to be printed and delivered later (a practice known as subscription publishing).[96] Traveling agents were employed as well within the abolitionist press.[97] Also crucial in the dissemination of reading matter was mail order: books and periodicals could be sent by mail to consumers or retail outlets (bookstores, general stores, etc.), and story papers were a form of fiction-rich periodical invented specifically to take advantage of reduced postal rates for newspapers.[98]

Especially after the Civil War, the strong identification of literature with trade publication fueled the belittlement of other forms of publication, which were treated as inherently unliterary. Even though Mark Twain founded his own subscription publishing company, subscription publishing was usually viewed with suspicion in literary culture, whose judgments lined up with the economic interests of trade publishers.[99] Trade publishers were also active in lobbying for postal regulations that would be disadvantageous to mail order publications such as storypapers.[100] Story papers, dime novels, and subscription books—along with any reading matter peddled rather than selected in a retail outlet or library—were categorically disparaged, anticipating the way in which pulps and mail-order book clubs would be treated in the twentieth century. In other words, the dominant interpretation of aesthetic autonomy—the belief that true literature was independent of religion and politics and that literature as art was only incidentally made available for sale—converged with the process by which literature was linked to trade publishing, and this association meant that the ways in which books and periodicals were likely to make first contact with new readerships were ritually disparaged within literary culture. The prickly tendency for lovers of literature to enforce the boundaries of literature with contempt was built into literature's association with trade publishing, adding to the unpleasant ways in which literature colluded with its commodification.

Books are marked by their life in civil society, including their legal status and their marketing. From the earliest traces of the modern idea of literature, literature was keyed primarily to the codex, even though written manuscripts, magazines, and newspapers have obviously been media in which works counted as literature could circulate. But every kind of print contributed to civil society—indeed, the abundance and variety of print was bound up with the sense of possibility that attended late eighteenth- and early nineteenth-century public life, which organized many hopes around the idea of civil society. People longed for literature to improve the collective thinking attributed to civil society without triggering state repression—and that longing may have rolled together wishes not to be punished with wishes not to have to watch the government operate repressively. They also longed for literature to be somehow insulated from the commercial circulation that was its lifeblood. These longings could not straightforwardly come true, but they shaped literary culture, catalyzing formulations about the nature of authorship, literary property, and aesthetic autonomy. Chapter 3 takes up the fervent hopes involved in one of the most remarkable—and least remarked—features of the modern idea of literature: the belief that literature was meant to be studied.

{ 3 }

Studying Literature

> There can surely be little doubt that women will occupy a much wider space in American literature during the next thirty years than they have done hitherto. Chautauqua circles, University Extension lectures, the innumerable literary, scientific, religious and charitable classes and clubs which young women are forming from Murray Hill to Montana ranches, are all doing a quickening work.
>
> —REBECCA HARDING DAVIS (1891)[1]

After the winnowed modern version of literature took shape, it was commonplace to believe that reading literature could be emotionally intense and vitally energizing, but most attempts to define what was valuable about literature emphasized also that it deserved careful attention and repeated reading: study. Literature was meant to be studied, and the study was often passionate. When Francis Bacon distinguished between books to be "tasted," books to be "swallowed," and the "few to be chewed and digested," he could not have anticipated how influential this alimentary metaphor would become.[2] The *OED*'s earliest instance of "consumption" to mean "the purchase and use of goods, services, materials, or energy" comes from a tax treatise from 1662, more than thirty years after Bacon's death, but this sense of consumption built on the more long-standing definition of consumption as "eating or drinking something, or... using something up in an activity," and the idea of something's being used up resonated powerfully in fears about consumerism.[3] Of course, berries gathered in the woods can be consumed with no money changing hands, but strongly judgmental treatments of consumerism were shaped by the awareness that a machinery of marketing stimulated artificial appetites; aspersions were cast on "bookmaking." Regardless of how the lines were drawn among Bacon's three categories, however, the point of the aphorism was for readers not to miss out on chewing and digesting valuable books. Study was an alternative to consumption and maybe an antidote.

The study of literature was central to literary culture, and it was pursued in a variety of ways. The educational zeal that gripped Americans during the long nineteenth century included formal education, but many other educational undertakings thrived.[4] Most histories of literary studies in the United States have concentrated on the development of English and American literature as academic fields in colleges and universities and sometimes in secondary education.[5] In histories of disciplinary literary studies, as in histories of other academic disciplines, it is customary to give some credit to energetic, gifted amateurs, even though English departments are presented as having been founded by academics. Such teleological accounts seriously misrepresent the scope of intellectual culture and scholarship in the nineteenth century, though, and they omit the ways in which the disciplines that were established within the research university model depended on intellectual infrastructures forged in public culture. This is especially the case for literary studies. The people whose work made academic English literary studies possible included university-based academics and teachers in various venues, but overall, the founders of literary studies in the United States would not be best remembered as academics, professional educators, or amateurs. They were all stakeholders in public literary culture, invested primarily in the value of literature and only secondarily in literature's development as the basis for an academic discipline.

Once academic English departments were established in the United States, by the end of the nineteenth century, a class of literary experts came into being, and the reorganization of knowledge that made them experts made everyone else into amateurs. Before that time, the study of literature in higher education and literature's development as a subject in secondary schooling were both outcroppings of public literary culture. Secondary schooling touched many people, many more than higher education, but the issue at stake in my emphasis on the transformation in higher education is not numbers of students but rather structures of authority.[6] What changed, toward the end of the century, was not only the organization of colleges and universities into discipline-based departments, together with other features of the research university model. The reorganization of knowledge embodied a new cultural valuation of expertise, which mainly operated through accreditation: academic degrees along with forms of professional credentialing that incorporated academic degrees. The importance of expertise was manifested as well by the development of uniform standards for school accreditation, models for uniform secondary curricula in various subjects, the development of schools of education, and the creation of professional organizations such as the National Education Association (founded in 1857) and the National Council of Teachers of English (founded in 1911).[7] Universities and the professional organizations of the university-educated acquired the power not just to make new knowledge but, more importantly, to authorize it. Earlier in the century, the teaching of literature in secondary schools was legitimized by public support, and mainstream periodicals paid attention to methods of instruction and textbooks. By the end of the century, literary study in school was legitimized because academically based, accredited experts in literature and education prescribed it.[8]

The era in public literary culture examined in this chapter and the next mainly preceded the ascendancy of expertise. (The last two chapters of this book examine what happened after expertise began to restructure literary culture.) Authoritative knowledge was valued in public literary culture, but authority could be gained in many ways, not only through academic credentialing. Without romanticizing intellectual life outside academia (although it began to be romanticized as soon as the dominance of expertise began to be legible), I want to give it its due, in part because it offers such a valuable example of what literary studies could accomplish without being organized as a discipline. The chapter does not exclude contributions to literary culture made by academics or in academic contexts, but I argue that they operated within public literary culture, not in the separate expert domains that would later be established.

Because Shakespeare was the exemplary modern literary author, I trace the contours of public literary culture by following Shakespeare. International admiration for Shakespeare made the strongest case for literary study, which was pursued in reading groups and informal schools as well as by individuals on their own. Shakespeare was also a gateway figure for academic literary study in the United States, serving as the subject of many of the earliest extramural lectures and college courses about literature and figuring prominently in almost every instructional venue that featured literature. In order to grasp the significance of literature's being studied, this chapter examines where and how Shakespeare was studied in the United States during the long nineteenth century, taking up as well the ways in which admiration for Shakespeare was caught up in the modern and antimodern dimensions of literature's conceptualization.

Many kinds of literary studies that thrived in public culture drew on philology and rhetoric, important intellectual traditions that did not become disciplines in the research university when literary studies did. This chapter traces some of the currents in popular culture that moved literary studies away from rhetoric in particular, even though literary studies drew heavily on rhetoric's resources. My attention to the interplay of philology, rhetoric, belles lettres, and the cultivation of taste in public literary culture culminates in the argument that the development of modern literature was shaped by public anxieties about the power of language, anxieties aggravated by increased importance of print in public life and by the unprecedented opportunities for literacy on offer. The paradoxical result is that literary study was developed to be both a fortification against literature's intimate power and a preparation designed to subject readers more thoroughly to this power. Chewing and digesting are active operations, but they also incorporate things into the self. Whereas the ethic of individualism grounded in capitalist self-interest encourages people to understand themselves as independent integers and bounded wholes,, literature's potential to wreak transformations challenged this bounded individualism.[9] Studying literature therefore involved ways in which readers tried to take control—harnessing literature to education and advancement, managing it through protocols of study and scholarship—as well as ways of surrendering. The chapter ends by considering Samuel Taylor Coleridge and Ralph Waldo Emerson as figures whose authorial examples and models of reading eased certain historical adjustments required for the coalescence of modern literature by appearing to safeguard readerly agency.

Shakespeare, Modern and Antimodern

As a guest at a U.S. expatriate's chateau near Paris, in the summer of 1817, George Ticknor somehow became embroiled in a literary competition in which he staked "Shakespeare and Milton against the whole body of French poetry," by way of asserting the "supremacy of English literature." Ticknor's rivals were two Frenchwomen with whom he had been having a charming time; other members of the house party judged the contest. The competition may have doubled as flirtation, but Ticknor did not hesitate to crow about his triumph in a letter to a friend back home:

> All the morning the ladies were in council with Voltaire, Racine, Corneille,— in short, a whole library. In the evening they covered the table with books till there was not room to put down a pin-cushion, and were a little abashed to find I took from my pocket nothing but your little 'Paradise Lost,' which alone exhausted their three great authors. In short, in four evenings they had no more passages of the *first* order of poetry to offer, and I had still Shakespeare's best plays in reserve, so that I prevailed on putting the vote, by four to two, without counting myself.[10]

The incident underlines how eager an American could be to claim the superiority of English literature, a phrase that hovered between England's literature, Britain's literature, and Anglophone literature (as it often does today). Ticknor, later to write the *History of Spanish Literature* (1849), was an important conduit between European and U.S. literary cultures, and his French adventure drives home the fact that U.S. literary culture was in many respects a set of U.S.-marked traces within transnational literary culture. The cultural processes that led to Ticknor's veneration of Shakespeare in 1817 did not originate in the United States, although Ticknor imbibed them there. They include the quarrel of the ancients and moderns, as I've mentioned, and the rise of Romanticism, a movement entangled from its beginnings with the love of Shakespeare.

This nineteenth-century promotion of Shakespeare, in which many U.S. readers were active, involved a double transformation: Shakespeare came to be understood and valued as an exemplar of literature, and what literature meant was affected by the ways in which Shakespeare was understood and valued. Other authors were involved in similar reciprocal relationships with literature, especially the authors of the supercanon, but at least in Anglophone culture, Shakespeare was paramount.[11]

The magnitude of the transformation can be glimpsed in the fact that Johann Gottfried Herder, who shared in the Sturm und Drang movement's fascination with Shakespeare, feared in the late eighteenth century that Shakespeare was on the verge of becoming too remote for readers to enjoy. Herder's concern is interesting because in other respects his essay is in tune with grand Romantic assertions of Shakespeare's enduring value. Herder declares that "the whole world is the body for this great mind: All movements of nature are the limbs of this body, just as all characters and ways of thinking are the features of this mind. The whole thing might be called Spinoza's great God, Pan! Universe!"[12] But in spite of his admiration, Herder sees Shakespeare growing more and more distant from readers:

> It is sadder and more important to think that this great creator of history and the human spirit is becoming more and more antiquated! We are already so far removed from these great ruins of knighthood, because the words and customs and genres of the period wilt and decay like leaves in autumn.... His drama [on the stage] will become the ruin of a colossus, of a period, at which everyone gazes in wonder but which no one understands. It is fortunate that you and I live in a period of time in which I can understand Shakespeare.[13]

His fears were not foolish: we ought to find it curious that Shakespeare did not grow more distant from readers over time but, rather, became more intimately cherished. Ancient drama and Aristotle's strictures about it continued to be accessible because they were central to the classical curriculum pursued in colleges and universities. Without comparable institutional supports—since no curriculum in 1773 was designed to keep Shakespeare accessible—Shakespeare's plays were in real danger of becoming obscure: linguistically and generically distant from late eighteenth-century readers, at odds with neoclassical aesthetics. Neither Herder nor Voltaire, who criticized Shakespeare for violating classical protocols for tragedy, wrote in ignorance of the fact that Shakespeare's plays were widely admired across Europe, but the understanding of Shakespeare that would make Herder's fears groundless and Voltaire's criticisms irrelevant was not yet robust. Shakespeare had not yet been welded firmly to the foundation of literature.

Margreta de Grazia's <u>Hamlet without Hamlet</u> charts a sea change in the play's reception during the late eighteenth century, one that seems likely to have been part of literature's becoming "Shakespearized" (Emerson's term in *Representative Men* [1850]).[14] Only at the end of the eighteenth century did *Hamlet* begin to be a play experienced by influential readers as vividly contemporary, with a protagonist who floated free of the design of the play and absorbed their attention. In contrast, the Earl of Shaftesbury had admired the play in 1711 in terms that had nothing to do with Hamlet's interior life and motives. He called the play "almost one continu'd *Moral*; a Series of deep Reflections, drawn from *one* Mouth upon the Subject of *one* single Accident and Calamity, naturally fitted to move Horrour and Compassion."[15] The nineteenth century's love affair with *Hamlet* was based on a new way of interpreting the play made famous (with variations) by Goethe, Schlegel, and Coleridge. Their obsession with whether Prince Hamlet's brooding distracted him from his revenge departed significantly from earlier treatments of the play as an ensemble piece full of action.[16]

The process by which Shakespeare became the face of literature is somewhat mysterious, since it was gradual and involved many factors. He was a prominent author before he became literary, and his literary prominence reworked some of the terms of his earlier prominence.[17] Ticknor's contest offers a reminder that Shakespeare's enlistment for literature was gradual and uneven. In 1817, at the time of the contest, Ticknor was a reader formed in some ways by Romanticism. He had met Byron and would soon meet Southey, Wordsworth, and Coleridge; within his generally wide reading, he was steeped in philosophical and imaginative writings associated with Romanticism.[18] Yet the literary contest proceeded by the principals' declaiming excerpted passages, apparently without much attention to the works' formal designs, a practice that resembles Shaftesbury's admiration for the play's "Series of deep Reflections." It all seems closer to an eighteenth-century rhetorical admiration for epigrammatic style, the kind underlying the veneration of Addison, than to characteristically Romantic concerns with organic form, imaginative visions, and the creation of powerful characters.[19] Literary culture was variegated in ways that don't fit our retrospective periodizations, which can only be provisional heuristics.

For readers in the United States, admiring Shakespeare offered one way of participating in the Republic of Letters, civilization, or other cosmopolitan modes of international culture. The exceptionalist belief that the United States was the most modern of nations also created the possibility that it needed Shakespeare's guidance the most, once Shakespeare's significance as an exemplary modern author began to be elaborated. The complex relationship between the United States and the British Empire tinged many discussions of U.S. readers' particular stake in Shakespeare. There were readers friendly to the Revolution who criticized Shakespeare for celebrating monarchical and aristocratic power, among them Thomas Paine, but this was a minority position.[20] Over the course of the long nineteenth century, two positions were forged that laid. claim to Shakespeare on behalf of the United States.

One position identified Shakespeare as a legacy for all English-derived people (as a prevailing ideological fantasy defined residents of the United States) and more specifically as an author friendly to the United States because he was sensitive to tyranny and friendly to liberty, especially the tradition known as

English liberty.[21] Michael Bristol has identified this stance in John Adams's *Discourses on Davila* (1790), where Adams notes that the plays detail the kinds of monarchical abuses that English constitutionalism and English liberty sought to combat, thereby implying that the U.S. Revolution carried forward England's Glorious Revolution.[22] The belief that Shakespeare's English was preserved in parts of the United States, especially in remote stretches of Appalachia where people who came from the British Isles were insulated from newer waves of immigration, reinforced the vague belief that the United States might have remained truer to certain English values than the United Kingdom did.[23] Coupled with the assumption that the primary cultural and ethnic connections operating in the United States were with England, the "mother" country, this position could devolve into white supremacist uses of Shakespeare to endorse Anglo-Saxonism; it paralleled also the peculiar antebellum tradition of assimilating U.S. slavery to serfdom in medieval England.[24] However, the understanding that Shakespeare was a friend to liberty also made it possible for African Americans opposing slavery and other groups protesting injustice to claim a special kinship with Shakespeare and England.[25] As Elisa Tamarkin has emphasized, Britain had a special place in the antislavery imaginary as a place where African Americans could enjoy equality and respect. Just as Anglophilia meant many things to white Americans, so it was complex for black Americans, but one strain that Tamarkin traces casts Britain as "a whole fantasized realm within which a cosmopolitan universalism gets realized."[26]

The other common way for people in the United States to claim Shakespeare was to identify with the national and imperial contexts for Shakespeare's greatness: "That Shakespeare was declared to rule world literature at the same time that Britannia was declared to rule the waves may, indeed, be more than a coincidence."[27] In sometimes subtle, sometimes flagrant ways, U.S. readers who emphasized the Elizabethan imperial projects operating in Shakespeare's lifetime linked Shakespeare to national and imperial ambitions that the United States might emulate.[28] For example, one of Peter Parley's popular textbooks in 1845 deplored the "colonial vassalage" of U.S. writers in relation to England but also celebrated the fact that the English language "seems destined to overspread the earth."[29] The beliefs that the United States kept alive the best version of English liberty and that the United States was destined to be a great empire could converge in the idea that the national or (proto)imperial greatness of the United States was embodied in its commitment to liberty, an ideological tenet still used to justify U.S. foreign policy today and rooted in the promotion of what Donald Pease has called "[i]mperial conquest as an Anglo-Saxon practice of freedom."[30]

Whether their investment in Shakespeare was cosmopolitan, republican, or national-imperial, U.S. readers were as interested as anyone else in the historical William Shakespeare. John Adams and Thomas Jefferson visited Stratford as tourists in 1786, after Adams had been appointed the first U.S. minister to

England. Like most visitors, they cut slivers from a chair advertised as Shakespeare's, but Adams complained in his diary about the tawdriness of this touristic access: "There is nothing preserved of this great genius...which might inform us what education, what company, what accident turned his mind to letters and drama."[31] By the time Washington Irving visited in 1815, Stratford had acquired an even deeper touristic patina. Irving writes in *The Sketch-Book* that on visiting Stratford he "dreamt all night of Shakespeare, the Jubilee, and David Garrick," the Jubilee being Garrick's 1769 celebration of Shakespeare in Stratford, which had amplified his fame and accelerated tourism.[32] Irving greeted the entire machinery of Shakespeariana with "resolute good humoured credulity," a stance perhaps akin to the "willing suspension of disbelief" that Coleridge offered as a hallmark of literary reading:[33]

> I am always of easy faith in such matters, and am ever willing to be deceived, where the deceit is pleasant, and costs nothing. I am therefore a ready believer in relics, legends, and local anecdotes of goblins and great men; and would advise all travellers who travel for their gratification to be the same. What is it to us whether these stories be true or false, so long as we can persuade ourselves into the belief of them, and enjoy all the charm of the reality?

Irving's account took for granted the fraudulent status of the much-whittled chair; he treated Shakespearean legends like other kinds of folklore, valuable precisely insofar as they were not susceptible to modern standards of evidence.[34] And unlike Adams, Irving delighted in the ways that the plays' fictiveness expanded into Shakespearean sites. He had earlier visited East Cheap in much the same spirit, half hoping to find traces of Shakespeare's Boar's Head Tavern and the characters who frequented it. Moreover, in an essay called "The Mutability of Literature," he delighted even in the fictive-seeming improbability of Shakespeare's extraordinary reputation, recounting his lively dialogue with a talking quarto volume two centuries old who was angrily incredulous to learn of the lasting fame of this "vagabond deer stealer... [and] man without learning."[35]

For Irving, tourism offered a pleasurable way of participating in Shakespeare's imaginary worlds. *The Sketch-Book* models an insouciant alternative to Shakespearean scholarship, which Irving treats as parasitic and destructive. Having described Shakespeare as an organic monument, "like giant trees" whose roots extend to the "very foundations of the earth," Irving goes on to assert that "even he, I grieve to say, is gradually assuming the tint of age, and his whole form is overrun by a profusion of commentators, who, like clambering vines and creepers, almost bury the noble plant that upholds them."[36] In contrast to Herder (forty years before), Irving assumes that only fussy scholarship makes Shakespeare seem old and distant.

Irving's fanciful investment constructed Shakespeare's value as primarily antimodern in the sense that he and his works resist empirical investigation and rational inquiry, similar to Keats's sense (set down a few years earlier) that Shakespeare was endowed with "*negative capability*, that is, when a man is capable of being in uncertainties, mysteries, doubts, without any irritable reaching after fact and reason."[37] The characters of Shakespeare's plays take on a folkloric quality for Irving. Just as Hawthorne would later link romance to the dreamy magic of moonlight rather than the demystifying empiricism of sunlight, Shakespeare's plays and characters seem for Irving to shelter forms of experience and belief that modernity put at risk—and an empirical, scholarly approach to the plays put them further at risk, Irving suggests.

However, Irving's account of Shakespeare and his times bore features also found in scholarly literary histories connecting Shakespeare's greatness with the characteristically modern achievements of the Elizabethan period. Irving argues that Shakespeare's writings "contain the spirit, the aroma... of the age in which he lives," an age that is somehow still vivid in Irving's time; Chaucer's writings, also valuable, are in contrast "antiquated" and have to be "renewed."[38] This idea that Shakespeare's age was especially available to nineteenth-century readers cropped up often. In countless capsule accounts, the genealogy of nineteenth-century modernity was traced back to a set of Renaissance beliefs, discoveries, and inventions. Empiricism, individualism, secularism, and Protestantism were frequently invoked; signature technologies such as the printing press were often made part of the story, as were the economic opportunities of empire.[39] An 1856 *Putnam's* review of William Prescott's *History of the Reign of Philip the Second, King of Spain* (1856–1858) offered an especially comprehensive capsule summary keyed to the modernity of Shakespeare's contemporary, Cervantes:

> The sixteenth century is, to the nations of the modern world, all, and more than all, that the age of Caesar was to the Roman Empire.
>
> The visible development of modern society dates from that epoch; modern politics, modern literature, modern philosophy, modern industry, all shot up in the sixteenth century to the light. The century was born to greatness; it inherited from its immediate predecessor such a legacy in the invention of printing and the discovery of the New World, as had been the portion of no previous era since the advent of Christianity.... Everywhere, the crystallization of nationalities was going on—the concentration of authority, the expansion of enterprise.... Life in the middle ages had been comparatively simple.... In the sixteenth century, life became suddenly richer, more varied: a thousand new desires, curiosities, aspirations, awoke in the hearts of men.... All that makes our modern life peculiar, first begins to appear distinctly, on the face of Europe, in the sixteenth century.[40]

This account proposes that modern times brought about a change in the quality of people's internal experience, a new intensity of self-awareness often summed up as individualism. As we've seen, the assumption that new technologies and political and economic opportunities were somehow conjoined with fundamental changes in people's self-understanding was the hallmark of the paradigm of modernity.

Henry N. Hudson in 1848 called Shakespeare's age "the birthday of modern civilization; the precise period when the powers that produced it, were in their highest vigor."[41] Barrett Wendell's *A Literary History of America* (1901) similarly declared, "In 1575 there was hardly such a thing as modern English literature; in 1625 that great body of English literature which we call Elizabethan was complete." Wendell pointed out that "the America with which we shall be concerned," the European settlements—at least acknowledged not to be the only "America"—came into being in Shakespeare's time.[42] In many literary histories that identified Shakespeare's lifetime as the onset of modernity, his vitality was linked to a capacity to interpret modern phenomena and experiences. Like Irving, champions of the Elizabethan era as the birthplace of the modern were likely to find earlier writers such as Chaucer remote by comparison. James Morgan Hart, a Cornell professor, proposed in the 1880s that students couldn't get a sense of "literary culture" from any author earlier than Chaucer and that even Chaucer didn't count as "one of us."[43] In this way, the modern understanding of literature was projected back onto the Elizabethan era, whereas earlier writings were treated as the prehistory of literature, valuable mainly for what they had set in motion. (Chapter 1 demonstrated that the omission or demotion of eighteenth-century writings was also conspicuous in these back-projections.)

Understood as a modern resource, literature was supposed to mirror back to readers their modernity and inform them about modern conditions by representing and investigating the world—not necessarily the contemporary world, but some world whose challenges resonated in contemporary life. In contrapuntal fashion, however, the Elizabethan era was also valued because of its proximity to the Middle Ages, so that Shakespeare's works could alternatively be valued for harboring antimodern elements. James Russell Lowell's "Shakespeare Once More" (1868) treated the Bard's lifetime as a watershed in which older resources had become newly available for modern purposes. Had he been born fifty years earlier, there would not have been an English "book-language...flexible enough" for his purposes, Lowell argues; the fact that Bacon wrote his *Novum Organum* (1620) in Latin indicated that English was not yet a language that lent itself to learned endeavors. Fifty years later, according to Lowell, political and religious disturbances would have challenged Shakespeare's equanimity, and English book language had lost some of its vitality because it had begun to diverge from spoken language. Instead, Shakespeare lived at just the right time. The recent memory of the Reformation meant also that Catholic beliefs and practices had in Shakespeare's time newly become an imaginative resource, which Lowell treats condescendingly: "Old forms of belief and worship still lingered, all the more touching to Fancy, perhaps, that they were homeless and attainted."[44] As Lowell's discussion shows, the elaboration of modernity tended to require the construction of its opposite or remainder, which was usually organized temporally as its past.

The best-known Romantic frames for Shakespeare, the poet of nature and the "myriad-minded," in Coleridge's phrasing, were constructed to assuage modern losses.[45] Schiller's account in 1795 of how hard he had found it, earlier in life, to learn to appreciate certain features of Shakespeare captures the tremendous reorientation that the plays required of readers schooled in neoclassical aesthetics:

> When I first became acquainted with Shakespeare at a very early age, I was shocked by his coldness, the lack of feeling which allowed him to joke in the midst of the greatest pathos, to break up the heart-rending scenes in *Hamlet, King Lear, Macbeth*, etc., by the introduction of a fool, which at times stopped him where my emotions rushed on, at times bore him cold-heartedly on where the heart would gladly have paused.... I was not yet capable of understanding nature at first hand. I could only bear her image filtered by the understanding and ordered by rules, and for this the sentimental French and also German writers of the years 1750 to approximately 1780 were just the right subjects.[46]

If art was a second nature, as Kantian aesthetics held, Shakespeare as poet of nature helped to close the gap. Here, Schiller also substantiates Herder's sense that Shakespeare might easily *not* have become the bosom author of nineteenth-century readers. If we suspend Schiller's assumption that Shakespeare simply wrote according to nature, we might infer instead that the emotional modulations in Shakespeare's plays were for Schiller's generation of Euro-American intellectuals an acquired taste, dependent on their developing an appreciation for tonal and emotional variation or complexity rather than for, say, the pleasure of deepening an emotional experience by prolonging it. Coleridge rebutted Voltaire's criticism that Shakespeare ruined tragic effects by his use of low scenes and commonplace dialogue, arguing instead that one of Shakespeare's compositional principles was to use comedy to offset dramatic intensities:

> [A]fter the mind has been stretched beyond its usual pitch and tone, it must either sink into exhaustion and inanity, or seek relief by a change.... Indeed, paradoxical as it may appear, the terrible, by a law of the human mind always touches on the verge of the ludicrous. Both arise from the perception of something out of the common order of things.[47]

Shakespeare the myriad-minded was also initially unsatisfying to Schiller, who wanted to commune with a more definite author. Omitted from the passage I quoted above were Schiller's failed efforts to find a specific voice and source of wisdom in the plays:

> Misled by my acquaintance with more modern poets to look first of all in the work for the author, to encounter *his* heart, to reflect on his subject-matter together *with him*, in short to look for the subject-matter in the person, it was unbearable to me that here the poet could nowhere be grasped, was nowhere answerable to me. He had already possessed my entire admiration and had been my study for several years before I learned to love his personality.[48]

Chastened and instructed by his incapacity to find Shakespeare in the plays, Schiller changed his understanding of how an author could be found and loved. His brief discussion here resonates with accounts that praise the range of Shakespeare's characterization, the capacity that marked for many readers his unequalled and unbiased understanding of human nature.

Shakespeare the poet of nature offered moderns estranged from nature a route of reconnection. The fact that he drew on earlier materials, not simply on observed "nature," meant that he could also be conscripted for Romantic nationalist efforts to "craft a shared national consciousness out of the relics and chronicles of a shared past."[49] Shakespeare the myriad-minded was a figure of human amplitude—an instance of the expanded individual possibilities coded as modern—who countered the danger that moderns were fundamentally self-divided or diminished, polarized into thought and feeling or distorted by modern requirements of specialization. Art could take on a prosthetic or therapeutic quality in such accounts: for instance, Schiller diagnoses a "split within man" that can be "healed" by art.[50] However, neighboring strands of aesthetic philosophy (especially Kant's) clashed with therapeutic understandings, which addressed only the historical organism. Kantian aesthetics credited art instead with putting people in touch with the absolute, with their own timeless significance and being, and with fundamental (but somewhat evanescent) human freedom.

Shakespeare's power to shelter antimodern values could be understood either historically or ahistorically (that is, as universal). He might offer a treatment for modern ailments, insofar as his works offered nineteenth-century readers regenerative access to the premodern as well as stimulating access to the early modern, understood as the early outcroppings of modern modes of thought and action. On the other hand, Shakespeare might be an instance of timeless genius, entirely independent of the era when he lived and wrote. Either of these positions might appear in isolation, but it was also common for authors to mingle them or move between them: indeed, if either position came up, the larger cultural conversation was likely to bring the alternative to bear, since the positions served as familiar rejoinders to each other. In this way, the author-work-period cluster, inflected by the metaperiodization of ancient and modern, was generatively yoked to the possibility of transcendent genius in a range of writings about Shakespeare.

Where Shakespeare Was Studied

A great deal of Shakespearean scholarship was in circulation by the time Irving bristled about it. Although eighteenth-century performances had liberally adapted the plays, eighteenth-century editions of the plays had begun to adopt the textual practices of editors of classical and biblical texts, seeking to establish the single best version of each play and to link those versions to Shakespeare's personal conception: his most direct authorial activity, uncontaminated by others' collaborative input or adaptations for specific performances.[51] The Tonson family publishing house (dubbed by Andrew Murphy the "Tonson cartel") retained its copyrights to Shakespeare's plays until 1772, and the Tonsons were responsible for setting up influential editions of the plays by Nicholas Rowe (1709), Alexander Pope (1725), and Samuel Johnson (1765), among others.[52] As Gary Taylor notes, the Tonsons "wanted editors who were already famous," and their prestige contributed to the accumulating cultural value of Shakespeare's writings.[53] Editions began to acquire biographical and bibliographical apparatuses. For example, by listing all known earlier editions of Shakespeare, Pope's 1725 edition made it possible for interested readers to "acquire, deliberately, large private collections of Shakespeariana."[54] Editors mainly established the canon (the authorized body of his work) not long before Shakespeare became the centerpiece of the modern literary supercanon and the English literary canon.[55] And new editions were plentiful, especially after the Tonsons lost control of the copyright: one historian counts forty-three British editions of Shakespeare between 1769 and 1800.[56] It was likely that anyone who read Shakespeare during the long nineteenth century would encounter editorial apparatuses emphasizing the scholarly labors of historical reconstruction, and anyone who tuned into these apparatuses would get a feel for the kinds of questions that occupied scholarly readers.

Shakespearean discoveries and controversies were also frequently reported in nineteenth-century U.S. magazines and newspapers, giving even people who didn't read Shakespeare or attend performances some sense of the historical, philological, and interpretive issues at stake in Shakespeare studies.[57] In the early national period, the *Massachusetts Magazine; or, Monthly Museum* gleefully published an "Account of, and Extracts from, the Newly Discovered Shakespeare Manuscripts" in 1796, although the so-called discoveries turned out to be forgeries.[58] (Forgeries and hoaxes in Shakespearean scholarship were always news.) In 1805, the *Literary Magazine, and American Register* published a series of articles, apparently from interested correspondents familiar with philological approaches, about whether the phrase "wrinkle of a smile" in *Troilus and Cressida* was inept or singularly adept.[59] The *Literary Magazine* disputants all worked in English, but a writer in 1809 complained about philological tendencies to privilege classical etymologies: "The commentators on Shakespeare have unfortunately been generally what the world calls learned men. We say *unfortunately*, because, when a difficult word or passage in his works has occurred, they have applied to the *dead* languages for explanation."[60] Also circulating in U.S. periodicals during the decades leading up to Irving's *Sketch-Book* were defenses of Shakespeare against Voltaire, assessments of Shakespeare's puns, reviews of the kinds of care required in expurgating Shakespeare's plays for family reading (Thomas Bowdler's notorious project), and prickly responses to heavy-handed editorial prefaces.[61]

As the century continued, the widely circulating questions of whether Hamlet shirked his duty and whether Hamlet was mad or just shamming disseminated a variety of ideas about how literary interpretation worked and why it mattered. The frequency of excerpting and reprinting increased the chances that print supports for literary culture would reverberate beyond their initial sites of publication, and literary events and gatherings were often advertised in advance and reported afterward. Although some of the reporting was cursory, it was not unusual for periodical accounts of Shakespearean events and publications to formulate the intellectual issues at stake. Consider, for example, a notice published in the *Cincinnati Daily Gazette* in 1869 about recent publications of the German Shakespeare society. The notice makes shorthand reference to Aristotle's theory of dramatic unities as well as competing approaches to textual editing:

> The German Shakespeare Society has published its third and fourth series (1868–1869), both of which (says the North German Correspondent [a German newspaper]) furnish abundant testimony of the industry and critical acumen bestowed by German scholars on the works of the great English bard. An article by N. Delius, entitled "Dryden and Shakespeare," deserves a passing notice. The writer, in referring to the attempts made by "glorious John" to "correct" and improve the great English dramatist according to the Frenchified taste of his day, observes that the signal failure of the eminent poet, than whom no man was better fitted for the task, should serve as an example to deter modern critics from mangling Shakespeare by ill-advised and vain attempts to make him conform to the "unities." The society consists of 180 members. The next meeting will be held in Weimar.[62]

Cincinnati's sizable German population may have inspired the *Daily Gazette*'s attention to German intellectual culture, but similar articles about Shakespearean scholarship can be found in many other newspapers outside the metropolitan Northeast. A Galveston newspaper in 1869 reported that a document purporting to date some of Shakespeare's plays had turned out to be a forgery; a San Francisco newspaper in 1874 reported the founding of the New Shakspere Society in London, launched "with a view to advance aesthetic rather than textual criticism"; and a Salt Lake City newspaper in 1867 described the interpretive significance of actress Isabella Glyn's rendering of some of

Othello's questions to Desdemona, in her public reading in London.[63] Many newspaper articles about Shakespeare were probably condensed from longer pieces in European or U.S. East Coast periodicals: the recycling of magazine pieces by newspapers extended the reach of events and ideas in literary culture.

Beyond the superficial news flashes and society items relating to Shakespeare clubs, general magazines and newspapers allowed stakeholders to keep abreast of what was happening in literary studies throughout the century. In addition, Shakespearean scholars communicated by undertaking private correspondence; by publishing monographs and reference works—and books about Shakespeare were legion in this era, including self-published books; by participating in published exchanges in general periodicals, as in the case of the discussion of "wrinkle of a smile"; by writing or following columns devoted to Shakespeare, such as Joseph Parker Norris's "Shakespearian Gossip" column in the *American Bibliopolist*; and, later in the century, by following or writing for specialized periodicals tilted toward book collecting and literary studies, about which I'll have more to say.[64] When literary studies began to become primarily an academic endeavor, journals such as *PMLA* (founded 1884) and *Modern Language Notes* (founded 1886) became sites where new theories about Shakespeare would be exchanged among experts before reaching the public through a transfer usually understood as popularization. Before academic control of literary studies was established (around the turn of the century), however, there were no structural barriers to anyone's contributing to scholarship and criticism about Shakespeare.

Textual scholars were hampered by the limitations of Shakespearean holdings in the United States, but whatever kinds of Shakespearean study U.S. scholars could viably undertake, they did. In 1879, Henry N. Hudson identified three people in the United States who counted as Shakespeareans "in an eminent sense," none of whom was an academic. The careers of these Shakespeareans offer a sense of the kinds of literary authority that nonacademic scholars could acquire.[65] One eminent Shakespearean was Horace Howard Furness, best known as founding editor of the Variorum Shakespeare. Furness, an attorney whose independent wealth allowed him to retire early, was a member of the Philadelphia Shakespeare Society, the most highly respected Shakespeare club in the United States, and the Variorum project began as an outgrowth of the society's studies.[66] Like many other Shakespearean scholars and critics, he was also a collector—publications such as the *American Bibliopolist* offered important information about new publications as well as Shakespeareana for sale. Furness never held an academic appointment, although he was active as a trustee for the University of Pennsylvania.[67] Having graduated from Harvard and studied in Germany, he was the only major Shakespearean in the postbellum United States who might count as "patrician" or a "gentleman scholar," two somewhat pejorative ways in which public literary scholarship has been retrospectively diminished. No one could diminish the Variorum, however, a scholarly achievement unequalled by university-based Shakespeareans in England or Germany (the nations preeminent in Shakespeare scholarship).[68]

A second eminent Shakespearean was Richard Grant White, who supported himself as a music critic, literary reviewer, and Shakespearean editor.[69] White, a graduate of New York University, made his reputation by a judicious contribution to Shakespearean scholarship, a skeptical evaluation of what turned out to be forged marginalia in a Shakespearean Folio.[70] The third and most unlikely eminent Shakespearean was Joseph Crosby, who owned and operated a grocery in Zanesville, Ohio, and also sold insurance. He had attended Queens College, Oxford, as a scholarship student before emigrating to the U.S. Like Furness, Crosby was a serious book collector as well as a scholar; the University of Michigan eventually purchased his private library. Crosby participated in networks of scholarly inquiry by corresponding extensively with other Shakespeareans and by publishing contributions on Shakespearean topics in the *American Bibliopolist*, *Shakespeariana*, the *Literary World*, and local newspapers.[71]

It was implicit in Hudson's pronouncement that he had some claim to being an eminent Shakespearean himself; a *Literary World* article reprinting his pronouncement confirmed that Hudson had "title to a fourth place in the list" and held "the first place as an aesthetic critic."[72] Like William J. Rolfe, a rival whom Hudson left off the list, Hudson was well known as an editor of Shakespeare's plays for use in schools. An Episcopalian minister, Hudson had made his reputation by delivering lyceum lectures about Shakespeare in the South and Midwest, ending up in Boston. Hudson and Rolfe both taught mainly in secondary schools but eventually had appointments as professors in schools of oratory; it was not unusual for educators in the era to move between secondary and collegiate appointments, since the missions of these institutions were not clearly differentiated.[73] And because secondary education was an important concern within public literary culture, editing Shakespeare for use in schools was respected. *Shakespeariana*'s series of articles about U.S. editors, in 1889–1890, included editors of school editions, such as Hudson and Rolfe, interspersed among other editors, such as Furness, noted for their scholarly editions.[74]

The compact biographies of these Shakespeareans point toward three axioms about public literary culture in the nineteenth-century United States:

1. Serious participants in nineteenth-century public literary culture valued and shared authoritative knowledge and forms of inquiry, but their reputations and channels of communication were not mainly academic. People with no university credentialing or ties to formal education, secondary educators, and university-based academics all collaborated in public literary culture.

In the latter half of the nineteenth century, a number of nonacademic but specialized periodicals allowed for exchanges beneficial to Shakespearean scholars, critics, serious readers, and collectors: chiefly, the *American Bibliopolist* (1869–1877), *Shakespeariana* (1883–1893, sponsored by the Shakespeare Society of New York), the *American Shakespeare Magazine* (1895–1898, sponsored by the Fortnightly Shakespeare Club of New York City and the Shakespeare Society of New York), and *Poet-Lore* (founded as a magazine devoted to Shakespeare and Browning studies; 1899–present). These specialized publications concentrated interests that had long circulated in general magazines. They capitalized as well on the growth of Shakespeare societies and clubs, which proliferated in the late nineteenth century and usually involved members' presenting scholarly, critical, and interpretive papers. Women were better represented among Shakespeareans than Hudson's list suggested, and probably the two most prominent were Charlotte Porter and Helen A. Clarke, the founding editors of *Poet-Lore*. They had met when Porter was editing *Shakespeariana* and Clarke was a contributor. In addition to shaping *Poet-Lore* and editing Robert Browning's and Elizabeth Barrett Browning's collected works, they published a highly regarded Shakespeare edition in the early twentieth century.[75] Porter had graduated from Wells College and taken courses at the Sorbonne, and Clarke had studied at the University of Pennsylvania without taking a degree. However, their Shakespearean education was necessarily conducted mainly in public literary culture, especially through the editing of *Poet-Lore*, which put them in touch with academic and nonacademic Shakespeare scholars.

The Philadelphia Shakespeare Society (which sponsored the Variorum) and the Shakespeare Society of New York (which published books and periodicals, operating as the Shakespeare Press and the Shakespeare Magazine Company) were the best known, but there were Shakespeare clubs throughout the United States. In the Northeast, Shakespeare clubs were numerous, and the most unlikely people ended up in them—even Emily Dickinson, before she became reclusive, and Charles Sanders Peirce, before he became famous as a philosopher and logician.[76] Shakespeare clubs could be supported even in new communities: for example, tiny Clarendon, Texas, had a Shakespeare club within a few years of its founding in 1878.[77] It was easy to find Shakespeare's plays in inexpensive editions, even in relatively remote areas, and clubs could also make use of textbooks and instructional editions designated for schools, clubs, and families.[78] Joseph Crosby endorsed an edition that was sold by subscription, and even agricultural periodicals advertised editions of Shakespeare.[79] Some Shakespeare clubs expanded their mission over time to include other kinds of literature, but Shakespeare could serve as a gateway to the rest of literary culture or an enduring challenge.

Outside of clubs, Shakespeare study was advanced by public lectures. Mechanics' Institutes began in Britain as organizations for workers pursuing "mutual education"; they soon sprang up in the United States and also inspired the lyceum movement. The lyceum movement began in Massachusetts but spread like wildfire during the 1830s, extending as far as Cincinnati, St. Louis,

Milwaukee, and Austin, and African American groups and women's groups adapted the (white and male-dominated) lyceum model.[80] Literary topics were from the beginning popular. Emerson was a frequent lyceum lecturer. Henry N. Hudson, as I've mentioned, and James Russell Lowell both gave lyceum lectures about Shakespeare.[81] Even Herman Melville delivered more than twenty Lyceum lectures, in cities from Boston to San Francisco, on the South Seas and on classical sculpture.[82] Lyceum lectures sometimes led to publications—for instance, Hudson compiled *Lectures on Shakespeare* from lectures he began giving in the South and West (in Huntsville and Mobile, Alabama, and Cincinnati, Ohio) before taking his lectures to Boston and making a reputation there; he dedicated the book to Richard H. Dana, who had delivered influential lectures about Shakespeare in Boston and other cities a decade earlier.[83] Hudson's published lectures and James Russell Lowell's were widely used as academic resources well into the twentieth century.[84] The Boston Lyceum published a journal, *Lyceum,* and lyceum lectures throughout the United States (like many events in public literary culture) were often summarized in newspapers or reprinted or excerpted in periodicals, so that the reach of these lectures extended beyond those who attended them.[85] By the 1880s, the lyceum movement was declining in popularity, but the earlier importance of lyceums was captured in Thomas Wentworth Higginson's 1868 characterization of a lyceum lecturer as "a living shuttle, to weave together this new web of civilization."[86]

Early university-based lectures on Shakespeare contributed to public literary culture, very much as lyceum lectures did. The earliest lectures on Shakespeare delivered in a U.S. institution of higher education were George Ticknor's at Harvard in the 1830s.[87] Ticknor was the Smith Professor of French and Spanish Literature and of Belles-Lettres (a position held afterward with slight variations in title by Henry Wadsworth Longfellow and James Russell Lowell, and one of the earliest professorial titles to reference "literature"), but his lectures about Shakespeare were extracurricular, as many early academic lectures on literature were.[88] Ticknor's were not published; Henry Reed's were. Henry Reed, professor of rhetoric and English literature at the University of Pennsylvania, offered a series of public lectures about English literature, "illustrated by Shakespeare," in the 1840s and early 1850s, explaining in his opening lecture that many students had requested his guidance about their personal reading, and that he realized any student was likely to make the "literature of his own language ... part of his thoughts and feelings."[89] He emphasized the importance of criticism in directing the reading of both men and women. As early as 1858, his lectures were being used as a text in one of the earliest college courses on English literature, taught at the University of Michigan.[90] It's amusing that Reed's lectures were used for formal instructional purposes, though, since he argued against "prescribed courses of reading" precisely because they afford too little scope for readers' choices and trajectories of development: "Our communion with books, to be intelligent, must be more or less spontaneous."[91]

Like many later writers about literature, Reed emphasized that it was most important for readers to acquire a "taste for reading": the refinement of that taste could come later.[92] Reed proposed that books lead to other books, so that readers often move in unpredictable ways.[93] In contrast, his lectures offered a periodized literary history, attentive to genres, movements, and the interplay of literature with events. Perhaps the lectures were meant to offer a map of a territory available for spontaneous individual exploration.

Other sets of extracurricular lectures and an occasional elective course on English literature were tried out in the 1840s and 1850s.[94] These early courses and lecture series undoubtedly helped prepare the way for the incorporation of English literature into core curricula in higher education. However, it isn't clear that they were more serious than many studies of literature undertaken apart from formal higher education or secondary schooling. The literary societies active in many colleges and universities were also important outposts of literary culture, and many of them had libraries or reading rooms that bypassed or supplemented the official curriculum.[95]

The lectures and discussion-based clubs lead to my second axiom:

2. Literature was identified primarily with print, but literary culture relied heavily on orality and performance.

In another early set of lectures about English literature, in 1858–1859, George P. Marsh called the United States a "nation of readers," a phrase that captured the powerful cultural investment in literacy that helped fuel public literary culture.[96] However, Marsh's reference to a "nation of readers" specifically celebrated the fact that people in the United States were likely to "pronounce [words] deliberately" and "assimilate the spoken to the written language."[97] A nation of readers was a nation of good speakers, Marsh believed. Whether or not reading improved pronunciation, many people read aloud (or listened) in the company of others.[98] The popularity of reading aloud meant that literary culture included even people who could not read (or could not read well), although it's hard to imagine that many nonreaders pursued literature in a sustained way.[99]

Literature's collaboration with speech and performance takes on some complexity with respect to Shakespeare, since one of the best-known Romantic manifestations of what George Bernard Shaw later called Bardolatry was the belief that Shakespeare was better encountered on the page than in performance.[100] "We do not like to see our author's plays acted, and least of all, Hamlet," wrote William Hazlitt in 1817. "There is no play that suffers so much from being transferred to the stage." Charles Lamb concurred:

> It may seem a paradox, but I cannot help being of opinion that the plays of Shakspeare are less calculated for performance on a stage, than those of almost any other dramatist whatever. Their distinguished excellence is a reason that they should be so. There is so much in them, which comes

not under the province of acting, with which eye, and tone, and gesture, have nothing to do.... I am not arguing that Hamlet should not be acted, but how much Hamlet is made another thing by being acted.[101]

Lamb's position emphasized the rich potentiality of the print text, of which any performance could render only a fraction; he especially railed against the instructional practice of having students declaim soliloquies out of context. However, his sense that performance diminishes the play conforms to the broader tendency to treat the plays like novels. He even contrasts Shakespeare in performance with the delight given by *Clarissa* in quiet reading.[102] The divorce of stage and page seems to have had no effect on the frequency with which Shakespeare's plays were produced, but it wove them into the assumption that literature was mainly found in books and that theatrical performances of plays were incidental, if not detrimental.[103]

The animus against performance may have been fueled partly by dismay about how drastically Shakespeare's plays had been adapted for performance until the late eighteenth century. This tendency clashed vividly with eighteenth-century textual editors' quest for the closest approximation to Shakespeare's personal intentions. Nahum Tate's adaptation of *King Lear*, in which Cordelia lives and marries Edgar, is the best-known instance of this liberal adaptation, and the nineteenth-century reinvention of Shakespeare as a literary touchstone discouraged any such riding roughshod over the Bard's intentions. Of course, an adaptation such as Tate's might also be understood as a way of treating Shakespeare's works as contemporary—available for engagement, open to accommodating new sensibilities—whereas the later insistence on honoring Bardic intentions risked turning the plays into artifacts suitable only for preservation.[104] Tate's adaptation of *Lear* brought the play back from the margins of the theatrical repertoire into regular performance.[105]

Lawrence Levine has famously demonstrated that commercial productions of Shakespeare during the first half of the nineteenth century attracted cross-class audiences, whereas in the latter part of the century Shakespeare performances were increasingly installed in elite-controlled spaces.[106] Levine and Paul DiMaggio have persuasively sketched a transition between the boisterous audiences of the early part of the century—those who rioted about competing performances of *Macbeth*—and the well-disciplined audiences of the high-culture theater circuit where Shakespeare was usually found toward the end of the century.[107] Professional Shakespearean theater became a mainly bourgeois space during the postbellum years; that's not to say that interlopers from other classes who cared about Shakespeare stayed away, though, and it's important to recognize that the East Coast metropolitan model examined by Levine and DiMaggio did not instantly become a national norm. Then as now, Shakespeare plays were also favorite choices for informal productions of various kinds. Even the Latter Day Saints' Social Hall, erected in 1853 in Salt Lake City, included a gilded bust of Shakespeare atop the arch over its stage.[108] Attendance at Shakespeare productions was undoubtedly impacted by the fact that so many readers knew Shakespeare in print, and evidence suggests that African Americans, working-class Americans, and women of all demographics could easily encounter Shakespeare in print, performance, or both.[109]

Shakespeare was also recited from memory or read aloud, since during the nineteenth century the art of expressive reading was widely valued, ubiquitous in schools and colleges (and developed especially in schools of oratory, such as the ones where Hudson and Rolfe taught) and pursued by many in later life. In 1836, George Ticknor came to know Ludwig Tieck, widely known as the "best reader in Germany," and heard Tieck read the whole of *Henry IV, Part I*; Ticknor also loved to read entire Shakespeare plays aloud to friends.[110] A number of Shakespearean actresses followed Fanny Kemble's lead in turning their dramatic abilities to the platform rather than the stage. Isabella Glyn, whose London reading from *Othello* was reported in a Salt Lake City newspaper, also toured in the United States.[111] Emily Dickinson attended a number of platform readings, probably including at least one featuring Shakespeare.[112] There were African American elocutionists throughout the century who were known for their readings of Shakespeare, one of the best known being Hallie Quinn Brown, who in her long career also became a secondary school teacher, a college professor, a university dean, and principal of Tuskegee Institute.[113] Platform readings appear to have been held mainly in elite cultural spaces, but the sheer number of Shakespearean cultural offerings in circulation suggests that they reached many people.

> 3. Public literary culture was shaped by a widespread belief in the potential for education to improve individuals' lives and the quality of collective life in the United States, although the organization of public literary culture also reflected and sometimes compounded economic and social inequalities.

The boundaries between education, class advancement, sociability, and discretionary pleasure were flexible in public literary culture. Clubs could be light or serious commitments. Many of them were designed to supplement formal education or to substitute for it. Indeed, there is a long tradition in British America and the United States of clubs furthering the education of those who had to leave school or had never been allowed to attend.[114] As a printer's assistant, Benjamin Franklin formed a club of friends who critiqued each other's compositions, and he later joined an early subscription library.[115] Charles Brockden Brown also supplemented his education through clubs. After completing a classical course of study at the Friends' Latin School in Philadelphia by age sixteen, Brown was apprenticed to a lawyer and joined a legal debating club. Around this time, in 1787 or so, he was also a member of a Belles Lettres Club whose members "first denominated themselves the rhetorical, then the literary Society," tracing in miniature a larger cultural shift.[116] Later, when he had given up the law and was living in New York City, he was active in the intellectually bold but politically conservative Friendly Club.[117] The Friendly Club, formed around 1793, emulated salon culture, emphasizing conversation and including women, although the women played circumscribed roles.[118] Hocquet Caritat, a bookseller and printer in New York who published and promoted some of Brown's work, was involved with the group, and his efforts to sponsor a Literary Assembly and several lecture series at his bookstore embodied a generative conjunction between print and salon-style cultural events.[119] A number of literary societies arose in the United States for the purpose of establishing subscription libraries and reading rooms, which in turn supported clubs, lecture series, and study groups.[120]

A generation or two after Brown, E. P. Whipple, later a renowned critic and essayist, left school at fifteen to become a bank clerk but pursued his literary studies through membership in the Boston Mercantile Library Association and a club called Attic Nights.[121] African American literary societies founded around that time, such as the New York Philomathean Society (founded in 1830) and the Minerva Literary Association of Philadelphia (founded in 1834), were similarly designed to give participants access to books and forms of mutual education that would substitute for schooling. These organizations also importantly affirmed African Americans' right of access to education and literary culture.[122] Indeed, efforts at self-education always doubled as efforts not to be shut out of certain conversations or to be marked as ignorant of them, just as the effects of formal education always included the capacities to take part in certain exclusive conversations and to identify others' areas of ignorance. Clubs that substituted for formal schooling or supplemented it might be understood as remedial: designed to fill deficiencies. Since there were many kinds of secondary schooling, though, and since higher education was undergoing long-term curricular transformations, mutual education in these groups was much more open-ended than the practice of earning a general equivalency diploma is today, and independent learners supported by clubs and libraries could get excellent educations. For example, club-educated Whipple became an important reviewer and literary critic; he has been credited with first naming "interpretation" as a specifically literary activity, in an 1846 essay about Coleridge in the *Whig Review*.[123] Literary study could spring from many motives and embody many ideas and hopes about education.

Zeal for adult self-education and mutual education built on possibilities that were historically new, galvanized by the belief that the United States was at the forefront of modern transformations. One reason why the United States never had to undertake the kind of centralized literacy campaign that many European nations did is because access to literacy was so widely supported. Ronald Zboray has called attention to the "worldwide recognition" of the "near-universal literacy" of (free, white) people in the United States during the antebellum period.[124] No doubt this achievement added to the national belief that the United States was exceptional and that remarkable things might be possible here. This cultural investment in literacy added to the oppressive force of laws against slave literacy and contributed to African Americans' investments in literacy and education.[125]

The Morrill Act of 1862 provided funding for land-grant colleges designed to make higher education more readily available, and even though the act emphasized agricultural education and teacher training, it was understood that the colleges were not to be merely vocational. (Rep. Morrill argued that passing the measure would do "[s]omething for every man who loves intelligence and not ignorance.")[126] A side effect of the Morrill Act may have been to increase the desire of those without college educations to sample kinds of learning that were becoming less exclusive. The year 1872 saw the publication of George Cary Eggleston's *How to Educate Yourself: With or without Masters*, for example.[127] Efforts at self- and mutual education were supported by the ways in which the networks of communication and transportation developed during the Civil War increased access to books and periodicals as well as to like-minded collaborators. Over the course of the century, higher education and secondary education became more homogeneous across regions and institutions, and even informal, discretionary outcroppings of literary culture were likely to be connected to kindred outcroppings in other places.

Indeed, the latter part of the nineteenth century was the golden age of informal adult education in the United States: informal in the sense that it was not regulated within a system of standardized credentialing, even if it was highly organized and even if it sometimes enhanced participants' qualifications for employment.[128] This was the case in part because opportunities for formal education, even high school education, were limited throughout the century: only 6.4 percent of the eligible age group had graduated from high school in 1899–1900, although no doubt many more had attended; only 4.0 percent of the eligible age group (assuming those graduating from high school went on immediately to college) had attended college in 1900.[129] One of the best-known informal educational institutions was Chautauqua, which originated as a summer institute for Methodist Sunday school teachers but soon became a major engine of adult education.[130] Infused by the community-building currents of the Social Gospel movement, the leading lights at Chautauqua founded the Chautauqua Literary and Scientific Circle (CLSC) in 1878. The CLSC operated through local study groups, a national publication (the *Chautauquan*), and summer residential programs at the original western New York campus as well as other sites. Chautauqua attracted a number of academics who taught and authored textbooks under its auspices, although its teachers also included ministers and other nonacademics. It represented an attempt (like the university extension movement, which flowered late in the century) to fold academic expertise into the educational currents of public literary culture—for example, it offered a four-year degree program, representing a personal achievement for those who completed it but carrying uncertain authority.[131] Andrew C. Rieser points out, "At the CLSC's height in 1887, its enrollment eclipsed that of the nation's largest universities: 4,468 people received diplomas for completing the four-year course of study, 18,000 were enrolled in the course, and untold tens of thousands more unreported (non-dues paying) readers were participating as ex officio circle members or as casual readers."[132]

English literature was part of the CLSC curriculum from the beginning. A notable Chautauqua textbook was Henry A. Beers's *An Outline Sketch of English Literature* (1886), a literary history organized primarily by the careers of Chaucer, Spenser, Shakespeare, and Milton as well as Sir Walter Scott, whose unusual prominence points to the fact that literary history was beginning to annex nineteenth-century novels.[133] Chautauqua also sponsored fan celebrations of literary authors (Bryant's day; a graduating class dedicated to Sidney Lanier).[134]

George Ticknor's daughter, Anna Eliot Ticknor, founded an influential correspondence study program that thrived around the same time as the CLSC. The Society to Encourage Studies at Home (1873–1896, known as SH) was modeled on an English organization of the same name, but unlike the original, Ticknor's society highlighted its design to "interest all classes."[135] (Further evidence of the transatlantic dimensions of literary culture was the fact that the United Kingdom's National Home Reading Union, organized in 1889, was modeled on Chautauqua, even offering a summer assembly at Blackpool.)[136] SH studies were organized into departments and sections on the emerging university model, and they were impressive in range. Within the sciences, the offerings gradually came to include botany, zoology, astronomy, mathematics, mineralogy, archeology, sanitary science, and psychology. English, German, and French literary studies were all on offer, as were Shakespeare courses. No doubt the extraordinary concentration of intellectual capital in the Boston area accounted for the range of offerings. Ellen T. Parkman (cousin of the nonacademic historian Francis) was a correspondent; Alice Longfellow, one of Henry's daughters, was the head of a section; Alice James, the famous sister of William and Henry, was one of the correspondents, and her lifelong companion (maybe partner) Katharine Peabody Loring was part of the founding oversight committee as well as a department head. Elizabeth Cary Agassiz, an educator whose husband, Louis, was the most eminent scientist at Harvard, also served on the oversight committee, and one of the correspondents in science was Mary W. Whitney, then a special postgraduate student at Harvard, later professor of astronomy at Vassar.[137] The SH in this respect followed in the tradition of Margaret Fuller's conversations and other ambitious informal courses taught by women whose education extended beyond their formal credentialing.[138]

Informal courses of many kinds helped satisfy the extraordinary public appetite for education in the liberal arts. The scarcity of cultural resources in many locations—together with widespread awareness of the cultural and educational ambitions encouraged in public culture nationwide—whetted this appetite, as in the case of an SH student who wrote from "a small town without lectures or lending libraries."[139] But this scarcity also encouraged people to take initiatives, to pool resources, and to make connections across social divides, so that people met as fellow learners or as learners and teachers who might not otherwise have encountered each other. The SH brought many educated women of the Northeast into contact with women far from this orbit—mainly white women in remote areas of the United States, it appears, but at least a couple of African American women and one Japanese student.[140] Since Chautauqua encouraged group study and was open to all comers, it was likely to bring together learners across class lines or at least across familiar social groupings. John Habberton's novel *The Chautauquans* (1891) registered the potential for cross-class community-building effects of CLSC, whether or not it was always fulfilled. The novel features a working-class woman, Mrs. Purkis, who joins a CLSC and ends up studying ancient Greek, tutored by a local college graduate; the aimless college man finds a direction because of the CLSC. Mrs. Purkis's Chautauqua experiences deepen her belief that women's minds are as good as men's—indeed, Chautauqua was overwhelmingly female in membership. And one of the marks of the egalitarian respect practiced at a summer Chautauqua is that she can assure her husband that if he attends, everyone will call him "Mr."[141] Although racially segregated Shakespeare clubs (and KKK-friendly Chautauquas, after World War I) testified that adult educational efforts did not always break down prejudices and social barriers, these efforts were valued for generating new kinds of social connections, and there is some evidence to suggest that they did.[142] For example, Hallie Quinn Brown graduated with a Chautauqua credential and later helped form the first British Chautauqua, in addition to being active throughout her life in the U.S. Women's Club Movement.[143]

Especially in the postbellum decades, liberal arts education was widely sought and invested with hopes for social and individual transformation. Chautauqua, the Society to Encourage Studies at Home, and similar institutions broadcast the importance and pleasure of studying modern literature, ancient literature, philosophy, theology, and other fields. Supported by infrastructures such as these, most of the people who acquired a liberal arts education in the late nineteenth century did so on their own.

How Literature Was Studied

As literature became more narrowly specified, there were ongoing efforts to delineate the kind of reading and study it deserved, and some of the most influential ideas derived from philology and rhetoric. Both philology and rhetoric were conspicuous features of higher education in the United States from the Revolutionary era until the later nineteenth century, but neither became a discipline within the research university model. In broad strokes, between 1800 and 1900, higher education in the United States moved from the model of the college—characterized by a uniform undergraduate curriculum based on classical texts, overseen by professors who taught broad swaths of the curriculum—to that of the research university—which adapted the specialization typical of graduate study for undergraduate education in the forms of majors and electives, and which was organized into discipline-based departments housing faculty members expert in the disciplines. Philosophy, broadly construed, was considered to be the unifying intellectual framework of the early college: moral, intellectual, political, and natural philosophy covered most of the curriculum, supplemented by rhetoric and mathematics.[144] Works that would come to count as literary—Sophocles's *Oedipus Rex* and Homer's *Odyssey* and Ovid's *Metamorphoses*—were taught in Latin and Greek courses in the early college, as were works such as Aristotle's *Poetics* that would become formative in literary culture, but they were taught alongside Tacitus's history, Lucretius's science, and Euclid's mathematics, all of which could be approached through philology and rhetoric. It is possible that neither became a discipline within the research university model precisely because they were associated with the classical curriculum and the intellectual sprawl of the early college.

Philology and rhetoric also circulated outside U.S. colleges. Although it was difficult for people who could not study at a Latin grammar school or a college to learn ancient languages, by the late eighteenth century it was taken for granted that both philology and rhetoric applied to texts in English and other modern languages. Before the widespread creation of professional publications devoted to specific branches of academic learning, a variety of magazines and newspapers reviewed new publications in these fields: as with Shakespeare studies, it was easy for people to take an interest in these fields, and people without academic credentials could become respected authorities.

Philology treats languages as historically dynamic, examining the cultural worlds in which they circulated. James Turner argues that philology was the seedbed of most current humanistic disciplines, in tandem with antiquarianism: the study of language and the study of human artifacts collaborated in shedding light on ways in which life was lived and meaning made at various places and times. Like rhetoric, philology has ancient roots; like rhetoric, it was distinguished from philosophy insofar as philosophy sought "universally valid generalizations" rather than understandings of particular cases (compositions, words, genres, practices, political cultures, and so forth).[145] But whereas rhetoric was the study of eloquence, oriented toward practice, philology was oriented toward research, haunting libraries and homing in on texts distant and complex enough to pose interpretive difficulties.[146]

By the late eighteenth century, philology had become standard equipment for understanding valuable legacy texts: sacred texts, in the case of the Bible, and sacralized texts, in the case of cherished classical writings. The Bible was understood to pose many of the same kinds of textual challenges posed by the *Iliad*, challenges best met by scholars who could use the earliest extant manuscript versions (varied by translation and transcription practices) to extrapolate features and wordings of still earlier, presumably more authentic versions that had probably been lost forever.[147] By the late seventeenth century, at least some editors recognized that Shakespeare's plays could benefit from the same philological procedures, since each play existed in several versions.[148] It is even possible that the textual complexities of Shakespeare's plays contributed to his status as a foundational modern literary author, since the task of establishing authoritative versions of the plays lent itself to the kinds of scholarly investigation practiced on other venerated texts.[149] Shakespeare's plays required the caretaking of textual editors, and this editorial attention led editors to dilate on the local and global attainments of Shakespeare's work. The elaboration of close reading as literary practice built on the philological practice of writing textual glosses, which could offer "flashes of textual insight" as well as "sustained interpretations."[150] And some of the earliest widely circulating instances of philologically inclined literary interpretation were Coleridge's published lectures on Shakespeare, which offered framing perspectives on the plays followed by running philological glosses on the significance of even slight and seemingly trivial wordings, such as "again," early in Hamlet, and "Hillo, ho ho," a little later.[151]

Many resources for literary interpretation derive from biblical philological scholarship, and controversies over the new wave of biblical criticism known as the higher criticism disseminated these resources.[152] The higher criticism held that biblical scribes had necessarily embedded divine messages in their own worldviews and linguistic genres, so that the Bible was shaped by the disparate contexts of its initial scribes in addition to registering the vagaries of oral and manuscript transmission. The higher criticism also proposed that many passages from scripture, perhaps even the whole story of Jesus's life, ought to be read as figurative or mythic. The emphasis on sacred truth that was not literally true—offering wisdom or insight, not empirical knowledge—set an important precedent for many claims made about literature and also laid the foundation for the study of the Bible as literature.

Many interpretive projects that became part of literary studies were developed first or simultaneously within biblical criticism, which was also informed by Jewish rabbinical studies. Most influential for literary studies was the project of extracting authorial intentions—divine inspiration, for believers—from the historical travels that counted as textual corruptions. Biblical criticism also offered methods for incorporating cultural contexts into interpretation (those scribal distortions) and models of textual unity appropriate even to a compendious text.[153] The allegorical interpretation of biblical persons and events was common among nineteenth-century Euro-American Christians, and Christian typological criticism assumed that key events and figures in the Old Testament prefigured those in the New Testament, given that all time was equally present for God. The belief that an Old Testament personage might be a forerunner or first draft of a New Testament revelation prepared the way for the literary interpretation of certain characters as foils for others (or versions of others), the presumption that certain characters might be more central than others to an author's or work's vision, and even the possibility that narrators who were not completely reliable—not fully aware of the significance of what they narrated—could nonetheless be immensely instructive.[154]

In attending so closely to the analysis of form and genre as a function of interpretation, philology drew on poetics. Indeed, the contact zone between public-oriented and aesthetic versions of literature might be traced back to rhetoric and poetics, a pairing authorized by Aristotle—and since so many Euro-American persons of letters were steeped in classical traditions, this genealogy cannot be wrong. It doesn't offer the whole story, however, since as we've seen, poetry and poetics were altered significantly by being reconfigured within the ensemble of literary genres and brought into contact with philology. Rhetoric had undergone an even more remarkable transformation since the classical era. Although rhetorical traditions were never completely forgotten, rhetoric languished between the classical era and the Renaissance because medieval Scholasticism privileged dialectics (effectively, logic) instead. Quintilian's *Institutes* were rediscovered in 1416, renewing interest in rhetoric, including its potential to inform dialectical disputation.[155] Rhetoric's prominence in the long nineteenth century resulted from a seventeenth-century French and Scottish refurbishing, which prepared the way for republican investments in rhetoric on the part of English Whigs and U.S. revolutionaries in the eighteenth century.[156]

The most obvious benefit of rhetoric during the Revolutionary era was its support for oratory, a crucial political practice. Eloquence can be valuable in public or private, but public oratory remained important in secondary and higher education throughout the nineteenth century, sometimes in the curriculum and always for ceremonial occasions. Commencements typically featured class orators as well as class poets, and this practice lasted long after the time of Barlow, Brackenridge, and Freneau. Bliss Perry, who studied at Williams College from 1877 to 1881, and Denton J. Snider, who was a student at Iberia College and Oberlin College in the 1850s, wrote memoirs in the early twentieth century about their collegiate ambitions to distinguish themselves as orators. Both men took for granted that their readers might not know that public speaking used to be so highly valued. "No one pays much attention to such contests now, but in our day crowds attended them," Perry recalled, mentioning a competition for graduating seniors at Williams. Similarly, Snider recreated the context in which "I, like every American boy, was ambitious to be an orator, and to speak before the people."[157] Notwithstanding their sense that oratory had lost prestige, David Gold's case study of three nonelite colleges in the late nineteenth century suggests that oratory remained important in many institutions of higher education throughout the century and was often supervised by English departments.[158] And oratory may have allowed some students to draw on traditions of eloquence that did not derive from ancient Greek and Rome: the Native American authors Charles Eastman and Zitkala-Sâ were both accomplished student orators.[159]

It's easy to spot the emerging version of literature in textbooks designed to support rhetoric and oratory. Many of these circulating in college and secondary schools brought together protoliterary arrays of readings, with Shakespeare prominent.[160] William Enfield's *The Speaker* (1774) and William Scott's *Lessons in Elocution* (1781), English textbooks that circulated and were reprinted in the United States, included numerous passages from Shakespeare, Pope, Milton, Dryden, and Addison, authors well on their way to literary canonization.[161] The difference between the contents of a textbook called a "speaker" and a textbook called a "reader" was not great, but the ones called readers signaled their orientation toward print, with McGuffey's *Fifth* and *Sixth Readers* serving as the introduction to literature—and to Shakespeare—for countless secondary school students during the nineteenth century.[162] Because students had to acquire these books, rather than being lent them by the school or buying them and selling them back at year's end, the books were likely to stay in students' lives.[163] Decades after he left Williams, Bliss Perry remembered the names of some of his textbooks. Growing up in Ohio in the 1850s, Denton Snider quarreled amicably with his father about the comparative virtues of Lindley Murray's *English Reader*, which had been his father's textbook, and the McGuffey readers used in his own schooling. Snider did not fail "to absorb" the *English Reader* in spite of his preference, presumably because it was a cultural touchstone.[164] Books used as course texts also circulated outside formal schooling, contributing to many projects of self-education and mutual education.[165] A sign of the traffic between instructional cultures and public literary culture was the fact that the examinations of two U.S. women college students who had competed well in a contest held by the New Shakspere Society of London were published as a book in 1883.[166]

Rhetorical textbooks could morph easily into literary textbooks because literature's conceptualization borrowed significantly from rhetoric. Many tropes prominent in rhetorical studies became standard equipment in literary studies (metaphor, metonymy, apostrophe, and so forth), and rhetorical criteria such as *decorum* (suiting speech to the speaker and the situation) shaped literary attention to speakers, narrators, and characterization. In keeping with rhetorical emphasis on genres, the discrimination of literary genres, subgenres, and modes became a prerequisite for literary interpretation and appraisal. Rhetorical frameworks for analyzing a skilled rhetor's effects on an audience were incorporated into rationales for literature's (public-oriented) potential to stimulate sympathy, promote virtue, and contribute to readers' understandings of social problems.

The fact that rhetoric and oratory were so prominent in the eighteenth century has led historians to ask what happened to rhetoric over the next century; the fact that literature carried forward so many rhetorical practices adds to the conundrum. As Robert Connors has posed the problem, John Quincy Adams served as Boylston Professor of Rhetoric at Harvard from 1806 to 1809 (an appointment embodying the link between rhetorical capability and public political life), whereas a century later, rhetoric was invisible in Harvard's curriculum and played a diminished role throughout U.S. higher education.[167] Instead of rhetoric, departments of English came to occupy a central place in the U.S. research university: that is, in the variety of institutions organized on the disciplinary model of the research university. Just as literary studies absorbed some of rhetoric's frameworks for analyzing texts, rhetoric's role as a framework for students' composing, in speech and writing, was transferred to composition. Since composition was for a long time devalued in English studies, relegated to the transmission of skills and cast as something that served rather than advanced the intellectual missions of the research university, the channeling of rhetoric into composition might be understood to have turned robust civic eloquence into administrative report writing, built on the dull foundations of the five-paragraph essay and multimodal rhetoric.[168]

Literature comes off badly in these accounts. The origin story of composition's devalued status is this: when Johns Hopkins tried to hire Francis Child, Harvard retained him by allowing him to teach literature, passing on all the teaching that required intensive marking of student essays to lower-status faculty members.[169] George Ticknor was similarly freed up from instructing students in foreign languages in order to lecture on literature.[170] In parallel with the separation of composition instruction from literary studies and composition's demotion, practitioners of speech and theater studies often felt marginalized within English departments, presumably by the literary contingent, before they left to form disciplines and departments of their own. (Joseph Roach has lamented theater history's "Babylonian captivity in departments of English.")[171] It is possible that even more than other new disciplines, modern language and literature departments rigorously patrolled their disciplinary center—literary studies—segregating and demoting anything that seemed preparatory or supplemental. Nevertheless, the politics and organizational cultures of English departments can't really take sole blame for the disappearance of rhetoric in higher education, because by the time the research university model was developed, literature had already established widespread public support, and rhetoric, as an area of study, was on the wane. As far as I know, there was no constituency pressing for the establishment of rhetoric as a core discipline in research universities when they were new.

The larger question is whether the decline in rhetoric's public prominence during the nineteenth century manifested—or caused or contributed to—public culture's diminishment. Some histories of rhetoric strikingly parallel Jürgen Habermas's argument that the politically vital culture of the eighteenth century declined in the nineteenth century, so that public culture became consumerist, privatized, and somewhat passive.[172] As Mark Longaker has summarized this tradition, it posits that a "golden age" of public deliberation "precedes a fall, sometimes into belletrism, sometimes into liberal individualism, sometimes into formalism."[173] Longaker has countered this narrative by pointing out that rhetorical instruction in early U.S. colleges was not necessarily a support for civic republicanism, in part because higher education was modeled on the elite educational traditions of the United Kingdom; this perspective aligns with civic republicanism's potential to fuel imperial ambitions and identifications with the ruling class.[174] Other scholars have argued that literature embodies everything that went wrong with public culture in the nineteenth century. Barbara Warnick has proposed that the emergence within rhetoric of belles lettres, premised on the receptive faculty of taste rather than the active work of composition, set in motion a Habermas-style descent, culminating in the privileging of passive, subjective literary studies and the rhetoric's marginalization in the research university.[175] Outside the history of rhetoric, Jared Gardner has similarly argued that the prestige accorded to the novel and its book format in nineteenth-century U.S. literary culture marked the loss of the lively, civic-oriented dialogic magazines that characterized the early national period.[176]

The largest purpose of *Literature in the Making* is to offer a history of the consolidation and institutionalization of literature, but it is really impossible to offer a comprehensive explanation for why rhetoric lost ground in the nineteenth century. Many factors can be identified, though. Connors has proposed that an important reason for this decline might be that German universities, so important as models in the United States, did not offer doctorates in rhetoric; Turner's sense that rhetoric had in earlier centuries been more closely aligned with teaching than scholarly research suggests why that was the case, and the research university's tendency to promote scholarship at the expense of teaching may have compounded rhetoric's subordination, once rhetoric became an infrastructure for composition instruction.[177]

Two additional factors that may have contributed to rhetoric's decline and literature's rise are worth considering more closely: U.S. culture's dependency on print and public fears of coercion and manipulation, both of which escalated in the nineteenth century. In spite of everyone's admiration for Joseph Addison's style, and in spite of the fact that a number of eighteenth-century instructional texts in rhetoric emphasized written composition, rhetoric remained strongly associated with oral eloquence. In modern (and eagerly modernizing) nations, in contrast, there was ever-growing reliance on written and print records and on print as a medium for disseminating information, analysis, and criticism. Writing during the late 1720s in France, Charles Rollin, in a chapter devoted to the "Eloquence of the Bar," included a discussion of legal report writing, noting that this branch of legal work "is of much more frequent use, and more extensive in our days than the eloquence of the bar."[178] Writing in Scotland later in the century, Hugh Blair also took for granted that oratory had declined in importance. He recycled the familiar claim that the most powerful eloquence was likely to be produced by citizens participating in healthy political cultures, but he implied that public speaking was less important than it used to be because print had taken over some of its functions.[179] Law had become so complex that just keeping on top of it had to be a lawyer's primary goal, with eloquence being demoted to a "secondary accomplishment." A further symptom of the decline of eloquence was that ministers had begun reading sermons rather than speaking from memory, leading to a very "different" and "inferior" kind of composition, Blair judged.[180]

Benjamin Franklin observed in 1782 that print was replacing oratory because it could reach so many more people.[181] Edward Larkin estimates that by 1791 Thomas Paine had sold more books than any single author in the history of publishing, and even beyond the enhanced influence of individual books and pamphlets such as *Common Sense*, colonial newspapers played a crucial role in circulating information about acts of anti-British resistance.[182] In-person deliberation was and is important in U.S. political life, but especially in the long nineteenth century (when print literacy and print outlets were expanding, and before cinema and television), a host of functions previously accomplished by speech were taken over by print. Evaluations of political officeholders and corporate and community leaders continued to prompt informal rhetorical analysis, especially of ethos, but comprehensive rhetorical traditions had to be rediscovered in late twentieth-century U.S. academic culture because they had come to be marginalized and underestimated in the late nineteenth century.[183]

Print became more widespread and consequential. It also fascinated people, and the cultural fascination with print's impact—often counted as modern—may have prepared the way for new modes of analysis that departed from rhetoric. The primacy of print should not be understood as print's displacing earlier cultural forms or making them obsolete, however. Ronald J. Zboray and Mary Saracino Zboray have pointed out the "nineteenth-century print culture surge" did not "replace earlier scribal and oral cultures" but rather reconfigured them: for example, Emerson characterized a writer as an "orator manqué."[184] In public literary culture, print, manuscript, speech, and performance were all interwoven, and things were continually being transferred from one medium to another. Literary texts were read aloud and performed, and like George Ticknor, many people wrote letters about the literary conversations they had and the performances they witnessed. (Ticknor's selected letters were published in 1877.) People who studied together often wrote papers they presented orally; some of them were later printed in books or periodicals, and others were summarized in newspapers. In addition to the circulation of creative works in manuscript, people copied passages from books and periodicals into letters and commonplace books, and sometimes handwritten copies of print texts were important channels of distribution: for example, some of Elizabeth Barrett's poems circulated in hand-copied form at Brook Farm before they were available in the United States in print.[185] Ballad and folklore collectors who were helping to equip nations with popular traditions transferred oral compositions to handwriting and then print.[186] Like scholarship about manuscript cultures, then, scholarship about oral and performance cultures has begun to reconfigure literary studies; the category "orature" has been proposed as a way to bring together written and oral compositions.[187]

For all that rhetoric has long been prized for supporting argumentation, another important factor in rhetoric's decline may have been the Enlightenment's obsession with rationality. The chief medium of rationality in U.S. political culture was language, especially print, as manifested in a written constitution achieved through deliberation; codified laws and records of government proceedings; and literacy-based education designed to form a citizenry capable of voting, holding office, and obeying laws. State reason depended on language's stability: effective communication across lines of party was assumed to be possible, and in this large-scale representative democracy, written texts had to be constant over time and across distances. Numbers were also a medium of governmental rationality, and rational language sometimes was envisioned on the model of arithmetic. One plus one always equaled two; Socrates's mortality, centuries after the contingent historical fact of his death, could still be logically deduced; and certain self-evident truths were so durable that they could become the permanent basis of a new regime. The desire for language to be stable and transparent—purely functional and communicative, not metaphoric and dynamic—reflected a desire for uncorrupted literal communication, and it informed attempts to distinguish poetry from prose, ornament from argument. It was also impossible to fulfill, and it points to the fact that rationality, or at least instrumental rationality—involving means and ends, profits and losses, checks and balances—was itself a kind of fantasy.[188]

Within this fantasy of perfect rationality, rhetorical persuasion was suspect. The relationship between persuasion and conviction had long posed difficulties for rhetoric: one can be convinced by a rational demonstration, even a syllogism, so what exactly does persuasion add?[189] This difficulty is prominent in Hugh Blair's *Lectures on Rhetoric and Belles-Lettres* (1783), arguably the most influential rhetorical guidebook in the United States during the period.[190] Blair fended off various "prevalent" "false notions" about eloquence, thereby recirculating them.[191] In countering the false notion that eloquence was a means of prettifying an argument and manipulating an audience, Blair posited a relationship between conviction and persuasion that was often reiterated by other writers: "Conviction affects the understanding only; persuasion, the will and the practice."[192] Ideally, eloquence would build on conviction to turn a justified intellectual conclusion into action. However, the idea that persuasion was responsible for moving people to action introduced the slippery problem that emotional responses were required for the operations of the will. Blair even refers to the "passions," which were usually treated as powerful, perhaps unruly, different in register from the emotional cultivation of sympathy or other sociable affects.[193] The mistrust that this model of persuasion could generate is marked by the fact that for the immensely influential Immanuel Kant, this gap between conviction and action ought never even exist. Rhetorical persuasion even for a good cause is nefarious, Kant held, "for it is not enough to do what is right, but it is also to be performed solely on the ground that it is right."[194]

Of course, it was possible for eloquence to be abused—like "every Art which ever has been studied among mankind," Blair pointed out—but Blair believed that modern Britons especially were "on the watch," "jealous of being deceived by Oratory" and well-prepared (especially if they knew Blair's *Lectures*) to detect insincere rhetors and specious arguments.[195] As Gordon Wood has observed about the new United States, "Republics demanded far more morally from their citizens than monarchies did of their subjects," and they demanded new forms of discernment as well.[196] Rhetoricians promoted the idea that it wasn't possible for rhetors to manipulate others' feelings effectively if they dissimulated: according to Rollin, "to affect others,... we must be deeply touched with the subject we treat of, be fully convinced of it, and be sensible of its whole truth and importance."[197] This idea that successful rhetors had to be sincere could only be stipulated, not demonstrated, and it was not universally believed. When Charles Brockden Brown was ambivalently considering a career in law, during the early 1790s, he worried that "the superior artifice or eloquence" of a silver-tongued lawyer might lead to injustice—in effect, he worried that he might be too effective an advocate.[198] His 1799 novel *Ormond* explored a different rhetorical danger. The eponymous villain was not a deceiving Machiavel but a self-deluded sociopath who believed that because the machinery of society is likely to make anyone a party to great evils, the only rational thing any man can do is pursue "his own good." Ormond's own good required a number of seductions and murders, which he justified with rational-sounding eloquence.[199] Syllogistic reasoning and rhetorical eloquence were both rendered monstrous in *Ormond*.

From this perspective, the fact that books were encountered separately from their authors' persons might contribute to their value, since readers' reflectiveness and distance from authors might protect them from being overwhelmed by authors' personal charisma. A strangely vehement case for the superiority of books to oratory cropped up in Frederick Beecher Perkins's *The Best Reading* (1872), and the vehemence suggests that oratory was still an

Studying Literature

enemy worth stabbing in 1872. Perkins, an influential early librarian and the absentee father of Charlotte Perkins Gilman, proposed the categorical superiority of books to oratory by identifying oratory with manipulation and coercion—the worst possibilities of rhetorical persuasion—in contrast to judicious readerly reflection:

> Now, Reading is the best means of nourishing Thought. Oratory, on the other hand, is the worst, since it depends on moving the feelings, which disturbs the reason. And even if the hearer can keep his feelings untouched, yet he may not object or question. He is to sit unresisting, and drink in whatever is put down his throat. This is well enough for young robins and babies, but it is a ludicrous way of dieting for a grown man—for an enlightened mind. Debating and conversation are better discipline than oratory, since they allow a comparison of views. Conversation especially, and most of all that form of it so highly prized by open minds, where one can resort to some wise friend and ask questions, and discuss them, is extremely useful. It is greatly superior to debate in this, that it is not so liable to excitements of the external sort, such as anger, desire to win, or desire to show off.
>
> But if only one of these kinds of mental exercise might be had, it should be books, books, books, a thousand times to one. Compared with books, public speaking is a war-dance, conversation a beating bushes for wild fruit; well enough for savages and strays, but having small place or power in the discipline of a cultivated mind.[200]

Perkins's stand was so extreme as to be ludicrous, but it crystallized the idea that books and oratory were in competition and that books promoted reflection, oratory impulsiveness.

As we've seen, aesthetic autonomy was initially formulated to protect literature from excessive patrolling on the part of the state and religious authorities. It also distanced literature from the marketplace, submerging its commodity status in a fantasy of direct communion with authors. In addition, the promotion of aesthetic autonomy constituted literary reading as a reflective encounter whose emotional intensities were qualitatively different from those inciting action. Literature as art operated at a remove from the world of action, which meant that literature was insulated from some of the dangers associated with rhetoric and oratory.

It's ironic that the power of oral eloquence was so mistrusted even though print was shaped by the indirect persuasions of consumer culture, class hierarchy, and party polarization. As I've recounted, though, print literacy was powerfully identified as a support for individuals' efforts to learn about the world and develop new competencies. It's possible also that the prevailing fantasy of private individual reading provided the imaginative means of being outside "Society" (that mystifying collective) and its performances: the fantasy may have had real effects, although they would be impossible to measure.[201] Literary culture's attention to reception, originating as Warnick has noted in concerns with "taste," may also have helped people formulate a discerning relationship to print at a time when its actual impact was greater than ever before.

Taste, Belles Lettres, and the Sublime

The practice of criticism included the cultivation of taste, an all-purpose category of readerly discrimination, and this development went hand in hand with the promotion of belles lettres. Belles lettres effectively began with the 1663 founding of France's Académie des Inscriptions et Belles-Lettres, which was charged with producing elegant Latin inscriptions for public monuments and medals, another collaboration between philology and antiquarianism.[202] Over the next century, the study of "beautiful writings" became a project attached to rhetoric, and it was taken up by Scottish rhetoricians like Blair who were influenced by Rollin; Rollin's *De la Manière d'enseigner et d'étudier les belles lettres* (1726–1728) was translated in 1734 as *The Method of Teaching and Studying the Belles Lettres*.[203] Rollin attended both to conventional forms of oratory and public eloquence and to belles lettres, chiefly poetry, which he took for granted that students would write as well as read.[204]

Belles lettres was often translated into English as "polite literature."[205] Politeness provided an ethic for eighteenth-century print culture, most obviously in the case of *Spectator*-style periodicals but perhaps also for books whose subtitles, prefaces, and other apparatuses seemed designed to offer courteous introductions to the strangers who took them up.[206] In the Republic of Letters, politeness and civility were emollients for transactions among people who met only through their correspondence or who inhabited very different social worlds; politeness also characterized social milieus in which the sexes mingled.[207] And just as civic republican and liberal discourses could amalgamate in the eighteenth century, discourses and philosophies of virtue could combine with concerns for politeness and civility.[208] The groundwork for belletrism's potential to merge with "republican political discourse" in British America and the early United States is already visible in Rollin's linking of taste with possibilities for personal worth and dignity that are detached from wealth and birth, a stance that makes sense because republican ideas and the expansion of higher education were also at work in eighteenth-century France.[209]

In spite of the republican roots of belles lettres, belles lettres came to be a keyword for the most aesthetically rarefied and least public-oriented understandings of literature after modern literature emerged. By 1904, the D. C. Heath Company had begun to publish a series of literary works and literary studies called "The Belles-Lettres Series: Literature for Literature's Sake," aligning belles lettres with late-century aestheticism.[210] In the same spirit, Henry Beers wrote in 1887 that "[p]ure literature, or what, for want of a better term we call *belles lettres*, was not born in America until the nineteenth century was well underway."[211] Ironically, his periodization excluded the eighteenth-century works written specifically under the rubric of belles lettres, offering another instance of the nineteenth century's suppression of eighteenth-century cultures of letters. Even more ironically, these eighteenth-century productions included many civic-oriented writings in literary genres, not literature for literature's sake. In the nineteenth century and after, belles lettres came to be associated with elitism and luxury, perhaps because French phrases in English are often associated with overrefined cultural arrogance: belles lettres got linked to French social artifice rather than Scottish civic-mindedness or German idealism.[212] Belles lettres signified an elevated concern with beauty and taste, and this elevated concern could carry class condescension or even class aggression.

The pairing of rhetoric with belles lettres was famously marked by Blair's *Lectures on Rhetoric and Belles Lettres* and cropped up often; we've seen it in the name of one of Charles Brockden Brown's clubs and in the lengthy title of George Ticknor's professorship. Blair's definition of poetry, the centerpiece of his discussion of belles lettres, emphasizes its catalytic power: poetry is "the language of passion, or of enlivened imagination, formed, most commonly, into regular numbers."[213] However, the fact that belles lettres takes its name from beauty may also have become a liability as the sublime, contrasted with beauty, began to name one of the best-known versions of literature's dynamism. Henry Reed's lectures of 1850–1851 offered a vigorous critique of belles lettres grounded in the assumption that belles lettres excluded the sublime:

> "Belles-lettres"—fine letters—polite literature—what thought do these terms convey but of luxuries of the mind, a refined amusement, but no more than amusement, confectionaries (as it were) of the mind, rather than needful, solid, healthy, life-sustaining food. If the term "*belles-lettres*" excludes the weighty and sublime productions of the mind, then is it a miserable substitute for what should be comprehended in such a term as "*literature*:" if it includes them, then is it a pitifully inapposite title. Now the mischief is just here: this dainty, feeble term leads people to suppose that literature is an easy, indolent cultivation, a sort of passive, patrician pleasure, instead of demanding dutiful and studious and strenuous energy. It lowers the great works of genius, as if they could be approached indolently, thoughtlessly, and without preparatory discipline.[214]

Reed's account (keyed, let's recall, to the activities of private readers, supported by informal extracurricular lectures) insists that reading literature is work, whereas the category of belles lettres reeks of leisure. He also draws on De Quincey's distinction between the "literature of knowledge" and the "literature of power" to disqualify the literature of knowledge from his primary categories of universality and timeless significance, since knowledge can be superseded.[215] Literature that combines both power and knowledge can be valuable, but "a nation's purest literature" is the literature of power, and power was the mark of the sublime rather than the beautiful.[216]

In practice, many discussions of belles lettres, including Blair's, had taken up the sublime in an admiring fashion, not registering any sense that it was out of place in a domain named for beauty. The sublime was not necessarily aligned with the disruptive or the unorthodox: indeed, it could take the form of religious awe, conducive to piety.[217] The sublime had become an important European aesthetic touchstone after Longinus's rediscovered treatise *On the Sublime* was translated by Nicolas Boileau into French in 1674 (into English in 1739).[218] There were competing attempts afterward to distill the sublime's fundamental nature and elaborate its significance, most notably by Edmund Burke (1757) and Immanuel Kant (1790), both of whom contrasted the sublime with the beautiful, as Longinus had not done. Kant's discussion is more complex than Burke's, but in both, the sublime is identified with dynamism and risk and coded as masculine, whereas beauty receives a condescending, misogynistic treatment as a quality characteristic of objects that lend themselves to pleasing—and conforming to—the senses.[219] Flowers are beautiful, whereas vast stormy oceans are sublime—except that Kant outdoes Burke by proposing that, really, only Ideas of Reason are sublime, since the sublime is characterized fundamentally by demanding the exercise of faculties surpassing the senses. (Kant concedes that vast stormy oceans may lead the mind to sublime contemplations, though.)[220] For Burke, the sublime is connected with genuine threats to self-preservation: the stormy ocean's objective dangers contribute to its sublime effect on us, even if we are not at sea and vulnerable. For Kant, it's just the opposite, since a threat to self-preservation might catalyze self-interest. We experience the sublime only when we are personally safe, Kant holds, but the sublime presents a challenge to the mind's power of engagement, a sense of its "limits and inadequacy," as well as an opportunity to "measure ourselves against the apparent all-powerfulness of nature" and become aware of our minds' distinct powers.[221] The sublime arises within the human mind, summons the mind's most valuable capacities, and ultimately affirms the mind's powers of apprehension and comprehension. "Dazzling and tremendous how quick the sunrise would kill me, / If I could not now and always send sunrise out of me," Whitman put it, folding erotic capacities into the circuit of sublime encounter.[222]

The sublime was often codified, but especially in the Kantian tradition it was paradoxically characterized as eluding codification. Kant identified the sublime with boundlessness.[223] In this way, the sublime was peculiarly compatible with the idealization of organic form (versus rule-bound classicism) that was influential in the development of modern literature, especially in relation to Shakespeare, the poet of nature.[224] Kant's account emphasizes the volatility of the sublime versus the repose—perhaps even stasis—of the beautiful: "The mind feels itself *moved* in the representation of the sublime in nature, while the aesthetic judgment on the beautiful in nature is in *calm* contemplation."[225] As Perkins's caricature of literature versus oratory indicated, however, literature and literary reading could also be aligned with the beautiful, described in registers consistent with Kant's account of the contemplative response elicited by beauty. Literary reading was often figured as withdrawn from the world, in keeping with the idea that art (in the strictest idealist formulations) was independent of public political life, collective social life, and ordinary existence in time and place.

But the centrality of the sublime in modern literary aesthetics reveals how deeply literature was also imbued with desires for transformative experience, desires that were partly the legacy of rhetorical theory and practice. The very patrolling of literature attested to its power. Strict constructions of aesthetic autonomy that banished not only the political regulation of literature but also authors' political convictions; formulations of literary taste that idealized a canon and displaced commodification onto print texts deemed subliterary; the preeminence of the author-function, which sought readerly protection in classical rhetoric's emphasis on ethos; the promulgation and institutionalization of protocols for proper literary reading; and the tendency to construct literary practices as devotional practices, borrowing from Protestant soul-searching, Catholic confession, and other forms of self-monitoring—all these ways of regulating literature registered the sense that literature was, or might be, overwhelmingly powerful. The forms of regulation may have effectively diluted literature's power for many readers, and the ways in which the regulation of literature perpetuated social hierarchy meant that literature (not just belles lettres) was sometimes an engine of class aggression or class aspiration. Nevertheless, the relentless obsession with the nature of agency in literary reading throughout the century might be understood as marking the deep ambivalence at work in such projects of cultivation, in which desires to open the self to possibilities of transformation strained against countering desires to preserve the self, patrol its boundaries, and rigorously control its interchanges with the world.

Coleridge, Emerson, and the Legacies of Moral Philosophy

The concerns I've described about readers' vulnerability led a number of literary readers to take guidance from two literary and religious authorities, Samuel Taylor Coleridge and Ralph Waldo Emerson. In different ways, these important thinkers forged ideas about how literature could be more or less secular while offering some of the comforts of religious authority and the power of the sacred. Both studied literature, but Coleridge offered models for literary analysis suited to modern ways of knowing, whereas Emerson continually urged readers to resist modern ways of knowing and being known. Both figures shaped public literary culture and have remained important in academic literary studies.

The cultural authority exercised by both Coleridge and Emerson drew on a surprising precedent: the stature of moral philosophy, as exemplified by its place in the early college curriculum. The Christian affiliations of many U.S. colleges, shored up by the cultural dominance of Protestant Christianity, and the youth of many college students (who might enter whenever they had acquired the prerequisites for entrance, even in their early teens) all contributed to the paternalistic climate of early colleges.[226] The capstone course for seniors was moral philosophy, usually taught by the college president, who was likely to be a minister and certain to be religiously orthodox, according to the brand of Protestantism holding sway. Moral philosophy was therefore a course in which an authoritative intellectual figure modeled ways in which philosophy, science, and other forms of intellectual inquiry could be reconciled with Christian orthodoxy as well as with established laws and conventional morality.[227] Moral philosophy as a subject matter emblematized the early college's religious and social functions, which may be why the discipline of philosophy later installed in research universities initially deemphasized ethics.[228]

The curricular prominence of moral philosophy in colleges was one outcropping of the widespread influence of Scottish intellectual and institutional models in the early United States.[229] Scottish higher education was strikingly innovative during the decades after the 1707 Act of Union, and some of the earliest lectures about English literature or its near predecessors were offered in Scottish universities.[230] As Neil Rhodes explains, "English literature was the medium through which the newly Britished Scots might become socially assimilated with England," assimilation that might further their chances of enjoying "the commercial benefits of the expanding British Empire." The fact that English literary studies developed on the peripheries of the British Empire as well as in dissenting academies in England meant that the earliest academic versions of English literary studies were set up to facilitate acculturation, including projects of social aspiration.[231] These factors applied in early U.S. colleges as well, since the United States had been a British colony and continued to be oriented culturally toward Europe. Whereas the classical curriculum had given elite men in the United States an education comparable to that available to elite Europeans, the study of English literature gave college students some access to English social life and tastes.

The Scottish way of grafting literary studies onto moral philosophy circulated in books readily available in North America, but it was also carried directly by Scottish academics who emigrated (such as John Witherspoon, who later became president of Princeton) and by graduates of Scottish universities who brought and promoted the books important to their intellectual formation (such as Francis Alison, a protégé of philosopher and rhetorician Francis Hutcheson and later vice provost of the University of Pennsylvania).[232] In 1729,

Alison's mentor Hutcheson had taken up a chair in moral philosophy at the University of Glasgow and became the first faculty member in the institution to teach in English rather than Latin, perhaps because he hoped the vernacular would make the course more directly applicable to students' lives. His *Inquiry into the Origin of Our Ideas of Beauty and Virtue* (1725), written while he taught in a private academy in Dublin, was an early work coordinating taste and ethics within the framework of Common Sense, and his teaching folded together rhetoric, belles lettres, and contemporary social and political issues.[233] Hutcheson's student Adam Smith offered some of the earliest lectures on English literature and elaborated, in *Theory of the Moral Sentiments*, how imaginative literature, especially fiction, could help stimulate and refine moral responses.

Not surprisingly, early literary studies in the United States often cropped up in close proximity to moral philosophy, whose professors were likely to add rhetoric or belles lettres to their subject areas, as in the case of an overloaded professorship of "Moral, Intellectual, and Political Philosophy, Rhetoric and Belles Lettres" at Columbia College (from 1818 to 1854) and a professorship in "Belles Lettres, and Moral and Mental Philosophy" at the University of Mississippi (from 1856 to 1868).[234] Henry Reed had been a professor of moral philosophy before becoming a professor of rhetoric and English literature by about 1835.[235] William H. McGuffey, of *McGuffey's Reader* fame, was in the late 1850s professor of moral philosophy at the University of Virginia.[236] Hiram Corson, who was by 1890 an influential professor of English literature at Cornell University, began his career as professor of moral science, history, and rhetoric at Girard College in 1856.[237]

These professorial titles are handy markers of the influence of moral philosophy on literature, which mainly took the form of the widespread assumption that literature was ethically valuable. Although didacticism was deemed unliterary, it usually designated excesses of ethical prescription or short-circuitings of ethical work that ought to be more robust. Invocations of "art for art's sake" late in the century were mainly pitched against the widespread idea that literature ought to promote morality. Many people who embraced some version of aesthetic autonomy nonetheless believed that literature undertook ethical missions—indeed, this belief provided an enduring rationale for literature, even when the ethical mission was pitched against social orthodoxy. Over the course of the nineteenth century, the most familiar public-oriented understandings of literature held that it made people morally better, usually by giving readers insights into what other people's inner and outer lives might be like. Especially, literature was credited with promoting altruism, which was charged with providing an antidote to economic self-interest. (Since the ability to grasp and pursue one's self-interest counted as a hallmark of rationality, as I've described, the promotion of altruism was circumscribed from the start.)

The designer of the most enduring alloy of aesthetic and ethical rationales for literature was Coleridge, whose influence in the United States was augmented by the cultural authority of the early college. Literary history has emphasized Coleridge's important role in adapting German philosophy for Anglophone literary culture, since his reading (and sometimes creative misreading) of Kant, Schelling, Fichte, Schiller, and other aesthetic philosophers informed his criticism and literary theory.[238] Coleridge's distinction between the imagination, as a faculty of original invention, and the fancy, as a subordinate, combinatory faculty, was taken to parallel the superiority of Romantic to neoclassical aesthetics and circulated widely. His elaboration of organic form, the counterpart of his insistence that literary criticism ought to begin by determining the nature of the work at hand, was also influential, and the vocabulary he developed for literary interpretation was widely adopted.[239] His adaptation of philological glosses became the basis of what he called practical criticism, and the glosses eventually became models in literary studies for explication or close reading. He also pursued a philological attention to the cultural factors at work in literary texts.[240] His lectures on Shakespeare, which circulated widely in his *Literary Remains* (1836) and as separate publications, recorded his way of addressing both large interpretive questions and local crafting in the plays, modeling a way of turning the ongoing process of literary reading into a record that could be shared.

Although Coleridge's engagement with German philosophy is better remembered, his criticism also made sense within the framework of the Christian-friendly Common Sense Philosophy dominant in U.S. higher education and circulating in public culture. His writings received momentum from his Anglican Christianity, a public Christian identity that was well known in the United States even before his *Literary Remains* gave readers full access to his aesthetic principles and critical practices. Indeed, Coleridge, a minister's son and erstwhile Unitarian preacher, was renowned in the United States not only for his poetry and for *Biographia Literaria* (published in the United States in 1817) but also for *Aids to Reflection*, which was published in the United States in an 1829 edition designed by James Marsh. (Blair was also a minister; his *Sermons* circulated alongside his lectures, and he also embodied a link between protoliterary approaches and religious orthodoxy.)[241] *Aids to Reflection* was a devotional text, opening with the address "Fellow-Christian!"[242] Coleridge had set out to edit a selection of writings by the seventeenth-century archbishop of Glasgow Robert Leighton, but he ended up enfolding selections from Leighton in expansive discussions of his own. Marsh reframed the text for a U.S. audience.[243] As the president of the University of Vermont, Marsh was perfectly positioned to offer guidance in moral philosophy, although his advice drew heavily on German idealist philosophy as well as the Scottish tradition.[244] His introduction to the volume culminated in the hope that it "would promote among us the interests, which cannot be long separated from each other, of sound philosophy and of true religion," a pairing fundamental within U.S. higher education at the time.[245] The Coleridge of *Aids to Reflection* (and of *The Friend*, which Marsh brought out in 1831) was framed very much within the tradition of early nineteenth-century moral philosophy, which treated imaginative literature as a practice ground for readers' ethical invigilation. The moralistic tendencies in some of Coleridge's literary interpretations, such as his heavy emphasis on Hamlet's failed "duty," were in tune with the character-forming implementation of Common Sense Philosophy in U.S. culture, although they also aligned with Kant's commitment to the uncompromising discernment of one's duty in the form of categorical imperatives.[246]

Coleridge offered a way of understanding literature as quasi-secular: not fully independent of the dominant Christian culture but existing outside organized religion; sacralized, but available to irreligious or dissenting readers. In this connection, it's important to recognize that the term "secular" was an invention of the Catholic Church: in the Middle Ages, secular clergy were distinguished from monastics and were the representatives of the church in the larger world. In the nineteenth century, "secularism" and "secularist" were terms introduced by European freethinkers who wished to avoid the opprobrium of being known as atheists.[247] The subsequent development of the word to designate a sphere independent of religion, or at least an ecumenical zone, was itself part of a modern paradigm in which religion was relegated to the many forms of outmoded tradition that could be individually accessed (like Schiller's sense of the naïve) but that were understood to operate independently of modern institutions and forms of knowledge.[248] Moral philosophy, as it affected Coleridge and entered into early literary studies, was a Christian endeavor, and ideas about modern literature were marked in this way (among others) by Christianity's dominance. There was a "seeping of biblical and religious norms, myths and logics into secular narratives."[249]

Coleridge's criticism showed that Shakespeare and other literary authors could serve Christian purposes, and his discussions of reading emphasized readers' conscious direction of this activity, guided by spiritual mentors such as Coleridge himself. Ralph Waldo Emerson's ideas about nature and literature offered a different way of safeguarding readers' intimate communing with authors and authors' openness to inspiration. Emerson was one of the most prominent spokespersons for the antimodern and unorthodox qualities of literature, and one of his special concerns was to guard his readers against insidious influences, especially the force of social orthodoxy. Very far from Coleridge's judicious counsel is Emerson's announcement, in "Self-Reliance," "I would write on the lintels of the door-post, *Whim*."[250] Yet contrasting Coleridge's espousal of self-discipline with Emerson's reckless independence belies the fact that Emerson's well-publicized life was much better regulated than Coleridge's. Coleridge's opium addiction was public knowledge even before his death in 1834, contributing to the incipient cultural tendency to identify poetic inspiration with other kinds of altered states, but like his adventurous poetry, his human struggles seemed to augment his authority as a spiritual advisor, indicating that he understood struggling sinners better than a more conventional virtuous minister or professor of moral philosophy might have. Emerson's background as a minister together with his reputation for irreproachable conduct meant that his writings—though unorthodox—could be assimilated to the idea that works of literature, like capstone courses in moral philosophy, carried the counsel or the personal moral influence of wise men (less often, women). As an active and beloved public lecturer, his career may also have bolstered the fantasy that print culture was simply an extension of an in-person relationship between author and audience.

Broadly speaking, Coleridge as critic (not necessarily as poet) stressed literature's modernity, its power to shape and influence modern (Christian) subjects and to align with other modern forms of institutional regulation.[251] Conversely, Emerson presented literature mainly as a resource that readers could use to keep modern forms of regulation at bay, pitting the modern commitment to individualism against the rest of the ensemble of modernity.[252] In keeping with the Common Sense tradition, Emerson valued visceral, strongly felt personal responses and believed they manifested important human capacities for discernment. The German aesthetic thinkers whom Emerson admired valued this quality in art, but (like the Scottish ones) they tended to be warier than he was about grounding personal conduct, especially unorthodox personal conduct, in vivid individual insights or revelations. Emerson shared with Kant a belief in the transcendent power of imaginative insight, but Emerson's sense of the irreducible singularity of human experience made him uninterested in formulating Kant-style ethical maxims. "If you are true, but not in the same truth with me, cleave to your companions; I will seek my own," Emerson warned, suggesting that there might be no way to negotiate incompatible truths, much less to formulate universal truths.[253]

As a result, Emerson insisted on the value of spiritual, perhaps unconscious connections among people even as he warned about the danger that people posed to each other in their guises as walking orthodoxies. In Emerson's view, literature offered glimpses of human greatness, which could properly be emulated only by readers who did not defer or imitate but rather sought to be loyal to comparable stirrings of greatness within themselves. Emerson's critique of "sycophantic" reading, in "Self-Reliance," correlates with his praise of Shakespeare's borrowings, since Shakespeare along with Homer and other earlier writers believed that "all wit was their wit": that those who recognized something genuine had a share in it, had a right to weave it into their own productions.[254] In this respect, Emerson's version of originality did not simulate individual property rights, another sense in which it departed from characteristically modern formulations.

Emerson wrote eloquently about the experience of reading and about some of the things he read, but he had no interest in presenting interpretive cases or modeling critical reading, as Coleridge did. Indeed, his authorial and reading practices both point to the longevity of the commonplacing tradition, which was at odds with Coleridge-style attention to genre, formal design, and characterization. Some critics have observed that the unit of composition for Emerson was the sentence, and it may have been the primary unit of his reading as well.[255] Emerson's skeptical remarks about Hegel, as Denton J. Snider remembered them, hinted as much: "'I cannot find,' said he in substance, 'any striking sentences in Hegel which I can take by themselves and quote. There is no period in him which rounds itself out into a detached thought, or pithy saying or rememberable metaphor.'"[256] The anecdote may not get at Emerson's full estimate of Hegel (and did Emerson really say "rememberable"?), but it points to one of his own strengths. He offered detachable thoughts and pithy sayings in abundance, and his particular kind of brilliance helped keep alive in modern literary culture the epigrammatic mode of reading that George Ticknor also valued.

Emerson took seriously the idea that art was a second nature, and he held that both nature and art nourished individuals. "Nature," in Emerson's sense, included most importantly the aesthetic and spiritual effects of being out-of-doors, the awareness that human life is part of a larger creation, and specific, symbolically resonant facts about nonhuman life forms and processes.[257] Inquisitive observation was at work in Emerson's engagement with nature (as well as transcendent receptivity), but observing natural processes led to wisdom—timeless ethical and spiritual insights, often generated through allegorical interpretation—rather than to knowledge, especially knowledge of the characteristically modern sort that requires experimental protocols and record keeping. In this way, Emersonian nature resists the modern modes of knowledge and value embodied in empirical science and capitalism.[258] At odds with modernity, nature in Emerson's sense is a domain of universal tradition, the site of a long-standing stabilizing experience increasingly valuable in a world with "things...in the saddle." Beyond this, Emerson's nature was framed as a good in itself, sacred.[259]

As Emerson presents it, the authentic experience of nature requires a special form of passive receptivity, which he captures in *Nature* (1836) as the fantasy of being a "transparent eye-ball."[260] The capacity to reconsolidate oneself as an individual agent is paradoxically refreshed and strengthened by surrender, which offers "a low degree of the sublime."[261] The precondition for this receptivity, as Emerson presents it, is the evacuation of the pressures of social life. Nature is trustworthy because it is a spiritual principle at work in humans and beyond and because it is devoid of any separate intention. The secondary operation of nature through great poets and thinkers makes possible an extension of this trust: art is "a nature, passed through the alembic of man." The artist-author's presence in the work—his genius, his authorial personality—guarantees the receptive reader's safety. And a sign that an author faithfully channels the kind of generative creative wisdom found in nature is the quality of the work, which for Emerson is the quality that makes a leaf as wonderful and as potentially inspiring as a tree or a forest.[262] This is the point of view from which a sentence can be the test of a writer's value. (For Coleridge, in contrast, this organic quality might inhere in the intricacy with which disparate roots and bark and sap and leaves all operate together to produce the whole that is "tree.")[263]

As a result, system and theory are hostile to art, maybe even dangerous, in Emerson's view. (They don't really fit Coleridge's organic aesthetic, either, although distinctions such as that between fancy and imagination can feed system-building tendencies.) In an author, marks of system or theory bespeak the lurking presence of a will that might exceed the reader's own.[264] In a critic, they imply a distortion or betrayal of the organic nature of art, and they risk overshadowing readers' experiences. Whereas for Coleridge deference to the author manifests a wholesome dimension of literary reading, for Emerson the assumption that great authors channel nature protects readers from the coercive power of authors' personal wills. The author counts for both Coleridge and Emerson as not just an interpretive principle but an ethical agent authorizing a mode of reading. The influence of both marked the robustness of a kind of spiritual-philosophical reading (Coleridge called his work "philosophical criticism," not in distinction to practical criticism but simply as another characterization of it) that was either Christian-friendly or in tune with influential departures from Christianity (such as deism) that bore its traces.

Recent scholarship about Renaissance texts emphasizes the enmeshment of Protestantism in Catholicism and of secular culture in Christian culture.[265] It is possible that another factor in Shakespeare's literary preeminence—his nineteenth-century value, not his sixteenth-century value—was his work's success in reframing religious questions to downplay controversy (and of course, some of the original controversies had faded since Shakespeare's time). Insofar as modern literature was presented as secular—a crucial precondition for its becoming the basis of an academic discipline—though readily available for many Christian purposes, literature was one of the routes by which the language of the sacred was adapted for uses not explicitly tied to a particular faith. Secularization used to be modeled as cultural translation, insofar as art was envisioned as addressing souls that were no longer defined theologically. I have emphasized instead that Christianity structured dominant Anglo-American versions of secularism: indeed, the Christian belief that Judaism was an earlier dispensation whose greatest contribution was Christianity offered a model for the way that modernity would manage the premodern. The oxymoron "human spirit" ideally suits the belief that a humanist theory of art would address spirituality in an all-purpose way, but in practice, in Christian-dominated Euro-American culture, the human spirit was often presented as a doctrinally vague rendition of the Christian soul.

"Like voodoo and hoodoo, the English classics help control the dead to serve the interests of the living," Joseph Roach has proposed. Roach's context is the performance of Shakespeare's plays, which ritualizes these devotions under the guise of the aesthetic, reconfiguring the spirit world into a secular mystery consistent with the physical and mental segregation of the dead. In this reinvention of ritual, performers become the caretakers of memory through many kinds of public action, including the decorous refinement of protocols of grief.[266]

Roach's polemic registers the difficulty of distinguishing between the secular appropriation of religion and religion's extension in the guise of aesthetics. As Jonathan Arac has pointed out, early Romantic writings about Shakespeare have "a feel of religious conversion," and Shakespeare elicits devotional language even today.[267] Nineteenth-century accounts of secular culture were often colored by the fearful or gleeful belief that orthodox religion was at risk, its influence perpetually waning, so they tended to cast literature's secular status as something borrowed from religion's declining stocks. Henry N. Hudson noted unhappily in 1881 the common tendency "to replace the Bible with Shakespeare as our master code of practical wisdom and guidance."[268] In fact, Shakespeare's works were often coupled with the Bible as twinned sources of authority, a conjunction facilitated by the fact that the most-quoted translation of the Bible, the King James version, shares Shakespeare's period style. Christianity and so-called secular literature reinforced each other's cultural authority at least as often as they competed.

Many aesthetic discussions about the relationship between "genius" or "inspiration" and the deliberate practices of authorial craft play out versions of theological debates about the relationship between divine omnipotence and human free will or the operations of grace and the potential for humans' cooperating will to invite it. Coleridge took Shakespeare as a preeminent object of "practical criticism" in the same stretch of *Biographia Literaria* in which he dubbed Shakespeare "myriad-minded," and his discussion emphasized that great poets also had to be great philosophers whose intellectual discipline informed their writing:

> What then shall we say? even this; that Shakespeare, no mere child of nature; no automaton of genius; no passive vehicle of inspiration, possessed by the spirit, not possessing it; first studied patiently, meditated deeply, understood minutely, till knowledge, become habitual and intuitive, wedded itself to his habitual feelings, and at length gave birth to that stupendous power, by which he stands alone, with no equal or second in his own class; to that power which seated him on one of the two glory-smitten summits of the poetic mountain, with Milton as his compeer not rival.[269]

Coleridge's vision fit a post-Calvinist emphasis on individual responsibility. Accounts of human agency and responsibility tended to fit modern paradigms, insofar as they underwrote modern fantasies of human capability as well as reliance on contract as a paradigmatic human action. In contrast, genius and inspiration indexed the ways in which literary authorship, like literary reading, involved being vulnerable to mysterious influences or collaborations beyond the self's control. If the fantasy of secluded reading was supposed to guarantee readers' self-possession, the countervailing fantasy that reading enabled an uncanny communing with authors made it important to establish (great) authors as benevolent or disinterested, worthy of readers' trust when they allowed authors into their intimate spaces. Studying authors as well as their works—and studying authors through their works—was part of an intricate transaction in which readers took charge of when and how they abandoned themselves.

{ 4 }

Lost Episodes from Public Literary Culture

> The railway, the magnetic telegraph, the steam-ship, the steam-press, with its journals, its magazines, its reviews, and its cheap literature of all kinds, the public library, the book-club, the popular lecture, the lyceum, the voluntary association of every kind—these are all but a part of that magnificent apparatus and means of culture which society is now putting in requisition in that great school of hers, wherein the universal man, rescued from infinite self-degradations, is now at last beginning his culture.
>
> —DELIA BACON (1856)[1]

One of the sneakiest things about the belief in the modern is that it presents the world as it is—or at least, the features of the world that count as modern—as the best possible outcome of what's gone before. Leibniz's proposal that we live in the best of all possible worlds, satirized by Voltaire in *Candide* (1759); Whig history; and a host of ways of identifying historical change with forward motion—through metaphors of progress and advance, especially—all suggest not just that things tend to get better, in the absence of direct political repression, but that things become more rational, more efficient, and more convenient unless they are somehow held back. Modernity is perpetually rescuing humanity from inferior and backward phases of existence by means of inventions of various kinds. Within the tacit framework of modernity, inventions that embodied alternate or dissenting vision—maybe antimodern visions, maybe just different ways of fulfilling modern possibilities—have often been dismissed or diminished in retrospect, once they have been abandoned or disallowed.

In any attempt to read against the grain of modern self-congratulation, failures and dead ends can be wonderfully instructive.[2] This chapter examines four failures and dead ends that indicate the quality of thought and intellectual commitment mustered in U.S. public literary culture before it was sorted into experts and amateurs. I've chosen what I hope will be somewhat surprising and impressive failures and dead ends, of course, but by considering four disparate examples, I want to make the case that public literary culture supported some valuable approaches to literary studies. The four episodes in public literary culture, which have been forgotten or misremembered, are (1) the St. Louis movement, mainly encountered now as a footnote in the history of philosophy; (2) the Browning Society, often dimly recalled as a club for genteel pretenders to literary culture; (3) the Shakespeare-Bacon authorship dispute, whose embarrassing wrongheadedness might seem to justify putting literary experts in charge; and (4) the *Library of American Literature*, an ambitious anthology mainly remembered today as the publishing project that bankrupted Mark Twain.

These episodes have several things in common. One is that they all involve Shakespeare, since the study of Shakespeare can serve as a diagnostic dye we can use to trace the capillaries of public literary culture. Another commonality is that they all registered investments specifically in literature but also presumed that literature could contribute to a number of fields of thought, especially philosophy. They indirectly shed light on the considerable effort that was required not only to make literature the basis of an academic discipline but also to segregate it from other disciplines. Unfortunately, this segregation meant that literature came to be cut off from some important registers of significance, which we would now consider interdisciplinary but which were at that time predisciplinary. Most importantly, all these failures and dead ends were impacted by the reorganization of knowledge around disciplinary expertise that distanced it from forms of literary study and literary authority operating in public culture.

The St. Louis Movement and the Concord School

Stanley Cavell's recovery of Emerson for philosophy indicates how powerful the founding tendency to segregate disciplines from each other was. To the extent that Emerson was an authorizing figure for U.S. literary studies—not just a figure who turned up sometimes in literary anthologies, as writers central to other disciplines have done—he seems to have been dismissed within philosophy, even though the wildly creative and speculative Nietzsche, who admired Emerson, was solidly established in the discipline.[3] The same disciplinary division of spoils filed the St. Louis movement as a (minor) philosophical curiosity, sometimes known as the St. Louis Hegelians, and the movement entered disciplinary histories of philosophy mainly because it led to the founding of the *Journal of Speculative Philosophy* (*JoSP*, 1867–1893), the first philosophy journal in North America. The journal lasted into the 1890s, providing translations of a number of Greek and German philosophical texts that had not previously been available in English as well as early, groundbreaking work by William James, Hugo Munsterberg, Charles Sanders Peirce, Josiah Royce, and other scholars who shaped the disciplines of philosophy and psychology.[4] But literary study was equally part of the St. Louis movement: for example, the first volume of the *Journal of Speculative Philosophy* included three contributions about Goethe and essays about Milton and Shakespeare as well as several essays about music and the visual arts.

The St. Louis movement was philosophical, but perhaps the most distinctive feature of the movement was a commitment to *Bildung* that led members to support free public education and lifelong informal education. According to the movement's own lore, it began in 1858 when William Torrey Harris met Henry C. Brockmeyer at a lecture or public discussion at the St. Louis Mercantile Library.[5] Harris, a New Englander, had studied for a couple of years at Yale without taking a degree and then became a high school teacher in St. Louis, or would become one soon after his meeting with Brockmeyer. Brockmeyer had left Prussia at age sixteen and ended up in St. Louis a few years later, managing along the way to take courses at Georgetown College in Kentucky and at Brown College (later University) as he supported himself, probably through manual labor, since by 1854 he worked as an iron molder for a stove company.[6] At some point after this meeting, Harris and Brockmeyer formed a philosophy club, initially a Kant club. What came to compel them was the study of Hegel, whom Brockmeyer had encountered in Hedge's *Prose Writers of Germany*. (Brockmeyer had met Hedge in the early 1850s. He might have bought the book or borrowed it from the St. Louis Mercantile Library, which had a copy.)[7]

The key Hegelian text for the St. Louis movement was *The Philosophy of Right* (1821), which lays out a set of institutions—the family, civil society, and the state—that both condition the possibilities for individual exercises of will and embody the outcomes of cumulative exercises of will. The movement's Hegel was civic-minded, positing collective life as the product and foundation of individual action and development (in contrast with the Emersonian dread of society's power to coerce and repress individuals). The Civil War was a crucial backdrop for their interest in the ways in which historical events might be understood as "dialectic in action." They were Union soldiers or sympathizers, but they hoped the conflicts that fueled the war could be resolved ethically and politically in national life, not simply by military victory.[8] Harris and Brockmeyer promoted active citizenship; they also believed in the state's responsibility toward its citizens, especially its responsibility to provide schooling. Harris became superintendent of the St. Louis Public Schools and later U.S. commissioner of education (1889–1906), and Brockmeyer, as lieutenant governor of Missouri (1877–1881), was responsible for helping to draft a state constitution for Missouri that made education mandatory for people under twenty.[9]

Many high school teachers and administrators were part of the St. Louis movement, but its signature educational commitment may have been to the kindergarten movement. The kindergarten movement, launched in Germany during the 1830s by Friedrich Fröbel, advocated educating the whole child, incorporating active play and preparing teachers to build on children's own initiatives rather than simply taking charge of them. It emphasized the intellectual, even philosophical, significance of children's early explorations of the world through play. Susan E. Blow and Anna Brackett, leading kindergarten theorists in the St. Louis group, brought Hegelian ideas about the importance of "self-estrangement" (through imaginative play and imaginative reading) as well as "self-activity" (Harris's term, broadly disseminated) to bear on kindergarten pedagogy.[10] Blow established "the nation's first continuous free kindergarten system" in St. Louis in 1873 and spent a year of further intensive study in Germany before launching a training school for kindergarten teachers in 1877.[11] Although most histories of the St. Louis movement have emphasized its famous men, many women were part of the movement, including many kindergarten teachers, and women published philosophical, pedagogical, and literary studies and translations in the *JoSP*.[12]

Permeating the St. Louis movement's commitments to philosophy and pedagogy—even to kindergarten—was the literary supercanon. Chapter 1 quotes Denton J. Snider, one of the most active members of the St. Louis movement, about his "Literary Bibles"—Homer, Dante, Shakespeare, and Goethe—but many in the St. Louis group taught, wrote, and published about the supercanon.[13] Harris published *The Spiritual Sense of Dante's "Divina Commedia"* with Appleton in 1889, after it had been excerpted in the *Journal of Speculative Philosophy*, which he edited.[14] Brockmeyer published "Letters on Goethe's *Faust*" in the *JoSP*, and Snider published numerous essays about Shakespeare there that were later incorporated into his books.[15] G. P. Putnam's Sons published Susan E. Blow's critical study of Dante in 1886. Snider remembered four different informal courses on Goethe's *Faust* that members of the movement offered in St. Louis between the 1860s and the 1880s, courses by Brockmeyer; Harris; F. L. Soldan, a secondary teacher in St. Louis and later superintendent of schools; and Thomas Davidson, a Scottish-born peripatetic philosopher, who later published a study of *Faust* and translated into English one of the best-known Italian studies of Dante.[16]

The St. Louis movement was, as at least one of its members insisted, a "great national movement," not limited to St. Louis, and everywhere it extended, literature and philosophy were likely to be fruitfully conjoined.[17] Its networks included philosophy clubs in the Midwest and beyond, some with their own philosophy publications friendly to literature, such as *Journal of the American Akademe* (1884–1892), a journal devoted to Plato published in Jacksonville, Illinois, and *The Platonist* (1883–1888, intermittently), based in Osceola, Missouri. Its networks also took in the kindergarten movement, especially the Chicago training school for kindergarten teachers that evolved into National-Louis University, and other circuits of educators who wrote, published, and conferred about pedagogy. The movement also reached countless people who participated in the many informal courses and clubs that it spawned, most of which had literary components.

The most famous informal school was the Concord School of Philosophy and Literature, which was collaboratively conducted in summers from 1879 to 1888 by Concord-based Transcendentalists, including Emerson, Bronson Alcott, and Elizabeth Peabody (another early kindergarten teacher), in collaboration with members of the expansive St. Louis network.[18] Founding members associated with the St. Louis Movement included Harris; Hiram K. Jones, a physician who led a Plato Club in Jacksonville, Illinois, and later founded the *Journal of the American Akademe*; and S. H. Emery, who held a managerial position at a stove foundry and led a Hegelian group in Quincy, Illinois.[19] Emery became the Concord School's director, Alcott being the dean; Alcott's death marked the end of the school. The Concord School brought together academics, secondary teachers, kindergarten teachers, and a host of others with serious interests in philosophy and literature, from William James to Julian Hawthorne.[20] Literature was prominent every year, with the seventh year of the school focusing on Goethe and the eighth year on Dante.[21] Dorothy G. Rogers notes that there was considerable "mentoring and networking" among the women who attended, who included Blow, Peabody (who lectured on *Paradise Lost* and Emerson), Ednah Dow Cheney (who lectured on the history of art, Goethe, Dante and Michelangelo, and seventeenth-century playwrights), Julia Ward Howe (who lectured on Emerson, Goethe, Dante, Plato's *Republic,* and Aristophanes and opened the 1881 course with her poem "On Leaving for a Time the Study of Kant"), Emma Lazarus (who read a sonnet in memory of Emerson at the opening of the 1884 school), Ellen M. Mitchell (who lectured on Aristotle's *Ethics*), Caroline K. Sherman (a kindergarten teacher who lectured on Goethe and "child-life"), suffragist Lucy Stone, astronomer Maria Mitchell, and philosophers Grace C. Bibb and Marietta Kies.[22] Kate Douglas Wiggin, who attended in 1880, founded the first free kindergarten in San Francisco plus a kindergarten training school before becoming famous as the author of *Rebecca of Sunnybrook Farm* (1903).[23]

Both Thomas Davidson and Denton J. Snider lectured at the Concord School, but their other educational projects targeted less privileged populations. During the 1890s, Davidson lived on the Lower East Side in New York City and organized the Breadwinners' College (supported by Joseph Pulitzer, whom he had gotten to know in St. Louis), which offered classes on evenings and weekends for working people, mainly Russian Jewish immigrants.[24] Davidson's working-class New Yorkers read Dante along with Aristotle and Hegel, and Davidson was active in helping to form the American Dante Society.[25] Visiting lecturers at the Breadwinners' College included prominent academic philosophers as well as members of the St. Louis Movement: William James, Josiah Royce (who lectured on Tolstoy as well as philosophy), and John Dewey along with Mary C. McCullough, one of the St. Louis kindergarten teachers (who organized a Literary School devoted to Dante), and Amelia C. Fruchte, who taught high school and normal school classes in St. Louis (and founded the St. Louis Shakespeare Club).[26] Davidson also operated the Glenmore Summer School for the Culture Sciences from 1888 to 1900, which brought a wide range of speakers and which some of his Breadwinners students visited or attended.[27]

Denton Snider also taught working adults. He offered courses on Shakespeare, Dante, Goethe, Homer, and Greek historians at the Chicago training school for kindergarten teachers (where Davidson and Harris also occasionally taught), and he was a speaker at the Shakespeare Club at Hull House as well as in other midwestern cities where he was invited.[28] For example, a Milwaukee Literary School, inspired by Concord, brought Harris to speak on Goethe's *Wilhelm Meister* and Snider on *Faust*.[29] It's not entirely clear how Snider supported himself after he resigned from high school teaching, but he traveled for a while in Europe before returning to St. Louis and offering, for the rest of his life, the free classes on literature, psychology, and philosophy he called his "Communal University."[30] He taught working people in the evenings, women who did not work outside the home in the afternoons.[31]

I've homed in on Davidson and Snider because they epitomize some of the antidisciplinary tendencies of the group, whose members included academics but whose leaders were not professors.[32] Although both Davidson and Snider supported public education, both of them were wary of the ways in which academic credentialing distorted what ought to be the lifelong pursuit of education. Both of them were born in poor or financially unstable circumstances; both of them had college degrees, Davidson's via a scholarship to University of Aberdeen and Snider's from Oberlin.[33] But both of them mistrusted what they saw happening in higher education at the end of the century. Davidson was a close friend of William James, who tried to secure for him a position at Harvard. Davidson torpedoed the plan by publishing a report in the *Atlantic Monthly* critical of Harvard's Greek scholarship and curriculum. Moreover, Davidson discouraged friends from taking up academic appointments; James later recalled Davidson's denunciation of "academicism."[34] Taking a similar stance, Snider pointedly argued that the St. Louis movement "had broken ground for the coming home-grown University, quite different from the traditional one imported from Europe," the research university model associated with Germany. For his own part, in spite of some friendly collaborations with academics, Snider "refused to be subject" to academia "or to submerge in it my own educative organism, small and incomplete though this be."[35]

In both cases, their mistrust of academia had a populist flavor, insofar as they mainly taught people who could not afford higher education. Davidson and Snider are not easy to classify politically; Davidson founded the London fellowship from which the Fabians splintered off, and both he and Snider appeared to be keenly interested in bridging the gap between haves and have-nots but reluctant to embrace specific political strategies or positions.[36] Still, both of them actively nurtured the educational ambitions of people at large, especially working people, and were reluctant to turn this work to profit. Snider claims to have barely broken even on the books he published himself, and a contributing factor must have been that he provided his books free of charge to his students. He published pieces in the *Western* and the *JoSP*, but in an autobiography written late in his life, he claimed that the only periodical piece he ever published for pay was a theater review.[37] Davidson appeared to take pride in barely getting by, and his Breadwinners' School was free.[38] Both Snider and Davidson held that professionally supervised formal higher education had taken a wrong turn. Davidson leaned in the direction that John Dewey would take when he pointed out to the Breadwinners that conventional higher education "stops with knowing, and does not go on into loving and doing. It therefore never is really appropriated, for knowing that does not pass into act and habit is never ours, but remains an external thing, a mere useless accomplishment, to be vain about."[39]

The same commons ethic that led Snider to teach for free seems to have led him to publish his own books, although he also mistrusted the concentration of power in the East Coast publishing industry. Midwesterners' resentment of East Coast authority was an undercurrent in the group, perhaps explaining why the movement's association with St. Louis stuck in spite of its broad geographic reach. The *Journal of Speculative Philosophy* was begun after the *North American Review* rejected a critique of Herbert Spencer submitted by Harris. It followed on an earlier publishing venture of the group, *The Western: A Review of Education, Science, Literature and Art* (1866–1881), which Davidson edited for three years.[40] The do-it-yourself ethic of *JoSP* and Snider's book-publishing venture exemplifies the way that print publication could operate as an extension of manuscript circulation. The St. Louis movement also circulated writings (and meeting reports) in manuscript, the most valuable manuscript being Brockmeyer's translation of Hegel's *Logic*, which was used by several philosophy clubs and even a course at Harvard.[41]

Snider's self-publication, like his informal teaching, was in keeping with his lifelong fascination with Johnny Appleseed, a model of idiosyncratic civic-mindedness. However, Snider's hostile opinions about commercial publishing—"the American publishing machine," "Eastern literary centralization, which seems to become more tyrannical and grasping every day," and so forth—suggest that he mistrusted it fundamentally: "A book never was primarily a commercial bantling with me, but a legitimate child of my brain, to whom I owed a duty; I was to endow my spiritual offspring with the best outfit for life that I might be able to furnish. The right of being printed and imparted every worthy book may well claim for its own sake, and even for the sake of its reader."[42] He may have been both paranoid and prescient in noting that even bookstores had deteriorated during his lifetime: his 1919 memoir noted how many had become annexed to department stores.[43]

In spite of having never earned an advanced degree or taught at the college level, and in spite of publishing his own books, Denton J. Snider had a national reputation, especially in Shakespeare studies.[44] As a lecturer at the Concord School, he was singled out by the *Boston Traveller* (reprinted in the *Washington Post*) as a chief draw in a year when President Noah Porter of Yale, President James McCosh of Princeton, President J. H. Seelye of Amherst, and other Transcendentalist and Hegelian luminaries were on the program.[45] H. H. Furness printed an excerpt from one of Snider's essays about Shakespeare in the Variorum *Hamlet*; Snider corresponded with Joseph Crosby, who read and admired some of Snider's publications in the *JoSP*, and probably with other Shakespeareans.[46] Crosby's friend J. Parker Norris, author of a column on Shakespeareana for the *American Bibliopolist*, wrote a review encouraging Snider to collect his essays in a volume so that they would be available to the "general reader."[47] Snider's *The System of Shakespeare's Dramas* (1877) was reviewed in national periodicals, although most of the reviews shared Crosby's wariness (following Emerson and Coleridge, as we've seen) of any literary approach that was defined as systematic.[48] Perhaps in response to these criticisms, Snider repackaged some of the material in separate volumes and dropped "system" from the titles.[49]

Most importantly, Snider's approach to the plays is worth reading. Although Hegel is never mentioned in *System of Shakespeare's Dramas*, Snider follows Hegel in framing the plays as taking up problems of individual freedom and action with respect to institutions, chiefly the family and the state, but also property (the lowest-priority institution, for Snider), the church, and (most Hegelian, but seldom addressed in Snider's analyses) the "world-historical spirit." With asperity, Snider casts aside any view that "moralizes" Shakespeare's plays "into pitiful lessons of good behavior"—and many nineteenth-century readings would betray this fault, certainly Coleridge's.[50] Shakespeare's higher fidelity was to these human institutions, thought Snider, and the conflicts he traces involve competing institutional loyalties or interpretations of loyalties, treated with subtlety because of the paradoxical fact that people's free, meaningful action depends even on institutions they oppose: "The Individual, in destroying institutions, destroys the very reality of his substantial, permanent self; still, this self, this subjectivity, is the primitive germ from which are developed and vitalized all institutions, and hence it is that which must be protected above everything else."[51]

In keeping with some German critics of Shakespeare—along with Henry N. Hudson—Snider emphasized that modern tragedies mainly involved conflicts between duties, versus Goethe's and Coleridge's much simpler sense that Hamlet had a straightforward duty to avenge his father's death that he put off.[52] Snider treated every play structurally, identifying key conflicts and delineating the chief movements of each play in relation to the elaboration, transformation, and resolution of these conflicts. (Snider's conflicts were not the simplistic pairs—man vs. man and so forth—that became pedagogical staples after the turn of the century, as chapter 5 discusses.) Like many nineteenth-century aesthetic critics, he elucidated the terms of each play's unity; unlike many aesthetic critics who focused on character, he held the most fundamental question about any literary work to be "What is the world in which it moves?," a question that informed his attention to authorial design and social and political analysis.[53]

Snider's bent is philosophically and psychologically analytic. Noting the "supernatural tinge" of *Macbeth*, for instance, Snider analyzes one way the effect is produced:

> In the first place, Nature, whenever it is introduced, is made to prognosticate moral or spiritual occurrences and conflicts; it exists only as the sign of the future deed; it is filled with human purposes. The raven, the owl, the cricket, betoken darkly what is to come; the wind and tempest, the raging elements, always foreshadow the struggles of men. The minor characters, in particular, manifest this tendency—to see in Nature their fears and premonitions, and thus show the popular consciousness.[54]

Snider goes on to point out that the converse tendency also at work in the play, in which people project their own "workings into external forms" or "phantoms," has a strange kind of authenticity: "it is a genuine attempt of the individual...to find or create some expression for what is true within him."[55] The dialectical premise that attempts at understanding are always partial, always seeking fuller expression, saves Snider from the moralism so evident in the best-known nineteenth-century Shakespeare criticism.

Snider's scholarship was not cited by A. C. Bradley, but Snider's *System of Shakespeare's Dramas* was probably the most important predecessor of Bradley's structural analysis in *Shakespearean Tragedy* (1904). Snider's treatment is in many respects preferable to Bradley's for readers who are not primarily invested in making moral evaluations of particular characters. Bradley acknowledged Hegel's importance for the study of tragedy but insisted that tragic conflicts were internal, "the expression of character"; Bradley's was the study that propelled the idea that every Shakespearean tragic hero has a tragic flaw, a "marked one-sidedness, a predisposition in some particular direction; a total incapacity, in certain circumstances, of resisting the force which draws in this direction; a fatal tendency to identify the whole being with one interest, object, passion, or habit of mind."[56] Perhaps Bradley did not know Snider's work, even though Furness's Variorum included it. More likely, though, he did not feel the need to cite it, since academic expertise was becoming dominant by 1904 and scholars like Snider were being relegated to amateurism. Chapter 6 examines more closely Bradley's role in filtering public literary culture out of Shakespeare scholarship. Very likely, if he knew it, Bradley would have found Snider's attention to institutions and to the political worlds of the plays hopelessly unprofessional.

Dueling Bards

Melville's Pierre shared the St. Louis movement's faith in the supercanon. Having only just learned about his secret half-sister, and stewing about how he could be loyal to her without giving away his dead father's secret, he opened two sacred books at random and sought their advice. The first book was Dante's *Inferno*, the advice devastating: "All hope abandon, ye who enter here." But the other volume, *Hamlet*, seemed to galvanize Pierre after the book opened to the well-known couplet "The time is out of joint;—Oh cursed spite, / That ever I was born to set it right!" Unfortunately, what galvanized Pierre was the Coleridgean view that Hamlet delayed when he should have acted swiftly. Melville's rendition of the lesson Pierre drew from the passage is riddled with sarcasm:

> If among the deeper significances of its pervading indefiniteness, which significances are wisely hidden from all but the rarest adepts, the pregnant tragedy of Hamlet convey any one particular moral at all fitted to the ordinary uses of man, it is this:—that all meditation is worthless, unless it prompt to action; that it is not for man to stand shilly-shallying amid the conflicting invasions of surrounding impulses; that in the earliest instant of conviction, the roused man must strike, and, if possible, with the precision and the force of the lightning-bolt.
>
> Pierre had always been an admiring reader of Hamlet; but neither his age nor his mental experience thus far, had qualified him either to catch initiating glimpses into the hopeless gloom of its interior meaning, or to draw from the general story those superficial and purely incidental lessons, wherein the painstaking moralist so complacently expatiates.

The narrator goes on to hint that further, "more final insights" would "reveal" not only "the depths" but also "some answering heights"; Pierre's agony, as he struggles with *Hamlet* and Dante's *Inferno*, might represent the pains of a reading that falls short of these insights.[57] As a result of consulting *Hamlet* and taking up Coleridge's moralizing assessment of the Danish prince, Pierre becomes "the grand self-renouncing victim" characterized by "disinterestedness" who acts immediately on his resolutions instead of shilly-shallying like Hamlet. A body count comparable to *Hamlet*'s is the end result.[58]

"Shilly-shallying" points to the problem with faulting Prince Hamlet for delay, as if a dutiful son would not blink at committing regicide. This is a reductive view of Coleridge's position, although both Coleridge and Wilhelm Meister (who in Goethe's novel also faults Hamlet for failing to take up his obligation more swiftly) may have been especially vehement in criticizing Hamlet because they displaced onto Hamlet concerns about themselves: Coleridge was recognized by himself and the world as having trouble with willpower, and Goethe's Wilhelm voices this criticism of Hamlet at a time when he has abandoned business obligations he was supposed to handle for his father and joined a troupe of actors instead. "There is no indecision about Hamlet, as far as his own sense of duty is concerned; he knows well what he ought to do, and over and over again he makes up his mind to do it," Coleridge diagnoses.[59] The idea that *Hamlet* was all about Prince Hamlet's delay circulated far and wide, carrying the potential to chastise thought, reflection, or intellectualism: "When it is said that Hamlet's reflection destroys his action, is it meant that we should never think before we act? Many have taken such to be the Poet's meaning," warned Snider, who did not agree.[60]

It's easy to imagine that Melville would have been equally impatient with this interpretation of *Hamlet*, in itself and as a familiar instance of the kind of moralizing reading of Shakespeare gaining ground. In 1850, in his famous essay "Hawthorne and His Mosses," he credited Hawthorne and Shakespeare with a "power of blackness" valued by "philosophers":

> But it is those deep far-away things in him; those occasional flashings-forth of the intuitive Truth in him; those short, quick probings at the very axis of reality—these are the things that make Shakespeare, Shakespeare. Through the mouths of the dark characters of Hamlet, Timon, Lear, and Iago, he craftily says, or sometimes insinuates the things, which we feel to be so terrifically true, that it were all but madness for any good man, in his own proper character, to utter, or even hint of them. Tormented into desperation, Lear the frantic King tears off his mask, and speaks the sane madness of vital truth.[61]

Melville's Shakespeare inclines toward paradox, unorthodoxy, and subversion, in this essay—and so did Melville himself when he unfolded the misery that ensued from Pierre's taking *Hamlet* to mean that he should abandon all his own desires and plans and instead devote his life to making up for his father's misdeeds.

There's no reason to think Melville doubted whether William Shakespeare wrote the plays attributed to him, but the contrast set up in "Mosses" and *Pierre* between deep, dark truths and more palatable but superficial lessons provides an important context for the Shakespeare-Bacon controversy of the middle and late nineteenth century. (Dante's injunction might also have led Pierre to hold back and resist the temptation of immediate action, if he had taken it in.) The idea that Francis Bacon wrote the plays attributed to Shakespeare has usually been taken for ignorant elitism, refusal to allow that the plays might have been written by a commoner. The Baconian theory was indeed premised on genuine ignorance, afflicting everyone, about how Shakespeare could have acquired the education and knowledge of the world manifested in the plays. Nevertheless, the initial target of the Baconians—although later they added others—was the tendency of some Shakespeareans to use the mysteries of Shakespeare's background to stoke theories of romantic genius that short-circuited interpretive engagement. Snider, who was not a Baconian, also objected to the ways that theories of genius precluded investigations of Shakespeare's methods and development: "It is an absurdity to declare that, in a world where thought alone is greatness, its greatest man was an unthinking prodigy."[62] Just as Melville prized Shakespeare but railed against the "blind, unbridled admiration that has been heaped upon Shakespeare," the Baconians' speculations were pitched first and foremost against the Bardolatry that discouraged inquiries into how Shakespeare had become Shakespeare.[63]

"This vast, magical, unexplained phenomenon which our own times produced under our own eyes"—in contrast to "literary miracles of antiquity"—"appears to be, indeed, the only thing which our modern rationalism is not to be permitted to meddle with," complained Delia Bacon in the lead essay of *Putnam's Monthly* for January 1856.[64] Bacon was the most famous debunker of William Shakespeare in the nineteenth century. Like Snider, Bacon was interested in the philosophical dimensions of the plays; more than Snider, she was interested in their political visions. Everything she valued in the plays clashed with the emerging orthodoxies of Shakespearean criticism. She proposed that the plays had been written by a "school" of brilliant men, including Walter Raleigh and Francis Bacon (from whom she did not claim to be descended, until late in her life under mental duress).[65] Thwarted by the close scrutiny and violent repression of the Elizabethan court, these men turned to writing plays as a way of leaking their dangerous political ideas to the people and protecting them for posterity. Hiding their authorship was essential because the plays would have been grasped as politically threatening—especially by Queen Elizabeth, King James, and audiences of courtiers—if their author had been recognized as someone politically powerful and strategically clever. The plays would have risked censorship or suppression; the authors would have risked the Tower. Indeed, Bacon emphasizes that the plays were written literally and figuratively in the shadow of the Tower, a place where some of the plays' team of authors were at one time or other imprisoned.[66]

Bacon's idea that the authorship was collective may have been influenced by currents in classical and biblical philology positing that the cumulative work of many lay behind names like Homer and Aesop.[67] More important was her sense that literary works provided safe houses for certain vulnerable ideas that could not safely be put into practice, a view akin to Annabel Patterson's idea that literature was shaped fundamentally by censorship.[68] The dangerous core of the plays, for Bacon, was their critique of monarchy, since they called into question artificial distinctions of rank. Her style is elliptical, sometimes paranoid, so it is hard to pin down all of her analysis. However, her commentary stresses the fundamental worth of all people, amounting to an endorsement of popular sovereignty (a version of English liberty) or perhaps a more radical critique of political hierarchy. Her analysis of *King Lear*, one of the three plays she examines at length in her published monograph, focuses on scenes that expose the arbitrariness of monarchical power and foreground the claims of those oppressed and suffering. For example, Lear's visit to the hovel of Tom of Bedlam (Edgar in disguise) leads Bacon to argue that it isn't the "king's great tragedy" that the author cares about, but the tragedy of those represented by Tom: "It is the tragedy of the Many, and not the One,—it is the tragedy which is the rule, and not the exception,—it is the tragedy that is common, and not that which is singular, whose argument this Poet has undertaken to manage."[69] Bacon argues that *Lear*'s repeated staging of the violence endured by those who speak up against monarchical tyranny (Cordelia, Kent, and Gloucester) is a record of the violence of Elizabeth's regime, not the depiction of a mythic past. "Down to its most revolting, most atrocious detail, it is still the Elizabethan civility that is painted here," Bacon sarcastically insists, suggesting also that Goneril's murder of her sister Regan parallels Elizabeth's execution of her kinswoman Mary, Queen of Scots.[70]

Despite Bacon's proposal that the plays were a collective effort, she paid the most attention to Francis Bacon, whose intellectual contributions she characterized repeatedly as "modern." She identified a familiar catalog of modernizing historical phenomena that catalyzed or manifested the philosophical advances registered in the plays: "the Printing press, and the revived Learning of Antiquity, and the Reformation, and the discovery of America, and the new revival of the genius of the North in art and literature, and the Scientific Discoveries which accompanied this movement on the continent."[71] Francis Bacon represented the possibility of a distinctively modern system of unified knowledge: not the ancient unity of the classical curriculum, but the unity of an intellectual approach that could embrace self-knowledge (in his *Essays*), the inductive development of scientific laws (in the *Novum Organum*), and the principled construction of a new political order (in the *New Atlantis*). In other words, positing Francis Bacon as the author of Shakespeare's plays meant that the plays were connected with bold and wide-ranging inquiries drawing together many fields of knowledge, rather than being cordoned off from the rest of intellectual life in a channel called "literature." Support for Francis Bacon's authorship implicitly bucked trends already at work toward specialization, trends that the research university would accelerate. Delia Bacon asserted that things that "come to us as *branches* of learning merely, do in fact meet and unite in one stem."[72] In this respect, her approach was designed to compensate for losses that accompanied the invention of literature: for the ways in which literature, by virtue of being refined as a particular kind of text requiring a particular kind of reading, risked being cut off from other domains of thought and knowledge. The longing to prove Francis Bacon's authorship of the plays was grounded, for Delia Bacon and some of her followers, in a desire to follow the plays' explorations of power and its institutions—more than a century before the New Historicists hit upon this approach, as Nina Baym has pointed out.[73]

It is usually assumed that anti-Stratfordians—those disputing William Shakespeare's authorship—doubt Shakespeare's authorship because of his limited education and knowledge of the world. Although Delia Bacon was skeptical about the adequacy of Shakespeare's small-town education, her animus mainly targeted Shakespeare's bourgeois success, not his humble beginnings. Bacon insisted that Shakespeare was the owner of the scripts, not their author, and in that role could serve as respectable frontman for the plays' real authors. The signs of his comfortable vanity she detested: for instance, his purchase of the "New Place" in Stratford, where he spent a quiet retirement without lifting a finger to put the plays in order or to supervise an authorized edition of them.[74] Indeed, Bacon polemically seized on the widespread belief that the youthful Shakespeare had poached deer—an allegation disputed or downplayed by many of Shakespeare's admirers—as the one detail that might rescue him from "hopeless stolidity." The fact that the records of Shakespeare's life had so much to do with property and status—his will, with the famous bequest of the "second-best bed" to his wife; his petition for a coat of arms; his penchant for lawsuits—provided further context for Bacon's assertion that the grasping, status-conscious William Shakespeare could not have been the idealistic and unorthodox thinker who wrote the plays.[75]

This aggressively bourgeois version of Shakespeare—"is not he a private, economical, practical man—this Shakespeare of ours—a plain, true-blooded Englishman, who minds his own business, and leaves other people to take care of theirs?"—was not something Delia Bacon made up.[76] It was a view of Shakespeare that had been taking shape for some time, and its chief U.S. spokesperson was Richard Grant White, one of the "eminent" Shakespearians mentioned in chapter 3. White, you'll recall, first made his reputation by spotting a Shakespearean hoax. He then published a collection of essays about Shakespeare in 1854 and produced a highly respected edition of Shakespeare (published between 1857 and 1866) that was based on the First Folio rather than received editorial traditions.[77] He used his authority as a bully pulpit to rail against the excesses, sometimes even the existence, of aesthetic criticism, and indeed of most forms of literary interpretation, implying that textual criticism was the business of scholars and that everyone else should just enjoy the plays. "Of criticism of what has been called the higher kind, I recommend the reading of very little, or better, none at all," he opined.[78]

White somehow combined extraordinary veneration for Shakespeare's artistry with the interpretive guideline that Shakespeare's plays could only have meant what his paying customers—apparently, his least discerning paying customers—were likely to grasp.[79] "People are apt to forget that Shakespeare wrote his plays to please the promiscuous public of London, at a time when the general diffusion of knowledge was infinitely less than it is now," White cautioned. "He wrote to make money by interesting such a public, and of course to be understood by it; and he was understood."[80] White's 1865 account of Shakespeare's life emphasizes Shakespeare's bourgeois respectability and comfort: his good income in retirement, the "records of the care with which he invested his money, and his willingness to take legal measures to protect himself against small losses."[81] Not surprisingly, White's Shakespeare lived in an England very different from Delia Bacon's: "From early manhood to maturity he lived, and labored, and throve, in the chief city of a prosperous and peaceful country, at a period of high intellectual and moral development."[82] Perhaps because he was especially eager to cast aspersions on Hamlet's speculative German intellectual formation (since many well-known German critics were aesthetic critics), White presents Hamlet as a superficial procrastinator, far inferior to Fortinbras: "He was too unstable and incontinent of soul even to keep his own great secret, but went about making others swear that they would keep it for him."[83]

White's 1854 book probably aggravated Bacon's contempt for Shakespeare the affluent manager, but her sarcastic treatment of this Shakespeare in the *Putnam's* essay may have made for her a dangerous enemy. White was the U.S. Shakespearean who had made British scholars sit up and pay attention; he was also a New York journalist well connected in the publishing industry. The *Putnam's* article in which Bacon first aired her views in print was supposed to be the first in a series by Bacon, and Wiley and Putnam had also expressed interest in publishing Bacon's larger argument in book form.[84] Using his connections, probably after he was consulted about the essay, White convinced *Putnam's* to back out of its plan to publish anything else by Bacon, and Wiley and Putnam followed suit.[85] By the time White confessed in print what he'd done, years later, he felt no need to apologize: Delia Bacon had died mentally ill, and she was notorious for having tried to dig up Shakespeare's grave in order to find hidden proofs of the plays' true authorship.[86] White left his readers to draw the conclusion that only crazy people doubted Shakespeare's authorship. Partly due to White, but also due to the ways in which Bacon's personal history undermined her credibility, Bacon's political approach to the plays was forgotten and only her dispute about the authorship was remembered.[87]

In spite of her work's eccentricity and her over-the-top antipathy to William Shakespeare, Bacon's work was part of a broader cultural investment in Shakespeare that was put at risk by approaches such as White's. Melville must have hated White's rendition of Shakespeare, if he paid attention to it. Bacon's friendly patrons included Ralph Waldo Emerson and Thomas Carlyle, whose writings, though studied now mainly in English departments, spanned (at least) literature, philosophy, and history. Like Hawthorne, who somewhat reluctantly underwrote the publication of Bacon's book and provided its introduction, Emerson and Carlyle did not doubt that William Shakespeare wrote the works attributed to him. However, Emerson and Carlyle believed that Delia

Bacon's work deserved public circulation: they were impressed by her learning and intelligence, and they took for granted that she was making a significant contribution to Shakespeare studies. Their support for her was personally gracious, but it also made sense.[88] Neither Emerson nor Carlyle thought of authorship as mainly commercial. Both insisted on the ways in which literary works could be both deeply distinctive and powered by forms of collective experience and wisdom. Delia Bacon depicted the plays' authors as men of action forced by circumstances to be men of letters; Carlyle's earlier writing about Shakespeare had prepared the ground for her, arguing, "The Poet who could merely sit on a chair, and compose stanzas, would never make a stanza worth much. He could not sing the Heroic warrior, unless he himself were at least a Heroic warrior too. I fancy there is in him the Politician, the Thinker, Legislator, Philosopher;—in one or the other degree, he could have been, he is all these."[89] Emerson had similarly emphasized a Shakespeare who channeled historical forces or experiences not fundamentally individual in nature.[90] Emerson, Carlyle, and Delia Bacon all treated Shakespeare's plays as having broad intellectual import. They were all committed to aesthetic criticism in philosophical veins, and Emerson and Bacon were active in public literary culture: Emerson as a renowned public lecturer, Bacon as a lecturer who taught ambitious private classes (similar to Margaret Fuller's) in New Haven and New York.[91]

Richard Grant White was opposed to public Shakespeare studies and made contemptuous comments about Shakespearean clubs as well as about all women readers of Shakespeare.[92] Although White made his living mainly as a journalist, writing especially about music, literature, and language, in his critical stance and in the kind of authority he claimed, he was aligned with an important camp in the emerging academic literary establishment.[93] White, author of *Words and Their Uses, Past and Present* (1870), sided in crucial ways with the textual critics and philologists who wanted to base the discipline of English literature on the highly empirical study of linguistic history. The study of Anglo-Saxon, which was promoted by philologically minded critics in English departments, was upheld as requiring the same mental discipline and historical precision as Latin and Greek. White's dismissal of Shakespeare clubs and of any literary interpretation not grounded in textual criticism and philology was, oddly enough, one of the earliest outcroppings in U.S. Shakespeare studies of the stark sorting of experts who were allowed to make literary knowledge from amateurs who could only admire it; White must have thought he could count as an expert if he operated like one. No wonder Joseph Crosby wrote gleefully to Norris that he had "discovered by 3 or 4 'infallible proofs,' that Grant White in editing his edition of Shakespeare did *not* have an original copy of the 1st Folio by him," in spite of basing his edition on the First Folio.[94] (White irritated Crosby because of his "*egotism & conceit.*")[95] White's protodisciplinary stance also highlighted the ways in which an obsession with textual accuracy carried "notions of property rights and rights of succession in respect of that property," as Michael Bristol has put it.⁹⁶ White's zeal in asserting property rights in Shakespeare against Bacon's incursions was a version of academic's power to marginalize and diminish authorities based in public literary culture, a power that has often channeled misogyny.⁹⁷

Hence the paradox: a number of proponents of Francis Bacon, the aristocrat, rather than William Shakespeare, the glover's son, were populist in sensibility because their real target was not Shakespeare but rather control of "Shakespeare," the author-function, by a cadre of experts. As Zachary Lesser shrewdly observes, all anti-Stratfordian theories "*rely on* dismissal by the establishment for much of their persuasive power," so that a populist stance is standard issue.⁹⁸ Mark Twain, who as a cub riverboat pilot began to doubt William Shakespeare's authorship after he heard or read Bacon's views, would fit this profile; so would Walt Whitman, who was a close friend of the Baconian William D. O'Connor.⁹⁹ Ignatius Donnelly, a congressman from Minnesota who by the 1890s would join the Populist Party, was also a Baconian, although his 1888 book, *The Great Cryptogram*, mainly searched for encoded evidence of the plays' hidden author.¹⁰⁰ (Indeed, the late-century anti-Stratfordian preoccupation with codes and ciphers strangely paralleled White's investment in empirical textual evidence.)¹⁰¹ But alongside the codebreakers, a wider range of discussion about the plays' authorship kept percolating. The controversy was so mainstream that Houghton Mifflin issued a series of "Books on the Shakespeare-Bacon Controversy" in the 1880s.¹⁰²

One kind of case often made against William Shakespeare's authorship was that the plays demonstrated various kinds of specialized knowledge that would have been hard for the historical Shakespeare to acquire. One of the most distinguished Baconians made this case: an interpretive critic, not a codebreaker. Nathaniel Holmes was a Harvard graduate who practiced as an attorney in St. Louis before joining Missouri's Supreme Court and ending his career as a law professor at Harvard.¹⁰³ Unlike Delia Bacon, he rejected the idea that the plays had more than one author; like Bacon, he had a special affinity for *Hamlet*, arguing that the play only became so prominent in the nineteenth century because Kant's philosophy helped readers recognize and appreciate the philosophical reflections that Francis Bacon had incorporated into the plays.¹⁰⁴ Holmes argued that the plays' detailed legal knowledge required an author with a thorough legal education.¹⁰⁵ His case for Francis Bacon in this way converged with a number of critical studies that formulated the kinds of specialized knowledge at work in the plays. Studies such as *Shakespeare's Legal Acquirements* (1859), by a lord chief justice of England, developed this interest, mainly taking Shakespeare's authorship for granted and proposing that he must have gained legal learning or other kinds of specialized knowledge during his lost years. It seems likely that the admiration many readers expressed for the range of Shakespeare's knowledge—and the skepticism expressed by others about what William Shakespeare could plausibly have known—were both prompted by the reorganization of knowledge in the nineteenth century. Because knowledge was becoming more specialized, it was becoming harder to credit that a middling layperson in the Elizabethan era could have acquired knowledge that now belonged only to specially educated experts. (Even Mark Twain thought the author of the plays must have been a practicing lawyer.)[106]

By the 1880s, Richard Grant White claimed that it really didn't matter who wrote Shakespeare's plays—that the very question was of interest only to "pene-literary people," the almost-literary. So long as the plays were "written by an Englishman, in London, between the years 1590 and 1610," the author's identity "affects in no way their literary importance or interest, their ethnological or their social significance, their value as objects of literary art, or their power as a civilizing, elevating influence upon the world."[107] There could be no clearer way of asserting that the Baconians had lost, in the view of the scholarly establishment: that the kinds of issues readers were authorized to find in the plays had already been settled, regardless of who their author was. Whitman's friend William D. O'Connor called White's bluff:

> Did he imagine that if Bacon were found to be the true Shakespeare, and the drama were put into collateral relation with him and his philosophy, it would not open up at once in new reaches of signification? Did he forget that its philosophic and artistic character and all its rich and lofty import were obscured for nearly a century by its merely being attributed to William Shakespeare, his vulgar and commonplace record having naturally limited the interpretation?[108]

Of course, we'll never know what the impact on literary studies might have been if the Baconians' concerns had gotten more traction or if (as happened subsequently) William Shakespeare's educational opportunities had been better understood, during these formative years of Shakespeare studies. Instead, the assumption that Shakespeare was an untutored and politically disengaged genius contributed to the process by which the repertoire of ethical and aesthetic questions that counted as literary narrowed.

The Browning Society in the United States

The organization of academic literary studies by national literatures has obscured the ways in which Robert Browning was a talismanic poet for many U.S. readers in the decades after the Civil War. Browning mattered in a way that no other nineteenth-century poet did because his work hosted the kind of widespread literary caretaking and collaborative thought that had previously been lavished on Shakespeare's plays. Browning's poetry became a favorite refueling station for late nineteenth-century U.S. readers who cared deeply about literature and believed it could change the world directly and rapidly—extra-disciplinary investments that compounded the condescension with which the Browning Society came to be treated within academic literary circles.

The generations coming of age around the Civil War knew Tennyson as poet laureate (1850–1892), an establishment figure; Matthew Arnold, author of *Culture and Anarchy* (1869) and a professor of poetry at Oxford, similarly claimed a traditional kind of cultural authority, although he exercised it polemically. Browning's reputation was not so high nor so firmly bolstered, and his position was also different from that of the U.S. poets who had made their reputations before the Civil War and who were gradually (and unfairly) remade into Schoolroom Poets or Fireside Poets after the Civil War: Longfellow, Whittier, and other *éminences grises*.[109] These poets became schoolroom staples precisely because they were loved and approved by postwar parents and teachers, whereas Browning's poetry, often faulted for obscurity, figured as a more intense stimulant sought by younger readers. Bliss Perry, who graduated from Williams College in 1881, discovered the poetry of Browning and Walt Whitman in college and became a lifelong admirer of both, eventually offering public lectures and graduate courses about Browning. "I was warned that [former Williams president] Mark Hopkins had declared that *he* could not understand Browning, but secretly I believed that the old gentleman had not made much of an effort," Perry recalled, underlining the generational divide.[110] Edith Wharton read Browning sometime after 1885 and counted him as one of her "great Awakeners."[111] Joaquin Miller, writing in 1886 about how he came to be a writer, grouped Browning with Shakespeare and the Bible as his three greatest influences.[112] Mark Twain loved Browning and declared that what Leo Tolstoy was to William Dean Howells—a signal inspiration—Browning was to him.[113]

If we look back in the wake of the twentieth century's canon building, Emily Dickinson and Walt Whitman loom as Browning's obvious rivals, the U.S. poets who departed most drastically and successfully from the Tennyson-Longfellow model. Since most of Dickinson's poetry was not published until after her death in 1886, and then with many startling features of her prosody smoothed away, her work's full import was not available to nineteenth-century readers. In contrast, Whitman was widely read and even more widely recognized as an unorthodox public figure (in spite of his late-century makeover into the Good Gray Poet). His formal innovations were bolder than Browning's, his sexual frankness and working-class cheekiness much more shocking to readers tuned to Tennyson and Longfellow. Whitman attracted counterculture attachments, and like Melville's less controversial postbellum poetry, Whitman's work vividly registered the seismic shifts of the Civil War. It's clear that Whitman and Browning were both important writers whose careers marked a break with antebellum models of poetry and poets, even though both of their careers began before the Civil War. However, an important difference between them is that Browning was not only read but also studied, and in ways that combined scholarly attention with expansive social speculation.

Browning was well aware that he had a large and lively readership in the United States; he is reported to have said that his poetry was better understood and appreciated in Chicago than anywhere else. Browning may even have been admired earlier and more intensely in the United States than in England.[114] In the experimental community of Brook Farm, William Henry Channing read the recently published *Paracelsus* to George William Curtis, Christopher Pearce Cranch, Margaret Fuller, Thomas Wentworth Higginson, and others; Fuller wrote an early review of Browning. Thomas Sergeant Perry remembered having in 1859 been part of a group of very young "Browningites" that included the teenaged William and Henry James, in Newport, Rhode Island. Henry James knew Browning personally in later life, heard him read his poetry many times, and attended Browning's burial service; William James wrote, late in his life, of Browning's value for strengthening the "backbone." Charles Francis Adams, Jr., and Sidney Lanier, Civil War soldiers north and south, took volumes of Browning to war with them. Emily Dickinson read a lot of both Brownings during the 1860s and wanted her friend Samuel Bowles to name his son "Robert" in the poet's honor.[115]

Browning clubs had close ties to Shakespeare studies. The Browning Society formed in England in 1881, and its members included William Rossetti, George Bernard Shaw, Eleanor Marx Aveling (Karl Marx's daughter), and Mary Gladstone (the prime minister's daughter). By 1882 a parallel organization sprang up in Chicago, followed by thirty-five or more Browning clubs in other U.S. cities. Frederick J. Furnivall, cofounder of the original London Browning Society, had previously founded the New Shakspere Society (1873), as well as the Early English Text Society (1864), the Chaucer Society (1868), and the Ballad Society (1873).[116] Compounding the association between Browning and Shakespeare, Robert Browning himself was a president of the New Shakspere Society.[117] In the United States, the convergence between Shakespeare studies and Browning studies was made especially explicit by the 1889 founding of the journal *Poet-Lore: A Monthly Magazine Devoted to Letters and to the Study of Shakespeare, Browning, and Comparative Literature*. Although *Poet-Lore* later shifted its emphasis and lost its hyphen, eventually becoming the journal of contemporary poetry still publishing today, *Poet-Lore*'s founding editors, Charlotte Porter and Helen A. Clarke, as noted earlier, met through their involvements in the magazine *Shakespeariana*.[118] *Poet-Lore* published a wide variety of essays about Browning and Shakespeare and also circulated news of Browning and Shakespeare organizations worldwide as well as news of interest to those communities.

There were several similarities between Browning and Shakespeare that underwrote this continuity. One was formal: Browning had written a number of plays (some of which were successfully produced) and a number of long poems structurally similar to plays or novels. Especially, though, he was well known for writing dramatic monologues—and a dramatic monologue, one critic explained, was like "Hamlet's soliloquy, if put out by itself as a complete poem, and if there were no play of 'Hamlet'."[119] Like Shakespeare, Browning took over many historical plots and characters but turned them to his own purposes. Both writers were prolific, and both had certain extraordinary technical capabilities—Shakespeare's vocabulary, which by the late nineteenth century had been identified as much larger than that of any other known writer, and Browning's range of meters, believed by some to set a record.[120] Perhaps no one called Browning "myriad-minded," but he deployed a multitude of characters of many stations, eras, and cultures, even taking up Shakespeare's Caliban. Many readers found Browning's scope of characterization ethically valuable, betokening an interest in many kinds of people, a desire to see from many points of view, even though his characters were usually considered less vividly individual than Shakespeare's. As was the case in the scripting of Shakespeare as modern, Browning's populous canvas was held to indicate a characteristically modern interest in the perceptions and springs of action of diverse individuals.[121]

For late Victorian readers, Browning as poet of growth could be as compelling as Shakespeare the poet of nature. Readers admired above all Browning's rendering of growth and development, which he treated as fundamental ethical and spiritual principles. The Harvard philosophy professor Josiah Royce, a member of the Boston Browning Society (also one of Thomas Davidson's guest lecturers), proposed that love for Browning included not just the "tenderer affections" but also

> the totality of human concerns, on their positive side, all passion, all human life, in so far as these tend towards growth, expansion, increasing intensity and ideality,—all these, however based their expressions may now seem, constitute, in us mortals, Love. Stress is laid, of course, upon this expanding, this positive and ideal tendency of love. This is the *differentia* of love amongst the affections.[122]

Another philosopher—Henry Jones, professor of moral philosophy at the University of Glasgow—examined Browning-style characterization in terms similar to Royce's: "For the primary truth about character—a truth which professed writers on morals have never forgotten except with calamitous results—is that it is a living process, an endlessly varying movement, a continuous new creation.... Even the freedom from which it derives its being is something never acquired, but is always being achieved."[123] This affirmation of growth, envisioned in an ethical and spiritual framework of love and acceptance, replaced the frightening aspects of evolution—"Nature, red in tooth and claw," as Tennyson put it—with a comforting but stimulating framework of open-ended transformation. In Charlotte Porter's version, this transformation was necessarily collective as well as individual. It is "expressed no less in the actions and history of the individual character than in the larger processes of a great social movement." Striking a note like Denton J. Snider's (and quoting him), Porter added, "Such movements, to a poet like Browning, are after all not impersonal but personal. They are the complex issue of many human wills."[124]

The veneration of Robert Browning seems to have fulfilled one of the longings that led Shakespeare's plays to be attributed to Francis Bacon: the longing to bridge the gap between Matthew Arnold's two cultures of art and science. Browning was held by some to be a scientific thinker insofar as he wrote about some of the epistemological and ethical problems raised by scientific methods. "Paracelsus," about a sixteenth-century physician and natural philosopher, was a case in point. Emma Endicott Marean proposed that "Paracelsus" "is at once a welcome to the new scientific ideal, and a recognition of the truth that man cannot live by science alone."[125] Josiah Royce took up the same poem as a more specific investigation of the worldview of "empirical mystics": men who "possess overwhelmingly clear intuitions of the divinest depth; but these always relate to the spiritual interpretation of particular physical facts."[126] These thinkers, among whom Emerson would have to be counted (although Royce does not name him), "find no facts 'hard,' as do the positivists, but all facts deep."[127] As Royce's approach indicates, Browning was credited with a philosophical interest in the nature of knowledge as well as ethics and theology; Percy Stickney Grant called Browning "a theologian with a genius for poetry."[128] This sense that his poetry was intellectually adventurous was connected for many readers with its difficulty. As Grant, an Episcopal clergyman, put it,

> The general readers of poetry have got into an expectant mood, and think that the art they enjoy should show a new development to correspond to the new knowledge and new experiences the world has gained,—that new wine should have new bottles. But when Browning constructs something to meet this need, the public at first laughs at his oddness, as though a new thing were not to be different from an old after all.[129]

Charles Carroll Everett (Unitarian minister and Harvard theology professor) believed there was some genuinely "bad writing" in some of Browning's poetry—that not all its obscurity was justified. However, he emphasized that other challenges presented by the poems result from Browning's seeing "relations more far-reaching than are commonly discerned." Evart also argued that obscurity can compel readers' attention and add "force" to a style, bringing shocks of recognition.[130]

Browning's difficulties—his syntactical obliquities, the uncertainties built into his compositional style, the intricacies of his historical references, and his allusions—meant that even though he was a contemporary poet, alive until 1891, the Browning Society had plenty to do. (Browning politely resisted resolving his readers' difficulties.) Their efforts were not limited to explication. Browning studies generated many apparatuses comparable to those of Shakespeare studies, including a range of published reference books. Like Shakespeare studies, Browning studies offered tremendous opportunities for pedantry as well as erudition. What was different about Browning studies was that Browning's difficulty and complexity were bound up with conditions of life in the nineteenth century. Browning was his readers' contemporary, so his readers counted on him to interpret their world and their inner life. Understood as a poet who affirmed and valued processes of human development, Browning was well suited to the educational improvisations of the late nineteenth-century United States. His poetry's support for the ethical underpinnings of cultural outreach was evident to admirers such as Charles Gordon Ames (a Unitarian minister), who drew from "Caliban upon Setebos" "a pathetic and powerful appeal or protest against all institutions, customs and doctrines that shut out individuals or masses from the helpfulness of light and love, and consign them to those 'dark places' which like Caliban's mind, are 'habitations of cruelty.'"[131]

Even though the Browning Society included men as well as women, it became a lightning rod for some of the late-century ambient misogyny swirling around women's clubs, especially privileged women's clubs with philanthropic leanings.[132] Max Beerbohm's cartoon of "Robert Browning, Taking Tea with the Browning Society" (1904) captured the society's reputation for status-seeking sociability, as well as the sense that the society's exchanges provided more of a ritual sipping than a full intellectual meal. The cartoon depicted men outnumbering women, but the setting appeared to be an effete women's world. Indeed, sendups of the Browning Society often implied that women in the Browning Society were swooning fans of the widower, not truly equipped to be good readers of poetry. Not surprisingly, the increasing polarization of expert and amateur often aligned with the master binary of gender: as literary clubs were coming to be structurally identified as amateur endeavors (no matter how serious their studies were or even whether academics were members), women's literary clubs attracted special contempt. This coding might be why E. M. W. Tillyard, after recounting Furnivall's intellectual accomplishments, declared that Furnivall's founding of the New Shakspere Society and the Browning Society "made him notorious."[133]

This context is important for considering Edith Wharton's "Xingu" (1911), a biting satire of the status-mongering pseudointellectualism of literary clubwomen. "Xingu" satirizes a women's club as an amateur organization whose members mistake superficial knowledge for the real thing. It was written after the consolidation of expertise in research universities, and it implies that clubs offered poor imitations of genuine, disciplinary academic knowledge. Wharton lampoons the club's feeble simulation of a university's division into departments of knowledge: Miss Van Vluyck covers "[p]hilanthropy and statistics" (a significant pairing, hinting at the emergence of Progressive forms of managerial sociology out of late nineteenth-century club work); Laura Glyde handles literature; and Mrs. Ballinger's "province" is "the Book of the Day," which means that she knows about whatever trendy volume is held to represent the "Thought of the Day."[134] An earlier Wharton story, "The Pelican" (1898), made a similar attack on superficial feminine learning in the person of Mrs. Amyot, who offered public lectures on Greek art, contemporary poets, Goethe (cribbed from George Lewes's work, the male narrator assures us), and science and religion. The combination's very eclecticism marks Mrs. Amyot's amateurism, compared to the disciplinary specialization of modern universities. Wharton's satires may have enacted her identification with professional authorship and expertise, which led her (like Richard Grant White) to share in experts' contempt for amateurs.

Women's literary clubs could be the engines of status and cultural hording, certainly. Charles W. Chesnutt's "Baxter's *Procrustes*" (1904), a satire of a men's club dedicated to collecting and producing beautiful limited-edition books, depicts an equally pretentious men's club that turns books into occasions for conspicuous consumption and conspicuous leisure (categories launched by Thorstein Veblen in 1899).[135] However, there's some irony in identifying literary clubs with shallow social climbing and displays of rank, in light of the fact that formal higher education was explicitly understood as a mechanism by which people could consolidate or improve their class positions. Formal education produced cultural capital directly, but the social consequences of informal study were much more unpredictable. The formation of the General Federation of Women's Clubs (1890), the National Association of Colored Women Clubs (1896), the Council of Jewish Women (1893), the National League of Women Workers (1897), and their many tributaries and offshoots built on generations of women's clubs, including many literary clubs.[136] Prejudice against women's clubs was compounded by the fact that women's education risked being reduced to an "ornamental accomplishment" precisely because women were not given opportunities to put it to use in the world.[137] Dorothy G. Rogers points out that the women philosophers involved in the Concord School for Philosophy were mainly excluded from the options for graduate study that would have equipped them for academic appointments, so they sought preparation in sites such as the Concord School and went on to be "teachers, public lecturers, social critics, and/or political analysts whose audience was almost exclusively female."[138] An 1898 history of the movement emphasized that women's clubs offered "postgraduate" education for women, although it wasn't clear whether postsecondary or postcollegiate education was meant.

As college became an option for more women, the women's club movement changed and literary education became less central to it, giving way to concerns about poverty and the living conditions of workers.[139] The women's club movement initially attracted women whose positions in the world gave them time for study and for philanthropy. Working Girls' Clubs were created as a form of outreach within the General Federation, having originally begun in conjunction with the New York State Aid Charity Association. By 1898, Working Girls' Clubs had thousands of members, and many of the clubs were becoming independent clubs (rather than sponsored offshoots) within the federation.[140]

Cultural or intellectual outreach, often disparaged as missionary work, is perhaps the feature of late nineteenth-century public literary culture most embarrassing to later scholars. Philanthropy is notoriously a mark of social privilege, and it would be easy to dismiss the women's clubs' efforts (like the many kinds of community education practiced by members of the St. Louis movement) as structurally serving class domination, no matter what the people involved on both sides hoped they were accomplishing. Indeed, some of the philanthropic volunteers feared as much. Margaret Sherwood, who was part of the settlement movement, wrote a novel in which a troubled do-gooding character working at a settlement house comments satirically, "we will elevate the masses by Swinburne and *frappee!*"[141] It isn't always easy to tell where philanthropy leaves off and solidarity begins, though. There were many kinds of sponsored literary education under way late in the century, even though all of them necessarily played out on terrains of uneven power and privilege. Browning Societies also attracted reformers and radicals.[142] Frederick Furnivall had been a founder of the London Working Men's College (1854), a Christian Socialist educational organization for working-class men; a women's branch was added later.[143] Among U.S. Browningites, Jenkin Lloyd Jones founded the Abraham Lincoln Centre in 1891 as an organ of community outreach for his Unitarian congregation in Chicago. Jones, a lecturer through the University of Chicago Extension Program, offered courses at the center on "Art in the Poetry of Robert Browning" and "Prophets of Modern Literature" (including Browning, of course).[144] The Boston Browning Society was rife with Christian socialists. Vida Dutton Scudder, a Wellesley colleague of Margaret Sherwood's who founded the College Settlement Association in 1890, was a Boston Browning Society member and taught Browning in her courses at Wellesley. There's no sign of Browning or Swinburne being an official offering at the Boston settlement house, but Shakespeare was.[145]

Pauline E. Hopkins's complex relationships with Boston-area clubs exemplify the clubs' double-edged character. Hopkins grew up in the relatively privileged and very active African American community of Boston's Beacon Hill; she became an actress and a playwright in the 1870s, working with well-respected African American theater companies. As Hopkins's biographer Lois Brown argues, Hopkins was a race writer for her whole career as a playwright, novelist, magazine editor, and highly versatile magazine writer. She presents in *Contending Forces* (1901) a critique of status climbing and influence brokering in an African American Boston women's club, reportedly modeling one overbearing member on Josephine Ruffin, the leader of Boston's New Era Club. Yet Hopkins was at the time of writing the novel an officer of the New Era Club, and she read portions of the novel in progress to two other Boston clubs (the

Woman's Era Club and a local set of members of the Colored National League). Brown argues that Hopkins's novel, which contrasted the women's club's efforts with the more direct help offered by a group of African American nuns, is very much in tune with Mary Church Terrell's call in 1901 for the National Association of Colored Women to "live up to the organization's credo of 'lifting as we climb...by coming into closer touch with the masses of our women.'"[146] The association, in which many writers and elocutionists from the turn of the century were active, had in 1901 already begun to campaign against lynching and went on to found schools, kindergarten programs, boarding houses, orphanages, and settlement houses.[147]

The interest in women's intellectual development and accomplishments that the women's club movement channeled points to another reason for Robert Browning's popularity. The hopes for social transformation and spiritual regeneration kindled by Browning Societies included transformations of gender relations and intimate life. Many admiring accounts of Robert Browning's poetry lingered over his marriage to Elizabeth Barrett, and critical discussions of Browning's poems about love and lovers often invoked his well-known admiration for his wife as a fellow practitioner (indeed, a poet initially more famous than he was). Robert Browning's treatment of gender and sexuality was scrutinized by many readers, just as Shakespeare's was, and some readers who homed in on these topics were gathering support for gender equality. Publishing in *Poet-Lore*, Scudder compared Shakespeare's and Browning's treatments of women, noting that Shakespeare studied women with "most reverential honor" but (according to Scudder) never made a woman character a "dramatic center."[148] Browning, in contrast, gave men and women equal treatment: "In Browning, they [women] are separated from the men by no sharp difference of function. They share in all the great activities of life. And the reason for this union is clear. They have neither peculiar goodness nor peculiar simplicity to set them in a class apart."[149] George Willis Cooke, a Unitarian minister and author of a critical study of George Eliot as well as a lecturer who spoke about "The Intellectual Development of Women," similarly credited Browning with modernizing romantic love, treating "woman" as "the object of his personal esteem, loved for her own sake and because he found in her a companionship that supplemented and revealed his own individuality."[150]

Browning's admirers included a number of women who partnered with other women and may have been lesbians. It is possible that their interest in his poetry was enhanced by the ways in which the Brownings' antipatriarchal elopement and the poets' equal commitments to their writing careers could point beyond the heteronormative. Charlotte Porter and Helen A. Clarke, editors of *Poet-Lore* and members of the Boston Browning Society, lived together and operated as partners; they produced an edition of Elizabeth Barrett Browning's poetry as well as a number of works relating to Robert.[151] Vida Dutton Scudder, who published about Browning's work in *The Life of the Spirit in the Modern English Poets* (1895), lived with editor and novelist Florence Converse. In Scudder's circle of colleagues at Wellesley College, there were a number of other women faculty members who lived in long-term relationships with women and were active in Browning studies. Margaret Sherwood, the novelist who wrote about settlement houses, was an English professor who later wrote about Browning in *Undercurrents of Influence in English Romantic Poetry* (1934); she lived with English professor Martha Hale Shackford, who edited a volume of Barrett Browning's letters. Katharine Lee Bates, long-time chair of Wellesley's English Department and a poet-scholar, wrote a poem about Browning, "In the Poet's Corner," and with economics professor Katharine Coman made use of Browning's work in their joint project *English History Told by English Poets* (1902). Bates and Coman lived together for decades, and Bates published a book of poetry (*Yellow Clover: A Book of Remembrance*) about Coman after her death.[152]

Browning's portraits of interesting women, his explorations of many intricate forms of love and desire, and his probing into conventional sexual mores might have appealed to anyone who wished to rewrite scripts of sex and gender. Mary E. Burt, in *Browning's Women*, unfolds the ironies of "A Light Woman," whose speaker has seduced the "light woman" who was attempting to seduce his friend, his motives a queasy amalgam of altruism and sexual competition. "Why should he criticise in her what he himself is guilty of," Burt asks, pointing out also that "[e]ven the little spark of soul in a 'Light Woman' ought to be respected." The case of Mildred, the young girl whose sexual transgression leads to death and tragedy due to her brother's rigid sense of honor in *A Blot in the 'Scutcheon*, prompts Burt to protest the logic by which only women, not men, could be "fallen."[153] My point is not that these interpretations of Browning's poetry are groundbreaking (or even necessarily wholly satisfying) but that Browning studies provided occasions for women and men to talk about gender equality and sexual power relations, just as such studies hosted critiques of wealth and economic power. Indeed, the Browning who emerges from the print record of Browning Societies is a figure who has much in common with Henrik Ibsen, whose "problem plays" galvanized audiences and readers in the United States around the same time. ("Ibsen Clubs are supplanting Browning Clubs," wrote a critic in 1890.)[154] When *Poet-Lore* expanded its brief, taking as its new subtitle *A Monthly Magazine of Letters*, it gave a lot of attention to Ibsen.

As this shift indicates, the joint career of Porter and Clarke offers a way of reframing the Browning Society as one of modernism's launch pads: an organization whose members cultivated a taste for obscurity, challenging new forms, and daring subject matter. Indeed, by the early twentieth century, *Poet-Lore* was a key site for translations of innovative European plays: works by Lagerlof, Strindberg, Gorki, Chekhov, D'Annunzio, Maeterlinck, Echegaray, and others.[155] *Poet-Lore* also published several translations of Noh plays. Porter and Clarke did not leave Shakespeare and Browning behind, producing in the early twentieth century a highly regarded edition of Shakespeare based on the First Folio.[156] They produced an edition of Robert Browning's works (1898, reissued in 1910) and study guides to his poetry along with an edition of Elizabeth Barrett Browning's works (1900). Their *Shakespeare Study Programs* (1915–1916, adapted or distilled from some of their work in *Poet-Lore*) were well respected.[157] They had collegial relations with other Shakespearean scholars, including H. H. Furness and college professors Richard Moulton and Hiram Corson.

Epitomizing some of the best tendencies of nineteenth-century public literary culture, Porter and Clarke combined scholarly seriousness, a taste for innovation, and fandom. They took for granted that public literary culture could be participatory as well as critical, in keeping with Roland Barthes's evocation of a nineteenth-century music culture "when, active amateurs being numerous (at least within a certain class), 'to play' and 'to listen' constituted a virtually undifferentiated activity," before the separation of roles between designated (professional) "interpreter" and "(passive) amateur."[158] Helen A. Clarke created musical settings for stretches of poetry by Shakespeare, Browning, Marlowe, and Spenser, and many of these arrangements were published in *Poet-Lore*.[159] Porter adapted Browning's tragedy *The Return of the Druses* for performance by the Boston Browning Society. They were unabashed literary enthusiasts who celebrated authors' birthdays and delighted in amateur theatricals, and they were also important players in a public literary culture that did not segregate scholarship from fan culture. A striking example of this fusion is George Dimmick Latimer's 1897 "A Browning Monologue," sixteen pages of prose structured, Browning-style, like a lopsided conversation in which we don't hear the interlocutor, only the speaker's responses and adjustments—a performance full of the pleasures of imitation but also shedding light on Browning's techniques.[160] The St. Louis movement generated similar creative responses, ranging from Denton J. Snider's poem "Shakespeare at Stratford" (1889)—read to the Chicago Kindergarten College in 1893—which whimsically responded to the authorship controversy by staging a visit from Francis Bacon to Shakespeare, to Snider's antiwar drama, *The Redemption of the Hamlets (Son and Father)* (1923), an ancestor of crossover fan fiction in which Hermione, from *The Winter's Tale*, turns Hamlet away from the idea of vengeance and the Ghost ends up embracing penitence rather than martial codes of honor.[161]

Browning societies brought together academics (including those in fields other than literature) and nonacademics on a mainly equal footing in the late nineteenth century, at a time when journals such as *PMLA* (1884) and academic presses such as Cornell University Press (founded 1869) had begun to create a print infrastructure for exclusively academic literary studies. Browning Societies also kept alive a literary commitment to the importance of hearing and speaking poetry, whereas the version of academic literary studies that would come to dominate in the twentieth century emphasized students' silent individual encounters with print texts. A number of Browning's best-known public readers were Browning Society members, performing sometimes for money but also for love: most notably, Levi Thaxter (husband of the writer Celia Thaxter; Browning wrote a poem on the occasion of Levi's death); Jenkin Lloyd Jones, founder of the Chicago Browning Society; the playwright Clyde Fitch; an actress called Sarah Cowell LeMoyne; and Cornell English professor Hiram Corson. Corson, who was also a Shakespeare scholar, read the entirety of Browning's *The Ring and the Book* to his students every year and began a Browning Club in 1877, well before the official society began in England.[162]

In their love of speaking and hearing poetry, of course, Browningites were characteristic products of a century in which performing poetry aloud was greatly valued. As Angela Sorby has observed, between 1839 and 1902 McGuffey's readers taught "more than 116 million children how to read with their voices, how to breathe while they read, and how to use their bodies as vehicles for performance."[163] The most unexpected testimonial to the pleasures of reading aloud might be Edith Wharton's account of a spontaneous performance by Henry James, worth quoting at length:

> One of our joys, when the talk touched on any great example of prose or verse, was to get the book from the shelf, and ask one of the company to read the passage aloud. There were some admirable readers in the group, in whose gift I had long delighted; but I had never heard Henry James read aloud—or known that he enjoyed doing so—till one night some one alluded to Emily Brontë's poems, and I said I had never read "Remembrance." Immediately he took the volume from my hand, and, his eyes filling, and some far-away emotion deepening his rich and flexible voice, he began:
>
>> Cold in the earth, and the deep snow piled above thee,
>> Far, far removed, cold in the dreary grave,
>> Have I forgot, my only Love, to love thee,
>> Severed at last by Time's all-severing wave?
>
> I had never before heard poetry read as he read it; and I never have since. He chanted it, and he was not afraid to chant it, as many good readers are, who, though they instinctively feel that the genius of the English poetical idiom requires it to be spoken *as poetry*, are yet afraid of yielding to their instinct because the present-day fashion is to chatter high verse as though it were colloquial prose. James, on the contrary, far from shirking the rhythmic emphasis, gave it full expression. His stammer ceased as by magic as soon as he began to read, and his ear, so sensitive to the convolutions of an intricate prose style, never allowed him to falter over the most complex prosody, but swept him forward on great rollers of sound till the full weight of his voice fell on the last cadence.
>
> James's reading was a thing apart, an emanation of his inmost self, unaffected by fashion or elocutionary artifice.[164]

The fact that even the high priest of the introspective novel designed for private silent reading loved chanting poetry, under the right conditions, offers a reminder of how variegated late-century literary culture was. There was a perpetual interplay between the appropriation of literature for the bourgeoisie and the invention of opportunities for others to join—or surpass—the bourgeoisie in enjoying it. But many people also believed that literature was an engine of transformation—spiritual, intellectual, social, and even political and economic. Many people loved opportunities to hold literature in common: to be in a room where poems or plays or stories were being read, or to be part of a reading; to be part of ongoing discussions about literary works, through discussion or a prepared paper, in venues of varying formality; to be part of a readership for a journal such as *Poet-Lore* that offered up the thinking of many about authors studied in common. In the Browning Society, in addition to the pleasures of close reading, philological inquiry, and allusion spotting, readers believed they were thinking together about some of the most urgent questions of the time, deriving hope and sustenance from Browning's poetry along the way. Browning's poetry offered a gathering place for many people who longed for change, a particular patch within the gathering place offered by literature at large during the last decades of the nineteenth century.

A Library of American Literature

> Literature is the fragment of fragments. The smallest part
> of what has been done and spoken has been recorded;
> and the smallest part of what has been recorded
> has survived.
>
> —JOHANN WOLFGANG VON GOETHE, A.D. 182–.[165]

The closest successor to the Duyckincks' two-volume *Cyclopedia of American Literature* was *A Library of American Literature from the Earliest Settlement to the Present Time*, a plush, eleven-volume set published between 1888 and 1890, edited by Edmund Clarence Stedman and Ellen Mackay Hutchinson and including selections by 1,207 authors.[166] The *Library* was a heroic undertaking, a thoughtful and wide-ranging anthology and literary-cultural history well suited to be a reference work within the public literary culture of the time; my epigraph borrows an epigraph from the *Library*'s last volume. Yet the *Library* did poorly commercially and was mainly forgotten within scholarly histories of U.S. literature in the twentieth century.[167] Both the ambitions embodied in the *Library* and its failures register some of the losses involved in literary scholarship's establishment as not only an expert domain but also a marketing sector within the publishing industry.

Stedman, the lead editor of the *Library*, was a reluctant stockbroker who preferred his work as a poet, critic, and periodical reviewer.[168] Ellen Mackay

Hutchinson was a published poet and a literary editor at the *New York Tribune*, where Stedman had published poems and reviews.[169] These poet-editors cared about aesthetics, but they understood literature capaciously, asserting in the final volume that the *Library* was neither a "Valhalla" including only masterpieces nor a "miscellany." Rather, they endorsed the comment by a reviewer of the earlier volumes who had characterized the editors' intentions as "historical rather than critical. They meant to exhibit the kind of composition which at this or that period was supposed by the American people, or a section of it, to belong to literature. A searching light would thus be thrown on the stage of taste and cultivation attained by our countrymen at a particular time."[170] In practice, the scope of the *Library* extended to examples of special eloquence, writings in the imaginative genres that would become literary staples, speeches and documents of historical importance, and influential works of scholarship, as well as works that were more closely aligned with the narrowed version of literature.

For the periods in which modern literature existed, a distinction between literary writings and disciplinary writings was observed, and the representation of disciplinary writings was accordingly diminished:

> It should be mentioned that, owing to the preponderance of theology, history, and politics in our early volumes, it was thought advisable to occupy the later chiefly with an exhibition of the modern rise of 'literature proper'—with essays, history, fiction, and poetry. Consequently the great concourse of recent savants, economists, and divines, eminent in the faculties of our colleges and institutes,—among them many near and honored friends of the editors,—is for the most part unrepresented.[171]

In the project as a whole, however, the editors construed "literature" in the broad sense that was often privileged in national literary histories: as a medium and record of collective thought and experience, a public-oriented sense of literature that resembled the pre-nineteenth-century sense of literature as learned writings. History was included in the narrower version of "literature proper," perhaps because histories were narrative projects in which stylistic distinction was especially valued. The *Library*'s historical writings are mainly by nonacademics, including major historians of midcentury such as William Prescott.

The periodization of the volumes tracks the history of the nation but does not attempt to create unifying themes or aesthetics: two volumes of colonial literature (earlier and later), one volume of literature of the Revolutionary period, and thereafter successive numbered volumes comprising the "Literature of the Republic." Writings about key events and phases in colonial and national history are included as well as speeches and documents of public significance: the New England synod's Platform of Church discipline, William Penn's "Letter to the Indians," George Washington's remarks on his appointment as commander in chief, a letter from Alexander Hamilton about the "Financial Condition and Prospects of the United States," a poem by Sarah Wentworth Morton about Aaron Burr's trial for treason, Charles Sumner's Senate oration "The Crime against Kansas," Lincoln's Gettysburg Address, General William T. Sherman's account of his march to the sea, and so forth. Collective and anonymous works are also sampled, such as "Verse of the French and Indian War," "Negro Hymns and Songs," and "Popular Ballads of the Civil War." A table in the final volume tracks the distribution of the selections among thirty-two topics ranging from "Anecdote" to "Witchcraft and Wonders." In the table, writings about war are broken into ten categories (about a single conflict, such as the Civil War, or a category, such as "Indian Troubles"); there are also categories for writings about "Manners and Customs," "Politics, Government, Etc.," and "Slavery, Abolition, Etc."[172]

The resulting compilation does not reflect a strong sense that history requires the testimony or responses of anyone besides the representatives of the ruling race and class, however. For example, of the many writings about slavery, only one is by an African American (two pages from *The Life and Times of Frederick Douglass*), and while there are countless writings by white Americans about Native Americans (ranging from John Smith's writing about Pocahontas to Mary Rowlandson's captivity narrative to Ojibwe lore collected by Henry Schoolcraft), writings by Native Americans are scarce (Red Jacket about Native American religion in volume 4; George Copway's memoirs in volume 11). Phillis Wheatley is represented by three poems in volume 3 (compared with eleven by Philip Freneau) plus the frontispiece illustration from her *Poems*.[173] Lucy Larcom, identified in her biographical note as a Lowell mill worker, was probably the only author marked as working-class, although other writers included may have been as well.[174] Women writers were well represented, but the blind spots around race and class are significant in a work explicitly committed to representing collective thought and feeling.[175]

The generic and intellectual range of the selections is nonetheless impressive. Volume 5, presenting "Literature of the Republic" from 1821 to 1834, includes writings by William Ellery Channing, John James Audubon, Washington Irving (Sydney Smith's question about "who reads an American book?" is one of the epigraphs to this volume), Emma Willard, James Fenimore Cooper, Catherine Sedgwick, Samuel F. B. Morse, Lydia Sigourney, Henry Schoolcraft, Samuel Goodrich, William Cullen Bryant, William Prescott, George Catlin, Sarah Josepha Hale, Horace Mann, and Amasa Walker.[176] Diverse historical writings, some in the form of memoirs, are included: excerpts from a biography of Thurlow Weed (about how Lincoln's cabinet was formed), from George Ticknor's *History of Spanish Literature* (1849), from the biography of a minister about time spent with Henry Thackeray during his U.S. tour, from a history of Boston about the Boston lecture as a cultural institution, from an account of the lost colony of Roanoke, and from Dunlap's *History of the American Theatre* (about the experiences of a working playwright). The volume also offers a lyric poem by Mirabeau Lamar (second president of the Republic of Texas), a defense of free trade, a scientific essay about "luminiferous ether," an account of the probable site of the Holy Sepulcher in Palestine, an essay calling for Christians to cultivate the "inner life," and a lecture by Francis Wayland (the first president of Brown University) about the philosophy of analogy.

The *Library* testifies amply to Shakespeare's importance in the United States. The editors' preface to the final volume describes the *Library* as ranging chronologically "from Shakespeare's time to our own," and a number of scholarly and critical writings about Shakespeare are featured throughout.[177] Volume 5 contains two excerpts from Gulian Verplanck's edition of Shakespeare's plays (1847), one "On the Madness of Hamlet" (taking up another of the best-known literary controversies of the nineteenth century) and one on the spelling of Shakespeare's name, a strangely heated topic in Shakespeare studies.[178] In the same volume is a comparison of Shakespeare and Schiller by Alexander Hill Everett (briefly an editor of the *North American Review*, otherwise mainly employed as a diplomat) denying that Shakespeare was in any sense a Romantic.[179] The Shakespeare-related selections demonstrate that the editors in practice gave more space to scholarly and disciplinary writings of the late nineteenth century than their official account of their methods suggested. Subsequent volumes include a discussion by George Marsh (diplomat and philologist) about Shakespeare's dramatic diction, emphasizing Shakespeare's use of "terms borrowed from every art and every science, from all theoretical knowledge and all human experience"; selections from Henry Norman Hudson and Richard Grant White on Shakespeare's characterization (offering slightly different spins on Shakespeare's being "myriad-minded"); and other Shakespearean writings by E. P. Whipple, H. H. Furness, William Torrey Harris, and Appleton Morgan. Denton J. Snider is represented by an excerpt from *A Walk in Hellas*, not his Shakespearean criticism, but William Torrey Harris's selection about Shakespeare takes an approach like Snider's, emphasizing the plays' philosophical resonance and their detailed presentation of the worlds in which characters' actions took on meaning. Most interestingly, an excerpt from Delia Bacon's *Putnam's* article contesting Shakespeare's authorship is included as well as an excerpt from her biography emphasizing that the authorship question was only a small part of her interest in the plays.[180] (An excerpt from Hiram Corson's *Introduction to the Study of Robert Browning's Poetry* rounded out the *Library's* representation of the three episodes in literary culture addressed previously in this chapter.)[181]

In a number of selections, Shakespeare's literary authority contributes to broader literary projects. Emerson's "Books and Reading," excerpted in volume 6, warns about the dangerous influence of genius ("The English dramatic poets have Shakespearized now for two hundred years") and pushes aside textual criticism in order to promote instead an emphasis on ascertaining Shakespeare's profoundest wisdom: "The discerning will read, in his Plato or Shakespeare, only that least part,—only the authentic utterances of the oracle; all the rest he rejects, were it never so many times Plato's and Shakespeare's."[182] Edward Tyrrel Channing, warning Harvard's graduating seniors about the hazards of "Literary Fame" in 1856, summed up the historical vicissitudes faced by the works of great writers in a way that would probably have brought Shakespeare to many readers' minds. Channing's account eloquently captured the disquieting features of canonization, summoning up its dangers in order to contrast them to the "life in the hearts, the experience and the wants of men" that he proposed as the true test of literary fame: "To be immortal as a writer is more than to have a place among the customary tenants of large libraries, to be hidden perhaps for ages; and, when brought to light, like an embalmed corpse of the East, for the examination of the curious,—to be wondered at chiefly for having lasted so long." Channing sketched the possibilities for revisionist history from the (dead) author's point of view, including one in which "[h]e is no longer to be a person, a unit, with a lawful name, but a set of ballad-singers, each with his own story upon the same great national subject." And the alternative was not much better: "an ample biography must be invented for him." Furthermore, the textual critics determined to "settle the text and explain obscurities" are "the most captious, assuming and quarrelsome set of men that ever claimed to be literary judges, or judges in any question": "A new reading, or the discovery of an old copy with alleged contemporary corrections, is received as a personal wrong, an invasion of some private right, and very soon the world is in arms. A pretty spectacle for a benign spirit...hailed...as the benefactor and glory of his race." In contrast with Samuel Johnson's fate—to be better known for the conversations reported by Boswell than for his own writings—Channing implies that Shakespeare's fate offered a cautionary tale of the ways in which the custodial machineries of literature encumbered as well as preserved.[183]

Shakespeare's role in authorizing an American literary tradition surfaces in Henry Theodore Tuckerman's 1857 essay about Charles Brockden Brown, entitled "The First American Novelist." Tuckerman uses Shakespeare's example to justify the "tendency to supernaturalism" (an early formulation of what was later called American Gothic) of U.S. writings in general and Brown's in particular. Throughout the excerpt, Tuckerman stresses Brown's successful way of combining not only "analytical with imaginative power" but also both of them with effective action. Tuckerman posited an "occult affinity between the achieving faculty and the sense of wonder" so that supernaturalism was not only compatible with purposeful accomplishment but somehow correlated with it: "Shakespeare has inwrought his grand superstitious creation amid vital energies of purpose and action, and thus brought into striking contrast the practical efficiency and spiritual dependence of our nature." Tuckerman went on to identify the American literary tendency toward introspection with Brown's power of analyzing "emotion" and describing "states of mind," his greatest strengths. Implicitly making the case for Brown's literary value, Tuckerman identifies these qualities as a Shakespearian infusion into fiction: "[I]n following out a metaphysical vein, in making the reader absolutely cognizant of the revery, fears, hopes, imaginings, that 'puzzle the will,' or concentrate its energies, he obeyed a singular idiosyncrasy of his nature, a Shakespearian tendency, and one, at that period, almost new as a chief element of fiction."[184]

The Stedman-Hutchinson *Library* provides ample evidence for the centrality of Shakespeare studies in U.S. public literary culture and for the public recognition granted to Shakespearean scholars and critics who have dropped out of the disciplinary memory of English literary studies. It also represents the continuing power of a public-oriented understanding of literature in an era better known for the emergence of aestheticism. In the case of the *Library*, a sense of literature's collective significance was mediated through the intellectual influence of Hippolyte Taine, the French critic sometimes considered the inventor of modern literary history. His four-volume history of English literature, published in 1864, was handicapped by the century's characteristic reliance on faux racial-cultural categories such as the Teutonic, but it addressed the emergence and transformations of literary genres as responses to collective material and intellectual conditions. Under the signs of history and culture, but not politics, Taine treated works of literature as the fossil remains of the "inner man," shaped by three collective conditions: race (a sprawling category, often identified with national character), milieu, and epoch.[185] Taine is not mentioned in the editorial apparatuses of the *Library*, but his influence was claimed on the very first page of Edmund Clarence Stedman's earlier *Victorian Poets* (1875).

Hutchinson has left few traces of her independent intellectual convictions, but Stedman's *Victorian Poets* and *Poets of America* (1885) combined a periodizing sense of the historicity of literature—"the insensible moulding of an author's life, genius, manner of expression, by the conditions of race, circumstance, and period in which he is seen to be involved"—with the insistence that genius transcended such historical circumstances—"great poets overcome all restrictions, create their own styles, and even may determine the lyrical character of a period, or indicate that of one which is to succeed them."[186] In other words, Stedman's criticism manifested the unresolved interplay between periodizing historicism and the ahistorical outcropping of genius (the favorite way of naming singular creative activity that was not solely the product and symptom of its historical conditions) that we saw in chapter 3. Stedman seems to have meant the national-historical approach he adapted from Taine to do for U.S. literature what Taine had done for British literature, and reviewers and well-wishers seem to have taken it for granted that the *Library* succeeded in demonstrating that the United States (projected backward onto relevant parts of British America) had a distinctive literature. John Greenleaf Whittier said in a letter to Stedman that the editors "are deserving of national thanks for demonstrating the fact that America has a Literature distinctly her own."[187]

However, the Stedman-Hutchinson *Library* was an expensive failure, best known today, as noted earlier, as a project that helped to bankrupt Mark Twain.

It was referenced as one of two recent "indispensable" "collections" but not treated at length as a forerunner by the editors of the *Cambridge History of American Literature*—who cite Rufus Griswold, the Duyckincks, and Charles F. Richardson, among others—and was not carried into the chief twentieth-century genealogies of U.S. literary studies and canon making.[188] It seems likely that the *Library*'s failure was partly due to its unusual mode of publication and partly by its having had nonacademic editors during an era when the authority of literary experts was being consolidated in academia.

The most obvious peculiarity of the *Library* was that it was published by subscription. Stedman and Hutchinson's volumes of poems and Stedman's earlier edited volumes had been published by trade presses with high literary reputations (Scribner, Houghton Mifflin, J. R. Osgood). However, the *Library* seems to have been the brainchild of a Cincinnati subscription publisher who recruited Stedman (who then recruited Hutchinson) but somehow failed to get any volumes into print.[189] By 1887, the project was taken up by Charles L. Webster and Co., the subscription publishing company that Mark Twain had founded in partnership with Webster, his nephew by marriage. Twain had become a convert to subscription publishing after the success of *Roughing It* (1872), which he had placed with a leading subscription publisher. *The Gilded Age* (coauthored with Charles Dudley Warner, published in 1873) and *Innocents Abroad* (1867) had been even bigger subscription hits, leading Twain to form his own subscription publishing company. Subscription publishing cut out the retail middleman and created a direct relationship between the press and its customers, both features that Twain found appealing. As chapter 2 explains, trade publishers such as Scribner dealt mainly with bookshops and other retail outlets, selling books to retailers who would mark them up and sell directly to the public. Subscription publishers instead sent out agents who would contract with customers directly to buy books, either books that had not yet been published or books that had been published but would be later delivered by the agents, perhaps in custom bindings selected by each customer. (*Huckleberry Finn* was available in "in blue cloth or green, in library leather or half-morocco, with a choice of plain, sprinkled, or marbled edges.")[190]

The decades after the Civil War were a busy period for subscription publishing, since there were still many customers who didn't have easy access to bookshops even though the infrastructure for getting agents and books to customers had been improved by wartime expansions to transportation networks. Subscription sales were often made on the installment plan, which made it possible for customers to undertake purchases that might have been impossible as single retail transactions; this was Webster's practice with the *Library*, and books in sets were especially well suited for subscription sales.[191] One estimate holds that books sold by subscription accounted for three-quarters of all book sales during the 1870s and 1880s.[192] As chapter 2 indicates, though, subscription publishing was treated as distinctly downmarket in the pages of the periodicals aligned with trade publishers that cultivated literary reputations.[193] Subscription books were often treated as "cheap books" regardless of what they cost.

Many subscription books looked different from trade books: they often featured elaborate and colorful bindings and lavish illustrations, and they cost more than comparable trade editions. Trade editions of serious literary books, especially novels, were likely to be in all-black type with at most a handful of illustrations. Subscription-printed novels were visually much richer: for example, Twain's edition of *Pudd'nhead Wilson* (1894) included playful marginal line drawings throughout.[194] Even though works by many standard authors (Shakespeare prominent among them) were sold by subscription, critics of subscription publishing charged that the books were sold more for the packaging than the contents and implied also that the packaging was vulgar, aimed at coffee-table display. Each volume of the *Library* included more than a dozen full-page portraits of authors accompanied by their autographs, and even though the portraits (black-and-white engravings) were in keeping with the sober aesthetics of trade books, the copiousness of illustration and the interplay of red and black print on each volume's cover page marked the livelier visual style of subscription publishing.

Charles L. Webster and Co. brought out the *Library* (including the final eleventh volume, which included biographical notes prepared by Stedman's son Arthur) between 1888 and 1890. Having previously had a number of successes—most notably Ulysses S. Grant's *Memoirs* (1885)—the company sank the profits into the *Library*. Unfortunately, the *Library* didn't sell well, apparently contributing to the firm's failure and Twain's bankruptcy. It's hard to be sure why the *Library* was a failure for Webster. William Evarts Benjamin bought the rights and continued to sell it, having some success.[195] Benjamin was a dealer in rare books, including Americana, who operated a modest publishing house, and it's possible that the association of the *Library* with rare and valuable Americana offset the negative associations of subscription books; apparently Benjamin had a reasonable return on his investment.

However, the *Library* may have floundered because it differed in important ways from other subscription books. Books that sold well by subscription included general reference works (especially encyclopedias); sets of works by standard authors (whose reputation was already made, so that a collected edition sold by subscription simply made available in new formats works already established in trade publishing); unscholarly compilations such as *Mark Twain's Library of Humor* (Charles L. Webster, 1888); and new nonfiction works, especially memoirs and biographies. (*The Life and Times of Frederick Douglass* was sold by subscription, in what may have been the first large-scale marketing strategy targeting African American readers.)[196] Stedman and Hutchinson framed the *Library* in part as a reference work offering "correct texts (sometimes differing from those usually accepted) of significant and historic sermons, speeches, public documents, and declarations"; sections of "Noted Sayings" served a similar purpose.

However, the *Library* was significantly more scholarly than the reference books and compilations that were subscription staples. The editors' account suggests that the project began as a casual and profit-oriented exercise in bookmaking that the editors decided to upgrade:

> It was thought by the business projector that the volumes could be made up with speed and ease, after the manner of various compilations for the subscription-trade. But we finally accepted his advances, because there seemed a chance to do something of real service, and only upon condition that we should work in our own way,—and thus doubled the labor and postponed our remuneration.[197]

The upgrading resulted in what the editors' promoted as an artisanal work: a "'handmade' Library...not a piece of 'machine-work'": "the product of the individual effort of two editors, consulting for years in harmony," with no other judgments intervening "to produce a confusion of tastes and methods."[198] Yet in the years in which Webster was marketing this exquisitely designed set, it was also promoting *The Legends and Myths of Hawaii* (1888), *Yanks and Johnnies; or, Laugh and Grow Fat* (1888), *The Life and Letters of Roscoe Conkling, Orator, Statesman, Advocate* (1889), *Biography of Ephraim McDowell, M.D., "The Father of Ovariotomy"* (1890), and a *Concise Cyclopedia of Religious Knowledge* (1890).[199] The editors' credentials and Twain's connection to the Webster Company supported the literary ambitions of the *Library*, but the eclecticism of the Webster list and the cultural coding of the subscription system did not.

The competition between subscription and trade publishing was only one result of the new forms of diversification and consolidation in the U.S. publishing industry in the wake of the Civil War. Indeed, trade publishing itself was just being stabilized as an industry defined by editing, selecting works to publish and shaping their published form; marketing, building a list that would augment the reputation of the house and organizing publicity on that basis; and retail distribution, to which marketing was tailored. Whereas subscription canvassers were understandably eager to create new book buyers, Ellen Gruber Garvey has pointed out that long-standing trade publishers were likely to envision their customer base as already-regular buyers of hardback books. Until about the 1920s, old-school literary publishers, especially, envisioned a "natural circle of readers" too discerning to be affected by aggressive advertising campaigns.[200] The publishers Garvey has in mind were most likely the same houses that had a "gentleman's agreement" to respect each other's arrangements with English authors, during the years before the United States finally and belatedly committed to international copyright in 1891: Harper and Houghton-Mifflin and Scribner and other houses named for the men or families in charge.[201] Most of these publishing houses owned monthly magazines whose character contributed to their literary standing and operated in collaboration with their book publication: magazines serialized novels en route to publication, ran short stories later published as collections, and offered reviews and critical articles that publicized the firms' books and authors.

In this context, the Stedman-Hutchinson Library might be understood as a trade book manqué whose subscription format jammed its signal to prospective buyers. Even though its canon was broad and "literature proper" only one strand of its project, it was keyed to the project of delineating national literary canons, identities, and trajectories that the trade publishers' magazines perpetually engaged, through topics such as literary realism was the best rubric for the nation's fiction. The *Library* may also have operated as an academic book manqué, since by the end of the century, it had become somewhat unusual for people other than academics to undertake major literary editions and literary histories in the United States. The literature of the United States was beginning to be taught in high schools, colleges, and universities toward the end of the nineteenth century, and there were a number of published histories of U.S. literature, many by college professors.[202] Moses Coit Tyler, identified on the title page by his academic title, published a two-volume *History of American Literature* in 1878.[203] John S. Hart, identified on the title page by his academic titles, published *A Manual of American Literature: A Text-Book for Schools and Colleges*, in 1872.[204] Charles F. Richardson published the two-volume history *American Literature, 1607–1885* in 1888; he was professor of Anglo-Saxon and English at Dartmouth College.[205] At the turn of the century, Barrett Wendell, professor of English at Harvard College, published *A Literary History of America* (1901).[206] None of these books was an anthology, the category we would probably use today for the *Library*.[207] All were expository histories that mainly quoted passages from literary works and sometimes included an entire short poem. However, these and similar histories were often used as textbooks in college literature classes, even though some professors believed strongly that entire literary works ought to be assigned instead or as well, and the work these books did in presenting legacy texts chronologically was comparable to the work of the *Library*.

Put otherwise: canon-setting efforts, within a national literature or in the corpus of an author, were increasingly likely to carry some kind of academic branding in the era of the *Library*. As a poet-critic, author of *Victorian Poetry* and *Poets of America*, Stedman had literary authority, but the kind of comprehensive literary history that he and Hutchinson attempted in the *Library* was moving closer to the domain of academic literary expertise. Another sign of this transformation is that editions of Shakespeare were beginning to be linked to universities and academic editors. The Shakespeare edition published by Macmillan but known as the Cambridge Shakespeare (1863–1866) was edited by two Cambridge fellows and a Trinity College librarian; the Arden Shakespeare launched not long after by Methuen was headed by Professor

Edward Dowden of Trinity College, Dublin. Henry N. Hudson's 1881 edition for Ginn, Heath, and Company appears to have been called the Harvard edition, following the English pattern, even though Hudson's edition was connected to Harvard mainly in that both its editor and publishing house were located in Boston. Furness's Variorum was the great exception to this trend, and it was eventually absorbed by the academy: in the twentieth century several academic editors joined the project, and in 1932 the MLA became its sponsor.[208]

No wonder that Charles Dudley Warner's *Library of the World's Best Literature, Ancient and Modern* (1896–1898) boasted an "Advisory Council" of twelve people, all of whom except for William Torrey Harris were faculty members at leading universities.[209] Even so, a reviewer gave it flak for "log-rolling" by including American writers who "have no standing whatever outside Home Reading Societies in the backwoods of Wisconsin."[210] Such jostling between broader and narrower canons was common, perhaps enacting intradisciplinary conflicts as well as drawing lines between experts and amateurs. There were many attempts like Stedman and Hutchinson's to distinguish "literature proper"—almost always defined in relation to the imagination—from broader understandings of literature; some critics sought to rule out the broader categories, others to include them. Historicism was almost always involved, usually not in a Hegelian mode but in a loosely evolutionary framework such as Taine's. The recognition that "literature proper" was a relatively recent invention cropped up often: for example, J. J. Halsey, reviewing Charles F. Richardson's *American Literature* for the *Dial,* proposed that literature in the United States "has not yet seen its three score and ten."[211] Hutcheson Posnett's *Comparative Literature* (1886) proposed also that understandings of literature had changed over time, and that only now, in the "conditions of art and science under which we live," did literature mean "works which, whether in verse or prose, are the handicraft of imagination rather than reflection, aim at the pleasure of the greatest possible number rather than instruction and practical effects, and appeal to general rather than specialized knowledge."[212] However, even Halsey, who cited this definition by Posnett approvingly, invoked it in order to quarrel with the space Richardson gave to colonial and early U.S. writers in *American Literature*, insisting that these sermons and works of oratory and history "are not literature, we assert."[213] Richardson's *American Literature, 1607–1885* had criticized Stedman's *Poets of America* for including too many "little rhymers and poetesses," but Richardson was in turn criticized by one stringent reviewer for including too much of everything:

> The tendency in writing such histories has been too strong for claiming as literature what does not really belong to it. The lines need to be more sharply drawn, and the classification made more exact.... If, as he [Richardson] says, 'practically our literature is only about eighty years

old,' the question will be asked, 'Does it then need two volumes of 500 pages each in order to give its history?'[214]

Barrett Wendell also declared summarily in his introduction, "we can instantly perceive that only…the Americans of the nineteenth century," as distinct from Americans of the previous two centuries, "have produced literature of any importance."[215] By this standard, of course, Stedman and Hutchinson's project had gone even further afield.

From the standpoint of those who understood literature as a purely aesthetic and imaginative category, the careful selection principles set out by Stedman and Hutchinson may have been overshadowed by the tendency for subscription publishing to proliferate compilations. And because the editors' selection principles were touched on only lightly in the prefatory materials, the *Library* did not squarely enter the conversation in which Posnett and Richardson were significant players—players, moreover, who had advanced degrees and professorial standing. The *Dial* did not usually speak for a large public, but it's easy to imagine that many readers invested in literature in the narrower sense might have joined in its reviewer's criticism of Richardson's *American Literature*, volume 1, to the effect that "[i]n a volume of five hundred and twenty pages more than one hundred and fifty are consumed before Franklin is discussed, and nearly half the book must be read before Irving is reached."[216] In Stedman and Hutchinson's *Library*, Franklin wasn't found until volume 3, Irving until volume 5.

About why the *Library* didn't sell better I can only speculate. The *Library* was a subscription book that tried to compete in a market sector dominated by trade publishers; the *Library* was a scholarly book edited by nonexperts; the *Library* was part of an intellectual movement toward evolutionary or scientific literary history but was not pitched to enter very clearly into contemporary controversies about canons. The *Library* was also in some ways suited to be a textbook, operating in a tertiary or secondary classroom whose instructor could fill in a historical understanding in keeping with the selection principles, except that it took up eleven hefty volumes.[217]

The fact that the *Library* was envisioned with care and reviewed with admiration suggests that its failures were not inevitable (and of course, that it was not in every sense a failure). The anomalies I've described may not have been obvious or more fundamentally debilitating because the trends I've mentioned can be identified only in retrospect. For instance, subscription publishing might have developed a different repertoire; indeed, if it's considered as an ancestor of the Book-of-the-Month Club, it did, but a few decades later. And in an era when Professor Richardson's literary history was widely deemed inferior to the histories of poetry produced by the "banker-poet" Stedman, there was room to gamble that academic standing might not yet be required for a project such as the *Library*. The very fact that Richardson's study was published by G. P. Putnam and Sons and reviewed in the *Dial* and the *Chap-Book* marks the fact that studies by academics had not yet moved into a separate domain of print culture in which they would be evaluated only by specialists. That change, however, was under way.

Collectively, these failures and dead ends point to literature's potential to be involved in many kinds of inquiries, as "literature of power" and "literature of knowledge."[218] Turning literature into a discipline-defining object meant that literature within academic literary studies became segregated from some of the inquiries and the other disciplines that had animated it or that it maintained a connection to other disciplines only by incorporating very limited versions of them (versions dominant and widely familiar in the final decades of the nineteenth century, for the most part). Arguably, the proliferation of literary scholars' interdisciplinary poaching in the twentieth century amounted to literature's attempting to upgrade the starter set of disciplinary contents it had incorporated from philosophy, psychology, and other neighboring disciplines. The St. Louis movement, the Shakespeare-Bacon controversy, the Browning Society, and the *Library of American Literature* all offered foundations for literary studies that departed from its disciplinary foundation.

{5}

Literary Species and Academic Toolkits

> [L]iterary criticism has no apparatus delicate enough
> to measure the currents, the depths and the tideways,
> the relations and interactions of literary forms.
>
> —BLISS PERRY (1903)[1]

Counterpointing the nineteenth-century belief that individual genius strikes unpredictably, like lightning, was the idea that literature was a product of collective life. Literary nationalism was shaped powerfully by ideas surfacing in Herder's work and the higher criticism about how a people's history and conditions—what we often now call "culture"—shaped their understanding and their language. Herder even proposed that a language shaped what could be thought in it, an idea complicating long-standing philosophical questions about whether human minds were equipped to understand the world around them (and each other) or whether approximation, distortion, and projection were inevitable.[2] In a cosmic irony, one of the century's boldest and most original ideas was Charles Darwin's theory of evolution, which was popularly understood to reduce individuals to epiphenomena of species existence.

Materialism was invoked throughout the century in a vague and spluttering way, as if it were an archvillain defying ordinary human understanding. By the latter part of the century, it often designated some combination of capitalism (pursuit of profits, consumer cravings) and science, especially the scientific study of evolution. Together, these elements were imagined to threaten spiritual life and its quasi-secular stand-in, ideality, which combined various hopeful beliefs about humans' nature and capacities with the vaguely Platonic sense that the truest reality existed in a dimension beyond the reach of science. Going back to Plato's Cave, versions of idealism had emphasized the difficulty or impossibility of humans' truly grasping the ideal forms dimly shadowed in our world of appearances. Yet perhaps because nineteenth-century idealism was often grafted onto Christianity, it could be softened by the belief that a benevolent God, creator of humans, controlled both real and ideal; maybe getting to heaven meant finally perceiving things-in-themselves.

Theories of capitalism, ranging from Marxism to garden-variety understandings of market forces and economic cycles, and theories of evolution threatened people's sense that they could lead meaningful lives more than idealism did, perhaps because these theories were harder to fold into Christianity, although capitalism (as Max Weber has shown) was made to fit. Nevertheless, even Adam Smith's "invisible hand" turning individual self-interest to the good of the market had pointed to the ways in which anyone operating within capitalism might not be fully aware of the conditions and consequences of his or her actions. The global circulation of goods and raw materials compounded the sense that everyone was part of systems whose further reaches they could not possibly be sure of. As advertising and marketing efforts multiplied before everyone's eyes, the potential for consumer desires to be induced or spread by contagion made it hard to know where individuals left off and markets began. Evolution posed a version of the same problem at a level that appeared even more fundamental, insofar as nineteenth-century thinkers liked to believe that individuals preexisted their encounters with markets and that class was merely an external constraint. Not only were most of the world's creation stories invalidated by evolutionary theory—creation stories that tended to draw a firm line between humans and the rest of creation—evolution also meant that humans' capacity to understand and act in the world had emerged contingently, through eons of interactions with environments and other species. Even what was most valued about being human might be accidental, shaped by the particular habitats to which humans had adapted.

Of course, a characteristically modern response to evolution was to try to understand it better in order to take control of it. This was Herbert Spencer's approach, which in its most egregious form held that any supports given to struggling humans would weaken the species, in contrast to Darwin's emphasis on the very long term and unconscious nature of evolutionary change. Even people who were not explicitly trying to take charge of evolution were left trying to take on board the interplay between what felt like individual free will and what looked in the aggregate like behavioral conditioning or even determinism. Literature was conscripted for these efforts, since one of its missions was to register and reflect on the quality of human experience. In retrospect, realist fiction has been celebrated for its assertion of individual agency, versus naturalism's exploration of biological and economic determinism. However, critics' eagerness to differentiate the two may reflect a desire to simplify problems of agency that works assigned to both modes treated with more complexity, insofar as many late-century novels juxtaposed scenes of decision making with renderings of circumstances and systems that conditioned or determined human action. As we've seen with respect to the paradoxes surrounding aesthetic autonomy and literature's separation from rhetoric and oratory, problems of agency rippled through nineteenth-century literature and literary theory, and differentiating will-fortifying realism from will-sapping naturalism may have been another way of managing a paradox.

In this context, experts effectively operated as a new and more powerful human species that could divide and conquer these problems. Of course, no one thought experts were biologically distinct, and especially during the early decades of the research university's implementation (a model that influenced most forms of higher education, as I've noted), it appeared as though new and more rigorous ways of knowing might be developed and practiced both inside and outside higher education. On this basis, Richard Grant White operated in concert with academic philologists and patrolled the borders of literary studies; on this basis, also, many literary authors embraced a version of professionalism, even though none of them believed that authorship ought to require standardized forms of education or licensing. In the case of authorial professionalism, authors' desires to be compensated well meant that they wished to be valued for their skills and experience, not just their inspiration. One conventional way of elevating authors as professionals was to identify and discredit amateurs, taking up informally the prerogative of professions to set standards for practitioners. Authors and critics who sorted professionals from amateurs were caught up in something that simulated the reorganization of knowledge around expertise, even though it did not rely on formal credentialing. Indeed, during the late nineteenth century and the early twentieth century, there was a fashion of calling men of letters (never women, never men of color) "deans," suggesting that the world of literature relied on seasoned arbiters to check youthful excesses and that the world of literature was a little like a college.[3]

As a result, critics who weren't academics as well as those who were tried out forms of disciplinary rigor, often borrowing models and language from the sciences. When Bliss Perry warned that literary critics had no instruments to measure the "currents, the depths and the tideways," of interactions among literary forms, he managed to suggest both that literary studies did not operate like an empirical science and that it could nonetheless be instructive to model the interplay of literary genres on a physical phenomenon subject to scientific investigation. More common were evolutionary metaphors that cast genres as species evolving from each other, developing alongside each other, or competing with each other—metaphors likely to rely on treating genres as empirically discrete, versus the fluidity Perry captured. In keeping with some of the loose understandings of evolution that circulated, critics sometimes practiced a functionalism that assigned genres certain tasks (implicitly on behalf of the human species, although the assignments were often cast as tasks necessary for the survival of the genre-species). Just as Darwin's theory of evolution as large-scale and unconscious, proceeding on the basis of unpredictable variations and contingencies, collided in public understandings with Spencer's urging people to take charge of natural selection and Lamarck's proposing that acquired characteristics could be inherited, loosely evolutionary treatments of literary genre ranged from stances of dispassionate observation to stances featuring strong advocacy and the desire to engineer outcomes.

By midcentury, as we've seen, an assemblage of genres had been forged that counted as "literature," a new entity that wasn't exactly poetry or belles lettres or the previous century's idea of literature and whose chief genres were drama, fiction, poetry, and certain kinds of essays. These genres, which were often treated in literary culture as if they were comprehensive and authoritative categories, were all homogenizing myths, a point that has been made forcibly in recent years about poetry but that has broader relevance.[4] But the assemblage was dynamic: new works were being written, new ways of defining and assigning genres were being developed, and new genres were coming into view within the complex of literature. (I'll use "genres" and "forms" interchangeably, not trying to sort genres from subgenres or genres from modes, in keeping with the flexible practice of the time.) Literature itself was therefore perpetually being adjusted. And because the generative potential of literature as a category depended on the tension between aesthetic and public-oriented understandings of literature, new literary works and new ideas about genre continually elaborated this founding contradiction, sometimes crafting local ways of resolving it and at other times managing the problem by distributing it across genres. The sense that literature ought to both shelter antimodern values and further modern endeavors could be spun into independent stories for each genre, providing a scaffolding for competitions among genres. Being more ancient and more culturally fundamental than other genres could mark a claim to cultural value, just as being more modern and unprecedented could.

In order to examine relations among literary genres in the late nineteenth and early twentieth centuries, this chapter takes up two important sets of transactions between genres. The first is the famous competition between novels and poetry in the late nineteenth century, which has usually been scripted as an upset in which novels somehow outstripped poetry even though, it is now recognized, poetry remained vital to virtually everyone throughout the century. The other is the surprising convergence between theories of drama and theories of the short story, whose shared aesthetic of streamlined structural integrity was prized as an evolutionary advance. Unfortunately, key ingredients of this advance—Gustav Freytag's pyramid and a set of conventional conflicts—became part of a standardized toolkit for academic literary studies that limited the scope of interpretation in the twentieth century, especially in college and high school literary classrooms. Literary readers often expressed desires to be bowled over by the great American novel or the representative American poet, yet these desires were at odds with the disciplinary imperative to stabilize and delimit what literature was and to establish interpretation as a standardized, reproducible procedure.

Clash of the Titans: Novels versus Poetry

It was long a commonplace of literary history that during the nineteenth century, in Anglophone culture, the novel continued its notorious rise and eclipsed, marginalized, or even menaced poetry, a baggy monster looming over a slender lyric. There can be no doubt that poetry was prized within the most elite registers of literary culture as well as in popular culture. But between the century's beginning and end, the novel grew more important and poetry's importance seemed to get vaguer. Novels ceased to be stigmatized, except perhaps in religious subcultures suspicious of all secular literature; a watershed in the novel's literary standing was the 1831 launching of British publisher Richard Bentley's Standard Novels series, which included Brown's *Edgar Huntly* and works by other British and U.S. authors ranging from Austen to Cooper.[5] By the end of the century, Bliss Perry at Williams College and Princeton, William Lyon Phelps at Yale, and other professors in U.S. universities were teaching courses on novels.[6] And novels continued to sell well—so well that Walter Besant, who claimed casually that "nine-tenths" of all books bought were novels, warned aspiring novelists in 1884 of the dangers of breaking into print too early. He also urged them to *"never,* never, NEVER pay for publishing a novel," highlighting the new role that editors of modern publishing houses played in patrolling the boundaries of literature.[7]

What changed was not that novels began to be widely read—they were widely read in 1800, although of course they kept finding new readers and readers in new places—but that the novel as a form became more thoroughly integrated into the conceptualization of literature, so that novels were poised to contend with poetry for literary primacy. Even though by midcentury it was clear that novels could be literary and that their style and construction could be admired, the powerful aesthetic discourse around novels that developed in the latter part of the century was an important innovation. Indeed, the discussion combined aesthetics and public significance, leading Andrew Lang to complain in 1885, "The whole world seems lately to have resolved itself into a commission on fiction.... [Novels] cannot contain, and they need not pretend to contain, the whole sum of mortal thought, knowledge, and experience, with a good deal of prophecy thrown in."[8]

The most obvious outcroppings of this discourse were Walter Besant's and Henry James's dueling accounts of "The Art of Fiction" (initially published in 1884), both of which focused on novels. Besant was a prolific English novelist whose work sold well. He had some scholarly credentials, since he had published a study of French poetry in 1868 and was for eighteen years the paid secretary of the Society for the Systematic and Scientific Exploration of Palestine.[9] His lecture emerged in the wake of some of William Dean Howells's earliest promotion of realism and continued Howells's prescriptive tendencies, though in a different direction.[10] Lecturing at London's Royal Institution, Besant made an oddly neoclassical case for fiction, laying out a set of "Laws which govern this Art" that might offset the problem of considering fiction writing a profession even though the art "has no lecturers or teachers, no school or college or Academy, no recognized rules, no text-books, and is not taught in any University." The laws he set out were fairly general, starting from the premise that fiction should be grounded in "personal experience and observation" and spelling out the kinds of care and precision that should be followed in transferring the fruits of observation to the page.[11] But his stance was admonishing, which may have prompted James's response; James may also have been able to distance himself discreetly from Howells's heavy-handed promotion of realism (for which Howells used James as an exemplar) by shrugging off Besant's attempt to legislate.

James made a Romantic intervention, agreeing wholeheartedly that fiction was an art and that its field was (as Besant held) "the whole of Humanity" but holding that artistic originality was better left unregulated: "A novel is in its broadest definition a personal impression of life; that, to begin with, constitutes its value, which is greater or less according to the intensity of the impression. But there will be no intensity at all, and therefore no value, unless there is freedom to feel and say."[12] Moreover, James argued, "the deepest quality of a work of art will always be the quality of the mind of the producer." He had already proposed that art was vitally dependent on an art culture that promoted ongoing reflection on artistic efforts undertaken: "Art lives upon discussion, upon experiment, upon curiosity, upon variety of attempt, upon the exchange of views and the comparison of standpoints."[13] Besant-style laws interfered with the unbounded dynamic of artistic innovation and reflection crucial to the artistic development of the novel form.

Between them, Besant and James played out a number of novels' modern and antimodern possibilities. The roots of fiction in ancient storytelling, invoked by Besant, meant that fiction could be cast as keeping alive something premodern; casting the novel as the modern successor to much older forms meant that it was linked to collective experiences (bards reciting epics and ritual drama, as well as the dim history of storytelling around ancient fires).[14] At the same time, the fact that the novel as a form was comparatively new, as its name announced, made a strong case for novels' modernity. I've pitched Besant's proposed laws for novels as neoclassical because he presented them as analogous to the laws of "harmony, perspective, and proportion"; as the rest of this chapter shows, toward the end of the century, laws for literature fared much better if they were framed as scientific rather than grounded in traditional aesthetics. At the same time, Besant was picking up on the novel's association with modern-coded empirical methods when he advised novelists "never to go beyond your own experience": for example, "a young lady brought up in a quiet country village should avoid descriptions of garrison life."[15] James's famous corrective was not antiempirical but may have pointed to the possibility that trained—inspired? expert?—observers could see what others could not: "Try to be one of the people on whom nothing is lost!"[16]

James's sense of novelists as receptive and absorptive meshed with the common idea that novels readily assimilated new ideas about psychology and social life. Novels, because they were prose, were believed to incorporate technical and disciplinary languages more readily than poetry. As one reviewer of Dickens put it (enacting also the rivalry between prose fiction and poetry),

> Prose is better adapted than poetry to our complex modern life. It is more flexible to our modes of thought, a fitter medium for our sophisticated habits, a finer analyser of civilized characters. The poetical genius of this time, who takes his inspiration from his own age, will be led to express himself rather in polished prose, than in any of the forms of versification known in the poetical craft.[17]

As the very term "realism" indicated, though somewhat disingenuously, the impossible premise of the realist novel was that reality could be reliably grasped through the medium of the realist novel, shaped lightly but unobtrusively. "The Art of Fiction" was the essay in which James called Trollope-style narrative intrusions, the kind that made readers aware of an author's shaping control, the "betrayal of a sacred office"—so he did not forgo admonishing entirely.[18] In spite of the popularity and critical acclaim of many long narrative poems, which required poets to experiment with developing durable, unobtrusive meters for this purpose, novels were usually defined as works in prose.[19] The most influential aesthetic vision of the novel—James's, with support from Howells—was strongly representational, grounded in the sense that prose was an inconspicuous medium conducive to subtleties of presentation.

Novels' more thorough assimilation into literature also took the form of their becoming more highly valued as indices of modern, implicitly national realities. Henry A. Beers, in a literary textbook developed for Chautauqua Literary and Scientific Circles, proposed that the novel of the present (1886) was to its readers what "the stage play was to the audiences of Elizabeth's reign, or the periodical essay, like the *Tatlers* and *Spectators*, to the clubs and breakfast-tables of Queen Anne's."[20] Versions of this idea circulated widely, and they contributed to the cultural obsession with producing the Great American Novel. Public esteem for British novelists such as Austen, Scott, Dickens, and Eliot—novelists whose successes were deeply identified with Scotland's and England's national histories and social tapestries—contributed to the sense that the United States needed both to rival Britain on its own terms and to succeed in being distinctive. Among the earliest occurrences of the phrase "Great

American Novel" were advertisements for Rebecca Harding Davis's *Waiting for the Verdict* (1867) in 1867–1868, part of a campaign that began before the novel was published and that cited Davis's previous works *Life in the Iron Mills* (1861) and *Margret Howth* (1861).[21] The ads printed below the book's title and its author's name the phrase "The Great American Novel." As a novel about interracial love and racial passing published just after the Civil War, *Waiting for the Verdict* was positioned in some ways to do for the struggle toward racial justice in the postwar United States what *Uncle Tom's Cabin* (1851) had done for abolition before the war: the advertising campaign announced a bold purpose. Nonetheless, Davis probably regretted the ads, since in 1891 she warned novelists never to "try to give to us that much longed for monstrosity—the Great American Novel."[22]

References to the Great American Novel grew increasingly common after 1867, generating the backlash one would expect. For instance, T. S. Perry complained that the phrase gave writers a "false aim" and critical readers a "defective standard."[23] But even in the course of dismissing the obsession in 1885, Charles F. Richardson implied that Americans needed to grapple with what their national character was: "Whether or not the 'great American novel' will ever be written is an unimportant question—what is *the* great American poem, history, essay? But if it shall be, it will be based on the character which has made the nation in the past, and which, if anything, will save it from future wreck."[24] Even when the phrase was deployed skeptically, it marked how deeply embedded novels were in nation-states. Novels captured the national reality and expressed the national character, or so the impossible wishes went. When bestsellers began to be tracked in the 1890s, most of them were novels, a phenomenon adding to the impression that novels were perpetually taking the public's pulse.[25] As Ellen Gruber Garvey puts it, "Fiction became enmeshed with issues found in it, making it difficult to discuss the issue without reference to the book, and making the book a natural segue for the issue."[26]

Realism's impact depended on the fact that it combined public-oriented and aesthetic claims to value. As Howells and other backers presented it, it required skillfully unobtrusive narration. Treated by reviewers as topical, realism was nonetheless valued for not promoting particular solutions or reforms. A highly literary novelistic treatment of a contemporary social problem staged the problem without presenting a solution more specific than the cultivation of sympathy or human connection. The polarization of realism and romance operating after midcentury identified realism with the public-oriented range of literature's operations, romance with the imaginative and aesthetic, but realism's promoters presented it as capable of tackling urgent public concerns while offering a character-driven approach compatible with aesthetic autonomy. Realism was most often valued for its power of vivid representation, epitomized by Henry James's conception of novels as fundamentally dramatic, but novels' role in stimulating and shaping public opinion could align the novel with essayistic forms of inquiry.[27] Richard G. Moulton, the University of Chicago professor who borrowed Snider's term "Literary Bibles," promoted the idea that the novel was a "vehicle of thought" in his publications and university extension courses in both England and the United States.[28] An 1891 extension course he organized in the United States was entitled "Stories as a Mode of Thinking," and in his 1915 work *The Modern Study of Literature*, Moulton emphasized that literature is "a function of thought," the modern novel having been fused in many respects with the essay. "It is part of the vitality of fiction as a literary form that it tends to become a floating literature of transient human interests," Moulton asserted.[29] Frank Norris took a similar stand, asking whether any novel could be written *without* a purpose and identifying the proper subject matter of the novel as "elemental forces, motives that stir whole nations."[30]

Moulton's view of the novel was keyed to the emergence of engaged but reflective reform literature toward the end of the century: novels that were not as straightforwardly committed to changing people's hearts as *Uncle Tom's Cabin* (1852) (a novel whose political and religious agendas were downplayed late in the century, Barbara Hochman has shown) but that clearly invited readers to perceive injustices and consider how they could be redressed.[31] Helen Hunt Jackson's *Ramona* (1884), which she intended to be the fictional companion piece to *A Century of Dishonor* (1881), might be a transitional work in this tradition; Bellamy's *Looking Backward: 2000–1887* (1887), an emotionally cool utopian novel that, as noted earlier, inspired many political clubs, moved further away from structuring the novel around readerly sympathy, inviting readers to invest instead in the challenge of reorganizing collective life.[32] Examples even closer to the essayistic aesthetic Moulton proposed were the Christian socialist novels of Margaret Sherwood and Florence Converse, whose Browning connections chapter 4 examines. Sherwood, who taught English Romantic poetry at Wellesley, wrote novels broadly designed to promote Christian compassion, but they recognized that individual changes of heart were not enough to bring about social improvements. *An Experiment in Altruism* (1895) even recounted a woman's traumatic experience as a twelve-year-old charity volunteer who confronted unspeakable misery but had only gingham aprons to dispense. "Since then, all of the charity work I have heard of has seemed as ironic as that," she concluded, although she did not abandon the work.[33] Florence Converse's *The Burden of Christopher* (1900) features a character whose senior thesis was entitled "Benevolence: Our Modern Crime."[34] These were novels issued by literary publishers (Macmillan, Houghton Mifflin) that overtly depicted economic injustice and urged systemic change, though not through revolutionary violence or any specific mode of political organizing. Somewhat abstractly characterized and stylistically understated, these novels offered plausible accounts of chronic injustices and people who suffered and witnessed them. Many of these novels registered both proto-Progressive impulses toward reform and suspicions of the psychological motives that issued in impulses toward reform.

By the last decades of the nineteenth century, the literary standing of novels had been revitalized. The novel as a form had been aesthetically refurbished, novels had been sewn more tightly to literary nationalism, and novels had expanded their repertoire of public functions. In contrast, the public understanding of poetry had not been refreshed. Casually evolutionary thinking urged the perpetual adaptation of life forms to new conditions, exacerbating the modern tendency to crave the new and improved; print culture markets rewarded literary movements such as realism that doubled as ways of branding innovations. On both counts, the belief that U.S. (indeed, Anglophone) poetry had been in a holding pattern since the Civil War meant that there was a crisis in poetry's renewal as a foundational literary genre.

It might seem perplexing that this concern about poetry emerged even though poetry was everywhere. The publication rate of volumes of poetry lagged behind that of novels, but poetry was a staple within a wide range of periodicals, even if it was diminished by serving sometimes as filler.[35] Poetry, recited or read aloud, remained prominent in public culture. Graduating from high school in 1891, Paul Laurence Dunbar was the class poet whose composition, set to music, was sung at commencement, and he advanced his reputation through public readings of his poems.[36] The year after Dunbar's graduation, Harriet Monroe, later the cofounder of *Poetry* magazine, wrote a "Columbian Ode" for the World's Fair, which was recited at the opening ceremonies by Sarah Cowell LeMoyne, a platform reader well known for her readings of Browning.[37]

Poetry's popular success may have detracted from its literary standing, however, not because it was so widely read but because it was so widely written. Stedman voiced the condescension and contempt that many established poets and critics expressed: "Since the heyday of the Della Cruscans never were so many neophytes and amateurs suffered to bring their work before the public."[38] The treatment of this phenomenon has often been loaded with misogyny and class condescension (less often racism, because the white literary establishment was so oblivious to most nonwhite writers) as well as the contempt of experts for amateurs I've been tracking. However, Angela Sorby has identified a dimension of the problem distinct from these predictable assertions of cultural privilege. More than novels or short stories or plays or essays, poetry was defined as expressive and central to public primary and secondary education. Sorby argues that the wide circulation of poetry together with loosely Romantic understandings of poetry as a rendering of feeling meant that "every reader [of poetry] was also—quite naturally—a competent writer." And whereas the writing of fiction, which was also widely read, was increasingly figured as a professional endeavor, the writing of poetry was not.[39] Even though writing poetry continued to be treated by many authors and critics as the highest and most intensely aesthetic literary ambition, in the late nineteenth century it may have been harder than ever before to determine what kinds of preparation or achievement ought to mark serious poetic ambitions.[40]

That poetry was in a holding pattern—more optimistically, an "intercalary" period or "interregnum"—was the surprising diagnosis of Edmund Clarence Stedman, who as we've seen was probably the most distinguished U.S. critic of poetry at the end of the century.[41] Stedman first announced his diagnosis in *Victorian Poets* (1875), writing in the introduction that he undertook this work out of a sense that the difficulties facing U.S. poets were shared by British poets: that a poetic period was coming to an end, and that there was uncertainty about what would come next.[42] Published in 1885, Stedman's *Poets of America* formulated a specifically U.S. version of this concern, arguing that no set of major poets or new poetic platform had come into prominence in the years since the Civil War. His diagnosis of a "twilight of the poets" took on a life beyond his argument, as Elizabeth Renker has documented, since it was picked up and recirculated in the same network of high-culture periodicals that had promoted realism.[43] His concern about what would come next betrayed the assumption that progress and innovation must be nonstop; it makes sense that *Poets of America* was published at the height of realism's promotion. Stedman's characterization of the holding pattern also illuminates some important tensions within the complex of literature in the decades after the Civil War.[44]

Stedman's *Poets of America* offered thoughtful, careful surveys of the careers of major poets (as Stedman viewed them: Bayard Taylor merits a chapter) as well as an overview of the conditions affecting national poetry and the outlook for the future. Stedman in this volume is quite strictly concerned with canonization on aesthetic grounds, not the more inclusive canon he inventoried as coeditor of the *Library of American Literature*. (For example, addressing the poetry Moses Coit Tyler compiled from the colonial and early national periods in his *History of American Literature*, Stedman in *Poets of America* complains that most poets before 1765 were "simply third-rate British rhymesters.")[45] Looking back at the decades around the Civil War in which poetry by U.S. authors flourished, a period in which long narrative poems and verse dramas thrived, he diagnoses an "interregnum" partly because all of the poets who merit individual chapters in *Poets of America* had launched their careers before the Civil War, most of them some time before; the latest-born of the group, Taylor, had died in 1878, and the others were more recently dead (Bryant, Emerson, Longfellow, Poe) or over sixty by the time of Stedman's writing. Implicit in his account is the sense that the war was a national watershed and that no new major poets have emerged to address postwar life. Implicit also is a charge that the greatest poets of this earlier generation no longer satisfy readers, or at least not readers' highest literary longings.

Formed by the poetry culture of the antebellum era, Stedman identifies verse drama as the target of the highest poetic aspirations and optimistically predicts that the United States is about to produce a strong verse drama once more.[46] An amusing historical detective novel might be spun about the search for a long-lost narrative poem by Walt Whitman—*Song of Mannahatta*, say, vying with Longfellow's *Song of Hiawatha* (1855)—or verse drama by Emily Dickinson—perhaps a Browning-style historical drama about the leader of Shays' Rebellion, who lived not far from Amherst. There's no reason to believe such works existed, but when Whitman (1819–1892), Dickinson (1830–1886), and Stedman (1833–1908) were coming of age as poets, narrative poetry and verse drama were the genres of poetic ambition. (Dickinson and Whitman strayed from these models, but most of Dickinson's work was unpublished when Stedman made his survey and Whitman, as we shall see, was not legible to Stedman as the pathbreaker we know today.) As late as the 1880s, after the young Edith Jones (later Wharton) published some short poems in the *Atlantic Monthly*, partly through the good offices of her brother's friend Allen Thorndike Rice, Rice encouraged her to work on an epic.[47] Book-length narrative and dramatic poems were extremely popular for most of the century: British works such as Byron's *Childe Harold's Pilgrimage* (1812–1818) and *Don Juan* (1819–1824); Tennyson's *The Princess* (1847), *Maud* (1855–1856), and *Idylls of the King* (1856–1885); and Barrett Browning's *Aurora Leigh* (1857); and works by U.S. authors such as Longfellow's *Evangeline* (1847), *Song of Hiawatha* (1855), and *The Courtship of Miles Standish* (1858); Bayard Taylor's *The Picture of St. John* (1866) and *Lars: A Pastoral of Norway* (1873); Richard Henry Stoddard's *The King's Bell* (1863); and Stedman's own *The Blameless Prince* (1869). Robert Browning's verse dramas and narrative poems, especially *The Ring and the Book* (1868–1869), were read and studied along with his shorter poems.

The peculiar transformation that turned Bryant, Whittier, Longfellow, Holmes, and Lowell into the Schoolroom Poets or Fireside Poets was under way, and in spite of Stedman's careful attention to the work of these poets, he appeared to find them outdated. His discussion of Longfellow is the most revealing. Aside from Tennyson, Stedman points out, Longfellow was the only poet whose long poems were as popular with readers as novels. Stedman assiduously traces the range of Longfellow's career, the heights of his poetic ambition, and the precision of his prosody, all features that Stedman values. However, he condescendingly identifies poems such as "The Children's Hour" as the "inimitable fireside songs that made this 'old moustache' the children's poet." Even Longfellow's translation of Dante's *Divine Comedy* is subtly undercut when Stedman describes Longfellow's method as translating "line for line, almost as literally as a class recitation." Moreover, he casts Longfellow as predictable: "His mode was perfectly obvious and unchanged, save by greater refinement, during fifty years."[48] Stedman's selective appraisal of Longfellow is evident here, since Longfellow made many technical experiments informed by his remarkable knowledge of modern and ancient European poetry.[49]

Sorby's landmark study of nineteenth-century U.S. poetry cultures has analyzed the process by which Longfellow and company came to be associated with childhood and domestic coziness, a side effect of this poetry's coming to be cast as pedagogical: identified primarily with the classroom and its oral poetry culture. As Sorby describes pedagogical poetry, its aesthetic was utterly at odds with Robert Browning's formal, syntactical, and intellectual difficulty: "The rules of poetry, as practiced by Longfellow, Whittier, Riley, Dodge, and Field, dictated that it be accessible by, and useful to, ordinary middle-class people; this meant that it should rhyme, that its meter should be regular, and that its language should be easy to understand, to remember, and to repeat."[50] James Whitcomb Riley, Mary Mapes Dodge, and Eugene Field were late-century additions to the earlier tradition, wildly popular poets whose writings often took up childhood (and were often published in venues directed at children) but who were also read and enjoyed by adults. It might even be the case that Longfellow and company were reframed in retrospect by the examples of Riley, Dodge, and Field, so that the memory of Longfellow the Harvard professor and translator of Dante was somehow eclipsed by Longfellow the author of "The Children's Hour" and "Psalm of Life," the latter a textbook staple.[51] By being associated with childhood—childhood taken to be a repository of everyone's personal past—the Schoolroom Poets and writers in their tradition were linked to nostalgia and cozy versions of history.

The contrast with novelistic realism could not be more vivid. The realist movement had created momentum by differentiating the realist novel from romance, associating the romance tradition with childhood and earlier phases of history assumed to be less modern. In spite of the constraints on realism—which were often misogynistically blamed on the need to protect young women readers—realism was cast as the mode of fiction that best informed adults about the modern world. Even realist novels not devoted to easily recognized social issues, such as James's late novels *The Wings of the Dove* (1902) and *The Golden Bowl* (1904), took up the economics of sexual intrigue in ways that counted as modern and mature, within this logic. Realism's agenda conflated modernity and maturity, suggesting that anything childish could not really be seriously literary, however pleasurable or well crafted it might be.[52] Within this logic, Stedman treats Longfellow not only as someone whose poems pleased children but also as someone who never grew up artistically.

By inverting the realist paradigm, however, it's possible to see that childhood and the past were also established as sites in which realist patrolling could be avoided—even sites from which rebellions could be launched. The ever-more-popular Schoolroom Poets (first and second generation); regionalist fiction, which was ideologically identified with the "past" of urban modernity; and a retooled version of romance were all important in late nineteenth-century literary culture, and all these writings were identified with childhood or with places and people coded as premodern or primitive. The new romance was epitomized by English writers who offered literary adventure: Robert Louis Stevenson, Rider Haggard, and Rudyard Kipling.[53] Like James Whitcomb Riley or Eugene Field, they were writers believed to cater to a child (usually gendered "boy") reader, but this reading position was one that could be occupied with pleasure by adults, even by women. Indeed, one of the most vocal U.S. proponents of a return to romance was the polemical essayist Agnes Repplier, who found realism emotionally impoverished. A subtext of Catholic impatience with elaborate Protestant self-denial may have been at work when Repplier argued powerfully that the business of fiction was pleasure, not ethics, and reasserted the foundation of aesthetics in emotional transport (in a piece called "Pleasure: A Heresy"). She endorsed the idea that "[t]he trained intelligence grasps its pleasures and recognizes them as such," identifying with puzzlement the tendency of the ethically obsessed to feel guilty about pleasure.[54]

One of the poetic pleasures that had become trickier, if not quite guilty, was rhyme, for reasons chapter 1 sets out. Emerson's spirited contribution to the question of whether poetry had to rhyme was to proclaim in 1844 that "not metres, but a metre-making argument,... makes a poem," something with "an architecture of its own."[55] This stimulating formulation inspired Whitman and no doubt many other poets, but it contributed to the Romantic downplaying of technique, even to a sense that the kind of attention required by intricate poetic forms headed toward ornament rather than organic aesthetics. Howells, verging on self-caricature, actually suggested that rhyme was not for respectable grown-ups: "There are black moments when, honestly between ourselves and the reader, the spectacle of any mature lady or gentleman proposing to put his or her thoughts and feelings into rhymes affects us much as the sight of some respected person might if we met him jigging or caracoling down the street, instead of modestly walking."[56] Stedman did not entertain this prejudice, but his assimilation of poetry to song bespoke a formal conservatism.[57] As Virginia Jackson has warned, the trope of song also framed the lyrical as a newly abstracted and individualized poetic mode on its way to becoming the twentieth century's epitome of poetry: "lyric as poetry writ large."[58]

Stedman admired Emerson's poetry and admired Whitman's even more, but he held against them the fact that they did not appear to have opened up routes for poetry that successors could follow.[59] Although he cites his own early sense of Whitman as a "real poet, one who stirred my pulses," he proposes that Whitman appeals mainly to those drawn to any form of radical experimentation, and he is mistrustful of Whitman for not demonstrating his gifts in established forms, such as blank verse. Worst of all, from Stedman's point of view, Whitman's followers "have produced little that has not seemed like parody, or unpleasantly grotesque," leading Stedman to conclude, "I suspect that the old forms, in endless combinations, will return as long as new poets arise with the old abiding sense of time and sound."⁶⁰ That Stedman was impervious to the promise of Whitman's innovations indicates how much he clung to the midcentury poetic aesthetics that Whitman and Dickinson abandoned, but Stedman was not alone: Whitman's reputation rose dramatically after his death in 1892.⁶¹

Not surprisingly, Stedman also mistrusted the "vogue of novel forms," the "[l]yrics, sonnets, canzonets, produced on every hand." Notwithstanding Stedman's skepticism, these forms could be vital and were turned to a variety of projects. For example, Paul Laurence Dunbar's "We Wear the Mask" (1895) was a rondeau, one of the French poetic forms made popular by the British poet Austin Dobson. Dobson was one of the most famous practitioners of society verse (*vers de société*), which Stedman identified as a specialty of Oliver Wendell Holmes and Bret Harte; like Dunbar, Harte alternated between the polished and the folksy. Stedman noted the surprising popularity of society verse in 1885, and in 1894 Brander Matthews defended it.⁶² In particular, Matthews defended Dobson's use of obscure forms, including the French forms the triolet, ballade rondeau, and rondel, and quoted Dobson's poetic defense of rhyme, which culminated:

> In the work-a-day world,—for its needs and woes,
> There is place and enough for the pains of prose;
> But whenever the May-bells clash and chime,
> Then hey!—for the ripple of laughing rhyme!⁶³

Stedman thought the formal experimentation bespoke "over-refinement," but his stance suggests that he shared Howells's assumption that the highest literary ambitions were serious and weighty—earnest, as Oscar Wilde lampooned.⁶⁴

Robert Browning would seem to have answered Stedman's longing for a strongly dramatic poet, but in addition to the fact that Stedman was constructing conventional national traditions, Stedman faulted Browning for offering too little beauty along the way. In faulting Browning's lack of musicality, Stedman failed to grasp what the Browning Society apparently understood: that something new might require an adjustment in the very forms of pleasure, and that a work of art might have reason to be abrupt or harsh when it was interrogating or suspending conventional ways of thinking. No wonder that Ezra Pound's *Cantos* harked back to the example of *Sordello*, notorious for being Browning's most difficult work; no wonder also that T. S. Eliot asserted that modern poetry was necessarily "difficult," although he did not find Browning to be difficult in this vivid and amalgamating way ("Tennyson and Browning are poets, and they think, but they do not feel their thought as immediately as the odour of a rose").⁶⁵ Stedman also mistrusted Browning's ethical vitalism, the idea (cherished by many of Browning's followers) that "our instincts have something divine about them," as Stedman put it, and that there was "[n]o sin like repression."⁶⁶

Stedman's ultimate discontent with all the poets on offer raises the possibility that no new style of poetry would have satisfied his longings. However, one reason his canon was narrow was because his sense of literature was so closely bound up with trade book publication and affiliated forms of periodical publication. Newspapers throughout the country were full of poetry, and those were the places where many of the poets outside Stedman's establishment published.[67] As Elizabeth Renker has argued, working-class poets who were in some ways aligned with realism published prolifically in sites Stedman never considered.[68] Stedman's selectiveness is a reminder that strong theories about genres were (and are) likely to be based on small canons, even if the critics putting forth the theories tack on lists of additional works that might fit the model. Moreover, even when authors outside the ruling class published in literary venues and were treated as literary, their works were not likely to be made defining samples of genres. When James Paul Allen wrote condescendingly that Paul Laurence Dunbar "reached, in some of his poems, the highest level that his race has yet attained in lyric form, and feeling," he allowed only that Dunbar's work included some of the best lyric poetry written by an African American, not that Dunbar's work helped to determine what the lyric could be.[69]

In spite of the far-reaching and active networks of public literary culture—or perhaps because of them—powerful gating mechanisms were at work among "deans" such as Stedman. Women were left almost entirely out of Stedman's search for the next great poet or the next great movement in poetry. In light of the extraordinary number of women poets working in the nineteenth century, from mainstream popular poets such as Lydia Sigourney to edgier but still widely admired poets such as Sarah Piatt, it can scarcely be believed that women receive so little space and so much condescension in *Poets of America*. (Sigourney's writings "answered to the simple wants of a primitive constituency," for example.[70]) Just after the release of the revised thirteenth edition of *Poets of America*, in 1888, an anonymous pundit lamented in verse:

> But, oh, Mr. Stedman, consider again,
> When your critical pages you're printing anew,
> That four hundred and seventy you give to the men,
> While the ladies are huddled together—in two![71]

The exclusion of women, the depreciation of poets linked to schooling, the anxious monitoring of male poets' masculinity (Poe's being "effeminate" vs. George Henry Boker's showing a "manly hand"), and the call for poetry to be above all "dramatic" converge in the idea that poetry ought to appeal to ruling-class men so that it can inform the way the world is run. Poetry is to be manly rather than effeminate, mature rather than childlike, and active rather than passive (or purely receptive, the danger raised by theories of inspiration); sentimental poetry, which brought people together as sufferers of loss and bearers of risk, represented the obverse of this aesthetic.[72] Precisely because poetry is the standard-bearer for the highest aesthetic possibilities, often summed up as the "ideal," its impact is uncertain. In *Victorian Poets*, Stedman had summed up Tennyson's practice and influence as the "idyllic," a category that made reading poetry sound like a vacation rather than a vital transformation: "The idyl is a picturesque, rather than an imaginative, form of art, and calls for no great amount of invention or passion. It invariably has the method of a busy, anxious age, seeking rest rather than excitement. Through restrained emotion, music, and picturesque simplicity it pleases, but seems to betoken absence of creative power."[73] Stedman had written early in the volume about the danger that poetry had shifted from being "the devil's frippery," for conservative Christians, to being a "mere pastime and amusement."[74] Given his lack of any sense that poetry ought to shake people up—to interrupt or challenge common feelings and thoughts rather than voicing them as song—poetry was put in a peculiar double bind.

In some respects, Stedman's *Poets of America* lays out the impossibility of having a strong national poetic tradition—in effect, of producing poetry that is aesthetically remarkable and also has a national public. The poetry so widely respected that it has become a schoolroom staple is too familiar and conventional—hence, it is insufficiently aesthetic, insufficiently committed to innovation. Highly intricate or stylized poetry—the society verse of Oliver Wendell Holmes and Bret Harte, as well as the sonnets and poems in other demanding forms that were popular in the last decades of the century—Stedman faulted for circulating only in university culture or among coteries.[75] Not only was Whitman formally too original for Stedman's tastes, Stedman believed he was not genuinely in tune with ordinary people, certainly compared with Whittier, the "truer type of the people's poet."[76] Whittier's national role before and during the Civil War made his work—or perhaps his career—a touchstone for Stedman. Stedman holds that even though the war itself was not good for poetry, "the moral and emotional conflicts preceding the war, and leading to it, were largely stimulating to poetic ardor."[77] Whittier embodied poetry's potential to galvanize people's convictions and energies. The highest poetry requires "devotion, repose, and calm" in the service of its "ideal," for Stedman, but it matters to him that Whittier's "songs touched the hearts of his people. It was the generation which listened in childhood to the *Voices of Freedom* that fulfilled their prophecies."[78]

Stedman seems divided against himself, not so much about Whittier but about whether it is most important for poetry to capture something timeless (amid repose and calm) or something quite timely, likely to register and inspire action. As he put it in *Victorian Poets*, "A craving for more dramatic, spontaneous utterance is prevalent with the new generation. There is an instinct that to interpret the hearts and souls of men and women is the poet's highest function."[79] Whitman, however, strikes Stedman as having tried to make the role of people's poet into a celebrity brand: "No poet, as a person, ever came more speedily within range of view. His age, origin, and habits were made known; he himself, in fastidiously studied and picturesque costume, was to be observed strolling up Broadway, crossing the ferries, mounting the omnibuses, wherever he could see and be seen, make studies and be studied."[80] With Whitman disqualified for aggressive publicity seeking and Whittier consigned to the fireside and schoolroom (and to an experience of civil war that no one wished to repeat), it is hard to envision what kind of poetic career would satisfy Stedman's wish for innovative but popular poetry.[81]

Like the critics looking for the Great American Novel, Stedman sought a poet who could do everything ("The greatest poet must be all in one"): work across genres, work in diversified forms and meters, and capture every imaginable phase of experience.[82] The desire for poets to be national representatives fueled Stedman's hopes and his disappointment. He did not grasp the ways in which poetry yoking familiar kinds of beauty to conventional ethics would become the object of modernist critique and disruption. But insofar as modernism was not only a literary movement (or a network of movements) but was, or included, an avant-garde, it was not only a revolt against the previous century's literary forms but also against their mode of institutionalization: the ways in which the collusion between aesthetic autonomy and saleability muffled the potential of art to galvanize change. Peter Bürger identifies the avant-garde, exemplified by Dadaism, as a movement seeking to reintegrate art into life ("praxis," Marxist-style) by protesting and disrupting art's status as consumer experience and discretionary pleasure.[83] An avant-garde, in this sense, offers not simply a new aesthetic or an add-on commitment to social engagement (as many public-oriented theories of literature did). Rather, an avant-garde in Bürger's sense attempts to challenge and change art's location: the places and forms in which art is found, the ways in which art is incorporated into the lives and worlds of its makers and audiences. An avant-garde acts on its awareness that art is shaped fundamentally by its institutionalization, assuming that any hopes for art or theories of art that ignore art's location are likely to be ineffectual.

No one would call Stedman avant-garde, but his understanding of poetry's impasse incorporated some of the concerns and perceptions that would culminate, before long, in avant-garde stances. The longing for a poet to channel collective experience ran aground on the problem that a popular poet was effectively a saleable poet. The sense that poetry needed to attempt new things jostled with the idea that poetry widely shared—because widely sold—was likely to conform to conventions. Conversely, poets who were too learned or difficult were associated with university culture or coteries, niche audiences defined precisely by *not* being part of a more general cultural mainstream. In prophesying a revival of verse drama—flying in the face of all evidence—Stedman may have longed for a renewed collective life for poetry, as well as for poetry that was not confined to the lyric task of capturing abstracted and isolated moments.[84] Howells appeared to believe that realist novels were doing exactly what they ought to be, overlooking the irony that realism itself had become a marketing category and that it had routinized the literary vending of certain kinds of social convictions. Stedman at least had the courage to be uncertain about what form poetry in his time could take, if it were to fulfill its highest possibilities.

Not just the commodification of books and periodicals but also the forms of generic marketing and regulation practiced within print culture meant that the most important literary innovation would be to find new locations and modes of circulation for literature. This is arguably what the little magazines of the late nineteenth and early twentieth centuries did. (In a different sense, this is also what the mass circulation magazines of the late nineteenth and early twentieth centuries did, nodding toward literature but aiming for bigger markets—creating a new cultural niche that fell between the old-guard magazines of literary standing and the older, less ambitious kinds of cheap publications.)[85] By resisting (at least for a while) vertical integration and economic conglomeration, and by differentiating themselves from both the academic culture of universities and the established literary culture of the major presses and their periodicals, the little magazines and fledgling book publishers of the early twentieth century distanced literary innovation from the most powerful machineries of corporate publishing and marketing (and the social strata aligned with them), though not of course from commodification itself. Self-published writers such as Denton Snider could not evade commodification, either, but they opted out of corporate packaging and marketing. The established cultural arbiter Edmund Clarence Stedman—poet and stockbroker—seems to have shared their longing to separate literature from the commercial and industrial matrix that shaped it so powerfully.

Crafting Conflicts

Many realist novels were big, but realist aesthetics privileged economy—hence James's differentiation of his own artistic practice from the "loose, baggy monsters" of an earlier novelistic generation. Realist composition involved paring away artifice, convention, excess, and digression, in most accounts. The term "streamlining" was not in common use until several decades into the twentieth century, but the idea that organic form entailed perfect adaptation to function would become central to the functionalist movement in architecture and design of the 1920s and 1930s, the culture in which streamlining was a central aesthetic and ethic. Louis Sullivan published his famous dictum that "form ever follows function" in 1896.[86] He was drawing in turn on the writings of sculptor Horatio Greenough, who at midcentury had formulated the primacy of structure and the undesirability of "embellishment," beliefs that would become dogma for modernist architects.[87] Like Emerson's "metre-making argument," emphases on structure rather than ornament fulfilled the Romantic desire for organic form. They also mimicked evolutionary accounts of the ways in which life forms could thrive by fitting efficiently into their habitats.

The premise of eugenics was that humans could direct or speed the course of evolution, increasing the proportion of the fit by decreasing the numbers of the unfit through birth control or sterilization. Eugenics and social Darwinism made evolutionary progress into a moral imperative, bolstered by the economic promotion of productivity and traditions of moral and spiritual perfectionism. It was as if humans were duty-bound to evolve the species as quickly as possible into its best form, which was determined by highly suspect criteria. Christina Cogdell argues that eugenicist ways of thinking shaped and animated functionalist ideologies of design. In addition to direct outcroppings of eugenicist beliefs on the part of designers, eugenics cropped up in the "application of biological evolutionary laws to product design"—as in Frederick Taylor's *Principles of Scientific Management* (1911)—and "the consideration of modern styling as evidence of racial superiority."[88] She explains that the proponents of streamlining in the 1920s found models in animals (dolphins, greyhounds, and other fast creatures)—organic form, in other words—but also in forms of modern transportation, such as "ships, zeppelins, and airplanes."[89]

Efficient design was often treated as a moral imperative in promotions of stylistic economy during the latter part of the century. Even Horatio Greenough's essay "Structure and Organization," published in the early 1850s, conveyed powerfully that keeping form true to function required—and deserved—strict discipline. Grounding this stance in divine practice, Greenough wrote, "If there be any principle of structure more plainly inculcated in the works of the Creator than all others, it is the principle of *unflinching* adaptation of forms to functions" (emphasis added).[90] Greenough treated ornament as a sign of degeneration: "When high art declined [his example of an architectural high point was the Parthenon], carving and embellishment invaded the simple organization. As the South Sea Islanders have added a variety to the human form by tattooing, so the cunning artisans of Greece undertook to go beyond perfection."[91] The notion that there was something primitive and insufficiently modern about ornament was widespread. To indulge in ornament or enjoy it was, it seemed, not to grasp fundamentals: a taste for ornament was allied with premodern forms of pseudoscience or myth, approaches to the world that were colorful and imaginative but didn't get at central and vital truths. (Howells's disapproval of rhyme struck the same note.) Around the same time, Herbert Spencer published his *Philosophy of Style* (1852), premised on the idea that readers had limited attention and that the most forceful utterances would be brief. His chief stylistic principle was the "principle of economy."[92]

The aesthetic worship of economy surfaced in accounts of realism's unobtrusive and impersonal narration and perhaps even in the reworking of poetry as fundamentally lyric, but the most intense commitments to paring down and stripping away were developed in theories of the drama and the short story: the drama first, the short story by extension. Indeed, much of the terminology and conceptualization of what in the twentieth century became known as the writer's craft were first developed in theories of the drama and the short story. In effect, many commonplaces of writers' workshops and literary instruction today are products of an evolutionary-inflected ideology of restraint and discipline that took shape at the end of the nineteenth century.

Henrik Ibsen's plays argued and embodied the belief that rotten conventions—formal as well as social—ought to be exposed so that they could be discarded.[93] Perhaps because *A Doll's House* (1879) was the first Ibsen play to be performed widely in Britain and the United States, a taste for Ibsen during the 1880s often accompanied an interest in reforming sexual politics (ground that Ibsen shared with Browning, as we've seen). George Bernard Shaw, who cantankerously preferred Ibsen to Shakespeare, set his play *The Philanderer* (1893) in the environs of an Ibsen Club, where only women who weren't womanly and men who weren't manly could be found.[94] Like Shaw's, Ibsen's plays were social problem dramas that touched on dangerous topics (such as venereal disease, in *Ghosts* [1881]). There were U.S. playwrights who also specialized in social commentary, such as James Herne, and who identified their practice as realist.[95] But even aside from the innovations of Ibsen's plots, productions of Ibsen's plays were credited with paring away conventions and embellishments that obscured reality. Ibsen's influence in Euro-America was especially remarkable given that his plays were encountered mainly in translation.

Although Ibsen wrote a few plays in verse, some of which were translated and performed, his dramas in prose were more successful; the English-language collections of the 1890s, *Ibsen's Prose Dramas* and *Prose Dramas of Ibsen*, drove home the point that his best works were in prose.[96] Having spent some years as a working theater director, Ibsen was credited with a good understanding of theater craft, and his admirers grasped the spareness and concentration of his plays as a new dramatic aesthetic. Comparing Ibsen's dramatic construction with Shakespeare's, for example, Thomas R. Price in 1892 ultimately preferred Shakespeare's—as is not surprising, since his essay was published in *Shakespeariana* after being delivered to the New York Shakespeare Society. What Price admires about Ibsen points to the development of a new dramatic sensibility, however. For example, Price praises Ibsen's choice to set all fifty-one scenes of *Hedda Gabler* in one place, Hedda's sitting room, because of the staging's economy and concentration: "The drama is to be reduced from the splendor of scenic display to the minute study of human emotion. In something of the same spirit, the story that spreads over ten years [that is, in its backstory] is concentrated within the time space of thirty-six hours." That the play employs only seven characters, many fewer than in Shakespeare's plays, concentrates and intensifies its effects. With approval, Price observes that "in unity of plan, in limit of time and in concentration of characters" Ibsen reverts to the method of the Greeks, although Price also notes several techniques Ibsen borrowed from Shakespeare.[97]

In spite of Price's loyalty to Shakespeare, he astutely identifies the core features of Ibsen's dramatic construction that by the end of the century had been ratified by theorists and critics of drama. Ibsen was credited with clearing out the underbrush: abandoned were "the lengthy soliloquy, the undisguised confidant [brought onstage simply to hear about a main character's situation], the stage aside," as one critic summed up in 1909.[98] The promotion of a schematic, economical approach to dramatic construction provided a new aesthetic for prose drama (a phrase on its way to redundancy).[99] This aesthetic was grounded in performance: it represented the belief that drama was based in the theater, not in the book and perhaps not even in literature. It's not surprising that theater history was becoming institutionalized around the same time. In 1891, a society was founded in honor of William Dunlap, a U.S. theater historian, stage manager, and playwright whose best-known play was *Andre* (1798). The Dunlap Society brought together actors, academics, theater critics, literary critics, and playwrights; early members included Joseph Jefferson, Brander Matthews, Augustin Daly, and Stedman. Its main object was to publish books related to drama: plays and studies of theater history, especially.[100] In keeping with this attention to performance, Brander Matthews—professor of dramatic literature at Columbia University—founded a Dramatic Museum of performance history. Matthews even pitched drama as an art form independent of literature, like painting or sculpture: an art with roots in pantomime, song, and dance rather than primarily in words.[101]

Oddly enough, this exuberant sense of drama's performative dynamism coincided with a resurgence of generic regulation and unprecedented forms of schematization. In addition to the evolutionary dimensions I've indicated, the interest in technique also manifested a late-century fascination with skilled handicrafts. Ideas from William Morris and John Ruskin reverberated through the dictums about fine craftsmanship in the drama and the short story. Indeed, one reason why drama was the genre most hospitable to the revival of rules and laws may have been that drama more than other literary genre could be linked to immediate consequences akin to those a woodworker would face in building a table or chair. For instance, manuals such as Alfred Hennequin's *Art of Playwriting* (1890) took it for granted that fledgling playwrights would benefit from advice about ways of coping with the machinery of the stage such as managing characters' entrances.[102]

It's remarkable how much the drama, a form explicitly valued at this time for highlighting characters' freedom to act and choose, was subjected to constraints and necessity. The assumption that every playwright needed to master certain conventional matters of technique or craft haunted these discussions. Brander Matthews endorsed the proposal of Francisque Sarcey, an influential French drama critic, that every dramatic subject carried certain scenes that a playwright was required to include, "*scènes à faire,* the scenes which had to be done," because "the spectator vaguely desires these scenes, and is dumbly disappointed if they take place behind closed doors and if they are only narrated." If drama is struggle, Matthews concluded, then the scenes in which "the contending forces are seen grappling with one another" must be *scènes à faire*. (Pauline Hopkins's novel *Contending Forces* marks another appropriation of dramatic power for fiction.)[103] The embrace of craft required a certain submission to necessity, even if new artistic decision points emerged as a result.

Given that many studies of the drama and short story were addressed to writers attempting work in these forms, attention to craft may also have channeled a renewed appreciation for lore about technique. As I've noted, the Romantic emphasis on genius didn't address the fact that writers have to learn many things about writing, sometimes in dogged rather than inspired ways. Like Besant's and James's proposals about the art of fiction, the forms of craft-related regulation that proliferated at the end of the century were aimed primarily at instructing writers, not guiding critics, even though some of the key promoters (such as Thomas R. Price and Brander Matthews, both professors in Columbia's English Department) were academics.

Two of the foundational theorists of the new, spare aesthetic were Gustav Freytag and Ferdinand Brunetière. Freytag was a German playwright and novelist (the author of *Debit and Credit* [1855], published in translation by Harper Brothers in 1858) and was for a while a *Privatdozent* at the University of Breslau; he also edited a liberal German weekly. His 1863 work *Technique of the Drama* was translated into English in 1894, when it was hailed as an authoritative work whose translation was long overdue.[104] Ferdinand Brunetière was a professor of French language and literature at the École Normale and, by the 1890s, editor of *Revue des Deux Mondes*. Like Hippolyte Taine, he was a literary historian who took an evolutionary approach. Much of his work was not translated into English or widely reviewed in the United States, but his short piece "The Law of the Drama," originally the preface to a French work of theater history (1894), gained currency in part because Brander Matthews addressed it in his 1902 study *Development of the Drama*. Brunetière toured the United States in 1897, delivering the Turnbull Lectures at Johns Hopkins University and speaking in several East Coast cities.[105]

The culmination of Thomas Price's analysis of *Hedda Gabler*, in the 1892 essay I examined above, is an examination of how Ibsen distributes the action of the play among five dramatic phases: "the *protasis* or exposition," "the *epitasis*" or "tightening of the plot," "the climax of the dramatic action," "the *catabasis* or downward movement of the action," and "the catastrophe." Whereas Shakespeare's plays gave roughly equal time to each phase, Price points out that Ibsen's *Hedda* has expanded the exposition to take up about half the play, so that the other phases are compressed and accelerated.[106] Price's five-phase schema was borrowed from Freytag, although Price's phrasings were Aristotelian. Freytag's presentation of the five phases, in *Technique of the Drama*, applied them to works by Sophocles, Shakespeare, Lessing, Goethe, and Schiller but presented them as fundamental to all good drama. Freytag rendered the schema as a pyramid whose segments were the introduction, rise, climax, return or fall, and catastrophe (in the terms used in the 1894 translation).[107] He looked past Shakespeare to classical authorities in justifying the schema, assimilating Shakespeare to the ancients when possible but usually siding with the ancients where there were differences. (For instance, Shakespeare changed scenes sometimes during the introduction, but Freytag cautioned dramatists of his own time against this practice.) Freytag even proposed that every scene in a play should properly include the same five phases on a smaller scale: like branches on a tree and branching veins within a leaf, the phases could be organically elaborated at more than one compositional level. Moreover, the analysis Freytag proposed was intended to allow authors, critics, and producers to discern the fundamental architecture of the play's development so that inessentials could be pruned. Once a scene's purpose is attained, in terms of the five-phase development, "then every useless word is too much."[108]

This five-phase pyramid was in circulation even before the 1894 translation of *Technique of the Drama*. Alfred Hennequin, a Belgian playwright on the faculty at the University of Michigan, made use of Freytag's pyramid, with the key terms translated slightly differently and without attribution, in his 1890 treatise *The Art of Playwriting*.[109] Even though Hennequin's book lists his Ph.D. on the title page, it's not a scholarly study: there are no footnotes and no attempt to identify where any of these ideas about drama had been previously developed. However, Hennequin knew Freytag and also Aristotle—he entered a Shakespearean controversy in the *Critic* in 1891 and elucidated Freytag's "height" or "climax" as corresponding to the "*peripeteia* of Aristotle's Poetics."[110] It seems likely that he didn't cite Freytag or anyone else because his book was a practical handbook, addressing the roles of theater personnel (the stage manager, the head usher, and so forth), stage plans, and basic kinds of stage movement as well as a range of basic compositional issues (such as "How to Determine the Length of an Act"). Precisely because Hennequin's book doesn't claim to present a highly original approach, it offers a sense of what analytic classifications were in use. For example, Hennequin delineates some common types of plays (social dramas, emotional dramas) in terms of theme, characters, plot, and style: theme was glossed only as a "topic of the day, social or political" and was therefore a straightforward premise, not yet an interpretive element (46). Hennequin uses a diagram of Freytag's pyramid (which for both Freytag and Hennequin is simply an upside-down V, with the phases marked at the bases, the apex, and along each side) and identifies the phases as the exposition, growth, height, fall, and close or catastrophe.[111]

What Brunetiére's *Law of the Drama* added was a schematic elaboration of the premise that drama was fundamentally about conflict. As Brander Matthews pointed out, Brunetière took this strand of Aristotle's and Hegel's theories of tragedy and made it into the foundational principle of drama.[112] August Schlegel had defined tragedy by its presentation of "the struggle between the outward finite existence, and the inward infinite aspirations."[113] Hegel had characterized drama, especially tragedy, as representing an action that "rests entirely on *collisions* of circumstances, passions, and characters."[114] He also insisted that dramatic action issues from an individual, proceeding from "the self-determination of the individual's character.... [I]t does not presuppose the epic ground of an entire world-view elaborated objectively in all its aspects and ramifications."[115] Brunetière presented the drama as a genre affecting the world and its rulers: "Men of action, Richelieu, Condé, Frederick, Napoleon, have always been fond of the theater."[116] Brushing aside all more elaborate rules of the drama, he identified the central element of drama as "the spectacle of a *will* striving towards a goal, and conscious of the means which it employs." To his way of thinking, which many novelists and novel readers would have disputed, the novel took the opposite approach, presenting instead "the influence which is exercised upon us by all that is outside of ourselves."[117]

Since the drama staged the will's encounter with obstacles, dramas could be classified according to the kind of obstacles encountered—and here was the feature of Brunetière's thought that came to be most widely influential. Dramatic conflicts might involve "laws of nature" or "decrees of Providence," in the case of tragedy; one's own passions or social factors, in the case of "romantic drama or social drama"; another's will, in the case of comedy; or the "irony of fortune" in its most ludicrous aspects, in the case of farce. Brunetière even integrated this will-centered theory of drama into nationalized literary traditions, proposing grandly that "it is always at the exact moment of its national existence when the will of a great people is exalted, so to speak, within itself, that we see its dramatic art reach also the highest point of its development": Greek tragedy was fueled by the Persian Wars; Cervantes and Lope de Vega and Calderón by Spanish conquest in Europe and the New World; and Lessing, Schiller, and Goethe by Frederick the Great's rule.[118] Hegel had laid the groundwork for this position, identifying the drama with specifically Western exercises of the will, whereas (in orientalist fashion) he held that the East lacks the "live conception of *individual* freedom" or "responsibility."[119] The eugenic and imperialist dimensions of drama-as-will were in place before Brunetière's writing, but Brunetière's schematic account efficiently packaged and disseminated the assumption that drama concerned Western-style individual wills confronting a world.

This zest for generic regulation was extended to the short story, which was being touted at the turn of the century as an utterly new literary phenomenon. A cluster of widely reviewed studies by academics all asserted the novelty and distinctiveness of the short story: Walter Morris Hart's *Hawthorne and the Evolution of the Short Story* (1900), Brander Matthews's *The Philosophy of the Short-Story* (1901), Henry Seidel Canby's *The Short Story* (1902), and Bliss Perry's *A Study of Prose Fiction* (1903), which included a chapter on short stories.[120] These works mainly compiled and formalized ideas that had already been circulating in periodical culture. All agreed that the short story was a form quite distinct from the novel rooted in an older form, the tale; Canby and Hart emphasized the influence of *Spectator*-style periodical sketches, although Matthews differentiated the sketch, as an essayistic form, from the short story, as a dramatic form ("while a sketch may be still-life, in a short-story something always happens").[121] But whatever the short story's origins, critics agreed that it had achieved its modern form in the writings of Poe and Hawthorne along with a few others (especially French writers—Maupassant and Merimée were often given credit).[122] Chekhov's short stories, published in the 1880s and 1890s, were translated into English by Constance Garnett after 1916, so Chekhov was only later retrospectively folded in to an Anglophone history and theory of the short story that had already been forged.

The short story was prized as a form in which U.S. writers excelled, contrasting with the sprawling British triple-decker novel.[123] Like the drama, the short story required artful economy. The short story's emergence was often described in terms that evoked the evolutionary adaptation of a life form to an environment. As Canby put it, the "modern Short Story seems to differ from the old tale by a very scientific adaptation of means to end, which end may be called vividness, and by a structure which, in its nice proportions and potentiality for adequate expression, is a more excellent instrument than anything the old tale can show." Identifying the novel and short story as "distinct instruments," Canby figures the short story as both efficient life form and streamlined technology.[124] Approaches like Canby's didn't simply hold that clean lines and economy were good. They treated ornament, embellishment, and digression as very bad indeed. An ideal of craft converged with an almost sadomasochistic avoidance of waste and excess.[125] There's a kind of brinksmanship—just how much can be trimmed?!—in Clayton Hamilton's proposal that "[t]he aim of a short-story is to produce a single narrative effect with the greatest economy of means that is consistent with the utmost emphasis."[126] Drawing on Poe's discussion of Hawthorne's stories, Matthews asserted that "the short-story must do one thing only, and it must do this completely and perfectly; it must not loiter or digress; it must have unity of action, unity of temper, unity of tone, unity of color, unity of effect; and it must vigilantly exclude everything that might interfere with its singleness of intention."[127] Matthews went on to elaborate the rigors of the craft ideal that obtained after Poe, in which a short story "was no longer to be accomplished by a lucky accident only; it could be achieved solely by deliberate and resolute effort. The restrictions were rigid, like those of the sonnet, and success was not easy; but the very difficulty of the undertaking was tempting to the true artist, ever eager for a grapple with technic."[128]

By 1904, Matthews—a crucial link between drama and the short story, since he promoted both—had identified society verse as another form at which U.S. writers excelled. A collection of *American Familiar Verse: Vers de Société* was the third publication in the series he edited (named The Wampum Library, oddly enough), each of whose volumes dealt "with the development of a single literary species, tracing the evolution of this definite form here in the United States, and presenting in chronological sequence typical examples chosen from the writings of American authors."[129] Matthews characterized familiar verse (his preferred term) by "brevity," "brilliancy," and "buoyancy," and his discussion and examples embraced technical playfulness. Works by all of the Schoolroom poets were included in Matthews's volume (Bryant, Holmes, Longfellow, Lowell, and Whittier) as well as poems by Eugene Field and Mary Mapes Dodge (two of the most prominent late-century poets of childhood identified by Sorby), Bret Harte, Edmund Stedman (whose pieces included "Pan in Wall Street," the stockbroker's fantasy), and a number of other active poets familiar to readers of literary monthlies. Matthews thought of familiar verse as "closely akin to what in prose is known as the 'eighteenth-century essay,'" perhaps because it was a sociable form.[130] It's interesting that, like Richard Moulton, he looked to the eighteenth century for a model of imaginative writing that circulated pleasurably without taking on monumental ambitions. In his essay on Dobson, however, Matthews praised the "utmost economy" of his verbal brushstrokes, making clear that no eighteenth-century prolixity was on offer.[131] Dobson formulated at the request of Matthews "Twelve Good Rules of Familiar Verse," somewhat tongue-in-cheek; the last rule enjoins against asking whether the author of the rules has followed them. But the rules amount to an aesthetic, one in which certain forms of artifice (such as inversions) are to be avoided and others (such as exact rhymes) are to be practiced—indeed, Dobson calls for rhymes to be "rigorously exact."[132]

Brevity, in short stories and lyric poetry, was a sign of concentration, heightened technique, and unified aesthetic effect, all of which amplified the works' power. Bliss Perry drove home the parallel: "The short story in prose corresponds, then, to the lyric in poetry; like the lyric, its unity of effect turns largely upon its brevity; and as there are well known laws of lyric structure which the lyric poet violates at his peril or obeys to his triumph, so the short story must observe certain conditions and may enjoy certain freedoms that are peculiar to itself."[133] The tendency to assimilate all poetry to the lyric model was reinforced to an incalculable extent by the rise of reading pedagogies geared to economism, even before the New Criticism. Charles Alphonso Smith argued that U.S. readers' preference for "brief intensity" was at work even in their taste for Browning's dramatic monologues, since the "dramatic monologue is in poetry what the short story is in prose."[134] The perfect short story was a powerful action, like the swing of a club or the firing of an arrow, and it was more powerful than a novel, its promoters alleged. Henry Seidel Canby argued that in creating a short story, "[w]e are selecting far more than in a novel...; we are looking only for what bears upon our narrow purpose, that the interest may be concentrated, and the conception vivified, beyond the power of a novel. The process is very artificial, but very powerful; it is like turning a telescope upon one nebula in the heavens."[135] Again and again, short story theorists emphasized the artifice of the short story, as if arguing against any naïvely representational version of realism, and held that the artifice added intensity. Henry James had already objected to intrusive narration, but Evelyn Albright moved even closer to the twentieth-century writing workshop prescription that showing is better than telling: "The genuine narrative method of portraying character is the dramatic one of making the characters talk and act. Description and exposition are valuable, but only as accessories."[136] This close attention to short story technique laid groundwork for the development of narratology. For example, Lewis Worthington Smith's *The Writing of the Short Story* (1902) offered elaborate protocols for examining short stories sentence by sentence, tracking features such as whether statements reveal "author's attitude toward the character."[137]

By the early decades of the twentieth century, Brunetière's conflicts and Freytag's pyramid had become fairly standard equipment in works about how to write plays and short stories. The era had forged a set of standardized literary terms that would be staples of literature and creative writing classrooms throughout the twentieth century. Characters, plots, and themes had become familiar features of plays and short stories, and these ingredients came to be treated as the building blocks of interpretation. It's easy to see the classroom beckoning as the environment in which short stories would take on their fully schematic significance. Albright, an instructor at Ohio Wesleyan University, wrote, "A good character, like a good story, has a *point*. This point is given by interpretation." The very concentration of short stories, together with the privileging of characterization, meant that characters tended to be isolated—"from family, from relatives, from past history, and from the distant future," as Albright put it—and that settings tended to be "structural" in significance, capable of setting "mood" or "tone" but envisioned primarily as backdrops for revelations about character.[138] William Archer, Ibsen's foremost English translator, made a similar point about plays: "Action ought to exist for the sake of character: when the relation is reversed, the play may be an ingenious toy, but scarcely a vital work of art."[139] The Coleridgean precept that *Hamlet* was about Prince Hamlet's internal struggle, for which the court at Elsinore was merely a backdrop, persisted in this approach. Indeed, Albright laid it out fairly explicitly:

Inner conflicts have assumed greater importance and greater interest. The modern hero has something worse to fight than an evil world and selfish men—he has the evil motives of his own heart arrayed against him. The stage of action in the story of character is not always the great world of events: more often the real stage is behind the scenes.[140]

This strategy moved far away from Denton J. Snider's attention to the world in which a literary work moves. Snider's approach allowed specific power relations (embodied in institutions and channeled by them) to be analyzed, versus the vacuousness of a Brunetière-style conflict between individual and society.

A side effect of economistic functionalism is that any element in a short story was presumed to have its justification, and formulating that justification became a standard classroom task. Clayton Meeker Hamilton revealed the oddly tautological nature of this kind of craft analysis when he recounted a short story writer's proper way of proceeding. According to Hamilton, "The initial problem of the writer of short-stories is to find out by intellectual means the one best way of constructing the story that he has to tell." How his creative process has previously arrived at the story to be told is left mysterious. Hamilton offers an analysis of Poe's "Ligeia," taking as a clue to the theme of the story its epigraph from Joseph Glanvill about the mysteries of the will and formulating the story's purpose as being "to exhibit a character with a superhuman will, and to show how, by sheer force of volition, this person conquered death." The resulting discussion, which proceeds very much in the manner of Poe's "Philosophy of Composition," unfolds all the things that Poe could not have done differently, given his artistic purpose and the "laws of the short-story."[141] The fact that the story in question is about the strength of the human will compounds Hamilton's emphasis on authorial control. In accounts such as Hamilton's, themes are presented as the motives and starting points of plays or stories, and interpretation is cast as the act of recovering them (which might or might not involve recovering the author's intentions or any reader's experience, in keeping with formalist approaches). Themes were usually phrased as general truths or dimensions of existence, so there might be a peculiar gap between the breadth of a theme ("appearance versus reality") and the intricate particulars of a literary work that could not possibly have been written any differently. It could also be hard to distinguish between a theme and a very abstract plot summary. For example, William Archer summed up the theme of *Hamlet* as "the hesitancy of a young man of a certain temperament in taking vengeance upon the seducer of his mother and murderer of his father."[142]

The interpretive work of discerning a theme repeated in some respects the hermeneutic circle, the dynamic interpretation of parts in relation to the whole and the whole in relation to the parts, except that the nature of the parts and the trajectory of the whole were loaded with assumptions—including the insistence that every possible creative integer (the theme, the plot, each character, the action) be unified. According to this logic, shorter works were bound to be better unified and therefore to exemplify higher-order crafting. Albright's view, influenced by one of her instructors at the University of Chicago, James Linn, is that "[t]he novel aims to show *growth* of character, with reaction of one character upon the other.... The short-story has to do with *change* in character—the cross-road, rather than the main road travelled."[143] Albright's especially normative presentation captures the tendency to identify a short story with the representation of a "crisis" (structured by a conflict) affecting one or more characters, one whose resolution is suggested rather than presented in detail.[144] Frank R. Stockton's "The Lady or the Tiger?" (1882) was one of the most celebrated U.S. short stories of the period, and its culmination in a cliffhanger crisis (in spite of the thinness of its characterization) took to an extreme the aesthetic Albright would later delineate. A more highly literary elaboration of this aesthetic would be James Joyce's *Dubliners* collection (1914), famous for organizing each story around an epiphany. Insofar as an epiphany or crisis is likely to convey or prompt an individual decision, perhaps in the form of a transformed understanding, the short story aesthetic is aligned with the tendency in Coleridge-style *Hamlet* criticism to focus on character: to scrutinize Hamlet's self-knowledge and Hamlet's will rather than the world in which Hamlet operates. The very idea that characters and setting are separate ingredients of plot implies that characters can easily be separated from the environments that provide the conditions of possibility for their actions.

By the early decades of the twentieth century, Freytag's pyramid was routinely referenced in writings about the short story as a genre. A measure of its cultural absorption was the publication in 1900 of a "literary study" of the book of Job that identified Freytag-like phases and a central conflict.[145] The pyramid was sometimes attributed to Freytag and sometimes presented as a self-evident apparatus, the names of the five phases varied, and the pyramid diagram was sometimes accompanied by a ritual warning that the structure might not fit all stories. However, the pyramid remained an instructional fixture.[146] Brunetière's emphasis on conflict similarly became standard equipment for literary instruction, but somehow the link to Brunetière was lost as the set of conflicts settled into a stable schematic form. As early as 1908, Cornelia Beare, an instructor at New York City's Erasmus Hall High School, prefaced her instructional edition of George Eliot's *Silas Marner* by outlining a set of conflicts, on the model of Brunetière's, that were likely to structure novels:

> The struggle of the individual against an obstacle constitutes plot. According to the type of novel, it may be man against nature, as in tales of exploration and discovery; man against man, as in stories of adventure, daring, and the greater number of romances; and finally man against himself, the working out of his higher or lower self, as in the so-called problem novels of today.[147]

Beare's is the earliest example I've found of the simplest binary schematization of conflicts (X against Y) that became widely promulgated, but probably no single person deserves credit for what seems to have been a collective effort to distill the possibilities for conflict in literature.[148] In 1910, Clayton Hamilton reshuffled Brunetière's conflicts into three periodized instances: the individual in conflict with fate, for which Greek tragedy was paradigmatic; the individual in conflict with his [sic] own faults, a type discovered by Marlowe and perfected by Shakespeare; and the individual in conflict with social conditions, typified by the "modern social drama" of Ibsen.[149] In Robert Wilson Neal's *Short Stories in the Making* (1914), Freytag's pyramid appears without attribution, and the set of conflicts harking back to Brunetière is further distilled: "the conscious struggle between man and the physical world, between man and man, between man and his own spiritual nature."[150] The array of conflicts was more schematic still in James Irving's guidebook (1919) to writing short stories and "photoplays" (film scripts): "man's struggle with nature, man against man, man against society, man against temptations."[151]

By 1910, J. E. Spingarn—now best known for establishing the NAACP's Spingarn Medal—attempted to launch a "new criticism" that discarded such apparatuses. Spingarn insisted on the singularity of any aesthetic creation.[152] Tracing the long interplay between purely personal, impressionistic criticism, on the one hand, and dogmatic criticism, emphasizing rules and judgments, on the other, Spingarn proposed that the expressive point of view offered an intelligent alternative to these extremes. Dogmatic criticism he attacked more fiercely, probably because it was in the ascendant. Countering the idea that attention to conventions and techniques is historical or scientific—two registers privileged as empirical—Spingarn argued that the rules and laws promulgated by Brunetière and company were mere superstitions: "The very conception of 'rules' harks backs to an age of magic, and reminds the modern of those mysterious words which the heroes of the fairy-tales are without reason forbidden to utter; the rules are a survival of the savage *taboo*."[153] Brushing aside genres as being anything but conveniences, he noted that the classical insistence on genres mainly involved the imperative that they "should not be mingled," whereas artists in practice perpetually mingled and morphed them.[154] (Jacques Derrida later made a similar point in "The Law of Genre.")[155] Spingarn insisted, "Every poet re-expresses the universe in his own way, and every poem is a new and independent expression."[156] He cited Benedetto Croce's understanding that art is expression and expression is everywhere, so that the things we call art are simply concentrations of expressivity. Spingarn wrote a separate essay targeting dramatic criticism, singling out his colleague Brander Matthews's "Dramatic Museum" as an example of everything wrong with drama criticism that focused on the institution of the theater. To presume that the circumstances of the theater meaningfully shaped the compositions of great dramatists would be to diminish or negate their aesthetic inspiration, according to

Spingarn. Sarcey, who formulated *scènes à faire*, was a particular villain for Spingarn, "responsible for so much of this cheap materialism of contemporary dramatic criticism."[157]

It was only the vague and spluttering kind of materialism at work again, though, not the attention to material practices and conditions we might value today. Indeed, Spingarn might better have called his enemy functionalism, rooted in vernacular evolutionary theory and grafting a love of handicraft onto an obsession with individual will, or even Taylorism, which James F. Knapp has identified as a range of scientific and economistic practices affecting culture as well as industry in the early twentieth century.[158] Freytag's pyramid and the paired conflicts adapted from Brunetière succeeded so well because they fulfilled the disciplinary imperative for the academic study of literature to simulate the empirical methods of the natural sciences.[159] The five-part narrative schema (exposition, rising action, and so forth) and schematized conflicts are alive and well in U.S. high school literature textbooks today, usually stripped of any connection to Freytag, Brunetière, or any other human agent and presented simply as fundamental features of narrative.[160] Like chemistry experiments, they are designed to produce predictable outcomes reproducible in any classroom.

Timothy Lenoir has suggested with respect to biochemistry, considered as a sample scientific discipline, "The common core of the discipline was not a commitment to a particular theory of life or a specific research agenda but rather a growing collection of techniques and problem solutions.... These techniques and associated instrumentalities were more stable than the different, and often conflicting, theories they supported."[161] In similar fashion, establishing a standard vocabulary for literary analysis and common interpretive procedures were signs that literary studies had become thoroughly disciplinary. Knapp argues that Taylorism served the "need for central management to appropriate the traditional knowledge which has always been possessed by the workers, thereby initiating a crucial division between knowledge (refined as the proper concern of management and its new servant, science), and practice, the machine-like execution by the workers of plans laid down by others."[162] The standardization of these highly schematic interpretive practices similarly meant that experts determined a set of protocols that could be executed by students who were not encouraged to assess the protocols themselves. As chapter 6 demonstrates, however, the disciplinarity of literary studies in the early twentieth century—and beyond—was not settled without considerable institutional struggle.

{6}

Disciplinarity and Beyond

> Here, then, is a fact of the greatest historical significance. Almost before society is aware of it there has come into existence an American system of public universities, at once the complement and the crown of an American system of public schools. In its creation, as in the creation of the latter, the State has joined hands with the nation.
> —GEORGE E. HOWARD (1891)[1]

> America is thus as a nation rapidly drifting towards a state of things in which no man of science or letters will be accounted respectable unless some kind of badge or diploma is stamped upon him, and in which bare personality will be a mark of outcast state.
> —WILLIAM JAMES (1903)[2]

Disciplinarity enables and constrains.[3] On the one hand, a discipline brings a set of people into a shared domain of inquiry that has some ground rules, focusing their attention on certain questions and offering frameworks for refining these questions. A discipline provides shared vocabularies, understandings, and protocols that make it possible to take up complex questions and investigations in ways that will be readily legible to others. It orchestrates local efforts and facilitates relationships among the discipline's participants, who may be far-flung. On the other hand, disciplinarity can routinize and standardize intellectual work in a way that merely manages intellectual questions. The imperative of innovation can lead scholars to overstate the novelty and significance of their work, and it tends to create trends, so that the value of something new or old gets distorted by the perpetual construction of the new-hot versus old-tired (complicated by the ongoing rediscovery of the old and its repackaging as new again).[4] The need to present fields as advancing (and one's own work as advancing a field) also promotes trend spotting and trend claiming. The ways in which scholars work in concert—because it's only through the collective work of scholars that a field assimilates new phenomena and constructs new possibilities—can be undervalued because of the need to present individual publications as original. By far the most insidious feature of disciplinarity at present is that it covers its tracks, hardening and patrolling boundaries that began as provisional. Insofar as departmentalized disciplines are forced to vie for precedence (and funding and students), they have strong incentives to idealize their founding gestures in order to emphasize their long-standing importance. The disciplinary requirement of innovation keeps us from being able to rely on the lazy justification that "we've always done it this way," but institutional insecurity creates reasons not to admit that "we happen to do it this way, and we don't have to."

A host of standardizing, instrumentalizing tendencies were at stake in the creation of professional academic expertise, tendencies that shaped every discipline, including literary studies. A repeated story of modernity involves the creation of modern, rational mechanisms to fend off earlier abuses of power, such as the system of competitive exams under the Pendleton Civil Service Reform Act of 1883 that was inaugurated to combat the spoils system.[5] Another repeated story of modernity involves the discovery that the modernizing solutions create new problems: inefficiency, inflexible forms of standardization, and a variety of instrumentalizing effects often summed up as dehumanization. The hope that modern solutions will offer handy ways of organizing the world more rationally belies the danger that standardizing, bureaucratizing solutions will pervade and transform what they organize. It's not that the old ways were better; it's that we need to recognize what some of our favorite innovations have wrought. The creation of experts, expert credentialing, and academic disciplines were understood (and celebrated) as modern ways of reorganizing intellectual life, but they altered it profoundly, not only for the better. During the early establishment of disciplinarity, there were enthusiastic embraces of the modern organization of literary studies as well as outcroppings of regret and dissent, and the two stances often paralleled the versions of modernity and antimodernity that were operating in literary culture.

There were gains and losses in the academic installation of literary studies, and because the losses have received less attention and have accumulated alarmingly, I emphasize them here. The disciplinary study of literature is getting the last word in part because this book is designed to contribute to academic literary studies and in part because academic literary studies so powerfully shaped the roles played by literature in the twentieth and twenty-first centuries—not least by constituting a new establishment to be resisted or rejected by stakeholders in public literary culture. However, in keeping with my attention to what academic literary studies left behind in public literary culture, what interests me most about the disciplinary study of literature is its generative instability. Academic literary studies, I argue, has been from the outset disciplinary, interdisciplinary, and antidisciplinary, and its interdisciplinary and antidisciplinary features may be especially important to examine as we consider its future.

Literature as Disciplinary

The struggle in early English departments between philologists and their opponents, who have usually been identified as generalists or belletrists, has featured prominently in histories of English studies, and it implies that literary studies succeeded by finding a middle way between the extremes of dogged empiricism and gushing or genteel impressionism. This polarization is not the best way to characterize the early dynamics within English literary studies. Moreover, this competition between elements still recognizably part of literary studies was probably less consequential than the processes that led to literary studies being differentiated from oral and dramatic performance, which gradually moved into their own departments during the first half of the twentieth century. Although modern literature and language departments have continued to teach plays and maintain interdisciplinary relationships with performance-oriented departments, the separation further distanced academic literary studies from some of the practices that had been widely valued and enjoyed in public literary studies. The virtual exclusion of performance from literary studies paralleled—and may have facilitated—the strict management of emotional engagement within literary studies, and it confirmed the tendency of early disciplinarity to privilege standard procedures and reproducible outcomes.

The story so far, sketched in chapter 3, is that the eighteenth-century model of the college, with its unified classical curriculum, was gradually replaced by the disciplinary and departmental organization of the modern research university, a model that affected many institutions of higher education, not just universities, and that also affected high schools, which also adopted departmental organization and which oriented their curricula toward entry requirements for college.[6] Before the advent of departmental organization, professorships had been designated in a variety of idiosyncratic ways. After departments became the key academic units, in the 1880s and 1890s, special named and endowed professorships were still established, but most professorships were located within departments, and garden-variety professorial appointments were simply identified by department ("professor of French"), as is still the case today.[7] The research university model was organized around facilitating advanced, specialized research on the part of graduate students and professors, with the PhD at the heart of the enterprise. Harvard president Charles William Eliot's embrace of the system of majors and minors, which adapted graduate-level specialization for undergraduates, helped to make it a norm within higher education.

Disciplines were organized into departments, which took on special responsibility for their majors along with their graduate students. However, the privileging of research built into the university model meant that education, especially undergraduate education, was often envisioned simplistically as the mere transfer of disciplinary content to learners, a process that unfolded more agreeably if professors were charismatic but that did not really deserve disciplinary attention. As Mariolina Rizzi Salvatori has documented, pedagogy was treated mainly as a practical rather than intellectual endeavor, and the work of normal schools was transferred to departments or schools of education, segregated from the work of the disciplines that were subjects of instruction.[8]

Some of the fields that became disciplines were long-standing, and others were new. Nevertheless, no field was guaranteed a place in the research university unless it could be organized as a discipline. Each discipline was defined by a set of objects, questions, and methods, and each discipline established standard, authoritative knowledge in its area, knowledge whose fundamentals were organized into an undergraduate curriculum. Since the purpose of disciplinarity was to advance knowledge, however, disciplines also perpetually generated new ideas, critiques of old ideas, and disputes. The division of labor among disciplines initially discouraged overlaps or blurry boundaries, even though it was taken for granted that there were relationships among disciplines: interdisciplinarity was born alongside the disciplines.

Although German universities were mainly credited as its inspiration, the research university model that became dominant in the United States was a new institutional plan that selectively combined elements of German universities with elements borrowed from Scottish and English universities.[9] The Morrill Act (1862) establishing land-grant colleges embodied the idea that higher education in the United States ought to be more widely available than in Europe. The Morrill Act, which provided for vocational components (linked especially to agriculture and teacher training) within a framework of education in the arts and sciences (and the emerging social sciences), also marked a commitment to making liberal arts education widely available, versus the European trend toward making university educations available to the few and vocational training to the many.[10] After about 1880, college enrollments in the United States expanded rapidly, business leaders came to dominate university boards of trustees, and foundations such as the Rockefeller Institute and the Carnegie Foundation for the Advancement of Teaching emerged to promote forms of modernization and standardization in higher education.[11] In keeping with these pressures to standardize higher education, even the vocationally focused elements of university education came to take the form of academic disciplines: clearly demarcated and well-justified courses of study designed to present the current state of knowledge in an area to students and to promote new scholarship and innovations in practice.

The research university not only drew on specific scientific practices but also made science the symbol of everything modern, progressive, rational, and efficient. Laboratory sciences became the model disciplines of the research university. Chemistry and physics were often cited as exemplary disciplines, perhaps because they were the sciences best suited to being advanced and taught by means of reproducible experiments under controlled conditions. (Harvard's President Eliot was a chemist.) Those promoting any study as disciplinary—even philosophy—tended to cast its significance as scientific or describe its practices as analogous to those of empirical science.[12] Arguing for the importance of studying novels in 1895, for example, Richard Moulton countered the charge that fiction is "made up" by pointing out that scientific experiments are also fabricated: "[D]oes not their whole value consist in the fact that they are artificial substitutes of the investigator or expositor for actualities of nature that could not serve his purpose?"[13]

Within the research university model, the modern language and literature departments (in conjunction with classics, effectively a department of ancient literature) became the sites of mainly nationalized literary studies, and comparative literature became a supplemental rubric for literary studies that crossed national boundaries but was still grounded in nationally organized literary scholarship and traditions.[14] Homing in on this disciplinary scientism and the resistance it provoked, historians of English literary studies have often sorted late nineteenth-century professors into two camps: the superempirical philologists and another, less rigorous set of scholars usually described as generalists or belles-lettrists.[15] Members of the former group would have recognized themselves as philologists, but the names applied to the latter group are misleading. It isn't clear what the term "generalist" means in a discipline whose scholarship and coursework has from the beginning been specialized (by period, genre, and author). Like the philologists, the so-called generalists often taught period courses and wrote works of scholarship designed to make new contributions to specialized areas of study. Likewise, the term "belles lettres" had by the end of the century come to signal either the narrowest, most refined of literary canons or a somewhat archaic and elitist investment in literature, as chapter 3 describes, so it was not a rallying point for literary academics, even though it occasionally formed an element in professorial titles heading toward literary studies. This second group of scholars might most accurately be identified with the practice of aesthetic criticism, which included interpretation as well as appreciation, both activities that they thought the more stringent forms of philology lacked. And by the early twentieth century, aesthetic criticism was poised to become dominant, its centrality clinched by Oxford's and Cambridge's appointments of aesthetic critics to its new professorships in English literature in the first decade of the twentieth century.[16]

The philological approach to literary studies, exemplified by Francis A. March at Lafayette College, examined changes in the English language in themselves and as they were registered in the literary canon; it was sometimes combined with appreciative, interpretive approaches to literature and sometimes not.[17] But aesthetic criticism and philology were not the only important formations in English studies at the time. Textual criticism in the service of textual editing, as we've seen in Shakespeare studies, was an important area of expertise in itself as well as a support for aesthetic criticism and philology. Literary history was commonly taught, sometimes in courses using specialized textbooks of literary history (which may or may not have been combined with the study of primary texts, as we've seen) and sometimes in courses presenting particular literary periods.

What all four of these strands—philology, textual criticism, literary history, and the best-known forms of aesthetic criticism—had in common was an orientation toward stable print texts as the object of literary studies. The key definitional element of an English department was the English literary canon, which provided disciplinary unity for a heterogeneous range of disciplinary practices, some of which meshed poorly with the aesthetic selection principles at work in the canon. The core canon of early English departments was an old and British canon that culminated in the Romantics, although more recent works of British literature (as in the courses on novels, short stories, and late nineteenth-century poets mentioned in the previous chapter) and U.S. literature were making appearances in college curricula by 1900.[18] One reason why philology gradually became less prominent in literary studies may have been that there was no reason why the texts of the literary canon were the best objects for investigating the history of the English language; the rise of linguistics departments in the mid-twentieth century gave the historical study of language another disciplinary base, which may have become especially desirable after New Criticism swept through English departments.[19]

Given the centrality of the canon, it is surprising that the dramatic performance and expressive reading of canonical literature did not become established features of academic literary studies. As we've seen, drama was a foundational literary genre, and Shakespeare was the chief modern literary author, but literary studies continued to distance page from stage. A theatrical production was understood as an interpretation, certainly, and attending performances, staging plays, and reading or reciting plays aloud were features of public literary culture, including student organizations in college and universities. Nevertheless, academic literary studies at the turn of the century mainly treated performance as incidental to the understanding of plays, which—perhaps as a result of this restrictive sense of drama—continued to occupy an anomalous place in literary studies, underrepresented in most canons and seldom counted as crucial determinants of literary historical periods other than the English Renaissance.[20] Although the occasional literary drama course featuring performance had appeared by the turn of the century, academic literary studies was mainly not equipped to take more than a casual interest in theatrical performances and productions, even of canonical works.[21]

Truly embracing the study of theatrical performance—including acting, lighting, sets, costumes, and the host of factors involved in any theater production—would have made enormous demands on literary studies, although it seems unlikely that turn-of-the-century literary scholars ever got as far as trying. More revealing of literary studies' resistance to performance is the fact is that even late-century versions of elocution designed as literary interpretation did not find a permanent place in English departments. Alongside oratory, which remained important in some institutions but not others, and alongside college debate, which began to be organized during the 1890s together with other kinds of public speaking, practices called "expression" and "oral interpretation" emphasized the interpretive significance of the expressive public reading of literary texts.[22] They were successors or variants of elocution, which was sometimes treated as a way of naming all expressive public reading or speaking but at other times treated as a specific earlier school of performance that expression and oral interpretation rejected or adapted.

It makes sense, of course, that elocution and its successors would be important in universities during the years when "speaker-reciters"—including many, many interpreters of Shakespeare—played to enthusiastic paying audiences.[23] David Gold has established that public speaking and oratory remained important throughout the century in higher education, just not mainly in the elite institutions that have often been privileged within academic histories.[24] Expressive reading—which built on traditions of reciting poetry and reading it aloud in primary and secondary schools—was closely associated with these practices, surfacing in a variety of academic departments and many kinds of institutions. The National Association of Elocutionists was formed in 1892. In the same year, Thomas Clarkson Trueblood was promoted to full professor and made the head of the new Department of Elocution and Oratory at the University of Michigan, one of the earliest departments in the field later to be known as speech.[25] Schools of oratory were formed at Ohio Wesleyan and the University of Southern California during the same decade.[26] "Shakespearean Readings" was one of the courses Trueblood offered early in his career; later in his career, in addition to courses in extemporaneous speaking and debate, he offered courses on Tennyson and Browning.[27]

In the latter decades of the nineteenth century, conservatory-style institutions offering instruction in vocal culture made literature prominent. A 1913 directory lists fifty "Schools of Oratory, Elocution, Physical Culture and Dramatic Art" in thirteen states plus the District of Columbia.[28] Henrietta Vinton Davis, an African American performer who began her career in 1883 interpreting Shakespeare's plays, studied at the Boston School of Oratory (founded as the Boston Conservatory of Elocution, Oratory, and Dramatic Art in 1880, and later absorbed into Emerson College), where Charles Wesley Emerson was promoting "expression."[29] William J. Rolfe, the editor of instructional Shakespeare editions who was Henry N. Hudson's chief rival, was on the faculty of the School of Oratory and became Emerson College's second president.[30] Hudson was on the faculty of Boston University and taught in its School of Oratory.[31] Anna Baright, a graduate of the Boston University School of Oratory, opened a School of Elocution and Expression in Boston in 1879 and changed the name to the School of Expression in 1882, a further sign that expression was overtaking elocution as the favored platform. She was joined by Samuel Silas Curry, formerly a professor of oratory at Boston University, whom she married; in the twentieth century, the school became Curry College. An index of the standing of the school was the fact that Alexander Graham Bell, formerly a professor of vocal physiology and elocution at Boston University, where he also taught classes for deaf-mute students, became chancellor of the School of Expression. His father had been an elocutionist, among other things, and Bell himself had operated a school of vocal physiology in Boston during the 1870s.[32] Serving on the School of Expression's board at various points were Henry N. Hudson, Charles W. Eliot, William Dean Howells, and Joseph Jefferson.[33]

Practitioners of expression and oral interpretation had strong literary commitments that adapted features of aesthetic philosophy. Their work was influenced by François Delsarte, who emphasized expression's aesthetic mission, although expression-friendly elocutionists such as Alexander Graham Bell also emphasized the importance of understanding scientific aspects of physiology and sound.[34] The practice of expression in the United States, wherever it was taught, was closely entwined with literature.[35] In Samuel Silas Curry's influential account, expression anticipated method acting's emphasis on the internal as well as the external work of dramatic interpretation, but it employed a spiritual vocabulary:

> Expression implies mystic activity causing action manifest to the senses.... Expression is the result not of physical but of psychic action at the moment of utterance. The physical actions are directly caused by mental action. Thinking before an audience to awaken thought in others is not the same as thinking alone, but it is not primarily a physical act.

Curry cast expression as a fundamental element of education, which involves both "the reception of truth and the manifestation of truth." He argued that the previous elocutionary dispensation's emphasis on exaggerated performance meant that "selections from the best authors" were seldom used for platform reading because of their subtlety. Instead, Curry cast expression as one of the fine arts, to be guided by the principles that guided other fine arts and to be distinguished from mere "entertainment." Expression ought to be grounded in emotion as well as thought, and the body was the "interpretative" means by which the soul was revealed.[36]

Schools of expression tended to include more contemporary works in their canon. Indeed, the canon at Toronto's Margaret Eaton School of Literature and Expression, which became part of the University of Toronto in the 1930s, sounds a lot like the canon of *Poet-Lore*, featuring Shakespeare, Browning, and contemporary literature in translation. Expressionists studied poems "as literary wholes," and they also pursued "the humanistic goal of developing the whole person, not just the mechanisms of voice and body," which is why physical culture and physical movement were usually part of the curriculum.[37] It should come as no surprise that Robert Browning was one of Curry's touchstone authors. The dramatic monologue was a favorite genre for platform reading—as Curry pointed out, it "can only be rendered by means of public reading; it cannot be acted"—so it makes sense that Browning's late-century popularity coincided with the flourishing of expression. Curry wrote an entire book about Browning's dramatic monologues, identifying them as examples of a new literary form, in an approach similar to contemporary treatments of the short story as a new form.[38]

The era of expression and oral interpretation was one in which oral performance, though often housed in English departments, was not nurtured there. Faculty members working in oral genres seceded from the National Council of Teachers of English in 1915 to form the organization (National Association of Academic Teachers of Public Speaking) that later became the Speech Association of America, mainly because they believed their work was not highly valued within English departments and would fare better elsewhere. The first PhD awarded in a department of speech, in 1922, marked an important watershed.[39] The separation of speech from English, accomplished gradually over a number of decades, intensified the identification of literature with books, analysis, and written culture, distancing academic literary studies further from public literary culture. Indeed, speech instructors' sense of their lower status within English departments may have been a byproduct of the deepening expert-amateur divide that privileged print. It wasn't just that academic literary studies and public literary culture had parted ways: academics also secured their expert status by disallowing features of public literary culture that might count as entertainment. (Shoring up the disciplinary standing of departments of speech, once they were formed, was an emphasis on vocal physiology as a conspicuously scientific part of the discipline.)[40]

Performance involves thought as well as feeling, as Curry and other proponents of expression emphasized, but the division of literary studies from performance seemed to align with the division of intellect from emotion. Susan Harris Smith has argued that the academic status of drama suffered precisely because of the "taint of emotion," which was linked to "the histrionic and the 'feminine'" as well as to "childhood if not also childishness."[41] More precisely, emotions were allowed to contribute to literary interpretation only if they could be valued (and contained) as aesthetic responses qualitatively different and separate from the rest of emotional life. Selden Lincoln Whitcomb, associate professor of English at the University of Kansas, was patrolling this border in 1905:

> Criticism attempts to distinguish between emotional effects which are truly aesthetic, and those which are not. To the first class belong delight

in the technical mastery of the artist, the sense of 'difficulty overcome,' imaginative pleasure in the picture of life, whether it be joyful or sad, etc.; to the second class, all emotions associated with the personal experiences, antipathies and sympathies of the individual reader. The properly aesthetic emotions do not lead to any external activity; they never become real passions.[42]

Whitman's formulation raises the problem we've encountered before: that in defining aesthetic experience as noninstrumental and declaring it to be qualitatively different from the garden-variety emotional and intellectual experiences of daily life, critics effectively cordoned off literature from the rest of life (even though they also insisted on literature's powerful effects). In contrast, oral interpreters were likely to connect the emotional experience of literature with the rest of emotional life. Curry presented reading aloud as a practice requiring students to encounter the emotional significance of what was read, countering the "cold, mechanical," and implicitly philological study of literature in which "[w]ords may be only so many facts to us and sympathies remain unstirred."[43] Like aesthetic critics, the proponents of oral interpretation were at odds with philology, not only for leaving aside (at least sometimes) larger questions of how passages fit into the whole but also for promoting a kind of examination that discouraged emotional engagement.

Not surprisingly, some of the most prominent interpretive critics who opposed philology, critics previously cast as generalists or belletrists, cultivated expressive oral reading. Bliss Perry, who began his academic career as an instructor of elocution and English and ended as professor of English literature at Harvard, promoted oral reading's interpretive significance (in relation to the key aesthetic criterion of unity) and its emotional element:

> The most perfect test of one's appreciation of the parts as related to the whole is doubtless to read the poem aloud. To do this adequately, as I have said elsewhere, "necessitates something more than a translation of the symbolism into terms of the understanding; it requires an interpretation of the emotional element in the poem, of that indeed which has made it a poem."[44]

Yet Perry privileged silent encounters with print texts when he went on to encourage readers, once they became good at reading aloud, to "read silently henceforward. The melodies unheard are sweeter!"[45] Richard Moulton, who in England and at the University of Chicago led university extension courses, made oratory and drama prominent in his conception of literature, pointing out that "oral poetry" addressed "the whole public" whereas print literature "disenfranchised" those who could not read.[46] Perhaps the strongest supporter of oral interpretation was Hiram Corson, professor of English at Cornell University. Corson was the author of *A Hand-Book of Anglo-Saxon and Early*

English (1871) and had translated Juvenal's *Satires*, but he was a stalwart opponent of the scientism he saw at work in philological studies of literature, which he identified with endless empirical accumulation rather than efforts to give students the "fullest command of [their] faculties."[47] Corson valued philological studies for establishing the proper pronunciation and voicing of early texts as well as for offering readers a deep historical understanding of how language operated, but he also advocated studying the physiology of the voice and cultivating expressive reading. Most importantly, he understood oral interpretation to be a form of literary interpretation that required harmonizing the reader's feelings with the piece read as well as understanding subtleties of language and formal unity.[48] Corson wrote somewhat skeptically about schools of oratory, but his understanding of literary studies overlapped with S. S. Curry's.

"Appreciation," the aesthetic critics' shorthand, could mean the cultivation of taste, but it could also mean emotional receptivity: indeed, receptivity was a capacity not readily assimilated to disciplinary paradigms promoting mastery.[49] As early as 1875, in a lecture about the future of universities, Corson had criticized the "Scientific Papacy" and advocated the need to develop not only students' analytic powers but also "this receptivity, this absorbent passivity," which he framed as a spiritual capacity.[50] Of course, the converse danger is that emphasizing receptivity can lead to intrusive pedagogical monitoring. Corson believed that it was less important for a student to pass an examination about previous published criticism about Gray's "Elegy Written in a Country Churchyard" than to show by his oral reading of the poem aloud "whether he had responded, to any extent, or not, to its sweet evening pensiveness, to the general tenor of the theme, [or] to the moulding of the whole."[51] It is hard to tell what place there might be in this pedagogy for principled resistance to a poem. Corson's idea of "appreciative reading" was elaborately developed, though, and was not simply the unintellectual enthusiasm often dismissed today as "appreciation."[52] Approaches like Corson's came to be deprecated not only because they emphasized the emotional labor of interpretation but also because they highlighted spirituality, even though they often invoked it in an unspecific way related to broadly humanist touchstones such as "the human spirit." The usage was not far from Emerson's, but it clashed with the independence that the modern research university sought from the forms of religious authority at work in the earlier college model.

Over the course of the twentieth century, the fine arts came to be integrated into the research university model, although creative fields have never fit seamlessly into academic models of hiring, tenure, and promotion designed to assess disciplinary scholarship. Creative writing became a standard domain within English departments. Arguably, once a framework of academic disciplines was established, the influence of the early scientific model could be countered by a competing tendency for higher education to claim comprehensive authority (and expand the purview of its credentialing) by offering an education in any valued cultural endeavor that was not merely a skill (as conventional understandings and devaluations of skills operated) and that had acquired a body of methods and theories. In the early years of academic literary studies, however, creative writing was only intermittently featured, and the pressures of disciplinarity were pitted against anything performative, perhaps because performance offered new and unprecedented renderings rather than outcomes of standard protocols.[53]

A tremendous irony of early disciplinarity lay in the fact the German university model was admired for espousing "*Lernfreiheit,* or the freedom of learning," which James Hart glossed as "the emancipation of the student from *Schulzwang*, compulsory drill by recitation."[54] Calling recitation "drill" implied that the new methods of academic assessment—written examinations and essays—would offer students more scope for taking initiatives and trying out distinctive approaches, yet one of the advantages of written forms of assessment was that they could be standardized, preserved for record keeping, and cross-checked. Essay assignments might have offered students opportunities for extended investigations and arguments, but the pressures toward standardization were at work in writing assignments, too, especially in the development of the special kind of academic composition known as a theme. The theme, geared to students' demonstrating their knowledge, analysis, and argumentation, was an apprentice version of the kind of professional academic essay that could be delivered at a conference or published in an academic journal as part of ongoing exchange among professional scholars.[55] Since themes were supposed to be original (in a way that lab reports were not), the themes that students were assigned to write hovered awkwardly between demonstrating students' mastery of disciplinary protocols and expressing students' individual experiences and views. Alexander Bain's 1866 composition manual identified the theme as a genre appropriate mainly to the sciences because of its emphasis on informational content, but the elaboration of academic disciplinarity extended the theme's range.[56] By the 1890s, Frank Norris complained that the themes required in English courses were virtually factory products. By his junior or senior year, Norris's hypothetical student "has learned to write 'themes' and 'papers' in the true academic style, which is to read some dozen text books and encyclopedia articles on the subject, and to make over the results in his own language." Not surprisingly, Norris notes, the student also "knows just where he can lay his hands upon some fifty to a hundred 'themes' written by the members of past classes, that have been carefully collected and preserved by enterprising students"—plagiarism being an adverse consequence of standard protocols and formats.[57]

Historians of composition have identified similar forms of standardization at work in late nineteenth-century composition instruction. Bain's 1866 textbook provided a schematization that became as influential as Freytag's pyramid and lists of literary conflicts: the delineation of four rhetorical modes—

narration, description, exposition, and argument. As Robert J. Connors has argued, the birth of multimodal rhetoric meant the demotion of argument, formerly the heart of rhetoric, to only one mode among others. Moreover, the kind of argumentation valued in composition instruction appears to have been mainly the kind Norris caricatured in literary courses, hobbled by implicit or explicit generic constraints and crude empiricism. Alongside multimodal rhetoric and the theme (requiring interpretation, research, or both), the personal essay emerged as a feature of composition instruction not so strongly aligned with professional academic writing, but the assumption that the personal had to be a domain remote from controversy or argument limited the range of this genre as well.[58] Norris's experience points to the extent to which student writing in literary studies was standardized, and Whitcomb's *The Study of the Novel* (1905) demonstrates how neatly the schematizing trends in literary and composition pedagogies could be combined. Whitcomb, who made use of Freytag's pyramid and Brunetière-style binary conflicts, also held that novels offered ample opportunities for "review of the formal rhetorical study of exposition, narration, and description."[59]

No one familiar with English literature (or composition) classrooms in the twentieth century would argue that students were deprived entirely of expressive oral reading, formal and informal performances of plays, or writing in a variety of genres. However, the disciplinary expulsion of performance and standardization of genres meant that performative exercises and creative writing assignments in literature courses were marked as less thoroughly and rigorously disciplinary. Arguably, they might sometimes have *been* less rigorous because they had to be freelanced by instructors rather than drawing on comprehensive disciplinary development. Creative and performative exercises could be merely fuzzy, or they could be pedagogically thoughtful; in some cases they might have been deepened by an instructor's independent knowledge of speech, drama, or creative writing. But performance was not developed as an important component of literary education, and college literature courses' forays into performance and a wider range of written genres have usually counted as enlivening pedagogical strategies rather than central disciplinary work. The self-segregation of literary studies from expressive reading and dramatic production represents another way in which academic literary studies was narrowed, in comparison with the variety of forms of literary engagement and study that had been pursued in public literary culture.

Literature as Interdisciplinary

"It is clear that the study of literature, by its inherent character, and in the nature of things, is one which must bring us in contact with many other distinct studies," Richard Moulton declared in 1915. He included in *The Modern*

Study of Literature a remarkable chart tracking the connections of literary genres to fields of study including hermeneutics, theology, mythology and folklore, philosophy, sociology, psychology, history, archeology, and philology (along with elocution and stage art).[60] As compositions in language and as representations, works of literature were necessarily entangled with objects, questions, and methods assigned to other disciplines. All disciplines have to work out overlaps, of course, but the best way to secure a new discipline was to claim for it a distinctive and exclusive object. For this reason, as I've noted, the literary canon was a crucial element in the disciplinary definition of literary studies, even though the methods of academic literary studies (including forms of literary history and philology) were from the start not completely aligned with the aesthetic rationale for canonicity. From the earliest academic institutionalization of literary studies, the discipline kept developing approaches and methods that exceeded or clashed with the aesthetic foundations of the literary canon, even after the discipline had filtered out some forms of literary studies that had operated in public literary culture. It seems likely that the expansion of the canon—and the gradual rethinking of the aesthetic criteria underlying canonicity—did not begin until the late twentieth century in part because of disciplinary inertia but also because institutional politics made it risky for literary scholars to call into question the object that named their field and held charismatic authority.

The close connection between literary studies and several other disciplines fueled what has been characterized ungenerously as literary scholars' tendency to poach. The chief disciplines in which literature had stakes were history, philosophy, and psychology, with sociology and anthropology following closely. In the case of the first three disciplines, literary studies incorporated certain features of these fields before they became disciplines—from history, the models of historical explanation that informed periodized literary history and periodized authors' careers; from philosophy, general ideas about ethics and metaphysics that shaped interpretations of particular characters and understandings of the potential thematic significance of literary works; and from psychology, ideas about human development and motivation as well as the nineteenth-century terrain of sanity and insanity (which in the twentieth century became the terrain of more complex diagnostic categories), all of which shaped discussions and characters' words and actions. Since literary studies had from its beginnings incorporated certain early features of these other disciplines, academic literary scholars sometimes wished to refresh literature's terms of engagement when they glimpsed new developments.

A. C. Bradley's *Shakespearean Tragedy* (1904) demonstrates that quite restricted versions of history, philosophy, and psychology were incorporated into academic literary studies and naturalized as components of literary analysis. Bradley became the Oxford Professor of Poetry in 1901, having been previously appointed a Regius Professor at the University of Glasgow.[61] *Shakespearean*

Tragedy was a threshold text between the (mainly nonacademic) literary criticism of the nineteenth century and the professionalized literary criticism of the twentieth.[62] It was one of the influential early texts to use Freytag's pyramid and draw on sets of conflicts consistent with the Brunetière tradition, and no doubt the continuing influence of Bradley throughout the twentieth century helped perpetuate these apparatuses.[63] In this study, Bradley rhetorically positioned himself in a literary culture bigger than the academy, apologizing that his notes would be of interest "only to scholars" and explaining that although he would cite some debts to earlier critics, he was not conscientiously tracking them: "most of my reading of Shakespearean criticism was done many years ago, and I can only hope that I have not often reproduced as my own what belongs to another."[64] However, Bradley's citations were conspicuously disciplinary. His scanty notes mainly acknowledged professors (Edward Dowden, Karl Werder, Hermann Ulrici, Richard Green Moulton), literary authors of high standing (Algernon Swinburne, who published *A Study of Shakespeare* in 1880, and Coleridge), and foundational figures in modern aesthetics (Hegel and Friedrich Schlegel). He cited few U.S. Shakespeareans and hardly any nonacademic scholars, even though many U.S. nonacademic scholars had made contributions to Furness's Variorum, which Bradley cited (Furness himself being a nonacademic whose contribution could not be overlooked).

In an artfully casual way, Bradley set out a domain of literary criticism that somehow homogenized what was brought into it. It wove in history in the form of Shakespeare's biography—for instance, Shakespeare had a "tragic period" that may have been a time when he was "heavily burdened in spirit"—but disavowed any knowledge of "Shakespeare's personal feelings and attitude."[65] The periodizing of Shakespeare's body of work was set out in a note as a convenience to readers, capturing what Bradley deemed a reasonable critical consensus.[66] Neither Shakespeare's personal religious beliefs nor the theology of the plays was significant for Bradley, though, since he stipulated that Elizabethan drama had been "secular" and took for granted that Shakespeare "confined his view to the world of non-theological observation and thought."[67] Separating Shakespeare's plays even further from the social and political world Shakespeare had inhabited, Bradley identified the true setting of the tragedies as a "tragic world" dominated by a system or order more powerful than individuals' intentions—a world suited to the genre and characters.[68] This stance also precluded any Snider-style attention to power relations and institutions.

Psychology was absorbed into the analysis of character, which Bradley made central and differentiated firmly from attention to anything "external," such as the politics of the Danish court, in the case of *Hamlet*. Following Aristotle, he attributed to each tragic protagonist a "tragic trait," "fatal" but also the source of "greatness," and without using the word "foil" he proposed that certain characters were designed "to throw the character of the hero into relief."[69]

Literary studies had incorporated psychology casually, while it was still an incipient discipline, a specialty in medicine and philosophy—indeed, Coleridge was one of the first to describe Shakespeare's characterization as "psychological."[70] Any representational understanding of literature's development of character meant that there were reasons for literature to engage the discipline of psychology and vice versa. One of the best-known literary questions of the nineteenth century was the controversy over whether Hamlet was mad (or insane, a diagnostic category keyed to questions of legal responsibility), and the enthusiasm with which alienists and physicians working at insane asylums entered into the question led many literary scholars to reclaim their authority over this question vehemently.[71] Bradley followed the mainstream literary insistence that Hamlet might be "melancholy," welcoming any "pathologist" who might diagnose the "species" of melancholy at work, but insisted that Hamlet was not insane, implying that no further contributions by pathologists and their ilk were needed.[72] Psychological interpretation that did not mark itself as the product of a specific school—that was not conspicuously disciplinary—could count as simply literary; incursions into psychology that had to be marked and explained or that were conducted by psychologists (as in the case of Ernest Jones's 1910 Freudian analysis of *Hamlet*) counted as interdisciplinary and posed challenges to literary authority.[73] The loose psychological understandings that had been incorporated into literary studies in the early disciplinary era held a default authority within literary studies, whereas new contributions risked being dismissed as alien grafts onto literature or literary studies.

Bradley also practiced a mode of ethical attention to literature that could be lopped off from larger philosophical investigations. The insistence that heroes, to be tragic, had to be morally responsible and therefore could not be insane had been sounded often in earlier debates about Hamlet's madness, and the point was directly connected to the ethical mission of literature, insofar as readers might identify with characters and their decisions. With considerable subtlety, Bradley argued that even though the tragic world does not practice anything like poetic justice—since what tragic protagonists suffer may not be what they deserve, and since we as readers are not in a position to decide what they deserve—it offers a standpoint that is not "indifferent to good and evil" but rather "akin to good and alien from evil." The sense of inevitability that tragedy might generate, "[giving] rise to the idea of fate," manifests the literary affirmation of a "moral order" consisting, in Kantian fashion, of laws nonetheless compatible with human freedom: "the moral order acts not capriciously or like a human being, but from the necessity of its nature, or, if we prefer the phrase, by general laws."[74] The preeminence of Kant in late nineteenth-century academic philosophy was in this way inscribed in moral understandings, or at least inscriptions of general moral tendencies, that could be treated as literary equipment requiring neither explanation nor direct engagement with philosophy.[75]

Bradley mainly left textual criticism aside, except for occasional notes referencing differences between quarto and folio versions of the plays, and any very technical discussion of such issues would have fit poorly into Bradley's approach. The analysis of character was his mainspring, and careful attention to imagery and other patterns of language contributed to his analysis of individual characters or groups of characters.[76] Within the terms of his analysis, Bradley was exhaustive: the attention to minutiae that L. D. Knights later criticized in *How Many Children Had Lady Macbeth?* (1933) served a critical approach that was psychological (though conducted utterly apart from the new academic discipline of psychology) and ethical (though conducted utterly apart from philosophy's subdiscipline of ethics) but not impressionistic, being grounded instead in the careful selection and treatment of textual evidence.[77] For example, having laid out his argument in lecture 3 that Hamlet, who had before his father's death been a man capable of decisive action, is presented to us only after he has been weakened by melancholy, Bradley begins lecture 4 by explaining that the only way "in which a conception of Hamlet's character could be proved true, would be to show that it, and it alone, explains all the relevant facts presented by the text of the drama"—as lecture 4 goes on to do.[78] *Shakespearean Tragedy* includes thirty-two appendix-style notes at the end working through Bradley's solutions to a host of traditional interpretive questions (and a few textual ones with big interpretive stakes), further demonstrating his empirical rigor.

Bradley's *Shakespearean Tragedy* was admiringly reviewed in the United States (and England, echoing across the Atlantic) when it was published. Another sense in which it was a threshold text is that it did not circulate only in the world of academic journals, then becoming a separate publishing domain, but was discussed and reviewed in newspapers and magazines.[79] *Shakespearean Tragedy* was one of the texts by which Oxbridge reclaimed academic authority about British texts, in spite of having been so late in developing English as a field of study, and it put forth within Shakespeare studies—the foundation of Anglo-American literary studies—a highly disciplinary, somewhat schematized, but textually nuanced version of aesthetic literary studies. Bradley's approach famously became a staple of exams, and its instructional afterlife in the United States and Great Britain has not yet ended.[80] As a supercanonical work of criticism about the chief author of the literary supercanon, it helped to demarcate the turf of literary studies, contributing to the definition of literary studies that compelled many literary scholars who wished to engage updated versions of historical, philosophical, and psychological questions to become poachers. Interdisciplinary scholarship and teaching need no special justification, but at least some of this poaching was designed to renovate the outposts of other disciplines embedded in the foundation of literary studies. Literary studies was from its beginnings closely intermeshed with a few neighboring disciplines, a circumstance that may have whetted literary scholars' appetite for interdisciplinary approaches.

Literature as Antidisciplinary

If literature was within Coleridge's tradition an important moral source—if it played an important role in developing fundamental human capacities, by providing unique subjective experiences that contributed to readers' self-regulation and self-understanding—then how could it also become the subject of exclusive credentialing?[81] If it was everyone's cultural legacy—"truth, not individual and local, but general, and operative," in Wordsworth's terms—how could it become the property of experts?[82] The idea that academic disciplines needed to take the physical sciences as their model was also at odds with the belief that aesthetic objects needed to be protected from disenchanting analysis (disenchantment being a favorite trope of antimodernism). Romantic understandings of literature tended to be antidisciplinary, and the sense that aesthetic experience is by its nature unpredictable continues to be important within literary studies. As a result, aesthetic value is necessarily difficult to formulate or standardize, and modes of instruction and scholarship that try to convey and elicit a sense of the aesthetic are likely to be different from modes of instruction and scholarship privileging empirical understanding. Aesthetic approaches to literature are based fundamentally on literature's capacity to offer a special way of knowing and experiencing the world, whereas things that can be empirically asserted about literature might not address its catalytic quality.

The English professors who were aesthetic critics, though often remembered as generalists, were not themselves unspecialized, but critiques of the particular mode of specialization involved in expertise were often launched from their position.[83] These critiques addressed ways in which literary studies has been from the outset antidisciplinary: resistant to specialization, to the expert-amateur divide created by disciplinarity, and to the tendency for undergraduate teaching to be devalued compared to research and graduate teaching. To grasp the antidisciplinary dimensions of literary studies, it is important to consider the structural effects of disciplinary expertise, as it has operated in the U.S. academy, as well as the related effects of academic professionalism.

In the research university model, the organization of disciplines serves credentialing: professional credentialing, for graduate and professional students, and the hazier credentialing of undergraduates earning bachelor's degrees. As a result, the intellectual construction of disciplines is enmeshed with this instrumental function.[84] The traditional professions—law, medicine, and theology—were fields requiring practitioners to acquire a command of authoritative bodies of knowledge, but before the onset of the research university model, there was no standardized method for accrediting practitioners. Prospective lawyers apprenticed informally with practicing lawyers, as Charles Brockden Brown did; Frank Norris's fictional dentist McTeague (in *McTeague* [1899]) had had a similarly informal career preparation, and that is why late-century licensing laws put him out of business. The reorganization of knowledge around the model of expertise was the transformation of fields of knowledge into disciplines and the vesting of universities and professional organizations with the power of credentialing, which was for some professions legally enforced (hence McTeague's plight). In the latter decades of the nineteenth century, numerous professions were created, formalized, or upgraded, and questions of professional standards and privileges were elaborated in relation to many forms of work that did not become full-fledged professions.[85]

Historians of professionalism have attributed the special authority of professionals to the persistence of a feudal structure of authority, with the power differential between feudal lords and subjects approximated by the power differential between professionals and clients who are vulnerable or in pain or crisis, perhaps made desperate and dependent.[86] The development of professions emphasized the discretionary judgment and expansive authority of professionals. Professionals are paid partly for what they know, even in some ways for who they are, even if their rate of pay is calculated on the basis of hours worked or professional tasks performed. Not all professionals thrive economically, but the gating mechanisms of credentialing and licensing (which require would-be professionals to invest in their educations) make it likely that professionals will be comparatively well off. This is the reason why humanities professors complain that they don't make as much money as physicians or attorneys, not plumbers (however highly paid plumbers might be): the whole machinery that makes income an indicator of social value leads professionals to expect to be part of an economic and social elite, partly because of their years of education but also because of the cultural value of what they provide.[87]

Viewed solely in economic terms, expert professionalism is a formation that allows practitioners to commodify and purvey an immaterial product, expertise: as Timothy Lenoir has proposed, "disciplines are embedded in market relationships regulating the production and consumption of knowledge."[88] Access to higher education determines access to professional status, and the liberal arts mission of higher education adds to the charismatic authority of academic professionals, reinforcing the idea that professors are learned people in an expansive sense, even if they have to specialize to be credentialed.[89] Underlying the invention of the research university, the transformation of fields of knowledge into disciplines, and the burgeoning of academic professionalism was the university's successful and profitable bid to become the pipeline to credentialing and therefore a powerful engine in the reproduction of class hierarchy. In the crudest terms, the construction of expertise in literary studies appropriated (and winnowed) the intellectual resources of the commons, resulting in a monopolistic formation that concentrated resources for scholarship and teaching but limited the public's access to them.

The humanities, whose value has traditionally been defined as noninstrumental in spite of the many purposes ascribed to them, have always resisted acknowledging the instrumental character of credentialing and the class privilege marked by access to higher education, even though elitism has never been alien to the pursuit of art and culture. Indeed, all fields of knowledge have had to navigate the paradoxes involved in advancing knowledge (according to the modern logic of progress embedded in the legitimation of higher education), a task that is supposed to be undertaken in the service of large collectives (the nation, the world, humanity), while charging for direct access and offering indirect access only through the inferior mode of popularization. ("To popularize usually means to superficialize," Denton Snider noted disapprovingly in the course of laying out his goal instead of "deepen[ing]" the "popularity" of the books he taught.)[90] These paradoxes are produced by capitalism, not by some failing unique to higher education, but they produce the greatest strains in undertakings for which the highest and most comprehensive forms of human value are claimed. My point is not that no one working in higher education should be paid or that they should be paid less but that academics need to recognize how deeply academic literary studies is impacted by the economics and politics of expert professionalism.

More than some other disciplines, literary studies was transformed and diminished in the course of becoming a specialist endeavor set apart from the public. Ordinary people who admire rocky outcroppings may not understand their geological significance, but geology as a discipline is not designed to elaborate the meaning or potential meaning of rocks to humans. To focus on that response would not be to deny the physical existence and properties of rocks and terrains, but it would reorient geology profoundly. In contrast, literary studies has always been designed at least partly to explain why and how certain texts matter to people and affect people, privileging the real or possible effects that include the range of amalgamated emotional-cognitive (and maybe spiritual) experiences we count as aesthetic. The grounds for expert understanding of literature are therefore more elusive and potentially controversial than the grounds for expert understanding of rock formations. The tacit formalism of literary studies, which even before the onset of disciplinarity often treated print (and manuscript) as if it operated independently of readers' activities, mystifies the nature of literary interpretation, although readers' literary educations may expand their repertoires as readers, offering them new reading experiences as well as additional material for reflection. Structurally, the creation of literary experts implied that lay readers might be reading wrong, or at least that only experts could determine the value of lay reading—which was very close to determining the value of lay reading experiences. It's no wonder that literary expertise has engendered resentment.

It's also no wonder that conjoined with the disparagement of amateurs around the turn of the century was a new regard for what was valuable about amateur—that is, nonexpert, unprofessional, not thoroughly disciplinary—approaches to literature. Deidre Shauna Lynch has called attention to academic readers' chronic fascination with amateur or lay readers, who are envisioned to enjoy pleasures that academics lose through excessive education.[91] It's possible that the fascination is chronic because the expert-amateur divide has so often been adjusted and reconceived, although of course every credentialed expert also negotiates the boundary personally. The tendency to romanticize amateur reading as wholly free and discretionary may also account for the tendency, in histories of academic English, to identify only the philologists with disciplinary professionalism, not the aesthetic critics: modernity's rational instrumentality can be abstracted as hostile to pleasure and embodied life, but the outcomes of instrumentality and disciplinarity must always include routings of pleasure and accommodations to embodiment. Nevertheless, deployments of the amateur also measure the institutional costs of expertise and may register as well the countervailing intellectual significance of the "heterogenous, unpredictable ways we encounter and make use of books and texts," as Stephanie Foote puts it.[92] Frank Norris's complaint about academic literary studies at the University of California in the 1890s posited the college sophomore as a figure sacrificed to standardized forms of literary instruction:

> "Classification" is the one thing desirable in the eyes of the professors of "literature" at the University of California. The young Sophomore, with his new, fresh mind, his active brain and vivid imagination, with ideas of his own, crude, perhaps, but first hand, not cribbed from text books. This type of young fellow, I say, is taught to "classify," is set to work counting the "metaphors" in a given passage. This is actually true—tabulating them, separating them from the "similes," comparing the results. He is told to study sentence structure. He classifies certain types of sentences in De Quincey and compares them with certain other types of sentences in Carlyle. He makes the wonderful discovery—on suggestions from the instructor—that De Quincey excelled in those metaphors and similes relating to rapidity of movement. Sensation![93]

Agnes Repplier's somewhat nostalgic idealization of child readers who could roam at will in libraries, part of her protest against Howells's creation of a realist orthodoxy, similarly suggested that readerly independence was put at risk, in this case not by academics but by a literary establishment that claimed an analogous kind of modern authority.[94] The Romantic sense that children are born "trailing clouds of glory" lost as they mature dovetailed with the Emersonian conviction that individuals are fundamentally at odds with "society" (a stance built into the Brunetière-style conflict between "man and society" examined in chapter 5). The Romantic child was the ur-version of Norris's sophomore, and the Romantic child, like the Romantic genius, was designed as the obverse of regimentation, standardization, and other instrumentalizing processes.[95]

Chapter 4 examines Wharton's biting satires of amateur literary studies in "Xingu" and "The Pelican," but over her lifetime Wharton struggled with the division between expert and amateur. Her first book, *The Decoration of Houses* (1897), coauthored with Ogden Codman, Jr., aligned the authors with experts, criticizing the "unscientific methods" of the "lay mind" insofar as lay people thought of decoration as mere ornament rather than as the extension and fulfillment of architectural design.[96] (Streamlining was in the offing here, as in contemporary studies of drama and short stories.) Wharton and Codman drew on the work of experts to advise private people who had the means to undertake innovations in décor—people whose uptake would make a difference. Structurally, the authors operated as popularizers, but Wharton and Codman were not credentialed experts. Wharton's *A Backward Glance* reveals that *The Decoration of Houses* faced initial skepticism at the press because most architects were not interested in decoration, nor was it clear that the public influenced by architects would be. Like Richard Grant White, Wharton operated as an ally or agent of credentialed professionals, but the position was precarious.

As an author who aspired to professionalism but did not have any institutional credentialing—and could not have been formally credentialed for authorship—Wharton was understandably ambivalent about the phenomenon.[97] Wharton's alignment with experts is also indicated in *A Backward Glance* when she describes her ongoing education in the visual arts, including her admiration for the "scientific accuracy" of art scholars such as Giovanni Morelli and Bernard Berenson, who developed scientific methods of attribution and authentication. This education in more scientific approaches to visual culture led to her becoming embarrassed about her earlier admiration for writers such as Walter Pater and John Addington Symonds (identified as practitioners of "literary 'appreciations'").[98] At another point in her memoir, though, she circles back to what was left behind by the rigors of expertise:

> The application of scholarly standards to the judgment of works of art certainly helped to clear away the sentimental undergrowth which had sprung up in the wake of the gifted amateur; but nowadays, as was almost certain to happen, the very critics who did the necessary clearing have come to recognize that, their task once done, there remains the imponderable something, the very soul of the work contemplated, and that this something may be felt and registered by certain cultivated sensibilities, whether or not they have been disciplined by technical training. There remains a field of observation wherein the mere lover of beauty can open the eyes and sharpen the hearing of the receptive traveler, as Pater, Symonds, and Vernon Lee had done to readers of my generation.[99]

Wharton's admiration for Harry Cust (a British member of Parliament renowned for his conversation, whom she called "one of the most eager and radio-active intelligences in London, unhappily too favoured by fortune to have been forced to canalize his gifts") and for the exquisite nonprofessional intellectual culture provided by Parisian hostesses also registered her attraction to the valuable intellectual and aesthetic contributions made outside professional formations.[100]

The lead essay in Bliss Perry's *The Amateur Spirit* (1904) confronted the new organization of knowledge more directly, seeking to reclaim the best of amateurism. The essays in the volume were written while Perry was editor of the *Atlantic Monthly*, where most of them were published, and was also teaching at Princeton University. *The Amateur Spirit* includes several essays that take a sociological approach to academia, analyzing university life and college professors for the wider audience of the *Atlantic* and beyond. Perry had studied at Strassburg University in the 1880s but had not pursued a PhD, writing of his generation studying abroad, "None of us dreamed, of course, that within the next thirty years American colleges would insist upon a Ph.D. degree as a requisite for promotion, that its commercial value would consequently be reckoned with the precision of an actuarial table, and that all the academic 'go-getters' would take it in their stride."[101] This was the phenomenon that William James criticized as the "[t]he Ph.D. Octopus" in the essay from which one of my epigraphs is taken, and James's account lambastes the institutional status seeking involved as well as the overvaluation of research at the expense of teaching ("Will any one pretend for a moment that the doctor's degree is a guarantee that its possessor will be successful as a teacher?").[102] Perry had become a college professor effectively through old boys' networks: as a Williams College graduate in 1881 (and the son of a Williams College professor), he was hired at Williams as an instructor and then promoted. He studied on his own to consolidate his knowledge in preparation for the position.[103] His interest in the figure of the amateur may well have been shaped by his experience having designed his own graduate education, between informal studies and his German coursework.

Perry's discussion, like Wharton's, loops backs to value the amateur from within a worldview in which the expert professional must take—indeed, has already taken—priority. Perry defines the amateur and the professional as types or tendencies, emphasizing the amateur spirit's power to curb "this special development—this purely professional habit of mind" which otherwise risks "[injuring] the symmetry of character" and "impairing the varied and spontaneous and abundant play of human powers which gives joy to life."[104] The professional represents the path of progress, fulfilling the requirements of modern competition; the amateur is the corrective, following the logic by which the aesthetic compensates for the specialization and hyperrationalization of modernity.[105] Perry's development of the figure was further invested with a special U.S. significance. Writing a little more than a decade after Frederick Jackson Turner announced the closing of the frontier, Perry connected the "amateur spirit" to the legacies of pioneers: "[v]ersatility, enthusiasm, freshness of spirit, initiative, a fine recklessness of tradition and precedent, [and] a faculty for cutting across lots."[106]

Perry presents amateurism and professionalism as intellectual and temperamental tendencies, playing out in the modern university but floating free of its determinants. Just as Schiller had formulated the naïve and the sentimental not as stark historical alternatives but as stances available to moderns, Perry converts the historical devaluation of the amateur (which, as I've noted, reduced all the uncredentialed to amateur status) into a plenitude of options: anyone might choose between the orientations that epitomize amateurism and professionalism or might combine the best of them. Indeed, Perry's most optimistic proposal was that that liberal arts education was coming to produce "amateurs without amateurishness, professionals untainted by professionalism," insofar as it offered not only "specialized training" and scientific methods, but also forms of intellectual nourishment that could offset or complement them: "unquenched ardor for the best things, spontaneous delight in the play of mind and character, a many-sided responsiveness that shall keep a man from hardening into a mere high-geared machine."[107] His account suggests that the rationale for the liberal arts, and especially the division among arts and sciences (later, among physical sciences, social sciences, and humanities), involved attributing modernizing functions to the sciences and social sciences, whereas the humanities were designed to cultivate capacities that offset modernity.[108]

Early aesthetic critics tended to be interdisciplinary, as we have seen, but also antidisciplinary, skeptical of features of the research university model and oriented toward public literary culture. Not all aesthetic critics admired Chautauqua circles, correspondence courses, and Shakespeare and Browning Societies, of course, but there was a good deal of traffic between aesthetic critics and those stretches of public literary culture. For instance, in addition to being active in the university extension movement, Richard G. Moulton of the University of Chicago lectured at the Kindergarten College, taught at Chautauqua, and contributed to the Boston Browning Society. Other Browning Society members or occasional participants included Hiram Corson and Bliss Perry, Professors Vida D. Scudder and Katharine Bates of Wellesley College, Professor William Lyon Phelps of Yale, and Harvard's James Russell Lowell (not, apparently, a very active member).[109] Corson's *The Aims of Literary Study* (1896) brought together essays previously published in *Poet-Lore*, and he also contributed to the *Chautauquan* (as did Katharine Lee Bates, who published a textbook, *American Literature*, for use in Chautauqua circles).[110]

These working academics did not, like the outsiders Thomas Davidson and Denton Snider in chapter 4, consider higher education fundamentally pernicious, but they worked to offset at least some of the things Davidson and Snider criticized by retaining an expansive sense of literature's intellectual connections and by operating to extend the university's resources and collaborate in public literary culture. Their antidisciplinarity was cast as concern and mistrust, not protest, but they identified many of the features of university-based literary studies that are still troubling: the potential for the credentialing mechanisms of universities to drive scholarship and undermine pedagogy; limited and unequal access to higher education; the overvaluation of the rational and empirical methods of the sciences (which do not constitute the full intellectual repertoire even of the sciences, of course) and the extension of these methods to fields of inquiry where they don't fit; and the creation of an artificial gulf between the credentialed and the uncredentialed, between disciplinary insiders and outsiders. It makes sense that academics with ties to public literary culture and nonacademic scholars would be in a position to notice the shortcomings of academic literary studies. They knew that literary studies could be practiced and promoted in other ways.

Coda

Since the 1960s, as a result of the influence of literary and cultural theory; the influence of cultural studies, popular cultural studies, middlebrow studies, studies of fan cultures, and performance studies; and the canon wars, academic literary studies has reclaimed and developed many of the possibilities that were foreclosed or marginalized during its early disciplinary life. The conglomerate known as "Theory" was a multiform challenge to disciplinary business as usual, offering opportunities not simply to poach but to rework and deepen literature's connections to political science and political philosophy (and more broadly to analyses of power), economics (building on decades of Marxist criticism, a stalwart minority tradition in literary studies), psychoanalysis and other forms of psychology, sociology (through new forms of reception studies and analyses of institutions), linguistics and philology, history, philosophy, and anthropology. Theory made the politics of knowledge a crucial consideration within disciplinary scholarship.[111] Omnivorous categories such as "discourse" and "textuality" allowed literary scholars to revisit the ways in which the dynamic circulation of language had always pressed against the boundaries of disciplinarity. The expansion of literary attention to new objects, named as the expansion or revision of the canon, weakened the glue of literary studies as a discipline, but since familiar forms of analysis and figures from older canons continued to appear in curricula and scholarship, the effects of the transformation were muffled.

What was treated in public culture as a great shake-up in literary studies did not bring drastic changes, in large measure because the machinery of disciplinarity was well equipped—perhaps too well equipped—to assimilate the new ingredients. One ironic consequence was that Theory, which carried the potential for radical critique of individual disciplines and the organization of the research university, became a domain for elite professional attainment, resulting in the disorienting development of a star system for rebels. The incongruity of this phenomenon contributed to the polarizing effects of Theory and no doubt inhibited its impact, although there is no doubt that Theory opened up important new territories for literary studies. Some important legacies of theoretical writings, along with the more general theoretical call to beware of our routines and comfort zones, operate in literary studies today more flexibly, without the elaborate performances of deference or citation formerly exacted.

English departments in the United States were famously (though not uniformly or unanimously) hospitable to Theory, and the history of the nineteenth-century invention of literature I've been recounting suggests why. The yoking of public-oriented and aesthetic-oriented understandings of literature meant that the discipline was founded on a contradiction, albeit one managed elegantly by the organization of a (somewhat) aesthetically derived canon within public-oriented literary periods. It's impossible for any discipline to be grounded in perfectly consistent rationality, of course, but this contradiction may have been especially provocative, alerting literary scholars to the fact that intellectual work isn't solely rational, that power relations and the sedimented histories of power relations impact it, and (in a deconstructive key) that language is both formative and invented. The interdisciplinary and antidisciplinary orientations of literary studies also provided reasons for scholars to be less invested in the singularity of aesthetic experience and in narrow versions of aesthetic autonomy, opening them to rethinking earlier grounds of canonicity.

Our discipline has been transformed, and, surprising as it might seem, in some ways we are closer to nineteenth-century public literary culture and early aesthetic critics than we are to A. C. Bradley. It's not that current literary scholarship is directly descended from Delia Bacon, Denton Snider, Richard Moulton, or Charlotte Porter and Helen A. Clarke. In the last few decades, though, literary studies and literary pedagogy have reincorporated a number of concerns that A. C. Bradley would have ruled out of bounds but that nineteenth-century public literary culture and the academics friendly to it entertained: the political work of literature, including its potential to shape political visions and energize activism; literature's potential to investigate subjective experience outside rationality or sanity; the emotional effects of literature, now reframed by affect studies; the importance of performance, now informed by scholarship about embodiment; the interpretive value of creative, fan-culture-style responses to literature; and the kind of expanded canon represented by the *Library of American Literature*, but made more genuinely inclusive. The nineteenth-century figures I have showcased were not ahead of their time. Rather, the narrow disciplinarity of the early research university set back literary studies, and we have only in the last few decades been catching up.

At present, we face new challenges. Fewer students are able to afford the cost of higher education on the liberal arts model, and public confidence in its credentialing value—especially for humanities majors—has ebbed. Tenured faculty lines, which are designed to be crucial to the research mission of the university, faculty governance, and the protection of academic freedom, are dwindling, and many of them are being converted to non-tenure-stream positions. There is no consensus about how to value (intellectually and institutionally) and compensate (financially) the contributions of non-tenure-stream faculty in relation to those of tenure-stream faculty, yet undergraduate literary education is being conducted increasingly by non-tenure-stream instructors whose teaching load frees up tenure-stream faculty members for research. There is uncertainty about how many humanities PhDs ought to be produced, and the backlog of PhDs looking for work has made it easy to hire non-tenure-stream faculty for modest, even exploitative salaries. These conditions, which have been widely publicized, affect universities at large.

Higher education has responded to these conditions in several ways, including the good strategies of promoting the value of undergraduate teaching in universities and in some cases improving non-tenured faculty pay and working conditions. A less constructive response has been an obsession with measurement, which has at its best required faculty members to think more about the specific impacts of their work but which has also encouraged the belief that rating something on a numeric scale is the most reliable way of assessing it and the most valuable currency of accountability. This obsession harks back to the early influence of laboratory sciences on disciplinarity itself, which marked a setback for literary studies. The humanities, including literary studies, have resources for offering an important critique of the assumptions about disciplinarity and professional credentialing at work in ratings and measurement, especially since the value of literary studies and other humanities disciplines has always been grounded partly in their capacity to resist instrumental rationality. (As we've seen, literature was also endowed with modernizing functions, and as I've argued throughout this book, the category of the modern is a tendentious one that should be taken with a grain of salt. The association of the humanities with qualitative analysis is nonetheless important to pit against the imperative to quantify.)

Resistance to these measures cannot rest on the charismatic expert professional authority of humanities professors, however, as if faculty members ought simply to be unaccountable to their institutions and their students. As I've suggested, resistance also can't rest on an appeal to centuries of unbroken academic practice, because that isn't true. The fact that literary studies doesn't fit well into instrumental rationales for higher education is a reminder that higher education has never been solely instrumental. Given how many academic majors do not provide direct preprofessional preparation, colleges and universities that feature the liberal arts need to do a better job of defining what kind of preparation a liberal arts major—any major—entails, rather than making particular liberal arts departments compete against each other for majors and compare placement figures. If university X determines that anyone who completes one of its liberal arts majors will have certain skills and intellectual resources, the credentialing function can be detached from the specious attempt to discover whether the experiences of writing, research, collaborative analysis, and exploration offered by anthropology, art history, or astronomy render graduates more employable. The university should not compel departments to compete against each other for majors and should not devalue the importance of providing elective courses, which can be as valuable for students as courses required for majors.

The erosion of the category of literature has made it more challenging to define and present the distinctive value of literary studies within the larger mission of the humanities or liberal arts. Yet public literary culture is thriving, in large measure because the Internet provides spaces for serious reflection and exchange outside academia. Reading groups and other forms of personal and print exchange about literature remain important in public culture, but the Internet's capacity to offer sites for large-scale exchange and collaboration outside expert control has allowed people to formulate and enact resistance to expert monopolies. As Elizabeth Renker argues, "We have entered an age of collective intellectual power, emblematized by Google, citizen journalism, peer-to-peer and open-source software, file-sharing applications, wikis,...and new kinds of games involving user-generated content."[112] There is a creative ferment at work that is mainly good for literature and public culture, even though it is changing the terms of academic authority.

On Goodreads and BookRiot, on countless Wikipedia sites and author fan sites, on fan fiction sites, and on Internet sites sponsored by print publications (the *Paris Review*, the *Los Angeles Review of Books*, and so on), people write about literature, in most cases not for money, a grade, or a professional credential. Some of the sites are friendly to older or newer academic traditions of interpreting and valuing literary works, but many Internet sites signal their commons ethos by distancing themselves from academic language and protocols, as the authors or site founders understand them. For example, the TV Tropes site distances itself not only from academia but even from the academic citation practices of Wikipedia, announcing, "We are not a stuffy encyclopedic wiki. We're a *buttload* more informal. We encourage breezy language and original thought. There is No Such Thing As Notability, and no citations are needed."[113] Targeting a literary divide likely to be identified with academic literary studies (though not consistently found there), Book Riot's mission statement declares, "We think you can like both J. K. Rowling and J. M. Coetzee and that there are smart, funny, and informative things to say about both and that you shouldn't have to choose."[114] These sites may circulate ways of thinking that also circulate in academia, but they don't defer to expert guidance.

As the name of the TV Tropes site suggests, what I'm calling public literary culture is not defined by a common literary canon or even an exclusive devotion to literature, in the nineteenth-century sense. TV Tropes, which began as a website devoted to *Buffy the Vampire Slayer*, brings together television, film, novels, fan fiction, video games, and other genres.[115] Its home page announces that it is a site for "*celebrating* fiction" and also provides a "catalog of the tricks of the trade for writing fiction," but its audience appears to comprise mainly people who are intense and thoughtful readers, viewers, or users of the cultural texts featured on the site. The site features distinctive genres such as the "liveblog"—a "detailed walkthrough of a work, usually done in installments," offering some of the pleasures of a close reading or a shot-by-shot analysis—and combines reviewing, narratology, genre analysis, and a variety of interpretive approaches. The term "literature," operating in many ways and usually not well defined, is alive and well on Internet sites about reading—see for example Jason Diamond's "The 25 Best Websites for Literature Lovers" on Flavorwire.[116] However, the strict delineation of a canon of valued texts, a set of genres, or even of a medium seems to be less important to these sites than a commonality in the way the participants care and think about these cultural texts. In other words, the sites examine objects that respond well to a set of shared approaches—by and large approaches that were developed within academic literary studies or that are legible within academic literary studies (or neighboring academic studies of cultural and media forms)—that are deployed on these sites casually, creatively, and with looser and more short-term obligations to previous contributions. Broadly speaking, what I'm calling contemporary public literary culture—to mark its continuities with the nineteenth-century version I've been examining—is the public practice of cultural studies, conducted by nonacademics (and some academics who join on the same basis as anyone else) in a variety of formats, many hosted on the Internet or supported by the Internet.

There is no reason to believe that the Internet will replace academic literary studies as a framework for research or teaching, although online courses, proprietary series of academic lectures, and peer-reviewed online publications have narrowed the gap. Much more than academic literary studies, Internet literary culture focuses on contemporary works: academic websites (many of them open source) and academic publications still offer the best resources for studying anything produced earlier than the twentieth century. The Internet hasn't taken up a serious share of higher education's role as caretaker for legacy texts. It also doesn't offer many good forums for long, complex, sustained discussions, and it doesn't offer anything like the experience of focused, graduated instruction and real-time responsiveness provided by an academic course. As was the case in nineteenth-century print channels of public literary culture, Internet literary culture often combines reflective (and affective) analysis with consumer reviewing; a new dimension of Internet culture, uncomfortably combining consumer satisfaction with public reflection, is the perpetual invitation to rate contributions ("How useful was this review?"). Internet culture is so new, so various, so decentralized, and so rapidly changing that its cumulative impact on literary culture cannot be easily assessed, but it clearly presents limitations as well as affordances.

It would be great for academics in literary studies to partner more often with secondary educators and developers of secondary curricula and textbooks, another common practice of nineteenth-century public literary culture that was diminished after disciplinarity set in. It would also be useful for academics to envision that many of our students bring to college some background in Internet literary culture (which is not, I reiterate, a unified domain). Likewise, Internet literary culture is likely to attract our graduates who are serious readers, including those who took reading practices as well as inspiration from their college courses. Rather than envisioning our courses as following and building on (or reframing) our students' high school courses and then sending them off into what we hope will be a life that includes private reading, we ought to keep in mind that undergraduate literary or cultural studies education will for many students be contextualized by their earlier and later experiences in a public literary culture hosted and shaped by the Internet. Academics can build on that culture, assess or criticize that culture, or contribute to that culture, but we will ignore it at our peril. We need to know about the public life of literary reading, which I understand to be reading that involves any of the practices developed within literary studies. We need to pay attention to public literary culture, especially its Internet infrastructure, so that we can learn more about public literary reading and about what nonacademic readers dislike or disparage about academic literary studies, justly or not.

Academic literary studies has no strictly delimited object any more—no limited set of genres, no canon with any weight beyond the set of texts often read, taught. and referenced today—but this isn't necessarily a problem. Literary studies, as it forms part of the broad repertoire of the study of language and culture, has developed valuable frameworks for examining a wide variety of cultural products, and its track records of interdisciplinary collaboration attest to its power to contribute to larger inquiries. For institutional purposes, it might make sense for scholars of alphabetic texts (manuscript, print, or digital) to continue to work together under a rubric such as literature, organized by national-imperial languages (as is mainly the case at present). But the practice of academic literary studies is bigger than the maintenance of national-imperial departments of literature and language, and new disciplinary configurations and collaborations ought to be considered. The emergence of transnational literary and culture studies suggests that at the very least we need to provide better ways for undergraduate and graduate students to work across national and linguistic boundaries. TV Tropes offers a reminder that there are reasons to look at conventional literary genres in the context of film, television, and video games—in keeping with the heritage of the sister arts that has long offered a rubric for transmedial studies.

In practice, most English departments have made room for many kinds of cultural products, and to a lesser extent so have other departments of modern languages and literatures, which are usually smaller and have less room for curricular experimentation. Nevertheless, the assumption that conventional literary genres and periods define literary studies has kept most departments from developing the implications of our expanded objects of study. Wai Chee

Dimock's *Through Other Continents: American Literature across Deep Time* (2008) is a recent influential work that points toward forms of literary study in which history is important but periodization is not, leaving room to hope that the academic job market in literary studies will not permanently be organized by historical periods and that our curricula might take on new shapes and structures.[117] The divisions between composition, rhetoric, creative writing, and literary studies within many English departments might also be reconsidered, within an understanding of academic literary studies that values a broader variety of ways of studying and engaging literature.

Nineteenth-century public literary culture and the early disciplinary period of literary studies are important for academic literary scholars to remember precisely because professional pressure to defend the current configuration of the discipline and the current organization of academic labor has been building. We need room to maneuver, rather than succumbing to the narrative that our field and our work must stay exactly as it is or that everything we care about will be lost. We need ways to hear the public dimensions of dissatisfaction with the humanities that are prompted by the monopolistic features of expertise and some deadening tendencies of disciplinarity, not merely by anti-intellectualism or disregard for the kinds of art and experience embodied in literature.

Literature as we know it was invented not so long ago, and it doesn't operate today as it operated when it was invented. The academic practices that seem entrenched today were also invented not so long ago, and there is room to experiment with them. It was not the discipline of English literary studies on its own but the whole reorganization of knowledge around professional expertise that weakened public literary culture: that turned many students and scholars and devotees and authorities (yes, and dilettantes) into amateurs and obliged them to defer to experts. The Internet is reworking that amateur-expert divide, and it is opening new possibilities for academics to partner with the public, not on the one-way street of popularization, but in more genuinely collaborative ways. Informed by this change, we may also find ways to rethink the relationships between tenure-stream and non-tenure-stream faculty, on the one hand, and instructors and undergraduate students, on the other. We may find ways to involve more people inside and outside the academy in literary research and literary education, broadly construed, and we may thereby enlist more people in the cause of making sure that the best possibilities of literary studies continue.

{ NOTES }

Introduction

1. Ludwig Wittgenstein, *Philosophical Investigations: The English Text of the Third Edition*, trans. G. E. M. Anscombe (Upper Saddle River, N.J.: Prentice Hall, 1958), 32. Terry Eagleton's dazzling opening chapter of *Literary Theory* is an important predecessor for my approach here, clearing ground as early as 1983 for literature to be both valued and recognized as "not a stable entity." Terry Eagleton, *Literary Theory: An Introduction* (Minneapolis: University of Minnesota Press, 1983), 11.

2. On "boundary-work" (which I've adapted without the hyphen), see David R. Shumway and Craig Dionne, introduction to the valuable anthology they edited, *Disciplining English: Alternative Histories, Critical Perspectives* (Albany: State University of New York Press, 2002), 6.

3. "Interesting" has been a keyword used to expand canons for some time: "The sentimental naturalist would claim the right to elect Ibsen instead of Horace simply because he finds Ibsen more 'interesting;' he thus obscures the idea of liberal culture by denying that some subjects are more humane than others in virtue of their intrinsic quality, and quite apart from individual tastes and preferences." Irving Babbitt, *Literature and the American College: Essays in Defense of the Humanities* (Boston: Houghton, Mifflin, 1908), 96.

4. For a powerful discussion of why education cannot solve the problems of poverty and inequality that we love to delegate to it, see John Marsh, *Class Dismissed: Why We Cannot Teach or Learn Our Way out of Inequality* (New York: Monthly Review Press, 2011).

5. On the "anachronistic retroprojection" of the "Lang-Lit paradigm," see Joep Leerssen, "Introduction: Philology and the European Construction of National Literatures," in Dirk Van Hulle and Joep Leerssen, eds., *Editing the Nation's Memory: Textual Scholarship and Nation-Building in 19th-Century Europe* (Amsterdam: Rodopi, 2008), 15.

The best recent transnational literary scholarship (most of which does not address literature as a specific formation within print and adjacent media) brings together geopolitical power relations and their histories, print history, and intertextual and generic flows: see, for example, Anna Brickhouse, *Transamerican Literary Relations and the Nineteenth-Century Public Sphere* (Cambridge: Cambridge University Press, 2004); and Sean X. Goudie, *Creole America: The West Indies and the Formation of Literature and Culture in the New Republic* (Philadelphia: University of Pennsylvania Press, 2006). Dominant transnational paradigms affecting the United States are primarily geopolitical: the hemispheric (Americas), the Atlantic and especially the Black Atlantic, and the Pacific Rim.

6. I don't mean to imply that other thriving disciplines are perfectly coherent: most disciplines are administrative agglomerations that have developed over time, after all. As Gerald Graff has proposed, it's not necessarily a problem if English departments do not possess a "single disciplinary definition," but it is a problem "if students and other nonprofessionals find the diverse activities of the English department mysterious and unintelligible." In a

similar spirit, I'm suggesting that the attraction of academic literary studies is waning in part because it's hard to make sense of how literary studies differs from (and connects to) cultural studies, communications, media studies, and other neighboring fields that may seem better equipped to assimilate new conditions and contents. Gerald Graff, "Is There a Conversation in this Curriculum? Or, Coherence without Disciplinarity," in James C. Raymond, ed., *English as a Discipline: Or, Is There a Plot in This Play?* (Tuscaloosa: University of Alabama Press, 1996), 11.

7. The study of popular genres is long-standing, and its place in U.S. literary studies was secured by studies such as Jane Tompkins, *Sensational Designs: The Cultural Work of American Fiction, 1790–1860* (New York: Oxford University Press, 1985); and Michael Denning, *Mechanic Accents: Dime Novels and Working-Class Culture in America* (New York: Verso, 1987). The study of middlebrow novels has gained prominence in literary studies more recently, building on Joan Shelley Rubin's *The Making of Middlebrow Culture* (Chapel Hill: University of North Carolina Press, 1992). Middlebrow culture is a twentieth-century phenomenon, but middlebrow studies has expanded our repertoire for examining texts that reverberate in the national culture or in particular subcultures. The terms on which Gordon Hutner considers twentieth-century novels resemble the public-oriented features of literature I locate in the nineteenth century: "These readers were attracted to this literature, I suggest, for its potential, not for escape, but for re-creation—the opportunity for refreshing themselves and their understanding of society, their civic identities as readers." Gordon Hutner, *What America Read: Taste, Class, and the Novel, 1920–1960* (Chapel Hill: University of North Carolina Press, 2009), 4. For an excellent discussion of how the middlebrow can be productively defined, see Beth Driscoll, *The New Literary Middlebrow: Tastemakers and Reading in the Twenty-First Century* (Basingstoke: Palgrave Macmillan, 2014).

8. Especially important here is Rita Felski's example of valuing "ordinary motives for reading—such as the desire for knowledge or the longing for escape—that are either overlooked or undervalued in literary scholarship." Felski's *The Uses of Literature* and Cristina Vischer Bruns's *Why Literature?* mark the same shift: neither of them is about canons but rather about literature and literary reading as phenomena. These studies and J. Hillis Miller's *On Literature (Thinking in Action)* are accessible accounts designed to invoke and value the unpredictable qualities of literary experience. Bruns's study, which is oriented toward literary pedagogy, culminates in a set of principles led by "[t]he priority of immersion in a text." Rita Felski, *The Uses of Literature* (Malden, Mass.: Blackwell, 2008), 14; Cristina Vischer Bruns, *Why Literature? The Value of Literary Reading and What It Means for Teaching* (New York: Continuum, 2011), 117; J. Hillis Miller, *On Literature (Thinking in Action)* (New York: Routledge, 2002).

Whereas these studies have mainly promoted to academics the value of lay reading, acknowledging also that academics may sometimes count as lay readers, Deidre Shauna Lynch uncovers the ways in which literary reading has always involved love and a host of other affective engagements, highlighting continuities between literature's life in nineteenth-century public culture and the affective life of literature in academic literary studies today. Deidre Shauna Lynch, *Loving Literature: A Cultural History* (Chicago: University of Chicago Press, 2015).

9. Many influential works of affect studies and scholarship about the commons have drawn on queer theory and critical race theory and have been shaped by activism as well as

political and cultural theory. Lauren Berlant's inspiring body of scholarship about U.S. literature exemplifies this convergence.

10. I also address philosophies of taste that were not identified by the name "aesthetics," a term that only entered widespread Anglophone usage in the middle decades of the nineteenth century. On British usage, see Jonathan Friday, introduction to Jonathan Friday, ed., *Art and Enlightenment: Scottish Aesthetics in the Eighteenth Century* (Exeter: Imprint Academic, 2004), 1. The American Periodical Series documents the emergence of the term "aesthetic" in U.S. print culture in the 1840s.

11. Important studies in this tradition are Gauri Viswanathan, *Masks of Conquest: Literary Study and British Rule in India* (New York: Columbia University Press, 1989); and Robert Crawford, ed., *The Scottish Invention of English Literature* (New York: Cambridge University Press, 1988).

12. Elizabeth Renker, *The Origins of American Literature Studies: An Institutional History* (New York: Cambridge University Press, 2007); David R. Shumway, *Creating American Civilization: A Genealogy of American Literature as an Academic Discipline* (Minneapolis: University of Minnesota Press, 1994).

13. About the imperial functions of English and British literature, see especially Viswanathan, *Masks of Conquest*; and Katie Trumpener, *Bardic Nationalism: The Romantic Novel and the British Empire* (Princeton, N.J.: Princeton University Press, 1997). For a strong polemic about the ways in which English literary education exercised social control in the service of the state, see Ian Hunter, *Culture and Government: The Emergence of Literary Education* (Houndsmill, England: Macmillan Press, 1988).

14. Anne Ruggles Gere, *Intimate Practices: Literacy and Cultural Work in U. S. Women's Clubs, 1880–1920* (Urbana: University of Illinois Press, 1997), 243.

15. As Steve Fuller argues, specifically in relation to the success of humanistic disciplines such as literary studies, "the success of a discipline's claims to worldly power is based largely on *folk* perceptions about the discipline's ability to transform the world," even if the discipline is "coy about being judged by the consequences of [its] practices." Steve Fuller, "Disciplinary Boundaries and the Rhetoric of the Social Sciences," in Ellen Messer-Davidow, David R. Shumway, and David J. Sylvan, eds., *Knowledges: Historical and Critical Studies in Disciplinarity* (Charlottesville: University Press of Virginia, 1993), 130.

16. An important discussion of the changed terrain of reading culture in an age of new "delivery systems" for books is Jim Collins's *Bring on the Books for Everybody: How Literary Culture Became Popular Culture*, which draws on media theory to analyze the new cultural locations of reading. Collins emphasizes the shift in cultural authority evidenced by widespread resistance to academic reading, even among academics. Jim Collins, *Bring on the Books for Everybody: How Literary Culture Became Popular Culture* (Durham, N.C.: Duke University Press, 2010).

17. Many scholars have urged this collaboration. See especially Renker, *Origins*, 142–143; Jeffrey J. Williams, "The Life of the Mind and the Academic Situation," in Jeffrey J. Williams, ed., *The Institution of Literature* (Albany: State University of New York Press, 2002), 219.

18. Considering "long" centuries makes use of century-based analyses but avoids overvaluing chronological divides between centuries. Eric Hobsbawm proposed a long nineteenth century in European history that stretched from the French Revolution (1789) to World War I (1914), but for my purpose, the long nineteenth century in the U.S. stretches

from the decade of the U.S. Revolution (1770s), the beginning of U.S. national laws and the official onset of nationalized cultural traditions, to the decade of World War I (1910s), when the research university model and the departmental organization of literary studies had become thoroughly established in the United States.

19. Rodrigo Lazo, "Migrant Archives: New Routes in and out of American Studies," in Russ Castronovo and Susan Gillman, eds., *States of Emergency: The Object of American Studies* (Chapel Hill: University of North Carolina Press, 2009), 36, 37.

20. In positioning British America and the United States as part of a larger set of exchanges among Europe and its former colonies, I follow the lead of scholarship such as that in Hugh Amory and David D. Hall, eds., *The Colonial Book in the Atlantic World*, vol. 1 of David D. Hall, ed., *The History of the Book in America*, 4 vols. (Cambridge: Cambridge University Press, 2000), which is centered in North America; and William St. Clair in *The Reading Nation in the Romantic Period* (Cambridge: Cambridge University Press, 2004), which is centered in Great Britain. Goudie focuses on U.S. relations to Europe's West Indian colonies, characterizing as "paranational" the early national pattern of commercial exploitation in the guise of spreading civilization (*Creole America*, 11–14).

21. Of course, there were other European conceptualizations circulating in the New World that were not prominent in Anglophone culture. Raúl Coronado's *A World Not to Come* demonstrates that New World Latino writing oriented toward Spain offered distinctive conceptual frameworks, such as ideas about modernity inflected by Spanish Catholicism, and different historical markers, such as transatlantic legislation in 1810 protecting freedom of the press in Spain and its American colonies. Raúl Coronado, *A World Not to Come: A History of Latino Writing and Print Culture* (Cambridge, Mass.: Harvard University Press, 2013), 8–11, 154–174.

22. The approach I take here has been informed by scholarship assessing the portability of many ways of thinking that were European in origin and whose significance in other parts of the world has been shaped by imperial and neoimperial power relations. As Dipesh Chakrabarty argues in a study designed to decenter European modernity, "The phenomenon of 'political modernity'—namely, the rule by modern institutions of the state, bureaucracy, and capitalist enterprise—is impossible to *think* of anywhere in the world without invoking certain categories and concepts, the genealogies of which go deep into the intellectual and even theological traditions of Europe." Dipesh Chakrabarty, *Provincializing Europe: Postcolonial Thought and Historical Difference* (Princeton, N.J.: Princeton University Press, 2000), 4. See also Talal Asad's account of the quasi-tautological nature of "European civilization" in *Formations of the Secular: Christianity, Islam, Modernity* (Stanford, Calif.: Stanford University Press, 2003), 165–170.

23. Jonathan Arac calls attention to the "disseminal powers" of English (on the basis of the rates at which works from English are translated into other languages, compared with rates of translation into English), powers augmented by the dissemination of English-language movies, TV, and music. Jonathan Arac, "Global and Babel: Language and Planet," in Wai Chee Dimock and Lawrence Buell, eds., *Shades of the Planet: American Literature as World Literature* (Princeton, N.J.: Princeton University Press, 2007), 23. In the same volume, Paul Giles argues that the globalization of U.S. culture has "also operated powerfully to disturb and dislocate the national identity of the United States itself." Paul Giles, "The Deterritorialization of American Literature," in Dimock and Buell, *Shades of the Planet*, 48.

24. Although I quote and reference usages that equate "America" with the United States and retain this usage in familiar compound terms such as "African American," otherwise I distinguish between the United States and North America or the Americas. The conflation of "U.S." with "American" is one of the mechanisms through which U.S. multilingualism was suppressed in the ideological establishment of Anglophone print culture as the domain of a national reading public. See Nancy Vogeley, *The Bookrunner: A History of Inter-American Relations—Print, Politics, and Commerce in the United States and Mexico, 1800–1830* (Philadelphia: American Philosophical Society, 2011), 22–23.

25. "Dramatic Literature," *Register of Pennsylvania*, 18 Sept. 1830, 86.

26. Christopher Hanlon, *America's England: Antebellum Literature and Atlantic Sectionalism* (Oxford: Oxford University Press, 2013); Meredith L. McGill, *American Literature and the Culture of Reprinting, 1834–1853* (Philadelphia: University of Pennsylvania Press, 2003); Elisa Tamarkin, *Anglophilia: Deference, Devotion, and Antebellum America* (Chicago: University of Chicago Press, 2008). In addition to these important studies reframing the U.S. relationship to British culture, which used to be dominated by the paradigm of autonomy-dependency, Paul Giles's formulation of "American literature as a 'bifocal' phenomenon"—constituted as an extension of British culture as well as attempting to define itself as national—characterizes my approach here as well. Paul Giles, *Transatlantic Insurrections: British Culture and the Formation of American Literature, 1730–1860* (Philadelphia: University of Pennsylvania Press, 2001), 3.

27. Fortunately, the literary movement called modernism plays only a small role in my study, so the potential confusion between modern*ist* literature—and I'll use "modernism" only to reference that movement—and the modern version of literature will be minimal within this account.

28. Although I'll be touching on some of the philosophers who most influentially theorized modernity, I won't be treating modernity in a philosophically rigorous way but rather as an interpretive framework and structure of feeling circulating in literary culture. A capsule summary of many features that I'll be identifying as modern—features explicitly or tacitly treated as modern within nineteenth-century literary culture—can be found in Anthony Giddens's *Modernity and Self-Identity: Self and Society in the Late Modern Age* (Stanford, Calif.: Stanford University Press, 1991), 14–21.

29. Michael Löwy and Robert Sayre refer to a specifically Romantic understanding of modernity, but my analysis draws in many respects on Romantic thinking without limiting its attention to the delineation of Romanticism. Michael Löwy and Robert Sayre, *Romanticism against the Tide of Modernity*, trans. Catherine Porter (Durham, N.C.: Duke University Press, 2001), 20.

30. Perry Anderson, "Modernity and Revolution," *New Left Review* 1, no. 144 (1984): 101; Marshall Berman, *All That Is Solid Melts into Air: The Experience of Modernity* (New York: Simon and Schuster, 1982).

31. Bruno Latour, *We Have Never Been Modern*, trans. Catherine Porter (Cambridge, Mass.: Harvard University Press, 1993), 76.

32. Asad, *Formations*, 13.

33. Raymond Williams, "Dominant, Residual, and Emergent," in *Marxism and Literature* (Oxford: Oxford University Press, 1977), 121–127.

34. Arjun Appadurai, *Modernity at Large: Cultural Dimensions of Globalization* (Minneapolis: University of Minnesota Press, 1996), 3.

35. The critique of the modern-traditional binary has been taken up especially in postcolonial theory. In relation to the functioning of "tradition" in western European contexts, see Michael McKeon, "Tacit Knowledge: Tradition and Its Aftermath," in Mark Salber Phillips and Gordon Schochet, eds., *Questions of Tradition* (Toronto: University of Toronto Press, 2004), 179; McKeon's discussion of tradition in *The Secret History of Domesticity* (Baltimore: Johns Hopkins University Press, 2005), xix–xx, 107–108; and Eric Hobsbawm and T. O. Ranger, eds., *The Invention of Tradition* (Cambridge: Cambridge University Press, 1992).

36. Talal Asad proposes that "[m]odern projects do not hang together as an integrated totality, but they account for distinctive sensibilities, aesthetics, moralities," and in this sense it is possible to characterize and analyze modern mindsets and phenomena without taking modernity on its own terms. Asad, *Formations*, 14.

37. Latour, *We Have Never*, 116, 133; Raymond Williams, "Structures of Feeling" in Williams, *Marxism and Literature*, 128–135.

38. Haunting the category of literature (and overlapping uncomfortably with ideas about modernity) is Romanticism, which is prominent throughout my discussion but used in a casual and conventional way to characterize writers, texts, and phenomena often associated with the movement. Since the era when literature cohered was the era later periodized within literary history as Romantic, it makes sense that many features of literature's conceptualization are aligned with Romanticism. But since literature was also established as a category projected backward in time, whereas Romanticism figured as a specific cultural movement and later (reductively) as the keynote of a literary period, literature cannot simply be equated with Romanticism. Because the task of addressing literature and modernity is already so big, I offer only local proposals about how works and ideas associated with Romanticism operated in literary culture.

39. Jürgen Habermas identifies Schiller's *Letters on the Aesthetic Education of Man* (1795) as "the first programmatic work toward an aesthetic critique of modernity." Jürgen Habermas, *The Philosophical Discourse of Modernity: Twelve Lectures*, trans. Frederick G. Lawrence (Cambridge, Mass.: MIT Press, 1996), 45. Here I focus on Schiller's closely related views in *On the Naïve and Sentimental in Literature* [1795], trans. Helen Watanabe-O'Kelly (Manchester, England: Carcanet, 1981).

40. Löwy and Sayre also emphasize the "particular tonality" of Romanticism, organized around the "experience of loss." Löwy and Sayre, *Romanticism*, 21.

41. Schiller, *On the Naive*, 82. Schiller identifies the abstracted naive stance with realism, which emphasizes necessity, and the abstracted sentimental stance with idealism, which emphasizes freedom.

42. Michael Bristol identifies the love of Shakespeare with the losses of modernity in *Shakespeare's America, America's Shakespeare*, within a framework for analyzing the modern somewhat different from mine. Michael Bristol, *Shakespeare's America, America's Shakespeare* (London: Routledge, 1990), 17.

43. Löwy and Sayre, *Romanticism*, 21.

44. On the prominence of Common Sense Philosophy in Continental Europe (and especially Germany) between 1760 and 1840, see Michel Malherbe, "The Impact on Europe," in Alexander Broadie, ed., *The Cambridge Companion to the Scottish Enlightenment* (Cambridge: Cambridge University Press, 2003), 298–301, 307–311.

45. Montesquieu's *The Spirit of the Laws* and a number of Herder's writings of the 1760s and 1770s worked out formulations of national character that influenced the national study of intellectual and cultural traditions.

Chapter 1

1. David D. Hall, "Readers and Writers in Early New England," in Hugh Amory and David D. Hall, eds., *The Colonial Book in the Atlantic World*, vol. 1 of David D. Hall, ed., *The History of the Book in America* (Cambridge: Cambridge University Press, 2000), 131.

2. Jon Klancher, *Transfiguring the Arts and Sciences: Knowledge and Cultural Institutions in the Romantic Age* (New York: Cambridge University Press, 2013), 165.

3. Sandra Gustafson, "Literature," in Bruce Burgett and Glenn Hendler, eds., *Keywords for American Cultural Studies* (New York: New York University Press, 2007), 145. My discussion here follows many of the same lines as Gustafson's and as Raymond Williams's history of the term "literature" in *Keywords*, which continues to be an extraordinary resource for critical historical scholarship. Raymond Williams, "Literature," *Keywords: A Vocabulary of Culture and Society*, rev. ed. (New York: Oxford University Press, 1983), 183–188.

4. Samuel L. Knapp, *Lectures on American Literature, with Remarks on Some Passages of American History* (Boston: Elam Bliss, 1829), 135, 29.

5. Klancher, *Transfiguring*, 1–12.

6. James Bowdoin, "A Philosophical Discourse Publickly Addressed to the American Academy of Arts and Sciences...," *Memoirs of the American Academy of Arts and Sciences* 1 (1 Jan. 1785): 3, 15. The address was delivered in 1780, the year that an American Academy of Arts and Sciences was formed in Massachusetts, and it was published and distributed privately by Bowdoin before it was included in the academy's first official volume of scholarship. Frank E. Manuel and Fritzie P. Manuel, *James Bowdoin and the Patriot Philosophers* (Philadelphia: American Philosophical Society, 2004), 151–156.

7. Bowdoin, "Philosophical Discourse," 3, 8, 6. Walter D. Mignolo's study of the cultures of knowledge at stake in European understandings of modernity and European imperial projects emphasizes the ways in which writing and especially the print form of the book were cast as the authentic currencies of knowledge, contributing to the reasons why the knowledge of colonized New World peoples didn't count. See Mignolo, *The Darker Side of the Renaissance: Literacy, Territoriality, and Colonization* [1995], 2nd ed. (repr., Ann Arbor: University of Michigan Press, 2003), 76, 127.

Remarks from Bowdoin's discourse quoted in the next paragraph are on page 20.

8. Adam Ferguson, "Of the History of Literature," *Royal American Magazine; or, Universal Repository of Instruction and Amusement*, Jan. 1774, 15.

9. See for example Sir Walter Scott, "Essay on Romance," in *The Miscellaneous Prose Works of Sir Walter Scott, Bart.*, 3 vols. (Edinburgh: Robert Cadell, 1841), 1: 554–575.

10. Lisa Hill, *The Passionate Society: The Social, Political, and Moral Thought of Adam Ferguson* (Dordrecht, the Netherlands: Springer, 2006), 223–224.

11. Ferguson, "Of the History," 20.

12. M. H. Abrams traces the Romantic belief that the earliest language was poetry and song to Vico, although it circulated broadly. M. H. Abrams, *The Mirror and the Lamp: Romantic Theory and the Critical Tradition* (New York: Oxford University Press, 1953), 78–84.

13. An influential source perpetuating the idea that poetry's main divisions were the epic, lyric, and dramatic (an Aristotelian grouping, versus the collection of genres Philip Sidney acknowledged) was Augustus William Schlegel's *Course of Lectures on Dramatic Art and Literature*, trans. John Black, rev. A. J. W. Morrison (New York: AMS Press, 1965; rept. from London: Henry G. Bohn, 1846), 43.

14. René Wellek, *The Rise of English Literary History* (New York: McGraw-Hill, 1966), 75.

15. Sir Philip Sidney, "Defence of Poesie," Electronic Text Center, University of Virginia Library (http://etext.virginia.edu/toc/modeng/public/SidDefe.html), accessed 27 Nov. 2011.

16. Aristotle, "On the Art of Poetry" (often translated as "The Poetics"), in *Classical Literary Criticism*, trans. T. S. Dorsch (New York: Penguin Books, 1982), 35.

17. With such confusion about whether poetry was an imitative project, an all-purpose enhancement of language, or a specific set of genres, no wonder that Sidney playfully displaces the problem onto readers, who must be dolts if they can't recognize poetry and its value for themselves. This approach has been often repeated and indexes also the belief that aesthetic experience is hard to formulate analytically, precisely because of its affective and somatic qualities: "But if—fie of such a but!—you bee borne so neare the dull-making Cataract of Nilus, that you cannot heare the Planet-like Musicke of Poetrie." Sidney, "Defence of Poesie."

18. William Wordsworth, "Preface to the Second Edition of *Lyrical Ballads* (1800)," in David Perkins, ed., *English Romantic Writers* (New York: Harcourt Brace Jovanovich, 1967), 320, 321.

19. "Poetry," *Christian's, Scholar's, and Farmer's Magazine*, Dec. 1789–Jan. 1790, 589.

20. Wordsworth's defense of ordinary language entailed that "there neither is, nor can be, any *essential* difference between the language of prose and metrical composition," although the "Preface" moves into analyzing the project of the poet without addressing whether prose writers could ever be included. Wordsworth, "Preface," 324.

21. Richard Green Moulton, *The Modern Study of Literature: An Introduction to Literary Theory and Interpretation* (Chicago: University of Chicago Press, 1915), 16.

22. A version of the poetry-prose distinction was at work in John Dunlop's *History of Fiction* (1814), which polemically contrasted fiction with poetry partly on the grounds of fiction's superiority in rendering a way of life: "Poetry is in general capable of too little detail, while its paintings, at the same time, are usually too much forced and exaggerated. But in Fiction we can discriminate without impropriety, and enter into detail without meanness. Hence it has been remarked [by Antonio Borromeo, who published an essay about Italian novels in 1797], that it is chiefly in the fictions of an age that we can discover the modes of living, dress, and manners of the period." John Dunlop, *The History of Fiction*, 3 vols. (Edinburgh: James Ballantyne, 1814), 1: x.

23. Knox's initial anthology of prose and most of the rest of the *Elegant Extracts* volumes announced in their subtitles their role as instructional texts: "Selected for the Improvement of Scholars at Classical & Other Schools in the Art of Speaking, in Reading; Thinking, Composing; and in the Conduct of Life." Vicesimus Knox, *Elegant Extracts; or, Useful and Entertaining Passages in Prose* (London: Charles Dilly, 1784). Coleridge in *Biographia Literaria* attested to the broad circulation of the volumes, which were also referenced frequently by Jane Austen. Samuel Taylor Coleridge, *Biographia Literaria; or, Biographical Sketches of My Life and Opinions*, 2 vols. (New York: Wiley and Putnam, 1847) 1: 179 n. 1; Susan Allen Ford, "Reading Elegant Extracts in Emma: Very Entertaining!" *Jane Austen Society of North America: Persuasions On-Line* 28, no. 1 (2007) (http://www.jasna.org/persuasions/on-line/vol28no1/ford.htm) accessed 30 June, 2014.

24. Longfellow's project helped construct cultural traditions that would authorize modern nations, but recirculating older literatures sometimes fueled radical "nationalist, autonomist or separatist movements" on the part of populations who dissented from the dominant national or imperial identity. Joep Leerssen, "Introduction: Philology and the European Construction of National Literatures," in Dirk Van Hulle and Joep Leerssen, eds.,

Editing the Nation's Memory: Textual Scholarship and Nation-Building in 19th-Century Europe (Amsterdam: Rodopi, 2008), 22–25.

25. Henry Wadsworth Longfellow, *Poets and Poetry of Europe: With Introductions and Biographical Notices* (Philadelphia: Carey and Hart, 1845), 688–692.

26. An earlier instance of the pairing of poetry and prose was George B. Cheever's *American Common-Place Book of Prose* [1828] (Boston: Carter, Hendee, 1833), designed for educational use, and his *American Common-Place Book of Poetry* [1831] (Philadelphia: H. Hooker, 1846).

The discrimination of poetry from prose was paralleled by the sorting of male from female authors (another development grounded in the primacy of the author-function). Notable anthologies of poetry by women from the mid-nineteenth century are T. Buchanan Read's *Female Poets of America* (1848), Caroline May's *American Female Poets* (1848), Griswold's *Female Poets of America* (1848), and John S. Hart's *Female Prose Writers of America* (1851). See Paula Bernat Bennett, *Poets in the Public Sphere: The Emancipatory Project of American Women's Poetry, 1800–1900* (Princeton, N.J.: Princeton University Press, 2003), 17–21.

27. Henry Reed, "Poetical and Prose Reading," in Evert A. Duyckinck and George L. Duyckinck, eds., *Cyclopaedia of American Literature*, 2 vols. (New York: Charles Scribner, 1855), 2: 492.

28. Griswold's introduction explained somewhat apologetically that he was more inclusive than some critics might prefer in order to represent authors who were "popularly known as poets." His own criteria for poetry were explicitly keyed to aesthetics of the sublime and the beautiful, however. Rufus Wilmot Griswold, preface to the first ed., *The Poets and Poetry of America* [1842], 6th ed. (Philadelphia: Carey and Hart, 1848), 7.

29. Duyckinck and Duyckink, preface to *Cyclopaedia*, 1: v.

30. The *Cyclopaedia* is an impressive accomplishment that notices, in addition to authors, institutions supporting literature such as the Redwood Library in Newport, the American Philosophical Society, and the Connecticut Academy of Arts and Sciences. Its broad net reaches writers mainly known for other accomplishments (such as the painter Washington Allston) and writers who lived in the United States for only a while (such as the Irish philosopher George Berkeley). It's notable also that some of the women and minority authors who were restored to the literary canon in the late twentieth century were included in the *Cyclopaedia*: Samson Occom, Phillis Wheatley, Mercy Warren, Susanna Rowson, and others. The *Cyclopaedia*'s inclusivity was probably facilitated by its having been chronological but not periodized, so that it was not constrained to fit authors, works, and institutions into homogenous period groupings.

31. See especially Virginia Jackson, *Dickinson's Misery: A Theory of Lyric Reading* (Princeton, N.J.: Princeton University Press, 2005), whose import chapter 5 addresses.

32. Henry Reed's discussion of prose and poetry concentrated mainly on shoring up the case for poetry (in the 1840s, for his students at Penn): "The neglect of poetical reading is increased by the very mistaken notion that poetry is a mere luxury of the mind, alien from the demands of practical life—a light and effortless amusement." Reed, "Poetical and Prose Reading," 492.

33. Chapter 3 traces an early version of periodized literary history to the elaboration of Shakespeare's Elizabethan context and to the need to connect literature with the fortunes of the nation, although of course periodization has also been elaborated in ways that are less nakedly ideological. For an account of the peculiar staying power of literary periods within the discipline of English, see Ted Underwood, *Why Literary Periods Mattered: Historical*

Contrast and the Prestige of English Studies (Stanford, Calif.: Stanford University Press, 2013). For a persuasive critique of periodization with ideas for renovation, see Eric Hayot, *On Literary Worlds* (New York: Oxford University Press, 2012), 147–188.

34. R. Lynn Matson, "Phillis Wheatley—Soul Sister?" *Phylon* 33, no. 3 (1972): 222.

35. Jonathan Arac argues that hypercanonization in U.S. literary studies began in the mid-twentieth century, elevating Twain's *Adventures of Huckleberry Finn* and a "limited canon of texts extravagantly praised and studied primarily through close reading." He points out that focusing academic instruction on the hypercanon has obscured "how limited an event nineteenth-century literary narrative was." Jonathan Arac, *Huckleberry Finn as Idol and Target: The Functions of Criticism in Our Time* (Madison: University of Wisconsin Press, 1997), 137.

36. For example, an 1856 reviewer of the Duyckincks' *Cyclopaedia of American Literature* (1855) approvingly cited the editors' attention to early writings selected because of "quaintness, from association with important public events, as characteristic of the times and the state of society, or as furnishing essential links in the chain of facts which indicate the progressive mental development of the nation." "Art. II—*A Cyclopaedia of American Literature*...," *North American Review*, Apr. 1856, 333.

37. Here I draw on John Beverley's important sense of *testimonio* as "a story that *needs* to be told"; Beverley's account of the tensions between *testimonio* and the institution of literature, which he analyzes as implicated in forms of national and imperial dominance, has been valuable for my work here. See especially "The Margin at the Center: On *Testimonio*" and "Second Thoughts on *Testimonio*" in Beverley's *Against Literature* (Minneapolis: University of Minnesota Press, 1993), 69–99. The phrase quoted is from "The Margin at the Center," 73.

38. Phillis Wheatley, "On Being Brought from Africa to America," *Complete Writings*, ed. Vincent Carretta (New York: Penguin, 2001), 13.

Terence Collins, "Phillis Wheatley: The Dark Side of the Poetry," *Phylon* 36, no. 1 (1975): 78. Henry Louis Gates discusses readings that fault Wheatley for being a "race traitor" in *The Trials of Phillis Wheatley: America's First Black Poet and Her Encounters with the Founding Fathers* (New York: Basic Books, 2003), 81.

Significantly, "On Being Brought..." and Wheatley's ode to the Earl of Dartmouth (which briefly references her having been kidnapped) are the texts by Wheatley included in a recent collection of politically engaged poetry. Carolyn Forché and Duncan Wu, eds., *Poetry of Witness: The Tradition in English, 1500–2001* (New York: Norton, 2014), 283–284.

39. June Jordan, "The Difficult Miracle of Black Poetry in America or Something like a Sonnet for Phillis Wheatley," *Massachusetts Review* 27, no. 2 (1986): 254.

40. James A. Levernier, "Phillis Wheatley's 'On Being Brought from Africa to America,'" *Explicator* 40, no. 1 (1981): 25–26; Matson, "Soul Sister?" 230.

41. Phillis Wheatley, "To Samson Occam (February 11, 1774)," *Complete Writings*, 152–153.

42. An early and especially explicit formulation of this problem can be found in J. Martin Favor, *Authentic Blackness: The Folk in the New Negro Renaissance* (Durham, N.C.: Duke University Press, 1999). Favor examines the effects that privileging certain "identities and voices" as authentic had on twentieth-century African American authors while they were writing, but his call to abandon a "'grand unified theory' of black identity" in favor of a "plurality of positions" applies to literary history as well (3, 152). Robert Dale Parker offers a similar analysis of the problems posed by making authors racial representatives: "Anticanonical polemics and routine, anticanonical assumptions sometimes represent an author's identity

so confidently that they assume it can predict the values in that author's writing." Robert Dale Parker, *The Invention of Native American Literature* (Ithaca, N.Y.: Cornell University Press, 2003), 173

43. Katy L. Chiles calls Wheatley's 1774 letter to Occom "a cornerstone of Wheatley scholarship that illustrates her poetry's antislavery sentiment." Katy L. Chiles, "Becoming Colored in Occom and Wheatley's Early America," *PMLA* 123, no. 5 (2008): 1398.

44. The scholarly introduction of the letter emphasized its publication history: Mukhtar Ali Isani, "'Gambia on My Soul': Africa and the African in the Writings of Phillis Wheatley," *Melus* 6, no. 1 (1979): 71 n. 9. Subsequent scholars who have noted that the letter was published in newspapers have not addressed the letter's status as a public document or have implied that Wheatley must not have sought or condoned its publication. For example, tying the letter directly to "On Being Brought," Charles W. Akers argued that the "letter affords a brief glimpse into her private thoughts concerning the institution that had torn her from the 'Pagan land' of her birth." Charles W. Akers, "'Our Modern Egyptians': Phillis Wheatley and the Whig Campaign against Slavery in Revolutionary Boston," in William H. Robinson, ed., *Critical Essays on Phillis Wheatley* (Boston: G. K. Hall, 1982), 165. Julian Mason's groundbreaking edition of Wheatley's writings correctly notes, "It is not known whether she knew the letter would be published. It is not in her 1779 Proposals" for a second book publication, but by calling the letter "her strongest and most direct publication against slavery," Mason registers the fact that the letter may have been designed for public circulation. Julian D. Mason, ed., *The Poems of Phillis Wheatley* [1966], rev. ed. (rept., Chapel Hill: University of North Carolina Press, 1989), 203.

45. Matson, "Soul Sister?" 230.

46. Collins, "Dark Side of the Poetry," 88.

47. Duyckinck and Duyckinck, *Cyclopaedia*, 1: 368.

48. Rufus Wilmot Griswold, *The Female Poets of America* (Philadelphia: Carey and Hart, 1852), 30-31. The Abbé Gregoire (Henri Gregoire) was a French priest and committed abolitionist who wrote about Wheatley's poetry in a pamphlet about the intellectual achievements of Negroes, *De la littérature des nègres*, (1808). Gregoire's estimate of Wheatley is reprinted in Robinson, *Critical Essays on Phillis Wheatley*, 48-51.

49. Much later in the century, Charles F. Richardson's 1887 *American Literature, 1607-1885*, excerpted by the *Dartmouth Literary Review* and reprinted by *The Critic* in 1888, noted that Wheatley's verses were "neatly turned according to the prevalent English fashion" and credited them some with "decided excellence," given the limitations of that fashion. C. F. Richardson, "Some Early American Poets," *The Critic*, 21 Jul. 1888, 34; Charles F. Richardson, *American Literature, 1607-1885*, 2 vols. (New York: G. P. Putnam's Sons, 1887).

50. For example, Edmund C. Stedman identified five or six of Freneau's lyrics such as "The Wild Honeysuckle" as virtually the only poems written in the wake of the Revolution possessing "the essential poetic spirit." Accordingly, Stedman's *American Anthology* omitted Freneau's closet dramas, Revolutionary-era poems of political aspiration and satire, and neoclassical efforts such as "Mars and Hymen" that resembled some of Wheatley's poems. Edmund C. Stedman, *Poets of America*, 2nd ed. (Boston: Houghton Mifflin, 1885), 35, and *An American Anthology: 1787-1900* (Boston: Houghton Mifflin, 1900).

51. The eighteenth-century conversation is surveyed by Donatus I. Nwoga, "Humanitarianism and the Criticism of African Literature, 1770-1810," *Research in African Literature* 3, no. 2 (1972): 171-179.

52. David S. Shields, *Civil Tongues and Polite Letters in British America* (Chapel Hill: University of North Carolina Press, 1997), xxii.

53. John C. Shields, "Phillis Wheatley's Struggle for Freedom in Her Poetry and Prose," in *The Collected Works of Phillis Wheatley*, ed. John C. Shields (New York: Oxford University Press, 1988), 252–267. Shields develops further his case for Wheatley's having been a pioneer or early adopter of Romantic aesthetics in *Phillis Wheatley and the Romantics* (Knoxville: University of Tennessee Press, 2010).

54. Virginia Jackson, "The Poet as Poetess," in Kerry Larson, ed., *The Cambridge Companion to Nineteenth-Century American Poetry* (Cambridge: Cambridge University Press, 2011), 59. Jackson builds on Paula Backscheider's work in *Eighteenth-Century Women Poets and Their Poetry: Inventing Agency, Inventing Genre* (Baltimore: Johns Hopkins University Press, 2005).

55. Paul Giles, "The Literary Culture of Colonial America," in *Transnationalism in Practice: Essays on American Studies, Literature, and Religion* (Edinburgh: Edinburgh University Press, 2010), 193.

56. One of the most important recent reconsiderations of the power dynamics of gender and race affecting Wheatley is Joanna Brooks's argument about Wheatley's somewhat coercive sponsorship by white women; the argument also productively shifts attention away from the watershed of book publication—which nineteenth-century literary culture emphasized more than eighteenth-century belletristic culture did—to Wheatley's ongoing navigation of her readership through manuscript circulation and periodical publication. Joanna Brooks, "Our Phillis, Ourselves," *American Literature* 82, no. 1 (2010): 1–28.

57. Duyckinck and Duyckinck, *Cyclopaedia*, 1: 367.

58. G. W. F. Hegel, *Aesthetics: Lectures on Fine Art*, trans. T. M. Knox, 2 vols. (Oxford: Clarendon Press, 1975), 2: 995–996.

59. William Hazlitt, *Lectures on the English Poets* (London: Taylor and Hessey, 1818), 318–319.

60. One sign of the flexible eighteenth-century sense of poetry's value was that turning poetry into prose or prose into poetry was a common compositional exercise. Elihu Hubbard Smith's anthology *American Poems, Selected and Original* (1793) included passages of prose turned into poetry, such as verse renditions of the biblical account of the fall of Babylon specifically cued to passages from Isaiah and Revelation. [Elihu Hubbard Smith, ed.], *American Poems, Selected and Original* (Litchfield, Conn.: Collier and Buel, 1793), 25–29.

61. See Eric Ashley Hairston, *The Ebony Column: Classics, Civilization, and the African American Reclamation of the West* (Knoxville: University of Tennessee Press, 2013), especially chapter 1, "The Trojan Horse: Phillis Wheatley," 25–63.

62. Bowdoin's published volume, *Paraphrase on Part of the Oeconomy of Human Life* (Boston 1759), was a poetic response to the prose work *Oeconomy of Human Life* (1750, commonly attributed to Robert Dodsley or Lord Chesterfield, although the pamphlet identified the work as "Translated from an Indian Manuscript, Written by a Bramin [sic]"). A few of his poems were also published in a volume popularly known as the "Harvard Verses" that was sent to George III on his accession to the throne: *Pietas et Gratulatio Collegii Cantabrigiensis Apud Novanglos* (Boston: Green and Russell, 1762). Gordon E. Kershaw, *James Bowdoin II: Patriot and Man of the Enlightenment* (Lanham, Md.: University Press of America, 1991), 133–136.

63. Wheatley also took an important initiative in publishing poetry under her own name rather than anonymously or pseudonymously. On the intricate relations between

print, manuscript, and women's public authorship, see Carla Mulford, "Print and Manuscript Culture," in Kevin J. Hayes, ed., *The Oxford Handbook of Early American Literature* (New York: Oxford University Press, 2008), 339–340.

64. Griswold, *Female Poets*, 31.

65. Wheatley, *Complete Writings*, 64–65. Bowdoin is identified as the likely author of the rebus on 183.

66. Roger Chartier, *The Order of Books: Readers, Authors, and Libraries in Europe between the Fourteenth and the Eighteenth Centuries*, trans. Lydia G. Cochrane (Stanford, Calif.: Stanford University Press, 1992), 65.

67. James Van Horn Melton, *The Rise of the Public in Enlightenment Europe* (Cambridge: Cambridge University Press, 2001), 165; Jean-Jacques Rousseau, *Letter to D'Alembert and Writings for the Theater*, vol. 10 of *The Collected Writings of Rousseau*, ed. and trans. Allan Bloom, Charles Butterworth, and Christopher Kelly (Hanover, N.H.: University Press of New England, 2004), 265–269.

68. Schlegel, *Dramatic Art*, 37, 39.

69. Nigel Cliff, *The Shakespeare Riots: Revenge, Drama, and Death in Nineteenth-Century America* (New York: Random House, 2007).

70. William Dunlap, *A History of the American Theatre* (New York: J & J Harper, 1832), 68–70, 210, 405.

71. The influential antitheatrical writings about Shakespeare were mainly English, and William Dunlap's account of English theaters in 1832 suggests that they (but not theaters on the Continent) were also sites of cross-class tensions: cursing and chucking orange peels are indicted, as well as the visibility of prostitutes (which was also a feature of U.S. theater, according to Dunlap). Dunlap, *History*, 365–366.

72. Smith summarizes her study's powerful claims: "I argue that for several reasons American drama has been shelved out of sight: in part because of a culturally dominant puritan distaste for and suspicion of the theatre; in part because of a persistent, unwavering allegiance to European models, slavish Anglophilia, and a predilection for heightened language cemented by the New Critics; in part because of a fear of populist, leftist, and experimental art; in part because of a disdain of alternative, oppositional, and vulgar performances; in part because of narrow disciplinary divisions separating drama from theatre and performance; and in part because of the dominance of prose and poetry in the hierarchy of genres studied in university literature courses and reproduced in American criticism." Susan Harris Smith, *American Drama: The Bastard Art* (Cambridge: Cambridge University Press, 1997), 3. I offer here a supplemental account of the production of the academic "hierarchy of genres."

73. Lawrence W. Levine, *Highbrow/Lowbrow: The Emergence of Cultural Hierarchy in America* (Cambridge, Mass.: Harvard University Press, 1990).

74. Schlegel, *Dramatic Art*, 36–37.

75. Jeffrey H. Richards clarifies more precisely *The Contrast*'s historical significance as "the first comedy written by a permanent resident of the United States to be mounted by a professional company." Jeffrey H. Richards, *Drama, Theatre, and Identity in the American New Republic* (New York: Cambridge University Press, 2005), 28.

76. Sir Walter Scott, "Essay on the Drama," in *Miscellaneous Prose*, 1: 583–597.

77. Scott, "Essay on the Drama," 596.

78. Scott, "Essay on the Drama," 596.

79. Thomas De Quincey, "The Literature of Knowledge and Literature of Power" [1847], in Perkins, *English Romantic*, 742–744.

80. Dunlap, *History*, 2.

81. Rufus Wilmot Griswold, preface to *The Prose Writers of America* [1852] (facsim., New York: Garrett Press, 1969), 5.

82. Henry Reed, *Lectures on English Literature, from Chaucer to Tennyson*, ed. William B. Reed, 5th ed. (Philadelphia: J. B. Lippincott, 1867), 30.

83. See for example A., "Thoughts on the Belles Lettres," *Western Monthly Magazine and Literary Journal*, June 1834, 310–316; and "On the Cycles of English Literature: In Four Parts—Part II," *Atheneum; or, Spirit of the English Magazines*, 15 Mar. 1830, 465–468.

84. Rufus Griswold, "The Intellectual History, Condition, and Prospects of the Country," in *Prose Writers*, 38.

85. "Walter Scott—Has History Gained by His Writings?" *The Anglo-American*, 2 Oct. 1847, 554.

86. William Ellery Channing, "Literature of the Age: From the Demands of the Age on the Ministry," in Griswold, *Prose Writers*, 167.

87. Melton, *Rise of the Public*, 94.

88. Anna Letitia Barbauld, "On Novel Writing," *Literary Magazine and American Register*, Dec. 1804, 693; Thomas Warton, *On the History of English Poetry from the Twelfth to the Close of the Sixteenth Century*, 3 vols. [1774–1781], London: J. Dodsley, 1774), 1: n. p.; John Dunlop, *The History of Fiction*, 3 vols. (Edinburgh: James Ballantyne, 1814), 1: 4–5; Sir Walter Scott, "Essay on Romance," in *Miscellaneous Prose* 1: 555, 558–559.

George Ticknor identified *Don Quixote* as the "oldest classical specimen of romantic fiction" in *The History of Spanish Literature* (1849), which was excerpted in the Duyckincks' *Cyclopaedia*, 2: 234.

89. J. Paul Hunter, *Before Novels: The Cultural Contexts of Eighteenth-Century English Fiction* (New York: W. W. Norton, 1990), 41.

90. Homer Obed Brown, *Institutions of the English Novel: From Defoe to Scott* (Philadelphia: University of Pennsylvania Press, 1997), 176.

91. Benjamin Franklin, *The Autobiography*, in *Benjamin Franklin: Writings*, ed. J. A. Leo Lemay (New York: Literary Classics of the United States, 1987), 1326. Vicesimus Knox's early editions of *Elegant Extracts* for prose made use of a similar category, "Narrative, Dialogue, Letters, Sentences, with Other Miscellaneous Pieces, Amusing and Instructive," which combined extracts from novelists (Fielding, Sterne) with essayistic or lightly narrative writings by Pope, Chesterfield, and others including himself.

92. Brown, *Institutions*, 168.

93. On the importance of considering eighteenth-century novels in relation to didactic and religious forms of popular reading, see Hunter, *Before Novels*, 226–304.

94. J. Paul Hunter identifies Clara Reeve's "The Progress of Romance" as an influential earlier definitional moment for the novel, but he notes that for Reeve, as in many later discussions such as Scott's, the novel and romance "appear cozily together, not to imply a distinction but rather to catch, between them, all known fiction and some long narratives whose factitiousness was uncertain." Hunter, *Before Novels*, 25.

The tendency to characterize the novel as a development of romance or beyond romance meant that the deleterious effects of mass culture could be projected onto the romance, whereas the novel could be left with a high-culture coding. Jonathan Brody Kramnick, *Making the English Canon: Print-Capitalism and the Cultural Past, 1700–1770* (Cambridge: Cambridge University Press, 1998), 42.

95. Sir Walter Scott, "Samuel Richardson," in *Miscellaneous Prose*, 1: 250, 251, and "Horace Walpole," in *Miscellaneous Prose*, 1: 306.

96. Scott, "Essay on Romance," 554, 555, 566.

97. Sir Walter Scott, "Henry Fielding," in *Miscellaneous Prose*, 1: 259, 253.

98. Richard Chase, *The American Novel and Its Tradition* (Baltimore: Johns Hopkins University Press, 1993), 10.

99. On the task of fiction as "recuperative," see Hunter, *Before Novels*, 162. Hunter posits new forms of curiosity, especially about the "radical contemporaneity" that had expanded the exploration of the internal consciousness, as the alternative dynamic to this recuperation (168).

100. Walter Scott, "Mrs. Ann Radcliffe," in *Biographical Memoirs*, vol. 3 of *Miscellaneous Prose*, 363, 364.

101. On the ways in which authors, genres, and literary stature operate as a form of branding within literary culture—since whatever else books may be, they are also commodities—see Nancy Glazener, "The Novel in Postbellum Print Culture," in Leonard Cassuto, Clare Virginia Eby, and Benjamin Reiss, eds., *The Cambridge History of the American Novel* (Cambridge: Cambridge University Press, 2011), 345–348.

102. Margaret J. M. Ezell, "Making a Classic: The Advent of the Literary Series," *South Central Review* 11, no. 2 (1994): 5.

103. Ezell, "Making a Classic," 6.

104. Ezell notes that an important early instance of this kind of periodizing and nationalizing literary anthology was Robert Dodsley's *Select Collection of Old English Plays*, initially published in 1744 and made possible because Dodsley had gained permission to publish manuscripts that at that time were available only in a private collection. For Dodsley, the value of the plays lay partly in their role of documenting "the history not only of the theatre, but also of the British nation and national temperament" (Ezell, "Making a Classic," 7).

105. As chapter 3 discusses, English poetry, drama, and other writings were beginning to be taught during the eighteenth century, and Hugh Blair's *Lectures on Rhetoric and Belles-Lettres* (which addressed ancient and modern writers) was in widespread use as a textbook. Some compilations were specifically designed for use in schools (such as Knox's *Elegant Extracts* volumes) but circulated more widely. More of the anthologies I've named might have been used as instructional texts in schools or for private study, but they weren't prepared and marketed specifically for such use in the way that a Norton or Heath anthology is today. On English translations of Quintilian's *Institutes*, which date back to 1756, see Lee Honeycutt, "The History of Quintilian's Texts," at the site *Quintilian's Institutes of Oratory* (http://rhetoric.eserver.org/quintilian/history.html), accessed 30 May 2015.

106. Kramnick, *Making the English Canon*, 8. Jayne Elizabeth Lewis persuasively argues that Augustan fable collections also marked a convergence between high-culture neoclassical advocates of the ancients and print-crazy pro-moderns, since both groups were eager to get fabulists such as Aesop into print, in *The English Fable: Aesop and Literary Culture, 1651–1740* (New York: Cambridge University Press, 1996), 51.

107. The editorship of *American Poems* has often been attributed to Smith, but there is reason to believe there was more than one editor involved. See John C. Frank, *Early American Poetry, 1610–1820: A List of Works in the New York Public Library* (New York: Bulletin of the New York Public Library, 1917), 5.

108. Rev. of *Lycée; ou, Cours de Literature, Ancienne et Moderne*, Port-Folio, 27 Nov. 1802, 372, continued 4 Dec. 1802, 381. In 1786, La Harpe began delivering a course of lectures on literature at a new academy in Paris called the Lycée; he continued developing these lectures as a professor at the École Normale and published them in 1799. These lectures were

collected and published in French in 1799. Daniel Brewer, "Political Culture and Literary History: La Harpe's *Lycée*," *Modern Language Quarterly* 57, no. 2 (1997): 163–184. La Harpe, a playwright and philosophe, was probably the French literary critic and historian most revered before C.-A. Sainte-Beuve.

The *Port Folio* review reprints a British review published earlier that year. Rev. of *Lycee; ou Cours de Literature, Ancienne et Moderne*, by J. F. La Harpe, *Anti-Jacobin Review and Magazine*, Jan.–Apr. 1802, appendix, 472–481.

109. Rev. of *Lycée; ou Cours de Literature, Ancienne et Moderne*, by J. F. La Harpe, *Port Folio*, July, 1819, 10. I've found no evidence of an English translation of *Lycée* in book form from around this time, but *Lycée* was republished in France in 1818 (Paris: Chez Deterville, Libraire), and perhaps that event prompted the review's second *Port Folio* appearance.

110. The Federalist *Port Folio* also probably sought to be aligned with La Harpe, who had initially supported the French Revolution but came to oppose it bitterly, a stance that would have resonated with editor Joseph Dennie's charge that Jeffersonian-style "democracy" meant chaos and disorder. Brewer, "Political Culture," 170. Chapter 2 discusses Dennie's trial for seditious libel because of his criticism of "democracy" in the *Port Folio*.

111. La Harpe's approach may have appealed to the *Port Folio* reviewer because its version of the new involved great admiration for the old. On La Harpe's position as an advocate for aesthetic understandings of literature, see Nanette C. Le Coat, "Philosophy vs. Eloquence: Laharpe and the Literary Debate at the École Normale," *French Review* 61, no. 3 (1988): 422; Brewer, "Political Culture and Literary History," 183. Several modern scholars use Le Coat's spelling of "Laharpe," but I will continue to use the spelling of the *Port Folio* reviewer and the early editions of La Harpe's work.

112. Rev. of *Lycée* (1819), 11.

113. La Harpe discusses Dante and Petrarch with admiration in a transitional section about the state of letters in Europe between the reign of Caesar Augustus and the reign of Louis XIV. Jean-François de La Harpe, *Cours de Littérature Ancienne et Moderne...*, 3 vols. (Paris: Firmin Didot Frères, 1840), 1: 426–440. Le Coat discusses La Harpe's unusual belief that Petrarch and Dante were important writers but notes that for him the Middle Ages were anomalous, neither ancient nor modern, and that the works of Petrarch and Dante were therefore not part of the teaching canon he promoted in the mid-1790s. Le Coat, "Philosophy vs. Eloquence," 422.

114. Douglas Lane Patey traces the beginnings of the modern Anglophone use of "canons" as selective lists of writers or works to the eighteenth century, and his discussion of the reconfiguration of genres deemed canonical offers a somewhat different account of phenomena I address here. Douglas Lane Patey, "The Eighteenth Century Invents the Canon," *Modern Language Studies* 18, no. 1 (1988): 17.

115. Emphasizing this same mechanism of institutional review, canon law names the body of ecclesiastical laws adopted by church councils.

116. Walter L. Reed, "Canonization and Its Discontents: Lessons from the Bible," in James C. Raymond, ed., *English as a Discipline: Or, Is There a Plot in This Play?* (Tuscaloosa: University of Alabama Press, 1996), 104.

117. The five chief divisions of rhetoric—*inventio* (invention), *dispositio* (arrangement), *elocutio* (style), *memoria* (memory), and *actio* (delivery)—were also called canons because they were essential features of rhetorical education.

A competing use of the term "canon" that interweaves the outcroppings of a "canon" as a body of valued text is the (etymologically fundamental) sense of a canon as a principle or standard. For example, an 1836 article delineating the poetical accomplishments of a writer whose poems were published mainly in newspapers acknowledged, "According to established literary canons, Mr. Little's poetical genius was not of the higher order"; an 1843 article identified the "canon of literature" with the "laws of taste," which in the eighteenth century were taken from the ideas of the French court. W. D. G. [W. D. Gallagher], "Literary Journal. Sketches of the Literature of the West. Number Two. Harvey D. Little," *Western Literary Journal and Monthly Review*, Nov. 1836, 361; "Minor French Poets," rept. from *Tait's Edinburgh Magazine*, *Campbell's Foreign Monthly Magazine*, 2 (Jan.–Apr. 1843), 271.

118. Robert Scholes, *The Rise and Fall of English: Reconstructing English as a Discipline* (New Haven, Conn.: Yale University Press, 1998), 106. An indication that the Alexandrian project was understood specifically as canonization can be found in an 1846 issue of the *Anglo American*, which published notes from a series of lectures delivered to Columbia College students by Charles Anthon, a professor of Greek and Latin. The published transcript asserts, "The principal feature in the Alexandrian age was the establishment of literary canons containing the best writers in each department of literature, and which were to be regarded as authorities in all matters of language." "On Grecian Literature," *Anglo American*, 16 Dec. 1843, 178. The Alexandrian critics also left as a legacy an array of literary genres. David Perkins, "Literary Classifications: How Have They Been Made?" in David Perkins, ed., *Theoretical Issues in Literary History* (Cambridge, Mass.: Harvard University Press, 1991), 254–255.

119. The Editor [Benjamin Franklin Tefft], "Literary Sketches: Joseph Addison." *Ladies Repository and Gatherings of the West*, Jan. 1847, 3. Frank Luther Mott identifies the editor in 1847 as Tefft in *History of American Magazines*, 5 vols. (Cambridge, Mass.: Harvard University Press, 1957), 2: 301.

120. Sarah Lawall, "Introduction: Reading World Literature," in Sarah Lawall, ed., *Reading World Literature: Theory, History, Practice* (Austin: University of Texas Press, 1994), 5; Charles Rollin, *The Method of Teaching and Studying the Belles Lettres*, 4th ed., 4 vols. (Dublin: M. Rhames, 1742), 1: 73; La Harpe, *Cours de Littérature*, 1: 3.

121. *Quintilian's Institutes of Oratory; or, Education of an Orator*, ed. John Selby Watson, 2 vols. (London: George Bell and Sons, 1899), 1: 72.

122. *Quintilian's Institutes*, 2: 251, 252.

123. For a fuller account of some ancient canons and their medieval perpetuation, see Wendell V. Harris, "Canonicity," *PMLA* 106, no. 1 (1991): 100–111.

124. As René Wellek notes, in the context of eighteenth-century literary histories, "Obviously, literature was not always studied by people with literary interests but a good deal by historians and antiquaries." Wellek's erudite study of literary history projects backward in time the modern idea of literature in a way that is at odds with my work here. Wellek, *Rise*, 65.

125. Thomas Warton, *The History of English Poetry: From the Eleventh to the Seventeenth Century*, repr. from the last London ed. (New York: G. P. Putnam & Sons, 1870), 759; Wellek, *Rise*, 177.

126. George Ticknor, *History of Spanish Literature*, 6th ed., 3 vols. (New York: Gordian Press, 1965), 1: 5.

127. Ticknor, *History*, 3: 234.

128. Ernest Renan, "What Is a Nation?" [1882], in Geoff Eley and Ronald Grigor Suny, eds., *Becoming National: A Reader* (New York: Oxford University Press, 1996), 41–55.

129. [Sydney Smith], rev. of *Statistical Annals of the United States of America*, by Adam Seybert, *Edinburgh Review*, Jan. 1820, 69–80.

130. Alok Yadav's study of England's eighteenth-century struggle to consolidate and legitimize its vantage point of cultural imperialism adds an additional dimension to the drama of U.S. struggles against cultural inferiority, since the U.S. struggles both emulated England's struggles and compounded England's success; Linda Colley has also examined the heavy cultural machinery required to forge Great Britain as a framework for belonging and cultural identity after the 1707 Act of Union. Alok Yadav, *Before the Empire of English: Literature, Provinciality, and Nationalism in Eighteenth-Century Britain* (New York: Palgrave Macmillan, 2004); Linda Colley, *Britons: Forging the Nation 1707–1837* [1992], 2nd ed. (repr., New Haven, Conn.: Yale University Press, 2005).

131. Andrew Burstein, *The Original Knickerbocker: The Life of Washington Irving* (New York: Basic Books, 2007), 109–132.

132. The supercanon was not always presented in precisely this grouping, but these authors regularly appeared. For example, George Ticknor, in assessing Cervantes, invoked a typical array: "[t]he greatest of the great poets—Homer, Dante, Shakespeare, Milton—have no doubt risen to loftier heights" (Duycknick, *Cyclopaedia*, 2: 234).

133. It is beyond the scope of this work to track the process by which each of these writers became a leading representative of modern literature, likely to appear in sculptures and inscriptions and stained glass windows in U.S. libraries, schools, and museums, but later chapters will trace some of the ways in which Shakespeare became literary and literature became Shakespeare-centered in the long nineteenth century. An example of the distinctive histories that are likely to be part of each author's trajectory in this supercanon is Dante's association with problems of national unification, which informed Americans' investments in his work from the early national period at least through the Civil War. Dennis Looney has tracked as well African American readers' attention to "segregation, migration, and integration" in Dante's work, beginning in the nineteenth century and extending to the present. Joshua Matthews, "The *Divine Comedy* as an American Civil War Epic," *J19: The Journal of Nineteenth Century Americanists* 1, no. 2 (2013): 315–337; Dennis Looney, *Freedom Readers: The African American Reception of Dante Alighieri and the Divine Comedy* (Notre Dame, Ind.: University of Notre Dame Press, 2011).

As John Guillory has argued, "there can be no *general* theory of canon formation that would predict or account for the canonization of any particular work, without specifying first the unique historical conditions of that work's production and reception." John Guillory, *Cultural Capital: The Problem of Literary Canon Formations* (Chicago: University of Chicago Press, 1993), 85.

134. Deidre Shauna Lynch, "Jane Austen and Genius," in *A Companion to Jane Austen*, ed. Claudia L. Johnson and Clara Tuite (Malden, Mass.: Wiley-Blackwell, 2009), 391–401; Scholes, *Rise* 105.

Deidre Shauna Lynch's *Loving Literature* explores many dimensions of the love readers felt for canonical authors and the kinds of love and tribute that literary canons exacted. See especially the chapters "Canon Love in Gothic Libraries" and "Poetry at Death's Door" in Deidre Shauna Lynch, *Loving Literature: A Cultural History* (Chicago: University of Chicago Press, 2015), 195–275.

135. Michel Foucault, "What Is an Author?" trans. Josué V. Harari, in *The Foucault Reader*, ed. Paul Rabinow (New York: Pantheon Books, 1984), 101–120.

136. Snider sometimes references particular works, such as *Paradise Lost*, as Literary Bibles, but he also identifies the Bibles as whole corpuses (in particular, all of Shakespeare's plays) designated by author. His supercanon, referenced throughout his work but laid out explicitly in one appendix, consists of Homer, Dante, Shakespeare, and Goethe. Denton J. Snider, *A Writer of Books: In His Genesis* (St. Louis: Sigma, [1910]), 629–654. Snider's phrase was borrowed, with acknowledgment, by Richard G. Moulton in *World Literature and Its Place in General Culture* (New York: Macmillan, 1911).

137. Denton J. Snider, *The St. Louis Movement in Philosophy, Literature, Education, Psychology, with Chapters of Autobiography* (St. Louis: Sigma, 1920).

138. Snider, *Writer of Books*, 54–58, 297–299.

139. These U.S. translations, together with C. P. Cranch's translation of Virgil's *Aeneid* and John Augustine Wilstach's translation of other works by Virgil, were all published by Houghton Mifflin, grouped together as "Translations of Great Classics," and advertised in related Houghton Mifflin books. See an example in the front matter of *The Odyssey of Homer*, trans. William Cullen Bryant (Boston: Houghton Mifflin, 1871), vol. 1.

140. Johann Wolfgang von Goethe, "On World Literature," in *Essays on Art and Literature*, ed. John Gearey, trans. Ellen von Nardroff and Ernest H. von Nardroff, vol. 3 of *Goethe's Collected Works* (New York: Suhrkamp, 1986), 224–228. Kant's "Toward Perpetual Peace" called for a *"league of nations"* to avert wars and protect the rights of nations on a worldwide scale. Immanuel Kant, "Toward Perpetual Peace" [1795], in *Practical Philosophy*, trans. and ed. Mary J. Gregor (Cambridge: Cambridge University Press, 1996), 326.

141. Kate Flint, "Is the Native an American? National Identity and the British Reception of *Hiawatha*," in Meredith L. McGill, ed., *The Traffic in Poems: Nineteenth-Century Poetry and Transatlantic Exchange* (New Brunswick, N.J.: Rutgers University Press, 2008), 63–80.

142. Longfellow, preface to *Poets and Poetry of Europe*, vi, v.

143. Snider, *St. Louis Movement*, 439.

144. Snider, *St. Louis Movement*, 441. Snider's discussion fits Paul Keen's proposal that the "ideal of the literary tradition," as it coalesced in Britain during the 1790s, "recuperated the universalist assumptions of the public sphere, but only to the extent that it remained securely within the cultural, rather than the political, domain. It was guided less by a reformist spirit of futurity than by a Burkean emphasis on tradition as a bulwark against unsettling social developments, but this conservatism did not deprive it of an active cultural role." Paul Keen, *The Crisis of Literature in the 1790s: Print Culture and the Public Sphere* (Cambridge: Cambridge University Press, 1999), 19–20.

145. Snider, *St. Louis Movement*, 439.

Chapter 2

1. "Article XXIV," review of *The Law of Libel and the History of its Introduction and Successive Alterations in the Law of England, &c.*, by Thomas Ludlow, and three other books, *Port Folio*, Jan. 1820, 185. An editorial note indicates that the review was translated from the original by J. Von Gentz in the *Vienna Quarterly Review* of Jan. 1818. It is not certain exactly what "civil society" entailed for the author, but since the topic was freedom of speech and the press, at least some of the dimensions that are emphasized in this chapter were at stake.

2. The Marxist tradition emphasizes the economic functions of civil society, whereas the liberal tradition has posited that civil society can operate independently of market relations. See Carolyn M. Elliott, "Civil Society and Democracy: A Comparative Review Essay," in Carolyn M. Elliott, ed., *Civil Society and Democracy: A Reader* (New Delhi: Oxford University Press, 2003), 7–8. In attributing to civil society both political and economic significance, I follow the practice of many scholars, including Charles Taylor's in "Modes of Civil Society," in Elliott, *Civil Society and Democracy*, 43–62.

3. This sense is schematically laid out in Hegel's *Philosophy of Right* (1820), which defined civil society as the zone between the family and the state, but versions of it circulated even earlier in Euro-American culture.G. W. F. Hegel, "The Civic Community," in *Philosophy of Right*, trans. S. W. Dyde (Amherst, N.Y.: Prometheus Books, 1996), 185–239.

4. Alexis de Tocqueville, *Democracy in America*, trans. Henry Reeve (New York: Bantam, 2000): 67.

5. Francis Bacon, "Of Studies," in *The Essayes or Counsels, Civill and Morall*, ed. Michael Kiernan (Cambridge, Mass.: Harvard University Press), 153.

6. Warner emphasizes that a public is not organized by particular texts but by "concatenations of texts through time." His work provides an inspiring account of print's role in forging publics that have the potential to transform collective life and state politics.Michael Warner, "Publics and Counterpublics," in *Publics and Counterpublics* (New York: Zone Books, 2002), 90.

7. Elizabeth Eisenstein points out that North Americans argued that a republic could be bigger than envisioned by political philosophers such as Montesquieu precisely because of print. Elizabeth L. Eisenstein, *Divine Art, Infernal Machine: The Reception of Printing in the West from First Impressions to the Sense of an Ending* (Philadelphia: University of Pennsylvania Press, 2011), 131. A striking European example of the ways in which the coordinated experience of print produced a sense of a unified, indeed standardized, national community is the report that a French minister of education during Napoleon's rule "is said to have looked at his watch and announced that at that very minute, every French schoolboy of a certain age was turning the same page of Caesar's *Gallic Wars*" (Eisenstein, *Divine Art*, 154).

Benedict Anderson has famously called attention to the way newspapers provide a sense of a national public organized temporally, as many people in a great anonymous public read the same newspaper at the same time (or read it later but know from its date how they relate to its initial time frame). Benedict Anderson, *Imagined Communities: Reflections on the Origin and Spread of Nationalism*, rev. ed. (New York: Verso, 2000), 32–36.

A counterargument is offered by Trish Loughran's *The Republic in Print: Print Culture in the Age of U. S. Nation Building, 1770–1870* (New York: Columbia University Press, 2007), which emphasizes the nonsimultaneous transmission of print and the variations among local print cultures during the Revolutionary and early national periods. Loughran's work instructively argues that an effective and nationally operating infrastructure for the distribution of print was not in place until the latter half of the nineteenth century, although she does not take into account the fact that books and periodicals circulated in far-flung ways even if not predictably. Her approach valorizes the "local category of place" over "more abstracted state- and region-based identities" (169).

8. According to J. G. A. Pocock, "The revolutionary effects of the introduction of public credit and the standing army [in Europe] included the recognition as a new and dominant

force in politics and history of what was termed 'commercial society' and later 'civil society'—that state of affairs, made possible very largely by trade, capital, and mobile property, in which exchange relations among human beings generated a wealth and civility proof against religious and civil warfare." J. G. A. Pocock, *The Machiavellian Moment: Florentine Political Thought and the Atlantic Republican Tradition* (Princeton, N.J.: Princeton University Press, 1975), 570. A famous elaboration of this analysis is Max Weber's *The Protestant Ethic and the Spirit of Capitalism* (1905), whose logic is beautifully previewed in a 1785 periodical piece asserting "[t]hat temperance; and that moderation, which the precepts of christianity [sic] require, are of great importance to civil society, and evidently tend to promote the public good." Thomas Reese, "Essay on the Influence of Religion in Civil Society" [1785], *American Museum; or, Universal Magazine,* Mar. 1791, 153. See Albert O. Hirschman's account of how "moneymaking" came to be understood as a "calm desire," in Francis Hutcheson's phrase, that could counteract more dangerous passions. Albert O. Hirschman, *The Passions and the Interests: Political Arguments for Capitalism before Its Triumph* (Princeton, N.J.: Princeton University Press, 1977), 65.

9. The legitimation of the state (which requires, in Antonio Gramsci's terms, the consolidation of a ruling group's hegemony) effectively happens in civil society, whose power of reflection and judgment was known as "criticism" in the eighteenth century. Antonio Gramsci, *Selections from the Prison Notebooks,* ed. and trans. Quintin Hoare and Geoffrey Nowell Smith (New York: International, 1971), 5.

10. Eisenstein, *Divine Art,* 119. William J. Gilmore has identified a significant investment in the idea of the Republic of Letters as late as the 1820s in the Connecticut River Valley communities he studied in *Reading Becomes a Necessity of Life: Material and Cultural Life in Rural New England, 1780-1835* (Knoxville: University of Tennessee Press, 1989), 19. See also Norman S. Fiering, "The Transatlantic Republic of Letters: A Note on the Circulation of Learned Periodicals in Early Eighteenth-Century America," *William and Mary Quarterly,* 3rd series, 33, no. 4 (1976): 644-647; and David D. Hall, "Learned Culture in the Eighteenth Century," in Hugh Amory and David D. Hall, eds., *The Colonial Book in the Atlantic World,* vol. 1 of David D. Hall, ed., *The History of the Book in America* (Cambridge: Cambridge University Press, 2000), 411-433.

11. References to a Republic of Letters go back at least as far as the fifteenth century, and Erasmus's advocacy of a "Commonwealth of Learning" important in the sixteenth century (Eisenstein, *Divine Art,* 62, 109-111). However, the effects of this ideal became important mainly in the seventeenth century, marked by publications such as the *Journal des Sçavans* (begun in 1665), whose announced goal was "[t]o give information concerning new happenings in the Republic of Letters." A French Huguenot who had fled to Rotterdam, Pierre Bayle began the journal *Nouvelles de la République des Lettres* in 1684, and the circulation of this publication in France embodied the association of the Republic of Letters with peaceable nonsectarian exchange that might incorporate political dissent: Eisenstein has identified the Republic of Letters with the promotion of a "Third Force" that would resist alignment with either Protestant or Catholic zealots. Dena Goodman, *The Republic of Letters: A Cultural History of the French Enlightenment* (Ithaca, N.Y.: Cornell University Press, 1994), 14-16; Fiering, "Transatlantic Republic of Letters," 644-647; and Eisenstein, *Divine Art,* 63. Eisenstein's work documents the many ways in which print invited "cross-fertilization" and "cross-cultural interchange": see Elizabeth L. Eisenstein, *The Printing Press*

as an Agent of Change: Communications and Cultural Transformations in Early-Modern Europe, 2 vols. (New York: Cambridge University Press, 1979), 1: 71–80.

12. On the importance of correspondence within the Republic of Letters, see Goodman, *Republic*, 17, 153, 160–161.

Goodman outlines the importance of sociability and politeness in Paris salons during the era leading up to the French Revolution (3, 9, 52). An instance of an equally boundary-crossing salon in North America is Archibald Home's salon in New Jersey, which "included Jews, Huguenots, Presbyterians, and Anglicans of both sexes in nearly equal number," according to David S. Shields, in "Eighteenth-Century Literary Culture," in Amory and Hall, *Colonial Book*, 456, 459–461.

13. Fiering, "Transatlantic Republic," 654.

14. Gordon S. Wood, *The Radicalism of the American Revolution* (New York: Vintage 1991), 220–222.

15. Paul G. Baton, "The Entrance of the Novel into Scottish Universities," in Robert Crawford, ed., *The Scottish Invention of English Literature* (New York: Cambridge University Press, 1988), 91.

16. Adam Smith was best known for *The Wealth of Nations* (1776), but he was a professor of moral philosophy at the University of Glasgow. His *Theory of Moral Sentiments* (1759) did not fit squarely within the Common Sense tradition, since it did not posit an innate moral sense, but it emphasized the moral significance of people's psychological orientation to other people's needs and judgments: to moral perceptions formed in a social matrix. See Adam Smith, *The Theory of the Moral Sentiments*, ed. E. G. West (Indianapolis: Liberty Classics, 1976), 265; see also 515–516.

17. Friedrich Schiller, *On the Aesthetic Education of Man in a Series of Letters*, ed. and trans. Elizabeth M. Wilkinson and L. A. Willoughby (Oxford: Clarendon Press, 1967), 56.

18. Gavin Budge argues that until German aesthetic philosophy (especially Kant) came to be widely read in England, around the 1860s, rather than grasped at second hand through interpreters such as Coleridge, the culture we retrospectively call Romantic was influenced by a "philosophical hybrid between Common Sense philosophy and German Idealism," very much the matrix I'm describing. Gavin Budge, "Introduction: Empiricism, Romanticism, and the Politics of Common Sense," in Gavin Budge, ed., *Romantic Empiricism: Poetics and the Philosophy of Common Sense* (Lewisburg, Pa.: Bucknell University Press, 2007), 22.

19. Terry Pinkard, *German Philosophy, 1760–1860: The Legacy of Idealism* (Cambridge: Cambridge University Press, 2002), 15.

20. James Van Horn Melton, *The Rise of the Public in Enlightenment Europe* (Cambridge: Cambridge University Press, 2001), 9. On the widespread fascination with "English Liberty" in Europe and North America, see Lee Ward, *The Politics of Liberty in England and Revolutionary America* (New York: Cambridge University Press, 2010).

21. T. J. Reed, "Coming of Age in Prussia and Swabia: Kant, Schiller, and the Duke," *Modern Language Review* 86, no. 3 (1991): 616.

22. By the eighteenth century, this censorship was postproduction—affecting works once they were published—in contrast to earlier forms of preproduction censorship that typically took the form of licensing requirements.Mark Rose, *Authors and Owners: The Invention of Copyright* (Cambridge, Mass.: Harvard University Press, 1993), 28–29, 32–33, 34–37; Eisenstein, *Divine Art*, 57; and Richard D. Brown, the section "The Shifting Freedoms

of the Press in the Eighteenth Century," in the chapter "Periodicals and Politics," in Amory and Hall, *Colonial Book*, 366–376, at 367.

23. Phillip H. Round, *By Nature and by Custom Cursed: Transatlantic Civil Discourse and New England Cultural Production, 1620–1660* (Hanover, N.H.: University Press of New England, 1999), 38–39; and Grantland S. Rice, *The Transformation of Authorship in America* (Chicago: University of Chicago Press, 1997), 1, 93.

24. Jeffrey L. Pasley, *"The Tyranny of Printers": Newspaper Politics in the Early American Republic* (Charlottesville: University Press of Virginia, 2001), 34–35; and Linde Katritzky, *Johnson and the Letters of Junius: New Perspectives on an Old Enigma* (New York: Peter Lang, 1996), 7.

25. "The Franklin case ended prior censorship and licensing of the press in Massachusetts," according to Murray N. Rothbard, *Conceived in Liberty* [1979] (Auburn, Ala.: Ludwig von Mises Institute, 2011), 643. Rothbard notes as well that the legislature was empowered to vote to punish James Franklin without an indictment or trial of any kind. See also David W. Conroy, *In Public Houses: Drink and the Revolution of Authority in Colonial Massachusetts* (Chapel Hill: University of North Carolina Press, 1995), 175–176.

26. Brown, "Shifting Freedoms."

27. June Eichbaum, "The Antagonism between Freedom of Speech and Seditious Libel," *Hastings Constitutional Law Quarterly* 5 (Winter 1978): 445–459.

28. Rothbard, *Conceived*, 643. Seditious libel was defined by its effects—its tendencies, or even its probable or envisioned tendencies—rather than inherent properties of the text, so it was terrifyingly flexible. Interestingly enough, this legal dimension drew attention to the power of reception, which was almost completely suppressed in the construction of literary property as owned (and by implication controlled) by authors. David Saunders and Ian Hunter have pointed out that obscenity laws have mainly followed this trajectory, addressing the "socioethical effects of the work's dissemination" rather than pursuing "hermeneutic procedures" that might be used to attribute "authorial intentionality." David Saunders and Ian Hunter, "Lessons from the 'Literatory': How to Historicise Authorship," *Critical Inquiry* 17, no. 3 (1991): 487. The key ruling influencing Anglo-American obscenity law until the 1933 Woolsey ruling that cleared *Ulysses* for U.S. publication was formulated by Alexander Cockburn in 1868 *Queen v. Hicklin*: "The test of obscenity is this, whether the tendency of the matter charged as obscenity is to deepen and corrupt those whose minds are open to such immoral influences, and into whose hands a publication of this sort may fall." Thomas L. Tedford, *Freedom of Speech in the U.S.* (New York: Random House, 1985), 162, cited by Paul S. Boyer, "Gilded-Age Consensus, Repressive Campaigns, and Gradual Liberalization: The Shifting Rhythms of Book Censorship," in Carl F. Kaestle and Janice A. Radway, eds., *Print in Motion: The Expansion of Publishing and Reading in the United States, 1880–1940*, vol. 4 of Hall, *History of the Book in America* (Chapel Hill: University of North Carolina Press, 2009), 282.

29. Phrasings are taken from an 1804 British verdict and a published essay by a British jurist, published in a Viennese review of British libel law. "Article XXIV," 194.

30. Neil Vidmar and Valerie P. Hans, *American Juries: The Verdict* (Amherst, N.Y.: Prometheus Books, 2007), 41–46.

31. Wood, *Radicalism of the American Revolution*, 82–86.

32. Paul Allen, *The Life of Charles Brockden Brown* (Delmar, N.Y.: Scholars' Facsimiles and Reprints, 1975), 37–38.

33. W. M. Verhoeven, "'This Blissful Period of Intellectual Liberty': Transatlantic Radicalism and Enlightened Conservatism in Brown's Early Writings," in Philip Barnard, Mark L. Kamrath, and Stephen Shapiro, eds., *Revising Charles Brockden Brown: Culture, Politics, and Sexuality in the Early Republic* (Knoxville: University of Tennessee Press, 2004), 7–40, at 27.

34. Melton, *Rise of the Public*, 268–269; and Bryan Waterman, *Republic of Intellect: The Friendly Club of New York City and the Making of American Literature* (Baltimore: Johns Hopkins University Press, 2007), 50–91.

35. On Britain's Seditious Societies Act of 1799 and its reassertion in 1881, see William St. Clair, *The Reading Nation in the Romantic Period* (Cambridge: Cambridge University Press, 2004), 311.

36. Melton, *Rise of the Public*, 109.

37. "Article XXIV," 210. See also Junius, preface to *The Letters of Junius: "Stat Nominis Umbra"* (London: W. Wilson, 1807), xii.

38. E. P. Thompson, *The Making of the English Working Class* (1963; New York: Vintage, 1966), 87, 132, 135, 469.

For an overview of the English political context shaping intellectual and print culture in the 1790s, see Paul Keen, *The Crisis of Literature in the 1790s: Print Culture and the Public Sphere* (Cambridge: Cambridge University Press, 1999). Pamela Clemit notes that William Godwin wrote the preface to *Caleb Williams* in response to Hardy's arrest but that the delayed publication of the novel separated it from that context. Pamela Clemit, *The Godwinian Novel: The Rational Fictions of Godwin, Brockden Brown, and Mary Shelley* (Oxford: Clarendon Press, 1993), 36.

39. Stacy Schiff, *A Great Improvisation: Franklin, France, and the Birth of America* (New York: Henry Holt, 2005), 406.

40. On aggravated forms of censorship and prosecution for sedition in World War I, see Boyer, "Gilded-Age Consensus," 287–288.

41. Donna Lee Dickerson, *The Course of Tolerance: Freedom of the Press in Nineteenth-Century America* (New York: Greenwood Press, 1990), 26. For the *Port Folio*'s report of the trial, which incorporated the original offending passage, see "Sketch of the Editor's Trial," *Port Folio*, 28 Dec. 1805, 402.

42. [William Cullen Bryant], *The Embargo; or, Sketches of the Times: A Satire* (Boston: n.p., 1808). On the title page, the author is identified only as "a youth of thirteen"; Bryant's father paid for the volume's publication. Charles H. Brown, *William Cullen Bryant* (New York: Charles Scribner's Sons, 1971), 24.

43. On British and U.S. Jacobin and anti-Jacobin novels of the late eighteenth century, see also Verhoeven, "'This Blissful Period.'"

44. Jonathan Arac, "Hawthorne and the Aesthetics of American Romance," in Leonard Cassuto, Clare Virginia Eby, and Benjamin Reiss, eds., *The Cambridge History of the American Novel* (New York: Cambridge University Press, 2011), 135–150. See also Jonathan Arac, "Literary Narrative," in *The Emergence of American Literary Narrative, 1820–1860* (Cambridge, Mass.: Harvard University Press, 2005), 121–180.

45. Clemit, *Godwinian Novel*, 8.

46. Robert S. Levine, *Dislocating Race and Nation: Episodes in Nineteenth-Century American Literary Nationalism* (Chapel Hill: University of North Carolina Press, 2008), 40–44.

47. Ian Watt, *The Rise of the Novel: Studies in Defoe, Richardson and Fielding* (Berkeley: University of California Press, 1957).

48. Jared Gardner, *The Rise and Fall of Early American Magazine Culture* (Urbana: University of Illinois Press, 2012), 39.

49. Gardner, *Rise and Fall*, 76–82.

50. In British America and the early United States, as in Great Britain, certain coffeehouses and taverns were headquarters for particular political parties or factions. Melton provides a wonderful discussion of the role of taverns and coffeehouses in British political culture (*Rise of the Public*, 212–252); and Conroy offers a similar account of taverns and similar establishments in colonial Massachusetts, including the role played by reading in these establishments (*Public Houses*, 180). On the significance of coffeehouses in British North American print circuits, see James Raven, "The Importation of Books in the Eighteenth Century," section 3 in chapter 5, "The Atlantic World," in Amory and Hall, *Colonial Book*, 192.

51. Thomas J. Schlereth, *The Cosmopolitan Ideal in Enlightenment Thought: Its Form and Function in the Ideas of Franklin, Hume, and Voltaire, 1694-1790* (Notre Dame, Ind.: University of Notre Dame Press, 1977), 87–88. On the special role Freemasons played in the development of civil society, in spite of their nonpartisan status, see Melton, *Rise of the Public*, 252–268; and David S. Shields, *Civil Tongues and Polite Letters in British America* (Chapel Hill: University of North Carolina Press, 1997), 187.

52. Here, also, manuscript circulation was an important way in which writing that wasn't print also served collective thinking: "Artisans' groups, private clubs, and Masonic organizations, all of which flourished in midcentury, sought privacy for their members, and so their materials—like their books—tended to circulate privately in the absence of printing." Carla Mulford, "Print and Manuscript Culture," in Kevin J. Hayes, ed., *The Oxford Handbook of Early American Literature* (New York: Oxford University Press, 2008), 338.

Jeffrey L. Pasley emphasizes the significance of partisan newspapers in U.S. history, and especially in relation to the development of key positions of early political parties: "There were no 'card-carrying' party members or 'registered voters' in eighteenth- or nineteenth-century America, but a subscription to a party newspaper, or a regular readership of one in a tavern or reading room, substituted for these more formal means of belonging. The party newspaper furnished a corporeal [*sic*] link to the party that could be obtained in few other ways." Pasley, *"Tyranny of Printers,"* 12. Richard L. Kaplan argues that U.S. newspapers did not seek to develop nonpartisan stances, including a journalistic code of ethics emphasizing objectivity, until the end of the nineteenth century. Richard L. Kaplan, "From Partisanship to Professionalism: The Transformation of the Daily Press," in Kaestle and Radway, *Print in Motion*, 133–134.

On the partisanship of British reviews, see Stefan Collini, *Common Reading: Critics, Historians, Publics* (Oxford: Oxford University Press, 2008), 225. David Higgins notes the strong partisanship of the early reviews, such as the Whiggishness of the *Edinburgh Review*, but he finds the next generation of *Reviews* (founded in the 1810s) to be considerably less partisan, characterized by a nonpartisan advocacy for "genius." David Higgins, *Romantic Genius and the Literary Magazine: Biography, Celebrity, and Politics* (London: Routledge, 2005), 13–28.

53. Edward Larkin, *Thomas Paine and the Literature of Revolution* (New York: Cambridge University Press, 2005), 26–30. Larkin identifies the *Pennsylvania Magazine* (1775) as the first such publication in British America.

54. "To the Patrons of the Port Folio," *Port-Folio*, May 1814, 1.

55. Tunis Wortman, *A Treatise concerning Political Enquiry, and the Liberty of the Press* (New York: George Forman, 1800), 270, 18, 177, 265–266. The title page announces that the

book was published by George Forman for the author, another reminder of the prevalence of private and subscription publication during this period.

56. Keen, *Crisis of Literature*, 56.

57. According to Higgins, the Lake Poets had all held "strongly Jacobinical views in the 1790s but had gone on to become supporters of the Tory government and beneficiaries of its patronage." Hazlitt was disappointed in what he considered their "apostasy" (Higgins, *Romantic Genius*, 102). Peter Kafer, *Charles Brockden Brown's Revolution and the Birth of American Gothic* (Philadelphia: University of Pennsylvania Press, 2004), 191–194.

58. William C. Dowling, *Literary Federalism in the Age of Jefferson: Joseph Dennie and "The Port Folio," 1801–1812* (Columbia: University of South Carolina Press, 1999), 69.

59. Baumgarten first introduced the term "aesthetics" (in Latin) in his 1735 work *Meditationes philosophicae de nonullis ad poema pertinentibus* (Philosophical meditations on some requirements of the poem), but his work *Aesthetica*, published in two volumes in 1750 and 1758, showcased the term. Kai Hammermeister, *The German Aesthetic Tradition* (Cambridge: Cambridge University Press, 2002), 4–6.

60. Anthony Ashley Cooper, third Earl of Shaftesbury, *Characteristics of Men, Manners, Opinions, Times*, ed. Lawrence E. Klein (New York: Cambridge University Press, 1999), 331

61. The espousal of disinterestedness could coincide with class privilege, however: for U.S. Federalists and British Whigs, disinterestedness was a special qualification that men of property brought to public office, since their wealth meant that they didn't need to seek profit from their positions. Wood, *Radicalism*, 104–106.

62. Immanuel Kant, *Critique of the Power of Judgment*, ed. Paul Guyer, trans. Paul Guyer and Eric Matthews (Cambridge: Cambridge University Press, 2007), 90–98.

63. Hammermeister, *German Aesthetic*, 22.

64. The analyses of Paul Keen and Grantland Rice have been important for my sense of the twin dangers of political censorship and commodification for early literary culture: Keen, *Crisis of Literature*, 115; Rice, *Transformation of Authorship*, 4.

65. Meredith McGill makes the intriguing argument that the use of authors' rights as stand-ins for publishers' rights might not be a ruse but rather might signal a "genuine difficulty" in conceptualizing responsibility for "mass-production." Meredith L. McGill, *American Literature and the Culture of Reprinting, 1834–1853* (Philadelphia: University of Pennsylvania Press, 2003), 55. See also John Feather, "The Book Trade in Politics," *Publishing History* 19, no. 8 (1980): 24, about antimonopolistic arguments against the Stationers' Company.

66. Richard D. Altick, *Lives and Letters: A History of Literary Biography in England and America* (New York: Alfred A. Knopf, 1965), 3, 16; St. Clair, *Reading Nation*, 122. Izaak Walton wrote biographical studies of several important figures, including the poets John Donne and George Herbert, in the mid-seventeenth century, and James Boswell's *Life of Samuel Johnson* (1791) clinched the significance of literary biography (Altick, *Lives*, 20, 60). On the long history of authors' portraits, see Roger Chartier, *The Order of Books: Readers, Authors, and Libraries in Europe between the Fourteenth and the Eighteenth Centuries*, trans. Lydia G. Cochrane (Stanford, Calif.: Stanford University Press, 1992), 52. Jayne Elizabeth Lewis analyzes the extraordinary interest in Aesop's image and biography exhibited in Augustan fable collections in *The English Fable: Aesop and Literary Culture, 1651–1740* (New York: Cambridge University Press, 1996), 71–98. In this context, David Shields argues for the significance of the verse memoir of Aquila Rose (a printer's apprentice briefly mentioned

in Franklin's *Autobiography*) that prefaced the edition of Rose's poems published by his son, an early example of a biographical preface presenting the author's works as illustrating episodes in his life story. Shields, "Eighteenth-Century Literary Culture," 439.

67. David R. Shumway has called this tendency "authorism" in *Creating American Civilization: A Genealogy of American Literature as an Academic Discipline* (Minneapolis: University of Minnesota Press, 1994), 125. Martha Woodmansee's work has influentially traced the process by which earlier European emphases on craftsmanship and inspiration were not keyed to purely individual agency and ownership; there were even forms of authorial compensation, honoraria and privileges, that were not predicated on a sense of the text as property and the author as proprietor. Martha Woodmansee, *The Author and the Market: Rereading the History of Aesthetics* (New York: Columbia University Press, 1994), especially 35–55. See also Rose, *Authors and Owners*, 88, 133. Michel Foucault, "What Is an Author?" trans. Josué V. Harari, in *The Foucault Reader*, ed. Paul Rabinow (New York: Pantheon Books, 1984), 101–120.

68. On authors' ownership of manuscripts alone, see Margaret J. M. Ezell, *Social Authorship and the Advent of Print* (Baltimore: Johns Hopkins University Press, 1999), 90.

69. For a comprehensive discussion of the Statute of Anne, see Feather, "Book Trade," 19–44.

70. Rose, *Authors and Owners*, 5, 42, 58; Rice, *Transformation of Authorship*, 74; St. Clair, *Reading Nation*, 84–121.

71. The statute mainly but not completely wrought this change: special arrangements allowed certain printers to retain extended copyright, as chapter 4 discusses in the case of Shakespeare.

72. *Oxford English Dictionary Online*, s.v. "Corpus" (http://www.oed.com.pitt.idm.oclc.org/view/Entry/41873?redirectedFrom=corpus), accessed 11 July 2014.

73. Ezell, *Social Authorship*, 125, 133.

74. Qtd. in Ezell, *Social Authorship*, 123.

75. On the history and significance of *Donaldson v. Becket*, see Mark Rose, "The Author as Proprietor: *Donaldson v. Becket* and the Genealogy of Modern Authorship," *Representations* 23 (Summer 1988): 51–85, and *Authors and Owners*, 92–112.

76. Margaret J. M. Ezell, "Making a Classic: The Advent of the Literary Series," *South Central Review* 11, no. 2 (1994): 9.

77. L. Bently and M. Kretschmer, eds., *Donaldson v. Becket, Primary Sources on Copyright (1450–1900)* (http://copy.law.cam.ac.uk/record/uk_1774, 953–1003), accessed 10 July 2014.

78. Bently and Kretschmer, *Donaldson v. Becket*, 988.

79. On Blackstone's formulations, see Rose, *Authors and Owners*, 63. N. N. Feltes argues that the *Donaldson* ruling established the commodity status of the text rather than the book, in *Modes of Production of Victorian Novels* (Chicago: University of Chicago Press, 1986), 7. Roger Chartier and Mark Rose agree that an earlier case, *Tonson v. Collins*, formulated many of the features of the understanding of literary property that would prevail in *Donaldson*. Since no ruling was issued in *Tonson v. Collins*, though, most scholars identify *Donaldson* as the watershed. Chartier, *Order of Books*, 36; Rose, *Authors and Owners*, 78–79.

80. John Milton, *Areopagitica*, ed. John W. Hales (1875; London: Oxford University Press, 1961), 7. Rose's landmark essay "The Author as Proprietor" makes the case that *Donaldson v. Becket* lays the groundwork for specifically literary authorship, a discussion elaborated in *Authors and Owners*.

Roger Chartier has identified this sacred conjunction as one of content with "form," although the ambiguous relation between form and genre makes this term equally hard to stabilize for legal purposes. Chartier, *Order of Books*, 36. Martha Woodmansee argues that Johann Gottlieb Fichte first formulated the understanding of "form" that became influential in copyright law and literary studies in "Proof of the Illegality of Reprinting: A Rationale and a Parable" (1793). Martha Woodmansee, "The Genius and the Copyright: Economic and Legal Conditions of the Emergence of the 'Author,'" *Eighteenth-Century Studies* 17, no. 4 (1984): 444. However, Mark Rose traces earlier versions of this understanding in English law (*Authors and Owners*, 131–132).

81. David Higgins offers evidence that the modern sense of genius (which he finds summarized in the *OED* definition "native intellectual power of an exalted type...instinctive and extraordinary capacity for imaginative creation, original thought, invention, or discovery") appeared around the beginning of the eighteenth century in British culture. Higgins, *Romantic Genius*, 1.

82. Woodmansee, *The Author*, especially 57–86; Rose, *Authors and Owners*, 6–7.

83. Bently and Kretschmer, *Donaldson v. Becket*, 999.

84. Bently and Kretschmer, *Donaldson v. Becket*, 1000.

85. McGill, *Culture of Reprinting*, 50.

86. Martin T. Buinicki, *Negotiating Copyright: Authorship and the Discourse of Literary Property Rights in Nineteenth-Century America* (New York: Routledge, 2006), 27, 109–112.

87. McGill, *Culture of Reprinting*, 3–4.

88. Peter Jaszi and Martha Woodmansee, "Copyright in Transition," in Kaestle and Radway,*Print in Motion*, 96–97.

89. McGill, *Culture of Reprinting*, 14.

90. Ralph Waldo Emerson, *Essays and Lectures*, ed. Joel Porte (New York: Literary Classics of the United States, 1983), 715.

91. Gilmore, *Reading Becomes*.

92. See Reinhard Wittmann, "Was There a Reading Revolution at the End of the Eighteenth Century?" in Guglielmo Cavallo and Roger Chartier, eds., *A History of Reading in the West* (Amherst: University of Massachusetts Press, 2003), 284–312; McGill, *Culture of Reprinting*, 3–4; and Deidre Shauna Lynch, *Loving Literature: A Cultural History* (Chicago: University of Chicago Press, 2015), 157.

93. Sarah Wadsworth, "A Blue and Gold Mystique," in *In the Company of Books: Literature and Its "Classes" in Nineteenth-Century America* (Amherst: University of Massachusetts Press, 2006), 161–191. On Beadle's Dime Novels" physical appearance, see Albert Johannsen, "Beadle's Dime Novels," *Northern Illinois University-University Libraries* (http://www.ulib.niu.edu/badndp/dn-a.html), accessed 11 July 2014.

94. Nancy Glazener, *Reading for Realism: The History of a U.S. Literary Institution, 1850–1910* (Durham, N.C.: Duke University Press, 1997).

95. David Paul Nord, *Faith in Reading: Religious Publishing and the Birth of Mass Media in America* (New York: Oxford University Press, 2004), 98, plus the rest of chapter 5, "The New Mass Media: Systematic Distribution," 89–112; Ronald J. Zboray and Mary Saracino Zboray, *Literary Dollars and Social Sense: A People's History of the Mass Market Book* (New York: Routledge, 2005), 129–139, 187–190.

96. About subscription publishing and other alternatives to retail sales in the antebellum era, see Zboray and Zboray, *Literary Dollars*, 130–143.

97. Trish Loughran argues that the abolitionist press played an important role around the 1830s in the development of a truly national U.S. public sphere (Loughran, "The Abolitionist Nation," *Republic in Print*, 303–361).

98. Scott E. Casper, "The Census, the Post Office, and Governmental Publishing," in Scott E. Casper, Jeffrey D. Groves, Stephen W. Nissenbaum, and Michael Winship, eds., *The Industrial Book, 1840–1880*, vol. 3 of Hall, *History of the Book in America* (Chapel Hill: University of North Carolina Press, 2007), 179–182. Because most publishers used the U.S. Postal Service to mail books or magazines to at least some distribution points or customers, postal regulations have been the conduit for the state regulation of obscene materials, which typically circulate discreetly. Modeled on legislation from the Civil War that targeted erotica mailed to soldiers, the Comstock Act of 1873 (and related state laws) made it illegal to distribute printed materials deemed obscene—including information about birth control and abortion—through the U.S. postal system. Under the Comstock laws, for example, there were successful prosecutions of booksellers and publishers who sold Zola's *La Terre* (1887) and Tolstoy's *Kreutzer Sonata* (1889).

99. "[A]n author of established reputation, who resorts to the subscription plan for the sake of making more money, descends to a constituency of a lower grade and inevitable loses caste," according to the anonymous author of "Subscription Books," *Literary World*, 1 Aug. 1874, 40. Many trade publishers maintained subscription departments in the late nineteenth century, however. Michael Winship, "The Rise of a National Book Trade System in the United States," in Kaestle and Radway, *Print in Motion*, 67.

100. See for example the coverage in *Publisher's Weekly*, a publication aligned with retail publishers, about the injustice of a postal bill that would allow dime reprints issued multiple times a week to benefit from bulk rate, while Harper's Select Novels would have to be mailed at ordinary book rates. The coverage is excerpted by John Tebbel in *The Expansion of an Industry, 1865–1919*, vol. 2 of *A History of Book Publishing in the United States*, 4 vols. (New York: R. R. Bowker, 1975), 39–40.

Chapter 3

1. Rebecca Harding Davis, "Women in Literature," *The Independent*, 7 May 1891, 1.

2. Francis Bacon, "Of Studies," in *The Essayes or Counsels, Civill and Morall*, ed. Michael Kiernan (Cambridge, Mass.: Harvard University Press), 153.

3. *Oxford English Dictionary Online*, s.v. "Consumption" (http://www.oed.com/view/Entry/39997?redirectedFrom=consumption#eid), accessed 25 July 2014.

4. The period saw the beginnings of the now-familiar U.S. belief that education—especially formal public education—is the solution to every social problem, according to William J. Reese in *America's Public Schools: From the Common School to "No Child Left Behind"* (Baltimore: Johns Hopkins University Press, 2005), especially 21–42. Lee Soltow argues that "[l]iteracy had become one of several virtues associated with progress while, at the same time, serving the conservative interests of social and political stability," so that it was universally promoted. Lee Soltow, *The Rise of Literacy and the Common School in the United States: A Socioeconomic Analysis to 1870* (Chicago: University of Chicago Press, 1981), 85.

5. The standard and smart studies of the institutionalization of U.S. and English literary studies in the United States are Elizabeth Renker, *The Origins of American Literature*

Studies: An Institutional History (New York: Cambridge University Press, 2007); David R. Shumway, *Creating American Civilization: A Genealogy of American Literature as an Academic Discipline* (Minneapolis: University of Minnesota Press, 1994); Gerald Graff, *Professing Literature: An Institutional History* (Chicago: University of Chicago Press, 1987); and Kermit Vanderbilt, *American Literature and the Academy: The Roots, Growth, and Maturity of a Profession* (Philadelphia: University of Pennsylvania Press, 1986). Another valuable resource is Gerald Graff and Michael Warner, eds., *The Origins of Literary Studies in America: A Documentary Anthology* (New York: Routledge, 1989).

6. Arthur N. Applebee recounts the gradual incorporation of studies of English usage and English literature in secondary education throughout the nineteenth century, culminating in the establishment of English as a standard (and standardizing) high school subject around the 1890s. Arthur N. Applebee, *Tradition and Reform in the Teaching of English: A History* (Urbana, Ill.: National Council of Teachers of English, 1974), 1, 13–14, 45. See also Jurgen Herbst, *The Once and Future School: Three Hundred and Fifty Years of American Secondary Education* (New York: Routledge, 1996), especially 42–47; and Reese, *America's Public Schools*.

7. Lawrence A. Cremin, "The Education of the Educating Professions," in Lester F. Goodchild and Harold S. Wechsler, eds., *The History of Higher Education*, 2nd ed. (Needham Heights, Mass.: Simon and Schuster, 1997), 403–415; and James W. Fraser. *Preparing America's Teachers: A History* (New York: Teachers College Columbia University, 2007), 135.

8. The development of uniform curricula for secondary schools accelerated in the wake of the Committee of Ten report of 1892, which sought to align high school curricula with college preparation; there was resistance from educators who wanted to preserve the integrity (and uniformity) of high school education as a common resource. See Reese, *America's Public Schools*, 185–188.

9. Amartya Sen has criticized the cultural acceptance of the idea that the pursuit of self-interest is a privileged sign of rationality; he argues that the scope of ethics was curtailed by the idea that economic analyses of human motivation were empirical and uncontroversial. Amartya Sen, *On Ethics and Economics* (New York: Basil Blackwell, 1987).

10. George Ticknor to Mrs. Walter Channing, 1 Aug. 1817, in George Ticknor, *Life, Letters, and Journals of George Ticknor*, 2 vols., 7th ed. (Boston: James R. Osgood, 1877), 1: 149.

11. For an account of another English author's foundational role in the development of literary studies, see Ian Reid, *Wordsworth and the Formation of English Studies* (Burlington, Vt.: Ashgate, 2004).

12. Johann Gottfried Herder, "Shakespeare," in *Against Pure Reason: Writings on Religion, Language, and History*, trans., ed., and intro. Marcia Bunge (Minneapolis: Fortress Press, 1993), 153.

13. Herder, "Shakespeare," 157.

14. Margreta de Grazia, *Hamlet without Hamlet* (Cambridge: Cambridge University Press, 2007), 169–173; and Ralph Waldo Emerson, "Shakspeare; or, The Poet," in *Essays and Lectures, e*d. Joel Porte (New York: Literary Classics of the United States, 1983), 715. De Grazia's study has been the chief source for my conceptualization of Shakespeare's central role within the modern version of literature.

15. Anthony Ashley Cooper, third Earl of Shaftesbury, extract from *Characteristicks of Men, Manners, Opinions, Times*, rept. In David Farley-Hills, ed., *Critical Responses to*

Hamlet, 1600–1790, vol. 1 of *Critical Responses to Hamlet, 1600–1900*, 5 vols. (New York: AMS Press, 1997), 38.

16. Johann Wolfgang von Goethe's *Wilhelm Meister's Apprenticeship* (published in German 1796; published in Carlyle's translation 1824) is excerpted and reprinted in David Farley-Hills, ed., *Critical Responses to Hamlet, 1790–1838*, vol. 2 of *Critical Responses to Hamlet, 1600–1900* (New York: AMS Press, 1996), 19–42; see also August Wilhelm Schlegel, *Lectures on Dramatic Art and Literature*, rept. in Farley-Hills, *Critical Responses to Hamlet, 1790–1838*, 49–52; and Samuel Taylor Coleridge, excerpted "Letters, Marginalia, Conversations," rept. in Farley-Hills, *Critical Responses to Hamlet, 1790–1838*, 53–90.

17. See Neil Rhodes, *Shakespeare and the Origins of English* (New York: Oxford University Press, 2004); Alden T. Vaughan and Virginia Mason Vaughan, *Shakespeare in America* (Oxford: Oxford University Press, 2012), 9; Gary Taylor, *Reinventing Shakespeare: A Cultural History, from the Restoration to the Present* (New York: Weidenfeld and Nicolson, 1989), 9–61; and Michael Dobson, *The Making of the National Poet: Shakespeare, Adaptation, and Authorship, 1660–1769* (Oxford: Clarendon Press, 1992), 12, 63–64, 80–85.

18. Ticknor, *Life*, 1: 54, 287, 88.

19. More than a century earlier, in the heat of the quarrel between ancients and moderns, it had become standard practice to reference a similar competition, perhaps apocryphal, in which Shakespeare's commonplaces were pitted against those of classical authors and Shakespeare won. The competition is referenced in the editions of Nicholas Rowe (1709) and Alexander Pope (1725). Rhodes, *Shakespeare and the Origins*, 173. On Shakespeare's role as representative modern pitted against the ancients, see Taylor, *Reinventing Shakespeare*, 114; and de Grazia, *Hamlet without Hamlet*, 10.

20. Taylor, *Reinventing Shakespeare*, 113. Paine may have been responding to the appropriation of Shakespeare by dominant cultural formations rather than to the plays themselves. See Heike Grundmann, "Shakespeare and European Romanticism," in Michael Ferber, ed., *A Companion to European Romanticism* (Malden, Mass.: Blackwell, 2005), 32.

21. Kim C. Sturgess cites Shakespeare's antimonarchical valences for U.S. audiences in *Shakespeare and the American Nation* (New York: Cambridge University Press, 2004), 56–57.

22. Michael Bristol, *Shakespeare's America, America's Shakespeare* (London: Routledge, 1990), 55–59. For Adams's treatment of Shakespeare, see [John Adams], *Discourses in Davila* [1790] (Boston: Russell and Cutler, 1805), 230.

23. The Duyckincks' *Cyclopedia* praised Gulian Verplanck's 1847 edition of Shakespeare for clarifying that some usages called "Americanisms" were simply "expressions…out of use in England, [that] have been preserved in this country." Evert A. Duyckinck and George L. Duyckinck, eds., *Cyclopaedia of American Literature* [1855], 2 vols. (New York: Scribner, 1866) 2: 70. Charles W. Stearns, *The Shakspeare Treasury of Wisdom and Knowledge* (New York: G.P. Putnam and Sons, 1869) 386–393, includes a chapter on "Americanisms in Shakspeare's Plays," helpfully subtitled "Words Obsolete in England, in Use in America," on the same topic.

24. Christopher Hanlon, *America's England: Antebellum Literature and Atlantic Sectionalism* (Oxford: Oxford University Press, 2013), 47–69. About the most glaring outcropping of this appropriation of Shakespeare, Charles Mills Gayley's *Shakespeare and the Founders of Liberty in America* (1917), see especially Coppelia Kahn, "Poet of America: Charles Mills Gayley's Anglo-Saxon Shakespeare," in Coppélia Kahn, Heather S. Nathans, and Mimi

Godfrey, *Shakespearean Educations: Power, Citizenship, and Performance* (Newark: University of Delaware Press, 2011), 201–215.

25. Douglas A. Jones, Jr., "Slavery, Performance, and the Design of African American Theatre," in Harvey Young, ed., *The Cambridge Companion to African American Theatre* (New York: Cambridge University Press, 2013), 23–28. About African American Shakespearean performers, see Vaughan and Vaughan, *Shakespeare in America*, 113–115.

26. Elisa Tamarkin, *Anglophilia: Deference, Devotion, and Antebellum America* (Chicago: University of Chicago Press, 2008), 196, and see also the rest of Tamarkin's chapter "Freedom and Deference: Society, Antislavery, and Black Intellectualism," 178–246.

27. Dobson, *National Poet*, 7; see also 228–230. The same logic informed George Ticknor's treatment of Spanish literary history. Wrote Ticknor, "In every country that has yet obtained a rank among those nations whose intellectual cultivation is the highest, the period in which it has produced the permanent body of its literature has been that of its glory as a state." In his examples, ancient and modern, state glory was marked by conquest. The capture of Granada from the Moors in 1492 and the far-flung imperial conquests of Charles V form the preconditions for the greatness of Cervantes, outweighing the more recent chilling influence of the Inquisition. George Ticknor, *The History of Spanish Literature*, 3 vols., 3rd American ed., corrected and enl. (Boston: Ticknor & Fields, 1863), 1:417, 417–432.

28. Sturgess, *Shakespeare and the American Nation*, 99–121. The U.S. special relationship with the United Kingdom also was at work in late nineteenth-century U.S. textbooks that linked dates in Shakespeare's life with events in North America. Malkiel Aron Choseed, "Representations of Teaching, Curriculum Reform, and the Formation of Collegiate English" (Ph.D. diss., University of Pittsburgh, 2007), 163. See also Curtis Breight, "Shakespeare on American Television and the Special Relationship between the UK and the USA," in Solange Davin and Rhona Jackson, eds., *Television and Criticism* (Bristol: Intellect, 2008), 37–48.

29. [S. G. Goodrich], *Literature, Ancient and Modern, with Specimens* (New York: John Allan, 1845), 335, 229.

30. Donald Pease, "Colonial Violence and Poetic Transcendence in Whitman's 'Song of Myself,'" in Kerry Larson, ed., *The Cambridge Companion to Nineteenth-Century Poetry* (New York: Cambridge University Press, 2011), 227.

31. David McCullough, *John Adams* (New York: Simon and Schuster, 2001), 359.

32. Charles Adams, *Memoir of Washington Irving* (New York: Carlton and Lanahan, 1870), 75. Washington Irving, *The Sketch-Book*, in *History, Tales, and Sketches*, ed. James W. Tuttleton (New York: Literary Classics of the United States, 1983), 983. On the Jubilee, see Vanessa Cunningham, *Shakespeare and Garrick* (New York: Cambridge University Press, 2008); and Christian Deelman, *The Great Shakespeare Jubilee* (New York: Viking Press, 1964).

33. Samuel Taylor Coleridge, chapter 14 of *Biographia Literaria*.

34. Irving, *Sketch-Book*, 985.

35. Irving, *Sketch-Book*, 862. On the importance of the fantasy that literary characters live beyond their texts of origin (and can be appropriated for new uses), see David A. Brewer, *The Afterlife of Character, 1726–1825* (Philadelphia: University of Pennsylvania Press, 2005).

36. Irving, *Sketch-Book*, 862.

37. John Keats to George and Tom Keats, December 21, 1817, in *The Romantics on Shakespeare*, ed. Jonathan Bate (New York: Penguin, 1992), 198.

38. Irving, *Sketch-Book*, 863. The obverse of this argument (which worked by similar logic) was William Godwin's claim that Chaucer's writings were especially valuable because they were truly from "times of barbarism," qualitatively different from the turn of the nineteenth century, whereas Shakespeare's time, "the age of queen Elizabeth[,] was a period of uncommon refinement" much closer to Godwin's own. William Godwin, *Life of Geoffrey Chaucer: The Early English Poet*, 2 vols. (London: Richard Phillips, 1803), 1: vi.

39. Craig Dionne identifies Jacob Burkhardt's *The Civilization of the Renaissance in Italy* (1860) as a scholarly work that clinched the identification of the Renaissance with the birth of individualism. Craig Dionne, "Period Making and the Discipline: A Genealogy of the Idea of the Renaissance in *ELH*," in David R. Shumway and Craig Dionne, eds., *Disciplining English: Alternative Histories, Critical Perspectives* (Albany: State University of New York Press, 2002), 83.

40. "Mr. Prescott's Philip the Second," *Putnam's*, Jan. 1856, 50.

41. H. N. Hudson, *Lectures on Shakspeare*, 2 vols. (New York: Baker and Scribner, 1848), 1: 103.

42. Barrett Wendell, *A Literary History of America* (New York: Charles Scribner's Sons, 1901), 4, 6.

43. James Morgan Hart, "The College Course in English Literature, How It May Be Improved," in Graff and Warner, *Origins*, 36.

44. James Russell Lowell, "Shakespeare Once More" [1868], in *The English Poets: Lessing, Rousseau* [1888] (Port Washington, N.Y.: Kennikat Press, 1970), 81–84. Denton J. Snider calls Catholicism the "Poetical Church," even for Protestants, in *System of Shakespeare's Dramas*, 2 vols. (St. Louis: G. I. Jones, 1877), 1: 23.

45. Margaret Cavendish called Shakespeare a "Natural Poet" and praised his representation of "Nature" in letter 123 of *Sociable Letters*. Margaret Cavendish, *Sociable Letters*, ed. James Fitzmaurice (New York: Garland, 1997), 131. On Cavendish's priority, see Rhodes, *Shakespeare and the Origins*, 212. John Dryden in 1668 also clinched the association of Shakespeare with nature: "he was the man who of all Modern, and perhaps Antient poets, had the largest and most comprehensive soul. All the images of Nature were still present to him." Dryden, "Of Dramatic Poesy: An Essay," in *Of Dramatic Poesy and Other Critical Essays*, ed. George Watson (London: J. M. Dent, 1962), 67.

Coleridge called Shakespeare "myriad-minded" (borrowing the term from an ancient source) in chapter 15 of *Biographia Literaria* (1817). On Shakespeare's "Protean" quality, see Jonathan Bate, *Shakespeare and the English Romantic Imagination* (Oxford: Clarendon Press, 1986), 15.

Garrick's Jubilee celebration circulated both versions of Shakespeare's greatness. Kate Rumbold, "Shakespeare and the Stratford Jubilee," in Fiona Ritchie and Peter Sabor, eds., *Shakespeare in the Eighteenth Century* (Cambridge: Cambridge University Press, 2012), 261–265. Bristol identifies the love of Shakespeare with the losses of modernity in *Shakespeare's America, America's Shakespeare*, within a framework for analyzing the modern somewhat different from mine; see especially 17.

46. Friedrich Schiller, *On the Naïve and Sentimental in Literature* [1795], trans. Helen Watanabe-O'Kelly (Manchester: Carcanet, 1981), 36.

47. Samuel Taylor Coleridge, *Literary Remains*, in Farley-Hills, *Critical Responses to Hamlet, 1790–1838*, 68; Voltaire, excerpts from *Lettres Philosophiques* (1733) and *Lettre à l'Académie Française* (1776), in Farley-Hills, *Critical Responses to Hamlet, 1600–1790*, 73–79.

48. Schiller, *On the Naive*, 36.

49. Kathryn Prince, "Shakespeare and English Nationalism," in Ritchie and Sabor, *Shakespeare in the Eighteenth Century*, 286.

50. Friedrich Schiller, *On the Aesthetic Education of Man In a Series of Letters*, ed. and trans. Elizabeth M. Wilkinson and L. A. Willoughby (Oxford: Oxford University Press, 1967), 45. Some thinkers, including Schiller, diagnosed a division between the intellect and other human capacities (emotion, intuition, sensory experience): to the extent that both reason and sensibility had cult followings, in the late eighteenth century, it appears that some shift took place, perhaps instigated by the idea that reason was a distinctively modern force of change. Art could develop "man's capacity for feeling," which Schiller believed strengthened thought. Schiller, *On the Aesthetic*, 53.

Offsetting modern specialized forms of work and education or training, Schiller expansively proclaimed that every person is fundamentally or potentially infinite and eternal and that art could kindle people's "complete awareness of [this expansive] human nature." Schiller, *On the Aesthetic*, 74–75, 95.

51. Taylor, *Reinventing Shakespeare*, 68–88.

52. Andrew Murphy, *Shakespeare in Print: A History and Chronology of Shakespeare Publishing* (New York: Cambridge University Press, 2003), 81; and Margreta de Grazia, *Shakespeare Verbatim: The Reproduction of Authenticity and the 1790 Apparatus* (Oxford: Clarendon Press, 1991), 192–201. Nicholas Rowe, less famous today than the other editors I've named, was a prominent man of letters who became poet laureate in 1715. On the significance of eighteenth-century editions of Shakespeare as well as the history of the earlier anthologization of Shakespeare's writings, see Rhodes, *Shakespeare and the Origins*, 170–184.

53. Taylor, *Reinventing Shakespeare*, 70.

54. Taylor, *Reinventing Shakespeare*, 87. See also Murphy's discussion of the contributions of each new edition of Shakespeare produced during the era of the Tonsons' monopoly (*Shakespeare in Print*, 57–86).

55. La Harpe's work attests that not all the initial stirrings of literariness were organized around Shakespeare, although Shakespeare is my focal point here. His discussion of Shakespeare, like Voltaire's, mainly faults Shakespeare for his irregularities and marvels at the English overvaluation of his work. Jean-François de La Harpe, *Cours de Littérature Ancienne et Moderne...*, 3 vols. (Paris: Firmin Didot Frères, 1840), 1: 435–436.

56. David Scott Kastan, *Shakespeare and the Book* (New York: Cambridge University Press, 2001), 20–21.

57. Although I analyze only Anglophone print traces of public culture, there is reason to believe that an expanded account of U.S. literary culture across languages will uncover similar evidence that newspapers and periodicals offered readers at large ideas about literary interpretation and textual criticism. Raúl Coronado's description of nineteenth-century Hispanic newspapers in the Americas identifies discussions and excerpts of supercanonical authors (Cervantes and Dante) as well as a host of other kinds of contemporary writings and reprints contributing to public literary culture. Raúl Coronado, *A World Not to Come: A History of Latino Writing and Print Culture* (Cambridge, Mass.: Harvard University Press, 2013), 332–333.

58. "Account of, and Extracts from, the Newly Discovered Shakespeare Manuscripts," *Massachusetts Magazine; or, Monthly Museum....*, May 1796, 279–280. The documents were forged by William Henry Ireland and exposed by Shakespearean editor Edmond Malone. Murphy, *Shakespeare in Print*, 95.

59. X, "Article 2," *Literary Magazine, and American Register*, Apr. 1805, 283-284; Y, "Shakespeare Vindicated," *Literary Magazine, and American Register*, May 1805, 373-374; and Crito, "Shakespeare Re-Examined," *Literary Magazine, and American Register*, June 1805, 432-433.

60. "Commentators on Shakespeare," *Something* Ed. by Nemo Nobody, Esq., 25 Nov. 1809, 20-21.

61. See, for example "Shakespeare," *The Stranger, a Literary Paper*, 4 Dec. 1813, 191-192; "Shakespeare," *Polyanthos*, 1 May 1807, 104-105; "Shakespeare," *New England Galaxy*, 6 Oct. 1820, 206; "Review 2," rev. of *The Family Shakespeare, Christian Observer....*, May 1808, 326-334; C., "Prefaces—Johnson's Shakespeare," *Boston Weekly Magazine, Devoted to Morality, Literature, Biography, History, the Fine Arts, Agriculture, &c. &c.*, 19 Feb. 1803, 70; and S., "On Prefaces," *Parterre, a Weekly Magazine*, 19 Apr. 1817, 121-123.

62. "The German Shakespeare Society," *Cincinnati Daily Gazette*, 3 July 1869.

63. Untitled, *Flake's Bulletin* [Galveston, Tex.], 31 Oct. 1868; "Literary Gossip," *San Francisco Bulletin*, 31 Jan. 1874; and "News Summary," *Salt Lake Daily Telegraph*, 18 Apr. 1867.

64. About Norris and his column, see John W. Velz and Frances N. Teague, preface to John W. Velz and Frances N. Teague, eds., *One Touch of Shakespeare: Letters of Joseph Crosby to Joseph Parker Norris, 1875-1878* (Washington: Folger Shakespeare Library, 1986), 18.

65. H. N. Hudson, "How to Use Shakespeare in School," in *Essays on Education, English Studies, and Shakespeare* [1879] (Boston: Ginn, Heath, 1884), v.

66. James M. Gibson, *The Philadelphia Shakespeare Story* (New York: AMS Press, 1990), 59. Furness's son, Horace Howard Furness, Jr., took over the Variorum project at his father's death (257).

67. Gibson, *Philadelphia*, 138-160.

68. These and similar characterizations of predisciplinary scholars have been widely used, but a couple of examples are John Higham's characterization of "amateur" historians as "patricians" and Laurence R. Veysey's account of the transformation by which the "professor" replaced "gentlemanly amateurism of spirit." John Higham, *History: Professional Scholarship in America* (Baltimore: Johns Hopkins University Press, 1983), 7, 9; and Laurence R. Veysey, *The Emergence of the American University* (Chicago: University of Chicago Press, 1965), 2.

69. White apparently turned down at least one offer of an academic position, Crosby believed because of embarrassment over a sexual scandal. Velz and Teague,*One Touch of Shakespeare*, 259, 287.

70. Richard Grant White, "Mr. Collier's Folio of 1632," *Shakespeare's Scholar* (New York: Appleton, 1854), 33-81.

71. John W. Velz and Frances N. Teague, introduction to Velz and Teague, *One Touch of Shakespeare*, 13-32.

72. "Mr. Hudson on American Shakespeareans," *Literary World*, 6 Nov.1880, 397.

73. Henry W. Simon, *The Reading of Shakespeare in American Schools and Colleges: An Historical Survey* (New York: Simon and Schuster, 1932), 108-119. Applebee notes that Rolfe was usually credited as introducing "the first regular high school instruction in literature," although it's hard to credit this claim in light of evidence presented by Applebee and others about widespread secondary teaching of English literature earlier in the century. Applebee, *Tradition and Reform*, 28. William J. Reese, *The Origins of the American High School* (New Haven, Conn.: Yale University Press, 1995), 127. At the end of his career, Rolfe was the president of the Emerson College of Oratory.

74. In 1889 and 1890, *Shakespeariana* ran a series of articles, "Shakespeare's American Editors," which profiles William J. Rolfe (Oct. 1889); Richard Grant White (Sept. 1889); Horace Howard Furness (Aug. 1889); Gulian Crommelin Verplank (usually spelled Verplanck) (Dec. 1889), identified as the first U.S. editor of Shakespeare; and Henry Norman Hudson (Oct. 1890).

75. Their edition was known as the Pembroke Shakespeare and was based on the First Folio; a number of individual plays were also issued separately: William Shakespeare, *The Complete Works of William Shakespeare*, ed. Charlotte Porter and Helen A. Clarke (New York: T. Y. Crowell, 1903). Murphy in *Shakespeare in Print* notes that the success (critical as well as popular) of their project seems to have contributed to Oxford professor Walter Raleigh's decision not to pursue an edition he had projected that would also have been based on the First Folio (164–165).

76. Paraic Finnerty, *Emily Dickinson's Shakespeare* (Amherst: University of Massachusetts Press, 2006), 15; and Louis Menand, *The Metaphysical Club: A Story of Ideas in America* (New York: Farrar, Straus, and Giroux, 2001), 221. Finnerty's study demonstrates that Dickinson (in common with most literary readers of the time) was steeped in Shakespeare, which she encountered in school, in the Shakespeare group, in performance, and in personal reading supported by a steady flow of Shakespearean-laced correspondence and camaraderie.

77. J. V. L., "Shakespeare Societies of America: Their Methods and Work," in *Shakespeariana*, Oct. 1885, 480–488; and Megan Seaholm, "Earnest Women: The White Woman's Club Movement in Progressive Era Texas, 1880–1920" (Ph.D. diss., Rice University, 1988), 212, qtd. in Elizabeth Long, *Book Clubs: Women and the Uses of Reading in Everyday Life* (Chicago: University of Chicago Press, 2003), 34. Long's study references the importance of easy access to Shakespeare and the preeminence of Shakespeare in the readings of Texas women's clubs (42, 45).

78. More than twenty separate U.S. editions of the complete plays were published before Gulian Verplanck's of 1847, but Verplanck's was often named as the first U.S. edition, perhaps because Verplanck took more editorial initiatives than his predecessors. Sturgess, *Shakespeare and the American Nation*, 19–21.

79. Velz and Teague, eds., *One Touch of Shakespeare*, 82.

80. On the Boston Mechanics' Institution, its library, and the lyceum movement it influenced, see Jesse H. Shera, *Foundations of the Public Library: The Origins of the Public Library Movement in New England, 1629–1855* (Chicago: Shoe String Press, 1965), 230–232; and Angela G. Ray, *The Lyceum and Public Culture in the Nineteenth-Century United States* (East Lansing: Michigan State University Press, 2005), 14, 21, 30–32. Racist exclusion of African Americans from some white-organized lyceums led them to form separate lyceums. Dorothy B. Porter, "The Organized Educational Activities of Negro Literary Societies, 1828–1846," *Journal of Negro Education* 5, no. 4 (1936): 557.

81. John Hampton Lauck, II, "The Reception and Teaching of Shakespeare in Nineteenth and Early Twentieth Century America" (Ph.D. diss., University of Illinois at Urbana–Champaign, 1991), 54, 230. Lauck argues that lyceum culture (especially in Boston) offered "the full beginning of Shakespeare study in America, and the full flowering of the aesthetic approach to that playwright which dominated the nineteenth century" (50).

82. Raymond M. Weaver, *Herman Melville: Mariner and Mystic* (New York: George H. Doran, 1921), 369–371.

83. H. N. Hudson, *Lectures on Shakspeare*, 2 vols. (New York: Baker and Scribner, 1848).

84. Lauck, "Reception," 77.

85. Ray, *Lyceum*, 40. This *Lyceum* journal was founded in 1869. An earlier *Family Lyceum* had been published from 1832 to 1833 (49).

86. Thomas Wentworth Higginson, "The American Lecture-System," *Macmillan's Magazine*, May 1868, 49.

87. Lauck, "Reception," 208–209.

88. Charles Henry Hart, *Memoir of George Ticknor, Historian of Spanish Literature* (Philadelphia: Collins, 1871), 8, 11.

89. Henry Reed, *Lectures on English History and Tragic Poetry, Illustrated by Shakespeare* [1855] (Philadelphia: E. Claxton and Col, 1881), 26. Ticknor urged Henry Reed's brother William to publish Reed's lectures on English literature after Reed died at sea (150).

90. For information about the course taught by Datus C. Brooks, assistant professor of rhetoric and English literature, see Simon, *Reading of Shakespeare*, 77; and Lauck, "Reception," 216.

91. Reed, *Lectures on English History*, 67.

92. Reed, *Lectures on English History*, 68.

93. Reed, *Lectures on English History*, 69.

94. James Russell Lowell's course in modern literature, taught at Harvard beginning in 1858, and the course on Shakespeare offered that same year at the University of Michigan were important early curricular offerings in English literary studies. Lauck, "Reception," 216, 230. On the gradual inclusion of Shakespeare in particular within U.S. college curricula, see Vaughan and Vaughan, *Shakespeare in America*, 84–86.

95. Monroe H. Little, "The Extra-Curricular Activities of Black College Students, 1868–1940," *Journal of Negro History* 65, no. 2 (1980): 135–148; and Mark Garrett Longaker, *Rhetoric and the Republic: Politics, Civic Discourse, and Education in Early America* (Tuscaloosa: University of Alabama Press, 2007), 46–47, 105–107, 189–190.

96. George P. Marsh, *Lectures on the English Language* (New York: Charles Scribner, 1860), 670. Marsh was an independent philologist who had no university appointment, but the trustees of Columbia College invited him to give a course of "Post-graduate Lectures" on the English language to "educated men and women" (vii).

97. Marsh, *Lectures*, 670.

98. "Reading aloud...appeared wherever leisurely social activity took place." Ronald J. Zboray and Mary Saracino Zboray, *Everyday Ideas: Socioliterary Experience among Antebellum New Englanders* (Knoxville: University of Tennessee Press, 2006), 137. Zboray and Zboray offer a wonderful inventory of the "oral dissemination" of reading matter.

99. On the relationship of illiterate users to books, a topic broached in passing by many historians of print culture, see Dominique Julia, "Reading and the Counter-Reformation," in Guglielmo Cavallo and Roger Chartier, eds., *A History of Reading in the West* (Amherst: University of Massachusetts Press, 2003), 266–268.

100. The term "Bardolatry" was coined by George Bernard Shaw in 1901, but the phenomenon he named was long-standing. Jonathan Bate, *Shakespearean Constitutions: Politics, Theatre, Criticism 1730–1830* (Oxford: Clarendon Press, 1989), 22. On some Romantics' preference for Shakespeare in book form, see Frederick Burwick, "Shakespare and the Romantics" in Duncan Wu, ed., *A Companion to Romanticism* (Malden, Mass.: Blackwell, 1998), 512–519; and Julie Stone Peters, "A Theatre Too Much with Us," *Theatre of the Book, 1480–1880: Print, Text, and Performance in Europe* (New York: Oxford University Press, 2000), 294–307.

101. Charles Lamb, "On the Tragedies of Shakespeare" [1811], in David Perkins, ed., *English Romantic Writers* (New York: Harcourt Brace Jovanovich, 1967), 571, 572.

102. Lamb, "Tragedies," 571.

103. This transformation also further effaced the context of performance in which the plays had been written. Stephen Orgel has influentially argued that the scripts of Shakespeare's plays were meant to be fluid and adaptable to the needs of disparate performances. Only publication raised the issue of establishing a single definitive text. Stephen Orgel, "The Authentic Shakespeare," *The Authentic Shakespeare and Other Problems of the Early Modern Stage* (New York: Routledge, 2002), 231–256.

104. Margreta de Grazia has documented the emergence of quotation marks in the late eighteenth century as another sign of the increased emphasis on individual and private ownership that coincided with the attempts of Shakespearean editors to identify words that were authentically Shakespeare's. De Grazia, *Shakespeare Verbatim*, 214–219.

105. On Tate's *Lear* and Garrick's use and adaptation of it, see Cunningham, *Shakespeare and Garrick*, 119–138. Cunningham emphasizes that "in the age of Garrick, eulogising the national Bard and paying 'serious attention' to his works was not thought by actors, critics or editors to be incompatible with altering his plays to suit the cultural preferences of the period" (11).

106. Lawrence Levine, *Highbrow/Lowbrow: The Emergence of Cultural Hierarchy in America* (Cambridge, Mass.: Harvard University Press, 1988).

107. Paul DiMaggio, "Cultural Entrepreneurship in Nineteenth-Century Boston, Part I: The Creation of an Organizational Base for High Culture in America," *Media, Culture and Society* 4, no. 1 (1982): 33–50, and "Cultural Entrepreneurship in Nineteenth-Century Boston, Part II: The Classification and Framing of American Art," *Media, Culture, and Society* 4, no. 4 (1982): 303–322; and Nigel Cliff, *The Shakespeare Riots: Revenge, Drama, and Death in Nineteenth-Century America* (New York: Random House, 2007).

108. John S. Tanner, "Shakespeare among the Saints," *Journal of Mormon History* 32, no. 1 (2006): 87.

109. Vaughan and Vaughan also propose that "Levine's emphatic binary between highbrow and lowbrow overlooks the myriad ways Shakespeare has influenced the lives of everyday Americans from the late nineteenth century to the present." Vaughan and Vaughan, *Shakespeare in America*, 191. For an overview of Shakespeare's wide circulation among African American, working-class, and female audiences and readers during the long nineteenth century, see Heather S. Nathans, "'A Course of Learning and Ingenious Studies': Shakespearean Education and Theater in Antebellum America," in Kahn, Nathans, and Godfrey, *Shakespearean Educations*, 54–70. Nathans argues that Shakespeare's works in the nineteenth century became "the *lingua franca* of... various racialized, classed, and gendered discussions" (55), an important claim, but a broader claim than my argument that a wide variety of people in the United States participated in the literary culture of which Shakespeare was the centerpiece. See also Kathryn Prince, *Shakespeare in the Victorian Periodicals* (New York: Routledge, 2008), esp. "Making Shakespeare Readers in the Early Working Class Press," 16–36. On the African Theatre, which staged Shakespeare in the 1820s in New York, see Jeffrey H. Richards, *Drama, Theatre, and Identity in the American New Republic* (New York: Cambridge University Press, 2005), 211–212. See also William Wells Brown's account of African American actor Ira Aldridge, who also played Hamlet, performing the lead in *Othello*: "William Wells Brown," James Shapiro, ed., *Shakespeare in America: An Anthology*

Notes to Pages 91–92

from the Revolution to Now (New York: Literary Classics of the United States, 2014), 142–147. On the remarkable number and variety of women's Shakespeare clubs in the United States, see Katherine West Scheil, *She Hath Been Reading: Women and Shakespeare Clubs in America* (Ithaca, N.Y.: Cornell University Press, 2012); chapter 4 discusses black women's clubs (95–116).

110. George Ticknor, *Life, Letters, and Journals of George Ticknor*, 7th ed. (Boston: James R. Osgood, 1877), 1: 473. Thomas Davidson, a freelance teacher of literature and philosophy who appears in chapter 4, also knew a great deal of Shakespeare by heart and once regaled a friend by performing most of *King Lear* during a walk. "[N]o one who had heard him read Shakespeare could fail to be impressed by his mastery of every shade and intricacy of meaning," according to his friend W. R. Dunstan. Wyndham R. Dunstan, "Recollections by William R. Dunstan," in *Memorials of Thomas Davidson: The Wandering Scholar*, collected and ed. William Knight (Boston and London: Ginn, 1907), 121.

111. John Joseph Knight, "Glyn, Isabella Dallas," *Dictionary of National Biography*, ed. Leslie Stephen and Sidney Lee, 63 vols. (New York: Macmillan, 1890), 22: 10 (https://play.google.com/books/reader?id=qSYJAAAAIAAJ&printsec=frontcover&output=reader&hl=en&pg=GBS.PA10), accessed 30 May 2015.

112. Richard Benson Sewall, *The Life of Emily Dickinson*, 2 vols. (Cambridge, Mass.: Harvard University Press, 2003), 2: 701.

113. On African American elocutionists, see James P. Danky, "Reading, Writing, and Resisting: African American Print Culture," in Carl F. Kaestle and Janice A. Radway, eds., *Print in Motion: The Expansion of Publishing and Reading in the United States, 1880–1940*, vol. 4 of Hall, *History of the Book in America* (Chapel Hill: University of North Carolina Press, 2009), 343. Susan Kates has emphasized the importance of Brown's performances' combining the dominant canon of white authors, such as Shakespeare, with works by African American authors. Susan Kates, *Activist Rhetorics and American Higher Education, 1885–1937* (Carbondale: Southern Illinois University Press, 2001).

114. Joseph Kett offers an analytic history of formal and informal programs of adult education, addressing many of the organizations I discuss here, in *The Pursuit of Knowledge under Difficulties: From Self-Improvement to Adult Education in America, 1750–1990* (Stanford, Calif.: Stanford University Press, 1994).

115. Benjamin Franklin, *The Autobiography*, in *Writings*, ed. J. A. Leo LeMay, Library of America Edition (New York: Literary Classics of the United States, 1987), 1340, 1361, 1362. On the early history of social, subscription, and commercial libraries, see Jesse H. Shera, *Foundations of the Public Library: The Origins of the Public Library Movement in New England, 1629–1855* (Chicago: Shoe String Press, 1965), 58, 129–130, 159–160.

116. Paul Allen, *The Life of Charles Brockden Brown* (Delmar, N.Y.: Scholars' Facsimiles and Reprints, 1975), 14, 27.

117. On Brown's participation in these clubs, see Allen, *Life*; Steven Watts, *The Romance of Real Life; Charles Brockden Brown and the Origins of American Culture* (Baltimore: Johns Hopkins University Press, 1994); Caleb Crain, *American Sympathy: Men, Friendship, and Literature in the New Nation* (New Haven, Conn.: Yale University Press, 2001); and two essays from Philip Barnard, Mark L. Kamrath, and Stephen Shapiro, eds., *Revising Charles Brockden Brown: Culture, Politics, and Sexuality in the Early Republic* (Knoxville: University of Tennessee Press, 2004): W. M. Verhoeven, "'This Blissful Period of Intellectual Liberty': Transatlantic Radicalism and Enlightened Conservatism in Brown's Early Writings" (7–40);

and Fredrika J. Teute, "A 'Republic of Intellect': Conversation and Criticism among the Sexes in 1790s New York" (149–181).

118. Bryan Waterman, *Republic of Intellect: The Friendly Club of New York City and the Making of American Literature* (Baltimore: Johns Hopkins University Press, 2007), 92–141.

119. George Gates Raddin, *Hocquet Caritat and the Early New York Literary Scene* (Dover, N.J.: Dover Advance Press, 1953), 41–76.

120. For example, the Boston Atheneum was founded in 1806 by the Monthly Anthology Club, which also published the *Monthly Anthology and Boston Review*. Josiah Quincy, *The History of the Boston Athenaeum* (Cambridge, Mass.: Metcalf, 1851), 6–7. Free or inexpensive libraries were crucial especially in the antebellum period, when books were too expensive for most working people to afford. Ronald J. Zboray, *A Fictive People: Antebellum Economic Development and the American Reading Public* (New York: Oxford University Press, 1993), 11–12.

121. Kett, *Pursuit of Knowledge*, 64.

122. Porter, "Negro Literary Societies," 555–576; Elizabeth McHenry, *Forgotten Readers: Recovering the Lost History of African American Literary Societies* (Durham, N.C.: Duke University Press, 2002), 50–52, 141; and Mary Kelley, *Learning to Stand and Speak: Women, Education, and Public Life in America's Republic* (Chapel Hill: University of North Carolina Press, 2006), 140–144.

123. M. D. Walhout, "The Hermeneutical Turn in American Critical Theory, 1830–1860," *Journal of the History of Ideas* 57, no. 4 (1996): 685; Edwin P. Whipple, "Coleridge as a Philosophical Critic," *Essays and Reviews*, 2 vols. (Boston: James R. Osgood, 1895) 1: 405–421.

124. Zboray, *Fictive People*, 83. Zboray also notes that literacy rates were clearly in excess of people's access to formal education in the antebellum period (96). Even though legislation after the Civil War aimed to make formal public education universal, it was no doubt widely understood that the reading public was still mainly informally educated, including through family commitments to literacy instruction and personal commitments to "self-culture" (84–88, 129–131).

On colonial education and support for literacy, see E. Jennifer Monaghan, *Learning to Read and Write in Colonial America* (Amherst: University of Massachusetts Press, 2005). On centralized literacy campaigns in other nations versus the growth of literacy in the United States, see Soltow, *Rise*, 58.

125. At the end of the Civil War, rates of African American illiteracy approached 95 percent. Reese, *America's Public Schools*, 71–75.

126. Justin Smith Morrill, *Speech of Hon. Justin S. Morrill, of Vermont, on the Bill Granting Lands for Agricultural Colleges* (Washington, D.C.: Congressional Globe Office, 1858), 15.

127. George Cary Eggleston, *How to Educate Yourself: With or without Masters* (New York: G. P. Putnam's Sons, 1872).

128. Significantly, this golden age began around the time when the reputations of U.S. colleges were especially low, in the 1850s and 1860s, before the revitalization brought about by the adoption of the research university model. Laurence R. Veysey, *The Emergence of the American University* (Chicago: University of Chicago Press, 1965), 5–10.

129. Kenneth A. Simon and W. Vance Grant, *Digest of Educational Statistics: 1968 Edition* (Washington, D.C.: National Center for Educational Statistics, 1968), 52; and Veysey, *Emergence*, 2.

130. Andrew C. Rieser, *The Chautauqua Moment: Protestants, Progressives, and the Culture of Modern Liberalism* (New York: Columbia University Press, 2003), 36–37, 34, 120.

131. On the flowering and withering of the university extension movement around the turn of the century, see Kett, *Pursuit of Knowledge*, 182–187. It was not clear exactly what material advantages were provided by degrees from colleges and universities, either, though. Roger L. Geiger, "The Era of Multipurpose Colleges in American Higher Education, 1850–1890," in Roger L. Geiger, ed., *The American College in the Nineteenth Century* (Nashville: Vanderbilt University Press, 2000), 152.

132. Rieser, *Chautauqua Moment*, 167. It is not clear whether Rieser's numbers include Canada, where Chautauqua circles were also popular. See Heather Murray, "Great Works and Good Works: The Toronto Women's Literary Club, 1877–83," *Historical Studies in Education/Revue de l'histoire de l'éducation* 11, no. 1 (1999): 81. In 1895, an official government report credited Chautauqua with "100,000 registered students, half of whom are between 30 and 40 years of age," and claimed that Chautauqua groups—presumably, CLSCs—were in every state and territory as well as a number of other countries. W. W. Willoughby, "History of Summer Schools in the United States," *Report of the Secretary of the Interior* (52nd Congress), 5 vols. (Washington: Government Printing Office, 1895), 5: part 2, 921.

133. Henry A. Beers, *An Outline Sketch of English Literature* (New York: Chautauqua Press, 1886), 112, 232.

134. "Weekly Program for Local Circle Work," *The Chautauquan*, Nov. 1884, 101; and "C.L.S.C. Outline and Programs," *The Chautauquan*, June 1898, 321.

135. Elizabeth Cary Agassiz, ed., *Society to Encourage Studies at Home…* (Cambridge, Mass.: Riverside Press, 1897), 9. On Chautauqua and Anna Ticknor's Society, see Kett, *Pursuit of Knowledge*, 147–181. Reversing the SH pattern, Christopher Hilliard holds that correspondence schools in general, especially schools for writing, thrived in the United States before they took hold in England. Christopher Hilliard, *To Exercise Our Talents: The Democratization of Writing in Britain* (Cambridge, Mass.: Harvard University Press, 2006), 22–24.

136. Robert Snape, "The National Home Reading Union," *Journal of Victorian Culture* 7, no. 1 (2002): 89–92.

137. "Mary W. Whitney," *Annual Report of the Maria Mitchell Association*, vol. 19, 10 (http://articles.adsabs.harvard.edu/full/1921MMAAR..19...10), accessed 30 May 2015.

138. Fuller held courses known as her "Conversations" in Elizabeth Peabody's bookstore in Boston from 1839 to 1844, some for women only and some including men; participants in 1841 included Peabody, Emerson, William Story, and George and Sophia Ripley, so it would be hard to position these courses in relation to our usual instructional classifications. Joel Myerson, ed., *Fuller in Her Own Time* (Iowa City: University of Iowa Press, 2008), especially 37–46, 55–62.

139. Agassiz, *Society*, 104, 117, 146. Both CLSC and SH thrived in the years before public libraries were well established throughout the nation; the first Carnegie-funded library was built in 1893, and the Carnegie grants not only helped to fund many libraries but, by requiring a guarantee of local support, lent force to the expectation that communities would fund libraries from taxes. Theodore Jones, *Carnegie Libraries across America: A Public Legacy* (New York: John Wiley and Sons, 1997), 26.

140. Agassiz, *Society*, 136.

141. John Habberton, *The Chautauquans* [1891] (New York: George D. Hurst, 1895), 285.

142. Ann Thompson and Sasha Roberts, eds., *Women Reading Shakespeare, 1660–1900: An Anthology of Criticism* (Manchester, England: Manchester University Press, 1997), 154;

Rieser, *Chautauqua Moment*, 159–280; and *Year Book of the Central Conference for American Rabbis, for 1895-5655* (Cincinnati: Central Conference of American Rabbis, 1895), 48–49. An 1895 report declared that there were "non-Christian" CLSC members but that the atmosphere was of "earnest Christianity." Willoughby, "History of Summer Schools," 930.

143. Ronald L. Jackson III and Sonja M. Brown Givens, *Black Pioneers in Communication Research* (Thousand Oaks, Calif.: Sage Publications, 2000), 68, 71–72.

144. Clifford Siskin, *The Work of Writing: Literature and Social Change in Britain, 1700-1830* (Baltimore: Johns Hopkins University Press, 1998), 69, 73.

145. James Turner, *Philology: The Forgotten Origin of the Modern Humanities* (Princeton, N.J.: Princeton University Press, 2014), 6.

146. Turner, *Philology*, 7–9.

147. Turner, *Philology*, 40–43. See also Geert Lernout, "The Angel of Philology," in Dirk Van Hulle and Joep Leerssen, eds., *Editing the Nation's Memory: Textual Scholarship and Nation-Building in Nineteenth-Century Europe* (Amsterdam: Rodopi, 2008), 45–61. On classical and biblical influences on Shakespearean textual editing in England, see Simon Jarvis, *Scholars and Gentlemen: Shakespearian Textual Criticism and Representations of Scholarly Labour, 1726-1765* (Oxford: Clarendon Press, 1995), esp. 17–18.

148. Turner, *Philology*, 80–81.

149. Turner, *Philology*, 151.

150. Andrew Elfenbein, *Romanticism and the Rise of English* (Stanford, Calif.: Stanford University Press, 2009), 13.

151. Coleridge, *Literary Remains*, 65, 73. Angela Esterhammer notes that most of what we know of Coleridge's critical opinions comes from his Shakespearean lectures delivered in London and Bristol between 1808 and 1819. Angela Esterhammer, "The Critic," in Lucy Newlyn, ed., *The Cambridge Companion to Coleridge* (Cambridge: Cambridge University Press, 2002), 142. Jon Klancher underlines the importance of the fact that Coleridge's lectures are only available to us in notes taken by students and (practiced but fallible) shorthand reporters, a "transmission failure [that] nonetheless produced an ideological success—the vast influence of Coleridge's discourse on Shakespeare and classics texts in history." Jon Klancher, "Transmission Failure," in David Perkins, ed., *Theoretical Issues in Literary History* (Cambridge, Mass.: Harvard University Press, 1991), 173–195. Klancher identifies the new style of institutions sponsoring lectures like Coleridge's as "an extraordinary device of social reproduction" (182).

According to Jonathan Bate, "Coleridge's most signal contribution to the history of Shakespearean criticism was to show how particulars, minutiae, are combined to produce the unified whole that is a Shakespearean drama. He analysed opening scenes in detail, as no one had before, because it was in openings that the germ of the whole could be discerned." Bate, *Shakespeare and the Romantic*, 13–14.

152. On historical criticism of the Bible and its public reverberations, see Jerry Wayne Brown, *The Rise of Biblical Criticism in America, 1800-1870: The New England Scholars* (Middletown, Conn.: Wesleyan University Press, 1969). On the emergence of biblical criticism in the context of Romantic philosophy and aesthetics, including the Romantic embrace of primitivism, see especially John Rogerson, *Old Testament Criticism in the Nineteenth Century: England and Germany* (London: Fortress Press, 1985); and Gillian M. Bediako, *Primal Religion and the Bible: William Robertson Smith and His Heritage* (Sheffield: Sheffield Academic Press, 1997). According to Turner, Johann Gottfried Eichhorn called his practice

the higher criticism "because it sought to decipher authorship, literary origins and form, date, composition, and ultimately meaning of the books of the Bible in original context," versus lower criticism that sought only to establish the most reliable text. Turner, *Philology*, 117.

153. Turner, *Philology*, 20–21.

154. On typological and allegorical interpretation (as well as the interweaving of religious and nonreligious reading traditions), see David Lyle Jeffrey, *People of the Book: Christian Identity and Literary Culture* (Grand Rapids, Mich.: William B. Eerdmans, 1996), 61–72; and Christopher Rowland, "The Literature of the Bible," in Rebecca Lemon, Emma Mason, Jonathan Roberts, and Christopher Rowland, eds., *The Blackwell Companion to the Bible in English Literature* (Malden, Mass.: Wiley-Blackwell, 2009), 18–20. See also two other chapters in Lemon, Mason, Roberts, and Rowland, *Blackwell Companion*: David Jasper's chapter on "Biblical Hermeneutics and Literary Theory" (26–28) calls attention to the importance of Friedrich Schleiermacher's and Samuel Taylor Coleridge's roles as biblical and literary interpreters making channels between the domains; and Graham Davidson's chapter, "S. T. Coleridge" (413–424), homes in on the modes of symbolic reading he developed in studying the Bible.

155. Turner, *Philology*, 35–36; Barbara Warnick, *The Sixth Canon: Belletristic Rhetorical Theory and Its French Antecedents* (Columbia: University of South Carolina Press, 1993), 129; and Herbert W. Simons, "Introduction: The Rhetoric of Inquiry as an Intellectual Movement," in Herbert W. Simons, ed., *The Rhetorical Turn: Invention and Persuasion in the Conduct of Inquiry* (Chicago: University of Chicago Press, 1990), 7.

156. Turner, *Philology*, 105–106.

157. Bliss Perry, *And Gladly Teach: Reminiscences* (Boston: Houghton Mifflin, 1935), 67; and Denton J. Snider, *A Writer of Books in His Genesis*. (St. Louis: Sigma, [1910]), 78, 124–126.

158. David Gold, *Rhetoric at the Margins: Revising the History of Writing Instruction in American Colleges, 1873–1947* (Carbondale: Southern Illinois University Press, 2008), 4.

159. Charles Eastman, *The Essential Charles Eastman (Ohiyesa): Light on the Indian World*, ed. Michael Oren Fitzgerald (Bloomington, Ind.: World Wisdom, 2007), 208; and Zitkala-Ša, *The School Days of an Indian Girl*, in Cathy N. Davidson and Ada Norris, eds., *American Indian Stories, Legends, and Other Writings* (New York: Penguin, 2003), 101–103. On African American oratory, see Gold, *Rhetoric at the Margins*, 20–21; and John Ernest, *Liberation Historiography: African American Writers and the Challenge of History, 1794–1861* (Chapel Hill: University of North Carolina Press, 2004), 219–276.

160. About Shakespeare's prominence in U.S. secondary education during the long nineteenth century, including in textbooks, see three essays in Kahn, Nathans, and Godfrey, *Shakespearean Educations*: Sandra M. Gustafson, "Eloquent Shakespeare" (71–94); Jonathan Burton, "Lay On, McGuffey: Excerpting Shakespeare in Nineteenth-Century Schoolbooks" (95–111); and Nan Johnson, "Shakespeare in American Rhetorical Education, 1870–1920" (112–127).

161. William Enfield, *The Speaker; or, Miscellaneous Pieces, Selected from the Best English Writers....*, new ed., corrected (London: J. Johnson, 1782); and William Scott, *Lessons in Elocution; or, Miscellaneous Pieces in Prose and Verse, Selected from the Best Authors, for the Perusal of Persons of Taste, and the Improvement of Youth* (Dublin: C. Talbot, 1781). Henry Simon notes that Enfield's selections from Shakespeare as well as his elocutionary scheme for organizing them were reproduced in many later textbooks. Simon, *Reading of Shakespeare*,

11–12. Another valuable resource for understanding the ways in which excerpts from Shakespeare operated in textbooks is Choseed, "Representations of Teaching."

162. Textbooks called "readers" were understood to support reading aloud, further narrowing the gap between a "speaker" and a "reader." Jean Ferguson Carr, Stephen L. Carr, and Lucille M. Schultz, *Archives of Instruction: Nineteenth-Century Rhetorics, Readers, and Composition Books in the United States*, Studies in Writing and Rhetoric Series (Carbondale: Southern Illinois University Press, 2005), 81.

Perhaps the most widespread circulation of Shakespeare in fragments was in textbooks such as the McGuffey readers, where, as Jonathan Burton has shown, passages from Shakespeare could be especially readily conscripted for the ideological purposes of the textbooks' producers. Burton, "Lay On, McGuffey." See also Henry H. Vail, *A History of the McGuffey Readers* (Cleveland: n.p., 1910), 78.

163. John A. Nietz, *The Evolution of American Secondary School Textbooks*.... (Rutland, Vt.: C. E. Tuttle, 1966), 36; and Lauck, "Reception," 93. William J. Gilmore notes that schoolbooks formed part of many family and public libraries (including the libraries of the poorest families with the fewest books), Lindley Murray's readers among them. William J. Gilmore, *Reading Becomes a Necessity of Life: Material and Cultural Life in Rural New England, 1780–1835* (Knoxville: University of Tennessee Press, 1989), 297. William Sanders Scarborough, a prominent African American professor of classics in the nineteenth century, recalled that when he and his wife traveled in Europe in the early 1900s, they harked back to pieces they remembered from *McGuffey's Fifth Reader*, which they may have known from their experience teaching in secondary school during the 1870s. William Sanders Scarborough, *The Autobiography of William Sanders Scarborough: An American Journey from Slavery to Scholarship*, ed. Michele Valerie Ronnick (Detroit: Wayne State University Press, 2005), 221.

164. Snider, *Writer of Books*, 53–54. Simon notes that Lindley excluded Shakespeare from his readers because of his disapproval of the drama, perhaps one reason for Snider's preferring McGuffey. Simon, *Reading of Shakespeare*, 13.

165. For an overview of the ways in which textbooks supported the development and refinement of literacy, inside formal schooling and out, see Carr, Carr, and Schultz, *Archives of Instruction*, especially 1–19, 87–93, 151–152.

166. Joseph Crosby reviewed the book for *Shakespeariana*, observing that the questions, which had been composed by H. H. Furness at the request of the students' instructor, were "divided into Historical and Bibliographical, Grammatical, Philological, and Aesthetic." Joseph Crosby, rev. of *Two Shakespeare Examinations: with Some Remarks on the Class-room Study of Shakespeare*, by William Taylor Thom (Boston: Ginn, Heath, 1883), *Shakespeariana*, Nov. 1883, 29–30.

167. Robert J. Connors, *Composition-Rhetoric: Backgrounds, Theory, and Pedagogy* (Pittsburgh: University of Pittsburgh Press, 1997), 171.

168. On the ascendancy of multimodal rhetoric and other ways in which rhetoric was diminished in the course of being retooled for composition instruction, see Connors, *Composition-Rhetoric*, 60–67.

169. Patricia Harkin, "Child's Ballads: Narrating Histories of Composition and Literary Studies," in Shumway and Dionne, *Disciplining English*, 21–37.

170. Turner, *Philology*, 148.

171. Joseph Roach, *Cities of the Dead: Circum-Atlantic Performance* (New York: Columbia University Press, 1996), 186.

172. Jürgen Habermas, *The Structural Transformation of the Public Sphere: An Inquiry into a Category of Bourgeois Society* [1962], trans. Thomas Burger with Frederick Lawrence (Cambridge, Mass.: MIT Press, 1991), 159–175.

173. Longaker, *Rhetoric and the Republic*, xii.

174. Longaker, *Rhetoric and the Republic*, 56–57. Walter Mignolo has pointed out that the Renaissance revival of classical learning in Europe offered cultural resources for imperialism, since the Roman Republic was also an empire. Walter D. Mignolo, *The Darker Side of the Renaissance: Literacy, Territoriality, and Colonization* [1995] (Ann Arbor: University of Michigan Press, 2003), vii.

175. Warnick, *Sixth Canon*, especially 95–131.

176. Jared Gardner, *The Rise and Fall of Early American Magazine Culture* (Urbana: University of Illinois Press, 2012), 77, 160–161.

177. Connors, *Composition-Rhetoric*, 178–179; and Turner, *Philology*, 7.

178. Charles Rollin, *The Method of Teaching and Studying the Belles Lettres*, 3rd ed., 2 vols. (London: C. Hitch, 1742), 2: 236.

179. Hugh Blair, *Lectures on Rhetoric and Belles-Lettres*, ed. Linda Ferreira-Buckley and S. Michael Halloran (Carbondale: Southern Illinois University Press, 2005), 344.

180. Blair, *Lectures*, 284–285.

181. "Now, by the press, we can speak to the nations." Benjamin Franklin to Richard Price, 13 June 1872, in *The Complete Works of Benjamin Franklin*, 10 vols. (New York: Putnam, 1877–1878), 8: 457, cited in Thomas J. Schlereth, *The Cosmopolitan Ideal in Enlightenment Thought: Its Form and Function in the Ideas of Franklin, Hume, and Voltaire, 1694–1790* (Notre Dame, Ind.: University of Notre Dame Press, 1977), 17.

182. Edward Larkin, *Thomas Paine and the Literature of Revolution* (Cambridge: Cambridge University Press, 2005), 7. Trish Loughran warns of the mythmaking implicit in the idea of *Common Sense* as an early bestseller, given how limited and uneven print circulation was in British America at the time, but newspaper reporting and the circulation of letters extended the reach of Paine's pamphlet just as they extended the reach of influential public speeches. Trish Loughran, *The Republic in Print: Print Culture in the Age of U. S. Nation Building, 1770–1870* (New York: Columbia University Press, 2007), 34–37; T. H. Breen, *The Marketplace of Revolution: How Consumer Politics Shaped American Independence* (New York: Oxford University Press, 2004).

183. Dilip Parameshwar Gaonkar has pointed out that "[e]ach putative revivalist of rhetoric"—including Gaonkar himself—"has to tell a tale of its glorious origins, its civilizing effects, its unjustified suppression, and its eventual demise and dispersion." He writes in particular about the hidden history of rhetoric surfaced (and continued) by Kenneth Burke, but his essay points toward the question of whether the measure of any tradition ought to be its suitability for being an academic discipline. Dilip Parameshwar Gaonkar, "Rhetoric and Its Double: Reflections on the Rhetorical Turn in the Human Sciences," in Simons, *Rhetorical Turn*, 351.

184. Ronald J. Zboray and Mary Saracino Zboray, "Nineteenth-Century Print Culture," in Joel Myerson, Sandra Harbert Petrulionis, and Laura Dassow Walls, eds., *The Oxford Handbook of Transcendentalism* (Oxford: Oxford University Press, 2010), 102–103. See also Sandra M. Gustason, "The Emerging Media of Early America," in Sandra M. Gustafson and Caroline F. Sloat, eds., *Cultural Narratives: Textuality and Performance in American Culture before 1900* (Notre Dame, Ind.: University of Notre Dame Press, 2010), 353.

185. Louise Greer, *Browning and America* (Chapel Hill: University of North Carolina Press, 1952), 15.

Commonplace books remained popular throughout the nineteenth century, and readers copied passages in the service of many kinds of reading practices. A related practice thriving into the twentieth century was the creation of scrapbooks incorporating clippings of things read. Zboray and Zboray, *Everyday Ideas*, 31–36; Ellen Gruber Garvey, *Writing with Scissors: American Scrapbooks from the Civil War to the Harlem Renaissance* (New York: Oxford University Press, 2012).

186. Katie Trumpener unfolds the significance of this Romantic nationalist activity in chapters 1 and 2 of *Bardic Nationalism: The Romantic Novel and the British Empire* (Princeton, N.J.: Princeton University Press, 1997).

187. Joseph Roach borrows the term "orature" from Ngũgĩ Wa Thiong'O, who borrowed it from a Ugandan linguist named Pio Zirimu. See Ngũgĩ Wa Thiong'O, "Oral Power and Europhone Glory: Orature, Literature, and Stolen Legacies," in *Penpoints, Gunpoints, and Dreams: Towards a Critical Theory of the Arts and the State in Africa* (Oxford: Clarendon Press, 1998), 105, 111; and Roach, *Cities of the Dead*, 11–12.

In addition to Roach's study, important works of scholarship embedding U.S. print literature in oral and performance cultures are Jay Fliegelman, *Declaring Independence: Jefferson, Natural Language, and the Culture of Performance* (Stanford, Calif.: Stanford University Press, 1993); Sandra M. Gustafson, *Eloquence Is Power: Oratory and Performance in Early America* (Chapel Hill: University of North Carolina Press, 2000); and Angela Sorby, *Schoolroom Poets: Childhood, Performance, and the Place of American Poetry, 1865–1917* (Durham, N.H,.: University of New Hampshire Press, 2005).

188. Jay Fliegelman explores the complex relations between print and speech as well as fantasies of natural (transparent) language in *Declaring Independence*.

Cornelius Castoriadis proposes, "But it is the economy that exhibits most strikingly the domination of the imaginary at every level—precisely because it claims to be entirely and exhaustively rational." Cornelius Castoriadis, *The Imaginary Institution of Society* [1975], trans. Kathleen Blamey (Cambridge, Mass.: Polity Press, 1987), 156.

189. Eugene Garver, "Arguing over Incommensurable Values: The Case of Machiavelli," in Simons, *Rhetorical Turn*, 188.

190. On Blair's circulation and influence in the United States, see Applebee, *Tradition and Reform*, 9; and Carr, Carr, and Schultz, *Archives*, 4–7, 33–43, 198.

191. Blair, *Lectures*, 264.

192. Blair, *Lectures*, 265.

193. Blair, *Lectures*, 265.

194. Immanuel Kant, *Critique of the Power of Judgment*, ed. Paul Guyer, trans. Paul Guyer and Eric Matthews (Cambridge: Cambridge University Press, 2007), 205. In contrast, Cornelius Castoriadis has proposed, "Historical reality is not wholly and entirely rational. If it were, *doing* would never be a problem, for everything would have already been *said*. Doing implies that reality is not rational through and through." Castoriadis, *Imaginary Institution of Society*, 79.

195. Blair, *Lectures*, 284. Some French writers wary of the uses to which eloquence had been put during the Revolution believed it was especially important to value and study eloquence in order to prepare people for more discriminating reception. Charlotte Hogsett, "The Causality of Reform and Counter-Reform," *French Review* 61, no. 3 (1988): 429.

Another reaction to the fear of what eloquence might wreak was that of the Marquis de Condorcet, who specifically endorsed print as an alternative to the demagoguery of public addresses and supported the Cercle Social, a French Revolutionary club devoted to creating print forums for public exchange. Elizabeth L. Eisenstein, *Divine Art, Infernal Machine: The Reception of Printing in the West from First Impressions to the Sense of an Ending* (Philadelphia: University of Pennsylvania Press, 2011), 149.

196. Gordon S. Wood, *The Radicalism of the American Revolution* (New York: Vintage, 1991), 105.

197. Rollin, *Method*, 2: 182. Blair took a similar stand: "The end of Popular Speaking is persuasion; and this must be founded on conviction" (*Lectures*, 295).

198. Allen, *Life of Charles Brockden Brown*, 40.

199. Charles Brockden Brown, *Ormond; or, The Secret Witness* [1799], vol. 6 of *Charles Brockden Brown's Novels* (New York: Burt Franklin, 1970), 110–111.

200. Frederick Beecher Perkins, *The Best Reading* (New York: G. P. Putnam and Sons, 1872), 232–233.

201. Many historians of reading have noted that even though cultural arbiters during the antebellum era often assumed that literary reading happened in silent solitude, there is ample evidence that a great deal of reading happened out loud and in company—that the literate and nonliterate encountered many texts by hearing them read aloud. On the "ideology of the solitary reader," see Elizabeth Long, "Textual Interpretation as Collective Action," in Jonathan Boyarin, ed., *The Ethnography of Reading* (Berkeley: University of California Press, 1993), 193.

202. Daniel Roche, "Natural History in the Academies," in N. Jardine, J. A. Secord, and E. C. Spary, eds., *Cultures of Natural History* (New York: Cambridge University Press, 1996), 127.

203. For information about the English translation and Scottish circulation of works by Rollin and other French belletrists, see Warnick, *Sixth Canon*, 5–15.

204. Rollin, *Method*, 1: 269.

205. An example of the translation is the title of Alexander Jamieson's *A Grammar of Rhetoric and Polite Literature* (New York: A. H. Maltby, 1824). George R. Cathcart translated *belles lettres* as "elegant letters" in *Cathcart's Literary Reader: A Manual of English Literature* [1874] (New York: American Book, 1892), xi.

206. Lawrence E. Klein, *Shaftesbury and the Culture of Politeness: Moral Discourse and Cultural Politics in Early Eighteenth-Century England* (Cambridge: Cambridge University Press, 1994), 13. Klein characterizes politeness as a gentlemanly ethos, but one that was taken up in many registers of public culture and which "assumed the equality of participants" (4). David Shields has similarly observed that the "manners and matters" of U.S. belles lettres, which was shaped in salon cultures, were taken up in print culture, especially periodicals. David S. Shields, "Eighteenth-Century Literary Culture," in Hugh Amory and David D. Hall, eds., *The Colonial Book in the Atlantic World*, vol. 1 of Hall, *History of the Book in America* (Cambridge: Cambridge University Press, 2000), 436.

207. Dena Goodman's scholarship about French salons suggests that in the great era of salons, the middle decades of the eighteenth century, many salons were devoted to the mildly meritocratic ethics of the Republic of Letters, in which polite sociability was cultivated in the service of navigating political conflicts and social inequalities. Politeness "could function as a bastion of the nobility," Goodman argues, but it was also "a response to the

monarchy's attempt to appropriate the definition of nobility to itself." Dena Goodman, *The Republic of Letters: A Cultural History of the French Enlightenment* (Ithaca, N.Y.: Cornell University Press, 1994), 114.

Caroline Winterer has traced some of the cultural and intellectual innovations made possible by the adoption of "salons and tea tables" in British America and the early United States: "Modeled on British precedents—which were modeled on French versions—this new colonial 'polite' society created a whole new arena for sociability between the sexes" and also created incentives and occasions for women to acquire classical learning. Caroline Winterer, "The Female World of Classical Reading in Eighteenth-Century America," in Heidi Brayman Hackel and Catherine E. Kelly, eds., *Reading Women: Literacy, Authorship, and Culture in the Atlantic World, 1500–1800* (Philadelphia: University of Pennsylvania Press, 2008), 106.

208. Klein, *Shaftesbury*, 150; and Paul Keen, *The Crisis of Literature in the 1790s: Print Culture and the Public Sphere* (Cambridge: Cambridge University Press, 1999), 80–84. Stephen Shapiro offers an excellent overview of recent scholarly interplay between liberalism and republicanism in *The Culture and Commerce of the Early American Novel: Reading the Atlantic World-System* (University Park: Pennsylvania State University Press, 2008), 2–18.

209. Rollin, *Method*, 1: 15, 44. Gordon Wood proposes that "liberal-minded" suspicions of government in the late eighteenth century meant that virtue was defined in relation to society, not just the state, with the result that politeness, sympathy, and other social virtues manifested this commitment to constructive participation. Wood, *Radicalism*, 217.

210. "Briefer Mention," *The Dial*, 1 Apr. 1904, 242. The slogan "Literature for Literature's Sake" appears in an advertisement at the back of Hiram Corson's *An Introduction to the Study of Shakespeare* (Boston: D. C. Heath, 1907).

211. Beers, *Outline Sketch*, 51.

212. Taking on T. H. Huxley's critique of literature from the vantage point of science, for example, Matthew Arnold argued that Huxley's real object was belles lettres, not literature. In this context Arnold defined literature expansively in a way that slid into "humane letters" and the humanities at large. Matthew Arnold, "Literature and Science," *The Works of Matthew Arnold*, 15 vols. (New York: AMS Press, 1970), 4: 339.

213. Blair, *Lectures*, 425.

214. Henry Reed, *Lectures on English Literature*, 2nd. ed. (Philadelphia: Parry and McMillan, 1855), 34–35.

215. Reed, *Lectures on English Literature*, 37.

216. Reed, *Lectures on English Literature*, 39.

217. William St. Clair, *The Reading Nation in the Romantic Period* (Cambridge: Cambridge University press, 2004), 133–134.

218. Warnick argues that Boileau's translation replaced Longinus's demystifying treatment of the sublime with an "aura of mystery and ineffability so that it was discernible only to a man of taste," contributing to aesthetic elitism; she sees Boileau's approach at work in writings by Blair and other rhetoricians in the belletristic tradition. Warnick, *Sixth Canon*, 79, 91.

219. Edmund Burke, *A Philosophical Inquiry into the Origin of Our Ideas of the Sublime and the Beautiful*, new ed. (Basil: J. J. Tourneisen, 1792), 54, 138.

220. Kant, *Critique of the Power of Judgment*, 144–145, 147.

221. Kant, *Critique of the Power of Judgment*, 140, 145.

222. Walt Whitman, section 25 of "Song of Myself."

223. Kant, *Critique of the Power of Judgment*, 128–129.

224. Rhodes, *Shakespeare*, 177–184.

225. Kant, *Critique of the Power of Judgment*, 141 (emphasis in original).

226. For example, Henry Reed attended the University of Pennsylvania, where he was later a professor, from age fourteen to seventeen. William B. Reed, "Introductory Notice," in H. Reed, *Lectures on English History*, xviii.

In England, the Anglican Church controlled most schooling until 1833, when the Factory Act of 1833 mandated a minimal amount of schooling for children working in factories. Reid, *Wordsworth*, 38. The fact that the Church of England and the Church of Scotland had great control over English and Scottish education may have served as important precedents for the Christian moral authority exercised in U.S. colleges. John A. Nietz has noted that an unusual number of ministers wrote textbooks before 1900, so the religious interpretation and control of academic subjects proliferated by that means in primary and secondary schooling as well. Nietz, *Evolution*, 9.

227. James Campbell, *A Thoughtful Profession: The Early Years of the American Philosophical Association* (Chicago: Open Court, 2006), 8–13.

228. Bruce Kuklick, *A History of Philosophy in America, 1720–2000* (Oxford: Oxford University Press, 2001), 171.

229. Franklin E. Court, "The Early Impact of Scottish Literary Teaching in North America," in Robert Crawford, ed., *The Scottish Invention of English Literature* (New York: Cambridge University Press, 1988), 134–163.

230. On eighteenth-century innovations in Scottish education and the general Scottish commitment to education, which contrasted dramatically with the doldrums of Oxford and Cambridge, see Siskin, *Work of Writing*, 89–94; Thomas P. Miller, *The Formation of College English: Rhetoric and Belles Lettres in the British Cultural Provinces* (Pittsburgh: University of Pittsburgh Press, 1997), 20–21, 144–170; and Robin Jarvis, *The Romantic Period: The Intellectual and Cultural Context of English Literature, 1789–1830* (London: Longman Pearson, 2004), 56–58, 84.

231. Rhodes, *Shakespeare*, 202; Gauri Viswanathan, *Masks of Conquest: Literary Study and British Rule in India* (New York: Columbia University Press, 1989), especially 119–128; and Miller, *Formation*, 63–67, 112.

On the forms of moral invigilation under state control practiced in the United Kingdom during the nineteenth century, see Ian Hunter, *Culture and Government: The Emergence of Literary Education* (Houndsmills, England: Macmillan Press, 1988), 106.

232. Miller, *Formation*, 149; Court, "Early Impact," 137–140. On Scottish publishers' aggressive marketing to North American readers, see St. Clair, *Reading Nation*, 106.

233. Court, "Early Impact," 135–136.

234. The two academic titles are mentioned in Perry Miller, *The Raven and the Whale: Poe, Melville, and the New York Literary Scene* [1956] (Baltimore: Johns Hopkins University Press, 1997), 28; and Donald K. Smith, "Origin and Development of Departments of Speech," in Karl R. Wallace, ed., *History of Speech Education in America: Background Studies* (New York: Appleton-Century-Crofts, 1954), 453. Miller's source for the first title is uncertain, but its holder, William McVickar, was initially appointed to a professorship in "Moral Philosophy, Rhetoric, and Belles-lettres" and later added the fields of intellectual philosophy and political cconomy. William A. McVickar, *The Life of the Reverend John McVickar, S.T.D.* (New York: Hurd and Houghton, 1872), 62.

235. Lauck, "Reception," 211.

236. Simon, *Reading of Shakespeare*, 79. McGuffey was personally involved with only the first four readers (Carr, Carr, and Schultz, *Archives*, 117), but his name persisted as a brand.

237. Simon, *Reading of Shakespeare*, 55.

238. Paul Hamilton, "The Philosopher," in Newlyn, *Cambridge Companion to Coleridge*, 170–186.

239. Henry Beers's history of English literature in 1886 summarized Coleridge's role in forging the vocabulary of criticism: "The terminology of criticism ... is in his debt for many of those convenient distinctions—such as that between genius and talent, between wit and humor, between fancy and imagination—which are familiar enough now, but which he first introduced, or enforced. His definitions and apothegms we meet every-where." Beers, *Outline Sketch*, 232.

240. Esterhammer, "The Critic," 152–154.

241. St. Clair, *Reading Nation*, 270–274. The British print history of Blair's works can be found in St. Clair's appendices, 580–581.

242. Samuel Taylor Coleridge, "The Author's Address to the Reader," in *Aids to Reflection* [1825] with preliminary essay by James Marsh, ed. Henry Nelson Coleridge (rept. Port Washington, N.Y.: Kennikat Press, 1971), 59. On Coleridge's parentage and Christian reading practices, see Jeffrey, *People of the Book*, 300–308.

243. Peter C. Carafiol, introduction to James Marsh, *Selected Works of James Marsh*, 3 vols. (Delmar, NY: Scholars' Facsimiles and Reprints, 1976), 1: xv–xvi.

244. James A. Good, *A Search for Unity in Diversity: The "Permanent Hegelian Deposit" in the Philosophy of John Dewey* (Lanham, Md.: Lexington Books, 2006), 57. Marsh had previously translated Herder's *The Spirit of Hebrew Poetry* (1833).

245. James Marsh, "Advertisement" to *Aids to Reflection*, reprinted in Marsh, *Selected Works*, 1: vi. John Beer recounts the important role that *Aids to Reflection* played in shaping Coleridge's reputation in England in *Romantic Influences: Contemporary—Victorian—Modern* (New York: St. Martin's Press, 1993), 150–151.

246. Coleridge, "J. P. Collier's Report," 54–59, particularly 55–57.

247. Talal Asad, *Formations of the Secular: Christianity, Islam, Modernity* (Stanford, Calif.: Stanford University Press, 2003), 23. On the etymological origins of the secular and the sacred, see 30–37.

248. Asad, *Formations*, 24. Asad productively argues that the secular is "neither continuous with the religious that supposedly preceded it (that is, it is not the latest phase of a sacred origin) nor a simple break from it (that is, it is not the opposite, an essence that excludes the sacred)," taking the secular to be rather "a concept that brings together certain behaviors, knowledges, and sensibilities in modern life" (25).

249. Jo Carruthers, *England's Secular Scripture: Islamophobia and the Protestant Aesthetic* (London: Continuum, 2011), 13. One of the most significant inquiries into secularism is that of Hans Blumenberg, who emphasizes that modern thinkers inherited many fundamental questions formulated in religious terms but that the result was not "the *transposition* of authentically theological contents into secularized alienation from their origin but rather the *reoccupation* of answer positions that had become vacant and whose corresponding questions could not be eliminated." Hans Blumenberg, *The Legitimacy of the Modern Age*, trans. Robert M. Wallace (Cambridge, Mass.: MIT Press, 1985), 65.

250. Ralph Waldo Emerson, "Self-Reliance," in *Essays and Lectures*, 262.

251. Coleridge's advocacy of the Clerisy, a national church that would oversee humanistic learning, is the fullest manifestation of his interest in literature's operation as part of a larger institutional apparatus. The tendency of Coleridge (along with other Romantic thinkers) to align literature with the state—and to theorize the individual's relationship to the state as a version of organic form—is worked out in fascinating ways by David Aram Kaiser as "aesthetic statism" and by Anne Frey as "state romanticism." See David Aram Kaiser, *Romanticism, Aesthetics, and Nationalism* (Cambridge: Cambridge University Press, 1999), 59–73; and Anne Frey, *British State Romanticism: Authorship, Agency, and Bureaucratic Nationalism* (Stanford, Calif.: Stanford University Press, 2010), 21–53.

252. Emerson's practice corresponds to Michael Löwy and Robert Sayre's discussion of Romantic individualism: "The development of the individual subject is directly linked to the history and prehistory of capitalism: the isolated individual emerges along with and because of capitalism. However, this is the source of a major contradiction in modern society, for the individual whom society has created cannot help being frustrated in the attempt to live in that same society and ends up revolting against it. The Romantic exaltation of subjectivity... is just one of the forms taken by the resistance to reification." Michael Löwy and Robert Sayre, *Romanticism against the Tide of Modernity*, trans. Catherine Porter (Durham, N.C.: Duke University Press, 2001), 25.

253. Emerson, "Self-Reliance," 273.

254. Emerson, "Shakspeare; or, The Poet," 714.

255. William B. Cairns, *American Literature for Secondary Schools* (New York: Macmillan, 1914), 136; F. O. Matthiessen, *American Renaissance* (Oxford: Oxford University Press, 1968), 64. Matthiessen points out that Emerson shared this intense appreciation for maxims and aphorisms with Coleridge.

256. Snider, *Writer of Books*, 329–330.

257. In *Nature*, Emerson emphasizes the human transformation of the world—"how is the face of the world changed, from the era of Noah to that of Napoleon!"—but never wavers from treating nature as a realm independent of human transformation. Ralph Waldo Emerson, *Nature,* in *Essays and Lectures*, 13.

258. The section titled "Commodity" in *Nature* involves human use of nature—including even sensory pleasures—and human invention. Amazingly, however, it makes no reference to economics or to the market conditions that turn goods into commodities.

259. Ralph Waldo Emerson, "Ode, Inscribed to William H. Channing," in Stephen E. Whicher, ed., *Selections from Ralph Waldo Emerson: An Organic Anthology* (Boston: Houghton Mifflin, 1966), 505. Charles Taylor addresses the Romantic-era establishment of nature as a "moral source" in part 4, "The Voice of Nature," *Sources of the Self: The Making of the Modern Identity* (Cambridge, Mass.: Harvard University Press, 1989), 305–390.

260. Emerson, *Nature*, 10.

261. Emerson, *Nature*, 34.

262. Emerson, *Nature*, 18–19.

263. Of poetry as a "living power" embodied: "a living body is of necessity an organized one—and what is organization but the connection of parts to a whole, so that each part is at once end and means!" Coleridge goes on to use the analogy of bark to tree. Samuel Taylor Coleridge, "On Organic form in Shakespeare's Plays...." [1812–1813], in *Coleridge's Criticism of Shakespeare*, ed. R. A. Foakes (Detroit: Wayne State University Press, 1989), 52.

264. David Simpson offers an instructive account of claims made in British literary culture either for literature's "immethodical" quality—which he links to its sublimity—or its being the "product of a method" that is elusive and exclusive in "System and Literature," in *Romanticism, Nationalism, and the Revolt against Theory* (Chicago: University of Chicago Press, 1993), 126–148.

265. See Stephen Greenblatt, *Hamlet in Purgatory* (Princeton, N.J.: Princeton University Press, 2001); and Jennifer Waldron, *Reformations of the Body: Idolatry in Early Modern Theater* (New York: Palgrave Macmillan, 2013).

266. Roach, *Cities of the Dead*, 77. Greenblatt's provocative claim about how he was drawn to Shakespeare gets at the same phenomenon: "I began with a desire to speak with the dead." Stephen Greenblatt, *Shakespearean Negotiations: The Circulation of Social Energy in Renaissance England* (Berkeley: University of California Press, 1988), 1.

267. Jonathan Arac, "The Impact of Shakespeare: Goethe to Melville," *Impure Worlds: The Institution of Literature in the Age of the Novel* (New York: Fordham University Press, 2011), 4. Sandra Gustafson describes Henry Clay Folger's "conversion" to Shakespeare—accomplished by hearing Emerson lecture about him—in "Eloquent Shakespeare."

268. Henry N. Hudson, "Preface to the Harvard Edition of Shakespeare," *Essays on English Studies* (Boston: Ginn, 1906), 97.

269. Samuel Taylor Coleridge, chapter 15, *Biographia Literaria*.

Chapter 4

1. [Delia Bacon], "William Shakespeare and His Plays; An Inquiry Concerning Them," *Putnam's Monthly*, Jan. 1856, 12.

2. Here I join many who have taken inspiration from Judith Halberstam's *The Queer Art of Failure* (Durham, N.C.: Duke University Press, 2011).

3. Stanley Cavell, *Emerson's Transcendental Etudes*, ed. David Justin Hodge (Stanford, Calif.: Stanford University Press, 2003), 2.

4. The most important recent scholarship about the St. Louis group is by philosophers James A. Good and Dorothy G. Rogers, who have brought out substantial series of reprints by the St. Louis group, a network that Good calls the Ohio Hegelians, and the women scholars of the St. Louis movement, who wrote about philosophy, pedagogy, and literature: Michael DeArmey and James A. Good, eds., *St. Louis Hegelians*, 2 vols. (Bristol, England: Thoemmes Continuum, 2001); William Torrey Harris, ed., *Journal of Speculative Philosophy*, intro. James A. Good, 22 vols. (Bristol, England: Thoemmes Continuum, 2002); James A. Good, ed., *The Ohio Hegelians,* 3 vols. (Bristol, England: Thoemmes Continuum, 2004); and Dorothy G. Rogers, ed., *Women in the St. Louis Idealist Movement, 1860–1925*, 4 vols. (Bristol, England: Thoemmes Continuum, 2003). See especially James Good, "The Value of Thomas Davidson," *Transactions of the Charles S. Peirce Society* 40, no. 2 (2004): 289–318; James A. Good, "A 'World-Historical Idea': The St. Louis Hegelians and the Civil War," *Journal of American Studies* 34, no. 3 (2000): 447–464; and Dorothy G. Rogers, *America's First Women Philosophers: Transplanting Hegel, 1860–1925* (New York: Continuum, 2005). Other important recent studies are Elizabeth Flower and Murray G. Murphy, "The Absolute Immigrates to America: The St. Louis Hegelians," in Elizabeth Flower and Murray G. Murphy, *A History of Philosophy in America*, 2 vols. (New York: Capricorn Books, 1977), 2: 463–516; and Matt Erlin, "Absolute Speculation: The St. Louis Hegelians and the Question

of American National Identity," in Lynne Tatlock and Matt Erlin, eds., *German Culture in Nineteenth-Century America: Reception, Adaptation, Transformation* (Rochester, N.Y.: Camden House, 2005), 89–106. *The Journal of Speculative Philosophy* published today is not the same journal.

    5. James A. Good, *A Search for Unity in Diversity: The "Permanent Hegelian Deposit" in the Philosophy of John Dewey* (Lanham, Md.: Lexington Books, 2006), 75; and Rogers, *America's First*, 21–22. Competing accounts of the origin story can be found in Erlin, "Absolute Speculation," 89; and Flower and Murphy, "Absolute," 472.

    6. Denys P. Leighton, "Brokmeyer, Henry Conrad," *Dictionary of Missouri Biography*, ed. Lawrence O. Christensen, William E. Foley, Gary Kremer, and Kenneth H. Winn (Columbia: University of Missouri Press, 1999), 117–119. As Leighton notes, Brokmeyer also spelled his name Brockmeyer, and he was mainly publicly known by this spelling in the United States during his lifetime.

    7. There are no borrowing records from the era, but an 1848 edition of *Prose Writers of Germany* is in the St. Louis Mercantile Library collection. Denton Snider records that Brockmeyer knew Hedge personally and that Hedge's book was Brockmeyer's introduction to Hegel. Denton J. Snider, *A Writer of Books* (St. Louis: Sigma, [1910]), 368–369.

    8. Rogers, *America's First*, 27; Good, *A Search for Unity*, 66–70.

    9. Good, "'World-Historical,'" 462.

    10. Rogers, *America's First*, 23.

    11. Rogers, *America's First*, 19, 53–54.

    12. Dorothy G. Rogers, introduction to *Assorted Articles and Essays by Anna C. Brackett, Grace C. Bibb, and Ellen M. Mitchell*, vol. 1 of Rogers, *Women in the St. Louis Idealist Movement*, ix–xxii.

    13. Snider sometimes called works, such as *Paradise Lost*, Literary Bibles, but he mainly identified the Bibles as a set of master authors. His supercanon, referenced throughout his work but laid out explicitly in one appendix, consists of Homer, Dante, Shakespeare, and Goethe. Snider, *Writer of Books*, 629–654. Snider's phrase was borrowed, with acknowledgment, by Richard G. Moulton in *World Literature and Its Place in General Culture* (New York: Macmillan, 1911). Denton J. Snider, *The St. Louis Movement in Philosophy, Literature, Education, Psychology, with Chapters of Autobiography* (St. Louis: Sigma, 1920), 555; and Rogers, *America's First*, 54.

    14. W. T. Harris, "The Spiritual Sense of Dante's 'Divina Commedia,'" *Journal of Speculative Philosophy* 21 (1888): 349–451, and *The Spiritual Sense of Dante's "Divina Commedia"* (New York: Appleton, 1889).

    15. H. C. Brockmeyer, "Letters on Goethe's *Faust*," *Journal of Speculative Philosophy* 21 (1888): 36–82, 151–188.

    16. Snider, *St. Louis Movement*, 342; Giovanni A. Scartazzini, *A Handbook to Dante*, trans. Thomas Davidson (Boston: Ginn, 1887); Thomas Davidson, *The Philosophy of Goethe's Faust*, ed. Charles M. Bakewell (Boston: Ginn, 1906).

    17. Louis J. Block, "The Philosophic Schools of St. Louis, Jacksonville, Concord, and Chicago," in D. H. Harris, ed., *A Brief Report of the Meeting Commemorative of the Early Saint Louis Movement in Philosophy, Psychology, Literature, Art and Education* (St. Louis: n.p., 1922), 17, 16. Available online at archive.org (http://archive.org/stream/cu31924028846835/cu31924028846835_djvu.txt), accessed 31 May 2015. Block's name has been spelled "Lewis" in many St. Louis histories.

18. The school was often known simply as the "Concord School of Philosophy," but both names circulated officially and unofficially, and literature was always prominent among the school's offerings. The most comprehensive discussions of the school (outside of the works about the St. Louis movement already identified) are Austin Warren, "The Concord School of Philosophy," *New England Quarterly* 2, no. 2 (1929): 199–233; Henry A. Pochmann, *New England Transcendentalism and St. Louis Hegelianism: Phases in the History of American Idealism* (Philadelphia: Carl Schurz Memorial Foundation, 1948); and Bruce Ronda, "The Concord School of Philosophy and the Legacy of Transcendentalism," *New England Quarterly* 82, no. 4 (2009): 575–607.

19. Jones, who had MD and MA degrees from Illinois College, was appointed at the college as a professor of philosophy from 1888 to 1900, probably as a result of his work in the Concord School. He shared the literary leanings of the St. Louis group, often connecting Plato's philosophy to the supercanon, and the Jacksonville Club entertained visitors and maintained correspondence with people in somewhat distant midwestern cities as well as with Concord-area Transcendentalists. Paul Russell Anderson, "Hiram K. Jones and Philosophy in Jacksonville," *Journal of the Illinois State Historical Society* 33, no. 4 (1940): 478–520. About Emery, see David F. Wilcox, "Samuel H. Emery, Jr.," *Representative Men and Homes, Quincy Illinois* (Quincy: Volk, Jones, and McMein, 1899), 27.

20. A detailed account of the offerings of the school can be found in Warren, "Concord School."

As Ronda notes, Bruce Kuklick considered the school to be "the last gasp of non-professorial philosophy in the Transcendentalist style." Bruce Kuklick, *The Rise of American Philosophy: Cambridge, Massachusetts, 1860–1930* (New Haven, Conn.: Yale University Press, 1977), 58. Cited by Ronda, "Concord School," 577.

21. W. W. Willoughby, "History of Summer Schools in the United States," *Report of the Secretary of the Interior* (52nd Congress), 5 vols. (Washington: Government Printing Office, 1895), 5: part 2, 909–912.

22. Dorothy G. Rogers, introduction to *Assorted Articles and Essays by Eliza R. Sunderland, Caroline K. Sherman, May Wright Sewall, and Lucia Ames Mead*, vol. 3 of *Women in the St. Louis Idealist Movement*, 11; and Pochmann, *New England Transcendentalism*, 88, 104. For each year's lecturers and lecture titles, see Kenneth Walter Cameron, ed., *Concord Harvest*, 2 vols. (Hartford, Conn.: Transcendental Books 1970), 2: 281–332.

23. Kate Douglas Wiggin, *My Garden of Memory: An Autobiography* [1923] (Boston: Houghton Mifflin, 1927), 146–158.

24. Good, "Thomas Davidson," 303. Davidson's ideal curriculum for the Breadwinners' College, which included courses in "Comparative Literature, including Theory of Criticism" and "Comparative Art, including Philosophy of Aesthetics," was laid out in the posthumous collection of some of his lectures, *The Education of the Wage-Earners*, ed. Charles M. Bakewell (Boston: Ginn, 1904), 76–77.

25. Flower and Murphy, "The Absolute," 485; and Snider, *St. Louis Movement*, 470.

26. Willoughby, "History," 912–914; Snider, *St Louis Movement*, 574.

27. Good, "Thomas Davidson," 299.

28. Snider, *St. Louis Movement*, 501.

29. Willoughby, "History," 914.

30. Snider, *St. Louis Movement*, 315–324, 523. Sources indicate that Snider's courses were free and that he often provided his self-published books to students as textbooks. Charles Perry (who spoke with people who had known Snider personally) indicates that after Snider

resigned from teaching high school, he made a living in real estate, perhaps as a real estate agent. Charles M. Perry, ed., *The St. Louis Movement in Philosophy* (Norman: University of Oklahoma Press, 1930), 43. On Snider's courses, see Mrs. D. H. Harris, "The Early St. Louis Movement and the Communal University," in D. H. Harris, *Brief Report*, 43.

31. Snider, *St. Louis Movement*, 255–256.

32. The most famous academic in the group—and the only academic involved substantially—was George Holmes Howison, who taught mathematics and political economy at Washington University during the 1860s but later moved into philosophy, eventually founding Berkeley's philosophy department.

33. Good, "Thomas Davidson," 290; Snider, *Writer of Books*, 13–38, 81.

34. Good, "Thomas Davidson," 294–295. Good has emphasized that Davidson represents "an example of the philosophical life that was marginalized by professionalization," an approach parallel to my interest here in the St. Louis movement (289). See also William James, "Thomas Davidson: Individualist" (1903), in William James, *Essays, Comments, and Reviews* (Cambridge, Mass.: Harvard University Press, 1987), 86–97.

35. Snider, *St. Louis Movement*, 261.

36. On Davidson's relations with the Fabians in London and on his political and philosophical views, see Good, "Thomas Davidson," 298–302. Some members of the St. Louis movement were somewhat centrist Hegelians, broadly progressive (and aligned with the Progressive movement's more specific focus on institutional solutions) but heavily interested in the importance of the state. Good, "'World-Historical,'" 447–464. Others were "left or left-center" Hegelians who supported feminism and Christian socialism. Rogers, *America's First*, 20–21, 35–36. Flower and Murphy identify the St. Louis Hegelians as middle-of-the-road Christian moderates, but Rogers points out that several members of the group were "religious radicals by just about any standard." Flower and Murphy, "Absolute," 471; Rogers, *America's First*, 20.

37. Snider, *Writer of Books*, 75.

38. Davidson, *Education of the Wage-Earners*, 99.

39. Thomas Davidson, "Lectures to the Breadwinners," *Memorials of Thomas Davidson, the Wandering Scholar*, ed. William Knight (Boston: Ginn, 1907), 83 (openlibrary.org), accessed 28 July 2014.

40. Frances A. B. Harmon, *The Social Philosophy of the St. Louis Hegelians* (Ph.D. diss., Columbia University, 1943), 5; Dorothy Rogers, rev. of *The Journal of Speculative Philosophy, 1867–1893*, ed. William Torrey Harris, new introd. James A. Good, in *Transactions of the Charles S. Peirce Society* 40, no. 3 (2004): 547; Perry, *St. Louis Movement*, 12. An index of the circulation of the *Western* in the East is the fact that the 1871 volume of the *Western Educational Review* digitized for Google is identified as being a gift to the Harvard Libraries of the Honorable Charles Sumner of Boston.

41. Good, *Search for Unity*, 79. On the circulation of notes from the Jacksonville Plato Club to a group in Quincy, see Anderson, "Jones," 493. Brockmeyer's translation was originally commissioned by two lesser-known members of the St. Louis movement, who funded Brockmeyer's modest living while he worked on it. Rogers, *America's First*, 27.

42. Snider, *Writer of Books*, 48; Snider, *St. Louis Movement*, 486; Snider, *Writer of Books*, 77; Snider, *St. Louis Movement*, 483. Some of Snider's early books identify in their front matter publishers other than Snider's Sigma Publishing Company, which became his imprint at some point after he published *The System of Shakespeare's Plays* with a local St. Louis publisher (Snider, *Writer of Books*, 483). Given his insistence in *Writer of Books* (not

contradicted in any of the writings of those who knew him that I've found) that he resisted commercial publication, it seems likely that these publishers were printers he employed. Snider, *St. Louis Movement*, 445–446; Snider, *Writer of Books*, 74–77. Snider had an agent in Chicago and may have had agents in other cities, however. Perry, *St. Louis Movement*, 73.

The Internet Archive's digitized version of Snider's long narrative poem, *Delphic Days*, in Snider's Sigma edition, was made from a copy in Oxford University's library, an indicator of the reach of Snider's self-published books (http://archive.org/details/delphicdays00snidgoog), accessed 16 May 2012. Denton J. Snider, *Delphic Days: A Greek Idyl* (St. Louis: Friedrich Roeslein, 1880). Late in his life, several of his works were published by the William Harvey Miner Company in St. Louis, Miner being a friend who may have served as Snider's printer or published the works as part of his antiquarian bookseller business (Perry, *St. Louis Movement*, 70; see the broadside "Announcement concerning the William Harvey Miner Company, Inc." [St. Louis, 1916] (http://library.duke.edu/digitalcollections/broadsides_bdsm021190/), accessed 28 July 2014.

Several of Snider's works were reprinted by established East Coast publishers during his lifetime, but they were apparently not submitted for editorial review. For example, *A Walk in Hellas* was reprinted by James R. Osgood in 1883; *Agamemnon's Daughter* by Osgood in 1885; *An Epigrammatic Voyage* was printed by Ticknor in 1886. London's Selwyn and Blount reprinted Snider's biography of Lincoln (one of his heroes) and the studies that made up *The System of Shakespeare's Drama* under the title *Shakespeare Commentaries* in 1925.

43. Snider, *St. Louis Movement*, 484.

44. Oberlin bestowed on Snider an honorary Litt.D. in 1899. *Annual Reports of Oberlin College*, *Bulletin of Oberlin College*, Mar. 1900, 38.

45. "Nothing on the programme, with the single exception of Dr. Harris' lecture[,] will be received with greater interest than Mr. Snider's brilliant and philosophical presentations. Mr. Snider's 'Walks in Hellas' [sic: *A Walk in Hellas*], a book the *Traveller* noticed editorially some time since, is growing in popular favor as it merits, and many high school libraries have added it as the best American work on modern Greece." "The Concord School," *Washington Post*, 18 Mar. 1883, 1. A *New York Times* article in 1880 detailing Snider's lecture on Shakespeare in a previous year had been similarly admiring. "The Sages at Concord," *New York Times*, 17 Jul 1880.

46. "D. J. Snider (1873)," Horace Howard Furness, ed., *Hamlet*, 2 vols., *A New Variorum Edition of Shakespeare*, 10th ed. (Philadelphia: J. B. Lippincott, 1877), 2: 182–184; Joseph Crosby to Joseph Parker Norris, 9 May 1875, 7 Aug. 1875, 6 Oct. 1875, and 11 June 1876, in John W. Velz and Frances N. Teague, eds., *One Touch of Shakespeare: Letters of Joseph Crosby to Joseph Parker Norris, 1875–1878* (Washington: Folger Shakespeare Library, 1986), 69–70, 95, 111, 163–164.

47. J. Parker Norris, "Shakespearean Gossip," *American Bibliopolist*, Dec. 1876, 120. On Norris, see Velz and Teague, introduction to *One Touch of Shakespeare*, 18. A reviewer (one of Snider's philosophical colleagues in St. Louis) who encountered *A Walk in Hellas* in its private printing warned that "[p]rivate printing means private reading," whereas he believed the poem deserved wider circulation; it was reprinted by James R. Osgood later that year. R. A. Holland, "A Yankee at Greek Doors," *The Dial*, Mar. 1883, 245.

48. The *Literary World*, in noticing Snider's *Delphic Days*, mentioned that his "*System of Shakespeare's Dramas* first brought him into prominence." "News and Notes," *Literary World*,

24 Apr. 1880, 144. See for example a review, presumably by William J. Rolfe, the editor of the column, in "Shakespeariana," *Literary World*, 7 May 1881, 168; a lengthy review in the *New York Times*, "New Publications: Shakespeare's System," *New York Times*, 28 Feb. 1878; and an unsigned review, which seems stylistically and intellectually likely to be by Richard Grant White, "Literature: More Shakespeariana," *The Independent*, 31 Jan. 1878, 10.

49. Denton J. Snider, *The Shakespearian Drama: A Commentary; The Tragedies* (St Louis: Sigma, 1887), *The Shakespearian Drama: A Commentary; The Comedies* (St Louis: Sigma, 1887), and *The Shakespearian Drama: A Commentary; The Histories* (St Louis: Sigma, 1889).

50. Denton J. Snider, *System of Shakespeare's Dramas*, 2 vols. (St. Louis: G. I. Jones, 1877), 1: 21, 25–26.

51. Snider, *System*, 1: 24.

52. Critics who suggested that Hamlet encountered a conflict of duties or a double bind included Julius L. Klein (whose name was truncated in Furness's *Variorum*), Hermann Ulrici, Henry N. Hudson, and Karl Werder. Hermann Ulrici, "Shakespeare's Dramatic Art," in David Farley-Hills, ed., *Critical Responses to Hamlet, 1839–1854* vol. 3 of *Critical Responses to Hamlet, 1600–1900*, 5 vols. (New York: AMS Press, 1999), 37–61; Henry N. Hudson, "(a) Lectures on Shakespeare 1845 (b) Shakespeare's Characters 1872," in Farley-Hills, *Critical Responses to Hamlet, 1839–1854*, 206–241, and "L. Klein (1846)" and "Karl Werder (1875)," in Furness,*Hamlet*, 2: 266–299, 354–371.

For an account of the dispute over Hamlet's "duty" and its links to the authorship question, see Nancy Glazener, "Print Culture as an Archive of Dissent: Or, Delia Bacon and the Case of the Missing Hamlet," *American Literary History* 19, no. 2 (2007): 329–349.

53. Snider, *System*, 1: 11.

54. Snider, *System*, 1: 170.

55. Snider, *System*, 1: 171.

56. A. C. Bradley, *Shakespearean Tragedy: Lectures on Hamlet, Othello, King Lear, Macbeth* [1904] (London: Macmillan, 1992), 14.

57. Herman Melville, *Pierre; or, The Ambiguities*, ed. William C. Spengemann (New York: Penguin, 1996), 168, 169.

58. Melville, *Pierre*, 173, 175.

59. Samuel Taylor Coleridge, "J. P. Collier's Report of Lecture 12 of the Series *Lectures on Shakespeare and Milton*, 1811–12," rept. in Farley-Hills, *Critical Responses to Hamlet, 1790–1838*, vol. 2 of *Critical Responses to Hamlet, 1600–1900* 5 vols. (New York: AMS Press, 1996), 55.

60. Snider, *System*, 1: 229.

61. Herman Melville, "Hawthorne and His Mosses," in "Reviews and Letters by Melville," Herman Melville, *Moby-Dick*, ed. Hershel Parker and Harrison Hayford, 2nd ed. (New York: Norton, 2002), 522.

62. Snider, *System*, 1: 4.

63. Melville, "Hawthorne," 523; Stephen Greenblatt, *Will in the World: How Shakespeare Became Shakespeare* (New York: Norton, 2004).

64. [D. Bacon], "William Shakespeare," 1.

65. Vivian C. Hopkins, *Prodigal Puritan: A Life of Delia Bacon* (Cambridge, Mass.: Harvard University Press, 1959), 252.

66. Delia Bacon, *The Philosophy of the Plays of Shakspere Unfolded*, preface Nathaniel Hawthorne (London: Groombridge and Sons, 1857; rept. New York: AMS Press, 1970).

Chapters 1 and 2 of Bacon's introduction (xvii–l) reference the Tower of London repeatedly in setting up the dangerous political situation of Elizabethan men of letters. Bacon and Raleigh were both imprisoned there.

67. Howard Felperin, "Bardolatry Then and Now," in Jean I. Marsden, ed., *The Appropriation of Shakespeare: Post-Renaissance Reconstructions of the Works and the Myth* (New York: St. Martin's Press, 1991), 129–144; and James Turner, *Philology: The Forgotten Origin of the Modern Humanities* (Princeton, N.J.: Princeton University Press, 2014), 118.

68. Annabel Patterson, *Censorship and Interpretation: The Conditions of Writing and Reading in Early Modern England* (Madison: University of Wisconsin Press, 1984).

69. D. Bacon, *Philosophy*, 222. For a recent account of Shakespeare's attentive presentation of many characters out of power or marked by difference, see Marianne Novy, *Shakespeare and Outsiders* (Oxford: Oxford University Press, 2013).

70. D. Bacon, *Philosophy*, 280.

71. D. Bacon, *Philosophy*, xxxi.

72. D. Bacon, *Philosophy*, xxii.

73. Baym is the author of the two best recent treatments of Bacon, which underline parallels between Bacon's thought and late twentieth-century Shakespeare criticism: "Delia Bacon: Hawthorne's Last Heroine," *Nathaniel Hawthorne Review* 20, no. 2 (1994): 1–10, and "Delia Bacon, History's Odd Woman Out," *New England Quarterly* 69, no. 2 (1996): 223–249. Baym's account of Bacon's adventurous thinking and the significance of the sponsors and sympathizers she found (who include Elizabeth Peabody) provides the best introduction to Bacon, and her interest in Bacon's anticommercial reading of Shakespeare has influenced my approach here. Another discussion of Bacon's achievement can be found in Juliet Fleming, "The Ladies' Shakespeare," in Dympna Callaghan, ed., *A Feminist Companion to Shakespeare* (Malden, Mass.: Blackwell, 2000), 3–20.

74. [D. Bacon], "William Shakespeare," 6. See David Scott Kastan, *Shakespeare and the Book* (Cambridge: Cambridge University Press, 2001), 53–54.

75. D. Bacon, *Philosophy*, 183, and "William Shakespeare," 9.

76. D. Bacon, "William Shakespeare," 7. Heike Grundmann has identified even earlier, in the wake of the French Revolution, an English "'gentrification' of Shakespeare, an ideological maneuver that turned a deer poacher into a prosperous middle-class businessman in Stratford-upon-Avon, who even applied for a coat-of-arms." Heike Grundmann, "Shakespeare and European Romanticism," in Michael Ferber, ed., *A Companion to European Romanticism* (Malden, Mass.: Blackwell, 2005), 31. Margreta de Grazia traces it in Malone's and Boswell's emphasis on Shakespeare's "respectability," in their 1790 edition. Margreta de Grazia, *Shakespeare Verbatim: The Reproduction of Authenticity and the 1790 Apparatus* (Oxford: Clarendon Press, 1991), 137. One of the strongest statements of this view of Shakespeare was Hartley Coleridge's discussion, which culminated in his claim that Shakespeare "saw and admired the whole structure of the British state, the most perfect system of representation ever devised." Hartley Coleridge, "Shakspeare a Tory and a Gentleman" [1828], in Jonathan Bate, ed., *The Romantics on Shakespeare* (New York: Penguin, 1992), 237.

77. Richard Grant White, "Mr. Collier's Folio of 1632," *Shakespeare's Scholar* (New York: D. Appleton, 1854), 33–81; on White's edition, see Jane Sherzer, "American Editions of Shakespeare: 1753–1866," *PMLA* 22, no. 4 (1907): 685–696.

78. Richard Grant White, "On Reading Shakespeare," *Studies in Shakespeare* (Boston: Houghton, Mifflin, 1886), 52.

79. Hilary Rowland notes that White attributed to Shakespeare "mercenary motives." Hilary Rowland, "Shakespeare and the Public Sphere in Nineteenth Century America" (Ph.D. diss., McGill University, 1998), 68. Sherzer also notes that White "entertains only utilitarian views of Shakespeare's motives," but her examples show she might as well have said "commercial": for instance, she quotes from White's *Introduction to King John*, "In writing the Histories he had the same purpose as in writing the Comedies and Tragedies; that purpose always being, to make a good play; and with him a good play was one which would fill the a theatre whenever it was performed" (qtd. in Sherzer, "American Editions," 689).

80. Richard Grant White, "Prefatory Letter," *Shakespeare's Scholar*, xv–xvi.

81. Richard Grant White, *Memoirs of the Life of William Shakespeare, with an Essay toward the Expression of His Genius, and an Account of the Rise and Progress of the English Drama* (Boston: Little, Brown, 1865), 111.

82. White, *Memoirs*, 1.

83. Richard Grant White, "The Case of Hamlet the Younger," in *Studies in Shakespeare*, 87. Of German critics of Shakespeare, White advises, "Avoid them. The German pretense that Germans have taught us folk of English blood and speech to understand Shakespeare is the most absurd and arrogant that could be set up. Shakespeare owes them nothing; and we have received from them little more than some maundering mystification and much ponderous platitude." White, "On Reading Shakespeare," 54.

84. Hopkins, *Prodigal*, 76.

85. Hopkins cites a letter by George William Curtis acknowledging that *Putnam's* was at fault for commissioning the articles and not publishing them, acknowledging also that *Putnam's* editors were "the indirect cause of her losing the publishers of the book." George William Curtis to J. A. Dix, 5 Aug. 1856, cited in Hopkins, *Prodigal*, 211. White's *Shakespeare's Scholar* was dedicated to Curtis, so Curtis's connection to White may have been a factor in the decision.

86. White recounted, "I returned the article to Mr. Putnam, declining the proposed honor of introducing it to the public, and adding that, as the writer was plainly neither a fool nor an ignoramus, she must be insane; not a maniac, but what boys call 'loony.' So it proved. She died a lunatic, and I believe in a lunatic asylum." White, *Studies in Shakespeare*, 181. The Hopkins biography and Bacon's brother Theodore establish that Bacon died with relatives, not in an asylum, but it is true that her mental and physical health declined drastically in her later life. Theodore Bacon, *Delia Bacon: A Biographical Sketch* (Boston: Houghton Mifflin, 1888), 314.

87. Louis J. Budd suggests that Bacon's approach played out to an extreme both Romantic ideas about Shakespeare and the tendency to "find in a work of belles-lettres the perfect synthesis of public and private wisdom." Louis J. Budd, "The Baconians: Madness through Method," *South Atlantic Quarterly* 54 (July 1955): 361.

88. Hawthorne, though publicly attached to Bacon because of his introduction to her book, appears to have been far less intellectually sympathetic to her, in keeping with his own work's tendency to position literature apart from public and political life. On Hawthorne's reluctant sponsorship of Bacon, see Baym's two essays cited in note 73.

89. Thomas Carlyle, *On Heroes and Hero-Worship* [1841] (London: Oxford University Press, 1965), 103.

90. Ralph Waldo Emerson, "Shakspeare; or, The Poet," in *Essays and Lectures*, ed. Joel Porte (New York: Literary Classics of the United States, 1983), 715. The remark of Emerson's

noted here sounds a lot like what Hawthorne wrote in a letter to Bacon, gingerly registering his skepticism about the need to find an author with broader experience of the world than William Shakespeare's: "We find thoughts in all great writers (and even in small ones) that strike their roots far beneath the surface, and intertwine themselves with the roots of other writers' thoughts; so that when we pull up one, we stir the whole, and yet these writers have had no conscious society with one another." Cited in T. Bacon, *Delia Bacon*, 184.

91. During the 1830s and 1840s, Bacon taught classes that, like Fuller's, were adventurous courses in literature, philosophy, and other areas. One of Delia Bacon's early New Haven courses included readings of Dugald Stewart, Thomas Reid, Victor Cousin, Coleridge, and Shakespeare, for example. Hopkins, *Prodigal*, 51–54, 68–69.

92. White's essay "On Reading Shakespeare" asserts that Shakespeare is best read by men ("Shakespeare is not a woman's poet"), and he warns against forming Shakespeare clubs, in keeping with his warning people away from undertaking any Shakespearean studies other than simply reading the plays. White, "On Reading Shakespeare," 2, 55. White was himself a member of the New York Shakespeare Society, so it seems likely that he distinguished between clubs dominated by educated men and other Shakespearean clubs.

93. The academic takeover of Shakespeare can be traced in the 1863–1866 Cambridge edition of Shakespeare, which was edited by three fellows of Trinity College, Cambridge; a series of Oxford editions followed, beginning in 1868. Gary Taylor, *Reinventing Shakespeare: A Cultural History, from the Restoration to the Present* (New York: Weidenfeld and Nicolson, 1989), 182–196.

94. Crosby to Norris, 12 Jan. 1876, in Velz and Teague, *One Touch of Shakespeare*, 130.

95. Crosby to Norris, 7 Apr. 1875, in Velz and Teague, *One Touch of Shakespeare*, 54. Crosby also deduced, apparently from following newspapers carefully, that White ended up not accepting the offer of a chair of English literature at Princeton (or perhaps having the offer withdrawn) because of damaging publicity from a sexual scandal (Crosby to Norris, 8 Feb. 1878, in Velz and Teague, *One Touch of Shakespeare*, 287).

96. Michael Bristol, *Shakespeare's America, America's Shakespeare* (London: Routledge, 1990), 95.

97. Claudia Stokes describes the somewhat parallel case of misogynistic treatments of Margaret Fuller that fault her for practicing undisciplined pre-professional criticism. Claudia Stokes, *Writers in Retrospect: The Rise of American Literary History, 1875–1910* (Chapel Hill: University of North Carolina Press, 2006), 123–137.

98. Zachary Lesser, "Mystic Ciphers: Shakespeare and Intelligent Design: A Response to Nancy Glazener," *American Literary History* 19 (Summer 2007): 351.

99. Mark Twain began taking an anti-Stratfordian position to play devil's advocate during his long Shakespearean conversations with riverboat pilot George Ealer, but he ended up falling in line with Delia Bacon's criticisms of William Shakespeare's petty mercenary ways, as they then appeared, and argued that the true author of the plays must have had legal training and might have been Francis Bacon. Mark Twain, "Is Shakespeare Dead? From My Autobiography," in Mark Twain, *1601, and Is Shakespeare Dead?* (New York: Oxford University Press, 1996), 50–120. Whitman's friend William D. O'Connor was the author of *Hamlet's Note-Book* (1886). In *November Boughs*, Whitman hinted at Baconian sympathies, asking if "a future age of criticism, diving deeper, mapping the land and lines freer, completer than hitherto, may discover in the plays named the scientific (Baconian?) inauguration of modern Democracy." Walt Whitman, "What Lurks behind Shakspere's Historical Plays" [1884], in Walt Whitman, *Collect and Other Prose*, vol. 2 of *Prose Works 1892*, 2 vols., ed.

Floyd Stovall (New York: New York University Press, 1964), 556. This position marked a shift from his earlier sense that Shakespeare's accomplishments were marred by manifesting the "principle of caste" (476). Walt Whitman, "Poetry To-day in America—Shakspere—the Future" [1881], in Whitman, *Collect*, 476–477.

100. Donnelly, though crediting Delia Bacon's influence, came to very different conclusions from hers—for instance, he found in the plays an aristocratic contempt for poor and working people, but he argued that the peasants of Francis Bacon's time were "sycophantic" and barbaric and deserved this contempt. Ignatius Donnelly, *The Great Cryptogram: Francis Bacon's Cipher in the So-Called Shakespeare Plays*, 2 vols. (London: Sampson Low, Marston, Searle, & Rivington, 1888; rept. New York: AMS Press, 1972), 1: 177.

101. Howard Felperin identifies Edward Dowden's heavily biographical periodizing treatment of Shakespeare's works in *Shakespeare: His Mind and Art* (1875) as a different kind of response to the need to "fill...the gaps" in our knowledge of Shakespeare. Felperin, "Bardolatry."

102. "Books on the Shakespeare-Bacon Controversy" published by Houghton Mifflin were advertised together and included William D. O'Connor, *Hamlet's Note-Book* (Boston: Houghton Mifflin, 1886); Mrs. Henry Pott, *The Promus of Formularies and Elegancies (Being Private Notes, circ. 1594, Hitherto Unpublished) by Francis Bacon, Illustrated and Elucidated by Passages from Shakespeare*, pref. by E. A. Abbott, (Boston: Houghton Mifflin, 1883); and Nathaniel Holmes, *The Authorship of Shakespeare*, new and enl. ed., 2 vols. (Boston: Houghton Mifflin, 1886).

103. Holmes's study, *Authorship*, was originally published in 1866. For Holmes's biography, see *Saint Louis: The Future City of the World* (St. Louis: Gray, Baker, 1875), available online through Southern Illinois University Libraries Online Digital Collections (http://lincoln-live.lib.niu.edu/islandora/object/niu-lincoln%3A37569), accessed 31 May 2015. I have found no link between Holmes and the St. Louis movement, although it seems likely there was contact.

104. Bacon argued that the author of the plays must have been someone like Hamlet—well educated, highly intellectual, and familiar with the intricacies of diplomacy and state politics; a later writer identified *Hamlet* confidently as Delia Bacon's "master-key." Appleton Morgan, *The Shakespearean Myth: William Shakespeare and Circumstantial Evidence* (Cincinnati: Robert Clarke, 1881), 190; and Holmes, *Authorship*, 2: 597.

105. Holmes, *Authorship*, 1: 11.

106. Twain, *Is Shakespeare Dead?* 66.

107. Richard Grant White, "The Bacon-Shakespeare Craze," in *Studies in Shakespeare*, 152.

108. O'Connor, *Hamlet's Note-Book*, 13.

109. Angela Sorby, *Schoolroom Poets: Childhood, Performance, and the Place of American Poetry, 1865–1917* (Durham, N.H.: University of New Hampshire Press, 2005).

110. Bliss Perry, *And Gladly Teach: Reminiscences* (Boston: Houghton Mifflin, 1935), 59.

111. Edith Wharton, *A Backward Glance* (New York: D. Appleton-Century, 1934), 66.

112. Louise Greer, *Browning and America* (Chapel Hill: University of North Carolina Press, 1952), 192.

113. Greer, *Browning*, 194.

114. William S. Peterson, *Interrogating the Oracle: A History of the London Browning Society* (Athens: Ohio University Press, 1969), 164; Yopie Prins, "Robert Browning, Transported by Meter," in Meredith L. McGill, ed., *The Traffic in Poems: Nineteenth-Century Poetry and Transatlantic Exchange* (New Brunswick, N.J.: Rutgers University Press, 2008), 205–230.

115. Greer, *Browning*, 16, 84, 102, 212, 156, 85; Susan Howe, *My Emily Dickinson* (New York: New Directions, 2007), 69–120.

116. John P. Farrell, "Interpreting the Oracle: The Browning Society in England and America," in David W. Thompson, ed., *Performance of Literature in Historical Perspectives* (Lanham, Md: University Press of America, 1983), 232–233.

117. Greer, *Browning*, 164.

118. About the biographies of Clarke and Porter and the founding of *Poet-Lore*, see Melvin H. Bernstein, "The Early Years of Poet Lore, 1889–1929," in *A Comprehensive Index of Poet Lore, Volumes 1–58: 1889–1964*, compiled by Alice Very with intro. by Melvin H. Bernstein (Boston: Branden Press, 1966), 9–32.

119. Percy Stickney Grant, "Browning's Art in Monologue," in *The Robert Browning Society Papers: Selected to Represent the Work of the Society from 1886–1897* (New York: Macmillan, 1897), 45.

120. H. A. Taine, *History of English Literature*, trans. H. Van Laun, 2 vols. (London: Chatto and Windus, 1878), 1: 310n; William J. Rolfe, "Browning's Mastery of Rhyme," in *Browning Society Papers*, 165; and Gamaliel Bradford, Jr., "The Return of the Druses," in *Browning Society Papers*, 286. Prins discusses the difficulty of his meters even for current scholars in "Robert Browning," 212–215.

121. A review of Browning's poetry from 1850 set out some of the terms in which he would continue to be appreciated. It noted that his poetry's "boldness of imagery" was like that of the "great dramatists of the age of Elizabeth," "those intellectual giants," and praised especially his creation of highly individualized and vital characters. The unconventional sensibility that the Browning Societies valued was marked in the reviewer's remark that Browning "possesses a keen and lively wit, a quiet humor, a decidedly sarcastic turn of mind, and a hearty dislike of all the conventional follies of our boastful age." C. C. S., "Art. II.—Browning's Poems," *Christian Examiner and Religious Miscellany*, May 1850, 261. The *Examiner* was a Boston-based Unitarian journal. C. C. S. may have been Charles Chauncy Shackford, later an English professor at Cornell University and a contributor to Browning scholarship.

122. Josiah Royce, "Browning's Theism," in *Browning Society Papers*, 23.

123. Henry Jones, "Browning as a Dramatic Poet," in *Browning Society Papers*, 206–207.

124. Charlotte Porter, "Dramatic Motive in Browning's 'Strafford,'" in *Browning Society Papers*, 192. Porter quotes Snider only about Shakespeare's conservatism, not the idea that institutions manifest the cumulative impact of acts of will.

125. Emma Endicott Marean, "The Nature Element in Browning's Poetry," in *Browning Society Papers*, 475.

126. Josiah Royce, "The Problem of Paracelsus," in *Browning Society Papers*, 230. On Browning's scientific tendencies, see also Daniel Dorchester, "Browning's Philosophy of Art," in *Browning Society Papers*, 99–117; Jenkin Lloyd Jones, "The Uncalculating Soul," in *Browning Society Papers*, 151; Bradford, "Druses," 287–288; and A. J. George, "The Optimism of Wordsworth and Browning, in Relation to Modern Philosophy," in *Browning Society Papers*, 323.

127. Royce, "Paracelsus," 232.

128. Grant, "Browning's Art in Monologue," 43.

129. Grant, "Browning's Art in Monologue," 39.

130. Charles Carroll Everett, "Sordello," in *Browning Society Papers*, 334–337.

131. Charles Gordon Ames, "Caliban upon Setebos," in *Browning Society Papers*, 80.

132. Anne Ruggles Gere, *Intimate Practices: Literacy and Cultural Work in U. S. Women's Clubs, 1880–1920* (Urbana: University of Illinois Press, 1997), 213–216. Joseph Kett notes that middle-aged women in the 1870s and 1880s were well aware of the educational opportunities they had missed and were the core supporters of educational women's clubs and Chautauquas. Joseph F. Kett, *The Pursuit of Knowledge under Difficulties: From Self-Improvement to Adult Education in America, 1750–1990* (Stanford, Calif.: Stanford University Press, 1994), 151.

133. E. M. W. Tillyard, *The Muse Unchained: An Intimate Account of the Revolution in English Studies at Cambridge* (London: Bowes & Bowes, 1958), 22. Tillyard misidentifies him as "E. J. Furnivall," but the profile makes clear that Frederick is intended.

134. Edith Wharton, "Xingu," in *Collected Stories 1911–1937*, vol. 2 of *Collected Stories*, 2 vols., ed. Maureen Howard (New York: Literary Classics of the United States, 2001), 7–8.

135. Charles W. Chesnutt, "Baxter's Procrustes," in *Stories, Novels, and Essays*, ed. Werner Sollors (New York: Literary Classics of the United States, 2002), 781–793; Thorstein Veblen, *The Theory of the Leisure Class* [1899], ed. Martha Banta (Oxford: Oxford University Press, 2007).

136. For further information about these groups, see Gere, *Intimate Practices*, 8. On segregation in the General Federation, see Daphne Spain, *How Women Saved the City* (Minneapolis: University of Minnesota Press, 2001), 19, 100.

"Up to 1894 the General Federation was an organization of literary clubs," proclaimed the introduction to the movement's 1898 history. Ellen M. Henrotin, introduction to Mrs. J. C. Croly (Jennie June), *The History of the Women's Club Movement in America* (New York: Henry G. Allen, 1998), ix.

137. Catherine E. Kelly, "Reading and the Problem of Accomplishment," in Heidi Brayman Hackel and Catherine E. Kelly, eds., *Reading Women: Literacy, Authorship, and Culture in the Atlantic World, 1500–1800* (Philadelphia: University of Pennsylvania Press, 2008), 124–143.

138. Rogers, *America's First*, 97.

139. By 1890, a total of 20,000 U.S. women were enrolled in collegiate courses, nearly half of them in women's colleges. Roger L. Geiger, "The 'Superior Instruction of Women,' 1836–1890," in Roger L. Geiger, ed., *The American College in the Nineteenth Century* (Nashville: Vanderbilt University Press, 2000), 183.

140. Henrotin, introduction, xi; Croly, *History of the Women's Club Movement*, 83, 82.

141. Margaret Sherwood, *An Experiment in Altruism* (New York: Macmillan, 1895), 73.

142. The heyday of the Browning Society was also the heyday of clubs catalyzed by Edward Bellamy's *Looking Backward* (1888), a utopian novel that inspired very direct social theorizing and attempts at political intervention. The two movements inspired by literature undoubtedly shared some overlapping members and goals, but Bellamy-inspired clubs (mainly known as Nationalist Clubs) were devoted to social visions and practices, not textual interpretation or an investment in literature. On Bellamy clubs and their associated periodicals, see Sylvia E. Bowman, *The Year 2000: A Critical Biography of Edward Bellamy* (New York: Octagon Books, 1979), 129–130.

143. Peterson, *Interrogating*, 22.

144. *The Abraham Lincoln Centre and All Souls Church Annual: Reports of 1908* (Chicago: Abraham Lincoln Centre, 1909), 25–26, 40.

145. Vida Dutton Scudder, *On Journey* (New York: E. P. Dutton, 1937), 157. On Scudder and the College Settlement Association, see Spain, *How Women*, 113–118.

146. Lois Brown, *Pauline Elizabeth Hopkins: Black Daughter of the Revolution* (Chapel Hill: University of North Carolina Press, 2008), 194, 218.

147. The National Association of Colored Women is one of the four organizations spotlighted throughout Spain's *How Women Saved the City*. Several other nineteenth-century African American authors who were active in women's clubs are profiled in Laurie F. Maffly-Kipp and Kathryn Lofton, *Women's Work: An Anthology of African-American Women's Historical Writings from Antebellum America to the Harlem Renaissance* (New York: Oxford University Press, 2010).

148. Vida Scudder, "Womanhood in Modern Poetry," *Poet-Lore*, Oct. 1889, 454. Many feminist readers of Shakespeare's plays have found his treatment of women characters more satisfying, although some have also criticized or struggled with the operations of gender in his work. About nineteenth- and twentieth-century women writers' engagements with Shakespeare, see Marianne Novy, *Engaging with Shakespeare: Responses of George Eliot and Other Women Novelists* (Athens: University of Georgia Press, 1994), and Novy, ed., *Women's Re-Visions of Shakespeare: On the Responses of Dickinson, Woolf, Rich, H.D., George Eliot and Others* (Urbana: University of Illinois Press, 1990).

149. Scudder, "Womanhood," 456.

150. George Willis Cooke, "Browning's Theory of Romantic Love," in *Browning Society Papers*, 97. On Cooke's lectures, see "Lectures," *The Unitarian*, Sept. 1888, 408.

151. Charlotte Porter and Helen A. Clarke, eds., *The Complete Works of Mrs. E. B. Browning*, 6 vols. (New York: Society of English and French Literature; Thomas Y. Crowell, 1900). Bernstein notes that they exchanged "token rings" and that Porter's collection of poetry, *Lips of Music* (1910), commemorated Clarke. Bernstein, "Early Years," 10.

152. Patricia Ann Palmieri offers a thorough discussion of the Wellesley faculty from this era and the many partnerships (known sometimes as "Wellesley marriages") among women faculty and students in her study *In Adamless Eden: The Community of Women Faculty at Wellesley* (New Haven, Conn.: Yale University Press, 1995).

153. Mary E. Burt, *Browning's Women* (Chicago: Charles H. Kerr, 1887), 94, 103. The book is dedicated to "Jenkin Lloyd Jones and His First Browning Club."

154. A. H. Bradford, "The Interpreter of Life," *The Independent*, 12 June 1890, [1].

155. Charlotte Porter's memorial essay about Helen A. Clarke offers an overview of their endeavors, including a list of some of the authors appearing in translation in *Poet-Lore*. Charlotte E. Porter, "A Story of Poet Lore," *Poet-Lore*, Autumn 1926, 432–453.

156. William Shakespeare, *The Complete Works of William Shakespeare*, ed. Charlotte Porter and Helen A. Clarke (New York: T. Y. Crowell, 1903); and Andrew Murphy, *Shakespeare in Print: A History and Chronology of Shakespeare Publishing* (New York: Cambridge University Press, 2003), 164–165.

157. Bernstein, "Early Years," 11.

158. Roland Barthes, "From Work to Text," in *The Rustle of Language*, trans. Richard Howard (New York: Hill & Wang, 1986), 63.

159. Prins discusses some musical settings composed by another Browning admirer in "Robert Browning," 217–223.

160. George Dimmick Latimer, "A Browning Monologue," in *Browning Society Papers*, 173–189.

161. Snider, *Writer of Books*, 631–654; Denton Jaques Snider, *The Redemption of the Hamlets (Son and Father)* (St. Louis: William Harvey Miner, 1923); and Willie John Abbot, "The Chicago Literary School," *Christian Union*, 21 Jan. 1893, 112.

162. Greer, *Browning*, 158, 166, 203, 167.

163. Sorby, *Schoolroom Poets*, xxix.

164. Wharton, *Backward Glance*, 184–186.

165. Qtd. in Edmund Clarence Stedman and Ellen Mackay Hutchinson, eds., *A Library of American Literature: From the Earliest Settlement to the Present Time*, 11 vols. (New York: Charles L. Webster, 1888–1890), 11: 2. (The epigraph includes the original attribution after Goethe's name.)

166. Evert A. Duyckinck and George L. Duyckinck, eds., *Cyclopaedia of American Literature*, 2 vols. (New York: Charles Scribner, 1855); Edmund Clarence Stedman and Ellen Mackay Hutchinson, "Preface to the Final Volume," in *Library*, 11: ix.

167. Karin Hooks offers an excellent account of the *Library* and previous scholarship about it. Her approach emphasizes the marks of its success: what it accomplished and how much it was admired. My emphasis here instead is on how quickly it was forgotten and how seldom it has been remembered. Karin Hooks, "Literary Retrospectives: The 1890s and the Reconstruction of American Literary History," (Ph.D. diss., Ohio State University, 2012), 24–67.

168. Edmund Clarence Stedman, *Victorian Poets* [1875] (Boston: James R. Osgood, 1876), 1.

169. Hooks provides a strong case that Hutchinson's shaping editorial role was not subordinate to Stedman's, even though later scholars have tended to give Stedman priority. Hooks, "Literary Retrospectives," 35–39; Karin L. Hooks, "Ellen Mackay Hutchinson," *Legacy* 30, no. 2 (2013): 373.

170. Stedman and Hutchinson, "Preface to the Final Volume," vi, viii. The review quoted is attributed to "M. W. H" of the *New York Sun*.

171. Stedman and Hutchinson, "Preface to the Final Volume," viii.

172. Stedman and Hutchinson, "Topical Analysis of Selections," in "Preface to the Final Volume," ix.

173. Phillis Wheatley Peters, "On Imagination," "On the Death of C.E., an Infant of Twelve Months," and "To the Right Honorable William, Earl of Dartmouth," in Stedman and Hutchinson, *Library*, 3: 504–505.

174. See for example Hugh Swinton Legaré, "Paper Money Beneficial to the Laboring Classes," in Stedman and Hutchinson, *Library*, 5: 462–464.

175. Stedman told Constance Fenimore Woolson that he deferred to Hutchinson about women writers, although there's no way to know whether this was true or a diplomatic ploy. Edmund Clarence Stedman to Constance F. Woolson, 2 Sept. 1889, in Laura Stedman and George M. Gould, eds., *Life and Letters of Edmund Clarence Stedman*, 2 vols. (New York: Moffat, Yard, 1910), 1: 140.

176. Stedman and Hutchinson, *Library*, 5: 2.

177. Stedman and Hutchinson, "Preface to the Final Volume," v.

178. Gulian Crommelin Verplanck, "On the Madness of Hamlet" and "Shakespeare's Name and Autographs," in Stedman and Hutchinson, *Library*, 5: 113–119.

179. Alexander Hill Everett, "Shakespeare and Schiller," in Stedman and Hutchinson, *Library*, 5: 253–255.

180. George Perkins Marsh, "The Dramatic Diction of Shakespeare and His Time," in Stedman and Hutchinson, *Library*, 6: 63–66; Henry Norman Hudson, "The Vision of a Great Poet," in Stedman and Hutchinson, *Library*, 7: 269; Richard Grant White, "Shakespeare the Dramatist," in Stedman and Hutchinson, *Library*, 8: 3–8; Edwin Percy Whipple, "The Shakespearian World," in Stedman and Hutchinson, *Library*, 7: 392–394; Horace Howard Furness, "A Kindred Dramatic Method, In Their Use of Double Time, Pursued by Aeschylus

and Shakespeare," in Stedman and Hutchinson, *Library*, 9: 61–70; William Torrey Harris, "Shakespeare's Historical Plays," in Stedman and Hutchinson, *Library*, 9: 334–336; Appleton Morgan, "Shylock's Appeal," in Stedman and Hutchinson, *Library*, 10: 342; Denton Snider, "At the House of Pindar," In Stedman and Hutchinson, *Library*, 10: 85–88; Delia Bacon, "Her Initiation of the Shakespeare-Bacon Controversy," in Stedman and Hutchinson, *Library*, 7: 117–120; Theodore Bacon, "Miss Bacon's Theory of the Shakespearian Plays," in Stedman and Hutchinson, *Library*, 11: 410–414.

181. Hiram Corson, "Spirituality a Test of Literature," in Stedman and Hutchinson, *Library*, 8: 406–408.

182. Ralph Waldo Emerson, "Books and Reading," in Stedman and Hutchinson, *Library*, 6: 142.

183. Edward Tyrrel Channing, "Literary Fame," in Stedman and Hutchinson, *Library*, 5: 225, 227, 228.

184. Henry Theodore Tuckerman, "The First American Novelist," in Stedman and Hutchinson, *Library*, 7: 225, 226.

185. Taine, *History of English Literature*, 1: 4, 10.

186. Stedman, *Victorian Poets*, 1–2.

187. John Greenleaf Whittier to Edmund Clarence Stedman, 18 Sept. 1888, in Stedman and Gould, *Life and Letters*, 1: 142.

188. Kermit Vanderbilt uses the *Cambridge History* forebears as a guide in his own study of the origins of literary studies, with the result that the *Library of American Literature* is also treated scantily and somewhat condescendingly, omitted from his main genealogy of the field in *American Literature and the Academy: The Roots, Growth, and Maturity of a Profession* (Philadelphia: University of Pennsylvania Press, 1986), 111–112. William Peterfield Trent, John Erskine, Stuart P. Sherman, and Carl Van Doren, preface to *The Cambridge History of American Literature* [1917], 4 vols. (New York: G. P. Putnam's Sons, 1923), 1: xi.

189. Bruce Michelson, *Printer's Devil: Mark Twain and the American Publishing Revolution* (Berkeley: University of California Press, 2006), 167. Hooks notes that Henry Wadsworth Longfellow, Oliver Wendell Holmes, John Greenleaf Whittier, James Russell Lowell, Ralph Waldo Emerson, and "Piatt" (probably J. J. Piatt rather than Sarah, since the other candidates were male) turned down the opportunity to edit the *Library* before Stedman accepted and recruited Hutchinson. Hooks, "Literary Retrospectives," 1.

190. Michaelson, *Printer's Devil*, 123–124.

191. Robert J. Scholnick, *Edmund Clarence Stedman* (Boston: Twayne, 1977), 142. On encyclopedias, see "Subscription Publishers and Underselling," *Trade Circular Annual* (1871), reprinted in Nancy Cook, "Reshaping Publishing and Authorship in the Gilded Age," in Scott E. Jasper, Joanne D. Chaison, Jeffrey D. Groves, eds., *Perspectives on American Book History: Artifacts and Commentary* (Boston: University of Massachusetts Press, 2002), 226.

192. James Hart, *The Popular Book: A History of American Literary Taste* (Berkeley: University of California Press, 1950), 151, cited in Michaelson, *Printer's Devil*, 84.

193. On the resurgence of subscription publishing after the Civil War and disapproval expressed in publications such as *Publisher's Weekly* and the *Literary World*, see Cook, "Reshaping Publishing," 224–230.

194. Mark Twain, *The Tragedy of Pudd'nhead Wilson and the Comedy Those Extraordinary Twins* (Hartford: American, 1894). For a further account of the literary coding of binding and illustration practices and a sample of the illustration practices in Twain's novels formatted for subscription sale, see Nancy Glazener, "The Novel in Postbellum Print

Culture," in Leonard Cassuto, Clare Virginia Eby, and Benjamin Reiss, eds., *The Cambridge History of the American Novel* (Cambridge: Cambridge University Press, 2011), 337–364.

195. On Benjamin's sales and the circulation of the *Library* while he held it, see Hooks, "Literary Retrospectives," 28–30. An advertisement identifies the *Library* as being sold by subscription only, even though the publisher, William Evarts Benjamin, had a retail shop. Ad, *Publisher's Weekly*, 7 Apr. 1894, 581. Benjamin's father was a prominent editor of literary magazines, and William had worked in Dodd and Mead's rare book department during the 1870s before setting up, with his brother Walter R. Benjamin, a bookshop specializing in Americana, English and American literature, autographs, and manuscripts. In partnership with William Bell, he formed Benjamin and Bell, a publishing concern. Donald C. Dickinson, "William Evarts Benjamin," *Dictionary of American Antiquarian Booksellers* (Westport, Conn.: Greenwood Press, 1998), 13–14.

196. Michaelson, *Printer's Devil*, 81.

197. Stedman and Hutchinson, "Preface to the Final Volume," vii.

198. Stedman and Hutchinson, "Preface to the Final Volume," v, vi.

199. Barbara Schmidt has compiled a list of Charles L. Webster and Co. titles from 1885 to 1894 drawn from Worldcat and advertising materials, "Mark Twain, Publisher," (http://www.twainquotes.com/websterco.html), accessed 31 May 2015.

200. Ellen Gruber Garvey, "Ambivalent Advertising: Books, Prestige, and the Circulation of Publicity," in Carl F. Kaestle and Janice A. Radway, eds., *Print in Motion: The Expansion of Publishing and Reading in the United States, 1880–1940*, vol. 4 of David D. Hall, ed., *A History of the Book in America* (Chapel Hill: University of North Carolina Press, 2009), 170.

201. Jeffrey D. Groves, "Courtesy of the Trade," in Scott E. Casper, Jeffrey D. Groves, Stephen W. Nissenbaum, and Michael Winship, eds., *The Industrial Book, 1840–1880*, vol. 3 of Hall, *History of the Book in America* (Chapel Hill: University of North Carolina Press, 2007), 139–147. Correspondence among Henry Holt, Henry Harper, Daniel Heath, and other publishers negotiating informal proprietary rights to particular authors and works can be found in Ellen D. Gilbert, ed., *The House of Holt, 1866–1946: A Documentary Volume*, vol. 284 of *The Dictionary of Literary Biography* (Detroit: Gale Research, 2003), 39–43.

202. For useful analyses of the major histories of American literature before 1910, see Stokes, *Writers in Retrospect*, 1–32; David R. Shumway, *Creating American Civilization: A Genealogy of American Literature as an Academic Discipline* (Minneapolis: University of Minnesota Press, 1994), 65–82; and Vanderbilt, *American Literature*.

U.S. literature became gradually incorporated into many high school curricula after midcentury. See William J. Reese, *The Origins of the American High School* (New Haven, Conn.: Yale University Press, 1995), 116.

203. Tyler is identified as "Professor of English Literature in the University of Michigan." Moses Coit Tyler, *History of American Literature* (New York: G. P. Putnam's Sons, 1878).

204. Hart is identified as "Professor of Rhetoric and of the English Language and Literature in the College of New Jersey, and Late Principal of the New Jersey State Normal School." John S. Hart, *A Manual of American Literature: A Text-Book for Schools and Colleges* (Philadelphia: Eldredge and Brother, 1872).

205. Charles F. Richardson, *The Development of American Thought*, vol. 1 of *American Literature, 1607–1885*, 2 vols. (New York: G. P. Putnam's Sons, 1888). These publications are distinct from earlier textbooks that were explicitly designed for secondary or sometimes primary use, such as N. K. [Noble Kibby] Royse, *A Manual of American Literature. Designed*

for the Use of Schools of Advanced Grades (Philadelphia: Cowperthwait, 1872). Royse was identified on the title page as "Principal of Sixth District Public Schools, Cincinnati, Ohio."

206. Barrett Wendell, *A Literary History of America* (New York: Charles Scribner's Sons, 1901).

207. Hooks details the changing usage of "anthology" in the period, which has complicated subsequent treatments of the *Library*. Hooks, "Literary Retrospectives," 10–11.

208. Murphy, *Shakespeare in Print*, 203, 206, 159.

209. Charles Dudley Warner, ed., *Library of the World's Best Literature, Ancient and Modern*, 30 vols. (New York: R. S. Peale and J. A. Hill, 1896–1898).

210. "Literary," *The Chap-Book*, 1 Nov. 1897.

211. J. J. Halsey, "American Literature," *The Dial*, Feb. 1887, 243.

212. Hutcheson Macaulay Posnett, *Comparative Literature* (London: Kegan, Paul, Trench, 1886), 18–19.

213. Halsey, "American Literature," 243.

214. Richardson, *Development*, 444; and "Richardson's American Literature," *New Princeton Review* 2 (Mar. 1887): 283.

215. Wendell, *Literary History*, 9.

216. Halsey, "American Literature," 243.

217. There is evidence that the *Library* was assigned in some high school and college courses, at least as recommended reading. Vanderbilt, *American Literature*, 112; and Evelyn Rezak Bibb, "Anthologies of American Literature, 1787–1964" (Ph.D. diss., Columbia University, 1965), 257, cited by Hooks, "Literary Retrospectives," 52.

218. Thomas De Quincey, "The Literature of Knowledge and Literature of Power" [1847], in David Perkins, ed., *English Romantic Writers* (New York: Harcourt Brace Jovanovich, 1967), 742–744.

Chapter 5

1. Bliss Perry, *A Study of Prose Fiction* (Boston: Houghton Mifflin, 1903), 331.

2. James Turner, *Philology: The Forgotten Origin of the Humanities* (Princeton, N.J.: Princeton University Press, 2014), 157.

3. Writers called deans of American letters, American literature, and so forth included William Dean Howells, of course, but also Charles Dudley Warner, Thomas Wentworth Higginson, Richard Henry Stoddard, and even Julian Hawthorne, somewhat later. "Richard Henry Stoddard," *The Independent*, 25 Mar. 1897, 10–11; Harry Thurston Peck, "A Note on Charles Dudley Warner," *The Bookman*, Dec. 1900, 368–371; "Miss Bellard's Inspiration," *Current Literature*, Aug. 1905, 214–215; Susan Hayes Ward, "Poetry," *The Independent*, 3 Dec. 1908), 1420–1421; and Lionel Stevenson, "Dean of American Letters: Julian Hawthorne," The Bookman, Apr. 1931, 164–172.

4. Practitioner-advocates of the new lyric studies have persuasively demonstrated that a lyric ideal overtook poetry criticism and poetry reading toward the end of the nineteenth century and became enshrined in twentieth-century theories of poetry, eliding and distorting the range of poetic forms alive in poetry culture. Since the lyric so monopolized the idea of poetry, Virginia Jackson has called into question also the status of "poetry" as an analytic and historical category. See for example Virginia Jackson, *Dickinson's Misery: A Theory of Lyric Reading* (Princeton, N.J.: Princeton University Press, 2005), and "Who Reads Poetry?" *PMLA* 123, no. 2 (2008): 181–187.

5. Pamela Clemit, *The Godwinian Novel: The Rational Fictions of Godwin, Brockden Brown, and Mary Shelley* (Oxford: Clarendon Press, 1993), 210. Clifford Siskin, who usefully distinguishes the novel's "*statistical* rise"—copies sold—from its "*generic* rise"—its literary standing—identifies the 1820s as a decade in which novels gained in literary stature in England, and the Bentley series may have marked a further advance. Clifford Siskin, *The Work of Writing: Literature and Social Change in Britain, 1700–1830* (Baltimore: Johns Hopkins University Press, 1998), 183.

6. Phelps's initial course on novels generated bad publicity, however, so he had to withdraw it for a few years. Bliss Perry, *And Gladly Teach: Reminiscences* (Boston: Houghton Mifflin, 1935), 128; William Lyon Phelps, excerpts from *Autobiography with Letters* (1839), in Gerald Graff and Michael Warner, eds., *The Origins of Literary Studies in America: A Documentary Anthology* (New York: Routledge, 1989), 165–166.

7. Walter Besant, "The Art of Fiction," in Walter Besant and Henry James, *The Art of Fiction* (Boston: Cupples, Upham, 1885), 10, 47.

8. Andrew Lang, "Literary Anodynes," *New Princeton Review* 5 (Sept. 1888): 145–153.

9. Walter Besant, *Studies in Early French Poetry* (London: Macmillan, 1868), 2, and *Autobiography of Sir Walter Besant*, prefatory note by S. Squire Sprigge [1902] (New York: Dodd and Mead, 1942), 132.

10. On the context of public disputation about novels, see Mark Spilka, "Henry James and Walter Besant: 'The Art of Fiction' Controversy," *Novel* 6, no. 2 (1973): 101–119.

11. Besant, "Art," 17, 8, 18.

12. Besant, "Art," 11; Henry James, "The Art of Fiction," in Besant and James, *The Art of Fiction*, 60–61.

13. James, "Art," 83, 52.

14. Besant, "Art," 9. "The novel has been called the epic poetry of the prosaic middle class of society," wrote William Torrey Harris, recycling a familiar point of view, in "Edward Bellamy's Vision," *Forum*, Oct. 1889, 199, rept. in William H. Goetzmann, ed., *The American Hegelians: An Intellectual Episode in the History of Western America* (New York: Knopf, 1973), 193.

15. Besant, "Art," 3, 18.

16. James, "Art," 66.

17. "The Genius of Charles Dickens," *Putnam's Monthly Magazine*, Mar. 1855, 263.

18. James, "Art," 55.

19. Edmund Clarence Stedman, *Poets of America* [1885] (Boston: Houghton Mifflin, 1893), 197.

20. Henry A. Beers, *An Outline Sketch of English Literature* (New York: Chautauqua Press, 1886), 262. In a similar vein, Frank Norris proposed that the novel was to the present day what great cathedrals were to the middle ages and what Shakespeare's and Marlowe's plays were to the Elizabethans, in *The Responsibilities of the Novelist*, vol. 6 of the *Complete Works of Frank Norris*, 6 vols. (New York: Doubleday, Page, 1905), 5.

21. Sample ads are in the *Christian Advocate*, 7 Nov. 1867, 360; *New York Observer and Chronicle*, 7 Nov. 1867, 255; and *The Independent*, 28 Nov. 1867, 6. For a slightly earlier use of the phrase, see the satirical reference "Sylvanus Slobb, Jr., will *not* contribute to our columns a great American novel to be called 'The Bloody Ferule, or the Bluebeard of the Village School,'" "Resident Editor's Department," *Massachusetts Teacher and Journal of Home and School Education* 17, no. 1 (1864): 15.

22. Rebecca Harding Davis, "Women in Literature," *The Independent*, 7 May 1891, 1.

23. T. S. Perry, "American Novels," *North American Review*, Oct. 1872, 366.

24. Charles F. Richardson, "The Moral Purpose of the Later American Novel," *Andover Review* 3, no. 16 (1885): 312.

25. Frank Luther Mott, *Golden Multitudes: The Story of Best Sellers in the United States* (New York: Macmillan, 1947), 204.

26. Ellen Gruber Garvey, "Ambivalent Advertising: Books, Prestige, and the Circulation of Publicity," in Carl F. Kaestle and Janice A. Radway, eds., *Print in Motion: The Expansion of Publishing and Reading in the United States, 1880–1940*, vol. 4 of David D. Hall, ed., *A History of the Book in America* (Chapel Hill: University of North Carolina Press, 2009), 186.

27. An article in *Littell's* reprinted from the *Quarterly Review* underlined the novel's having absorbed some of the functions of drama, so that the "problem of English literature, now grown world-wide and rooted in the very language of three continents," might be "to make a prose Shakespeare possible." "English Realism and Romance," *Littell's Living Age*, 16. Jan. 1892, 131.

28. The phrase was used by J. U. Barrow, secretary of a novel-reading organization in a mining village in the northeast of England, in accounting for his group's work, but within the context of Moulton's repeated use of similar phrasings, I'm inferring that the phrase was not Barrow's invention but part of the working vocabulary of the organization, perhaps initially Moulton's. The group's studies were published in a volume edited by Moulton, who had taught in the university extension movement in England before becoming a professor of literature in English at the University of Chicago. J. U. Barrow, "Backworth Classical Novel-Reading Union," in Richard G. Moulton, ed., *Four Years of Novel Reading: An Account of an Experiment in Popularizing the Study of Fiction* (Boston: D. C. Heath, 1895), 26.

29. Richard Green Moulton, "Stories as a Mode of Thinking," American Society for the Extension of University Teaching, 1891, digitized online at googlebooks (https://play.google.com/books/reader?id=r5vfAAAAMAAJ&printsec=frontcover&output=reader&authuser=0&hl=en&pg=GBS.PA8), accessed 28 May 2015, and *The Modern Study of Literature: An Introduction to Literary Theory and Interpretation* (Chicago: University of Chicago Press, 1915), 93, 161.

30. Frank Norris, "The Novel with a 'Purpose,'" in *Responsibilities of the Novelist*, 26–27. Sydney Bufkin reconstructs a canon of novels praised or criticized for having purposes during the height of this controversy about the novel with a purpose in "Reviewing the Purpose Novel: Reception, Social Reform, and the Limits of Persuasion in Turn-of-the-Century American Fiction" (Ph.D. diss., University of Texas at Austin, 2013).

31. Barbara Hochman, *Uncle Tom's Cabin and the Reading Revolution: Race, Literacy, Childhood, and Fiction, 1851–1911* (Amherst: University of Massachusetts Press, 2011), 132, 147.

32. Sylvia E. Bowman, *The Year 2000: A Critical Biography of Edward Bellamy* (New York: Octagon Books, 1979), 123–135.

33. Margaret Sherwood, *An Experiment in Altruism* (New York: Macmillan, 1895), 31–32.

34. Florence Converse, *The Burden of Christopher* (Boston: Houghton Mifflin, 1900), 30.

35. On poetry's significant public and political role during the nineteenth century, see Paula Bernat Bennett, *Poets in the Public Sphere: The Emancipatory Project of American Women's Poetry, 1800–1900* (Princeton, N.J.: Princeton University Press, 2003); Mary Louise Kete, *Sentimental Collaborations: Mourning and Middle-Class Identity in Nineteenth-Century America* (Durham, N.C.: Duke University Press, 2000); and Joan Shelley Rubin, *Songs of Ourselves: The Uses of Poetry in America* (Cambridge, Mass.: Harvard University

Press, 2007). Rubin cites Harriet Monroe's fear that poetry was devalued by being used as filler in periodicals (38).

Two important studies of the important role played by spoken poetry in education (a topic also addressed by Rubin) are Angela Sorby, *Schoolroom Poets: Childhood, Performance, and the Place of American Poetry, 1865–1917* (Durham, N.H.: University of New Hampshire Press, 2005); and Catherine Robson, *Heart Beats: Everyday Life and the Memorized Poem* (Princeton, N.J.: Princeton University Press, 2012), which emphasizes British experience but also sheds light on poetry's role in U.S. primary and secondary education. Rubin addresses the difficulty poets faced getting volumes of poetry published by the turn of the century, even though new volumes of poetry continued to be published (38–46).

36. Lida Keck Wiggins, *The Life and Works of Paul Laurence Dunbar* (Boston: Dodd Mead, 1907), 29.

37. Sarah Ehlers, "Making It Old: The Victorian/Modern Divide in Twentieth-Century American Poetry," *Modern Language Quarterly* 73, no. 1 (2012): 44; and Rubin, *Songs of Ourselves*, 34–35.

38. Stedman, *Poets of America*, 43.

39. Angela Sorby, "Who Wrote 'Rock Me to Sleep'? Elizabeth Akers Allen and the Profession of Poetry," *Modern Language Quarterly* 72, no. 3 (2011): 427, 438.

40. Elizabeth Renker, "The 'Twilight of the Poets' in the Era of American Realism, 1875–1900," in Kerry Larson, ed., *The Cambridge Companion to Nineteenth-Century Poetry* (New York: Cambridge University Press, 2011), 136.

41. After long neglect, Stedman's importance has been reaffirmed by recent scholars. Following Christopher Ricks, in his introduction to *The New Oxford Book of Victorian Poetry* (Oxford: Oxford University Press, 1987), Joseph Bristow has argued that Stedman originated "'Victorian' as a widely-accepted period designator." Bristow admires *Victorian Poets* as "one of the most inclusive pieces of research ever to map English poetry between the mid-1830s and mid-1870s," constructing along the way a "major Victorian canon" and in later, revised editions an influential set of chronological phases within the period. Joseph Bristow, "Whether 'Victorian' Poetry: A Genre and Its Period," *Victorian Poetry* 42, no. 1 (2004): 90, 91–93. Michael Cohen accords Stedman even greater significance, arguing that "*Victorian Poets* and *Poets of America*...serve as foundational works not only for their respective poetic fields of study, but for the modern practice of literary criticism itself—a practice characterized by, among many other things, a reliance on periodization, national fields, and literary theories." Michael Cohen, "E. C. Stedman and the Invention of Victorian Poetry," *Victorian Poetry* 43, no. 2 (2005): 167.

42. Edmund Clarence Stedman, *Victorian Poets* [1875] (Boston: James R. Osgood, 1876), xiii.

43. Stedman, *Poets of America*, 215; and Renker, "'Twilight,'" 135.

44. I emphasize here the extent to which public understandings of evolution shaped ideas about whether particular genres were thriving, setting poetry's problems in a late nineteenth-century frame. However, Lynch points to ways in which, before and since, poetry has counted as ghostly or posthumous. Deidre Shauna Lynch, chapter 6, "Poetry at Death's Door," *Loving Literature: A Cultural History* (Chicago: University of Chicago Press, 2015), 235–275.

45. Stedman, *Poets of America*, 33.

46. Stedman, *Poets of America*, 466.

47. Edith Wharton, *A Backward Glance* (New York: Appleton-Century, 1934), 74–75.

48. Stedman, *Poets of America*, 194, 211, 214.

49. Stephen Burt, "Longfellow's Ambivalence," in Larson, *Cambridge Companion to Nineteenth-Century Poetry*, 157–178.

50. Sorby, *Schoolroom Poets*, 185. Sorby traces the print infrastructure of school textbooks and magazines for children (most notably *St. Nicholas*, edited by Dodge and published by the literary-branded Scribner and Company) that circulated the work of these poets ever more widely, toward the century's end, but mainly to children.

51. Sorby, *Schoolroom Poets*, 13. Rubin has noted that the schoolroom poets may also have seemed "more approachable, and hence more emotionally available, than was consistent with the ethos of professionalism." Rubin, *Songs of Ourselves*, 32.

52. The promotion of realism involved wishful thinking, among other things about the extent to which realism (or any other practice) provided a stable and controlled mode of representation for the restless and divisive culture under examination. For a discussion of the ways in which late-century literature sought containment, see Nancy Bentley, "Literature and the Museum Idea," in *Frantic Panoramas: American Literature and Mass Culture, 1870–1920* (Philadelphia: University of Pennsylvania Press, 2009), 22–68. Bentley also notes that literary experience was insistently defined against "anything resembling mass pleasure or panic" within literary culture (226).

53. Nancy Glazener, *Reading for Realism: The History of a U.S. Literary Institution, 1850–1910* (Durham, N.C.: Duke University Press, 1997), 147–188.

54. Agnes Repplier, "Pleasure: A Heresy," *Atlantic Monthly*, Mar. 1891, 397.

55. Ralph Waldo Emerson, "The Poet" [1844], in *Essays and Lectures*, ed. Joel Porte (New York: Literary Classics of the United States, 1983), 450.

56. William Dean Howells, "Editor's Study," *Harper's New Monthly Magazine*, Mar. 1886, 647. The context was Howells's sense that he was not necessarily sorry to hear that Stedman believed "we are at the end of our great poets for the present." On the tensions between Stedman and Howells, see Robert J. Scholnick, *Edmund Clarence Stedman* (Boston: Twayne, 1977), 104–105.

57. Renker, "'Twilight,'" 138–139.

58. Jackson, *Dickinson's Misery*, 43.

59. Stedman, *Poets of America*, 169, 179.

60. Stedman, *Poets of America*, 357, 385–386, 377.

61. John Timberman Newcomb, *How Did Poetry Survive? The Making of Modern American Verse* (Urbana: University of Illinois Press, 2012), 10.

62. Stedman, *Poets of America*, 460; Brander Matthews, "Austin Dobson," *Century*, Oct. 1884, 912.

63. Matthews, "Austin Dobson," 916.

64. Stedman, *Poets of America*, 2: 459.

65. T. S. Eliot, "The Metaphysical Poets," in *Selected Prose of T. S. Eliot*, ed. Frank Kermode (New York: Harcourt Brace Jovanovich; Farrar, Straus & Giroux, 1975), 64.

66. Stedman, *Victorian Poets*, 301, 332.

67. See the following chapters in Larson, *Cambridge Companion to Nineteenth-Century Poetry*: Mary Louise Kete, "The Reception of Nineteenth-Century American Poetry," 28; Robert Dale Parker, "American Indian Poetry in the Nineteenth Century," 37; Eliza Richards, "Weathering the News in US Civil War Poetry," 113; and Ivy G. Wilson, "The Color Line:

James Monroe Whitfield and Albert Allson Whitman," 212. Karen A. Weyler's study of outsider authors in the early United States confirms that hardly any of them published their writings in or as books: Karen A. Weyler, *Empowering Words: Outsiders and Authorship in Early America* (Athens: University of Georgia Press, 2013).

68. Renker, "'Twilight,'" 141–142.

69. Wiggins, foreword to *Dunbar*, 20.

70. Stedman, *Poets of America*, 43.

71. Stedman, *Poets of America*, 43; and "The American Muses [Lines Written in Depression on the Fly-leaf of 'Poets of America,' by Edmund Clarence Stedman]," *St. James Gazette*, rept. in *Puck*, Feb. 1888, 401.

72. Stedman, *Poets of America*, 255, 57. 466; Kete, *Sentimental*, 32.

73. Stedman, *Victorian Poets*, 269.

74. Stedman, *Victorian Poets*, 12.

75. Stedman, *Poets of America*, 460. Three collections of U.S. sonnets were published around 1890: William Sharp, ed., *American Sonnets* (London: Walter Scott, 1890); T. W. Higginson and E. H. Bigelow, eds., *American Sonnets* [1891] (Boston: Houghton Mifflin, 1891); and Charles H. Crandall, *Representative Sonnets by American Poets* (Boston: Houghton Mifflin, 1890). Crandall's collection included "notable sonnets from other literatures" as well.

76. Stedman, *Poets of America*, 385.

77. Stedman, *Poets of America*, 29.

78. Stedman, *Poets of America*, 105.

79. Stedman, *Victorian Poets*, 31.

80. Stedman, *Poets of America*, 359.

81. Stedman believed "true national poetry should speak to and for the people, and its failure to do so in the late decades of the nineteenth century accounted for poetry's tenuous place in the hierarchy of genres." Cohen, "E. C. Stedman," 172. Cohen understands Stedman to have been seeking also to define the kind of American identity that could sustain a distinctive tradition of poetry; his approach differs from mine in that he emphasizes Stedman's efforts in finding a "non-lyrical reading practice for poetry" because of his attention to forms such as ballads (184).

82. Stedman, *Poets of America*, 178.

83. Peter Bürger, *Theory of the Avant-Garde*, trans. Michael Shaw (Minneapolis: University of Minnesota Press, 1984), 22–23.

84. A review entitled "The Twilight of the Poets" echoed Stedman's conclusion to *Poets of America*. "The voices that one hears to-day are solitary and isolated; they sing of things personal and individual, and not of things common and universal," the writer continued. "The Twilight of the Poets," *Christian Union*, 17 Sept. 1885, 3.

85. Richard Ohmann argues that the magazines helped to define a new professional managerial class that had consolidated by 1910. Richard Ohmann, *Selling Culture: Magazines, Markets, and Class at the Turn of the Century* (New York: Verso, 1996), 119, 173.

86. Louis Sullivan, "The Tall Office Building Artistically Considered," *Lippincott's Magazine*, Mar. 1896, 403–409.

87. Horatio Greenough, "Structure and Organization," in *Form and Function: Remarks on Art, Design, and Architecture*, ed. Harold A. Small (Berkeley: University of California Press, 1947), 118, 125.

88. Christina Cogdell, *Eugenic Design: Streamlining America in the 1930s* (Philadelphia: University of Pennsylvania Press, 2004), 32.

89. Cogdell, *Eugenic*, 8–9, 61.

90. Greenough, "Structure," 118.

91. Greenough, "Structure," 125.

92. Herbert Spencer, *Philosophy of Style*, together with T. S. Wright, "Ann Essay on Style," intro. and notes by Fred M. Scott (Boston: Alyyn and Bacon, 1894).

93. "Henrik Ibsen Dead; Norway in Mourning," *New York Times*, 24 May 1906.

94. Miriam Alice Franc, *Ibsen in England* (Boston: Four Seas, 1919), 41; and George Bernard Shaw, *The Philanderer: An Unpleasant Play* (New York: Brentano's, 1913), 26.

95. Marc Robinson, *The American Play, 1787–2000* (New Haven, Conn.: Yale University Press, 2009), 117–118. Robinson notes that plays in the realist movement could put pressure on conventional theatrical craft (110–111); I'm offering here not a full account of late nineteenth-century drama in the United States but an analysis of an influential discourse about craft and aesthetics.

96. Franc, *Ibsen*, 65–66.

97. Price disapproves of the play's pacing and also criticizes the drama for lacking beauty (or nobility) and for substituting complex for simple emotions, which he thinks cannot be so effectively presented in drama. Thomas R. Price, "Ibsen's Dramatic Construction Compared with Shakespeare's," *Shakespeariana*, Jan. 1892, 7–8.

98. Archibald Henderson, "Evolution of Dramatic Technique," *North American Review*, Mar. 1909, 444. Toril Moi's analysis suggests that increasing skepticism about language and a desire to keep characters' internal lives obscure—as they are in real-life encounters—may have contributed to this famous economy on Ibsen's part. Toril Moi, *Henrik Ibsen and the Birth of Modernism: Art, Theater, Philosophy* (New York: Oxford University Press, 2006), 319–320.

99. It's possible also that Hegel's influence on Ibsen provided a natural connection to the theories of dramatic conflict identified with Hegel. See Brian Johnston, *The Ibsen Cycle: Design of the Plays from "Pillars of Society" to "When We Dead Awaken"*, rev. ed. (University Park: Pennsylvania State University Press, 1992), 27–97. Johnston's discussion of the dialectical development within the plays bears many similarities to Denton J. Snider's Hegelian reading of the structures of Shakespeare's plays.

100. "The Dunlap Society Reorganized," *New York Times*, Feb. 5, 1896.

101. Brander Matthews, "The Art of the Dramatist," *North American Review*, Feb. 1903, 200.

102. Alfred Hennequin, *The Art of Playwriting* (Boston: Houghton Mifflin, 1890), 67.

103. Brander Matthews, *The Development of the Drama* (New York: Charles Scribner's Sons, 1902), 24–25; Pauline E. Hopkins, *Contending Forces: A Romance Illustrative of Negro Life North and South* (New York: Oxford University Press, 1988).

104. Gustav Freytag, *Technique of the Drama: An Exposition of Dramatic Composition and Art* [1894], trans. Elias J. MacEwan (Chicago: S. C. Griggs, 1895). Freytag's career and the fact that this is the first English translation are established in the "Biographical Note" (vii–ix). Another mark of Freytag's currency is that his novel *The Lost Manuscript* was being serialized in *Open Court* in 1888. On the translation being long overdue, see "The Drama," *The Critic*, 20 Jul. 1895, 49. An advertisement for *Technique of the Drama* included blurbs from two college professors who implied that they already knew and valued the work in German. "Freytag's Technique of the Drama," *Literary World*, 1 Dec. 1894, 434.

105. "M. Brunetière's Visit to America," *Review of Reviews*, June 1897, 694–695. Brunetière's *Manuel de l'Histoire de la Littérature française* was addressed in an 1898 review of histories of literature, which also mentioned Brunetière's lecture tour. W. P. Trent, "Recent Histories of Literature," *Forum*, Apr. 1898, 246.

106. Price, "Ibsen's Dramatic Construction," 12–15. Price is listed as having produced in collaboration with George Edward Woodberry and A. V. Williams Jackson a syllabus for the New York University Extension Department, "The English Drama: Its Rise and Development to the Closing of the Theaters" (http://www.archive.org/stream/englishdramaitsroopricrich/englishdramaitsroopricrich_djvu.txt), accessed 28 May 2015.

107. Freytag, *Technique*, 115.

108. Freytag, *Technique*, 120, 217, 214.

109. Hennequin, *Art of Playwriting*.

110. Letter from Alfred Hennequin to the editors of the *Critic*, 15 Jan. 1891, in W. J. Rolfe, ed., "Shakespeariana," *The Critic*, 21 Feb. 1891, 97.

111. The basic diagram is on 99 but elsewhere in the book, for example on 122, variations are diagrammed. Hennequin notes that *"dénouement"* is often used incorrectly as a synonym for the catastrophe, but that it is really an "untying" that "includes all between the height and the close." Hennequin, *Art of Playwriting*, 99.

112. Brander Matthews, "Notes," in Ferdinand Brunetière, *The Law of the Drama* (New York: Dramatic Museum of Columbia University, 1914), 91.

113. August Wilhelm Schlegel, *Lectures on Dramatic Art and Literature*, trans. John Black, 2nd ed., ed. A. J. W. Morrison (London: George Bell and Sons, 1892), 177. The lectures were delivered around 1805, published in 1809 and 1811. "A. W. Schlegel," *Stanford Encyclopedia of Philosophy* online (http://plato.stanford.edu/entries/schlegel-aw/), accessed 28 May 2015.

114. G. W. F. Hegel, *Aesthetics: Lectures on Fine Art*, trans. T. M. Knox, 2 vols. (Oxford: Clarendon Press, 1975), 2: 1159.

115. Hegel, *Aesthetics*, 2: 1161.

116. Brunetière, *Law*, 85.

117. Brunetière, *Law*, 73, 75–76.

118. Brunetière, *Law*, 77, 78, 79, 81–82, 82–83.

119. Hegel, *Aesthetics*, 2: 1205. Brander Matthews also followed this cue: "The drama has no place in the existence of the weak-willed Egyptians; but it is likely to have a place of honor among the more determined nations, more particularly in the years that follow hard upon the most abundant expression of their vitality. And this is why we find the golden days of the drama in Greece just after Salamis; in Spain not long after the conquest of Mexico and Peru; in England about the time of the defeat of the Armada; and in France when Louis XIV was the foremost king of Europe." Matthews, *Development of the Drama*, 23.

120. Walter Morris Hart, *Hawthorne and the Evolution of the Short Story* (Berkeley: University [of California] Press, 1900); Brander Matthews, *The Philosophy of the Short-Story* [1901] (New York: Longman's Green, 1917); Henry Seidel Canby, *The Short Story* (New York: Henry Holt 1902); and Perry, *Study of Prose Fiction*.

121. Matthews, *Philosophy*, 35.

122. Brander Matthews, ed. with intro., *The Short-Story: Specimens Illustrating Its Development* (New York: American Book, 1907), 25, 28, 29.

123. Matthews, *Philosophy*, 59.

124. Canby, *Short Story*, 27, 30. Hart also introduced his discussion by noting that "literary forms and types" were "phenomena probably not unlike those which the evolutionist finds in the material world." Hart, *Hawthorne*, 3

125. Matthews, *Specimens*, 31.

126. The definition, which Hamilton put forward as early as 1904, is offered in Clayton Meeker Hamilton, *Materials and Methods of Fiction* (New York: Baker and Taylor, 1908), 173.

127. Matthews, introduction to *Specimens*, 25–26. Poe's review of Hawthorne's *Twice-Told Tales* considered Hawthorne's genre as the tale, but Poe's strict differentiation of tale from essay and his stringent prescriptions made clear that he had in mind a new print genre— "requiring from a half-hour to one or two hours in its perusal"—quite different from the tale as an oral form sometimes rendered in print. Edgar Allan Poe, rev. of *Twice-Told Tales*, *Graham's Magazine*, May 1842, 298–300.

The argument that Poe perfected or best theorized the modern short story and that his approach was grounded in respect for the classical unities can be seen also in Charles Sears Baldwin, *American Short Stories* [1904] (New York: Longmans Green, 1921), 19.

128. Matthews, *Short-Story*, 28.

129. Brander Matthews, "General Editor's Note," in Brander Matthews, ed., *American Familiar Verse: Vers de Société* (London: Longman's, Green, 1904), viii.

130. Matthews, introduction to *American Familiar Verse*, 1.

131. Matthews, "Austin Dobson," 914.

132. The twelve rules are printed in Matthews, "Austin Dobson," 918.

133. Perry, *Study of Prose Fiction*, 306. Canby similarly credited the short story with "the greatest nicety of form to be found outside the domain of poetry." Canby, *Short Story*, 29.

134. Charles Alphonso Smith, *The American Short Story* (Boston: Ginn, 1912), 42.

135. Canby, *Short Story*, 25–26.

136. Evelyn May Albright, *The Short Story: Its Principles and Structure* (New York: Macmillan, 1908), 118.

137. Lewis Worthington Smith, *The Writing of the Short Story* (Boston: D. C. Heath, 1902), 28. Smith is identified on the title page as being at "Drake University, Des Moines, Iowa," and the book offers topics for themes and other instructional aids.

138. Albright, *Short Story*, 103, 105, 153.

139. William Archer, *Play-Making: A Manual of Craftsmanship* [1912] (Boston: Small, Maynard, 1918), 24.

140. Albright, *Short Story*, 124.

141. Hamilton, *Materials and Methods of Fiction*, 184, 189, 191.

142. Archer, *Play-Making*, 75.

143. Albright, *Short Story*, 104.

144. One of the leading exponents of "crisis" was William Archer, who developed it for playwriting and who viewed it as an advance over Brunetière's emphasis on conflict, which Archer did not think held true for many great plays in history. See Archer, *Play-Making*, 36.

145. William E. Smyser, "Art. I.—A Literary Study of the Book of Job," *Methodist Review*, Nov. 1900, 6.

146. For an example of a feeble caveat, see William Patterson Atkinson, *The Short-Story* (New York: Allyn and Bacon, 1916), xviii–xix.

147. Cornelia Beare, "The Structure of the Novel," in George Eliot, *Silas Marner*, ed. Cornelia Beare (New York: Charles E. Merrill, [1908]), 19.

148. A number of Internet and print sources attribute codified binary conflicts (usually, seven of them) to Sir Arthur Quiller-Couch, the British writer whose pen name was Q and who was appointed King Edward VII Professor of English Literature at Cambridge University in 1912. The conflicts may be laid out somewhere in his voluminous body of work; I have yet to find them, and the sources that credit Quiller-Couch do not cite a particular work by him. He was partial to rules and formulas, in spite of his puckish persona, so it would not be surprising if he had somewhere listed a set of conflicts. But citing any one source for this innovation would be misleading, given that Brunetière set the list in motion but that several others adapted it. The institutional processes that turned Freytag's pyramid and Brunetière's treatment of conflict into standard literary apparatuses also expanded their purview from drama to short stories and then to novels and beyond.

149. Clayton Hamilton, *The Theory of the Theatre and Other Principles of Dramatic Criticism* (New York: Henry Holt, 1910), 134–137.

150. Robert Wilson Neal, *Short Stories in the Making* (New York: Oxford University Press, 1914), 74, 48. Neal was also the author of *Today's Short Stories Analyzed: An Informal Encyclopedia of Short Story Art as Exemplified by Contemporary Magazine Fiction for Writers and Students* (New York: Oxford University Press, 1918), 150.

151. James Irving, *The Irving System: A New Easy Method of Story and Photoplay Writing* (Auburn, N.Y.: Authors' Press, 1919), 125.

152. Spingarn's lecture "The New Criticism" was originally delivered 9 Mar. 1910. J. E. Spingarn, "The New Criticism," in *Creative Criticism: Essays on the Unity of Genius and Taste* (New York: Henry Holt, 1917), 3–46.

153. Spingarn, "New Criticism," 24.

154. Spingarn, "New Criticism," 26.

155. Derrida's essay opens proclaiming the orthodoxy to be investigated: "Genres are not to be mixed." Jacques Derrida, "The Law of Genre," trans. Avital Ronell, *Critical Inquiry* 7, no. 1 (1980): 55–81.

156. Spingarn, "New Criticism," 29.

157. J. E. Spingarn, "Dramatic Criticism and the Theatre," in *Creative Criticism*, 47, 80.

158. James F. Knapp, *Literary Modernism and the Transformation of Work* (Evanston, Ill.: Northwestern University Press, 1988), 129.

159. Indeed, these schemas began very early to be extended to other genres in works such as Selden Lincoln Whitcomb, *The Study of a Novel* (Boston: D. C. Heath, 1905), which references Brunètiere and Freytag; and Carroll Lewis Maxcy, *The Rhetorical Principles of Narration* (Boston: Houghton Mifflin, 1911), which extends the categories of Freytag's pyramid to novels as well as short stories (but does not foreground the structural centrality of conflict). Both Whitcomb and Maxcy relate novels to rhetorical modes of narration, exposition, argumentation, and description. Whitcomb uses Freytag's schema to diagram *Silas Marner* and *Pride and Prejudice* and credits Freytag (58). Whitcomb also outlines "motivating forces" that resemble the types of conflict commonly invoked: "nature, society, individual character, the supernatural or superhuman...." (63–64).

160. Freytag's key terms or variants thereof are key terms in the glossaries of tenth-grade literature textbooks used as recently as 2013 by McGraw-Hill, Pearson–Prentice-Hall, and Holt-McDougal, and each glossary's entry for "Plot" references a version of the five-step sequence (with very little variation). All the glossaries define conflict primarily as "internal"

or "external," but the entries for "Conflict" offer as example the kinds of factors (usually called "forces") broken out in the early twentieth-century schemas. For example, the *Prentice-Hall Literature* textbook (published by Pearson) explains that an outside force might be "another character," "the standards or expectations of a group," or "nature itself." The schema still presumes that the conflict will always be primarily experienced by an individual character, not a group, and it still offers very little opportunity to analyze the kinds of pressures exerted on individuals by a "group" or society. *Prentice-Hall Literature* teacher's ed., grade 10, Common Core ed. (Columbus, Ohio: Pearson, 2012).

161. Timothy Lenoir, "The Discipline of Nature and the Nature of Disciplines," in Ellen Messer-Davidow, David R. Shumway, and David J. Sylvan, eds., *Knowledges: Historical and Critical Studies in Disciplinarity* (Charlottesville: University Press of Virginia, 1993), 81.

162. Knapp, *Literary Modernism*, 5.

Chapter 6

1. George E. Howard, "The State University in America," *Atlantic Monthly*, Mar. 1891, 336.

2. William James, "The Ph.D. Octopus," in *Essays, Comments, and Reviews* (Cambridge, Mass.: Harvard University Press, 1987), 69.

3. My analysis here follows Michel Foucault's sense of power as both productive and restrictive and draws especially on the approach of David R. Shumway and Craig Dionne, who identify "the academic discipline" as "the perfect instance of modern power," in Foucault's sense: lacking a clear "sovereign or center," operating through "micro-judgments," "micro-rewards and micro-penalties," and being internally enforced via new practitioners' internalization of "values, norms, and standards." David R. Shumway and Craig Dionne, introduction to David R. Shumway and Craig Dionne, eds., *Disciplining English: Alternative Histories, Critical Perspectives* (Albany: State University of New York Press, 2002), 3.

4. As Michael Berubé remarks, "[T]he hardest thing I've had to learn—or unlearn—is how thoroughly conditioned I am by the imperative to say something new." "Bite Size Theory: Popularizing Academic Criticism," in *Public Access: Literary Theory and American Cultural Politics* (London: Verso, 1994), 166–167.

5. For a defense of modern projects and the need to keep working to offset their limitations, see Jürgen Habermas, "Modernity—An Unfinished Project," trans. Seyla Benhabib, in Hal Foster, ed., *The Anti-Aesthetic: Essays on Postmodern Culture* (New York: New Press, 1998), 1–15. My analysis here invokes familiar versions and critiques of modernity, but I want to underline that modernity here, as I described in my introduction and in earlier chapters, operates as a paradigm that organized (and still recognizably organizes) a controversy, not as an analytic category I straightforwardly endorse. The critique of rationalizing instrumentality can operate independently of the idea that modernity is an epoch or a force, in keeping with the postmodern or amodern approaches offered by Latour, Asad, and Löwy and Sayre in my introduction.

6. Harvard University instituted an entrance exam in 1874. As of 1888, the New England Commission of Colleges set a preparatory reading list for college-bound students, and in 1893 the Association of Colleges and Preparatory Schools of the Middle States and Maryland set uniform entrance exams that included knowledge of certain "English masterpieces." The National Education Association's Committee of Ten in 1894 formulated recommendations for secondary school curricula that included four years of English, whose goals were

"composition training and literary appreciation," a separation corresponding to the deepening division between these areas. In the wake of the Committee of Ten's report, pedagogical texts for high school English teachers also began to be published. See David R. Russell, "Institutionalizing English: Rhetoric on the Boundaries," in Shumway and Dionne, *Disciplining English*, 50; and Arthur N. Applebee, *Tradition and Reform in the Teaching of English: A History* (Urbana, Ill.: National Council of Teachers of English, 1974), 45.

Denise Albanese has demonstrated the importance of these entrance requirements for the continuing presence of Shakespeare in twentieth- and twenty-first-century public culture. Denise Albanese, *Extramural Shakespeare* (New York: Palgrave Macmillan, 2010). See also Elizabeth Renker, "Shakespeare in the College Curriculum, 1870–1920," in Coppélia Kahn, Heather S. Nathans, and Mimi Godfrey, eds., *Shakespearean Educations: Power, Citizenship, and Performance* (Newark: University of Delaware Press, 2011), 131.

7. David Bartholomae's online "History of the Department of English" at the University of Pittsburgh offers in accessible public form a chronology of this process at one private but not elite university. Departments were organized at this university in the 1880s, and a Department of Rhetoric and English Literature was formed in 1882, transformed in 1886 into a Department of English (http://www.english.pitt.edu/history), accessed 4 June 2015.

8. Salvatori has tracked especially the late nineteenth-century conversation about whether pedagogy was an art or a science, an opposition that was also implicitly at work in many disagreements about literary studies. Her immensely valuable collection shows that the impasse was produced by the assumption that art and science were incompatible, versus the potential (which she identifies in Josiah Royce's ideas about pedagogy) for theorizing "a fruitful dialectical relationship between art and science." Mariolina Rizzi Salvatori, ed., *Pedagogy: Disturbing History, 1819–1929* (Pittsburgh: University of Pittsburgh Press, 1996), 240.

9. The research university model was overwhelmingly identified with Germany, an idea promoted in the United States by James Morgan Hart's *German Universities: A Narrative of Personal Experience* (New York: G. P. Putnam's Sons, 1874), which was excerpted in U.S. periodicals. However, Hart's account offers a somewhat misleading picture of German academia, in keeping with the selective and adaptive use that U.S. universities made of German academic practice. U.S. students in German universities during the nineteenth century tended to pursue coursework in the service of the Dr. phil. degree, which in Germany was a degree leading to an academic career, whereas the majority of the German students were preparing for civil service examinations. Moreover, German professors taught in research universities, not in gymnasia, which offered a closer equivalent to U.S. undergraduate education. James Turner and Paul Bernard, "The German Model and the Graduate School: The University of Michigan and the Origin Myth of the American University," in Roger L. Geiger, ed., *The American College in the Nineteenth Century* (Nashville: Vanderbilt University Press, 2000), 221–241; Jurgen Herbst, *The German Historical School in American Scholarship: A Study in the Transfer of Culture* (Ithaca, N.Y.: Cornell University Press, 1965), 22; Laurence R. Veysey, *The Emergence of the American University* (Chicago: University of Chicago Press, 1965), 126–133; Robert J. Connors, *Composition-Rhetoric: Backgrounds, Theory, Pedagogy* (Pittsburgh: University of Pittsburgh Press, 1997), 177.

Roger Paulin points out also that even though assertions of academic freedom have a long history in Germany (that is, the collection of states that in 1871 formed the modern nation-state of Germany), going back to statutes in 1694 guaranteeing "'libertas philosophandi,' the freedom to teach and do research," German rulers and government officials continued to intervene in German academic culture well into the nineteenth century. Roger Paulin, "Goethe, the Brothers Grimm, and Academic Freedom," inaugural lecture delivered 9 May 1990 (Cambridge: Cambridge University Press, 1991), 7, 19–20.

According to Konrad H. Jarausch, during the nineteenth century, German universities themselves changed in ways that brought them closer to the U.S. research university model. University enrollment "grew between five and ten times," the student body becoming "more cosmopolitan, urban, modern trained, and female" as well as more diverse in class. Emphasis also shifted from older fields of study to "newer, research-driven studies." Veysey also notes that laboratory sciences increased greatly in importance in German universities during the nineteenth century and that the seminar model may have begun in German universities as recently as 1830 (125, 153). Konrad H. Jarausch, "American Students in Germany, 1815–1914: The Structure of German and U.S. Matriculants at Göttingen University," in Henry Geitz, Jürgen Heideking, and Jürgen Herbst, eds., *German Influences on Education in the United States to 1917* (Cambridge: Cambridge University Press; Washington D.C.: German Historical Institute, 1995), 201.

On the merger of German and British models, see Connors, *Composition-Rhetoric*, 174–176.

10. Elizabeth Renker, *The Origins of American Literature Studies: An Institutional History* (New York: Cambridge University Press, 2007), especially 97–98.

11. Magali Sarfatti Larson, *The Rise of Professionalism: A Sociological Analysis* (Berkeley: University of California Press, 1977), 149, 152–153. On the tremendous growth in students enrolled in higher education after 1870, see also Arthur M. Cohen, *The Shaping of American Higher Education: Emergence and Growth of the Contemporary System* (San Francisco: Jossey-Bass, 1998), 98 (and for the period just before, see an analogous set of statistics, 51). Cohen calls 1870–1944 the "University Transformation Era" and notes, "Most of the change in institutional form occurred in the first forty years, and the largest growth in enrollment in the last thirty-five years" (103). Cohen's approving account of this transformation emphasizes features of modernization criticized by other scholars, including the university's role in creating "liaisons with incipient professional groups" and its increased success in acquiring funds from "the public treasury and from wealthy donors" (103–104, 107). A more critical account of the increased power of wealthy donors (including their role as trustees) is Peter Dobkin Hall, "Noah Porter Writ Large? Reflections on the Modernization of American Education and Its Critics, 1866–1916," in Geiger, *The American College*, 214.

12. James Campbell, *A Thoughtful Profession: The Early Years of the American Philosophical Association* (Chicago: Open Court, 2006), 28. On persistent scientism in humanities disciplines, see Veysey, *Emergence*, 173–174; on the symbolic masculinity of science, in contrast to the feminized humanities and especially the modern languages and literatures, see Elizabeth Renker, "Resistance and Change: The Rise of American Literature Studies," *American Literature* 64, no. 2 (1992): 347–349.

13. Richard G. Moulton, *Four Years of Novel Reading: An Account of an Experiment in Popularizing the Study of Fiction* (Boston: D. C. Heath, 1895), 4. The sense that literature was somehow accountable to scientific models was under way even earlier in the century, before the research university's advent. For example, a reviewer of Edwin Whipple's lectures offered a polemic similar to Moulton's in 1850: "Is not a book as truly a fact as a paving stone, or the fossil jaw of a grizzly bear? Is not the *physiology* of the soul as important a study, as its anatomy? Shall we deliberately deem it of less importance to cast and demonstrate the orbit

of a genius than the orbit of a planet?—to detect a law of art than a law of mineralogy?" T. S. K., "Art. V. Whipple's Lectures," *Universalist Quarterly and General Review*, Jan. 1850, 79.

14. For a history of world literature, universal literature, comparative literature, and other curricular predecessors of transnational literary studies, attending closely to nineteenth-century academic precedents and discussions, see John Pizer, *The Idea of World Literature: History and Pedagogical Practice* (Baton Rouge: Louisiana State University Press, 2006).

15. Gerald Graff and Michael Warner, eds., introduction to *Origins of Literary Studies in America: A Documentary Anthology* (New York: Routledge, 1989), 5–6; and Gerald Graff, *Professing Literature: An Institutional History* (Chicago: University of Chicago Press, 1987), 68–96. David Shumway's distinction between the "philologists" and "men of letters" has the advantage of capturing the fact that the latter role could be held by nonacademics as well and could involve a "critical" though not quite "oppositional" role. Shumway also traces the significance of literary history as a foundation within English studies. Graff, *Professing*, 14–15; David R. Shumway, *Creating American Civilization: A Genealogy of American Literature as an Academic Discipline* (Minneapolis: University of Minnesota Press, 1994), 51–53, 61–95.

Irving Babbitt offers evidence for the hostility between the two groups, quoting an unnamed philologist who said of a colleague, "He is almost a dilettante—he reads Dante and Shakespeare." Babbitt went on to distance himself from both philologists and dilettantes, revealing also the insidious gendering at work: "The man who took literature too seriously would be suspected of effeminacy.... One can already see the time when the typical teacher of literature will be some young dilettante who will interpret Keats and Shelley to a class of girls." Irving Babbitt, *Literature and the American College: Essays in Defense of the Humanities* (Boston: Houghton, Mifflin, 1908), 114, 119.

16. The backlash against philology can be discerned in the early appointments that Oxford and Cambridge made when they finally appointed professors of English literature. Cambridge's King Edward VII Chair of English Literature had been endowed by a newspaper magnate who specified that the chair should be occupied by a professor who would "treat this subject on literary and critical rather than on philological and linguistic lines." E. M. W. Tillyard, *The Muse Unchained: An Intimate Account of the Revolution in English Studies at Cambridge* (London: Bowes & Bowes, 1958), 38, quoted in Terence Hawkes, "Entry on Q," in Christy Desmet and Robert Sawyer, eds., *Shakespeare and Appropriation* (London: Routledge, 1999), 37. The best-known early holder of the chair, Arthur Quiller-Couch, was a novelist who "effectively had no learned publications to his credit and no experience of university teaching" (Hawkes, "Q," 37). At Oxford, the Merton Professorship of English Language and Literature had been created in 1885, and the first appointee, Arthur S. Napier, was a scholar of Anglo-Saxon philology who occupied the chair until 1916, but in 1904 a separate professorship of English literature was created, and Walter A. Raleigh was appointed. Raleigh was a scholar and teacher of English literature, having published on Milton and Wordsworth and held other professorships in modern literature and English language and literature. D. J. Palmer, *The Rise of English Studies* (London: Oxford University Press, 1965), 118–122.

17. The versions of philology prominent in U.S. instruction during this period had been narrowed considerably from philology's scope in European Enlightenment culture. Graff, *Professing*, 69; and Albert S. Cook, "The Province of English Philology," in Graff and Warner, *Origins*, 96–102.

18. See Renker, *Origins*; Shumway, *Creating*; Kermit Vanderbilt, *American Literature and the Academy: The Roots, Growth, and Maturity of a Profession* (Philadelphia: University of Pennsylvania Press, 1986).

19. Nadia Altschul, "What Is Philology? Cultural Studies and Ecdotics," in Sean Gurd, ed., *Philology and Its Histories* (Columbus: Ohio State University Press, 2010), 148–163.

20. Susan Harris Smith, *American Drama: The Bastard Art* (New York: Cambridge University Press, 1997), 114–158; and Applebee, *Tradition and Reform*, 61–64.

21. Giles Wilkeson Gray, "Some Teachers and the Transition to Twentieth-Century Speech Education," in Karl R. Wallace, ed., *History of Speech Education in America: Background Studies* (New York: Appleton-Century-Crofts, 1943), 429–430.

22. Marie Hochmuth and Richard Murphy, "Rhetorical and Elocutionary Training in Nineteenth-Century Colleges," in Wallace, *History of Speech*, 160.

23. Many public readers who included Shakespeare prominently among their offerings are mentioned in the essays in David W. Thompson et al., *Performance of Literature in Historical Perspectives* (Lanham, Md.: University Press of America, 1983); and in Nan Johnson, "Shakespeare in American Rhetorical Education, 1870–1920," in Kahn, Nathans, and Godfrey, *Shakespearean Educations*, 112–127.

24. Gold's study focused on a traditionally black college, a women's college, and a normal school, types of institutions that affected many more students than Princeton and Harvard. David Gold, *Rhetoric at the Margins: Revising the History of Writing Instruction in American Colleges, 1873–1947* (Carbondale: Southern Illinois University Press, 2008).

25. Gray, "Some Teachers," 423, 425.

26. Donald K. Smith, "Origin and Development of Departments of Speech," in Wallace, *History of Speech*, 461.

27. Gray, "Some Teachers," 425; and Lilla Heston, "Early Graduate Education: Michigan, Northwestern, Wisconsin," in Thompson et al., *Performance of Literature*, 317–357.

28. Harry J. Myers, compiler, *American College and Private School Directory*, 10 vols. (Chicago: Educational Aid Society, 1914), 7: 176–178.

29. "Henrietta Vinton Davis," *Who's Who of the Colored Race: A General Biographical Dictionary of Men and Women of African Descent*, ed. Frank Lincoln Mather, (Chicago: Frank Lincoln Mather, 1915), 87; and James P. Danky, "Reading, Writing, and Resisting: African American Print Culture," in Hugh Amory and David D. Hall, eds., *The Colonial Book in the Atlantic World* vol. 1 of David D. Hall, ed., *The History of the Book in America* (Cambridge: Cambridge University Press, 2000), 343.

30. "Emerson College" (http://en.wikipedia.org/wiki/Emerson_College), accessed 2 Mar. 2013.

31. Carrie J. Preston, *Modernism's Mythic Pose: Gender, Genre, Solo Performance* (New York: Oxford University Press, 2011), 103.

32. Robert V. Bruce, *Bell: Alexander Graham Bell and the Conquest of Solitude* (Boston: Little, Brown, 1973) 98, 162.

33. F. C. Blanchard, "Professional Theatre Schools in the Early Twentieth Century," in Wallace, *History of Speech*, 626.

34. A foundational physiological text was *Philosophy of the Human Voice* (1827), written by Benjamin Rush's son James. See Genevieve Stebbins, *Delsarte System of Expression*, 2nd ed. (New York: Edwin Werner, 1887); and Leland H. Roloff and John C. Hollwitz, "Performance

and the Body: Gilbert Austin and François Delsarte," in Thompson et al., *Performance of Literature*, 477–498.

35. See Judy Baker Goss, "'Expression' in the Popular Culture of Dallas in the Early 1900s," David Bartine, "'Key-Word' Theories of Reading from Elocution to Interpretation," and Paul C. Edwards, "The Rise of 'Expression,'" in Thompson et al., *Performance of Literature*, 259–281, 497–508, and 529–548.

36. Samuel Silas Curry, *The Province of Expression: A Search for Principles Underlying Adequate Methods of Developing Dramatic and Oratoric Delivery* (Boston: Expression, 1891), xi, 30, 31, 59, 139. Charles Wesley Emerson, the influential founder of the Boston School of Oratory, also emphasized the aesthetic expression of the soul but through attention to the physiology of voice. Charles Wesley Emerson, *Psycho Vox; or, The Emerson System of Voice Culture* (Boston: Emerson College of Oratory Publishing Department, 1903).

37. Edwards, "The Rise of 'Expression,'" 543–544. On this point, see also Edyth Renshaw, "Five Private Schools of Speech," in Thompson et al., *Performance of Literature*, 301–325. On the Margaret Eaton School, and for an intelligent and far-reaching analysis of the relationship between early English departments and schools of expression, see Heather Murray, *Working in English: History, Institution, Resources* (Toronto: University of Toronto Press, 1996), 46–67.

38. S. S. Curry, *Browning and the Dramatic Monologue: Nature and Interpretation of an Overlooked Form of Literature* (Boston: Expression, 1906), 137, 203.

39. Gray, "Some Teachers," 440. On the secession, see Smith, "Origin and Development"; and Steven Mailloux, *Disciplinary Identities: Rhetorical Paths of English, Speech, and Composition* (New York: Modern Language Association of America, 2006), 10–16.

40. Mailloux, *Disciplinary*, 10–15.

41. Smith, *American Drama*, 156.

42. Selden Lincoln Whitcomb, *The Study of a Novel* (Boston: D. C. Heath, 1905), 213.

43. Samuel Silas Curry, *Spoken English: A Method of Improving Speech and Reading by Studying Voice Conditions and Modulations in Union with Their Causes in Thinking and Feeling* (Boston: Expression, 1913), 279.

44. Bliss Perry, "Poetry," in H. Morse Stephens et al., *Counsel upon the Reading of Books*, intro. Henry Van Dyke (Boston: Houghton, Mifflin, 1900), 250.

45. Perry, "Poetry," 250.

46. Richard Green Moulton, *The Modern Study of Literature: An Introduction to Literary Theory and Interpretation* (Chicago: University of Chicago Press, 1915), 22.

47. Hiram Corson, *The Voice and Spiritual Education* (New York: Macmillan, 1904), 39.

48. Corson, *Voice*, 98.

49. Corson, *Voice*, 58–59.

50. Hiram Corson, *The University of the Future: An Address Delivered before the Alumni of St. John's College at the Annual Commencement, July 7th, 1875* (Annapolis, Md.: St. John's College, 1875), 18, 21.

51. Corson, *Voice*, 58–59.

52. Corson, *Voice*, 79.

53. Most educational institutions at the turn of the century gave credit for students' knowing the "history and theory of art and music" but not for performance. Karen J. Blair, *The Torchbearers: Women and Their Amateur Arts Associations in America, 1890–1930* (Bloomington: Indiana University Press, 1994), 25.

54. James Morgan Hart, excerpt from *German Universities: A Narrative of Personal Experience* (1874), in Graff and Warner, *Origins*, 18.

55. On the history of the essay, including and beyond its life as an academic genre, see Tara Lockhart, "Revising the Essay: Intellectual Arenas and Hybrid Forms" (Ph.D. diss., University of Pittsburgh, 2008). Fred Lewis Pattee in 1900 traced the complicated status of the essay, differentiating the origins of the form in Montaigne's deliberately unsystematic explorations from the essay's later increasing systematization through Addison and beyond. He identified the original, less systematic form with the personal essay, its more systematic development as the "literary" or "popular" essay, a conjunction probably explained by the fact that Addison also made the essay a staple of periodical publication. Pattee's account also registers the impact of multimodal rhetoric, since he begins by identifying the essay as a species of writing within the expository mode. Fred Lewis Pattee, "Critical Studies in American Literature. II. An Essay: Emerson's 'Self-Reliance,'" *The Chautauquan*, Mar. 1900, 628.

56. Alexander Bain, *English Composition and Rhetoric: A Manual* [1866] American ed., rev. (New York: Appleton, 1873), 6.

57. Frank Norris, "The 'English Courses' of the University of California," *The Wave*, 28 Nov. 1896, 2–3, rept. in *The Apprenticeship Writings of Frank Norris, 1896–1898*, ed. Joseph R. McElrath and Douglas K. Burgess (American Philosophical Society, 1996), 180.

58. Connors, *Composition-Rhetoric*, 61, 64–66.

59. Whitcomb, *Study of a Novel*, x.

60. Moulton, *Modern Study*, 93, 94.

61. Joan H. Pittock, *Henry Birkhead: Founder of the Oxford Chair of Poetry: Poetry and the Redemption of History* (Lewiston, New York: Edwin Mellen Press, 1999), 128.

62. Katharine Cooke, *A. C. Bradley and His Influence in Twentieth-Century Shakespeare Criticism* (Oxford: Clarendon Press, 1972), 80, 79.

63. For Bradley's adaptation of Freytag's schema (without attribution), see A. C. Bradley, *Shakespearean Tragedy: Lectures on Hamlet, Othello, King Lear, Macbeth* (London: Macmillan, 1904), 40–41; he summarizes potential conflicts on 17.

64. Bradley, *Shakespearean*, viii, vii.

65. Bradley, *Shakespearean*, 81.

66. Bradley, *Shakespearean*, 79–80n. 1.

67. Bradley, *Shakespearean*, 25.

68. Bradley, *Shakespearean*, 26.

69. Bradley, *Shakespearean*, 21, 90.

70. Margreta de Grazia, *Hamlet without Hamlet* (Cambridge: Cambridge University Press, 2007), 13.

71. The Variorum included an entire section of criticism on the topic "Is Hamlet's Insanity Real or Feigned?" William Shakespeare, *A New Variorum Edition of Shakespeare*, ed. Horace Howard Furness, vol. 4, *Hamlet*, 2 vols. (Philadelphia: J. P. Lippincott, 1877), 2: 195–235. See also Benjamin Reiss, *Theaters of Madness: Insane Asylums and Nineteenth-Century American Culture* (Chicago: University of Chicago Press, 2008).

72. Bradley, *Shakespearean*, 118, 121.

73. Ernest Jones, *Hamlet and Oedipus* (New York: Norton, 1949).

74. Bradley, *Shakespearean*, 32, 33, 36.

75. Philosophy was involved in reciprocal boundary work, as James A. Good has remarked: "The Kantian conception of philosophy flourished in the new research universities because it concedes ground to academic disciplining by placing limits upon the topics philosophers can justifiably examine as philosophers." James A. Good, *A Search for Unity in Diversity: The "Permanent Hegelian Deposit" in the Philosophy of John Dewey* (Lanham, Md.: Lexington Books, 2006), xx.

76. Bradley, *Shakespearean*, 94, 21, 90.

77. L. C. Knights, *How Many Children Had Lady Macbeth?* (Cambridge: Cambridge University Press, 1933).

78. Bradley, *Shakespearean*, 129.

79. For example, a review in *Current Literature* cites the previous rave reviews of the New York *Evening Post* and the London *Spectator*. "The Principles Underlying Shakespearean Tragedy," *Current Literature*, Oct. 1905, 427–428.

80. On the continued influence of *Shakespearean Tragedy*, see Terence Hawkes, *That Shakespeherian Rag: Essays on a Critical Process* (London: Methuen, 1986), 31–42.

81. Charles Taylor, *Sources of the Self: The Making of the Modern Identity* (Cambridge, Mass.: Harvard University Press, 1989).

82. William Wordsworth, "Preface to the Second Edition of *Lyrical Ballads*" [1800], in *English Romantic Writers*, ed. David Perkins (New York: Harcourt Brace Jovanovich, 1967), 325.

83. David Shumway identifies two groups of oppositional intellectuals, left and right, who criticized either the professoriate or the research university model in the early decades of the twentieth century and whom he relegates to the "preprofessional era": the "literary radicals" (Van Wyck Brooks and others) and the New Humanists (Irving Babbitt and others). These formations emerged at the end of the period I'm examining; I'm attending rather to ways in which, even earlier, academics and public literary authorities registered the new division between experts and amateurs, whether or not they formulated deliberate opposition to it. Shumway, *Creating*, 53–60.

84. Clifford Siskin, *The Work of Writing: Literature and Social Change in Britain, 1700–1830* (Baltimore: Johns Hopkins University Press, 1998), 20.

85. Burton J. Bledstein, *The Culture of Professionalism: The Middle Class and the Development of Higher Education in America* (New York: W. W. Norton, 1976), 80–128.

86. Magali Sarfatti Larson, "The Production of Expertise and the Constitution of Expert Power," and Peter Dobkin Hall, "The Social Foundations of Professional Credibility," in Thomas L. Haskell, ed., *The Authority of Experts: Studies in History and Theory* (Bloomington: Indiana University Press, 1984), 28–80, 107–141; and Bledstein, *Culture*, 92–100.

87. On the peculiar nature of the exchange relations that govern professional services, see Larson, *Rise*, 9–18.

88. Timothy Lenoir, "The Discipline of Nature and the Nature of Disciplines," in Ellen Messer-Davidow, David R. Shumway, and David J. Sylvan, eds., *Knowledges: Historical and Critical Studies in Disciplinarity* (Charlottesville: University Press of Virginia, 1993), 82.

89. Larson traces the transformation by which education moved from being a mark or privilege attending (preestablished) elite status to becoming a credential, as the complex of professionalism generated a new path for becoming elite (a new "collective mobility project"). Larson, *Rise*, 4, 66–79.

90. Denton J. Snider, *The St. Louis Movement/in Philosophy, Literature, Education, Psychology, with Chapters of Autobiography* (St. Louis: Sigma, 1920), 441.

91. Deidre Shauna Lynch, *Loving Literature: A Cultural History* (Chicago: University of Chicago Press, 2015), 2, 274–275.

92. Stephanie Foote, "Lost Books and a History of Reading Them," *J19: The Journal of Nineteenth Century Americanists* 2, no. 1 (2014): 40.

93. Norris, "'English Courses,'" in *Apprenticeship*, 179–180.

94. Nancy Glazener, *Reading for Realism: The History of a U.S. Literary Institution, 1850–1910* (Durham, N.C.: Duke University Press, 1997), 149–158.

95. In keeping with the paradoxes of modernity I've been examining, however, the very positing of the child as a distinctive and valuable identity (and projective identification) meant that childhood could be both "an adult imaginary kingdom and…an adult research institution." Judith Plotz, *Romanticism and the Vocation of Childhood* (New York: Palgrave, 2001), 3.

96. Edith Wharton and Ogden Codman, Jr., *The Decoration of Houses* (New York: Charles Scribner's Sons, 1897), xx. Italics in the original omitted here.

97. Amy Kaplan, *The Social Construction of American Realism* (Chicago: University of Chicago Press, 1988), 65–87.

98. Edith Wharton, *A Backward Glance* (New York: Appleton-Century, 1934), 141.

99. Wharton, *Backward Glance*, 141–142.

100. Wharton, *Backward Glance*, 220, 290.

101. Bliss Perry, *And Gladly Teach: Reminiscences* (Boston: Houghton Mifflin, 1935), 113. The German-language Strassburg University in Alsace later became the French University of Strasbourg.

102. James, "Ph.D. Octopus," 70.

103. Perry, *And Gladly Teach*, 72, 82–83.

104. Bliss Perry, *The Amateur Spirit* (Boston: Houghton Mifflin, 1904), 26.

105. Elisa Tamarkin has noted that Perry's figure of the amateur also harks back to the college culture that thrived a few decades before, implicitly Anglophilic and characterized by an "aimlessness" that combined the anti-instrumentalism of the liberal arts, the leisure of aristocrats, and a commitment to the cultivation of "sensibility." Here I'm calling attention instead to the ways in which Perry's amateur converges with Norris's sophomore. Elisa Tamarkin, *Anglophilia: Deference, Devotion, and Antebellum America* (Chicago: University of Chicago Press, 2008), 252–286.

106. Perry, *Amateur*, 13–14.

107. Perry, *Amateur*, 31–32.

108. The Rockefeller Foundation's creation of separate divisions of the Social Sciences, Natural Sciences, and Humanities (along with the Medical Sciences) in 1928 marked the operational consolidation of the humanities and its definition in distinction from these other domains. Elizabeth A. Wilson, "A Short History of a Border War: Social Science, School Reform, and the Study of Literature," in Shumway and Dionne, *Disciplining English*, 60.

109. About Browning Society members, see Louise Greer, *Browning and America* (Chapel Hill: University of North Carolina Press, 1952). A number of Browning Society members (especially in the Boston society) were academics but not professors of literature, signaling the interdisciplinary orientation of the group. For example, Daniel G. Brinton, professor of linguistics and archeology at the University of Pennsylvania, was a devoted Browning Society member but not a professional literary scholar, as was

the case for Josiah Royce of Harvard's Philosophy Department and Dr. Ralph Kendrick Smith, professor of orthopedics at Massachusetts College. Charles Carroll Everett, another active member, was Bussey Professor of Theology at Harvard but published *Poetry, Comedy, and Duty* (Boston: Houghton Mifflin, 1888), which addressed some examples from Browning.

Richard G. Moulton initially participated in the extension movement in England and published about the experiment in *Four Years of Novel Reading*. On his role in university extension education at the University of Chicago, see Joseph F. Kett, *The Pursuit of Knowledge under Difficulties: From Self-Improvement to Adult Education in America, 1750–1990* (Stanford, Calif.: Stanford University Press, 1994), 183–185.

110. Hiram Corson, *The Aims of Literary Study* (New York: Macmillan, 1895). Bates published a series "A Reading Journey in English Counties" in the *Chautauquan* from Dec. 1906 to May 1907. Her *American Literature* (New York: Chautauqua Press, 1897) was by 1911 republished by Macmillan, an indication perhaps of Bates's growing stature and the decline of Chautauqua.

111. The strange legacies of High Theory for the humanities today have yet to be adequately grasped, but alongside Theory's exposure and critique of lurking forms of power and control was an unsettling tendency for theorists to operate as a new kind of international supercanon. I'm capitalizing the spectral monolith of "Theory" because I'm sketching its aggregate effects on the practice of literary studies. Key representatives of Theory were the French intellectuals Jacques Derrida, Michel Foucault, Jacques Lacan, and Claude Lévi-Strauss, French intellectuals, but many other European and U.S. thinkers (including many feminist women thinkers) affiliated with Theory.

112. Renker, *Origin*, 136–137. I am seconding here and adding to Renker's recommendations about the importance of thinking "bottom-up" (127), from students' needs and circumstances, and her exhortation that literary studies faces "undiscovered terrain" rather than an "abyss" (143).

113. See the TV Tropes site (http://tvtropes.org/pmwiki/pmwiki.php/Main/HomePage), accessed 17 Aug. 2014.

114. See the Book Riot site (http://bookriot.com/about/), accessed 18 Aug. 2014. On the discrediting of academic literary authority within public literary culture today, see Jim Collins, *Bring on the Books for Everybody: How Literary Culture Became Popular Culture* (Durham, N.C.: Duke University Press, 2010), 35.

115. Kurt Cagle, "From Mary Sue to Magnificent Bastards: TV Tropes and Spontaneous Linked Data," 1 Apr. 2009 (semanticweb.com), accessed 19 Aug. 2014. Of course, I found out about this source through Wikipedia.

116. Jason Diamond, "The 25 Best Websites for Literature Lovers," 5 Aug. 2013 (http://flavorwire.com/407418/the-25-best-websites-for-literature-lovers), accessed 17 Aug. 2014.

117. Wai Chee Dimock's *Through Other Continents: American Literature across Deep Time* (Princeton, N.J.: Princeton University Press, 2006).

{ INDEX }

Abolition and slavery
 abolitionist press, 69
 slavery, 30–31, 34–36, 77, 150
Abrams, M. H., 231n12
Académie des Inscriptions et Belles-Lettres, 106
Act of Union (1707), 110
Adams, Charles Francis, Jr., 138
Adams, John, 77, 78
Adams, John Quincy, 100
Addison, Joseph, 40, 46, 55, 101
The Adventures of Huckleberry Finn (Twain), 154, 234n35
Aeneid (Virgil), 243n139
Aesop, 130
Aesthetica (Baumgarten), 63
Aesthetics. *See also* Realism; Romanticism
 aesthetic autonomy, 54–70, 105–106, 109, 111, 168
 affect studies and, 7
 canonicity and, 206
 neoclassical, 34, 112
 organic, 116, 180
 the sublime, 23, 33, 107–109, 115, 272n218
 taste, 15, 20, 21, 25, 27, 44–45, 49, 55–57, 73, 89, 101, 106–109, 156, 203, 227n10
Aesthetic philosophy. *See* Philosophy
African Americans. *See also* Abolition and slavery
 as authors, 5, 30–36, 143–144, 150, 176, 234n42, 288n147
 education of, 92–93
 in literary culture, 88, 91, 92, 95, 199, 143–144, 242n133, 260n80, 262n109, 263n113
 Shakespeare and, 77, 91
Agassiz, Elizabeth Cary, 94
Agency
 in drama, 182–183
 in popular sovereignty, 60–61
 of readers, 74, 116–118
 in realism and naturalism, 162–163
Aids to Reflection (Coleridge), 112
The Aims of Literary Study (Corson), 216
Akers, Charles W., 235n44
Albanese, Denise, 303n6
Albright, Evelyn, 188, 190
Alcott, Bronson, 123

Aldridge, Ira, 262n109f
Alien and Sedition Acts (1798), 59
Alison, Francis, 110
Allen, James Paul, 176
Amateurs. *See* Experts and Expertise
The Amateur Spirit (Perry), 215
American Academy of Arts and Sciences, 22, 35
American Bibliopolist, 85–87
American Dante Society, 123
American Familiar Verse: Vers de Société (ed. Matthews), 187
American Literature (Bates), 216
American Literature, 1607–1885 (Richardson), 157–159, 235n49
American Literature and the Culture of Reprinting, 1834–1853 (McGill), 12
American Philosophical Society, 233n30
American Poems, Selected and Original (Smith), 44, 236n60
American Shakespeare Magazine, 87
American Tract Society, 69
America's England: Antebellum Literature and Atlantic Sectionalism (Hanlon), 12
Ames, Charles Gordon, 141
Anderson, Benedict, 244n7
Anderson, Perry, 13
Andre (Dunlap), 182
Anglophilia: Deference, Devotion, and Antebellum America (Tamarkin), 12
Anthon, Charles, 241n118
Anthologies, 30, 31, 43–44, 48, 292n207
Anthropology, 206, 217
Anti-modernity. *See* Modernity
Appadurai, Arjun, 13
Applebee, Arthur N., 254n6, 259n73
Arac, Jonathan, 30, 59, 60, 117, 228n23, 234n35
Archeology, 206
Archer, William, 188, 189, 300n144
Aristophanes, 123
Aristotle, 25, 26, 38, 75, 96, 98, 123, 184, 185
Arnold, Matthew, 15, 137, 140, 272n212
Arthur Mervyn (Brown), 60
"The Art of Fiction" (Besant & James), 165, 167
The Art of Playwriting (Hennequin), 182, 184
Asad, Talal, 13, 230n36, 274n248
Astor Place Riot (1849), 37

Attic Nights (club), 92
Audubon, John James, 150
Aurora (newspaper), 59
Aurora Leigh (Barrett Browning), 172
Austen, Jane, 61, 167
Authors and authorship, 58–59, 64, 82, 97, 130–131, 189. *See also* Copyright *and specific authors*
Aveling, Eleanor Marx, 138

Babbitt, Irving, 305n15
Bache, Benjamin Franklin, 59
A Backward Glance (Wharton), 214
Bacon, Delia, 119, 130–134, 151, 218, 284n91, 285n104
Bacon, Francis, 20, 54, 128–136, 140, 146
Baconians. *See* Shakespeare
Bain, Alexander, 204
Baright, Anna, 199
Barlow, Joel, 35, 59
Barrow, J. U., 294n28
Barthes, Roland, 146
Bartholomae, David, 303n7
Bate, Jonathan, 266n151
Bates, Katharine Lee, 145, 216
Baumgarten, Alexander, 63
"Baxter's Procrustes" (Chesnutt), 142
Bayle, Pierre, 245n11
Baym, Nina, 132, 282n73
Beadle and Adams, House of (publisher), 69
Beare, Cornelia, 190, 191
Beauties of Poetry, British and American (Carey), 44
Beerbohm, Max, 141
Beers, Henry A., 94, 106, 167, 274n239
Bell, Alexander Graham, 200
Bell, John, 43, 65
Bellamy, Edward, 287n142
Belles lettres, 23, 32, 45, 73, 101, 106–109
"The Belles-Lettres Series: Literature for Literature's Sake" (D.C. Heath Co.), 106
Benjamin, Walter R., 291n195
Benjamin, William Evarts, 155, 291n195
Bentley, Richard, 165
Berenson, Bernard, 214
Berkeley, George, 233n30
Berman, Marshall, 13
Bernstein, Melvin H., 288n151
Besant, Walter, 165, 166, 183
The Best Reading (Perkins), 104
Beverley, John, 234n37
Bibb, Grace C., 123
Bible, 5, 46, 47, 68, 69, 97–98, 117, 137, 190–191
Biographia Literaria (Coleridge), 112, 117
Biography of Ephraim McDowell, M.D., "The Father of Ovariotomy" (Webster Co.), 156

Blackstone, William, 57
Blair, Hugh, 102–104, 107, 239n105
The Blameless Prince (Stedman), 172
Blow, Susan E., 122
Blumenberg, Hans, 274n249
Boileau, Nicolas, 108, 272n218
Boker, George Henry, 176
BookRiot, 220
Books, 22, 36, 53–54, 179. *See also* Print culture
"Books and Reading" (Emerson), 151
"Books on the Shakespeare-Bacon Controversy" (Houghton Mifflin), 135
Borromeo, Antonio, 232n22
Boston Atheneum, 264n120
Boston Lyceum, 88
Boston Mercantile Library Association, 92
Boston School of Oratory, 199, 307n36
Boston Traveller, 126
Boston University School of Oratory, 200
Boswell, James, 250n66
Bowdler, Thomas, 84
Bowdoin, James, 22–24, 35, 36, 231n6, 236n62
Brackenridge, Hugh Henry, 35
Brackett, Anna, 122
Bradley, A. C., 127, 206, 207, 209, 218
Breadwinners' College, 123, 125
Bring on the Books for Everybody: How Literary Culture Became Popular Culture (Collins), 227n16
Brinton, Daniel G., 310n109
Bristol, Michael, 77, 135, 230n42
Bristow, Joseph, 295n41
Britain. *See* Great Britain
British America. *See* Great Britain
Brockmeyer, Henry C., 121, 122, 277n6
Brooks, Joanna, 236n56
Brown, Charles Brockden, 12, 58–61, 63, 91, 104, 107, 144, 152, 210
Brown, Hallie Quinn, 91, 95
Brown, Homer Obed, 41
Brown, Lois, 143
Brown, William Wells, 262n109
Browning, Elizabeth Barrett, 87, 103, 144, 146, 172
Browning, Robert, 12, 18, 87, 136–148, 170, 172, 173, 175, 188, 200, 201
"A Browning Monologue" (Latimer), 146
Browning Society, 18, 120, 136–148, 160, 175, 216, 286n121, 310n109
Browning's Women (Burt), 145
Brunetière, Ferdinand, 183, 185, 188, 190, 191, 205
Bruns, Cristina Vischer, 226n8
Bryant, William Cullen, 50, 59, 150, 172, 187
Budd, Louis J., 283n87

Budge, Gavin, 246n18
Bufkin, Sydney, 294n30
Bunyan, John, 41
The Burden of Christopher (Converse), 169
Bürger, Peter, 178
Burke, Edmund, 108
Burkhardt, Jacob, 257n39
Burr, Aaron, 150
Burt, Mary E., 145
Burton, Jonathan, 268n162
Byron, George Gordon, Lord, 76, 172

Cambridge History of American Literature, 154, 290n188
Camden, Charles Pratt, Earl of, 66, 67
Canada, 67, 265n132
Canby, Henry Seidel, 186, 188
Candide (Voltaire), 119
Canons and canonicity
  canonicity, 6, 16, 21, 43–52, 176, 198, 206, 241nn117–118
  canon wars, 7, 33, 217
  national canons, 45–49, 198
  supercanon, 45, 47, 49, 50, 122, 128, 209
Canterbury Tales (Chaucer), 49
Cantos (Pound), 175
Capital (Marx), 5
Carey, Mathew, 44
Caritat, Hocquet, 92
Carlyle, Thomas, 133, 134
Carnegie Foundation for the Advancement of Teaching, 196
Castoriadis, Cornelius, 270n188, 270n194
Catlin, George, 150
Cavell, Stanley, 120
Cavendish, Margaret, 257n45
Censorship, 17, 31, 54–63, 130, 246n22
A Century of Dishonor (Jackson), 169
Cervantes, Miguel, 11, 28, 49, 50, 185
Chace Act (International Copyright Act of 1891), 67–68
Chakrabarty, Dipesh, 228n22
Channing, Edward Tyrrel, 152
Channing, William Ellery, 38, 41, 150
Channing, William Henry, 138
Chap-Book (periodical), 160
Charles L. Webster and Co., 154, 155
Chartier, Roger, 36, 251n79, 252n80
Chase, Richard, 42
Chaucer, Geoffrey, 49, 64, 80, 94, 257n38
Chaucer Society, 138
Chautauqua
  Chautauqua Literary and Scientific Circle (CLSC), 71, 93–95, 167, 216, 265n132
  The Chautauquan (publication), 93, 216

The Chautauquans (Habberton), 95
  history of, 93–94
Chekhov, Anton, 145, 186
Cheney, Ednah Dow, 123
Chesnutt, Charles W., 5, 12, 142
Child, Francis, 100
Childe Harold's Pilgrimage (Byron), 172
"The Children's Hour" (Longfellow), 172, 173
Chiles, Katy L., 235n43
Christians and Christianity. *See also* Bible
  Anglicanism, 112, 273n226
  canons, 46–47, 49
  Catholics, 46, 80, 109, 113, 116, 174
  Christian Socialism, 143, 169–170
  Coleridge and, 112–114, 117–118
  Deism and, 23
  Methodists, 34
  modernity and, 13, 79
  publishing, 69
  secularism and, 23, 79, 116–118, 161, 274n248
  reading and, 109–110
  Wheatley and, 30, 34
Cibber, Colley, 44
Civil Service Reform Act of 1883, 194
Civil society, 16, 39, 53–118, 138
Civil War, U.S., 70, 93, 121, 136–137, 154–155, 170, 171, 177, 178
Clara Howard (Brown), 60
Clarke, Helen A., 10, 19, 87, 138, 144–146, 218, 288n155
Class, 6, 37, 90–91, 95, 101, 105, 107, 132–133, 142–143, 148, 150, 160, 170, 173, 176, 211–212. *See also* Working-class culture
Classical Languages and Classical Studies. *See also* specific authors
  classical education, 35, 96, 134 ck for missing entry
  classical texts, 65, 130
  philology and, 130–131
Clay, Henry, 67
Clemit, Pamela, 248n38
Cobbett, William, 59
Cockburn, Alexander, 247n28
Codman, Ogden, Jr., 214
Cogdell, Christina, 180
Cohen, Arthur M., 304n11
Cohen, Michael, 295n41
Coleridge, Hartley, 282n76
Coleridge, Samuel Taylor, 12, 26, 33, 63, 74, 76, 78, 81, 97, 109–118, 126, 128, 129, 207, 208, 210, 232n23, 257n45, 275n251
College Settlement Association, 143
Colley, Linda, 242n129
Collins, Jim, 227n16
Collins, Terence, 32

Colonial America. *See* Great Britain
Columbia College, 111
"Columbian Ode" (Monroe), 170
Coman, Katharine, 145
Commentary on the Laws of England (Blackstone), 57, 66
Common Sense (Paine), 102
Common Sense Philosophy. *See* Philosophy
Comparative Literature (Posnett), 158
Comstock Act of 1873, 253n98
Concise Cyclopedia of Religious Knowledge (Webster Co.), 156
Condorcet, Marquis de, 271n195
Concord School of Philosophy and Literature, 123, 126, 142, 278n18
Connecticut Academy of Arts and Sciences, 233n30
Connors, Robert J., 100, 101, 205
Conroy, David W., 249n50
Consumer culture. *See* Economics
Contending Forces (Hopkins), 143, 183
The Contrast (Tyler), 37
Converse, Florence, 145, 169
Cooke, George Willis, 144
Cooper, James Fenimore, 150
Copway, George, 150
Copyright
  intellectual property, 17, 54, 64–67, 68
  international copyright, 67
  legislation, 64–69
Cornell University, 111
Cornell University Press, 146
Coronado, Raúl, 228n21, 258n57
Corson, Hiram, 111, 146, 147, 151, 202–203, 216
Council of Trent (1546), 46
The Courtship of Miles Standish (Longfellow), 172
Cranch, Christopher Pearce, 138, 243n139
Creative writing as field of study, 188, 203–205, 223
Criticism, literary
  aesthetic criticism, 112, 116, 117, 132, 134, 197–198
  literary history, 11, 30, 37, 47, 48, 50, 80, 89, 94, 112, 153, 157, 159, 198, 206
  textual criticism, 17, 46, 83, 84, 85, 90, 97, 132, 134, 135, 151–152, 197–198, 209
Croce, Benedetto, 191
Crosby, Joseph, 86, 87, 126, 134, 268n166
Culture and Anarchy (Arnold), 137
Cunningham, Vanessa, 262n105
Curry, Samuel Silas, 200, 201, 203
Curry College, 200
Curtis, George William, 138, 283n85
Cust, Harry, 214

Cyclopedia of American Literature (Duyckincks & Duyckincks), 28, 32, 148, 233n30, 234n36, 255n23

Daly, Augustin, 182
Dana, Richard H., 88
Dante, 11, 45, 49–50, 122–123, 128, 172, 240n113, 242n133
Darwin, Charles, 161
Davidson, Thomas, 19, 122, 123, 139, 216, 263n110, 278n24
Davis, Henrietta Vinton, 199
Davis, Rebecca Harding, 71, 168
D.C. Heath Company, 106
Debit and Credit (Freytag), 183
The Decoration of Houses (Wharton & Codman), 214
"A Defence of Poesie" (Sidney), 25, 27
Defoe, Daniel, 41
De Grazia, Margreta, 75, 254n14, 262n104
De Grey, William, 66
Delphic Days (Snider), 280n42
Delsarte, François, 200
Dennie, Joseph, 59, 240n110
De Quincey, Thomas, 38, 39, 107
Derrida, Jacques, 191, 311n111
Development of the Drama (Matthews), 183
Dewey, John, 124, 125
Diamond, Jason, 221
Dickens, Charles, 6, 67, 167
Dickinson, Emily, 87, 91, 137, 138, 172, 175
Dictionary of the English Language (Johnson), 65
DiMaggio, Paul, 90
Dime novels, 69–70
Dimock, Wai Chee, 222, 223
Dionne, Craig, 257n39, 302n3
Disciplines and disciplinarity. *See also* Professionalism, Experts and expertise
  anti-disciplinarity, 210–217
  credentialing, 72–73, 86–87, 124, 127–128, 148, 157–158, 159, 163, 170, 194, 203, 210–211
  disciplinarity, 7–8, 18, 193–205, 217
  disciplinary boundaries, 100, 120–121, 194
  interdisciplinarity, 205–209
Discourses on Davila (Adams), 77
Divine Comedy (Dante), 50, 172
Dobson, Austin, 175
Dodge, Mary Mapes, 173, 187
Dodsley, Robert, 236n62, 239n104
A Doll's House (Ibsen), 181
Donaldson v. Becket (1774), 65, 67, 251n79
Don Juan (Byron), 172
Donne, John, 250n66
Donnelly, Ignatius, 135, 285n100
Don Quixote (Cervantes), 41, 49

Dowden, Edward, 158, 207, 285n101
Dowling, William C., 63
Drama, performance, and theater. *See also* specific plays
  drama, 15, 25, 36–43, 75, 90, 126, 181–184
  in literary culture, 89–91
  performance, 36–38, 182, 199, 205
"Dramatic Museum" (Matthews), 191
Dubliners (Joyce), 190
Dunbar, Paul Laurence, 170, 175, 176
Dunlap, William, 37, 38, 182, 237n71
Dunlap Society, 182
Dunlop, John, 232n22
Duyckincks, Evert & George, 28, 32, 148, 154
Dwight, Timothy, 59

Eagleton, Terry, 225n1
Early English Text Society, 138
Eastman, Charles, 99
Economics, 13, 55, 71, 72, 105, 115, 142, 162, 189
Edgar Huntly (Brown), 60, 165
Education. *See also* Higher education
  informal, 92–95, 121
  liberal arts, 95, 196, 216, 218
  literacy education, 6
  public education, 18, 121, 124, 253n4
  secondary education, 72, 73, 86
  self-education, 18, 92, 93
Eggleston, George Cary, 93
Eichhorn, Johann Gottfried, 266–267n152
Eisenstein, Elizabeth, 244n7, 245n11
Elegant Epistles (Knox), 27
Elegant Extracts: Or, Useful and Entertaining Pieces of Poetry (Knox), 27, 44
Elegant Extracts: Or Useful and Entertaining Passages in Prose (Knox), 27
"Elegy Written in a Country Churchyard" (Gray), 203
Eliot, Charles William, 195, 200
Eliot, George, 144, 190
Eliot, T. S., 167, 175
Elizabeth I (Queen), 130
Ellis, Edward S., 69
Elocution and vocal culture
  elocution, 191–203, 206
  expression, 91, 191–203
  oratory, 22, 39, 98–99, 102–103, 149–150, 163, 191–203
  platform reading, 91, 170, 200–201
  vocal physiology, 201
Eloquence, 96, 98, 100, 101, 103–105, 270n195
Emerson, Charles Wesley, 199, 307n36
Emerson, Ralph Waldo, 12, 68, 74, 75, 109–118, 123, 133, 134, 151, 174, 180, 275n257
Emery, S. H., 123

Emotions and affect, 203–204
Encyclopaedia Britannica, 42
Enfield, William, 99
England. *See* Great Britain
English, Departments of, 9, 72, 100, 198, 203, 218, 222–223
English History Told by English Poets (Bates & Coman), 145
English Reader (Murray), 99
Enlightenment, 4, 55, 103
Enquiry concerning Political Justice (Godwin), 60
Essays
  as school assignments, 204
  familiar verse and, 187
  novels and, 168–169
  as prose genre, 39–40
An Essay Concerning Human Understanding (Locke), 55
"Essay on the Drama" (Scott), 38
Esterhammer, Angela, 266n151
Ethics. *See* Philosophy
Euclid, 96
Evangeline (Longfellow), 50, 172
Everett, Alexander Hill, 151
Everett, Charles Carroll, 140, 311n109
Evolution
  evolutionary theories, 18, 161, 162, 180
  eugenics, 180
An Experiment in Altruism (Sherwood), 169
Experts and expertise, 9. 72–73, 86–87, 127–128, 148, 159, 163, 170, 211–212, 215–216, 223. *See also* Disciplines and Disciplinarity
Expression. *See* Elocution and vocal culture
Ezell, Margaret, 43, 239n104

Fabians, 279n36
Factory Act of (1833, UK), 273n226
Fan fiction, 220
Faust (Goethe), 50, 122, 124
Favor, J. Martin, 234n42
Felperin, Howard, 285n101
Felski, Rita, 226n8
Feltes, N. N., 251n79
Female Poets of America (Griswold), 32
Ferguson, Adam, 23, 24
Fichte, Johann Gottlieb, 112, 252n80
Field, Eugene, 173, 174, 187
Fielding, Henry, 41–43
Finnerty, Paraic, 260n76
Fitch, Clyde, 147
Flavorwire, 221
Fliegelman, Jay, 270n188
Folger, Henry Clay, 276n267
Fortnightly Shakespeare Club of New York City, 87

Foucault, Michel, 50, 64, 302n3, 311n111
Franklin, Benjamin, 40, 41, 55, 57, 58, 91, 102
Franklin, James, 57, 58, 247n25
Frederick II of Prussia, 57
France
  belles lettres in, 45, 98, 106–107
  literary history, 45–46
  French Revolution, 35, 58, 60, 63, 227n18, 240n110, 270n185
  French poetry, 29, 74, 165, 175
  represented in supercanon, 49
  short stories, 186
  French theater, 37–38
Freneau, Philip, 28, 32, 35, 59, 150
Frey, Anne, 275n251
Freytag, Gustav, 164, 183, 184, 188, 190–192, 204, 205, 207, 298n104
The Friend (Coleridge), 112
Friendly Club, 92
Friends' Latin School, 91
Fröbel, Friedrich, 122
Fruchte, Amelia C., 124
Fuller, Margaret, 94, 138, 265n138, 284n97
Fuller, Steve, 227n15
Furness, Horace Howard, 85, 86, 126, 146, 151, 158, 207, 260n74, 268n166
Furnivall, Frederick J., 138, 141, 143

Gaonkar, Dilip Parameshwar, 269n183
Gardner, Jared, 61, 101
Garnett, Constance, 186
Garrick, David, 78
Garvey, Ellen Gruber, 156, 168
Gender and sexuality. *See also* Women
  in Browning's life and work, 144–146
  in genre, 42–43
  queer theory, 226n9
  in Shakespeare's works, 144
General Federation of Women's Clubs, 142
Genius, 24, 50, 117, 118, 130, 161, 183
Genres, 4, 5, 7, 15, 16, 20, 21, 22, 25–30, 33–47, 89, 97–99, 107, 149, 153, 161–192, 205, 206, 220, 221, 222, 226n7, 231n13, 237n72, 240n14, 241n118. *See also specific genres*
Gentz, J. Von, 243n1
Gere, Anne Ruggles, 8
Ghosts (Ibsen), 181
The Gilded Age (Twain & Warner), 154
Giles, Paul, 34, 228n23, 229n26
Gilman, Charlotte Perkins, 105
Gilmore, William J., 68, 245n10, 268n163
Ginn, Heath, and Company, 158
Girard College, 111
Gladstone, Mary, 138
Glanvill, Joseph, 189

Glenmore Summer School for the Culture Sciences, 124
Glyn, Isabella, 91
Godwin, William, 60–62, 248n38, 257n38
Goethe, Johann Wolfgang von, 11, 49, 50, 76, 121, 122, 124, 126, 128, 129, 142, 148, 184, 185
Gold, David, 99, 199, 306n24
The Golden Bowl (James), 173
Good, James A., 276n4, 279n34
Goodman, Dena, 246n12, 271n207
Goodreads, 220
Goodrich, Samuel, 150
Goudie, Sean X., 228n20
G.P. Putnam and Sons, 122, 160
Graff, Gerald, 225n6
Gramsci, Antonio, 245n9
Grant, Percy Stickney, 140
Grant, Ulysses S., 155
Great Britain
  academic institutions and culture, 8, 110, 137, 157–158, 197, 206–209
  British America, 23–24, 32, 41, 57–58, 91, 102, 106, 153, 171, 249n50, 271n207
  censorship legislation
  copyright legislation, 64, 65
  influence on U.S. law, 57, 58–59, 64–65, 67
  influence on U.S. literary culture, 11–12, 44, 48, 62–63, 67–68, 74, 77, 167, 172, 175, 186
The Great Cryptogram (Donnelly), 135
Great Instauration (Bacon), 20
Greenblatt, Stephen, 276n266
Greenough, Horatio, 179, 180
Gregoire, Abbé, 32, 235n48
Grimms' Fairy Tales, 49
Griswold, Rufus Wilmot, 27, 28, 32, 35, 40, 41, 154, 233n28
Grundmann, Heike, 282n76
Guillory, John, 242n133
Gustafson, Sandra, 21, 231n3, 276n267

Habberton, John, 95
Habermas, Jürgen, 101, 230n39
Haggard, Rider, 174
Haitian Revolution (1791–1804), 58, 60
Hale, Sarah Josepha, 150
Halsey, J. J., 158
Hamilton, Alexander, 149
Hamilton, Clayton Meeker, 186, 189, 191
Hamlet (Shakespeare), 76, 84, 128, 129, 135, 188–190, 207, 208
Hamlet without Hamlet (De Grazia), 75
A Hand-Book of Anglo-Saxon and Early English (Corson), 202–203
Hanlon, Christopher, 12

Hardy, Thomas, 59
Harper, Henry, 291n201
Harris, William Torrey, 10, 121–125, 151, 158
Hart, James Morgan, 80, 204, 303n9
Hart, John S., 157, 291n204
Hart, Walter Morris, 186
Harte, Bret, 175, 177, 187
Harvard University, 85, 88, 100, 124, 302n6
Hawthorne, Julian, 123, 292n3
Hawthorne, Nathaniel, 5, 40, 59, 60, 79, 129, 133, 186, 300n127
Hawthorne and the Evolution of the Short Story (Hart), 186
Hazlitt, William, 35, 89, 250n57
Heath, Daniel, 291n201
Hebrew. *See* Bible
Hedda Gabler (Ibsen), 184
Hedge, Frederic H., 28, 121, 277n7
Hegel, G. W. F., 18, 35, 54, 55, 115, 121, 123, 126, 185, 207, 244n3, 298n99
Hennequin, Alfred, 182, 184, 299n111
Henry IV, Part I (Shakespeare), 91
Herbert, George, 250n66
Herder, Johann Gottfried von, 15, 75, 81, 161, 230n45
Herne, James, 181
Higgins, David, 250n57, 252n81
Higginson, Thomas Wentworth, 88, 138, 292n3
Higham, John, 259n68
Higher criticism. *See* Bible
Higher education
  academic freedom, 218, 303n9
  access to, 6, 93, 101, 124, 142, 196, 211–212, 216, 218
  liberal arts, 19, 95, 196, 216, 218, 219–220
  literary studies in, 4, 6–7, 8, 9, 18, 72, 88–89
  research university model, 9, 11, 39, 72, 89, 93, 96, 100, 101, 110, 124–125, 131–132, 195–197, 203, 210, 216, 219
Hilliard, Christopher, 265n135
Hirschman, Albert O., 245n8
Hispanic literature and culture, 41, 47–48, 49, 50, 79, 151, 185, 228n21, 258n57, 299n119
History of American Literature (Tyler), 157, 171
History of Civil Society (Ferguson), 23
History of English Poetry (Warton), 47
History of Fiction (Dunlop), 232n22
History of Spanish Literature (Ticknor), 47, 74, 150
History of the American Theatre (Dunlap), 38, 150
History of the Reign of Philip the Second, King of Spain (Prescott), 79
The History of the Works of the Learned (periodical), 55

Hobsbawm, Eric, 227n18
Hochman, Barbara, 169
Holmes, Nathaniel, 135
Holmes, Oliver Wendell, 172, 175, 177, 187
Holt, Henry, 291n201
Homer, 11, 45, 49, 50, 96, 130
Hooks, Karin, 289n167, 289n169, 290n189, 292n207
Hopkins, Mark, 137
Hopkins, Pauline E., 12, 143, 144, 183
Horace, 25
Houghton Mifflin, 135, 243n139
The House Behind the Cedars (Chesnutt), 5
Howard, George E., 193
Howe, Julia Ward, 123
Howells, William Dean, 12, 137, 166, 168, 174, 179, 200, 213, 292n3, 296n56
Howison, George Holmes, 279n32
How Many Children Had Lady Macbeth? (Knights), 209
How to Educate Yourself: With or without Masters (Eggleston), 93
Hudson, Henry Norman, 80, 85, 86, 88, 117, 126, 151, 158, 199, 200, 260n74
Hunter, Ian, 247n28
Hunter, J. Paul, 237n94
Hutcheson, Francis, 15, 55, 110, 111, 245n8
Hutchinson, Ellen Mackay, 148, 149, 154, 155, 157–159
Hutner, Gordon, 226n7
Huxley, T. H., 272n212

Iberia College, 98
Ibsen, Henrik, 12, 181, 182, 184, 298n99
Idylls of the King (Tennyson), 172
Iliad (Homer), 50, 97
Imagination, 21, 33, 56, 63, 112, 116, 122
Imlay, Gilbert, 32
Imperialism, 4, 5, 6, 7, 8, 10–11, 23, 39, 77, 101, 185, 222, 227n13, 228n22, 231n7, 232n24, 234n37, 242n130, 256n27, 269n174
Individualism, 13, 15, 79, 257n39, 275n252
Inferno (Dante), 128
Innocents Abroad (Twain), 154
Inquiry into the Origin of Our Ideas of Beauty and Virtue (Hutcheson), 111
Institutes of Oratory (Quintilian), 44, 46, 98
Intellectual property. *See* Copyright
International Copyright Act of (1891, Chace Act). *See* Copyright
Internet, 9, 220–223
"In the Poet's Corner" (Bates), 145
Introduction to the Study of Robert Browning's Poetry (Corson), 151
Irving, James, 191

Irving, Washington, 12, 40, 48, 49, 78, 79, 83, 84, 150

Jackson, A. V. Williams, 299n106
Jackson, Helen Hunt, 169
Jackson, Virginia, 33, 174, 292n4
Jaczi, Peter, 67
James (King), 130
James, Alice, 94
James, Henry, 12, 138, 147, 165–168, 173, 179, 183, 188
James, William, 121, 123, 124, 138, 193, 215
Jane Talbot (Brown), 60
Jarausch, Konrad H., 304n9
Jefferson, Joseph, 182, 200
Jefferson, Thomas, 32, 77
Johns Hopkins University, 100, 183
Johnson, Samuel, 42, 43, 65, 83
Jones, Edith, 172
Jones, Ernest, 208
Jones, Henry, 139
Jones, Hiram K., 123, 278n19
Jones, Jenkin Lloyd, 143, 147
Jordan, June, 30
Journal of Speculative Philosophy (JoSP), 120–122, 125
Journal of the American Akademe, 122, 123
Joyce, James, 190
Judaism and Jewish-Americans
  Breadwinners' College, 123
  Council of Jewish Women, 142
  Judaism, 15, 97, 116
Junius (pseudonym), 57, 59
Juvenal, 203

Kaiser, David Aram, 275n251
Kant, Immanuel, 16, 33, 56, 57, 63, 64, 81, 82, 104, 108, 112–114, 135
Kaplan, Richard L., 249n52
Kates, Susan, 263n113
Keats, John, 79
Keen, Paul, 62, 243n144
Kemble, Fanny, 91
Kett, Joseph, 263n114, 287n132
Kies, Marietta, 123
Kindergarten movement, 122–123, 124, 146
King Lear (Shakespeare), 90, 131
The King's Bell (Stoddard), 172
Kipling, Rudyard, 174
Klancher, Jon, 20, 22, 266n151
Klein, Julius I., 281n52
Klein, Lawrence E., 271n206
Knapp, James F., 192
Knapp, Samuel L., 22
Knights, L. D., 209

Knox, Vicesimus, 27, 44, 232n23, 237n91
Kramnick, Jonathan Brody, 44
Kuklick, Bruce, 278n20

Lacan, Jacques, 311n111
"The Lady or the Tiger?" (Stockton), 190
La Harpe, Jean-François de, 44–46, 239n108, 240n113, 240nn110–111, 258n55
Lamar, Mirabeau, 150
Lamarck, Jean-Baptiste, 164
Lamb, Charles, 89, 90
Land-grant colleges, 93, 196
Lanier, Sidney, 94, 138
Larcom, Lucy, 150
Larkin, Edward, 102
Lars: A Pastoral of Norway (Taylor), 172
Larson, Magali Sarfatti, 309n89
Latimer, George Dimmick, 146
Latour, Bruno, 13
Lauck, John Hampton, II, 260n81
"The Law of Genre" (Derrida), 191
Law of the Drama (Brunetière), 183, 185
Lazarus, Emma, 123
Lazo, Rodrigo, 10
Lectures on American Literature (Knapp), 22
Lectures on Rhetoric and Belles Lettres (Blair), 103, 107
Lectures on Shakespeare (Hudson), 88
Lectures on the English Poets (Hazlitt), 35
The Legends and Myths of Hawaii (Webster Co.), 156
Leibniz, Gottfried Wilhelm von, 119
Leighton, Denys P., 277n6
Leighton, Robert, 112
LeMoyne, Sarah Cowell, 147, 170
Lenoir, Timothy, 192, 211
Lesser, Zachary, 135
Lessing, Gotthold Ephraim, 184
Lessons in Elocution (Scott), 99
"Letters on Goethe's *Faust*" (Brockmeyer), 122
Letters on the Aesthetic Education of Man (Schiller), 230n39
Levine, Lawrence, 90
Levine, Robert S., 60
Lévi-Strauss, Claude, 311n111
Lewes, George, 142
Lewis, Jayne Elizabeth, 239n106, 250n66
Liberal arts. *See* Higher education
Liberalism, 60, 101, 106, 244n2, 272n208
Library of American Literature (eds. Stedman & Hutchinson), 120, 148–160, 171, 218
Library of Humor (Twain), 155
Library of the World's Best Literature, Ancient and Modern (Warner), 158

The Life and Letters of Roscoe Conkling, Orator, Statesman, Advocate (Webster Co.), 156
The Life and Times of Frederick Douglass (Douglass), 150, 155
Life in the Iron Mills (Davis), 168
The Life of the Spirit in the Modern English Poets (Scudder), 144–145
"Ligeia" (Poe), 189
Lincoln, Abraham, 150
Linguistics, 198, 217
Linn, James, 190
Literary clubs and societies. *See* Literary culture, public
Literary Bibles, 51, 122, 169, 243n136, 277n13
Literary culture, public, 8–9. 12, 16, 17–18, 56–57, 69, 72–74, 86–95, 119–160, 218–223
A Literary History of America (Wendell), 80, 157
Literary Magazine, and American Register, 83
Literary Remains (Coleridge), 112
Literary World (periodical), 86
Literature
   books and, 22, 36–37, 179
   canons of, 43–52
   disciplinarity and, 195–205
   as learned writings, 4, 21–23
   "literature of knowledge" vs. "literature of power," 5, 38, 107, 160
   oral, orature, 4, 103
   other media and, 6
   manuscript culture and, 4, 103
   as modern and antimodern, 12–16, 21, 42–43, 74–83, 114–116
   rhetoric and, 25, 29, 39, 48, 64, 73, 91–92, 96, 98–106, 109, 110–111, 163, 223
   study of, 17–18, 71–118
   trade publication and, 69–70
   world, 4, 50, 77
"Literature of the Age" (Channing), 41
Lives of the English Poets (Johnson), 65
Lives of the Poets (Johnson), 43
Locke, John, 55
Long, Elizabeth, 260n77
Longaker, Mark, 101
Longfellow, Alice, 94
Longfellow, Henry Wadsworth, 10, 27, 50–51, 55, 69, 88, 137, 172–173, 187, 232n24
Longinus, 108, 272n218
Looking Backward: 2000–1887 (Bellamy), 169, 287n142
Looney, Dennis, 242n133
Loring, Katharine Peabody, 94
Los Angeles Review of Books, 220
Loughran, Trish, 244n7, 253n97, 269n182
Loving Literature (Lynch), 242n134

Lowell, James Russell, 40, 80, 81, 88, 172, 187, 216, 261n94
Löwy, Michael, 13, 229n29, 230n40, 275n252
Lucretius, 20, 96
Lyceum (journal), 88
Lyceum movement, 87, 88, 260n80
Lynch, Deidre Shauna, 212, 226n8, 242n134
Lyrical Ballads (Wordsworth & Coleridge), 26
Lyric poetry. *See* Poetry

Macbeth (Shakespeare), 127
Magazines, 61, 62, 69, 85, 157, 179. *See also specific titles*
The Making of Middlebrow Culture (Rubin), 226n7
Mann, Horace, 150
A Manual of American Literature: A TextBook for Schools and Colleges (Hart), 157
March, Francis A., 197
Marean, Emma Endicott, 140
Margaret Eaton School of Literature, 200
Margret Howth (Davis), 168
Marlowe, Christopher, 191
Marsh, George P., 89, 151, 261n96
Marsh, James, 112
Marx, Karl, and Marxism, 5, 138, 162, 178, 217, 244n2
Mason, Julian, 235n44
Massachusetts Magazine, 83
Mather, Cotton, 55
Matson, R. Lynn, 30, 32
Matthews, Brander, 175, 182, 183, 185, 187, 299n119
Maud (Tennyson), 172
Maupassant, Guy de, 186
Maxcy, Carroll Lewis, 301n159
McCosh, James, 126
McCullough, Mary C., 124
McGill, Meredith L., 12, 67, 68, 250n65
McGuffey, William H., 111
McGuffey's Readers, 99
McKeon, Michael, 230n35
McVickar, William, 273n234
Mechanics' institutes. *See* Working-class culture
Melton, James Van Horn, 37, 41, 57, 249n50
Melville, Herman, 12, 88, 128–130, 133, 137
Memoirs (Grant), 155
Merimée, Prosper, 186
Metamorphoses (Ovid), 96
The Method of Teaching and Studying the Belles Lettres (Rollin), 106
Mickiewicz, Adam, 49
Middlebrow literature, 7, 42, 226n7
Mignolo, Walter D., 231n7, 269n174
Miller, J. Hillis, 226n8

Miller, Joaquin, 137
Miller, Perry, 273n234
Milton, John, 11, 33, 34, 49, 50, 66, 67, 94, 121
Milwaukee Literary School, 124
Miner, William Harvey, 280n42
Minerva Literary Association of Philadelphia, 92
Mitchell, Ellen M., 123
Mitchell, Maria, 123
Modernism, 145–146, 178–179, 180, 229n27
Modernity
    antimodernity and, 13, 15, 21, 42–43, 80–82, 114–116, 119, 165, 166–168, 172, 194, 216
    emotion and, 14–15
    Europe and, 5, 14, 15, 29–30, 79–80, 228n21, 228n22, 231n7
    as epoch, 5, 12–14, 24, 29–30, 79–80, 119, 131–132, 194
    organization of knowledge and, 20–21, 131–132, 162–163, 213, 215
    as paradigm, 12–16, 229n28, 302n5
    progress and, 119–120
    Quarrel of Ancients and Moderns, 13, 14, 66, 74
    Shakespeare and, 15, 29, 79–81
Modern Language Association, 13
Modern Language Notes (journal), 85
The Modern Study of Literature (Moulton), 27, 169, 205–206
Moi, Toril, 298n98
Molière, 45, 49
Monroe, Harriet, 170
Montesquieu, 15, 230n45
Moral philosophy. *See* Philosophy
Morelli, Giovanni, 214
Morgan, Appleton, 151
Morrill Act (1862), 93, 196
Morris, William, 182
Morse, Samuel F. B., 150
Morton, Sarah Wentworth, 149
Moulton, Richard G., 27, 146, 169, 187, 197, 202, 205, 207, 216, 218, 294n28
Munsterberg, Hugo, 121
Murphy, Andrew, 83
Murray, Lindley, 99
"The Mutability of Literature" (Irving), 78

Nair, Mira, 6
Napier, Arthur S., 305n16
Nations and nationalism, 10–12, 28, 68, 74–80, 161, 165
National Association of Academic Teachers of Public Speaking, 201
National Association of Colored Women, 142, 144
National Association of Elocutionists, 199
National Council of Teachers of English, 72, 201

National Education Association, 72, 302n6
National Home Reading Union, 94
National League of Women Workers, 142
National-Louis University, 123
Native Americans and Native American cultures, 31, 50, 99, 149–150, 234n42, 296n67
Nature (Emerson), 115, 275n257
Neal, Robert Wilson, 191
New England Commission of Colleges, 302n6
New-England Courant, 57
New Era Club, 143
New Shakspere Society of London, 84, 99, 138, 141
Newspapers, 22, 31, 58, 59, 62, 69, 85, 86, 102–103, 176. *See also specific titles*
New York Philomathean Society, 92
New York Shakespeare Society, 181
New York State Aid Charity Association, 143
New York University, 86
Nietz, John A., 273n226
Nietzsche, Friedrich, 120
Norris, Frank, 12, 169, 204, 210, 213, 293n20
Norris, Joseph Parker, 85, 126
North American Review, 125
Novels. *See also* Realism
    Great American Novel, 167–168, 178
    as modern and antimodern, 166–168, 172
    poetry vs., 164–179
    value of, 40–42
Novum Organum (Bacon), 80, 131

Oberlin College, 98, 124
Occom, Samson, 31, 233n30
O'Connor, William D., 135, 136, 284n99
Odyssey (Homer), 50, 96
Oedipus Rex (Sophocles), 20, 96
"Of the History of Literature" (Ferguson), 23
Ohio Wesleyan University, 199
Ohmann, Richard, 297n85
On the Aesthetic Education of Man (Schiller), 56
"On Being Brought from Africa to America" (Wheatley), 30, 31
"On Imagination" (Wheatley), 33
"On the Madness of Hamlet" (Verplanck), 151
On the Nature of Things (Lucretius), 20
"On Reading Shakespeare" (White), 284n92
On the Sublime (Longinus), 108
Oratory. *See* Elocution and vocal culture
Orgel, Stephen, 262n103
Ormond (Brown), 60, 104
Osgood, James R., 280n42
Othello (Shakespeare), 91
An Outline Sketch of English Literature (Beers), 94
Ovid, 96

Paine, Thomas, 59, 76, 102, 255n20
Palmieri, Patricia Ann, 288n152
Pamela (Richardson), 41
"Pan in Wall Street" (Stedman), 187
Paracelsus, 138
Paradise Lost (Milton), 34, 67
Paraphrase on Part of the Oeconomy of Human Life (Bowdoin), 35, 236n62
Paris Review, 220
Parker, Robert Dale, 234n42
Parkman, Ellen T., 94
Parley, Peter, 77
Pasley, Jeffrey L., 249n52
Pater, Walter, 214
Patey, Douglas Lane, 240n114
Pattee, Fred Lewis, 308n55
Patterson, Annabel, 130
Paulin, Roger, 303n9
Peabody, Elizabeth, 123, 265n138, 282n73
Pease, Donald, 77
Peirce, Charles Sanders, 87, 121
"The Pelican" (Wharton), 142, 213
Pendleton Civil Service Reform Act of 1883, 194
Penn, William, 149
Percy, Thomas, 48
Performance. *See* Drama, performance, and, theater
Periodicals. *See* Newspapers, Magazines
Perkins, Frederick Beecher, 104, 105, 109
Perry, Bliss, 98, 99, 137, 161, 163, 165, 186, 187, 202, 216
Perry, Charles, 278n30
Perry, Thomas Sergeant, 138, 168
Petrarch, 240n113
Phaedrus (Plato), 5
Phelps, William Lyon, 165, 216, 293n6
Philadelphia Shakespeare Society, 85, 87
The Philanderer (Shaw), 181
Philology, 73, 96–98, 106, 112, 163, 195–198, 203, 206, 217
Philosophy. *See also specific philosophers and* St. Louis movement
  as academic discipline, 39, 110, 197
  aesthetic philosophy, 8, 15–16, 29–30, 45, 56–57, 63–64, 81–82, 112, 135, 200, 246n18
  Common Sense Philosophy, 15–16, 45, 55–57, 63–64, 112–114
  ethics, 10, 110, 111, 140, 175, 178, 206, 209, 254n9
  informing literary studies, 18, 120–128, 130, 133–134, 135, 139–140, 151, 160, 206–208
  moral philosophy, 26, 48, 56, 96, 109–118
  political philosophy, 48, 217
"Philosophy of Composition" (Poe), 189
The Philosophy of Right (Hegel), 121, 244n3

Philosophy of Style (Spencer), 180
Philosophy of the Human Voice (Rush), 306n34
The Philosophy of the Short Story (Matthews), 186
Piatt, Sarah, 176
The Picture of St. John (Taylor), 172
Pilgrim's Progress (Bunyan), 41
Platform readings. *See* Elocution and vocal culture
Plato, 5, 26, 38, 122, 123
The Platonist (journal), 122
"Pleasure: A Heresy" (Repplier), 174
PMLA (periodical), 85, 146
Pocahontas, 150
Pocock, J. G. A., 244–245n8
Poe, Edgar Allan, 176, 186, 189, 300n127
Poetics (Aristotle), 96, 164
Poet-Lore journal, 87, 138, 144, 145, 148, 200, 216
Poetry and poetics. *See also specific poets and works*
  bardic origin of, 24
  free verse, 29
  lyric, 29, 31, 33, 165, 174, 176, 178–179, 181, 187–188
  as modern literary genre, 24–37, 43,
  narrative, 172
  novels vs. poetry, 164–179
  poetics, 25, 98
  prose vs. poetry, 17, 24, 25, 26–28, 28–29, 103, 175, 232n22, 233n26, 236n60
  vers de société (society verse), 175
  verse and, 26–27, 28–29, 174, 175, 180, 181
The Poets and Poetry of America (Griswold), 27, 28
The Poets and Poetry of Europe (Longfellow), 27, 28, 50, 55
Poets of America (Stedman), 153, 158, 171, 176, 177
The Poets of Great Britain: Complete from Chaucer to Churchill (Bell), 43, 65
Pope, Alexander, 30, 32, 35, 83, 255n19
Porter, Charlotte, 10, 19, 87, 138, 140, 144–146, 218, 288n155
Porter, Noah, 126
Port Folio (periodical), 44, 45, 62, 240n110
Posnett, Hutcheson, 158
Pound, Ezra, 175
Prescott, William, 79, 149, 150
Price, Thomas R., 181–184, 298n97
The Princess (Tennyson), 172
Princeton University, 165
Principles of Scientific Management (Taylor), 180
Print culture, 7, 8, 54–63, 102

Professionalism, 194, 211–212, 215. *See also* Experts and expertise
Prose, 17, 24, 25, 26–28, 28–29, 38–39, 41, 42, 48, 103, 167, 181–182, 187, 232n22, 233n126, 236n60. *See also* Essays, Novels, Short Stories
Prose Dramas (Ibsen), 181
Prose Writers of America (Griswold), 28, 40
Prose Writers of Germany (Hedge), 28, 121
"The Prospect of Peace" (Barlow), 35
Proverbs, 48
"Psalm of Life" (Longfellow), 173
Pseudonyms, 57, 236n63
Psychology, 94, 121, 124, 160, 167, 206–209, 217
Publishing industry *See also* Censorship, Copyright, Print culture
  academic sector of, 96, 146, 154, 158, 160, 204, 209, 221
  literature and, 4, 5, 8, 11, 65–66, 68–69, 165, 169, 179
  postal regulations and, 69, 253n98
  printers, 64–70
  reprinting, 67
  self-publication, 5, 85, 125, 179
  subscription publishing, 69–70, 154–157, 159
  trade publishing, 69–70, 156–157, 179
Publius (pseudonym), 57
Pulitzer, Joseph, 123
Putnam's Monthly, 130, 133, 151

Quebec, Battle of (1759), 35
Queens College, Oxford, 86
Quiller-Couch, Arthur, 301n148
Quintilian, 44, 46, 98

Race
  authorship and, 30–32, 34, 143–144, 152, 176, 236n56
  critical race theory, 226n9
  in literary history, 48, 150, 153
Radcliffe, Ann, 30, 43, 61
Raleigh, Walter, 130
Ramona (Jackson), 169
Reading for Realism (Glazener), 69
Realism, 162, 166–168, 173, 174, 176, 179, 181, 296n52
Rebecca of Sunnybrook Farm (Wiggin), 123
The Redemption of the Hamlets (Son and Father) (Snider), 146
Red Jacket, 150
Redwood Library, 233n30
Reed, Henry, 28, 39, 88, 89, 107, 111, 233n32, 261n89, 273n226
Reed, William, 261n89
Reeve, Clara, 237n94
Reid, Thomas, 15, 55

Reliques of Ancient English Poetry (Percy), 48
Renker, Elizabeth, 171, 176, 220
Repplier, Agnes, 174, 213
Representative Men (Emerson), 68, 75
Republics and republicanism
  civic republicanism, 54, 57, 60, 67–68, 77, 98, 101, 104, 106, 149–150, 272n208
  print and, 54–55, 67–68, 244n7, 269n182
  Republic of Letters, 20, 55, 76, 107, 245n11, 271n207
Republic (Plato), 123
The Return of the Druses (Browning), 146
Revolutions
  French, 35, 58–59, 60, 63, 227n18, 240n110, 270n185
  Glorious Revolution (England), 57, 77
  Haitian Revolution (1791–1804), 58, 60
  U.S., 10, 24, 55, 57–58, 60, 61, 77, 149, 228n18
Revue des Deux Mondes (periodical), 183
Rhetoric
  belles lettres and, 106–109, 110–111
  composition and, 100, 204–205, 223
  literature and, 25, 29, 39, 48, 64, 73, 91–92, 96, 98–106, 109, 110–111, 163, 223
  multimodal, 204–205, 268n168
  as persuasion, 103–105
  poetics and, 26, 98
  print culture and, 101–103
  rhetorical canons, 46–47, 240n117
  textbooks, 99–100, 239n105
Rhodes, Neil, 110
Rice, Allen Thorndike, 172
Richards, Jeffrey H., 237n75
Richardson, Charles F., 154, 157–159, 168, 235n49
Richardson, Samuel, 41–43
Ricks, Christopher, 295n41
Rieser, Andrew C., 94, 265n132
Riley, James Whitcomb, 173, 174
The Ring and the Book (Browning), 147, 172
Ripley, George, 265n138
Ripley, Sophia, 265n138
"The Rising Glory of America" (Brackenridge), 35
Roach, Joseph, 100, 116, 117, 270n187
"Robert Browning, Taking Tea with the Browning Society" (Beerbohm), 141
Robinson, Marc, 298n95
Rockefeller Institute, 196
Rogers, Dorothy G., 123, 142, 276n4
Rolfe, William J., 86, 199, 260n74
Rollin, Charles, 102, 106
Romanticism,
  aesthetics, 24, 29, 31, 32, 76, 112, 166, 174, 180, 210

Index

genius and, 66–67, 130, 183, 213
modernity and, 14, 229n29, 230n38
nationalism and, 49
periodized, 24, 29–30
Shakespeare and, 74–76, 81–82, 89–90, 117, 130, 151
Wheatley and, 33–36
Rose, Aquila, 250–251n66
Rose, Mark, 66, 251n79
Rossetti, William, 138
Rothbard, Murray N., 247n25
Roughing It (Twain), 154
Rousseau, Jean-Jacques, 37
Rowe, Nicholas, 83, 255n19, 258n52
Rowland, Hilary, 283n79
Rowlandson, Mary, 150
Rowson, Susanna, 233n30
Royal American Magazine, 23
Royce, Josiah, 121, 124, 139, 140, 311n109
Rubin, Joan Shelley, 226n7, 294–295n35
Ruffin, Josephine, 143
Rush, James, 306n34
Ruskin, John, 182

St. Louis movement, 18, 120–128, 143, 146, 160, 276n4
St. Louis Shakespeare Club, 124
Salvatori, Mariolina Rizzi, 196, 303n8
Sappho, 45
Sarcey, Francisque, 183, 192
Satires (Juvenal), 203
Saunders, David, 247n28
Sayre, Robert, 13, 229n29, 230n40, 275n252
Scarborough, William Sanders, 268n163
The Scarlet Letter (Hawthorne), 5, 59
Schelling, Friedrich Wilhelm Joseph, 112
Schiller, Friedrich, 14, 16, 56, 81, 82, 112, 151, 184, 230n39, 230n41, 258n50
Schlegel, August, 37, 185, 231n13
Schlegel, Friedrich, 76, 207
Schoolcraft, Henry, 150
The School for Scandal (Sheridan), 37
School of Elocution and Expression, 200
Science
   arts and sciences, 22–23, 158, 196, 216
   contrasted with literature, 29, 115, 140, 162
   as disciplinary model, 163–164, 192, 196–197, 204, 210, 216, 219, 303n8, 303n9
   included in literature, 21–22, 26, 38, 44–45
   modernity and, 24, 115, 196–197, 216
   study of, 94, 96
Scott, Walter, 37, 38, 41–43, 94, 167
Scott, William, 99
Scudder, Vida D., 143, 144, 216
The Seasons (Thomson), 65

Secularism. *See* Christians and Christianity
Sedgwick, Catherine, 150
Seditious libel, 58, 59, 247n28
Seelye, J. H., 126
Select Collection of Old English Plays (Dodsley), 239n104
"Self-Reliance" (Emerson), 113, 114
Sen, Amartya, 254n9
Shackford, Charles Chauncy, 286n121
Shackford, Martha Hale, 145
Shaftesbury, Anthony Ashley Cooper, Earl of, 55, 63, 76
Shakespeare, William. *See also* Hamlet
   Bacon-Shakespeare authorship dispute, 18, 120, 128–136, 151, 160
   Browning clubs and, 138–140, 141, 146
   Coleridge on, 12, 81, 112, 113, 117–118, 129, 208
   as dramatist, 37–38, 89–91, 97, 198
   editions, 83, 85–86, 87, 157–158
   modernity and, 15, 29–30, 79–81
   Romanticism and, 37–38, 74–76, 81–82, 89–90, 117, 130, 151
   St. Louis movement and, 50, 121–122, 124–126
   Shaw on, 181
   Snider on, 50, 126–128
   study of, 73–95, 120, 150–152
   supercanonical, 11, 12, 18, 29–30, 49–50, 73, 122, 152, 200, 18, 153
Shakespearean Tragedy (Bradley), 127, 206, 209
"Shakespeare at Stratford" (Snider), 146
Shakespeare Magazine Company, 87
"Shakespeare Once More" (Lowell), 80
Shakespeare Press, 87
Shakespeare Society of New York, 87
Shakespeare Study Programs, 146
Shakespeariana, 86, 87, 181, 260n74
"Shakespearian Gossip" column (Norris), 85
Shaw, George Bernard, 89, 138, 181, 261n100
Sheridan, Richard, 37
Sherman, Caroline K., 123
Sherman, William T., 150
Sherwood, Margaret, 143, 145, 169
Sherzer, Jane, 283n79
Shields, David, 32, 250n66, 271n206
Shields, John C., 33
Short stories, 179–192
Short Stories in the Making (Neal), 191
The Short Story (Canby), 186
Shumway, David R., 251n67, 302n3, 309n83
Sidney, Philip, 25–27, 232n17
Sigma Publishing Company, 279n42
Sigourney, Lydia, 5, 150, 176
Sketch (genre), 39, 40, 49, 186,
Silas Marner (Eliot), 190

Simon, Henry, 267n161, 268n164
Simpson, David, 276n264
Siskin, Clifford, 293n5
The Sketch-Book (Irving), 40, 48, 78, 84
Smith, Adam, 15, 56, 111, 162, 246n16
Smith, Charles Alphonso, 187
Smith, Elihu Hubbard, 44, 58, 236n60
Smith, John, 150
Smith, Lewis Worthington, 188
Smith, Ralph Kendrick, 311n109
Smith, Susan Harris, 37, 201, 237n72
Smith, Sydney, 48, 150
Smollett, Tobias, 43
Snider, Denton J., 10, 19, 50, 51, 98, 99, 115, 122–127, 130, 140, 146, 151, 179, 189, 212, 216, 218, 243n136, 277n7, 279–280n42
Social Darwinism, 18, 180
Social Gospel movement, 93
Society to Encourage Studies at Home, 94, 95
Sociology, 141, 206, 217
Soldan, F. L., 122
Song of Hiawatha (Longfellow), 50, 172
Song of Mannahatta (Whitman), 172
Sophocles, 20, 49, 96, 184
Sorby, Angela, 147, 170, 173, 187, 296n50
Spain, Spanish literature. *See* Hispanic literature and culture
The Speaker (Enfield), 99
Spectator (periodical), 40
Speech. *See also* Elocution and vocal culture
    as academic subject, 100
    Departments of, 199, 201
    Speech Association of America, 201
Spencer, Herbert, 125, 162, 164, 180
Spingarn, J. E., 191, 192
Spinoza, Baruch, 75
The Spirit of Laws (Montesquieu), 230n45
The Spiritual Sense of Dante's "Divina Commedia" (Harris), 122
Stedman, Edmund Clarence, 148, 149, 153–155, 158, 159, 170–172, 174–179, 182, 187, 235n50, 297n81
Stevenson, Robert Louis, 174
Stockton, Frank R., 190
Stoddard, Richard Henry, 172, 292n3
Stokes, Claudia, 284n97
Stone, Lucy, 123
"Stories as a Mode of Thinking" (Moulton), 169
Story, William, 265n138
"Structure and Organization" (Greenough), 180
A Study of Prose Fiction (Perry), 186
A Study of Shakespeare (Swinburne), 207
The Study of the Novel (Whitcomb), 205
Sturm und Drang movement, 75
Sublime, the. *See* Aesthetics
Sullivan, Louis, 179

Sumner, Charles, 150
Swinburne, Algernon, 207
Symonds, John Addington, 214
System of Shakespeare's Dramas (Snider), 126, 127

Tacitus, 96
Taine, Hippolyte, 153, 183
Tamarkin, Elisa, 12, 77, 310n105
Taste. *See* Aesthetics
Tate, Nahum, 90
Tatler, 40
Taylor, Bayard, 50, 171, 172
Taylor, Frederick, 180
Taylor, Gary, 83
Technique of the Drama (Freytag), 183, 184
Tennyson, Alfred, 137, 172, 177
Terrell, Mary Church, 144
Thackeray, Henry, 150
Thaxter, Celia, 147
Thaxter, Levi, 147
Theater. *See* Drama, performance, and theater
Theobald, Lewis, 44
Theology, 62, 95, 140, 149, 206, 207, 210. *See also* Bible
Theory of the Moral Sentiments (Smith), 111, 246n16
Things as They Are; or, Caleb Williams (Godwin), 60
Thomson, James, 65
Through Other Continents: American Literature across Deep Time (Dimock), 223
Ticknor, Anna Eliot, 94
Ticknor, George, 10, 47, 48, 68, 74, 76, 88, 91, 100, 102, 107, 115, 150, 237n88, 256n27
Tieck, Ludwig, 91
Tillyard, E. M. W., 141, 287n133, 305n16
Tocqueville, Alexis de, 54
Tolstoy, Leo, 137
Tom Jones (Fielding), 42
Tonson publishing firm, 83
Tragedy, 47, 49, 75, 131, 185, 191, 207–208. *See also* Shakespearean Tragedy
The Tragedy of Numancia (Cervantes), 28
The Tragedy of Pudd'nhead Wilson (Twain), 155
Transcendentalists, 109–118, 114, 123, 126
Translation, 10, 12, 46, 50, 97, 106, 108, 121, 122, 125, 145–146, 172–173, 181, 183, 184, 186, 188, 200, 203, 228n23, 243n139
Treatise concerning Political Enquiry, and the Liberty of the Press (Wortman), 62
Trueblood, Thomas Clarkson, 199
Tuckerman, Henry Theodore, 152
Tuesday Club of Annapolis, 61
Turner, Frederick Jackson, 215
Turner, James, 96, 101

TV Tropes site, 220, 222
Twain, Mark, 12, 70, 120, 135–137, 153, 155, 156, 234n35, 284n99
"Twelve Good Rules of Familiar Verse" (Matthews), 187
"The 25 Best Websites for Literature Lovers" (Diamond), 221
Twice Told Tales (Hawthorne), 300n127
Tyler, Moses Coit, 157, 171, 291n203
Tyler, Royall, 37

Ulrici, Hermann, 207
Uncle Tom's Cabin (Stowe), 168, 169
Undercurrents of Influence in English Romantic Poetry (Sherwood), 145
United States. *See also* Literary culture
  censorship, 58–59
  copyright laws, 67–68
  cultural nationalism, 10, 28, 30, 37, 38, 48–49, 50, 51, 74, 76–78
  literature, 8, 10, 12, 17, 37, 50
  revolution, 10, 24, 54, 55, 57–58, 60, 61, 77, 149, 228n18
University of Aberdeen, 124
University of Chicago, 202
University of Glasgow, 111
University of Michigan, 86, 88, 199
University of Mississippi, 111
University of Pennsylvania, 85, 87, 88
University of Southern California, 199
University of Vermont, 112
University of Virginia, 111
The Uses of Literature (Felski), 226n8

Vanderbilt, Kermit, 290n188
Variorum (Furness), 85, 158, 207
Vaughan, Alden T., 262n109
Vaughan, Virginia Mason, 262n109
Veblen, Thorstein, 142
Verplanck, Gulian, 151, 255n23, 260n74, 260n78
Veysey, Laurence R., 259n68
Victorian Poetry and Poets of America (Stedman), 157
Victorian Poets (Stedman), 153, 171, 177
Virgil, 243n139
Voltaire, 75, 81, 84, 119

Waiting for the Verdict (Davis), 168
Walker, Amasa, 150
A Walk in Hellas (Snider), 151, 280n42, 280n45, 280n47
Walton, Izaak, 250n66
Wampum Library, 187
Warner, Charles Dudley, 154, 158, 244n6, 292n3
Warner, Michael, 54
Warnick, Barbara, 101, 106, 272n218

Warren, Austin, 278n18
Warren, Mercy, 233n30
Warton, Thomas, 47
Washington, George, 149
Watt, Ian, 61
Wayland, Francis, 151
The Wealth of Nations (Smith), 246n16
Weber, Max, 162, 245n8
Weed, Thurlow, 150
We Have Never Been Modern (Latour), 13
Wellek, René, 25, 47, 241n124
Wellesley College, 145, 169
Wells College, 87
Wendell, Barrett, 157
Werder, Karl, 207
The Western: A Review of Education, Science, Literature and Art (journal), 125
"We Wear the Mask" (Dunbar), 175
Wharton, Edith, 12, 137, 141, 142, 147, 213, 214
Wheatley, Phillis, 12, 21, 28, 29–36, 150, 233n30, 234n39, 235n44, 236n63
Wheaton v. Peters (1834), 67
Whedon, Joss, 6
Whipple, E. P., 92, 151, 304n13
Whitcomb, Selden Lincoln, 201, 205, 301n159
White, Richard Grant, 86, 132–136, 151, 163, 214, 260n74, 283n83, 284n92
Whitefield, George, 34
Whitman, Walt, 5, 135, 137, 172, 174, 175, 178, 202, 284n99
Whitney, Mary W., 94
Whittier, John Greenleaf, 137, 153, 172, 177, 178, 187
Why Literature? (Bruns), 226n8
Wieland (Brown), 60
Wiggin, Kate Douglas, 123
Wilde, Oscar, 175
"The Wild Honeysuckle" (Freneau), 32, 235n50
Wilhelm Meister (Goethe), 124
Willard, Emma, 150
William Harvey Miner Company, 280n42
Williams, Raymond, 13, 231n3
Williams College, 98, 165, 215
Wilstach, John Augustine, 243n139
The Wings of the Dove (James), 173
Winterer, Caroline, 272n207
Witherspoon, John, 110
Wittgenstein, Ludwig, 4
Woman's Era Club, 144
Women. *See also* specific individuals
  as authors, 32–34, 35, 150, 176, 233n26, 236n63
  education of, 88, 99, 124, 142, 144, 303n9
  in public literary culture, 9, 71, 87, 92, 94, 95, 122, 123, 124, 134, 141–144, 144–145, 145–146, 173, 174, 262n109, 271n207

Women's Club Movement, 95, 144
Wood, Gordon S., 55, 104, 272n209
Woodberry, George Edward, 299n106
Woodfall, Henry, 59
Woodmansee, Martha, 66, 67, 251n67, 252n80
Woolson, Constance Fenimore, 289n175
Words and Their Uses, Past and Present (White), 134
Wordsworth, William, 26, 35, 63, 76, 232n20
Working-class culture
   authors, 33, 137–138, 150, 176
   Breadwinners' College, 123, 125
   in literary culture, 91, 95, 124–125, 226n7, 262n109, 264n120
   London Corresponding Society, 59
   London Working Men's College, 143
   Mechanics' Institutes, 87

Working Girls' Clubs, 143
A World Not to Come (Coronado), 228n21
Wortman, Tunis, 62
The Writing of the Short Story (Smith), 188

"Xingu" (Wharton), 141, 213

Yadav, Alok, 242n129
Yale University, 165
Yanks and Johnnies; or, Laugh and Grow Fat (Webster Co.), 156
Yellow Clover: A Book of Remembrance (Bates), 145

Zboray, Mary Saracino, 102
Zboray, Ronald J., 102, 264n124
Zirimu, Pio, 270n187
Zitkala-Sâ, 99

www.ingramcontent.com/pod-product-compliance
Ingram Content Group UK Ltd.
Pitfield, Milton Keynes, MK11 3LW, UK
UKHW042005230426
12048UKWH00009B/573